Knowledge-based questions present challenging material in a multiple-choice format. Answer treatments not only explain why the correct options are right, they also tell you why the incorrect answers are wrong.

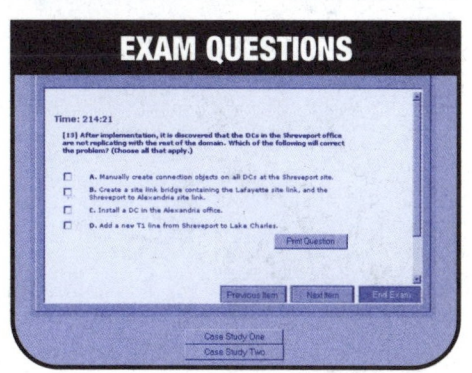

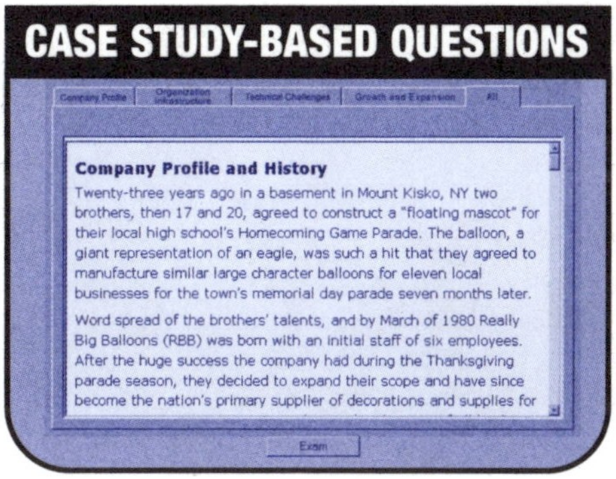

Realistic Designing Windows 2000 **Case Study-based** questions challenge your ability to analyze and synthesize complex information in realistic scenarios similar to those on the actual exams.

- Complete hyperlinked **e-book** for easy information access and self-paced study

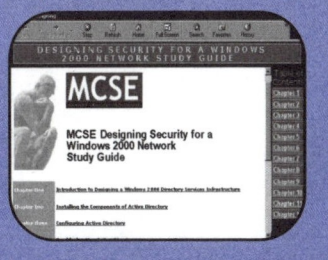

- **DriveTime** audio tracks offer concise review of key exam topics for in

The **Score Report** provides an overall assessment of your exam performance as well as performance history.

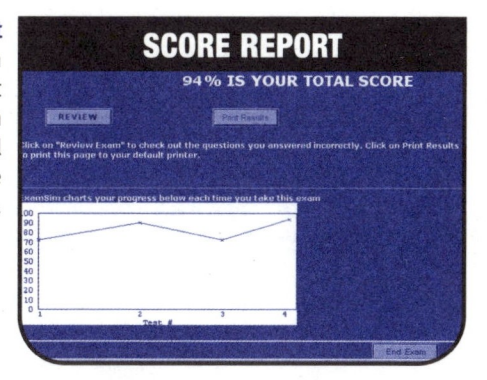

MCSE Designing Security for Windows® 2000 Study Guide

(Exam 70-220)

MCSE
MICROSOFT CERTIFIED SYSTEMS ENGINEER

MCSE Designing Security for Windows® 2000 Study Guide

(Exam 70-220)

Syngress Media, Inc.

Microsoft is a registered trademark of Microsoft Corporation in the United States and other countries. Osborne/McGraw-Hill is an independent entity from Microsoft Corporation, and not affiliated with Microsoft Corporation in any manner. This publication may be used in assisting students prepare for a Microsoft Certified Professional Exam. Neither Microsoft Corporation, its designated review company, nor Osborne/McGraw-Hill warrants that use of this publication will ensure passing the relevant exam.
  Use of the Microsoft Approved Study Guide Logo on this product signifies that it has been independently reviewed and approved in complying with the following standards:

- Acceptable coverage of all content related to Microsoft exam number 70-220, entitled Designing Security for a Microsoft® Windows® 2000 Network.
- Sufficient performance-based exercises that relate closely to all required content; and
- Technically accurate content, based on sampling of text.

Osborne/McGraw-Hill
Berkeley New York St. Louis San Francisco Auckland Bogotá Hamburg London Madrid Mexico City
Milan Montreal New Delhi Panama City Paris São Paulo Singapore Sydney Tokyo Toronto

Osborne/**McGraw-Hill**
2600 Tenth Street
Berkeley, California 94710
U.S.A.

For information on translations or book distributors outside the U.S.A., or to arrange bulk purchase discounts for sales promotions, premiums, or fund-raisers, please contact Osborne/McGraw-Hill at the above address.

MCSE Designing Security for Windows® 2000 Study Guide (Exam 70-220)

Copyright © 2000 by The McGraw-Hill Companies. All rights reserved. Printed in the United States of America. Except as permitted under the Copyright Act of 1976, no part of this publication may be reproduced or distributed in any form or by any means, or stored in a database or retrieval system, without the prior written permission of the publisher, with the exception that the program listings may be entered, stored, and executed in a computer system, but they may not be reproduced for publication.

1234567890 AGM AGM 019876543210

Book P/N 0-07-212495-4 and CD P/N 0-07-212496-2
parts of
ISBN 0-07-212497-0

Publisher Brandon A. Nordin	**Editorial Assistants** Tara Davis Jessica Wilson	**Indexer** Valerie Robbins
Vice President and Associate Publisher Scott Rogers	**VP, Worldwide Business Development Global Knowledge** Richard Kristof	**Computer Designers** Lauren McCarthy Gary Corrigan
Editorial Director Gareth Hancock	**Series Editors** Dr. Thomas W. Shinder Debra Littlejohn Shinder	**Illustrator** Michael Mueller
Associate Acquisitions Editor Timothy Green	**Technical Editor** Robert Aschermann	**Series Design** Roberta Steele
Editorial Management Syngress Media, Inc.	**Copy Editors** Lynette Crane Beth Roberts	**Cover Design** Greg Scott
Project Editor Patty Mon	**Proofreader** Pat Mannion	
Product Line Manager Mark A. Listewnik		

This book was published with Corel VENTURA™ Publisher.

Global Knowledge and its logo are a registered trademark of Global Knowledge Network, Inc.

Information has been obtained by Osborne/**McGraw-Hill** from sources believed to be reliable. However, because of the possibility of human or mechanical error by our sources, Osborne/**McGraw-Hill**, or others, Osborne/**McGraw-Hill** does not guarantee the accuracy, adequacy, or completeness of any information and is not responsible for any errors or omissions or the results obtained from use of such information.

FOREWORD

From Global Knowledge

At Global Knowledge we strive to support the multiplicity of learning styles required by our students to achieve success as technical professionals. In this series of books, it is our intention to offer the reader a valuable tool for successful completion of the MCSE Windows 2000 Certification exams.

As the world's largest IT training company, Global Knowledge is uniquely positioned to offer these books. The expertise gained each year from providing instructor-led training to hundreds of thousands of students worldwide has been captured in book form to enhance your learning experience. We hope that the quality of these books demonstrates our commitment to your lifelong learning success. Whether you choose to learn through the written word, computer-based training, Web delivery, or instructor-led training, Global Knowledge is committed to providing you the very best in each of those categories. For those of you who know Global Knowledge, or those of you who have just found us for the first time, our goal is to be your lifelong competency partner.

Thank you for the opportunity to serve you. We look forward to serving your needs again in the future.

Warmest regards,

Duncan Anderson
President and Chief Executive Officer, Global Knowledge

The Global Knowledge Advantage

Global Knowledge has a global delivery system for its products and services. The company has 28 subsidiaries, and offers its programs through a total of 60+ locations. No other vendor can provide consistent services across a geographic area this large. Global Knowledge is the largest independent information technology education provider, offering programs on a variety of platforms. This enables our multi-platform and multi-national customers to obtain all of their programs from a single vendor. The company has developed the unique Competus™ Framework software tool and methodology which can quickly reconfigure courseware to the proficiency level of a student on an interactive basis. Combined with self-paced and on-line programs, this technology can reduce the time required for training by prescribing content in only the deficient skills areas. The company has fully automated every aspect of the education process, from registration and follow-up, to "just-in-time" production of courseware. Global Knowledge, through its Enterprise Services Consultancy, can customize programs and products to suit the needs of an individual customer.

Global Knowledge Classroom Education Programs

The backbone of our delivery options is classroom-based education. Our modern, well-equipped facilities staffed with the finest instructors offer programs in a wide variety of information technology topics, many of which lead to professional certifications.

Custom Learning Solutions

This delivery option has been created for companies and governments that value customized learning solutions. For them, our consultancy-based approach of developing targeted education solutions is most effective at helping them meet specific objectives.

Self-Paced and Multimedia Products

This delivery option offers self-paced program titles in interactive CD-ROM, videotape and audio tape programs. In addition, we offer custom development of interactive multimedia courseware to customers and partners. Call us at 1-888-427-4228.

Electronic Delivery of Training

Our network-based training service delivers efficient competency-based, interactive training via the World Wide Web and organizational intranets. This leading-edge delivery option provides a custom learning path and "just-in-time" training for maximum convenience to students.

ARG

American Research Group (ARG), a wholly-owned subsidiary of Global Knowledge, one of the largest worldwide training partners of Cisco Systems, offers a wide range of internetworking, LAN/WAN, Bay Networks, FORE Systems, IBM, and UNIX courses. ARG offers hands on network training in both instructor-led classes and self-paced PC-based training.

Global Knowledge Courses Available

Network Fundamentals
- Understanding Computer Networks
- Telecommunications Fundamentals I
- Telecommunications Fundamentals II
- Understanding Networking Fundamentals
- Implementing Computer Telephony Integration
- Introduction to Voice Over IP
- Introduction to Wide Area Networking
- Cabling Voice and Data Networks
- Introduction to LAN/WAN protocols
- Virtual Private Networks
- ATM Essentials

Network Security & Management
- Troubleshooting TCP/IP Networks
- Network Management
- Network Troubleshooting
- IP Address Management
- Network Security Administration
- Web Security
- Implementing UNIX Security
- Managing Cisco Network Security
- Windows NT 4.0 Security

IT Professional Skills
- Project Management for IT Professionals
- Advanced Project Management for IT Professionals
- Survival Skills for the New IT Manager
- Making IT Teams Work

LAN/WAN Internetworking
- Frame Relay Internetworking
- Implementing T1/T3 Services
- Understanding Digital Subscriber Line (xDSL)
- Internetworking with Routers and Switches
- Advanced Routing and Switching
- Multi-Layer Switching and Wire-Speed Routing
- Internetworking with TCP/IP
- ATM Internetworking
- OSPF Design and Configuration
- Border Gateway Protocol (BGP) Configuration

Authorized Vendor Training

Cisco Systems
- Introduction to Cisco Router Configuration
- Advanced Cisco Router Configuration
- Installation and Maintenance of Cisco Routers
- Cisco Internetwork Troubleshooting
- Cisco Internetwork Design
- Cisco Routers and LAN Switches
- Catalyst 5000 Series Configuration
- Cisco LAN Switch Configuration
- Managing Cisco Switched Internetworks
- Configuring, Monitoring, and Troubleshooting Dial-Up Services
- Cisco AS5200 Installation and Configuration
- Cisco Campus ATM Solutions

Bay Networks
- Bay Networks Accelerated Router Configuration
- Bay Networks Advanced IP Routing
- Bay Networks Hub Connectivity
- Bay Networks Accelar 1xxx Installation and Basic Configuration
- Bay Networks Centillion Switching

FORE Systems
- FORE ATM Enterprise Core Products
- FORE ATM Enterprise Edge Products
- FORE ATM Theory
- FORE LAN Certification

Operating Systems & Programming

Microsoft
- Introduction to Windows NT
- Microsoft Networking Essentials
- Windows NT 4.0 Workstation
- Windows NT 4.0 Server
- Advanced Windows NT 4.0 Server
- Windows NT Networking with TCP/IP
- Introduction to Microsoft Web Tools
- Windows NT Troubleshooting
- Windows Registry Configuration

UNIX
- UNIX Level I
- UNIX Level II
- Essentials of UNIX and NT Integration

Programming
- Introduction to JavaScript
- Java Programming
- PERL Programming
- Advanced PERL with CGI for the Web

Web Site Management & Development
- Building a Web Site
- Web Site Management and Performance
- Web Development Fundamentals

High Speed Networking
- Essentials of Wide Area Networking
- Integrating ISDN
- Fiber Optic Network Design
- Fiber Optic Network Installation
- Migrating to High Performance Ethernet

DIGITAL UNIX
- UNIX Utilities and Commands
- DIGITAL UNIX v4.0 System Administration
- DIGITAL UNIX v4.0 (TCP/IP) Network Management
- AdvFS, LSM, and RAID Configuration and Management
- DIGITAL UNIX TruCluster Software Configuration and Management
- UNIX Shell Programming Featuring Kornshell
- DIGITAL UNIX v4.0 Security Management
- DIGITAL UNIX v4.0 Performance Management
- DIGITAL UNIX v4.0 Intervals Overview

DIGITAL OpenVMS
- OpenVMS Skills for Users
- OpenVMS System and Network Node Management I
- OpenVMS System and Network Node Management II
- OpenVMS System and Network Node Management III
- OpenVMS System and Network Node Operations
- OpenVMS for Programmers
- OpenVMS System Troubleshooting for Systems Managers
- Configuring and Managing Complex VMScluster Systems
- Utilizing OpenVMS Features from C
- OpenVMS Performance Management
- Managing DEC TCP/IP Services for OpenVMS
- Programming in C

Hardware Courses
- AlphaServer 1000/1000A Installation, Configuration and Maintenance
- AlphaServer 2100 Server Maintenance
- AlphaServer 4100, Troubleshooting Techniques and Problem Solving

ABOUT THE CONTRIBUTORS

About Syngress Media

Syngress Media creates books and software for Information Technology professionals seeking skill enhancement and career advancement. Its products are designed to comply with vendor and industry standard course curricula and are optimized for certification exam preparation. You can contact Syngress via the Web at www.syngress.com.

Contributors

Jeffrey W. Bahnsen (MCSE+I, MCT, CTT, CLP, PCLP, CNA, A+) is a Technical Officer for Chase Manhattan Bank, Global Investor Services in Dallas, Texas. In addition, Jeffrey is also a technical trainer, consultant, and a freelance author for his company Bahnsen Technology Services. Prior to working for Chase Manhattan Bank, Jeffrey was employed with Caterpillar, Micron Electronics, and ZEOS Computers.

Jeffrey has six years of experience in designing and implementing Windows NT and 2000 and Lotus Notes/Domino solutions with an enterprise-level scope. Jeffrey enjoys downhill skiing, scuba diving, flying, and spending time with his wife, Janet, and his three children, Erik, Ian, and Lauren. He can be reached at jbahnsen@hotmail.com.

Steve Juntunen is a research analyst for Sosinsky & Associates Inc., an analysis provider for the technology industry. Steve has more than five years' experience as a systems analyst using multiple platforms including Windows, UNIX, and Netware. In addition, he has designed and implemented mobile software applications. Steve lives in Boston.

Chris Rima (M.S., MCSE+I, MCT) is the Technical Programs Administrator for the Southern Arizona Campus of the University of Phoenix, the nation's largest private university. Chris administers a Microsoft Authorized Academic Training Partner (AATP) program and teaches Windows NT, Windows 2000, A+, and Network+ courses. As a member of the University's MCSE steering committee, he develops MCSE teaching materials and provides overall program guidance. Chris is a master-certified instructor for Microsoft's New Employee Support Training (NEST), Windows 95/98, and FrontPage 98 support curriculums. Chris formerly worked at Microsoft and Keane Inc. in Tucson, Arizona, where he started a Microsoft Certified Technical Education Center (CTEC).

Barrie Sosinsky is currently the Research Editor for *Windows 2000 Magazine*, where he served as news editor in 1998–1999. His Industry Trends column appears in the *Windows 2000 Magazine*, and he is a frequent contributor to the *Windows 2000 Magazine* Web site (http://www.win2000mag.com), where a body of his news and analysis may be found. In total, he has written more than 300 magazine articles for a variety of publications on topics as diverse as operating systems, hardware, application software, databases, collaboration and groupware, and the Internet. His consulting company, Sosinsky and Associates (Medfield, Massachusetts), does industry research for companies such as EMC, Data Return, and Anysoft.

Barrie is a longtime book author who has been lead author on more than 25 book titles and a contributor to more than a dozen others. His last book was *Teach Yourself Windows 2000 in 24 Hours* from Sam's Publishing (Macmillan). Other books have included: *The Windows NT 4 Answer Book* (Wiley), *The Warp Book* (Prima), *The BackOffice Bible* (IDG), *Building Visual FoxPro 5 Applications* (IDG), and *The Web Page Recipe Book* (PTR). His company specializes in custom software (database and Web related), training, and technical documentation. He can be contacted at barries@killerapps.com.

Debra Littlejohn Shinder (MCSE, MCP+I, MCT) is an instructor in the AATP program at Eastfield College, Dallas County Community College District, where she has taught since 1992. She is Webmaster for the cities of Seagoville and Sunnyvale, Texas, as well as the family Web site at www.shinder.net. She and her husband, Dr. Thomas W. Shinder, provide consulting and technical support services to Dallas area organizations. She is also the proud mom of a daughter, Kristen, who is currently serving in the U.S. Navy in Italy, and a son, Kris, who is a high school chess champion. Deb has been a writer for most her life and has published numerous articles in both technical and non-technical fields. She can be contacted at deb@shinder.net.

Thomas W. Shinder, M.D. (MCSE, MCP+I, MCT) is a technology trainer and consultant in the Dallas/Ft. Worth metroplex. Dr. Shinder has consulted with major firms, including Xerox, Lucent Technologies, and FINA Oil, assisting in the development and implementation of IP-based communications strategies.

Dr. Shinder attended medical school at the University of Illinois in Chicago and trained in neurology at the Oregon Health Sciences Center in Portland, Oregon. His fascination with interneuronal communication ultimately melded with his interest in internetworking and led him to focus on systems engineering. Tom works with his wife, Deb Shinder, to design elegant and cost-efficient solutions for small and medium-sized businesses based on Windows NT/2000 platforms.

Susan Snedaker (MCSE, MCP, MCT, MBA) has been involved with information systems technology for more than ten years. She is currently President and CEO of Virtual Team (www.vteam.cc), a consulting firm working with high-tech startups. During her career, Susan has worked for both hardware and software vendors. Prior to founding Virtual Team, Susan worked for a software startup firm as Vice President of Client Services. She has also worked for Microsoft, Honeywell, and Keane in key executive and technical roles.

Gene Whitley (MCSE, CNE, CCA) started his IT career in 1992 with Microsoft, earning his MCSE in 1994. He has been the lead consultant on many NT and BackOffice designs for Fortune 500 companies. He is currently a Solutions Consultant, specializing in Windows 2000/Active Directory Design and Implementation for TEKsystems in Charlotte, North Carolina. Gene holds a BSBA in Management Information Systems from The University of North Carolina at Charlotte.

Series Editors

Debra Littlejohn Shinder (MCSE, MCP+I, MCT) is an instructor in the AATP program at Eastfield College, Dallas County Community College District, where she has taught since 1992. She is Webmaster for the cities of Seagoville and Sunnyvale, Texas, as well as the family Web site at www.shinder.net. She and her husband, Dr. Thomas W. Shinder, provide consulting and technical support services to Dallas area organizations. She is also the proud mom of a daughter, Kristen, who is currently serving in the U.S. Navy in Italy, and a son, Kris, who is a high school chess champion. Deb has been a writer for most her life and has published numerous articles in both technical and non-technical fields. She can be contacted at deb@shinder.net.

Thomas W. Shinder, M.D. (MCSE, MCP+I, MCT) is a technology trainer and consultant in the Dallas/Ft. Worth metroplex. Dr. Shinder has consulted with major firms, including Xerox, Lucent Technologies, and FINA Oil, assisting in the development and implementation of IP-based communications strategies. Dr. Shinder attended medical school at the University of Illinois in Chicago, and trained in neurology at the Oregon Health Sciences Center in Portland, Oregon. His fascination with interneuronal communication ultimately melded with his interest in internetworking and led him to focus on systems engineering. Tom works with his wife, Deb Shinder, to design elegant and cost-efficient solutions for small and medium-sized businesses based on Windows NT/2000 platforms.

Technical Editors

Robert Aschermann (MCSE, MCP, MCT, MBA) has been involved with information systems as an IS professional for nearly ten years. During his career he has worked in technical support, systems design, consulting, and training. He has been an MCSE for almost five years now and has passed more than 15 Microsoft certification exams.

Currently Robert works for a large computer manufacturer based in Austin, Texas. His job responsibilities include systems engineering, project management, and business analysis. As a project manager, he has led large Windows 2000, Windows NT, and Windows 95 operating system migrations and many small- to medium-sized client/server development projects.

As a systems engineer and architect, his responsibilities include identifying business processes that need improvement, drafting design specifications for solutions, and building systems that meet those design specifications. He routinely works with Microsoft development tools such as Windows 2000, Microsoft SQL Server 7.0, Access, IIS 4.0, Visual InterDev, Visual Basic, and the Microsoft Solutions Framework.

Stace Cunningham (CMISS, CCNA, MCSE, CLSE, COS/2E, CLSI, COS/2I, CLSA, MCPS, A+) operates SDC Consulting in Biloxi, Mississippi. He has assisted several clients, including a casino, in the development and implementation of its networks, which range in size from 20 nodes to more than 12,000 nodes. Stace has been heavily involved in technology for more than 14 years. During that time he has participated as a Technical Contributor for the IIS 3.0 exam, SMS 1.2 exam, Proxy Server 1.0 exam, Exchange Server 5.0 and 5.5 exams, Proxy Server 2.0 exam, IIS 4.0 exam, IEAK exam, and the revised Windows 95 exam. Stace was an active contributor to The SANS Institute booklet *Windows NT Security Step by Step*.

In addition, he has coauthored 18 books published by Osborne/McGraw-Hill, Microsoft Press, and Syngress Media. He has also served as technical editor for eight books published by Osborne/McGraw-Hill, Microsoft Press, and Syngress Media. Recently, an article written by Stace appeared in *Internet Security Advisor* magazine. His wife, Martha, and daughter Marissa are very supportive of the time he spends with the computers, routers, and firewalls in his "lab." He would not be able to accomplish the goals he has set for himself without their love and support.

ACKNOWLEDGMENTS

We would like to thank the following people:

- Richard Kristof of Global Knowledge for championing the series and providing access to some great people and information.
- All the incredibly hard-working folks at Osborne/McGraw-Hill: Brandon Nordin, Scott Rogers, Gareth Hancock, and Tim Green for their help in launching a great series and being solid team players. In addition, Tara Davis, Jessica Wilson, Patty Mon, and Lisa Theobald for their help in fine-tuning the book.
- Monica Kilwine at Microsoft Corp., for being patient and diligent in answering all our questions.

CONTENTS AT A GLANCE

1	Introduction to Designing Security for a Windows 2000 Network	1
2	Analyzing the Existing and Planned Business Models	49
3	Analyzing Business Requirements	97
4	Analyzing End-User Computing Requirements	135
5	Analyzing Technical Requirements	191
6	Designing a Security Baseline for a Windows 2000 Network	229
7	Analyzing Security Requirements	289
8	Designing a Windows 2000 Security Solution	351
9	Understanding Policies	391
10	Data Security	441
11	Designing a Security Solution for Access Between Networks	527
A	About the CD	601
B	About the Web Site	607
	Glossary	609
	Index	677

CONTENTS

Foreword .... *v*
About the Contributors .... *ix*
Acknowledgments .... *xv*
Preface .... *xxxi*
Introduction .... *xxxvii*

1 Introduction to Designing Security for a Windows 2000 Network 1
    Correlation Between the Windows 2000 and NT 4.0 Exams .. 2
    Purpose of the Design Exams 3
  What is Designing Security for a Windows 2000 Network? 3
    Security Planning Strategies 5
    Security Planning Structure 10
  Overview of Exam 70-220 13
    Analysis Issues 13
    Design Issues 22
  What We'll Cover in This Book 25
    Analyzing Existing and Planned Business Models: Chapter 2 .. 26
    Analyzing Business Requirements: Chapter 3 26
    Analyzing End User Computing Requirements: Chapter 4 26
    Analyzing Technical Requirements: Chapter 5 27
    Designing a Security Baseline: Chapter 6 28
    Analyzing Security Requirements: Chapter 7 28
    Designing a Security Solution: Chapter 8 28
    Understanding Group Policies: Chapter 9 29
    Designing and Implementing Group Policy Strategies:
        Chapter 10 30
    Designing a Security Solution for Access Between Networks:
        Chapter 11 31

What You Should Already Know 32
    Security Terminology 32
    Security Fundamentals 34
    Basic Windows 2000 Networking Concepts 36
    ✓ Two-Minute Drill 38
Q&A Self Test 40
    Self Test Answers 44

2 Analyzing the Existing and Planned Business Models .. 49

Analyze the Company Model and Geographical Scope 51
    Exercise 2-1: Create the Organizational Charts 52
    Regional Model 57
    Exercise 2-2: Install Active Directory for Spring Valley
      Air Cargo 62
    Exercise 2-3: Create an OU in the Active Directory for
      Spring Valley Air Cargo 69
    National Model 70
    International Model 71
    Subsidiary Model 72
    Branch Office Model 73
Analyze Company Processes 74
    Information Flow 75
    Communication Flow 76
    Exercise 2-4: A communication flow example 76
Life Cycles 77
    Service Life Cycle 77
    Product Life Cycle 78
    Decision-Making 80
    ✓ Two-Minute Drill 82
Q&A Self Test 84
    Lab Question 88
    Self Test Answers 89
    Lab Answer 92

3 Analyzing Business Requirements ... 97

Analyze the Existing and Planned Business Models and
   Organizational Structures ... 99
      Geographical Scope ... 99
      Management Model ... 100
      Company Processes ... 101
      Company Organization ... 102
      Vendor Relationships ... 103
      Partner Relationships ... 106
      Customer Relationships ... 107
      Acquisition Plans ... 107
      Eliminating or Integrating Other IT Departments ... 108
      Defining Security Standards ... 109

Analyze Factors That Influence Company Strategies ... 109
      Company Priorities ... 110
      Projected Growth and Growth Strategy ... 110
      Relevant Laws and Regulations ... 110
      Company Tolerance for Risk ... 112
      Total Cost of Operations ... 113
      Exercise 3-1: Building a TCO model for your
         Security Strategy ... 113

Analyze the Structure of IT Management ... 114
      Administration ... 114
      Outsourcing ... 115
      Decision-Making Process ... 116
      Change-Management Process ... 116
      Exercise 3-2: Develop a Decision Tree ... 117
      Security Risks ... 118
  ✓ Two-Minute Drill ... 121
  Q&A Self Test ... 123
      Lab Question ... 127
      Self Test Answers ... 128
      Lab Answer ... 133

4 Analyzing End-User Computing Requirements 135

Analyze Business and Security Requirements for the End User 136
    Business Classes 136
    User Communities 140
    User Location 142
    Exercise 4-1: Dial up permissions 145
    User Applications 149
Analyze the Current Physical Model and Information Security Model .. 152
    Physical Security 153
    Data Protection 160
    Exercise 4-2: Setting Password Policy 162
    Security Risks 171
✓ Two-Minute Drill 177
Q&A Self Test 179
    Lab Question 184
    Self Test Answers 185
    Lab Answer 189

5 Analyzing Technical Requirements 191

Evaluate the Company's Existing and Planned Technical Environment. . 192
    Company Size 193
    User Distribution 194
    Resource Distribution 195
    Assess Available Connectivity Between the Geographic
       Location of Work Sites and Remote Sites 196
    Assess the Net Available Bandwidth 198
    Analyze Performance Requirements 200
    Analyze the Method of Accessing Data and Systems 201
    Analyze Network Roles and Responsibilities 202
    Exercise 5-1: Choosing an Appropriate Level
       of Cryptography 208
Analyze the Impact of the Security Design on the Existing and
    Planned Technical Environment 210
    Assess Existing Systems and Applications 210
    Identify Existing and Planned Upgrades and Rollouts 212

	Analyze Technical Support Structure	212
	Analyze Existing and Planned Network and Systems Management	213
	Exercise 5-2: Developing a Network Plan	213
✓	Two-Minute Drill	216
Q&A	Self Test	218
	Lab Questions	222
	Self Test Answers	223
	Lab Answers	227

6 Designing a Security Baseline for a Windows 2000 Network 229

Domain Controllers 230
    Exercise 6-1: Making a Windows 2000 Server into the First Domain Controller of a New Forest and Domain 231
Operations Masters 240
    Schema Master (One per Forest) 242
    Domain Naming Master (One per Forest) 242
    Relative ID Master (RID) (One per Domain) 244
    Primary Domain Controller (PDC) Emulator (One per Domain) 246
    Infrastructure Master (One per Domain) 248
    Exercise 6-2: Off-loading a PDC Emulator Role to a Domain Controller 250
Servers 252
    Memory 253
    Processor 253
    Disk Subsystem 253
    Network Subsystem 254
    Application Servers 257
    File and Print Servers 258
    RAS Servers 259
Group Policy Scenarios 260
    Installing the Scenarios 261
    Desktop Computers 265

	Laptop Computers	267
	Kiosks	270
	Implementing the Low TCO Desktop Scenario	272
✓	Two-Minute Drill	274
Q&A	Self Test	276
	Lab Question	280
	Self Test Answers	283
	Lab Answer	286

7 Analyzing Security Requirements ... 289

Identify the Required Level of Security for Each Resource ... 290
    Printers ... 291
    Files ... 292
    Shares ... 292
    Internet Access ... 293
    Dial-in Access ... 294
    Exercise 7-1: Evaluating the Security of
    Network Resources ... 295
Active Directory Concepts ... 296
    Directory Service ... 297
    Schema ... 298
    Global Catalog ... 298
    Trust Relationships ... 299
    Namespace ... 300
    Sites ... 301
    Exercise 7-2: Default-First-Site and New Sites ... 302
    Organizational Units ... 305
    Replication ... 305
    Group Policies ... 307
Active Directory Planning Considerations ... 310
    Namespace ... 310
    Sites ... 312
    Exercise 7-3: Site Link and Replication Configuration ... 316
    Organizations Units ... 317
    Group Policies ... 318

Securing the Active Directory 320
    Permissions Inheritance 320
    Exercise 7-4: View the Permissions for an Active
        Directory Object 323
    Object Ownership 326
    Delegating Administrative Control 327
    Exercise 7-5: Using the Delegation of Control Wizard 329
    Customized Administrative Control 333
✓ Two-Minute Drill 335
Q&A Self Test 337
    Lab Question 342
    Self Test Answers 344
    Lab answers 349

8 Designing a Windows 2000 Security Solution 351

Design the Placement and Inheritance of Security Policies 352
    Sites 353
    Domains 353
    Organizational Units 354
Design an Encrypting File System (EFS) Strategy 355
    Exercise 8-1: Encrypting a Folder Using EFS 356
Design an Authentication Strategy 357
    Select Authentication Methods 358
    Design a Security Group Strategy 365
    Exercise 8-2: A Defined Policy Conflict 366
Design a Public Key Infrastructure 369
    Design Certificate Authority (CA) Hierarchies 370
    Identify Certificate Services Roles 370
    Manage Certificates 371
    Exercise 8-3: Using Certificate Authorities and Digital
        Certificates Together in a Transaction 371
    Integrate with Third-Party CAs 373
Design Windows 2000 Network Services Security 374
    DNS Security 374
    RIS Security 375
    SNMP Security 375

	Terminal Services Security	377
	Exercise 8-4: Deciding to Run Terminal Services	377
	✓ Two-Minute Drill	379
	Q&A Self Test	381
	Lab Question	384
	Self Test Answers	386
	Lab Answer	389

9 Understanding Policies 391

Overview of Group Policy and the Microsoft Management Console	392
The Group Policy MMC	392
Group Policy Object	393
Group Policy Container	394
Group Policy Template	395
Exercise 9-1: Deploying the Group Policy Editor Microsoft Management Console Snap-In	396
Applying Group Policy	401
Order in Which Policies Are Applied	401
Configuring Group Policy	405
Scripts	405
Guidelines for Implementing Group Policy	405
Exercise 9-2: Assigning a Script to Run at User Logon	406
Designing an Audit Policy	407
Overview of Windows 2000 Security Auditing	408
Planning your Auditing Strategy	409
Security Templates	412
Configuring Security	414
Exercise 9-3: Creating and Configuring a Security Template	421
Creating and Applying New Security Templates	423
Exercise 9-4: Applying a Custom Template to OU Policy	424
✓ Two-Minute Drill	427
Q&A Self Test	430
Lab Questions	434
Self Test Answers	435
Lab Answers	438

10 Data Security 441
Design a Delegation of Authority Strategy 442
Access Control 443
Design Basics 445
Creating OUs to Delegate Administration 447
Delegation Methodology 450
Delegation Procedures 454
Exercise 10-1: Delegating Administration for an OU 456
Disaster Recovery 463
Fault Tolerant Volumes 465
Backup Utility 469
Emergency Repair 475
Exercise 10-2: Creating a Windows 2000 Emergency
Repair Disk 479
Design an Encrypting File System Strategy 481
EFS Overview 484
Encryption and Decryption 486
Exercise 10-3: Encrypting a Folder on a Local Machine ... 488
Exercise 10-4: Decrypting a Folder on a Local Machine ... 492
Exercise 10-5: Encrypting a Folder on a Remote Server 494
Cipher Command 497
Exercise 10-6: Copying an Encrypted Folder Between
Windows 2000 NTFS Volumes 497
Exercise 10-7: Using the Cipher Command to Encrypt
and Decrypt a Folder 500
EFS Backup and Recovery Operations 501
Exercise 10-8: Backing Up and Restoring an
Encrypted Folder 502
EFS Security Considerations 508
Recommended Best Practices 509
✓ Two-Minute Drill 512
Q&A Self Test 514
Lab Question 519
Self Test Answers 521
Lab Answer 525

11 Designing a Security Solution for Access Between Networks 527

Provide Secure Access to Public Networks from a Private Network 528
    Exercise 11-1: Connecting RRAS to the Internet 529
Provide External Users with Secure Access to Private
    Network Resources 539
        Basic RAS Setup 540
        Basic Setup of VPN 541
        Exercise 11-2: Enabling Remote Access on an Internet
            Connection Server 542
Provide Secure Access Between Private Networks 546
        Within a LAN 547
        Within a WAN 547
        Across a Public Network 547
        Creating an Enterprise Root CA 547
        Exercise 11-3: Creating an Enterprise Root CA 548
Design Windows 2000 Security for Remote Access Users 550
        Managing by User Account 551
        Managing Access by Policy 551
        Exercise 11-4: Managing Access by Policy 551
        Exercise 11-5: Setting up RAS Rights with Policies in a
            Mixed Mode Domain 552
        Authentication Protocols 554
        Inbound Connections 559
        Outbound Connections 562
        Exercise 11-6: Connecting to a VPN 562
        Remote Access Policies 563
Design an SMB Signing Solution 565
    Exercise 11-7: Implementing an SMB Signing Solution ... 566
Design an IPSec Solution 568
        Secure Servers 572
        Lockdown Servers 572
        Testing your IPSec Policy 583
        IPSec Encryption Scheme 585
        IPSec Management Strategy 586

		Negotiation Policies	586
		Security Policies	586
	✓	Two-Minute Drill	589
	Q&A	Self Test	591
		Lab Question	595
		Self Test Answers	596
		Lab Answer	599

A About the CD ... 601

Installing CertTrainer ... 602
    System Requirements ... 602
CertTrainer ... 602
ExamSim ... 603
    Saving Scores as Cookies ... 604
E-Book ... 604
CertCam ... 604
DriveTime ... 605
Help ... 606
Upgrading ... 606

B About the Web Site ... 607

Get *What* You Want *When* You Want It ... 608

Glossary ... 609

Index ... 677

PREFACE

This book's primary objective is to help you prepare for the MCSE Designing Security for a Microsoft Windows 2000 Network exam under the new Windows 2000 certification track. As the Microsoft program transitions from Windows NT 4.0, it will become increasingly important that current and aspiring IT professionals have multiple resources available to assist them in increasing their knowledge and building their skills.

At the time of publication, all the exam objectives have been posted on the Microsoft Web site and the beta exam process has been completed. Microsoft has announced its commitment to measuring real-world skills. This book is designed with that premise in mind; its authors have practical experience in the field, using the Windows 2000 operating systems in hands-on situations and have followed the development of the product since early beta versions.

Because the focus of the exam is on application and understanding, as opposed to memorization of facts, no book by itself can fully prepare you to obtain a passing score. It is essential that you work with the software to enhance your proficiency. Toward that end, this book includes many practical step-by-step exercises in each chapter that are designed to give you hands-on practice as well as guide you in truly learning how to design security for a Microsoft Windows 2000 network, not just learning *about* it.

In This Book

This book is organized in such a way as to serve as an in-depth review for the MCSE Designing Security for a Microsoft Windows 2000 Network exam for both experienced Windows NT professionals and newcomers to Microsoft networking technologies. Each chapter covers a major aspect of the exam, with an emphasis on the "why" as well as the "how to" of working with and supporting Windows 2000 as a network administrator or engineer.

On the CD

The CD-ROM contains the CertTrainer software. CertTrainer comes complete with ExamSim, Skill Assessment tests, CertCam movie clips, the e-book (electronic version of the book), and Drive Time. CertTrainer is easy to install on any Windows 98/NT/2000 computer and must be installed to access these features. You may, however, browse the e-book direct from the CD without installation. For more information on the CD-ROM, please see Appendix A.

In Every Chapter

We've created a set of chapter components that call your attention to important items, reinforce important points, and provide helpful exam-taking hints. Take a look at what you'll find in every chapter:

- Every chapter begins with the **Certification Objectives**—what you need to know in order to pass the section on the exam dealing with the chapter topic. The Objective headings identify the objectives within the chapter, so you'll always know an objective when you see it!

- **Exam Watch** notes call attention to information about, and potential pitfalls in, the exam. These helpful hints are written by authors who have taken the exams and received their certification—who better to tell you what to worry about? They know what you're about to go through!

- **Practice Exercises** are interspersed throughout the chapters. These are step-by-step exercises that allow you to get the hands-on experience you need in order to pass the exams. They help you master skills that are likely to be an area of focus on the exam. Don't just read through the exercises; they are hands-on practice that you should be comfortable completing. Learning by doing is an effective way to increase your competency with a product. The practical exercises will be very helpful for any simulation exercises you may encounter on the MCSE Designing Security for a Microsoft Windows 2000 Network exam.

- The **CertCam** icon that appears in many of the exercises indicates that the exercise is presented in .avi format on the accompanying CD-ROM. These .avi clips walk you step-by-step through various system configurations and are narrated by Thomas W. Shinder, M.D., MCSE.

- **On The Job** notes describe the issues that come up most often in real-world settings. They provide a valuable perspective on certification- and product-related topics. They point out common mistakes and address questions that have arisen from on the job discussions and experience.

- **From The Classroom** sidebars describe the issues that come up most often in the training classroom setting. These sidebars highlight some of the most common and confusing problems that students encounter when taking a live Windows 2000 training course. You can get a leg up on those difficult to understand subjects by focusing extra attention on these sidebars.

- **Scenario and Solution** sections lay out potential problems and solutions in a quick-to-read format:

SCENARIO & SOLUTION

Is Active Directory scalable?	Yes! Unlike the Windows NT security database, which is limited to approximately 40,000 objects, Active Directory supports literally millions of objects.
Is Active Directory compatible with other LDAP directory services?	Yes! Active Directory can share information with other directory services that support LDAP versions 2 and 3, such as Novell's NDS.

- The **Certification Summary** is a succinct review of the chapter and a restatement of salient points regarding the exam.

- The **Two-Minute Drill** at the end of every chapter is a checklist of the main points of the chapter. It can be used for a last-minute review.

- The **Self Test** offers questions similar to those found on the certification exams. The answers to these questions, as well as explanations of the answers, can be found at the end of each chapter. By taking the Self Test after completing each chapter, you'll reinforce what you've learned from that chapter while becoming familiar with the structure of the exam questions.

- The **Lab Question** at the end of the Self Test section offers a unique and challenging question format that requires the reader to understand multiple chapter concepts to answer correctly. These questions are more complex, and more comprehensive than the other questions, as they test your ability to take all the knowledge you have gained from reading the chapter and apply it to complicated, real-world situations. These questions are designed to be more difficult than what you will find on the exam. If you can answer these questions, you have proven that you know the subject!

The Global Knowledge Web Site

Check out the Web site. Global Knowledge invites you to become an active member of the Access Global Web site. This site is an online mall and an information repository that you'll find invaluable. You can access many types of products to assist you in your preparation for the exams, and you'll be able to participate in forums, online discussions, and threaded discussions. No other book brings you unlimited access to such a resource. You'll find more information about this site in Appendix B.

Some Pointers

Once you've finished reading this book, set aside some time to do a thorough review. You might want to return to the book several times and make use of all the methods it offers for reviewing the material:

1. *Re-read all the Two-Minute Drills*, or have someone quiz you. You also can use the drills as a way to do a quick cram before the exam. You might want to make some flash cards out of 3 x 5 index cards that have the Two-Minute Drill material on them.

2. *Re-read all the Exam Watch notes.* Remember that these notes are written by authors who have taken the exam and passed. They know what you should expect—and what you should be on the lookout for.

3. *Review all the Scenario & Solution sections* for quick problem solving.

4. *Re-take the Self Tests.* Taking the tests right after you've read the chapter is a good idea, because the questions help reinforce what you've just learned. However, it's an even better idea to go back later and do all the questions in the book in one sitting. Pretend that you're taking the live exam. (When you go through the questions the first time, you should mark your answers on a separate piece of paper. That way, you can run through the questions as many times as you need to until you feel comfortable with the material.)

5. *Complete the Exercises.* Did you do the exercises when you read through each chapter? If not, do them! These exercises are designed to cover exam topics, and there's no better way to get to know this material than by practicing. Be sure you understand why you are performing each step in each exercise. If there is something you are not clear on, re-read that section in the chapter.

INTRODUCTION

MCSE Certification

This book is designed to help you pass the MCSE Designing Security for a Microsoft Windows 2000 Network exam. At the time this book was written, the exam objectives for the exam were posted on the Microsoft Web site, and the beta exams had been completed. We wrote this book to give you a complete and incisive review of all the important topics that are targeted for the exam. The information contained here will provide you with the required foundation of knowledge that will not only allow you to succeed in passing the MCSE Designing Security for a Microsoft Windows 2000 Network exam, but will also make you a better Microsoft Certified Systems Engineer.

The nature of the Information Technology industry is changing rapidly, and the requirements and specifications for certification can change just as quickly without notice. Microsoft expects you to regularly visit their Web site at **http://www.microsoft.com/mcp/certstep/mcse.htm** to get the most up-to-date information on the entire MCSE program.

	Core Exams	
Candidates Who Have <u>Not</u> Already Passed Windows NT 4.0 Exams All Four of the Following Core Exams Required:	OR	Candidates Who Have Passed 3 Windows NT 4.0 Exams (Exams 70-067, 70-068, and 70-073) Instead of the Four Core Exams on Left, You May Take:
Exam 70-210: Installing, Configuring and Administering Microsoft® Windows® 2000 Professional		**Exam 70-240**: Microsoft® Windows® 2000 Accelerated Exam for MCPs Certified on Microsoft® Windows NT® 4.0. The accelerated exam will be available until December 31, 2001. It covers the core competencies of exams **70-210, 70-215, 70-216,** and **70-217.**

Core Exams
Exam 70-215: Installing, Configuring and Administering Microsoft® Windows® 2000 Server
Exam 70-216: Implementing and Administering a Microsoft® Windows® 2000 Network Infrastructure
Exam 70-217: Implementing and Administering a Microsoft® Windows® 2000 Directory Services Infrastructure
PLUS—All Candidates—*One of the Following Core Exams Required:*
*****Exam 70-219**: Designing a Microsoft® Windows® 2000 Directory Services Infrastructure
*****Exam 70-220**: Designing Security for a Microsoft® Windows® 2000 Network
*****Exam 70-221**: Designing a Microsoft® Windows® 2000 Network Infrastructure
PLUS—All Candidates—*Two Elective Exams Required:*
Any current MCSE electives when the Windows 2000 exams listed above are released in their live versions. **Electives scheduled for retirement will not be considered current.** Selected third-party certifications that focus on interoperability will be accepted as an alternative to one elective exam.
*****Exam 70-219**: Designing a Microsoft® Windows® 2000 Directory Services Infrastructure
*****Exam 70-220**: Designing Security for a Microsoft® Windows® 2000 Network
*****Exam 70-221**: Designing a Microsoft® Windows® 2000 Network Infrastructure
Exam 70-222: Upgrading from Microsoft® Windows® NT 4.0 to Microsoft® Windows® 2000
*Note that some of the Windows 2000 core exams can be used as elective exams as well. An exam that is used to meet the design requirement cannot also count as an elective. Each exam can only be counted once in the Windows 2000 Certification.

Let's look at two scenarios. The first applies to the person who has already taken the Windows NT 4.0 Server (70-067), Windows NT 4.0 Workstation (70-073), and Windows NT 4.0 Server in the Enterprise (70-068) exams. The second scenario covers the situation of the person who has not completed those Windows NT 4.0 exams and would like to concentrate *only* on Windows 2000.

In the first scenario, you have the option of taking all four Windows 2000 core exams, or you can take the Windows 2000 Accelerated Exam for MCPs if you have already passed exams 70-067, 70-068, and 70-073. (Note that you must have passed those specific exams to qualify for the Accelerated Exam; if you have fulfilled your NT 4.0 MCSE requirements by passing the Windows 95 or Windows 98 exam as your client operating system option, and you did not take the NT Workstation Exam, you don't qualify.)

After completing the core requirements, either by passing the four core exams or the one Accelerated exam, you must pass a "design" exam. The design exams include Designing a Microsoft Windows 2000 Directory Services Infrastructure (70-219), Designing Security for Microsoft Windows 2000 Network (70-220), and Designing a Microsoft Windows 2000 Network Infrastructure (70-221). One design exam is *required*.

You also must pass two exams from the list of electives. However, you cannot use the design exam that you took as an elective. Each exam can only count once toward certification. This includes any of the MCSE electives that are current when the Windows 2000 exams are released. In summary, you would take a total of at least two more exams, the upgrade exam and the design exam. Any additional exams would be dependent on which electives the candidate may have already completed.

In the second scenario, if you have not completed, and you do not plan to complete the Core Windows NT 4.0 exams, you must pass the four core Windows 2000 exams, one design exam, and two elective exams. Again, no exam can be counted twice. In this case, you must pass a total of seven exams to obtain the Windows 2000 MCSE certification.

How to Take a Microsoft Certification Exam

If you have taken a Microsoft Certification exam before, we have some good news and some bad news for you. The good news is that the new testing formats will be a true measure of your ability and knowledge. Microsoft has "raised the bar" for its Windows 2000 certification exams. If you are an expert in the Windows 2000 operating system, and can troubleshoot and engineer efficient, cost-effective solutions using Windows 2000, you will have no difficulty with the new exams.

The bad news is that if you have used resources such as "brain-dumps," boot-camps, or exam specific practice tests as your only method of test preparation, you will undoubtedly fail your Windows 2000 exams. The new Windows 2000 MCSE exams will test your knowledge and your ability to apply that knowledge in more sophisticated and accurate ways than was expected for the MCSE exams for Windows NT 4.0.

In the Windows 2000 exams, Microsoft will use a variety of testing formats, which include product simulations, adaptive testing, drag-and-drop matching, and possibly even fill-in-the-blank questions (also called "free response" questions). The test-taking process will measure your fundamental knowledge of the Windows 2000 operating system rather than your ability to memorize a few facts and then answer a few simple multiple-choice questions.

In addition, the "pool" of questions for each exam will significantly increase. The greater number of questions combined with the adaptive testing techniques will enhance the validity and security of the certification process.

We will begin by looking at the purpose, focus, and structure of Microsoft certification tests and examine the effect that these factors have on the kinds of questions you will face on your certification exams. We will define the structure of exam questions and investigate some common formats. Next, we will present a strategy for answering these questions. Finally, we will give some specific guidelines on what you should do on the day of your test.

Why Vendor Certification?

The Microsoft Certified Professional program, like the certification programs from Cisco, Novell, Oracle, and other software vendors, is maintained for the ultimate purpose of increasing the corporation's profits. A successful vendor certification program accomplishes this goal by helping to create a pool of experts in a company's software and by "branding" these experts so companies using the software can identify them.

We know that vendor certification has become increasingly popular in the last few years because it both helps employers find qualified workers and it helps software vendors, like Microsoft, sell their products. But why vendor certification rather than a more traditional approach like a college degree in computer science? A college education is a broadening and enriching experience, but a degree in computer science does not prepare students for most jobs in the IT industry.

A common truism in our business states, "If you are out of the IT industry for three years and want to return, you have to start over." The problem, of course, is *timeliness*; if a first-year student learns about a specific computer program, it probably will no longer be in wide use when he or she graduates. Although some colleges are trying to integrate Microsoft certification into the curriculum, the problem is not really a flaw in higher education, but a characteristic of the IT industry. Computer software is changing so rapidly that a four-year college just can't keep up.

A marked characteristic of the Microsoft certification program is an emphasis on performing specific job tasks rather than merely gathering knowledge. It may come as a shock, but most potential employers do not care how much you know about the theory of operating systems, networking, or database design. As one IT manager said, "I don't really care what my employees know about the theory of our network. We don't need someone to sit at a desk and think about it. We need people who can actually do something to make it work better."

You should not think that this attitude is some kind of anti-intellectual revolt against "book learning." Knowledge is a necessary prerequisite, but it is not enough. More than one company has hired a computer science graduate as a network administrator, only to learn that the new employee has no idea how to add users, assign permissions, or perform the other day-to-day tasks necessary to maintain a network. This brings us to the second major characteristic of Microsoft certification that affects the questions you must be prepared to answer. In addition to timeliness, Microsoft certification is also job-task oriented.

The timeliness of Microsoft's certification program is obvious and is inherent in the fact that you will be tested on current versions of software in wide use today. The job-task orientation of Microsoft certification is almost as obvious, but testing real-world job skills using a computer-based test is not easy.

Computerized Testing

Considering the popularity of Microsoft certification, and the fact that certification candidates are spread around the world, the only practical way to administer tests for the certification program is through Sylvan Prometric or Vue testing centers, which operate internationally. Sylvan Prometric and Vue provide proctor testing services for Microsoft, Oracle, Novell, Lotus, and the A+ computer technician certification. Although the IT industry accounts for much of Sylvan's revenue, the company provides services for a number of other businesses and organizations, such as FAA preflight pilot tests. Historically, several hundred questions were developed for a new Microsoft certification exam. The Windows 2000 MCSE exam pool is expected to contain hundreds of new questions. Microsoft is aware that many new MCSE candidates have been able to access information on test questions via the Internet or other resources. The company is very concerned about maintaining the MCSE as a "premium" certification. The significant increase in the number of test questions, together with stronger enforcement of the NDA (Non-disclosure agreement) will ensure that a higher standard for certification is attained.

Microsoft treats the test-building process very seriously. Test questions are first reviewed by a number of subject matter experts for technical accuracy and then are presented in a beta test. Taking the beta test may require several hours, due to the large number of questions. After a few weeks, Microsoft Certification uses the statistical feedback from Sylvan to check the performance of the beta questions. The beta test group for the Windows 2000 certification series included MCTs, MCSEs, and members of Microsoft's rapid deployment partners groups. Because the exams will be normalized based on this population, you can be sure that the passing scores will be difficult to achieve without detailed product knowledge.

Questions are discarded if most test takers get them right (too easy) or wrong (too difficult), and a number of other statistical measures are taken of each question. Although the scope of our discussion precludes a rigorous treatment of question analysis, you should be aware that Microsoft and other vendors spend a great deal of time and effort making sure their exam questions are valid.

The questions that survive statistical analysis form the pool of questions for the final certification exam.

Test Structure

The questions in a Microsoft form test will not be equally weighted. From what we can tell at the present time, different questions are given a value based on the level of difficulty. You will get more credit for getting a difficult question correct, than if you got an easy one correct. Because the questions are weighted differently, and because the exams will likely use the adapter method of testing, your score will not bear any relationship to how many questions you answered correctly.

Microsoft has implemented *adaptive* testing. When an adaptive test begins, the candidate is first given a level three question. If it is answered correctly, a question from the next higher level is presented, and an incorrect response results in a question from the next lower level. When 15 to 20 questions have been answered in this manner, the scoring algorithm is able to predict, with a high degree of statistical certainty, whether the candidate would pass or fail if all the questions in the form were answered. When the required degree of certainty is attained, the test ends and the candidate receives a pass/fail grade.

Adaptive testing has some definite advantages for everyone involved in the certification process. Adaptive tests allow Sylvan Prometric or Vue to deliver more tests with the same resources, as certification candidates often are in and out in 30 minutes or less. For candidates, the "fatigue factor" is reduced due to the shortened testing time. For Microsoft, adaptive testing means that fewer test questions are exposed to each candidate, and this can enhance the security, and therefore the overall validity, of certification tests.

One possible problem you may have with adaptive testing is that you are not allowed to mark and revisit questions. Since the adaptive algorithm is interactive, and all questions but the first are selected on the basis of your response to the previous question, it is not possible to skip a particular question or change an answer.

Question Types

Computerized test questions can be presented in a number of ways. Some of the possible formats are used on Microsoft certification exam and some are not.

True/False

We are all familiar with True/False questions, but because of the inherent 50 percent chance of guessing the correct answer, you will not see questions of this type on Microsoft certification exams.

Multiple Choice

The majority of Microsoft certification questions are in the multiple-choice format, with either a single correct answer or multiple correct answers. One interesting variation on multiple-choice questions with multiple correct answers is whether or not the candidate is told how many answers are correct.

EXAMPLE:

Which two files can be altered to configure the MS-DOS environment? (Choose two.)

Or

Which files can be altered to configure the MS-DOS environment? (Choose all that apply.)

You may see both variations on Microsoft certification exams, but the trend seems to be toward the first type, where candidates are told explicitly how many answers are correct. Questions of the "choose all that apply" variety are more difficult and can be merely confusing.

Graphical Questions

One or more graphical elements are sometimes used as exhibits to help present or clarify an exam question. These elements may take the form of a network diagram, pictures of networking components, or screen shots from the software on which you are being tested. It is often easier to present the concepts required for a complex performance-based scenario with a graphic than with words.

Test questions known as "hotspots" actually incorporate graphics as part of the answer. These questions ask the certification candidate to click on a location or graphical element to answer the question. For example, you might be shown the diagram of a network and asked to click on an appropriate location for a router. The answer is correct if the candidate clicks within the hotspot that defines the correct location.

Free Response Questions

Another kind of question you sometimes see on Microsoft certification exams requires a free response or type-in answer. An example of this type of question might present a TCP/IP network scenario and ask the candidate to calculate and enter the correct subnet mask in dotted decimal notation.

Simulation Questions

Simulation questions provide a method for Microsoft to test how familiar the test taker is with the actual product interface and the candidate's ability to quickly implement a task using the interface. These questions will present an actual Windows 2000 interface that you must work with to solve a problem or implement a solution. If you are familiar with the product, you will be able to answer these questions quickly, and they will be the easiest questions on the exam. However, if you are not accustomed to working with Windows 2000, these questions will be difficult for you to answer. This is why actual hands-on practice with Windows 2000 is so important!

Knowledge-Based and Performance-Based Questions

Microsoft Certification develops a blueprint for each Microsoft certification exam with input from subject matter experts. This blueprint defines the content areas and objectives for each test, and each test question is created to test a specific objective. The basic information from the examination blueprint can be found on Microsoft's Web site in the Exam Prep Guide for each test.

Psychometricians (psychologists who specialize in designing and analyzing tests) categorize test questions as knowledge-based or performance-based. As the names imply, knowledge-based questions are designed to test knowledge, while performance-based questions are designed to test performance.

Some objectives demand a knowledge-based question. For example, objectives that use verbs like *list* and *identify* tend to test only what you know, not what you can do.

EXAMPLE:

> **Objective:** Identify the MS-DOS configuration files.
>
> Which two files can be altered to configure the MS-DOS environment? (Choose two.)
>
> A. COMMAND.COM
>
> B. AUTOEXEC.BAT
>
> C. IO.SYS
>
> D. CONFIG.SYS
>
> **Correct answers: B, D**

Other objectives use action verbs like *install*, *configure*, and *troubleshoot* to define job tasks. These objectives can often be tested with either a knowledge-based question or a performance-based question.

EXAMPLE:

> **Objective:** Configure an MS-DOS installation appropriately using the PATH statement in AUTOEXEC.BAT.
>
> **Knowledge-based question:**
> What is the correct syntax to set a path to the D: directory in AUTOEXEC.BAT?
>
> A. SET PATH EQUAL TO D:
>
> B. PATH D:
>
> C. SETPATH D:
>
> D. D:EQUALS PATH
>
> **Correct answer: B**

Performance-based question:

Your company uses several DOS accounting applications that access a group of common utility programs. What is the best strategy for configuring the computers in the accounting department so that the accounting applications will always be able to access the utility programs?

A. Store all the utilities on a single floppy disk and make a copy of the disk for each computer in the accounting department.

B. Copy all the utilities to a directory on the C: drive of each computer in the accounting department and add a PATH statement pointing to this directory in the AUTOEXEC.BAT files.

C. Copy all the utilities to all application directories on each computer in the accounting department.

D. Place all the utilities in the C: directory on each computer, because the C: directory is automatically included in the PATH statement when AUTOEXEC.BAT is executed.

Correct answer: B

Even in this simple example, the superiority of the performance-based question is obvious. Whereas the knowledge-based question asks for a single fact, the performance-based question presents a real-life situation and requires that you make a decision based on this scenario. Thus, performance-based questions give more bang (validity) for the test author's buck (individual question).

Testing Job Performance

We have said that Microsoft certification focuses on timeliness and the ability to perform job tasks. We have also introduced the concept of performance-based questions, but even performance-based multiple-choice questions do not really measure performance. Another strategy is needed to test job skills.

Given unlimited resources, it is not difficult to test job skills. In an ideal world, Microsoft would fly MCP candidates to Redmond, place them in a controlled environment with a team of experts, and ask them to plan, install, maintain, and troubleshoot a Windows network. In a few days at most, the experts could reach a valid decision as to whether each candidate should or should not be granted MCDBA or MCSE status. Needless to say, this is not likely to happen.

Closer to reality, another way to test performance is by using the actual software and creating a testing program to present tasks and automatically grade a candidate's performance when the tasks are completed. This *cooperative* approach would be practical in some testing situations, but the same test that is presented to MCP candidates in Boston must also be available in Bahrain and Botswana. The most workable solution for measuring performance in today's testing environment is a *simulation* program. When the program is launched during a test, the candidate sees a simulation of the actual software that looks, and behaves, just like the real thing. When the testing software presents a task, the simulation program is launched and the candidate performs the required task. The testing software then grades the candidate's performance on the required task and moves to the next question. Microsoft has introduced simulation questions on the certification exam for Internet Information Server 4.0. Simulation questions provide many advantages over other testing methodologies, and simulations are expected to become increasingly important in the Microsoft certification program. For example, studies have shown that there is a very high correlation between the ability to perform simulated tasks on a computer-based test and the ability to perform the actual job tasks. Thus, simulations enhance the validity of the certification process.

Another truly wonderful benefit of simulations is in the area of test security. It is just not possible to cheat on a simulation question. In fact, you will be told exactly what tasks you are expected to perform on the test. How can a certification candidate cheat? By learning to perform the tasks? What a concept!

Study Strategies

There are appropriate ways to study for the different types of questions you will see on a Microsoft certification exam.

Knowledge-Based Questions

Knowledge-based questions require that you memorize facts. There are hundreds of facts inherent in every content area of every Microsoft certification exam. There are several keys to memorizing facts:

- **Repetition** The more times your brain is exposed to a fact, the more likely you are to remember it.
- **Association** Connecting facts within a logical framework makes them easier to remember.
- **Motor Association** It is often easier to remember something if you write it down or perform some other physical act, like clicking on a practice test answer.

We have said that the emphasis of Microsoft certification is job performance, and that there are very few knowledge-based questions on Microsoft certification exams. Why should you waste a lot of time learning filenames, IP address formulas, and other minutiae? Read on.

Performance-Based Questions

Most of the questions you will face on a Microsoft certification exam are performance-based scenario questions. We have discussed the superiority of these questions over simple knowledge-based questions, but you should remember that the job-task orientation of Microsoft certification extends the knowledge you need to pass the exams; it does not replace this knowledge. Therefore, the first step in preparing for scenario questions is to absorb as many facts relating to the exam content areas as you can. In other words, go back to the previous section and follow the steps to prepare for an exam composed of knowledge-based questions.

The second step is to familiarize yourself with the format of the questions you are likely to see on the exam. You can do this by answering the questions in this study guide, by using Microsoft assessment tests, or by using practice tests on the included CD-ROM. The day of your test is not the time to be surprised by the construction of Microsoft exam questions.

At best, performance-based scenario questions really do test certification candidates at a higher cognitive level than knowledge-based questions. At worst, these questions can test your reading comprehension and test-taking ability rather than your ability to use Microsoft products. Be sure to get in the habit of reading the question carefully to determine what is being asked.

The third step in preparing for Microsoft scenario questions is to adopt the following attitude: Multiple-choice questions aren't really performance-based. It is all a cruel lie. These scenario questions are just knowledge-based questions with a story wrapped around them.

To answer a scenario question, you have to sift through the story to the underlying facts of the situation and apply your knowledge to determine the correct answer. This may sound silly at first, but the process we go through in solving real-life problems is quite similar. The key concept is that every scenario question (and every real-life problem) has a fact at its center, and if we can identify that fact, we can answer the question.

Simulations

Simulation questions really do measure your ability to perform job tasks. You must be able to perform the specified tasks. There are two ways to prepare for simulation questions:

1. Get experience with the actual software. If you have the resources, this is a great way to prepare for simulation questions.

2. Use the practice test on this book's accompanying CD-ROM; it contains simulation questions similar to those you will find on the Microsoft exam. This approach has the added advantage of grading your efforts. You can find additional practice tests at **www.syngress.com** and **www.osborne.com**.

Signing Up

Signing up to take a Microsoft certification exam is easy. Sylvan Prometric or Vue operators in each country can schedule tests at any testing center. There are, however, a few things you should know:

1. If you call Sylvan Prometric or Vue during a busy time, get a cup of coffee first, because you may be in for a long wait. The exam providers do an excellent job, but everyone in the world seems to want to sign up for a test on Monday morning.

2. You will need your social security number or some other unique identifier to sign up for a test, so have it at hand.

3. Pay for your test by credit card if at all possible. This makes things easier, and you can even schedule tests for the same day you call, if space is available at your local testing center.

4. Know the number and title of the test you want to take before you call. This is not essential, and the Sylvan operators will help you if they can. Having this information in advance, however, speeds up and improves the accuracy of the registration process.

Taking the Test

Teachers have always told you not to try to cram for exams because it does no good. If you are faced with a knowledge-based test requiring only that you regurgitate facts, cramming can mean the difference between passing and failing. This is not the case, however, with Microsoft certification exams. If you don't know it the night before, don't bother to stay up and cram.

Instead, create a schedule and stick to it. Plan your study time carefully, and do not schedule your test until you think you are ready to succeed. Follow these guidelines on the day of your exam:

1. Get a good night's sleep. The scenario questions you will face on a Microsoft certification exam require a clear mind.

2. Remember to take two forms of identification—at least one with a picture. A driver's license with your picture and social security or credit card are acceptable.

3. Leave home in time to arrive at your testing center a few minutes early. It is not a good idea to feel rushed as you begin your exam.

4. Do not spend too much time on any one question. You cannot mark and revisit questions on an adaptive test, so you must do your best on each question as you go.

5. If you do not know the answer to a question, try to eliminate the obviously wrong answers and guess from the rest. If you can eliminate two out of four options, you have a 50 percent chance of guessing the correct answer.

6. For scenario questions, follow the steps we outlined earlier. Read the question carefully and try to identify the facts at the center of the story.

Finally, we would advise anyone attempting to earn Microsoft MCDBA and MCSE certification to adopt a philosophical attitude. The Windows 2000 MCSE will be the most difficult MCSE ever to be offered. The questions will be at a higher cognitive level than seen on all previous MCSE exams. Therefore, even if you are the kind of person who never fails a test, you are likely to fail at least one Windows 2000 certification test somewhere along the way. Do not get discouraged. Microsoft wants to ensure the value of your certification. Moreover, it will attempt to do so by keeping the standard as high as possible. If Microsoft certification were easy to obtain, more people would have it, and it would not be so respected and so valuable to your future in the IT industry.

MCSE
MICROSOFT CERTIFIED SYSTEMS ENGINEER

1

Introduction to Designing Security for a Windows 2000 Network

CERTIFICATION OBJECTIVES

1.01	What is Designing Security for a Windows 2000 Network?
1.02	Overview of Exam 70-220
1.03	What We'll Cover in This Book
1.04	What You Should Already Know
✓	Two-Minute Drill
Q&A	Self Test

Welcome to Windows 2000 and one of Microsoft's most important new elective topics for the Windows 2000 Microsoft Certified Systems Engineer (MCSE) certification track. With almost universal connectivity becoming a reality, and horror stories of hacker invasions making the front page of the newspaper on a regular basis, security is on the minds of everyone involved in computer networking today. Microsoft has recognized and addressed these concerns in designing Windows 2000. Understanding how to create a secure network environment is essential to performing the duties of an administrator in today's business world, and should be mastered by those intending to work as a certified systems engineer in any organization that deals in any way with sensitive or confidential information.

Exam 70-220 is one of the three Design electives, along with Designing a Windows 2000 Network Infrastructure and Designing a Windows 2000 Directory Services Infrastructure. You are required to pass one of the three in order to complete the Windows 2000 certification track. Because there is a growing market for security specialists, the Security Design exam is an excellent choice for enhancing your marketability in the workplace. Others will choose this exam as their Design elective because it is the only one of the three that explores a new topic area not covered in any of the four core exams. (Directory services and network infrastructures are the subject of both an *implementing/administering* core *and* a *designing* elective, whereas this is the only exam that focuses on security issues.)

This exam covers a wide range of security-related topics, encompassing concepts that are part of Active Directory as well as those involved in designing and implementing the network infrastructure. For that reason, we recommend you first study and test on the core topics, prior to tackling this Design exam. This might, at first glance, seem to be a backward approach; after all, you must *design* the security for a network *before* you implement and administer the network. However, Microsoft sees the Design exams as topics requiring a higher level of knowledge and expertise, with the ability to gather the appropriate data, analyze and evaluate requirements and specifications, and conceptualize the "big picture" being the task of a true enterprise architect, a step beyond the duties of the engineer in the field who carries out those plans after they've been formulated.

Correlation Between the Windows 2000 and NT 4.0 Exams

Although it is possible to draw some sort of correlation between the Windows 2000 core exams and their Windows NT 4.0 counterparts (for instance, the Windows 2000 Professional and Windows NT Workstation exams, or the two Server exams, or even the combination of Networking Essentials and TCP/IP compared to the Implementing and Administering a Network Infrastructure exam), it is impossible to map the Windows 2000 Design exams to anything in the Windows NT MCSE certification track.

You can expect the question format to be significantly different from the Windows NT 4.0 exams. The Design exams, especially, are expected to include case study questions that will require the exercise of analytical skills to a degree not found in more traditional question formats.

Purpose of the Design Exams

It has been rumored that the design exams are part of a long-range plan by Microsoft to create an "upper tier" MCSE certification, perhaps conferring the title *enterprise architect*. Whether or not this occurs, it is obvious that the company desires to raise the bar for the Microsoft Certified Systems Engineer certification itself, making it more difficult for the so-called "dumpers and crammers" (those who memorize test questions and answers from "brain dumps" distributed on the Internet or who cram "quick review" books as their primary source of study for the exams) to pass the exams.

CERTIFICATION OBJECTIVE 1.01

What is Designing Security for a Windows 2000 Network?

The American Heritage Dictionary defines *security* as "something that gives or assures safety," and goes on to specify that in the context of computer science, the term means "prevention of unauthorized use of a program or device."

The same source tells us that *design* means "to plan out in systematic, usually graphic form" or, as a verb, "to make or execute plans" and "to have a goal or purpose in mind."

Designing security, then, involves creating and implementing a plan with the goal or purpose of preventing unauthorized use of our network resources—keeping them safe.

Why an entire exam devoted to designing a network security plan? Is security really such a big deal that it warrants its own examination? The answer is obvious to those who have worked in an organization where data that travels across the network is sensitive. Security is important for confidential patient records in medical offices, client documents in law offices, trade secrets in manufacturing companies, secret formulae and code in intellectual property businesses, classified information in governmental agencies, financial data, the list goes on.

With the advent of the Internet as a major means of communication, company networks have been opened up, literally, to the world. Vulnerability to both accidental and malicious access by unauthorized personnel is a real and growing worry for organizations whose business viability, in many cases, depends on networked communications. Taking all that sensitive data offline is not an option, so methods must be devised to protect the integrity and privacy of information stored on networked computers or transmitted over network connections.

Although many of these security concerns and issues are the same ones encountered with Windows NT 4.0 networks, the Windows 2000 operating system family provides many new security functionalities with which you can address them. There are completely new features such as Kerberos, IPSecurity (IPSec), Active Directory object security, and file level encryption with the Encrypting File System (EFS). And vast improvements have been made to many of the security functions that were available in Windows NT, such as NTFS permissions, public key certificates, and virtual private networking. Windows 2000 is changing the world of networking, and the options administrators have for securing their network communications are changing and expanding as well.

To implement an effective security program on an enterprise level network, you must have a thorough understanding of how Windows 2000's security features work. Then you must go a step further. To pass the Security Design exam, you will need to know more than the technical aspects of security mechanisms; you will also need to understand business models and company processes, and how the organization's policies fit into the security plan. You should be able to analyze the existing network structure and identify security requirements, create a security baseline, and develop strategies that will balance the need for protection of sensitive data against the need for fast and easy accessibility.

Specifically, you will be expected to demonstrate the ability to design audit policies, authentication strategies, and plans for delegating administrative authority, applying group policy in the context of securing resources, and coming up with solutions for specific security-related scenarios.

The exam is comprehensive, covering security issues that arise in both local area networking and wide area networking environments, and addressing the special security needs associated with the growing practice of providing secure access to private networks over the very public Internet. Remote access connections are a popular means of keeping "in the loop" when employees are working at home or on the road, and maintaining security over Remote Access Service (RAS) connections will be another area of focus for this exam. Windows 2000 has also made it easy to implement terminal services as an alternative to upgrading old hardware, and the special considerations for securing the connections of terminal clients to the network through the terminal server will also be addressed.

Finally, areas that might not be traditionally thought of as security-related must be factored in. Domain Name System (DNS) security, security issues connected with Remote Installation Service (RIS), and security considerations when using the Simple Network Management Protocol (SNMP) and other monitoring tools must be factored into the design of the overall security plan. This book will cover each of these areas in detail.

Security Planning Strategies

Planning security for an enterprise network is not—or should not be—the sole province of one security expert. In order for the plan to be effective and workable, it must be a team effort, with input from different factions in the organization. A thorough understanding of both the risks and vulnerabilities of the organization and its needs and priorities is essential to developing a security strategy that helps, rather than hinders, the overall operation of the company's network. Rarely does one person, regardless of how intelligent or technically competent he or she may be, have the complete big picture perspective necessary to accomplish this alone.

The security plan and its implications and implementation should be considered from both an administrative and a technical point of view, so it makes sense at the very least to involve representatives from those two areas of the organization in the process.

In most companies, there is a great deal of specialization. Those in management positions are there because of their business administrative skills, and may not be technically savvy or even aware of what is or isn't possible, or the cost and time factors involved in implementing various network security options. Technical personnel tend to be more focused on the *how* rather than the *why*, and may be oblivious to, for instance, the psychological effects that a particular security plan may have on employees (thus impacting overall company productivity).

A good security planning *team* will work together, tossing out ideas, questioning, challenging, and playing devil's advocate, with the knowledge and viewpoint of each member complimenting that of the others. A team that works in this manner is more likely to end up with a security plan that truly meets the company's needs than an outsider called in to set up a turnkey security solution. Even if consultants are hired to do the bulk of the work, company personnel should insist on being involved in the analysis and design phases (and if you are the consultant, you should welcome and emphasize to them the importance of their involvement).

on the job

IT consultants find that clients often demand the impossible—and this is especially true in the area of network security. The ideal network environment is one in which all users who need access to resources can gain that access quickly and easily—and in which no one who shouldn't have access can possibly "get in." As I have explained on many occasions, security and ease of access are, in many ways, at opposite ends of a continuum. Prior to making a career change to network engineering several years ago, the author was a police officer and police academy defensive tactics trainer. Weapon security was an area of major concern. In the wake of numerous incidents in which police officers have had their own guns taken from them, they are always looking for the ultimate security holster that will keep their weapon secure. I continually reminded them that any holster that completely prevented a "bad guy" from removing the gun would also prevent the officer from being able to draw and use the gun when needed. Security, I told them, is always a trade-off, and I now find myself telling clients the same thing about computer and network security. The only way to ensure that unauthorized users absolutely have no chance of accessing data will also prevent authorized users from accessing it too.

Security Planning from the Management Point of View

Company managers who are responsible for the success or failure of the organization must concern themselves with many different factors, some of which are sure to be in conflict. Management ultimately decides on policies that impact the organization's financial well being, its customers' desire to do business with the company (or not), and the job satisfaction of its employees. As if all this weren't enough, managers must be acutely aware of the legal ramifications of their actions, both in terms of criminal law and civil lawsuits.

Although they have the broadest perspective and perhaps the best basis to know what needs to be accomplished in terms of securing the network, they often have no idea how to go about getting to that result.

Managers must juggle risk against cost: both monetary cost and the cost in terms of employee time, company morale, and perhaps internal political considerations.

The People Principle   If it weren't for people, security measures would not be necessary. Unfortunately, no organization operates without people (at least, not yet). The people who work there are an organization's biggest asset, and its greatest liability, or at least its greatest potential liability.

In developing security policies for an organization, managers must consider the people (the *human resources*, in popular terminology, or, to the technical folks, the *users*). How will the security policies and implementation of those policies impact the people who use the network? The users' level of knowledge and capability to function with the new security system in place must be considered. If many of the network's users may be unable to remember complicated security codes and procedures, perhaps smart card access or technologies such as fingerprint recognition would be more viable alternatives.

A somewhat delicate dilemma is how a sudden tightening of security will affect employees' relationship with management. Part of developing the new security plan involves planning how it will be presented within the company. If done properly, employees can be made to understand the benefits of increased security to the organization and even to them personally. If presented poorly, or as often happens, not really *presented* at all but merely handed down as an edict from on high, the policy's changes will be seen as insults to the employees' integrity and evidence that they don't have the trust of management. This is not just a matter of not wanting to hurt feelings; employees who feel unfairly mistrusted are more likely to rebel and attempt to circumvent what they see as unreasonable security measures, thereby creating a security risk that would not have otherwise existed.

Company Priorities   Although most companies (aside from non-profit organizations) are in business to make money, different companies have different priorities and philosophies. One company may wish to present itself to the public as a rock of stability; another may wish to be seen as innovative, risk-taking, on the cutting edge. Likewise, companies have different philosophies when it comes to security issues. Corporation A may put a priority on "team spirit." Internally, the attitude is "we're all just one big happy family and we don't keep secrets from one another." In other organizations, the "sibling rivalry" between departments or project teams may border on paranoia.

Priorities may also be dictated by law, government administrative regulations, or professional oversight associations. For instance, attorneys are prohibited from revealing confidential client information, thus a law firm *must* place a high priority on securing files that contain that information, whether secrecy is in keeping with the firm's personal philosophy or not. This leads us to the next factor.

Legal Considerations   It may not be a bad idea to have a member of the company's legal staff involved in the network security planning process. It is important to be cognizant of local, state, and federal laws that pertain to computer security, including those pertaining to unauthorized access. If yours is an international company, you must also consider those laws regulating exportation of encryption technologies and the applicable laws in the countries in which your company operates.

Growth Strategies   Managers must always be looking ahead, taking the long-term approach. IT professionals are used to constant change and quick obsolescence. They may be less inclined to plan for what may happen years down the road, as they work in a field where it's almost impossible to predict what new hardware and software solutions may be available in the near future.

The company's projections in terms of near- and long-term growth will affect the network and may influence the decisions concerning the best and most cost effective security strategies. Some factors to be taken into account include the nature of the expected growth; different security strategies may be more appropriate, depending on whether all the growth is from within the company or due to a merger or an acquisition.

Special security issues are created when you attempt to combine existing networks into one. It is likely that company policies will not be identical, and even if the basic security levels and access policies *are* the same, the implementation may differ. Additionally, this type of growth is large and sudden, and its impact is thus more apparent than the gradual growth that comes from within. For these reasons, it is important to take extra care in formulating your design plan in this situation.

Bottom Line Factors   Traditionally, of course, management's overriding concern has been the "bottom line" on the Profit and Loss statement. Careful planning will allow the security planning team to assess just what the true impact on the bottom line will be. They must take into account both the potential savings that can be attributed to the security plan as well as the cost of its implementation.

A security plan should be viewed somewhat like an insurance policy; you hope it will never be needed, but when it is, you're very glad you have it.

Security Planning from the Technical Point of View

Technical personnel, such as the network administrators and security specialists, are likely to have a somewhat narrower (but more in depth) point of view than the company's managers. As an IT professional, you may be more interested in the details of implementing a security plan than assessing why one is needed. Most IT workers enjoy implementing new hardware and software just for the fun of it. The technician must take care to keep the company's needs in mind, and remember that the very biggest and best is not always necessary or even desirable for every situation.

Ease of Implementation   Technical professionals will want to consider how easy a particular solution is for the IT staff to implement, and how long it will take to do so. Ease of implementation is especially important when the IT department is working to a tight, usually management-imposed, deadline.

Continued ease of maintenance, administration, and upgrading will also be factors in the decision-making process for those approaching security planning from the technical point of view.

Cost of Implementation   Those in charge of the IT budget will be aware of cost factors and how they impact the total funds allocated to the department. Cost in this case may also refer to the cost in terms of manpower that will be taken away from other IT projects in order to implement and maintain the security plan.

IT Administrative Structure   It will be important to consider the network administrative structure, that is, whether it is centralized in one IT department or whether administrative authority is distributed throughout the organization based on geographic location, department, or other divisions of responsibility. Other considerations include company relationships with partners or subsidiaries, how much work is outsourced, and so forth.

The administrative model will influence how the security programs are implemented and the number of people who must be trained in the new technologies, and thus will impact the total cost of operations.

Performance Factors   Finally, technical personnel would have difficulty, even if they wanted to, disregarding the issue of whether and how much security implementations will decrease network performance. Because the *need for speed* is a major concern in many of today's fast-paced environments (at least in the minds of the network's users), an analysis and cost-benefits comparison in this area is not only irresistible, it's prudent.

Security Planning Structure

The structure and schedule of the security planning team will vary depending on the company and its priorities, workload, and staffing considerations. Each team member should have defined areas of responsibility, and the team should meet on a regular basis during the analysis and design phase.

Each organization will customize the planning process to fit its own needs, but breaking the team's mission into specific phases, and tasks within those phases, will make for a smoother flow and easier transition to the new security model. It is likely that, whether formally defined or not, the planning process will go through the following steps:

- Information gathering and identification of needs and problems.
- Analysis of the existing structures and the administrative and technical requirements.
- Design of the new security solutions.
- Implementation of the plan.
- Assessment and evaluation (and revision, if necessary).

Information Gathering and Identification Phase

The first step in the establishment of any major policy is to gather information and identify the strengths and weaknesses of the current way of doing things and the areas where improvement is needed. This can be done by observing, by interviewing company personnel, by reviewing written records, or more likely by a combination of all three. Some of the information you will want to gather includes:

- What are the security measures currently in place?
- Have there been security breaches, and if so, of what nature (unauthorized access, denial of service attacks, IP spoofing, and so on)?
- What are the particular vulnerabilities of your network?
- What is the sensitivity level of the data stored on and transferred across the network?
- What are the accessibility requirements?

Analysis Phase

During the analysis stage, you put together the information gathered during phase one and draw conclusions based on the totality of the data. In the analysis phase, you determine what the problems are.

Design Phase

The design phase is where you put forth a solution or solutions to the problems identified in phase two. How can you best address the issues within the parameters of your organization's budget, philosophy, and priorities?

There may be more than one possible solution, and you will need to assess the pros and cons of each and decide on a plan of action. It is a good idea to also have in place a contingency plan if Plan A doesn't work.

Implementation Phase

The implementation phase is the phase in which you actually put the plan into action. Implementation may require hiring outside personnel, or you may be able to implement your plan with your current IT staff.

on the job — *Although presented here as one phase in the overall design process, the implementation phase itself may have to be divided into phases, especially if you are making several major changes to strengthen the security on the network. There are many practical reasons for this. The budget may not allow for implementing all of your new security measures at the same time, or the "human factor" may dictate that users will more readily accept the changes if they are introduced gradually instead of in one big lump.*

Assessment and Evaluation Phase

Often forgotten, the last and very important phase is the assessment and evaluation phase. In this phase, you test the security plan you've set in place and determine whether you have accomplished your goals, and whether the cost (both monetary and otherwise) of the higher security level is justified by the benefits to the company.

The evaluation phase may result in the pronouncement that the implementation of your security plan was a rousing success—or it may result in a trip back to the drawing board to revise and fine-tune, or even scrap the original plan and start over.

SCENARIO & SOLUTION

Why should the security plan be developed by a team rather than one individual?	It is highly unlikely that one person will have the broad perspective necessary to consider all aspects of implementing an enterprise-wide security policy. The plan should be approached with consideration for both the business and the technical points of view.
Who should be included as members of the security planning team?	Members of company management, members of IT administration, technicians, and perhaps legal experts and a representative of the end users.
How should the planning team gather information to form the basis of their analysis of the existing network security structure?	By observing, by interviewing network users and technical personnel, and by referring to written documentation.

CERTIFICATION OBJECTIVE 1.02

Overview of Exam 70-220

The Microsoft Windows 2000 exams, more than ever, attempt to measure your ability to perform the job rather than just how well you memorize factoids. This is particularly challenging in the network design area, since the topics are less technical and perhaps a bit more subjective in nature than those covered by the core implementation and administration exams.

You will notice, when you examine Microsoft's stated objectives for this exam, that about half of the objectives use the verb *analyze* and the other half uses the verb *design*. This is a clue that your analytical skills will be very important. This is further supported by the new "case study" question format, demonstrated on Microsoft's Web site. You *must* be able to read through a lot of information quickly, decide what is relevant and what can be discarded, and make decisions based on the information given. The scenario questions in the Windows NT 4.0 exams that asked you to determine whether a solution met required and desired results were Microsoft's earlier attempt to measure these same skills; the tabbed case study format takes this to new heights. You can expect questions of this type on all the Design exams.

exam
Watch

Before taking any of the Windows 2000 exams, and especially the Design electives, be sure you check out the new case study question format. You can download a demo of a case study sample question at http://www.microsoft.com/trainingandservices/default.asp.

Analysis Issues

Your analytical skills will be tested in specific areas. We will discuss each area in this section, and provide a few tips for preparing to answer the exam questions.

Analyzing Business Requirements

The first step in designing your network security plan has little to do with the network itself, and everything to do with the organization as a whole. As a network security designer, you function somewhat like a physician conducting a thorough physical examination. Unlike a doctor whose patient has come in with specific symptoms, you must step back and take a look at your "patient" (the network) as a whole, and assess where security issues might arise. Then you can practice preventative medicine in developing a plan that will head off problems later on.

You will need to analyze the existing model and also take into consideration any planned changes. A *business model* refers to the ways in which a company conducts its business. You will hear talk of the *digital business model* or the *networked business model* or the *e-commerce model*. Analysis of the model includes processes such as how information flows within the company, and the communication methods in place. Are interoffice communiqués disseminated through printed memoranda, e-mail, or accessed on an intranet Web site? Other questions to ask:

- What products or services does the company market?
- What are the life cycles of those products and services (that is, how often is a new version or model introduced)?
- How does the decision-making process work within this organization?

Geographic Model Where are the company's resources located and how are they distributed among the locations? Determine which of the following describes the company's scope of operations (a few years down the road, we may have to add *interplanetary* and *intergalactic*, but these are the current geographic models):

- **Local** The "mom and pop" corner store model, in which all or most business comes from members of the immediate neighborhood or community, or within a city.
- **Regional** The company operates within a confined area comprised of a state or specific region of the country.
- **National** The company does business all over the country, but rarely or never conducts business outside the national boundaries.
- **International** A global enterprise that does business in more than one country and perhaps has offices in different nations as well.

Remember to take into account where branch offices and subsidiaries are located, and the relationships of those offices to each other and to the company headquarters.

Management Model An important facet of the overall business model is the company's management model. How does the "chain of command" work within the company? Is management paternalistic, where control emanates from one person who may see him or herself as a benevolent dictator? Is the management style more team-oriented, where a group of upper level employees run the show (management by committee)?

Does the company's management style fit one of the following two popular management theories?

Theory X Theory X is the so-called traditional model, often used in government agencies, where there is a strict chain of command that employees are expected to follow. Going "over the heads" of superiors is frowned upon, or even formally prohibited, and the structure of the organization is paramilitary in nature. Employees are expected to follow the rules that are handed down from above.

Theory Y Theory Y is the modern management theory that offers a kinder, gentler atmosphere in which employee input in decision-making is encouraged or even required. The company presents itself as one big, happy family where each member is equally valued (although not, of course, equally compensated in monetary terms). Creativity is considered a more valuable asset than going "by the book."

Other Management Models Other management "styles" or models that have been popularized in recent years include Management by Objectives (MBO) and Total Quality Management (TQM). Each of these theories or styles will impact how decisions are made in the organization and how information flows (or doesn't), and thus directly or indirectly influences the process of designing a secure computer network.

Relationships Model Another consideration involved in analyzing the business requirements of your organization hinges on the company's relationships with the *outside world*—business partners, vendors, and customers. This is especially important if the company wishes to make information available to some or all of these through direct access to the company's network.

Factors That Influence Company Strategies Keep in mind that there are always a great many factors that influence company strategies. These must be identified during the information gathering and analysis stages of the planning process. Otherwise the plan you develop, regardless of how technically brilliant it may be, may not meet your organization's needs. Some common factors include:

- Company priorities
- Projected growth and the company's growth strategy
- Relevant laws and regulations
- The company's tolerance for risk
- The total cost of operations

Also, remember that although managers will ultimately make the decisions, much of the success of your security plan will depend on whether it is embraced by the end users, so you must not forget to analyze business and security requirements for the users.

The structure of IT management, in addition to the company's overall management, should be considered as well, especially in terms of the administration. Is administration of the network centralized or decentralized? What is the funding model? How much of the IT work is outsourced to consultants? Also consider the decision-making process and the change-management process as they relate to the company's information systems.

Analyzing the Physical Model

Assess the physical infrastructure of the network, and determine where the security issues exist and what can be done to address them. Your first line of defense against network intrusion is to physically secure your servers, the workstations that have access to those servers, the network media, and the network connectivity devices. The latter two categories are of special interest in a high-sensitivity environment.

Security of Network Media Types and Hardware Devices   Be aware that different media types offer more or less protection against "tapping" in and stealing data. Fiber optic cable is much more secure than copper wire; however, it is possible to insert an *optical splitter* in fiber cable to tap in and eavesdrop on the packets being transmitted.

on the Job *It is sometimes possible to detect that a tap has been made (with either copper or fiber cable) by measuring the strength of the signal. If the signal has been split, this will weaken it, and the change can be detected by using a TDR (Time Domain Reflectometer) or for fiber optic media, an OTDR (Optical TDR). Of course, you must have previously established a baseline measurement against which you can compare the current signal strength.*

Switches are more secure than hubs, because with a hub the communications go out every port, so by tapping into just one length of cable, all messages to all computers connected to the hub could be intercepted. With a switch, messages are sent out only on the port attached to the computer to which the packet is addressed.

Using optical cable and switches will provide a greater level of physical security. Because it is impossible to completely ensure that no one will be able to steal the packets, the next logical step is to create a situation in which even if those packets are intercepted, they can't be read by unauthorized personnel. That's where data encryption comes in. When the intruder attempts to read the message inside the packet, it will be scrambled and unreadable.

Securing the Servers and Central Connection Points It goes without saying that network servers should be in rooms that are locked and accessible only to authorized IT personnel. You should likewise lock the doors to wiring closets, labs, and other locations where hubs or routers are located.

Analyzing the Internal and External Security Risks

Security risks can come from either outside or inside the organization. It is important that you assess the level of risk from each, and prepare a plan that addresses both.

Protecting the Network from Outside Intrusion In planning protection from outsiders, take a tip from firms specializing in home and office protection, and establish several security *rings* or lines of defense, one inside the other. Don't depend on just one security solution to protect highly sensitive or critical data. You might put up an electrified fence to keep intruders off your property, but you would probably not think that because you had the fence, you could leave the front door to the house unlocked. If someone gets past the fence, he still has another barrier preventing access to the house. And within the house, you might establish yet another perimeter in the form of a locked safe where you store your real valuables.

Similarly, you should create several layers of security to protect your network. These could include:

- Locks on doors to server closets, the use of secure media, and other physical security measures.
- Firewalls between the internal network and the public Internetwork.
- Strict access control, including the enforcement of strong password policies, closing of unneeded ports, and limitations on remote access to the network.
- Limited assignment of administrative privileges and delegation of authority.
- File level encryption using Windows 2000's EFS or a third party product.
- Auditing to ensure accountability and detect breaches of security.

Microsoft Proxy Server 2.0 can be used with Windows 2000 to provide some firewall functions, both to protect internal resources and to limit the access of LAN users to the Internet. Proxy uses packet filtering to minimize risks on computers connected to the public network. If the local network is large or there is a great deal of traffic, multiple Proxy servers can be used in chains or arrays to handle the volume.

One popular option for creating a secure perimeter between the internal network and the outside world is to set up an area in the network infrastructure referred to as the demilitarized zone (DMZ), in which you place servers that are accessible from the public network and which do not have access to the internal network resources.

Protecting the Network from Internal Threats Security breaches often originate inside the organization, with persons who have legitimate physical access to the premises. This includes company employees, contract workers, maintenance personnel, and service workers. Internal security breaches may be intentional or accidental; either way, they should be addressed.

Remember that if a person has access to a client computer on the network, it becomes much easier for him to gain access to resources without authorization.

Again, strong password policies, encryption, and judicious assignment of administrative permissions will help protect against security threats that come from the inside, and auditing will help to make you aware of the problem if it does occur.

Another way in which an intruder can intercept packets without having to physically tap into the cable is by using "sniffing" software (many such programs are available as free downloads on the Web). These programs are capable of setting the network adapter to run in "promiscuous" mode, if supported by the network interface card (NIC), so that all packets traversing the network—not just those going to or from the particular machine on which the software is installed—can be captured and analyzed. Again, the key is to provide an "interior perimeter" using encryption technology so that even if an intruder gets this far, the packets that he or she captures will be useless.

Analyzing Technical Requirements

Another area in which you must be able to apply your analytical skills is that of the technical requirements associated with the company's network, and how security measures will impact the technical aspects (performance, stability) of the network infrastructure.

First you should evaluate the company's existing and planned technical environment, taking into account such factors as:

- Company size
- User and resource distribution
- Available connectivity between the geographic location of work sites and remote sites
- Net available bandwidth
- Performance requirements
- Methods in use for accessing data and systems
- Network roles and responsibilities (that is, administrative, user, service, resource ownership, and application)
- Technical support structure
- Existing and planned network and systems management

After you assess the existing systems and applications and identify existing and planned software and hardware upgrades and rollouts, you should attempt to predict the impact of the security design on the existing and planned technical environment.

Analyzing Security Requirements

Now that you have done a thorough analysis of the company's business and technical requirements, you can finally get down to the heart of the matter—analyzing the organization's security requirements.

The first step in this process is to establish a security baseline for your Windows 2000 network. A *baseline* is a reference point, measured before changes are made, that then allows you to compare the effects of the new design to the extant security model. This should include domain controllers, operations masters, application servers, file and print servers, RAS servers, desktop computers, portable computers, and kiosks.

Then, tedious as it may sound, the team should identify the required level of security for each resource. Examples of network resources include printers, scanners, modems, shared files and folders, Internet connections, and dial-in connections.

on the Job

If your network is large or complex, it may require more than one security plan. This is especially true if the network encompasses different geographic locations, or consists of different user groups that need distinctly different security policies.

Determining Types of Security Risks   In analyzing the requirements of your organization, you should determine what types of security risks you want to protect against, and establish priorities. Common types of security risks in a corporate environment include:

- **Identity interception**   In which unauthorized access is gained by using the valid credentials of someone else.
- **Impersonation**   Which is the ability of an unauthorized person to present credentials that appear to be valid (see *replay attack*).
- **Replay attack**   In which the unauthorized user records the exchange of packets between an authorized user and the server, and plays back the records later.

- **Masquerading**   Where an unauthorized user uses the IP address of a trusted system account or device.
- **Data interception**   Which consists of monitoring and capturing data as it is transferred across the network.
- **Manipulation**   Which means unauthorized modification of unencrypted data.
- **Repudiation**   In which the identity of the sender cannot be verified.
- **Denial of service attacks**   In which the server is flooded with numerous requests that use all the bandwidth or resources so that the server cannot communicate.
- **Trojan horse**   Which is a virus or malicious program that is disguised as a harmless program.

SCENARIO & SOLUTION

What is a *social engineering attack*?	This is the term used for breaking into a network by simply "outwitting" employees and convincing them to reveal their passwords. Often the intruder pretends to be with the company's IT department and tells the users that he is verifying their password or that there is a problem with their network account.
What is meant by *malicious code*?	This is a method of attacking a network by embedding ActiveX, VBScript, or a Java applet in a Web page or e-mail message, which when executed will provide the intruder with a way to access information on the network which he or she is not authorized to access.
What are macro viruses?	Macros are small programs that run inside other programs; for example, macros can be written to automate commonly used functions in Microsoft Word and other word processing programs. A macro virus uses this capability to invade a system and cause damage or gain unauthorized access to data.

Design Issues

The second half of the exam objectives address design issues. Specifically, you need to be able to demonstrate the following skills:

- Design a Windows 2000 Security Solution
- Design a Security Solution for Access between Networks (Internetworking)
- Design Security Solutions for Communication Channels (with an emphasis on Server Message Block signing and IPSec)

Let's take a look at each of those in a bit more detail.

Designing a Windows 2000 Security Solution

Auditing, to monitor the results of your security implementations, is an important part of any security policy. You will be expected to design an effective audit policy for an enterprise network.

A new feature in Windows 2000's new Active Directory domain structure is the ability to *delegate administrative authority*. You can assign administrative permissions over objects in an organizational unit (OU) to a user without making him or her an administrator elsewhere in the domain. The exam requires that you be able to design a strategy for delegating administrative authority.

Active Directory's group policy feature is a major player in the Windows 2000 security model. You will need to know how to *design and plan the placement of security policies* for sites, domains and OUs, and how to control (force or block) inheritance of policies by child containers from the parent containers in which they reside.

The *Encrypting File System* (EFS) is another security feature that is new in Windows 2000. You will need to understand how EFS works and how to best plan a strategy for the use of file level encryption in your organization's network communications.

Authentication of a user's or system account's credentials is a key element in securing the network. You will need to be familiar with common authentication methods available in Windows 2000, including:

- Certificate-based authentication
- Kerberos authentication
- Use of clear-text passwords
- Digest authentication

- Smart card authentication
- NTLM (NT LAN Manager) authentication
- Remote Authentication Dial-In User Service (RADIUS)
- Secure Sockets Layer (SSL)

Additionally, you will need to be able to design an authentication strategy for integration with other operating systems and platforms.

Windows 2000 uses *security groups* for more efficient assignment of permissions. Exam 70-220 requires that you be able to design a sound strategy for the use of security groups.

on the Job

The entities called "security groups" in Windows 2000 terminology serve the same function as plain old "groups" in Windows NT. However, Windows 2000 distinguishes between two types of groups: security groups, to which access permissions can be assigned; and distribution groups, which are used for sending messages to multiple users and which do not have a security function. Security groups in Windows 2000 can be one of three types: domain local groups, global groups, and (if the domain is running in native mode) universal groups.

A *public key infrastructure* (PKI) is a system of digital certificates, certificate authorities, and other registration authorities that verify and authenticate the validity of each party involved in an electronic transaction. This is done using *public key cryptography,* in which a public key, published and made widely available, is used to encrypt data and a corresponding private key, kept secret, is used for decryption. This exam requires you to be able to design a public key infrastructure, including the design of certificate authority (CA) hierarchies, identification of certificate server roles, management and mapping of certificates, and integration with third-party certificate authorities.

Windows 2000 is built around its *network services;* after all, networking is what the new operating system was made to do. The sharing of resources on a network, however (and especially implementation of sophisticated services designed to enhance connectivity and access), always presents a security risk. In order to pass Exam 70-220, you will need to understand Windows 2000 networking concepts and have a good grasp of network services, especially the following:

- Domain Name System (DNS) structure and implementation

- Remote Installation Service (RIS)
- Simple Network Management Protocol (SNMP)
- Windows 2000 Terminal services

You will need to demonstrate your ability to provide solutions for securing all of the preceding connection types.

Designing a Security Solution for Access Between Networks

Internetworking refers to connecting two or more networks. This concept is the foundation of the global Internet, as well as private large enterprise networks. With Internet connectivity becoming a necessity rather than a luxury, and most major (and many, many minor) companies "on the net," it is important to know how to secure your internal, private LAN from unauthorized access originating on the public network to which it is connected.

You must be able to provide authorized external (remote) users the ability to establish a secure connection and access the resources of the private network, while preventing other users of the public network from gaining access without authorization. You must be able to connect two private networks in a secure manner that protects the confidentiality of the communications. It is also essential that you be able to provide for secure access within a local network, as well as across a wide area network. Designing a security plan that will give remote users the access they need while protecting the integrity of the network's security can be a special challenge. All of these issues are addressed in the objectives for Exam 70-220.

Designing Security for Communication Channels

Finally, the exam will focus on designing a plan for establishing secure communication channels. The emphasis will be on two areas: SMB signing and IPSec.

SMB is the *Server Message Block protocol,* used in Windows networks for file sharing across the network, and sometimes referred to as the *core protocol.* SMB signing requires that every packet be signed for and verified. This guards against *man-in-the-middle* attacks, where an intruder intercepts packets in transit and changes the security credentials to *administrator,* thereby allowing administrative functions on the server. Designing an SMB signing solution will be a part of the Security Design exam.

on the Job *Since SMB signing requires that every packet in the stream be verified, enabling SMB signing can result in decreased performance on the server. This may be an acceptable tradeoff in an environment where sensitive data is subject to attack, but is a side effect of which you should be aware if your network's functions require optimum performance.*

Internet Protocol Security (IPSec) is a suite of protocols that is designed to allow for secure encrypted communications over a network that is *not* itself secure. IPSec encrypts the data at the network layer, unlike higher-level encryption protocols that require that applications be aware of and support the encryption method. IPSec uses a special algorithm to generate a "shared secret" (that is, the same encryption key at each end of the connection). This means the key itself is never transmitted over the network. IPSec can protect your network against data manipulation, interception, and replay attacks.

For Exam 70-220, you will need to be able to demonstrate your ability to design an IP Security solution, including an IPSec encryption scheme and management strategy. Further, you will need to be able to design negotiation policies. IPSec communications begin security negotiations using a protocol called the Internet Key Exchange (IKE) protocol, and then the two computers involved in the secure connection will exchange authentication information based on the method designated in the security rule. This could be Kerberos, public key certificates, or a pre-shared key value. IKE establishes *security associations* between the computers and generates a shared secret key for each association.

You should know how to plan the implementation of and configure IPSec filters, with which you can specify exactly which types of incoming TCP/IP traffic are processed for each IP interface. Each filter defines a particular subset of inbound or outbound network traffic that should be secured.

CERTIFICATION OBJECTIVE 1.03

What We'll Cover in This Book

Each of the exam objectives discussed in the preceding sections of this chapter will be covered in detail in the chapters of this book.

Analyzing Existing and Planned Business Models: Chapter 2

Chapter 2 will address the analysis of your company's business model, including the analysis of the geographic model (local, regional, national, or international), and the company processes and information flow patterns. This chapter will also deal with communication processes, life cycles of products and services, and the decision-making process.

Analyzing Business Requirements: Chapter 3

In Chapter 3, we will continue the discussion of the analytical skills required for the exam by examining methods for analyzing the company's business requirements. This will include the analysis of existing and planned organizational structures, management models, and company organization. We will explore the implications of the company's relationships with vendors, partners, and customers. In this chapter, we discuss acquisition plans, and how IT departments can be eliminated or integrated in the acquisition process. We will also talk about how to define security standards for the organization.

We will provide information on how you can analyze the many factors that influence company strategies. This includes company priorities, projected growth and the strategies that have been developed for handling that growth, the importance of relevant laws and the rules of regulatory agencies, and the company's tolerance for risk, along with how the total cost of operations is impacted.

Other topics addressed in Chapter 3 include how to analyze the structure of the company's IT management, and understanding different IT administrative models (centralized versus decentralized). We will talk about outsourcing, the decision-making process, and the change management process within the IT structure. Finally, we will wrap up with a discussion of both internal and external security risks.

Analyzing End User Computing Requirements: Chapter 4

In Chapter 4, we take a look at the needs and requirements of the network's users. We will focus on analyzing both the business requirements and the security requirements of end users, and will define classes of users, such as executives, technical personnel, and administrative personnel.

We will discuss how the user's physical location influences his or her needs, and how the requirements of local users differ from those of remote users. We will also talk a little about user applications, the roles they play, and the requirements of common applications.

Next we turn to an examination and analysis of the physical model and the existing information security model. We will discuss physical security, including facilities issues, protection of servers and the data center, and how to secure user workstations. We will also discuss protection of the data on local hard disks and on the servers, as well as the special problem of protecting data created by or accessed by remote users.

> **exam** ⓦatch
>
> *The authentication methods supported by Windows 2000 for remote access include Point to Point Protocol (PPP) challenge/response; Custom Extensible Authentication Protocol (EAP) for stronger authentication using token cards, smart cards, or biometric hardware; and EAP Transport Layer Security (EAP-TLS) based on digital certificates and smart cards.*

Analyzing Technical Requirements: Chapter 5

Our focus changes in Chapter 5, moving away from the business aspects to the technical aspects of providing security for our Windows 2000 network. Here we will discuss how to evaluate a company's existing technical environment, as well as any planned changes to that environment. Some considerations we will address include the size of the company, distribution of its users and resources, and the status of connectivity between onsite and remote locations.

We will explore a topic near and dear to the heart of most network professionals—network bandwidth—and we'll talk about how to assess the available net bandwidth. We will share methods of analyzing performance requirements based on the applications and usage of the network, and we will discuss how to analyze the methods used in the company to access the data and systems.

Then we will address the important topic of network roles and responsibilities, including the administrative role, the role of users, and the issues of network services, resource ownership, and applications.

We will learn to analyze the impact of the security design on the technical environment, both existing and planned.

Designing a Security Baseline: Chapter 6

Chapter 6 will focus on the concept of security baselines and how to establish them. In this chapter, we will establish a framework for understanding the details of establishing and using a baseline. Specifically, we will discuss the baseline as it applies to domain controllers, operations masters, and other Windows 2000 servers, including application servers, file servers, print servers, and remote access servers. We will also look at how the baseline applies to desktop computers (workstations), portable/mobile computers, and special-purpose computers such as kiosks.

Analyzing Security Requirements: Chapter 7

Chapter 7 will introduce you to the process of determining what level of security is required for each resource on the network. We will address the security issues involved in sharing printers, files, and other shares, as well as those involved in sharing Internet or dial-in access connections.

This chapter will cover Active Directory concepts related to security, including the basic operation of the directory services, the roles of the schema and global catalog in a Windows 2000 network, how trust relationships work in a Windows 2000 domain structure, and the security implications of the Active Directory namespace. We will look at Active Directory security boundaries, including sites, domains, and organizational units (OUs). We will talk about directory replication from the security standpoint, and how group policies can be used to secure access to network resources.

We will talk about how to use Active Directory permissions to secure the directory, controlling permissions inheritance, the implications of object ownership, and how administrative control can be delegated and even customized.

Designing a Security Solution: Chapter 8

In Chapter 8 we will address some important security concepts applicable to Windows 2000. Specifically, we'll discuss how the placement of security policies impacts the network, and how policies are inherited, as well as how you can change the default inheritance behaviors.

We will discuss the design of an authentication strategy and how to select from among the authentication methods supported by Windows 2000. The pros and cons and characteristics of each authentication method will be examined. Methods include certificate-based authentication, Kerberos, clear-text password authentication, digest authentication, the use of so-called *smart cards* for authentication, NTLM authentication (as used with older Microsoft operating systems), RADIUS authentication for remote users, and Secure Sockets Layer (SSL) authentication for secure Web transactions. We will talk about how to design an authentication strategy for integration with other operating systems and platforms, and the compatibility issues involved.

> **exam**
> **Watch**
>
> *Smart card authentication is called a "two factor authentication method." This refers to the fact that a user must do two things: present a physical object (the card) and supply a password. The most common example of this type of technology is the ATM card, which you "swipe" through the card reader; you then enter a PIN (personal identification number).*

Next, we will look at how to design a public key infrastructure, including the structuring of Certificate Authority hierarchies. We will identify the roles of certificate servers, and discuss the management and mapping of certificates. We'll also look at how to integrate Windows 2000 certificate services with third-party certificate authorities.

Finally, we will talk about Windows 2000 network services and how they can be secured. This discussion will cover security issues involving DNS, RIS, SNMP, and terminal services.

Understanding Group Policies: Chapter 9

In Chapter 9 we will attempt to give you an overview of how group policies work. This chapter will focus on the technical aspects of group policy, in preparation for the design details in the following chapter.

Chapter 9 will discuss audit policies, the Active Directory structure, and the use of Active Directory permissions for securing object access. The use of organizational units and how user and computer accounts fit into the group policy strategy will also be covered. We will talk about how to design a strategy for using security groups to control access, and this will include discussion of group types and scopes, and how to create and delete groups. We will explore best practices and strategies for implementing security groups based on such factors as the organizational structure, the administrative model, and the application model.

We will talk about security templates and how to use them, the Microsoft Management Console (MMC) group policy snap-in and how it works, the role of local policies, and how to use the Event Log and the Registry in conjunction with group policy implementation. We will discuss how to design a group policy, and how to configure group policy settings. We'll discuss group policy objects, containers, and templates, and we'll explore the rules of group policy inheritance and the processing order of multiple policies. Then we will explore how to apply group policies, including creation of a GPO, managing permissions and inheritance, using the group policy console, and how to use templates and scripts.

Designing and Implementing Group Policy Strategies: Chapter 10

Chapter 10 will build on the technical information in Chapter 9, focusing on strategy. Delegation of administrative authority, ownership and inheritance, access control entries, and assignment of the special NTFS permissions will all be discussed.

Then we will look at an often-overlooked aspect of security planning: disaster recovery. We will look at the options Windows 2000 provides for creating fault tolerant volumes on dynamic disks. We will also discuss how to use the built-in backup utility, and how to create and use an Emergency Repair Disk.

The next section of this chapter deals with the design of a strategy for implementing the Windows 2000 Encrypting File System (EFS) on your network. We will provide an overview of EFS concepts, discuss encryption and decryption methods, and explore the cipher command included in Windows 2000. We will also talk about using the Recovery Agent, which gives administrators the ability to recover encrypted files.

exam
Watch
In order to implement EFS, there must be a public key infrastructure established on the network. At least one administrator must have an EFS data recovery certificate. In order to encrypt a file, the author must have an EFS certificate. Finally, only files and folders located on NTFSv5 drives can be encrypted with EFS. If an EFS encrypted file is moved or copied by the owner to a FAT16 or FAT32 partition, the encryption will be lost.

Designing a Security Solution for Access Between Networks: Chapter 11

The last chapter of this book will cover issues pertaining to securing internetworked connections. We will talk about how to provide secure access to public networks, such as the global Internet, from a private network, such as a company LAN. We will also address ways to provide external users (for example, employees working from a remote location) with secure access to the resources of the private network. Then we will discuss how to establish a secure link between two or more private networks, to allow for secure transfer of traffic between the two.

We will talk about security issues with the local area network and security issues within a wide area network, as well as how to provide for secure private connections across a public network, using virtual private networking with the Point-to-Point Tunneling Protocol (PPTP) or Layer 2 Tunneling Protocol (L2TP) supplied with Windows 2000.

We will learn to design secure connections for remote access users, and we will discuss the protocols used in establishing secure RAS connections and authenticating remote users. This includes both inbound and outbound connections, and addresses both virtual private network (VPN) and dial-in connectivity.

Wrapping up this chapter, and the book, we will discuss SMB signing as a security solution, and we will look at an exciting new protocol suite that provides IP security—IPSec.

SCENARIO & SOLUTION

What protocols does Windows 2000 support for VPN connections?	Point-to-Point Tunneling Protocol (PPTP) and Layer 2 Tunneling Protocol (L2TP)
Which of the tunneling protocols was also supported in Windows NT 4.0?	PPTP
Which of the tunneling protocols works with IPSec to ensure secure end-to-end communications?	L2TP

exam
⊕atch

IPSec policies can be defined separately for each domain or OU on the network. You can also set local IPSec policies for computers that do not have domain IPSec policies assigned to them.

CERTIFICATION OBJECTIVE 1.04

What You Should Already Know

Before you embark on your journey through this book, there are some fundamental terms and concepts with which you should be familiar.

Security Terminology

A good grasp of the terminology associated with computer security issues will be helpful in understanding the concepts and practices discussed in this book. Following are a few of the terms with which you should be familiar before plunging into the technical chapters of this book:

- **Authentication**   The process of validating the identity of a user or a device such as a server or router. There are a number of different methods of authenticating identity, including Kerberos, NTLM, RADIUS, and others.
- **Certificate**   A message that has a digital signature that is associated with the private key of a trusted third party, and confirms that a particular public key belongs to the party (user or device) that claims to own it.
- **Certificate authority**   An entity, such as Verisign, that is entrusted with the authority to sign digital certificates confirming the identity of a user or device.
- **CHAP (Challenge Handshake Authentication Protocol)**   A protocol used for authentication over a Point to Point Protocol (PPP) connection.
- **Cipher**   An algorithm used to encrypt text to make it unreadable to unauthorized persons. The word comes from the Arabic word *sifr*, which means *empty* or *zero*.

- **Cryptography** The study of creating and deciphering encoded or encrypted messages. The word comes the Greek *kryptos,* which means *hidden.*
- **DES (Data Encryption Standard)** A method of cryptography that uses a secret (private) key, originated by IBM and later adopted by the U.S. government.
- **Encryption** Scrambling of information so that it will not be readable until it is *decrypted.*
- **Firewall** Either hardware or software that provides a security boundary or barrier between two networks by filtering incoming and outgoing packets.
- **Hash (hashing algorithm)** A mathematical calculation applied to a string of text, resulting in a string of bits of a fixed size, which cannot be done in reverse to arrive back at the original source data.
- **IPSec (IPSecurity)** A set of protocols used to protect packets produced by the Internet Protocol (IP), which works at the Network layer of the Open Systems Interconnection (OSI) model, thus allowing security to be handled without requiring awareness by user applications.
- **Kerberos** A network authentication protocol that uses a secret (private) key, which was developed by the Massachusetts Institute of Technology (MIT) and is an important component of Windows 2000's new security system.
- **Password** A string of characters (text, numbers, or symbols) that is kept private and used to authenticate a user's identity.
- **PAP (Password Authentication Protocol)** A simple authentication method used over PPP connections, which is less secure than CHAP.
- **Private key** A digital code that can be used to decrypt information, which works in conjunction with a corresponding *public key.*
- **Public key** A digital code used to encrypt information, which is then decrypted by a private key.
- **RADIUS (Remote Authentication Dial-In User Service)** A client/server protocol used for authentication of dial-in clients that allows centralized authentication and control of remote users.

- **Secret key** A digital code or password shared by two parties, used for both encryption and decryption of messages.
- **SSL (Secure Sockets Layer)** A protocol that provides security at the socket level and is used for securing Web access.
- **Smart card** A device similar to a credit card, which contains an embedded chip (also called a *token*) that stores digital certificates and is used for authentication.
- **Trust relationship** A logical relationship established between Windows domains to allow pass-through authentication, in which a trusting domain honors the logon authentications of a trusted domain.

Security Fundamentals

Before you start your study of security design in earnest, you will find the topics covered on this exam much easier to understand if you review some fundamental networking security concepts. These include:

- The elements of a secure networking environment
- Cryptography basics

The Elements of a Secure Networking Environment

Network security consists of both *physical* and *logical* security. That is, in order to secure network communications, physical access to the network computers, cable or other media, and network devices must be controlled. Logical security barriers, such as user authentication methods, encryption, and so on, should also be in place. Another way to think of these two divisions is *hardware security* and *software security*.

Windows 2000 provides for *distributed security*. This means the operating system includes numerous security functions that work together or separately to provide for a secure network environment.

Some basics of secure networking include:

- **Single Sign-on** The ability of users to provide one username and password to access all authorized network resources rather than having to be authenticated separately for multiple servers and applications.

- **Access Control**   The method of protecting resources by assigning or denying permissions.
- **Data Integrity**   Protecting network data against tampering and modification or destruction.
- **Data Confidentiality**   The ability to encrypt data before it is transferred over the network so that it cannot be read by someone eavesdropping or "tapping" the network.
- **Physical Security**   Protection of the network's physical assets (servers, workstations, cable, hubs, and so on) from intruders.
- **User Education**   The best security plan in the world will fail if users are not educated to keep their passwords secret and guard against distribution of confidential information.

Cryptography Basics

Cryptography is the study of writing and reading messages that are encoded to prevent unauthorized users from understanding them. Cryptographic methods use *algorithms,* which are mathematical functions or formulae, along with a value known as a *key*. The key is a string of bits, and the longer the key, the more difficult it will be to break the code by guessing the value.

There are various types of encryption:

- **Secret key encryption (also called symmetric encryption)**   Both parties use the same shared secret key to encrypt and decrypt the data.
- **Public key encryption (also called asymmetric encryption)**   Two different but corresponding keys (called a *key pair*) are used; one—the public key—is used to encrypt the data and is not kept secret but is published to all wishing to send an encrypted message to the owner. The second key—the private key—is known only by the owner and is used to decrypt data that was encrypted with the corresponding public key.
- **Digital signatures**   These are message digests that are hashed and attached to a document, and used to verify the identity of the sender and the fact that the data in the document has not been tampered with.

Basic Windows 2000 Networking Concepts

Be sure, before you attempt to take Exam 70-220, that you also have a good grasp of the following basic Windows 2000 networking concepts:

- Active Directory Security and Administrative Concepts
    - Active Directory Domain Structure
    - Group Policy
- Authentication methods
    - Certificate-based authentication
    - Kerberos authentication
    - NTLM authentication
    - Clear-text password authentication
    - Smart card authentication
    - RADIUS
    - Secure Sockets Layer (SSL)
- Windows 2000 Public Key Infrastructure
- Windows 2000 Network Services
    - Domain Name System (DNS)
    - Remote Installation Service (RIS)
    - Simple Network Management Protocol (SNMP)
    - Windows 2000 Terminal Services
- Windows 2000 Remote Access Service (RAS)

CERTIFICATION SUMMARY

In this chapter, we provided an overview of what is to come as you work your way through the book and prepare yourself for Exam 70-220, Designing Security for a Windows 2000 Network. We've given you some ideas about security planning, both from the manager's and the technical point of view, and discussed the formation and operation of a security planning team. We examined the phases of the typical planning process: information gathering, analysis, design, implementation, and assessment/evaluation.

We went into an overview of the exam itself, based on Microsoft's examination objectives. We talked about how to analyze business requirements, the physical model, and the technical requirements of a particular organization in relation to its network. This led us naturally to the analysis of the security requirements.

We provided a brief synopsis of what will be covered in each chapter of this book, and then added some tips on what you should already know before you tackle the individual content chapters, including security-related terminology, fundamentals of network security and cryptography, and Windows 2000 networking basics.

✓ TWO-MINUTE DRILL

What is Designing Security for a Windows 2000 Network?

- ❑ Designing security involves creating and implementing a plan with the goal or purpose of preventing unauthorized use of network resources.
- ❑ The Windows 2000 operating system family provides many new security functionalities that were not included in Windows NT 4.0, such as Kerberos, IPSec, Active Directory security, and the Encrypting File System (EFS).
- ❑ Planning security for an enterprise network should be a team effort, incorporating personnel who can provide the points of view of both management and IT.
- ❑ The management viewpoint is broader, taking into account the *people principle*, overall company priorities, legal considerations, growth factors, and the ever-popular "bottom line" on the financial statement.
- ❑ The technical point of view is more focused and specialized, but must consider ease of implementation, cost of implementation (both in terms of money and manpower allocation), the IT administrative structure, and performance factors.
- ❑ Security planning can, and usually should, be done in phases: information gathering and identification of needs and problems; analysis of existing structures and the administrative and technical requirements; design of the security solutions; implementation of the plan; and assessment and evaluation of the outcome (including revisions, if necessary).

Overview of Exam 70-220

- ❑ The stated objectives for Exam 70-220 can be divided into two broad categories: those addressing analysis issues, and those addressing design issues.
- ❑ A business model refers to the ways in which a company conducts business, and includes the geographic model, the management model, relationships with other entities, and factors that influence company strategies.

- ❑ Some of the factors that influence strategy include the company's priorities, projected growth and growth strategies, relevant laws and regulations, tolerance for risk, and the total cost of operations.

What We'll Cover in This Book

- ❑ The first line of defense in a security plan involves physically securing the network's computers (both servers and workstations), cable or other media, connectivity devices, and other hardware components.
- ❑ Security threats can be divided into two types: internal and external. Each must be addressed in order to provide for secure communications over the network.
- ❑ Designing a security plan requires the establishment of a security baseline for your network which includes domain controllers, operations masters, application servers, file and print servers, RAS servers, desktop and portable machines, and special purpose computers such as kiosks.
- ❑ Key elements in security design that take advantage of Windows 2000's built-in security features include auditing, delegating of authority, authentication, encryption, security groups, the public key infrastructure, and the network services.

What You Should Already Know

- ❑ Terms with which you should be familiar before reading further in this book include authentication, certificate, certificate authority, CHAP, cipher, cryptography, DES, encryption, firewall, hash algorithm, IPSec, Kerberos, Password, PAP, private key and public key, RADIUS, secret key, SSL, smart card, and trust relationship.
- ❑ Basics of secure networking are: single sign-on (SSO), access control, data integrity, data confidentiality, physical security, and user education.
- ❑ Secret key encryption uses the same shared key for encrypting and decrypting, whereas public key encryption uses key pairs—two different, but related keys—with a public key used to encrypt and a private key used to decrypt.

SELF TEST

The following questions will help you measure your understanding of the material presented in this chapter. Read all of the choices carefully, as there may be more than one correct answer. Choose all correct answers for each question.

What is Designing Security for a Windows 2000 Network?

1. Which of the following are security features incorporated into Windows 2000 that were not part of the Windows NT operating system out-of-the-box? (Choose all that apply.)

    A. NTLM authentication

    B. IPSec

    C. Kerberos authentication

    D. File level permissions

2. Which of the following is true of designing a security plan for an enterprise organization?

    A. One person should do the work of analyzing and designing, in order to maintain consistency.

    B. The duties should be divided between two persons, one who does the analysis tasks and one who does the design tasks.

    C. Both analysis and design should be undertaken as a team effort, with representatives from management, IT, and perhaps the legal department.

    D. The design phase is the last phase in security planning.

3. Which of the following usually is a concern from the *management* point of view in developing a security plan? (Choose all that apply.)

    A. The effect of tightened security on company employees' relationship with management.

    B. The effect of security measures on network bandwidth and throughput.

    C. The monetary cost of implementing security measures.

    D. How security measures fit into the current IT structure.

4. Observing, interviewing company personnel, and consulting written records are key elements of which phase of the security planning process?

A. Information gathering and identification phase
   B. Analysis phase
   C. Design phase
   D. Implementation phase

5. The "way in which a company conducts its business" is the definition of which of the following?
   A. Business cycle
   B. Business model
   C. Security model
   D. Management model

What We'll Cover in This Book

6. The geographic model refers to which of the following? (Choose all that apply.)
   A. How large the company is in terms of number of employees.
   B. Where the company's branch offices and subsidiaries are located.
   C. Whether the company does business on a local, regional, national, or international basis.
   D. How the company's headquarters offices are laid out.

7. Which of the following is defined as the traditional business model, in use in most government agencies, where a strict chain of command is followed and employees are expected to follow rules without question and go "by the book?"
   A. Management by objectives (MBO)
   B. The theory X management model
   C. The theory Y management model
   D. Total Quality Management (TQM)

8. Which of the following is true of fiber optic cabling?
   A. It is less secure than copper cabling.
   B. It is harder to "tap" into than copper, but it is possible to do so.
   C. It is impossible to "tap" into and thus is completely secure.
   D. It offers about the same security as copper cable.

9. Why do switches provide more data security than hubs?
   A. Switches use only optical cable, which is inherently more secure than the copper cable used by hubs.
   B. Switches have fewer ports than hubs, thus less of the total network traffic is exposed.
   C. Switches send messages out only on the ports associated with the destination address, whereas hubs send every message out of every port.
   D. Switches do not provide more data security than hubs.

10. Which of the following is a popular way of securing communication between the internal local network and the connection to the public Internet? (Choose all that apply.)
    A. Set up a proxy server between the LAN and the Internet.
    B. Establish a DMZ (demilitarized zone) in which the servers accessible to the "outside" are placed.
    C. Ensure that every computer on the LAN has its own registered IP address rather than using address translation to connect.
    D. Use commercial firewall software on the server that connects to the Internet.

11. The reference point that includes the company's domain controllers, operations masters, application servers, file and print servers, RAS servers, desktop computers, portable computers, and special purpose computers is called which of the following?
    A. Security model
    B. Security reference
    C. Security design
    D. Security baseline

What You Should Already Know

12. Which of the following is a security risk in which data is monitored and captured, then analyzed, by unauthorized personnel?
    A. Masquerading
    B. Interception
    C. Impersonation
    D. Manipulation

13. Which of the following describes an attack in which the unauthorized user records the exchange of packets between a user and server?

    A. Replay attack
    B. Denial of service attack
    C. Identity attack
    D. Trojan horse attack

14. A system of digital certificates and certificate authorities that verify and authenticate the validity of parties involved in electronic transactions is which of the following?

    A. Domain Name System
    B. Public Key Infrastructure (PKI)
    C. Address Resolution Protocol
    D. IP Security

15. Which of the following is defined as the study of creating and deciphering encoded messages?

    A. Cipher
    B. DES
    C. Cryptography
    D. Hashing

SELF TEST ANSWERS

What is Designing Security for a Windows 2000 Network?

1. ☑ **B and C.** Both IP Security and industry-standard Kerberos authentication are included in Windows 2000, but were not a part of the Windows NT 4.0 operating system.
   ☒ **A** is incorrect because NT LAN Manager (NTLM) authentication is the method used by Windows NT. **D** is incorrect because Windows NT provided for file level assignment of permissions to shares located on NTFS partitions.

2. ☑ **C.** Best practice is to create a security planning team, consisting of members of various departments in the organization who can provide different perspectives.
   ☒ **A** is incorrect because designing a security plan for an enterprise organization should not be the province of only one person. **B** is incorrect because dividing the tasks this way would be inefficient and ineffective because the two parts of the process are dependent upon one another. **D** is incorrect because after the design phase comes the implementation phase, and after that you must assess and evaluate the effectiveness of the plan.

3. ☑ **A and C.** Managers must consider how the tightened security will impact employees psychologically, because this can affect worker productivity and even determine whether the security plan works or becomes something to circumvent. The monetary cost of implementing security measures as it affects the company's bottom line is also a concern of management.
   ☒ **B** is incorrect because bandwidth and throughput are technical issues that are of more concern to IT personnel than to managers. Likewise, **D** is incorrect because the way security measures will fit into the current IT structure is usually more of a concern at the departmental level, rather than from the broader perspective of company management.

4. ☑ **A.** Observing, interviewing, and consulting written records are part of gathering the necessary information on which an analysis can be based.
   ☒ **B, C, and D** are incorrect because although these activities may be performed at any phase in the process, they are less prominent parts of the later phases. The key element of analysis is sorting through all the data gathered; the key element of design is developing a solution based on the analysis; and the key element of implementation is actually putting the plan into practice.

5. ☑ **B.** The business model refers to the overall conduct of business, or the strategy a business has adopted for success; an example would be the e-commerce model in which the business uses the Internet for most or all of its customer transactions.

☒ A is incorrect because a business cycle refers to the seasonal changes in the financial status of the business. C is incorrect because the security model refers to how the business protects its assets, and may impact how it conducts business but is not focused on it. D is incorrect because the management model is only a subset of the overall business model, which refers to the chain-of-command structure within the organization.

What We'll Cover in This Book

6. ☑ **B and C.** The geographic model refers to the scope of the business: local, regional, national, or international, and its branch offices and subsidiaries.
☒ A is incorrect because, although company size and number of employees may increase as the geographic scope broadens, these factors do not determine the geographic model. D is incorrect because the layout of company headquarters would be a facilities design issue, not a part of the overall geographic model.

7. ☑ **B.** The theory X management model is the paramilitary model followed by government agencies and "old fashioned" companies.
☒ A and D are incorrect because MBO and TQM are modern management models designed to address specific issues. C is incorrect because the theory Y model is a more open, team-oriented approach to management in which employee input and challenges are solicited and welcomed.

8. ☑ **B.** Fiber optic cable is more secure than copper cable because it is more difficult to physically "tap" into the line and steal the data; however, it can be done with an optical splitter.
☒ A and D are incorrect, because they contradict the correct answer. C is incorrect because fiber optic does not offer complete security, just more security than traditional copper wire.

9. ☑ **C.** Switches send messages out only on the ports associated with the destination address, whereas hubs send every message out of every port.
☒ A is incorrect because switches can use copper cable. B is incorrect because switches do not have fewer ports, and even if they did, this would provide no data security. D is incorrect because switches are in fact more secure than hubs.

10. ☑ **A, B, and D.** A proxy server provides both address translation and some firewall protection from outside access. Creating a DMZ is a popular way to set up a perimeter barrier between the LAN and the Internet. Commercial firewall software is available that filters incoming and outgoing traffic to provide security for communications between the LAN and the WAN.

☒ C is incorrect because ensuring that each computer has a registered IP address will not increase security and will, in fact, make the LAN computers more vulnerable if some other protective measures are not in place.

11. ☑ **D.** The reference point that includes the company's domain controllers, operations masters, application servers, file and print servers, RAS servers, desktop computers, portable computers, and special purpose computers is called the security baseline.
☒ A is incorrect because the security model refers to the overall security strategy or way of providing security. B is incorrect because *security reference* is not a commonly used term. C is incorrect because security design encompasses all aspects of both physical and logical security issues.

What You Should Already Know

12. ☑ **B.** Data interception refers to monitoring, capturing, and analyzing data without authorization.
☒ A is incorrect because masquerading is the use of the IP address of a trusted system or device to gain access. C is incorrect because impersonation is the presentation by an unauthorized person of credentials that appear to be valid. D is incorrect because manipulation refers to unauthorized modification of data.

13. ☑ **A.** A replay attack consists of recording the exchange of packets between a user and the server, and playing it back later to gain unauthorized access.
☒ B is incorrect because a denial of service attack refers to flooding the server with an overload of requests that use all its resources. C is incorrect because an identity attack, or identity interception, describes using the valid credentials of someone else to gain unauthorized access. D is incorrect because a Trojan horse attack involves sending a malicious program or a virus disguised as a harmless utility.

14. ☑ **B.** PKI is a system of digital certificates and certificate authorities that verify and authenticate the validity of parties involved in electronic transactions.
☒ A is incorrect because the Domain Name System (DNS) is a means of resolving fully qualified domain names to IP addresses. C is incorrect because the Address Resolution Protocol (ARP) is used to match IP addresses with Media Access Control (MAC) addresses. D is incorrect because IPSec is a means of providing secure end-to-end communications over an IP connection using encryption at the network layer.

15. ☑ **C.** Cryptography is the study of creating and deciphering encoded messages.
☒ **A** is incorrect because a cipher is the algorithm used to encrypt text. **B** is incorrect because Data Encryption Standard (DES) is a cryptography method developed by IBM and later adopted by the U.S. government. **D** is incorrect because hashing refers to applying a mathematical computation to a string of text to produce a fixed length result which can be compared to that of the original, and cannot be reverse engineered to determine the original text string.

2
Analyzing the Existing and Planned Business Models

CERTIFICATION OBJECTIVES

2.01	Analyze the Company Model and Geographical Scope
2.02	Analyze Company Processes
2.03	Life Cycles
✓	Two-Minute Drill
Q&A	Self Test

This chapter deals with how to research, analyze, and recommend various strategies for implementing Windows 2000 and Active Directory Service based on a business's company model, its geographical scope, and the interrelations of company processes and procedures as they relate to business requirements for information technology.

One of the most critical processes in designing a secure network is to analyze and understand the organizational structure and locations where business-computing activity takes place. During this discovery process, the information that is compiled should be used to produce various working documents. These documents should include an organizational chart, a network resource diagram that describes the physical sites and their link speeds, and various documents that define the administrative roles and responsibilities.

The organizational chart is a logical description of the structure of a business organized by groups, divisions, and, often, individuals. This structure is depicted in the context of who performs the work, who manages the workers, who manages the managers, and so on. Equally important is how each business unit, division, department, and so on, fits into the "Big Picture" of how the business as a whole operates. The structure of a company can be as simple as a manager and a few employees at a single site, to a multinational corporation with thousands of employees broken down into business units, divisions, and departments. Organizational charts should be used as working documents when implementing security, since they will assist you in designing a domain structure that is secure and compatible with your business processes. It will be your job to translate business requirements for data into file shares with access control lists (ACLs); and employees, departments, divisions, and business units into users, groups, organizational units (OUs), domains, trees, and forests.

The network resource diagrams will show all of the physical sites, the link type and speed between sites, the Local Area Network (LAN) type and speeds at each site, the protocols that are used, the resources located at each site, the number of users at each site, and the total number of users in the company. This document will be useful when planning the Windows 2000 site architecture. This document will be useful for planners to graphically depict where the current resources are deployed: Primary Domain Controllers (PDCs), Backup Domain Controllers (BDCs), file servers, print servers, printers, Domain Name System (DNS), Windows Internet Naming Service (WINS), Dynamic Host Configuration Protocol (DHCP), and so forth. Each resource has an associated amount of network traffic that it uses in normal operation.

In the course of your research, certain documents should be created that formally define the administrative roles and responsibilities of the various support organizations. This will include whether the business will take a centralized approach, a decentralized approach, or a hybrid of the two. A document should exist that defines what groups are responsible for the design and administration of the Active Directory. You should also document which group is responsible for the creation, modification, and deletion of users, groups, and OUs. The document should include what group will handle first-level support calls, a.k.a. the "Help Desk." There should be a document that defines who is responsible for the creation of file shares, applications support, and for the resources at each physical site. In addition, there should be a document that defines the naming standards for all of the directory objects.

CERTIFICATION OBJECTIVE 2.01

Analyze the Company Model and Geographical Scope

The first step you should perform when analyzing the company model and geographic scope is to research your business. Unless you are new to your company, you probably already know or have access to most of the information you will need to securely configure a Windows 2000 environment. It will be your job to identify how Windows 2000 Server's Active Directory can be implemented to complement your business model. It is always good to start with the basic questions about various company processes and procedures at various stages/states: essentially, the Who, What, When, Where, How, and Why of the operation. As Rudyard Kipling wrote, "I keep six honest serving-men (They taught me all I knew); their names are What and Why and When and How and Where and Who."

Questions to ask when researching your company's Access Control policies are

- Who is responsible for data and resources?
- Who is responsible for support and administration?
- What types of data exist, and are they Public Access, Internally Confidential, or Secret?
- What type of access to data and resources should each type or group of users be granted?

52 Chapter 2: Analyzing the Existing and Planned Business Models

EXERCISE 2-1

CertCam 2-1

Create the Organizational Charts

You have been assigned to work on a team that will recommend the security standards that will be used corporatewide in regard to Windows 2000 and Active Directory Services. This task requires you to investigate and document your current environment, research your organization, and obtain the information necessary to create an organizational chart. This is the first task in creating a set of working documents that will assist you when implementing and optimizing your Windows 2000 design.

Questions to ask when researching your company's structure:

- Who are the workers, and how are they logically grouped in the organization?
- What functions do the workers perform?
- Where are the locations at which work is physically performed?
- Are the workers at the location employees, contractors, or business partners?

The information that you will receive will then be used to create an organizational chart as shown here:

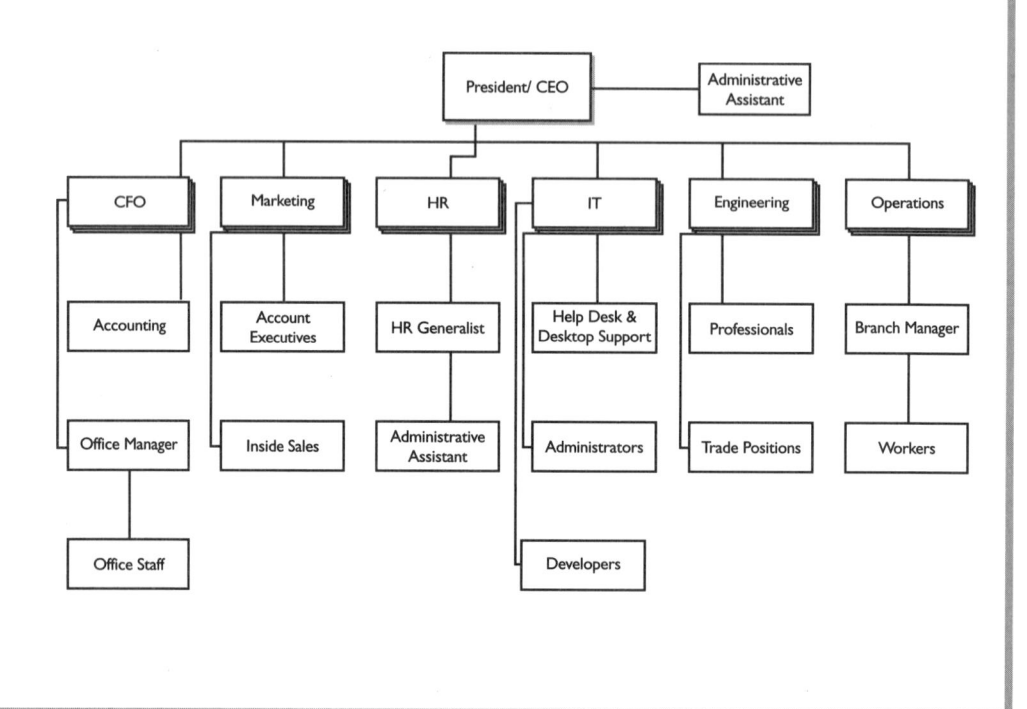

```
                          President/CEO ─── Administrative Assistant
                                │
    ┌──────┬──────────┬─────────┼──────────┬──────────────┐
   CFO   Marketing   HR         IT       Engineering   Operations
    │       │        │          │            │             │
Accounting Account  HR      Help Desk &  Professionals  Branch Manager
          Executives Generalist Desktop Support
    │       │        │          │            │             │
Office    Inside   Administrative Administrators Trade Positions Workers
Manager   Sales    Assistant
    │                          │
Office Staff                Developers
```

The Active Directory's structure should closely resemble the organizational chart. Workers will then be translated into users. Business units, divisions, and departments, if applicable, become OUs, and if required can also become groups for security and delegation of Active Directory authority. When you create an organizational chart that is listed by function, it can be used in the creation of groups and group policies. Also, this will be useful in designing the deployment of resources and related servers to optimize performance. The locations at which work is performed can assist when developing Windows 2000 sites, and in assigning or denying access rights to resources by physical location.

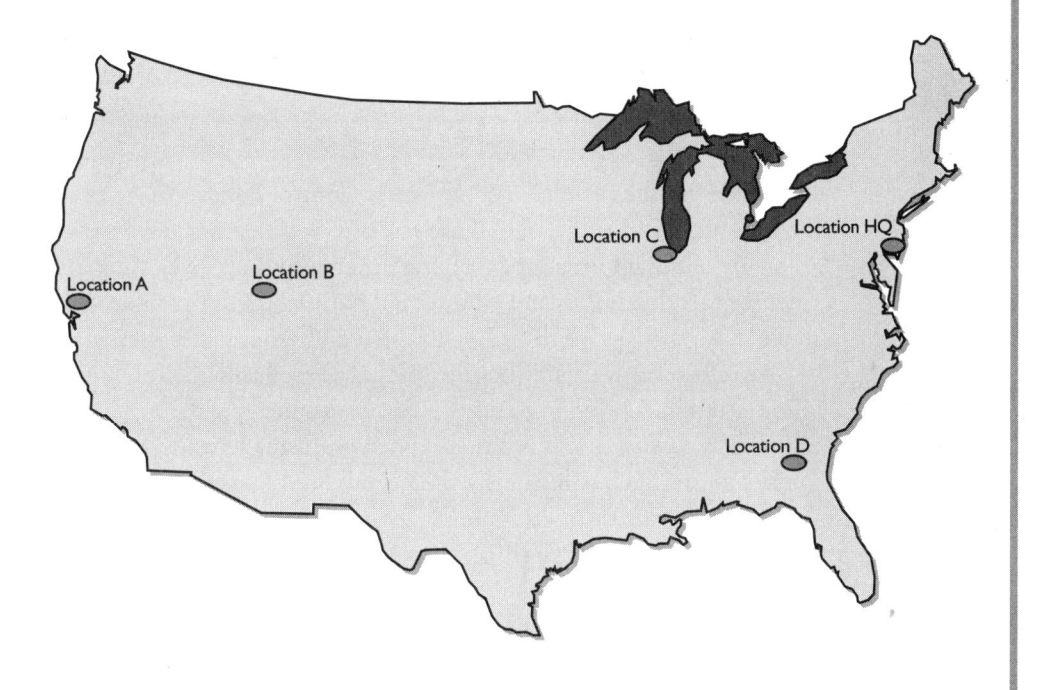

The knowledge of whether a worker is an employee or contractor can allow for the creation of users by type of employee. A related baseline security profile may be more restricted for a contractor than for an employee. A chart of the Active Directory with domain and organizational unit structure is pictured in the following illustration.

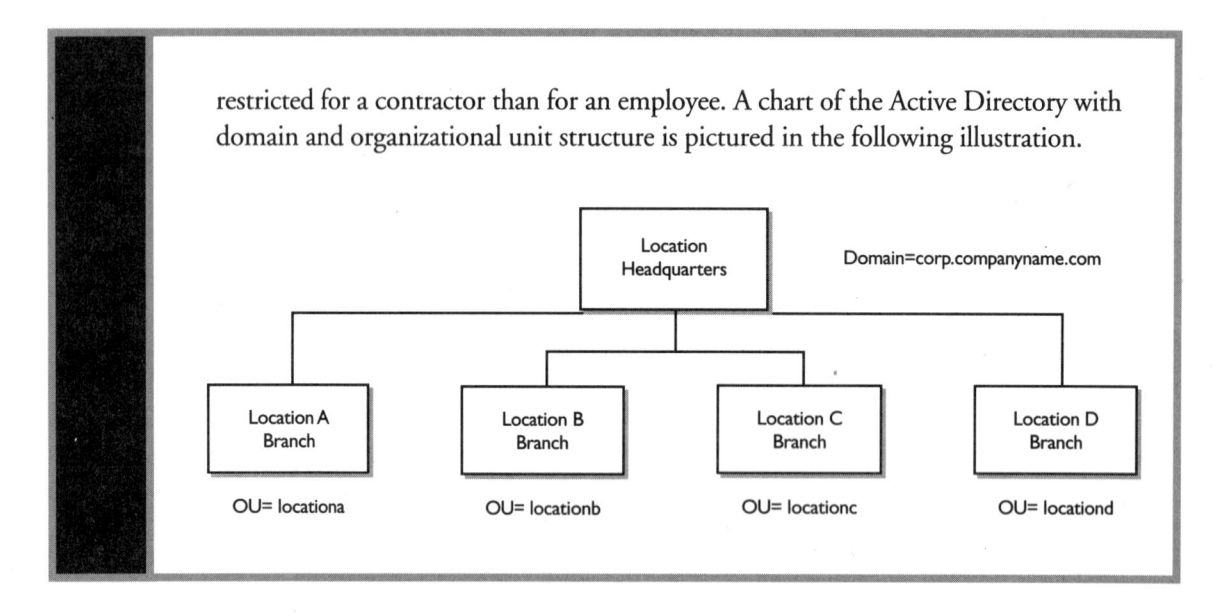

```
                        ┌──────────────┐
                        │   Location   │    Domain=corp.companyname.com
                        │ Headquarters │
                        └──────┬───────┘
           ┌───────────────┬───┴────────────┬───────────────┐
    ┌──────┴─────┐  ┌──────┴─────┐  ┌──────┴─────┐  ┌──────┴─────┐
    │ Location A │  │ Location B │  │ Location C │  │ Location D │
    │   Branch   │  │   Branch   │  │   Branch   │  │   Branch   │
    └────────────┘  └────────────┘  └────────────┘  └────────────┘

    OU= locationa    OU= locationb    OU= locationc    OU= locationd
```

This begins the definition of an Access Control Policy. An Access Control Policy is useful when auditing usage. If the resource is a file share, a person is identified as an owner of the information, and that person can then make a determination as to what the information is, and who should have access to the shared data. This control should always be performed through the use of groups, and normally not by user.

The information determines the roles and responsibilities of Windows 2000 administration. Common items that are determined are the person or group that is called for a password reset, printer-related problem, access to a resource, and so forth. Your research will identify the various levels of security, and can be used in group management.

A common requirement is that access is granted to groups and not individuals. This means a person must be a member of a group to access a particular resource; for example, a user must be a member of the "Secret_HR_Readers" group to access the Human Resources (HR) file share that contains the résumés of prospective clients. This can allow for different groups being assigned different rights, and eases the administrative burden. The access control list can either grant or deny access to a resource based on the following attributes: Full Control, Modify, Read & Execute, Read, Write, or, if applicable, List Folder Contents.

Questions to ask when researching your company's data administrative processes are

- ■ What unique resource naming convention is in place?

- How will the users authenticate?
- When do users access resources: 9 A.M.–5 P.M., anytime, or are there multiple shifts?
- When are production hours, and when is scheduled downtime for maintenance and backup?

A unique naming convention that incorporates things such as the physical location and/or business structure is a good descriptive way to identify a resource when browsing the Active Directory. A unique naming convention for users provides for easily remembered logon names, such as the last name + first initial + middle initial (John Test Doe would be doejt in NT and doejt@company.com in Windows 2000). Windows 2000 allows authentication to take place by user account and password being typed in or the use of smart cards. Currently, Windows 2000 does not support biometrics-based authentication. Knowing when a user's normal shift occurs is useful in defining logon hours in a user profile. Acquiring and documenting the information for scheduled downtime and outages is useful when setting business users' expectations for system availability. It provides a window for the systems to be unavailable to users and not be considered as downtime. Don't be surprised if this time is defined during late nights and weekends.

Questions to ask when researching your company's technology infrastructure are

- What type of PC is currently in service: a workstation, server, or domain controller?
- What types and versions of operating systems exist in your environment?
- What type of hardware will be used: PCs, servers, network printers, scanners, etc?
- What protocols will your network use?
- What additional TCP/IP services are implemented: DHCP, WINS, DNS, and Dynamic-DNS?

Once the type of machine is identified, the appropriate Windows 2000 template can be applied. Windows 2000 comes with the following predefined templates for four security levels: basic, compatible, secure, and highly secure. Identifying other operating systems allows for planning migration strategies if Microsoft based, and if not, then for the installation of optional services such as for Macs and UNIX platforms. The knowledge of the number of devices and their type can help an administrator plan the site topology. This is useful when optimizing the placement of Windows 2000 for file and print services, DHCP, DNS, and the placement of domain controllers (DCs). The type of protocols in use will definitely include TCP/IP, but possibly others such as IPX/SPX, Data Link Control (DLC), System Network Architecture (SNA), and AppleTalk. This will allow Windows 2000 to interact with other platforms in a mixed environment. Since most platforms support TCP/IP, knowledge of the additional TCP/IP services and how they have been deployed will allow an administrator to plan the type and location of servers in the environment, identify if static or dynamic assignment of IP addresses should occur, and what means of resolving host names to IP addresses or, if necessary, NetBIOS names to IP addresses.

Here are some questions to ask when researching your company's network topology:

- Where are various server resources located, and what are the link speeds of the infrastructure that connects internal servers and workstations?
- Is there a need for external business connectivity, and if so, is this connectivity public such as the Internet, or private such as a dedicated connection?
- Is the data that is transmitted publicly over the Internet sensitive?
- Are users in a single location, located in offices across the United States, in different time zones, or are they working around the globe 24 hours a day?

This can help in the creation of business location diagrams, which will normally mirror the network infrastructure diagram. This is useful for determining the Windows 2000 sites and optimizing the various Windows 2000 services, such as domain controllers for login, DHCP for IP address assignment, and DNS for name resolutions. Understanding the requirements of a business for remote access will allow an administrator to determine the need for a Remote Access Service (RAS) server and possibly a virtual private network (VPN) connection. The requirements will allow you to justify the implementation of either Point-to-Point Tunneling Protocol (PPTP) or Layer 2 Tunneling Protocol (L2TP) over IPSec for the creation of a VPN.

These are the first of many questions that you should ask yourself. The answers will provide you with requirements that will enable you to effectively implement Windows 2000 Server and the Active Directory Service (ADS). You will next see how various business models could produce different requirements. These requirements will be the driving force for deciding how to structure ADS for your company. Should you decide on a domain tree and a hierarchy of multiple domains and OUs, a single domain with separate OUs, or no domain at all?

Windows NT Server 4.0 Directory Service can manage approximately 30,000 users in a single master domain, and each resource domain is used to delegate local resources and the associated administrative duties as displayed in Figure 2-1. If a company has more than 30,000 employees, a multiple master domain with trust relationships has to be created and maintained.

FIGURE 2-1

Master and resource domain diagram

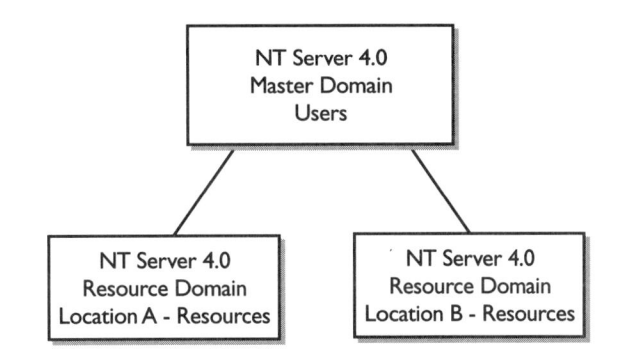

```
              NT Server 4.0
              Master Domain
                  Users
              /            \
   NT Server 4.0          NT Server 4.0
   Resource Domain        Resource Domain
   Location A - Resources Location B - Resources
```

Often times, a business is required to implement many domains and a complex assortment of associated trusts. The single master domain model is often used by both regional and national businesses. This implementation model uses a master domain for centralized control of users, and resource domains for decentralized control of resources. The Active Directory Service in Windows 2000 Server is no longer limited to approximately 30,000 users. ADS can scale up to millions of users in a single domain. ADS also introduces a new design object—organizational units—which are simply logical containers that organize domain resources. ADS uses OUs to delegate administrative control and the rights to the various objects within the domain. The design of multiple domains because of size restrictions or for delegation of administrative duties is no longer necessary with the introduction of Windows 2000 Active Directory Services.

exam
Watch

You will need to know that the core unit of logical structure in the Active Directory is the domain. The Active Directory Domain is a unit of partitioning in that it groups objects under a single name. The Active Directory Domain is also a security boundary in that security policies and ACLs do not cross between domains. It is also an administrative boundary in that the administrator of a domain has rights to set policies only in that domain.

Regional Model

A company is operating with a regional business model if it has operations that are located in multiple parts of a state or a country. These sections will serve as a case study regarding a fictional company that is regionally based.

The fictional company is known as Spring Valley Air Cargo. The core business of the company is the transportation of freight by airplane and the short-term storage of this freight prior to pick-up by truck. Spring Valley Air Cargo, SVAC, has its headquarters, maintenance facility, and main warehouse in Dallas, Texas. The company has branch offices with warehouses and receiving/shipping docks that are located at airports in Austin, Houston, and San Antonio. SVAC only has a receiving/shipping dock and branch office in Oklahoma City, Oklahoma. SVAC employs 71 people in Texas and 15 people in Oklahoma. The company contracts temporary workers from an employment agency for dockworkers. The number of dockworkers varies monthly, based on the time of year and market conditions regarding the volume of goods that are shipped. SVAC works in partnership with multiple truck lines at each location to coordinate the final delivery of freight by truck to its destination.

SVAC uses a custom MS SQL Server database to track its packages. SVAC has a registered Internet domain name of springvalleyaircargo.com. It uses Internet Information Service IIS for its internal and external Web server and Exchange Server for both internal and external e-mail. The IIS server has Web pages that are designed to allow the public to query information in real time from the SQL server regarding the status of where packages are and the expected time of arrival. This Web site is used primarily by the end customers. The SVAC Web site also has features that allow external authenticated users to update the status of freight being delivered, and view more detailed and confidential information than what is available to the public. This type of internally confidential information is available to the dockworkers and all internal employees. There is information that is available only to the office workers, such as accounts payable and receivables, sales contacts, freight schedules, and airplane maintenance records. There is also information that is secret, and its access is limited to those with a need to know: for example, HR information, business contracts, and so forth.

The office employees work a single shift from 8 A.M. to 6 P.M. The pilots, mechanics, warehouse personnel, and dockworkers perform their tasks during one of three shifts, 24 hours a day. The salespeople's work hours are dynamic, since they are home based and have territories in the states of Texas and Oklahoma. They remotely access the network by modem at varying times of the day. SVAC headquarters and branch offices have a five-day business week, and do not operate on Saturday or Sunday. The weekend is used by the IT staff as the time for performing scheduled maintenance to the IT infrastructure. The archiving of data to a tape backup begins at midnight and ends a few hours later.

The headquarters of SVAC has a LAN/WAN infrastructure as follows: The SVAC has a T1 connection to the Internet, and T1 lines connecting Dallas to Austin, Houston, and San Antonio. The Dallas HQ has a 56K Frame Relay connection with Oklahoma City. This is depicted in Figure 2-2.

Every desktop PC has Windows 2000 Professional. The HQ and each branch office have 10/100 switches for its LAN, and every PC has a 10/100MB NIC. The Dallas Headquarters has six network-enabled laser printers. Each branch office has

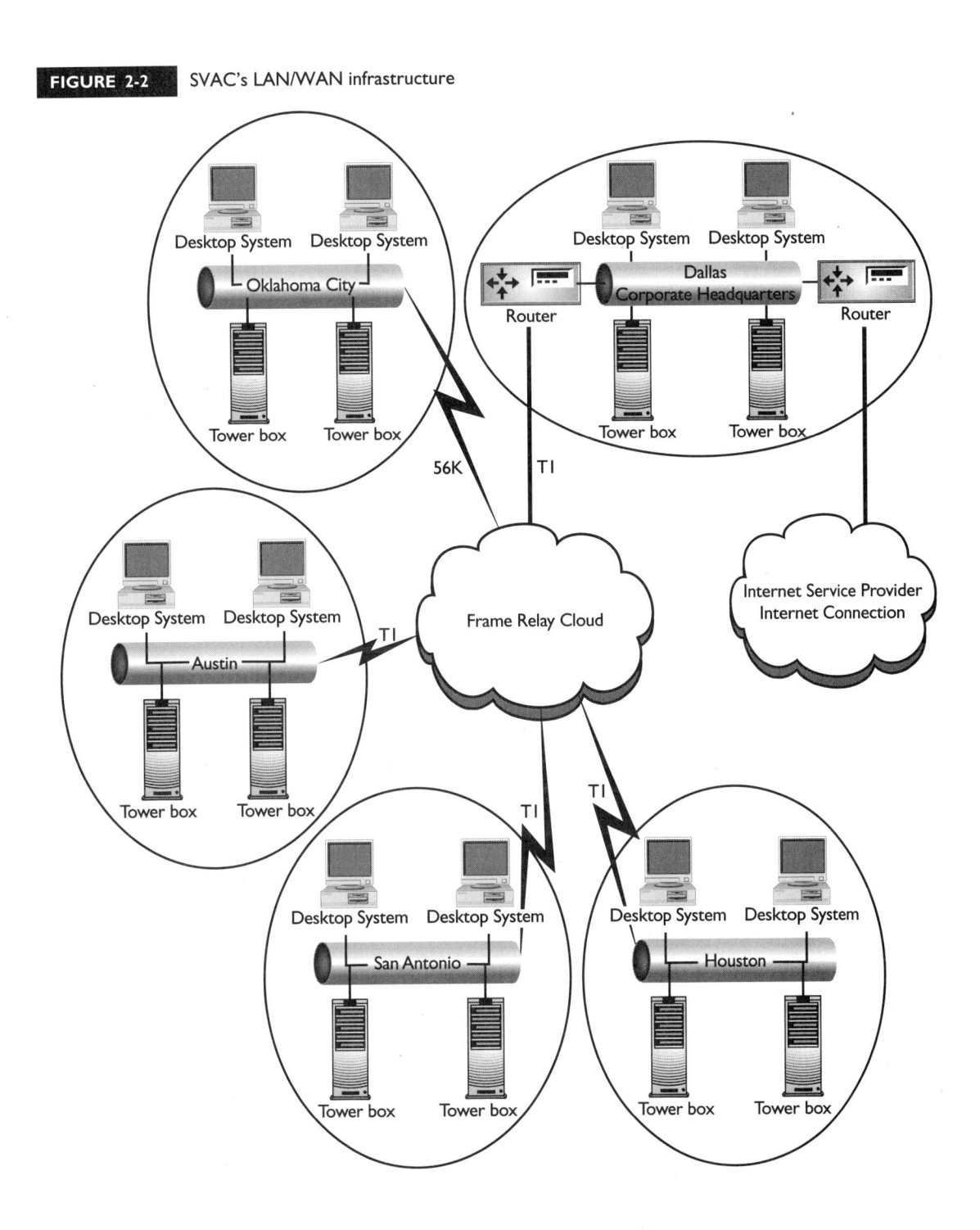

Analyze the Company Model and Geographical Scope

FIGURE 2-2   SVAC's LAN/WAN infrastructure

two laser printers: one in the office and one on the dock. The laptops are the only PCs that have modems, except for a single RAS server that is located in Dallas. The Texas branches came into existence through planned business expansion. The Texas and Oklahoma branches were each assigned an OU so that each site had control over its resources through delegation from within the ADS. The entire environment only uses the TCP/IP protocol. The headquarters in Dallas has five Windows 2000 servers, two domain controllers, a member server with DHCP, WINS, and DNS installed, a member server for IIS, and a member server for SQL Server. Each remote branch office has a single 2000 server set up for file and print sharing, except for Oklahoma City, which has two servers: one is a DC with WINS and DHCP enabled and the other is a member server that is set up for file and print sharing.

Figures 2-3, 2-4, and 2-5 are examples of working documents that would be created from the scenario describing SVAC.

FIGURE 2-3 An organizational chart of Spring Valley Air Cargo

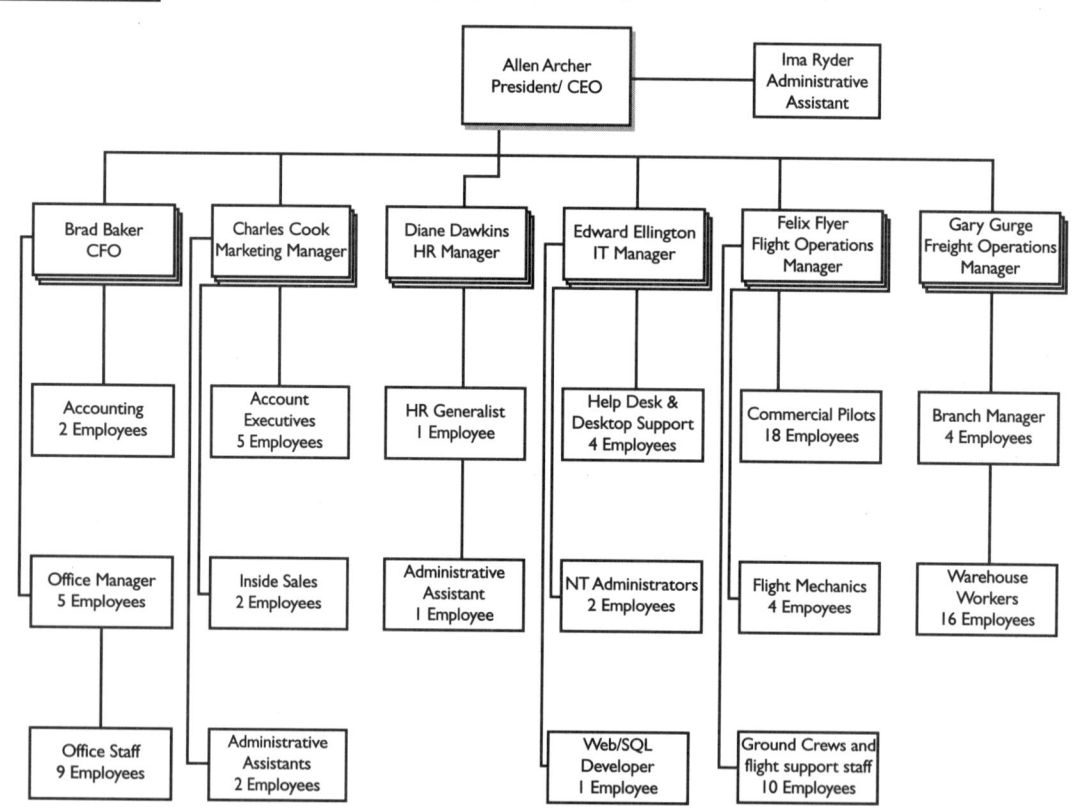

```
                    Allen Archer            Ima Ryder
                    President/ CEO          Administrative
                                            Assistant

Brad Baker    Charles Cook      Diane Dawkins   Edward Ellington   Felix Flyer           Gary Gurge
CFO           Marketing Manager HR Manager      IT Manager         Flight Operations     Freight Operations
                                                                   Manager               Manager

Accounting    Account           HR Generalist   Help Desk &        Commercial Pilots     Branch Manager
2 Employees   Executives        1 Employee      Desktop Support    18 Employees          4 Employees
              5 Employees                       4 Employees

Office Manager Inside Sales     Administrative  NT Administrators  Flight Mechanics      Warehouse
5 Employees    2 Employees      Assistant       2 Employees        4 Empoyees            Workers
                                1 Employee                                               16 Employees

Office Staff   Administrative                   Web/SQL            Ground Crews and
9 Employees    Assistants                       Developer          flight support staff
               2 Employees                      1 Employee         10 Employees
```

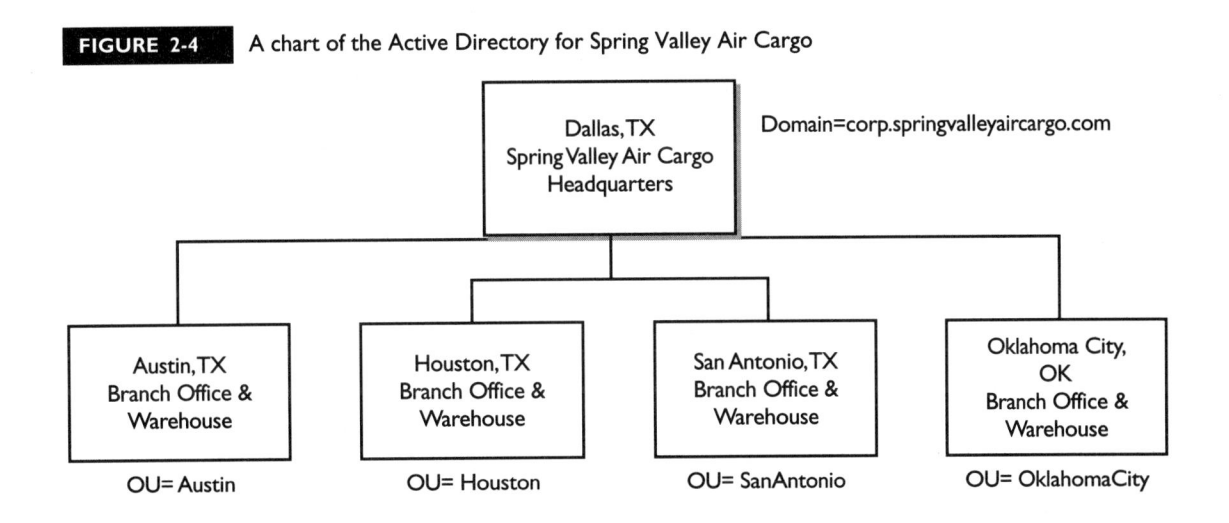

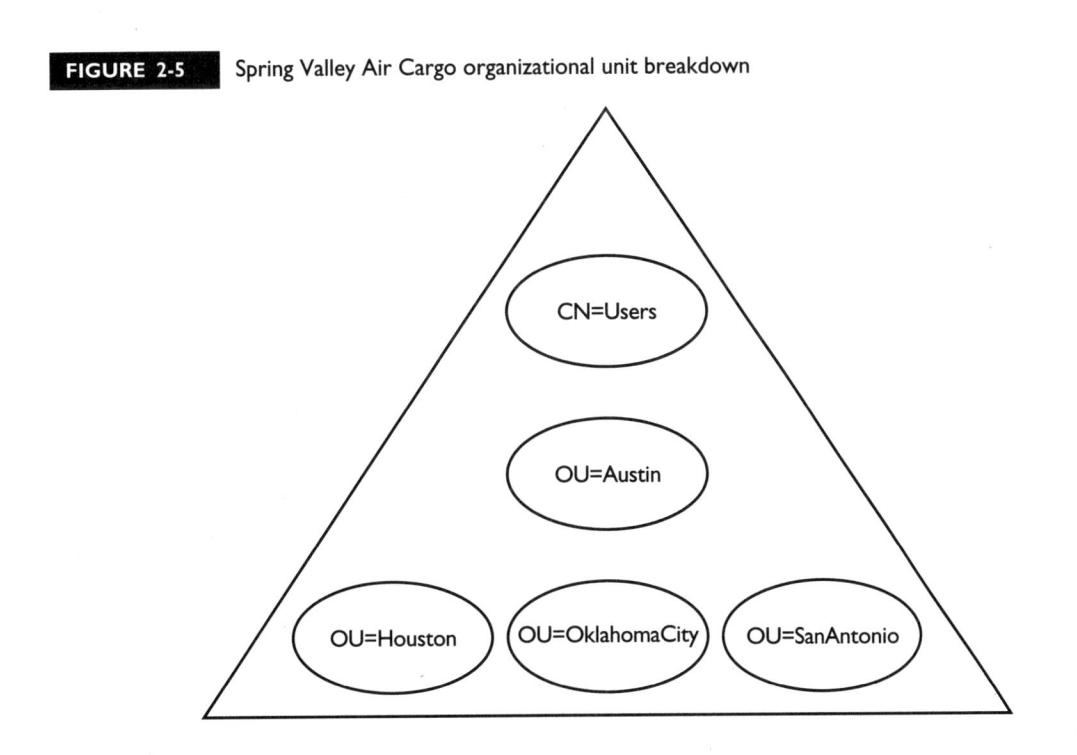

Analyze the Company Model and Geographical Scope **61**

FIGURE 2-4 A chart of the Active Directory for Spring Valley Air Cargo

Dallas, TX
Spring Valley Air Cargo
Headquarters

Domain=corp.springvalleyaircargo.com

- Austin, TX — Branch Office & Warehouse — OU= Austin
- Houston, TX — Branch Office & Warehouse — OU= Houston
- San Antonio, TX — Branch Office & Warehouse — OU= SanAntonio
- Oklahoma City, OK — Branch Office & Warehouse — OU= OklahomaCity

FIGURE 2-5 Spring Valley Air Cargo organizational unit breakdown

- CN=Users
- OU=Austin
- OU=Houston
- OU=OklahomaCity
- OU=SanAntonio

EXERCISE 2-2

Install Active Directory for Spring Valley Air Cargo

This exercise will cover the installation of Active Directory.

1. Click Next on the Active Directory Installation Wizard.

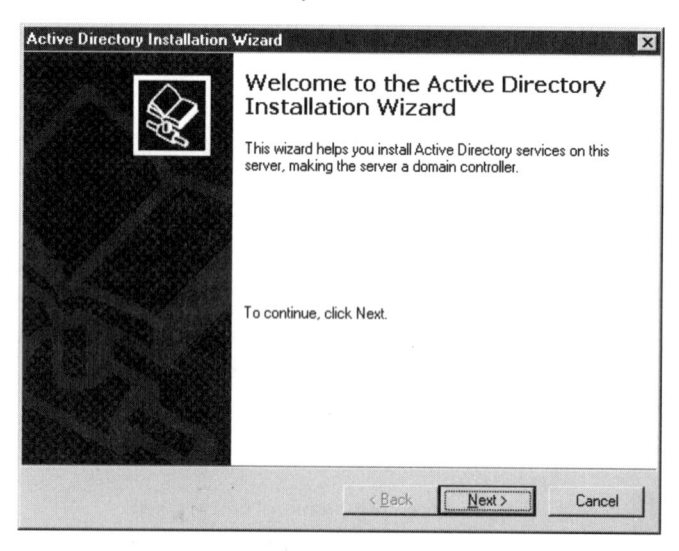

2. Select "Domain controller for a new domain," and then click Next.

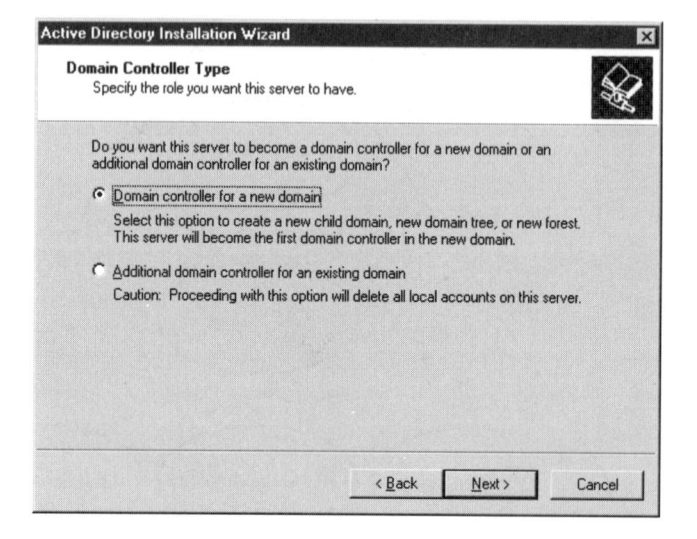

3. Select "Create a new domain tree" and click Next.

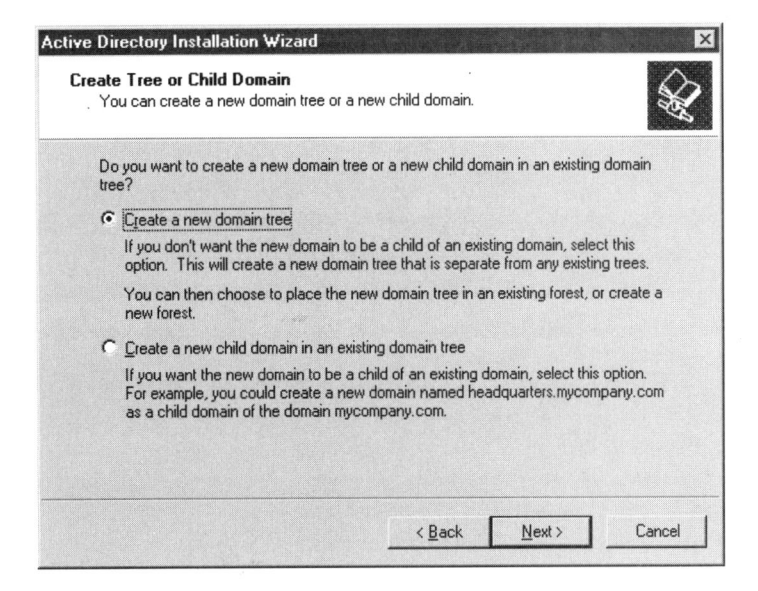

4. Select "Create a new forest of domain trees," and click Next.

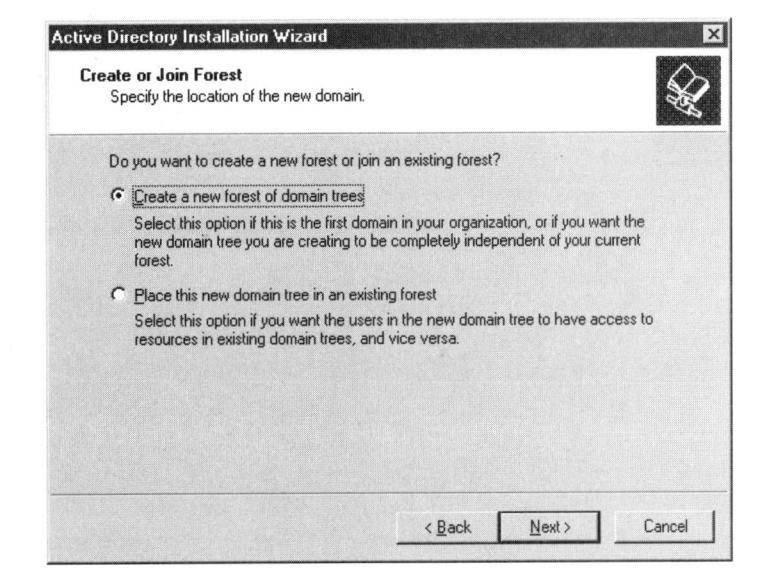

5. Select "No, just install and configure DNS on this computer," and then click Next.

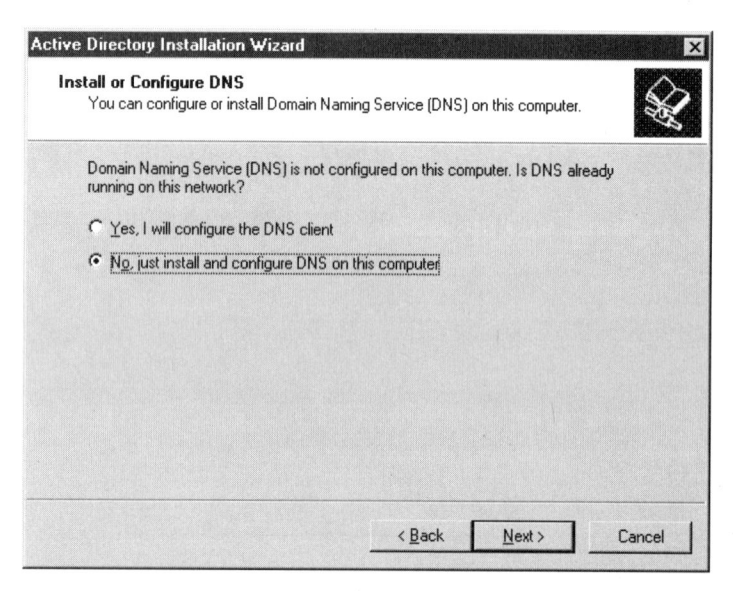

6. Type **corp.springvalleyaircargo.com**, and then click Next.

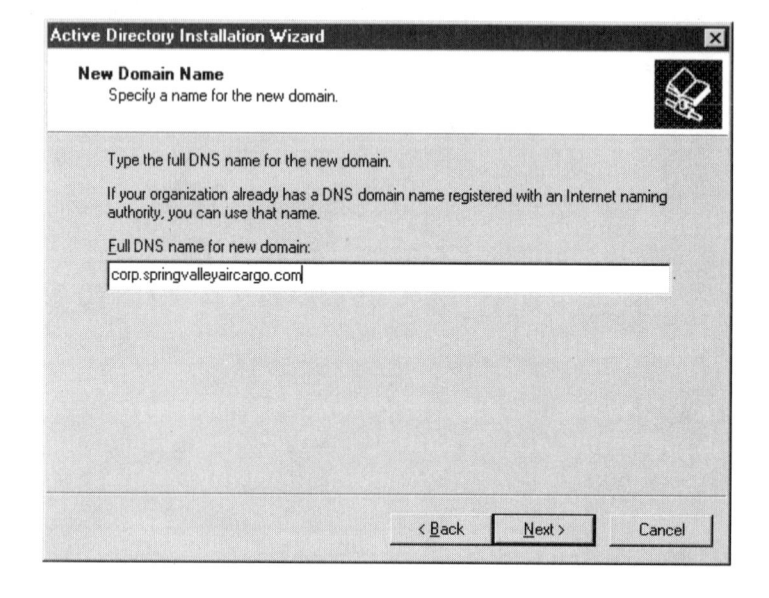

Analyze the Company Model and Geographical Scope 65

7. Accept CORP, and then click Next.

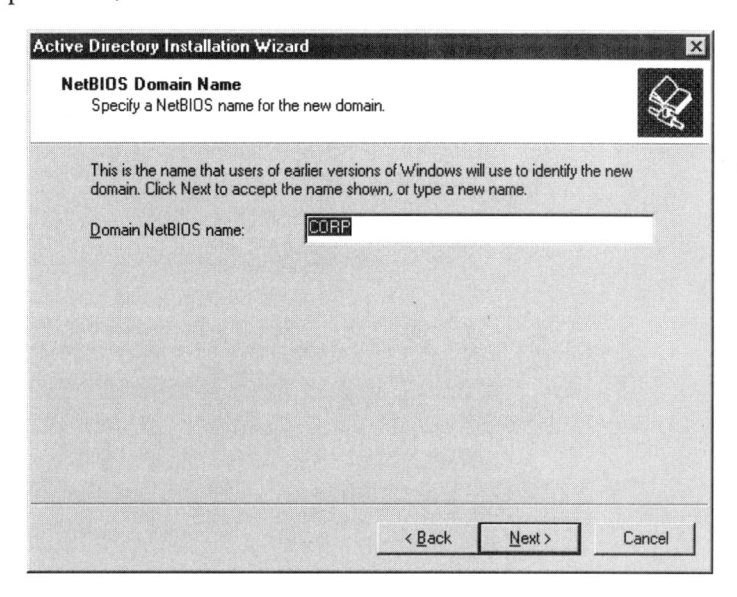

8. Accept the default locations for the database locations and the log location, and then click Next.

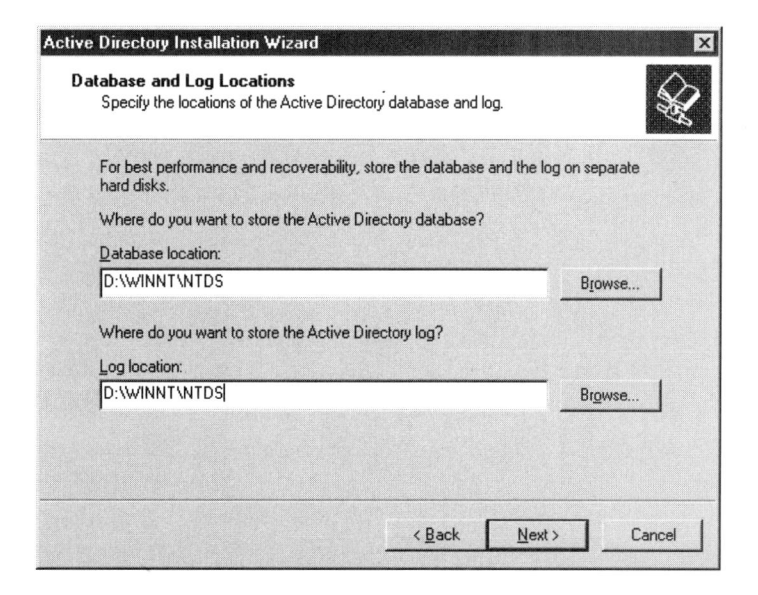

on the job *If you want the best performance, select a separate hard disk for the database and log, and, if possible, a separate controller for each disk.*

9. Accept the location for the SYSVOL, and click Next.

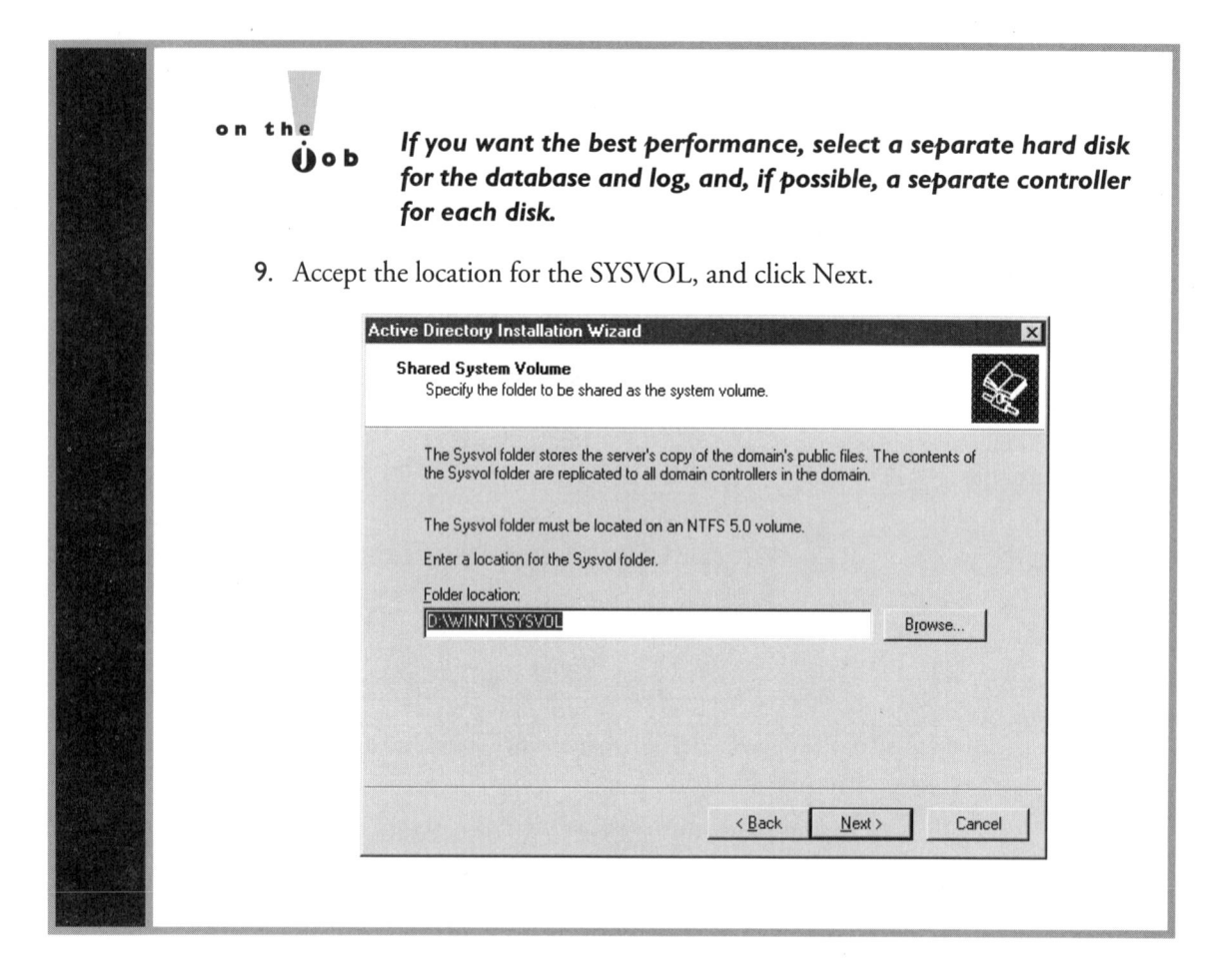

Active Directory Installation Wizard

Shared System Volume
Specify the folder to be shared as the system volume.

The Sysvol folder stores the server's copy of the domain's public files. The contents of the Sysvol folder are replicated to all domain controllers in the domain.

The Sysvol folder must be located on an NTFS 5.0 volume.

Enter a location for the Sysvol folder.

Folder location:
D:\WINNT\SYSVOL   Browse...

< Back   Next >   Cancel

10. Select "Permission compatible with pre-Windows 2000 servers" and click Next.

11. Type in the password for the server's Administrator account; in this case, it's *password*.

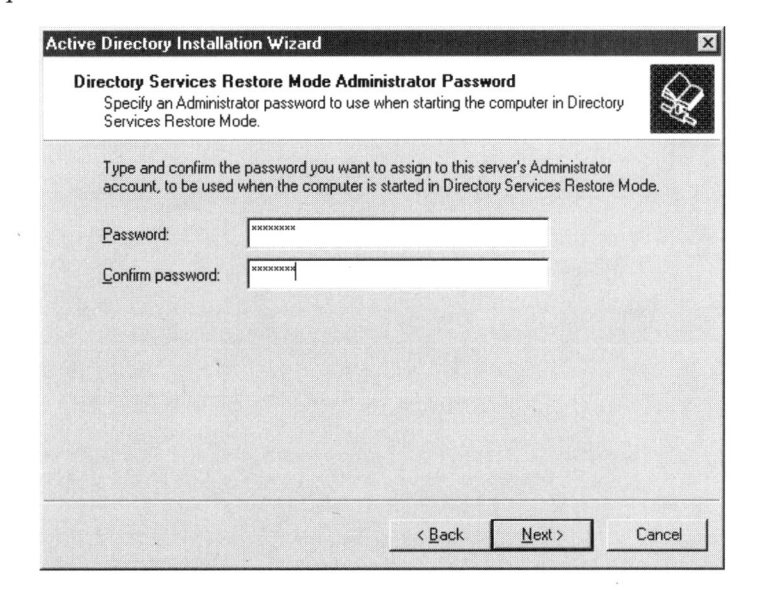

12. Review and Confirm the options, and click Next.

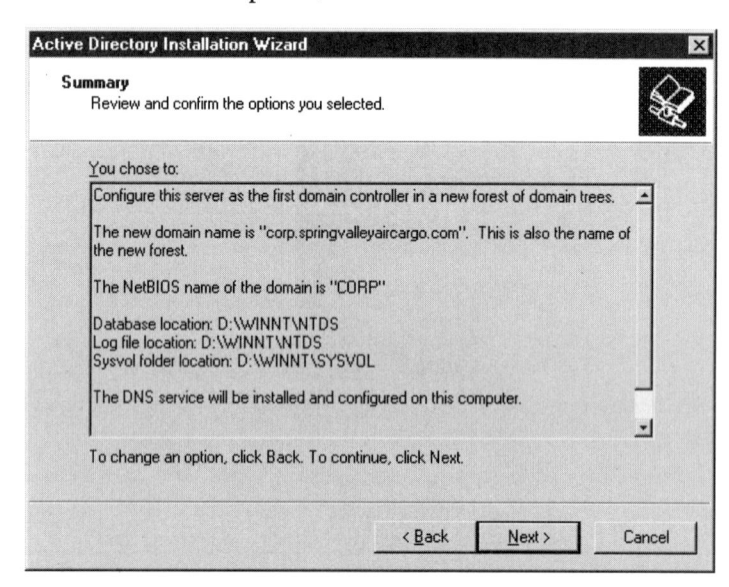

13. The wizard will configure the Active Directory.

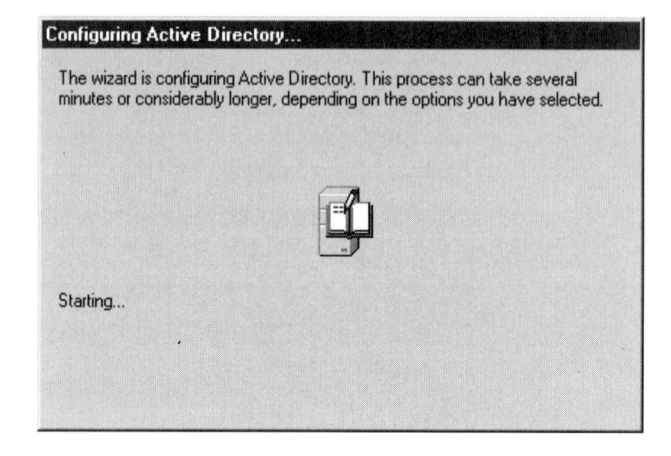

Analyze the Company Model and Geographical Scope **69**

14. Complete the installation of the Active Directory Installation Wizard, and click Finish.

EXERCISE 2-3

CertCam 2-3

Create an OU in the Active Directory for Spring Valley Air Cargo

1. Select Start | Programs | Administrative Tools | Active Directory Users and Computers.
2. Select the Domain to update.
3. Select Action | New | Organization Unit.
4. Type in the name for the new OU, and click OK.

National Model

A company is operating with a national business model if it has operations that are located in multiple distinct locations across a single country that are not merely regional in nature. The company will have business operations that consist of a corporate headquarters, regional offices, and production and distribution facilities located in multiple regions of a country.

Windows NT 4.0 had a number of weaknesses when implemented in a company with a national business model. If the business had an IT structure that was very centrally organized, then a single master domain model was implemented, and this was relatively easy to manage. If the company had merged recently, or if it was very large, then a multiple master domain or complete trust model was typically implemented. This meant that many trust relationships had to be identified, created, and maintained with many domains.

The lack of effective scalability and delegation of administrative controls were weaknesses in the design of Windows NT 4.0 directory services. These weaknesses have been addressed in Windows 2000 with the introduction of Active Directory Service's ability to scale to more than 1 million objects. What this means is that an administrator now has the ability to simplify the design of a current Windows NT architecture from multiple domains into a single Windows 2000 domain with OUs. One no longer has to create domains because of how many users and computers are in a company.

In very large national companies with Windows NT 4.0, one often has to implement a multi-master domain structure. With an account domain in Windows NT 4.0, all changes occur at the primary domain controller (PDC). This means that whenever a person changes his or her password, the change is actually processed only on the PDC. When the PDC has a change, it has to replicate this to every backup domain controller (BDC). What ends up happening is that whenever passwords are required to be changed, the network runs a little slower. This is due to all of the traffic being generated to and from a single point, the PDC. In very large environments, this has been a problem when using Windows NT 4.0 for authentication.

This problem is addressed in Windows 2000 with the Active Directory's use of multi-master replication. This means that there are no primary or backup domain controllers; every domain controller is equal. In Windows 2000, every domain controller can accept changes to Active Directory, and send those changes out for the other domain controllers to accept. Based on the last time that updates were made, replication of changes occurs until all domain controllers are brought up to date and synchronized. In the Windows NT 4.0 days, if you installed a server as a member server and later wanted to make it a BDC, a reinstall of the operating system was required. Windows 2000 Server has another improvement in that it can become a domain controller without having to reinstall the operating system. Likewise, a Windows 2000 domain controller can be "demoted" to a member server without a reinstall.

exam
Watch

Be sure you understand concepts relating to sites, how they reflect network topology. In this you obviously must take into account the fact that the physical locations are connected at various speeds. It's also important to know intersite replication of domain controllers, which is configured by links and a schedule for replication, and intrasite replication which is automatic and happens between domain controllers in the same site.

International Model

A company is operating with an international business model if it has operations that are located in more than one country. The company will have business operations that consist of a worldwide headquarters, possibly divisional headquarters that are based around the country or continent that is being serviced, offices, and production and distribution facilities located to take advantage of the economic advantages of being located in multiple international locations.

When planning a Windows 2000 implementation, one of the challenges is the cost of bandwidth from country to country and from continent to continent. It can be very expensive. What often happens is that in an effort to minimize costs, low connection speeds are implemented between major sites or countries. Low connection speeds present challenges when implementing Windows 2000. Another challenge is that different languages are spoken in the various countries, which can complicate the deployment of applications. In addition, the plan must take into account the different time zones in which the servers are located. Differences in time zones and the related production hours can complicate scheduling tape backups, and Active Directory replication between sites. The design choices are to create separate domains so that replication of the Active Directory needn't occur. If a single domain with OUs is chosen, then the creation of Windows 2000 sites by physical location and the scheduling of Active Directory replication is an option.

In addition, locating the following services at each international site will greatly improve users' experience by making it unnecessary for network traffic to traverse the slow international links.

- DNS, for local name resolution
- DHCP, for local assignment of IP Addresses
- A Windows 2000 DC for local authentication
- A local e-mail server such as Exchange Server
- A local Windows 2000 member server for file print services

on the Job

It is often common in companies that are located internationally to have multiple domains based on location, but are still part of the same tree. This means that replication does not have to take place at all, yet the ability exists to use resources by authenticating using transitive trusts.

Subsidiary Model

A subsidiary model is one in which there exists a parent company that owns, in whole or in part, other companies. The core business that each subsidiary services can be completely different, or subsidiaries can be in competition with each other. A company that has a subsidiary model will typically choose to implement Active Directory with multiple domains in a single tree. The reasons for this are that each subsidiary will probably want complete control over its environment. With the creation of multiple domains, each subsidiary can maintain it own autonomy. They are able to deploy their own set of requirement for their users. The following is a list of things that separate domains can allow each subsidiary:

- Unique Internet domain names
- Replication control of the subsidiary domain controllers
- Different password requirements for length, expiration time, etc.
- Decentralized administration of resources by each subsidiary
- The control of data shares and resources based on internal political requirements

exam watch

Subsidiary models are often designed and implemented as multiple domain trees. The individual domain trees are then joined together in a forest. That way, data and resources can be shared from one domain tree and any of its child domains with the other domain tree and its child domains by the use of transitive trusts.

Branch Office Model

The branch office model is one in which there is a primary office or headquarters, and multiple small branch offices that are distributed across a region. The main difference between this and a regional model is that the connectivity that is employed is typically on-demand LAN connectivity. Each site has a LAN, where the primary connectivity with the main office is accomplished via a modem, Digital Subscriber Line (DSL), or cable modem connection to an ISP using either PPTP or L2TP to create a secure VPN connection. When a user needs to submit an e-mail or access a file on a server that is located at the main office, the following steps occur:

1. A request is made for a file share on a server.
2. The servers host name is translated to an IP address by DNS.
3. The IP address is compared with the current machine's LAN segment and it is found to not be a local address.
4. The machine then sends the connect request to the gateway, which in this case is a Windows 2000 machine that is set up as an on-demand router.
5. The on-demand router sees how it must connect to the resource, and places a call to the branch office.

PPTP is a proprietary Microsoft security model that encrypts TCP/IP packets for use across a public connection like the Internet.

L2TP is an open standards security protocol that also encrypts TCP/IP packets for use across a public connection like the Internet.

exam watch

You will need to understand the concepts of virtual private networks and how companies can leverage the wide availability and low cost of connections to ISPs. You will need to know how to create a VPN and configure Windows 2000 as an on-demand router.

CERTIFICATION OBJECTIVE 2.02

Analyze Company Processes

The analysis of company processes is useful when creating security policies for access control of information. Just about every facet of a company uses information technology. It is critical to understand how the business units, divisions, and departments use the various types of data and resources. From the result of this discovery, a set of access controls is produced that has resources controlled by groups and users as members of the appropriate groups. One process that is commonly found in companies large and small is the HR process of hiring an employee. This is illustrated in Table 2-1.

Another process that commonly exists in every environment is the process whereby administrators provide access to data and resources.

TABLE 2-1 Hiring Process Steps	HR	How Information Technology Is Used
	A need is identified for an employee.	A requisition or document of some type is produced that defines job requirements, salary ranges, location, available posting date, etc.
	Management approves this need and recruitment begins.	A document is produced.
	The recruiting effort produces resumes from candidates for the position.	These documents will need to be accessible and limited to HR management, etc.
	An interview is performed.	The resume is accessed and printed, and results of the interview are recorded by the manager for use by the HR department.
	An offer is extended.	An offer letter is created and sent to the candidate; copies of the letter must be retained.

SCENARIO & SOLUTION

Who owns the data and resources available on the network?	The owner of the data will know who should or should not have access to the data.
Who assigns access to data and resources?	What group or subgroup has administrative control over resources? The delegation of administrative duties by OU is a major feature of Windows 2000 Active Directory.
Who needs access to the data and resources on the network?	The users that should be entered into the group; the information for this comes from the data owner.

Information Flow

A thorough understanding of how information flows throughout a company will be the basis for setting requirements for resources, and depending upon the nature of the information, will determine the appropriate security settings. The ability for computers to ease the creation, modification, and reporting of data is one of the reasons that so many corporations have adopted technology. The information contained in the data can be analyzed, and trends and predictions can be made. The flow of information begins with input from a user to a computer; the computer processes the information, optionally stores the data, and then displays a result. An example of information flow for a transaction is as follows:

A customer enters a store. The customer inquires about the features of a product to determine the advantages and benefits of the product and the product price. If the product meets the customer's needs, a request is made to purchase the product. The vendor determines if this is a new or existing customer. If new, the vendor creates a customer record for tracking the current purchase. The vendor then determines if the product is available and fulfills the order and delivers the product, or places a backorder for the product and confirms the order. Once an agreement is confirmed, an invoice is created, the customer is billed, and collection of money for the product is initiated.

Communication Flow

The flow of communication from Windows 2000 clients and server is an inherent process that must be understood in detail to enable proper planning to occur. There exists the communication of Windows 2000 domain controllers with each other to determine if changes have been made since the last time the servers communicated. There is the communication from Windows clients to the Windows 2000 DHCP server, which assigns IP addresses automatically and dynamically registers the host with DNS information in the Active Directory.

EXERCISE 2-4

A communication flow example

An example of the communication flow between a Windows client and a Windows 2000 DHCP and Dynamic DNS server is as follows:

1. At boot-up, a Windows 2000 client broadcasts its fully qualified domain name (FQDN), its Media Access Control (MAC) address, and its need for an IP address.
2. A DHCP server responds to the computer by MAC address, and after an offer and acceptance provides the client with a unique IP address, subnet mask, and usually other information such as default gateway and DNS server information.
3. The DHCP server registers the forward lookup information in the Account Resource Record (A RR) with the Dynamic DNS.
4. The DHCP server registers the reverse lookup information in the Pointer Resource Record (PTR RR) with the Dynamic DNS.

on the job

In Windows 2000 clients, the DHCP client updates Account Resource Records with the Dynamic DNS, not the DNS client. In Windows (Non-W2K) clients, the DHCP client registers with the Windows 2000 DHCP server. The DHCP server registers on behalf of the Windows client with Dynamic DNS.

CERTIFICATION OBJECTIVE 2.03

Life Cycles

The phases that a business will go through when implementing a change from the beginning to the end of use is known as the *life cycle*. Depending on the topic, a process goes through various phases until it begins to repeat itself. Products tend to go through various stages such as new technology, state of the art; advanced; mainstream; mature; and obsolete. Products are typically referred to using models and versions. Services are the culmination of processes and typically go through multiple iterations and are constantly being improved upon. The service life cycle follows the product life cycle. Windows 2000 needed to be released before service organizations could consult, implement, or respond to events related to Windows 2000.

Service Life Cycle

The services to be performed are often defined in a *service level agreement* (SLA). The SLA is a document created by the IT department that describes the roles and responsibilities of the IT department, outlines the scope of services to be performed, and attempts to set expectations for the end user. The SLA should address the following topics:

- User population supported.
- Equipment: Servers, PCs, network infrastructure supported.
- Software: OS, common desktop applications, custom applications.
- Support windows: Production hours, scheduled maintenance, network uptime.
- Help Desk telephone numbers, problem escalation procedures, response times guarantees.
- Definition of metrics for reports to track levels of service provided.

The service life cycle will go through the following phases. This methodology is followed by most IT service organizations.

1. End user experiences a service event.
2. End user notifies service provider.
3. Assessment of event by service provider.
4. Development of possible solutions by service provider.
5. Service provider acts on the event.
6. Service provider analyzes results of action.
7. Service provider documents event and outcome.

A typical example is as follows:

1. An event occurs; the user can't print.
2. The user calls the Help desk.
3. The Help desk person opens a ticket and questions the user regarding the problem.
4. The Help desk person identifies a possible solution and takes action to fix the problem.
5. The Help desk then asks the user to try to print again.
6. If the fix works, then the Help desk will document the solution and close the ticket. If the fix doesn't work, the Help desk will try another solution or escalate to a more knowledgeable associate.
7. The Help desk person then closes the ticket.
8. Tickets will be analyzed for trends in problems.

Product Life Cycle

The life cycle for implementing Windows 2000 and configuring Active Directory securely will go through the following phases:

1. Definition of requirements
2. Solution proposal

3. Planning of design
4. Proof of concept
5. Production implementation
6. Daily operations and monitoring
7. Optimization and maintenance
8. Retirement

The *definition of requirements* is the first step in the process. A person or team will acquire information from the end users on what needs they have. These needs are translated into tangible objectives. An example would be the ability for users at a branch office in Chicago to be able to use the internal HR Web site that is located in New York. Another requirement might that a file share only be accessible to managers. The system engineers would then analyze these requirements.

Solution proposal is the process that uses the knowledge of the system engineers. There are multiple options and ways for meeting the requirements. Based on the design goals, the physical locations, the business model, internal politics, and level of security needed, there will be various options available. From the various proposals, a consensus will be obtained that will allow the system engineers to recommend a plan for implementation to management. In an effort to minimize the associated risks of change, managers typically request that this solution be tested and demonstrated to work as planned.

The *proof of concept* is the stage where a solution is implemented on a limited scale for a subset of the total population and typically in a single site. The intent of this stage is to flush out any problems, and to refine processes and procedures prior to a full implementation. A common approach is to include power users and key representatives of various departments and divisions, so that the users can experience the solution and, if necessary, refine the requirements for the areas they represent.

The *production implementation* begins when the various team members begin the rollout of the solution for the production environment. The design plan will typically have various tasks assigned to different groups that have certain dates and times for implementation. During the implementation, there will be certain phases such as the implementation of Dynamic DNS that will be critical deliverables. Other processes and procedures can be carried out concurrently, such as the creation of user accounts and the remote installation of Windows 2000 Professional. Each team member will be responsible for executing his or her section of the plan, confirming that the section is operational, and monitoring the change until the plan is fully implemented and a final production environment is achieved.

Daily operations and monitoring is the phase after the full implementation in which the technology is used for the business purposes. Some of the activities include users' accounts being added, modified, and deleted. In addition, desktop computer accounts and servers are created, and their continued performance is maintained. These types of operations can typically be performed by less senior administrators.

Optimization and maintenance is the phase during which engineers preserve and sustain the technical infrastructure. This includes the testing and implementation of service packs for the operating system, release updates for the various installed services, and the updating of systems' BIOS and device drivers. Another important aspect is the review of logs and the generation of reports for use in security and infrastructure analysis. Engineers will often capture and analyze data on account activity, resource usage, and network traffic patterns in an effort to optimize the environment. Logs are analyzed to identify system, security, and application events. Reports are generated from data that is gathered from various system tools that can measure server and network performance.

Retirement is the phase in which a product has reached its useful life and will be decommissioned. The choice to retire a product such as Windows NT 4.0 and migrate to a new one such as Windows 2000 is a major undertaking. The retirement plan is usually part of an overall migration. The new product will then have its own requirements, and the cycle will begin again.

Decision-Making

The method in which IT decisions are made depends a great deal on how the IT department is categorized in the business model. Is the IT department viewed as a cost center, a profit center, or a business catalyst? If the business is a profit center, and management understands that there exists a clear correlation between a properly working IT environment and the company's profit, then new technology, software, and processes deployment will be policy and the debate will center around which solution to choose. On the other hand, if your IT department is considered a fixed cost, and the efficiency gains of technology are difficult to quantify in either costs deferred or profit produced, then expect resistance to new equipment, software, and processes. I prefer to think of technology and the IT department as the catalyst for a business to increase efficiency and productivity. The decision to implement a change such as implementing Windows 2000 and Active Directory and all of the associated aspects that are required for a successful deployment, including security design, systems administration, PCs, servers, and network support, is a daunting task. The decision process for a business usually begins with the formation of a workgroup comprised of key management representatives, end users, and IT staff. This group is tasked to produce a detailed report that recommends of the current and future needs of the organization. The report provides information on how business objectives and growth projections for the business were taken into account, which solutions exist, and recommends one strategy on how Windows 2000 can be deployed. Contained within the report will be recommendations for the entire structure of the Windows 2000 Active Directory. Senior management typically reviews the report and, if approved, then a project will be started, funds allocated, and a timeline for the project completion determined.

CERTIFICATION SUMMARY

This chapter requires the systems engineer to create a number of documents that will be used in designing a secure network. It requires the engineer to study in detail the business model and to realize the organizational and political structure. An understanding will be developed regarding the impact that the physical locations and connectivity speeds between locations have on the design of Windows 2000 and Active Directory. The data that is arranged will then be adapted to generate an organizational chart, a network resource diagram, definition of administrative roles and responsibilities, and service levels to be provided.

We identified various businesses models and discussed how Windows NT 4.0 does not always scale well to large environments. NT 4.0 often required multiple domains with various trust relationships to accommodate a combination of centralized account management and decentralized resource management. Windows 2000 has simplified the engineering of large environments through the introduction of Active Directory. The Active Directory's implementation of organizational units, use of group policy objects, multi-master replication, and the introduction of sites that account for network topology are all improvements and are features to consider when designing or migrating to Windows 2000.

✓ TWO-MINUTE DRILL

Analyze the Company Model and Geographical Scope

- ❑ *Research and document the composition of workers in the organization.* This can be used to create organizational charts that will ease the creation of user accounts, OUs, and domains.
- ❑ *Research and document the physical locations of the company.* An understanding of the locations can assist in the creation of OUs and is useful for network diagrams.
- ❑ *Research and document the network topology.* This is used for the creation of *sites*.

Analyze Company Processes

- ❑ *Identify and understand the political and functional divisions in the company, and the associated roles and responsibilities for various groups.* This will be used for creating group policies, determining if multiple domains are necessary, and delegation of administration.
- ❑ *Identify and document the unique naming convention for a domain.* This will be used to provide a common identifiable and unique structure for users, computers, and groups.
- ❑ *Identify and understand the core competencies of the business.* This will be useful in determining data access levels, global and local groups, and policies.
- ❑ *Understand the flow of information that enables your business to sell its products or services.* This will allow for a better architecture of where resources are located, what the most likely requirements are for access to data, redundancy of operations, and will provide information regarding how data should be secured.

Life Cycles

- ❑ *Understand and identify the life cycles for products.* This will allow you to prepare for the changes that occur from one stage to another as a product goes from its initial release to retirement.

❑ *Understand the life cycles for service.* This will allow you to prepare for the various steps that the service process goes through, from the initial event occurrence to the final solution.

❑ *Understand how decisions are made for technology implementation.* This will allow you to understand how often time management decisions are based on the business principles of profit. It will be your job to explain how the technology is aligned with the business strategy, and how this new technology will enable it to maximize revenues or minimize losses.

SELF TEST

The following questions will help you measure your understanding of the material presented in this chapter. Read all of the choices carefully, as there may be more than one correct answer. Choose all correct answers for each question.

Analyze the Company Model and Geographical Scope

1. Which of the following is not true about domains within Active Directory Services?
    A. Domains provide a method for structuring your network to reflect your business model.
    B. A domain can span multiple physical locations.
    C. A domain maps the physical structure of a business's network.
    D. Domain administration can be delegated.

2. Of the following objects, which can be created under an organizational unit? (Choose all that apply.)
    A. Domains.
    B. Computers.
    C. Users.
    D. Organizational units.

3. XYZ is a national company with 3000 employees nationwide. XYZ uses Windows 2000 Server and has configured Active Directory Services. The headquarters are located in New York, with regional offices located in Dallas and San Francisco. Each site has a 10/100MB LAN. The regional offices are connected by T1 connections. How many sites should be created in the Active Directory with this configuration?
    A. 1
    B. 2
    C. 3
    D. 4

4. Organizational units can be implemented for which of the following reasons? (Choose all that apply.)
    A. To structure a domain by hierarchical organizational structure.
    B. To structure a domain by business location.

    C. To delegate authority to administrators for subsets of resources.

    D. All of the above.

5. Which of the following protocols must be installed on the network before Active Directory can be installed?

    A. DHCP

    B. DNS

    C. WINS

    D. RIP

6. What tool is used to create a new organizational unit in a domain in Windows 2000?

    A. Active Directory Users & Computers

    B. Active Directory Domains & Trusts

    C. User Manager

    D. Server Manager

7. Which protocols can be used to establish a virtual private network (VPN) across the Internet? (Choose all that apply.)

    A. PPP

    B. PPTP

    C. DHCP

    D. L2TP

    E. RSVP

Analyze Company Processes

8. What types of trust relationships can be created with the MMC snap-in Active Directory Domain Users and Trusts? (Choose all that apply.)

    A. Implicit

    B. Explicit

    C. Full

    D. Transitive

    E. Shortcut

9. Which of the following protocols is an extension of Point-to-Point Protocol and is used for authentication?

   A. PPTP
   B. EAP
   C. RIP
   D. L2TP

10. An insurance agency has agents located in three remote offices in various suburbs of a major city. Each of the remote offices has a Windows 2000 server and a dial-up connection to an ISP. The remote sites are connected to the main office by on-demand LAN connectivity that employs a VPN. Which of the following models best describes the company?

    A. Regional
    B. National
    C. International
    D. Branch office

11. Which of the following objects is a security boundary in Active Directory Service?

    A. Forest
    B. Domain Tree
    C. Domain
    D. Organizational unit

12. Which of the following situations would make it necessary to have more than one domain when implementing Active Directory?

    A. The company has 55,000 users.
    B. The organization of the IT department is centralized.
    C. The company has multiple business units that have different DNS domain names.
    D. The company wants to reflect its organization by divisions and departments.

Life Cycles

13. Which of the following is NOT a reason to create an OU?

    A. To administer access rights to files
    B. To delegate administration duties

- C. To replace resource domains in NT 4
- D. To apply group policies

14. ABC company has a UNIX non-dynamic DNS server that processes all DNS requests for the abc.com DNS domain. It also has a Windows NT 4.0 domain known as dom1. The company has decided to migrate to Windows 2000. Which of the following options are viable solutions?
    - A. Continue to have the root domain abc.com served by the UNIX server, create a new zone known as dom1.abc.com, and migrate the NT 4.0 domain into the Active Directory domain of dom1.abc.com. Install Windows 2000 Dynamic DNS service to resolve requests for the dom1.abc.com domain.
    - B. Eliminate the UNIX DNS server since it is not dynamic. Install the Windows 2000 Active Directory as abc.com, and create an OU that contains the resources and users that were found in the NT 4.0 domain dom1.
    - C. Update the UNIX DNS server to a version that is dynamic and compatible with Windows 2000 Active Directory. Then create a domain dom1.abc.com and OUs that contain the resources and users that were found in the NT 40 domain dom1.
    - D. Continue to use the existing UNIX DNS server and implement WINS, which dynamically resolves IP addresses to NetBIOS names.

15. According to Microsoft, how many OUs can you create before performance degrades in Active Directory?
    - A. 4
    - B. 6
    - C. 8
    - D. 10

16. Which two types of replication are available in Active Directory?
    - A. Interdomain
    - B. Intradomain
    - C. Intrasite
    - D. Intersite

17. Company XYZ has a domain, xyz.com, which has three domain controllers. Company XYZ has a business unit, Research, that wanted complete control of their resources, so a child domain was created, research.xyz.com. The Research business unit has two domain controllers

installed for fault tolerance at their site. One of the domain controllers has failed due to a hardware failure. Which of the following options can an administrator perform?

A. The administrator can promote a member Windows 2000 server to a domain controller.

B. The administrator will need to reinstall Windows 2000 as a domain controller on an existing member server.

C. The administrator can take a domain controller from the xyz.com, demote it from a domain controller of xyz.com, move it to Research, and promote it to a domain controller in the research.xyz.com domain.

D. The administrator can promote a Windows 2000 Professional workstation to a domain controller.

LAB QUESTION

Spring Valley Air Cargo is located in Dallas. It has a single Windows 2000 domain known as springvalleyaircargo.com. The company obtained new offices through a recent acquisition in Oklahoma City. The users in Oklahoma City would like to retain local administrative control over their resources. Management has decided that the following design requirements must be met when integrating them into the Windows 2000 domain.

- The new users must adhere to the password policies for the company.
- Local administration of resources is approved.
- The new users must be a part of the same contiguous namespace springvalleyaircargo.com.

Create an organizational unit in the Active Directory on a Windows 2000 server. We will then delegate complete control of the administration of an organization unit to a local group of OKCAdmins. To follow is a list of steps to make the process fully operational.

SELF TEST ANSWERS

Analyze the Company Model and Geographical Scope

1. ☑ **C.** Domains map the physical structure of a business's network.
   ☒ **A, B,** and **D** are incorrect. Sites map the physical structure of a business's network. A network's physical structure and its domain structure are independent of each other.

2. ☑ **B, C, D.** An Organizational unit can contain computers, groups, contacts, organizational units, printers, users, or shared folders.
   ☒ **A** is incorrect. An organizational unit cannot contain other domains.

3. ☑ **C.** The company has three regional physical locations. A site is a localized high-speed connection and is defined by subnet ranges. A site can be identified when a connection leaves a LAN and switches to WAN connection.
   ☒ For the reasons stated above, **A, B,** and **D** are incorrect. Although the T1 connections are fast, they are still WAN connections, and replication traffic between locations can be optimized by the use of sites.

4. ☑ **D.** All of the above are possible reasons to implement organizational units.

5. ☑ **B.** Active Directory requires DNS. The DNS service that ships with Windows 2000 supports dynamic updates. If another vendor's DNS package is used, that DNS must support the service resource record (SRV RR), as described in the Internet draft, "A DNS RR for specifying the location of services (DNS SRV)," and dynamic updates in DNS, as described in RFC 2136.
   ☒ DNS is the only protocol of those listed that must be installed; thus **A, C,** and **D** are incorrect.

6. ☑ **A.** In Windows 2000, the Microsoft Management Console (MMC) snap-in Active Directory Users & Computers is used create a new user. It can be used to create computers, groups, contacts, organizational units, printers, users, or shared folders.
   ☒ **B** is incorrect because this snap-in is used to create explicit trusts between domains. C is the tool used in Windows NT 4.0 for user and group account management. **D** is the tool used for management of workstations, servers, and domain controllers in Windows NT 4.0.

7. ☑ **B, D.** PPTP, or Point-to-Point Tunneling Protocol, is a proprietary Microsoft protocol that is supported by Windows 2000 for creating VPN connections. Windows 2000 supports

L2TP, Layer 2 Tunneling Protocol, which is an open standards based method for encapsulating data packets for use across the Internet.

☒ A is incorrect because PPP, Point to Point Protocol, is a communication protocol and is not used for VPNs. C is incorrect because DHCP, Dynamic Host Configuration Protocol, is used for assignment of IP addresses. E is incorrect because RSVP is the Resource Reservation Protocol used for Quality of Service (QoS).

Analyze Company Processes

8. ☑ A, C, D, E. Trust relationships can be created with the MMC snap-in Active Directory Domain Users and Trusts.
☒ B is incorrect. The term *explicit trust* does not exist.

9. ☑ B. EAP, which is an acronym for Extensible Authentication Protocol, is an extension of PPP.
☒ A, C, and D are incorrect. PPTP and L2TP are protocols used to create VPNs. RIP is a routing protocol.

10. ☑ D. The branch office model is characterized by the on-demand LAN access and use of low-cost VPNs.
☒ A, B, and C are incorrect. The regional model typically employs permanent versus on-demand connections. A regional model is typical of a mid-sized business whose sites are located within a state or section of a country. Regional, national, and international will all take advantage of VPN, but will also use and can afford permanent connections because of the need for a certain amount of WAN traffic. National model deals with organizations located across a country, and international deals with a company that has operations in multiple countries.

11. ☑ C. A domain is a security boundary. Security policies, ACLs, and administrative rights are applicable only to the domain in which they are applied; they do not cross from one domain to another.
☒ A, B, and D are incorrect. A domain tree is a hierarchical organization of domains that share a contiguous namespace. A forest is an organization of domain trees that do not share a contiguous namespace. Organizational units are containers used to logically organize objects in a domain.

12. ☑ C. If the company has different business units that each have unique DNS domain names, then this will require multiple Active Directory domains.
☒ A is incorrect because the Active Directory is designed to handle over 1 million objects.

B is incorrect because delegation of administrative function is possible with OUs, and the ability to centrally administer objects is available to members of the domain administrators group. **D** would not require more than one domain when implementing Active Directory, so it is incorrect as well.

Life Cycles

13. ☑ **A.** The ability to administer access rights to files can only be granted to users, groups, or computers. This is the same access security found in NT 4.0.
    ☒ **B, C,** and **D** are all reasons to create an OU.

14. ☑ **A, B, C.** There are three different choices when implementing DNS. To use the Windows 2000 DNS server exclusively, to implement Windows 2000 DNS server as a subdomain, or to use a Dynamic DNS solution that is compatible with Windows 2000.
    ☒ **D** is incorrect. Dynamic DNS is a requirement of Active Directory, while WINS is a service that is included for backward compatibility for NetBIOS to IP address name resolution.

15. ☑ **D.** The maximum suggested number of OUs is 10. Real-world testing has found that the fewer the better, with five showing little signs of performance degradation. It has been observed that with seven to eight OU levels, there is a noticeable slowdown in Active Directory queries.

16. ☑ **C, D.** Sites are created to reflect the network topology. When domain controllers share a common site, this implies that they share relatively fast connections between domain controllers. Since the connections are fast, directory information is updated frequently and automatically. When domain controllers are located in different sites with relatively slow connections, then you would configure a link from one domain controller to the other and determine how often replication should occur.
    ☒ **A** and **B** are incorrect. Replication is controlled at the site level, not between domains.

17. ☑ **A, C.** A Windows 2000 member server can be promoted from a domain controller. Any member server can be promoted to a domain controller, and any domain controller can be promoted to a member server without a reinstall.
    ☒ **B** is incorrect because in Windows NT, changing from a member server to a primary or backup domain controller required a reinstall. **D** is incorrect because a domain controller must be a server and cannot be from Windows 2000 Professional, which is designed as a client OS.

92 Chapter 2: Analyzing the Existing and Planned Business Models

LAB ANSWER

1. Click Start | Programs | Administrative Tools | Active Directory Users and Computers.

2. In the left pane, right-click oklahomacity, and then click Delegate Control (Figure 2-6). The Delegation of Control Wizard Welcome page appears (Figure 2-7).

3. Click Next.

4. From the Users, Computers, or Groups page, select OKCAdmins (Figure 2-8).

5. Click OKCAdmins, click Add, and then click Next (Figure 2-9).

6. On the Tasks to Delegate page, select all of the tasks to delegate, and then click Next (Figure 2-10).

7. Review the delegation settings. If everything is correct, click Finish (Figure 2-11).

Did you notice that there is a step missing in the process outline above?

FIGURE 2-6

Delegating control

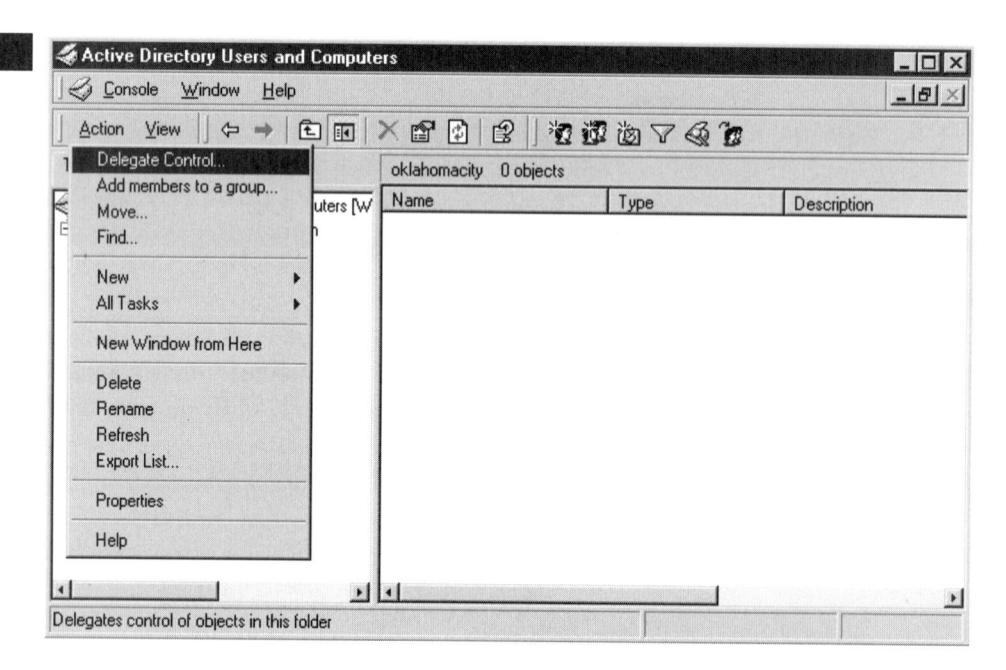

FIGURE 2-7

The Delegation of Control Wizard

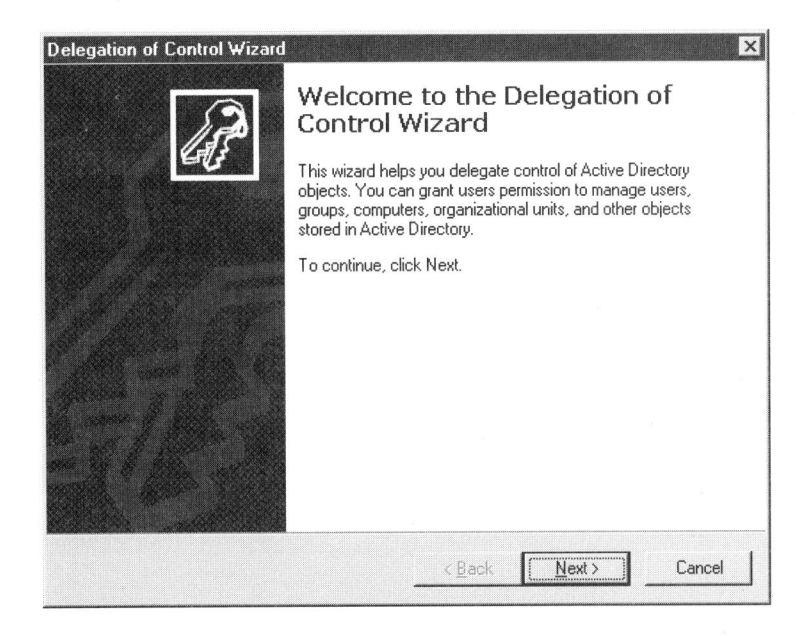

FIGURE 2-8

Users, Computers, or Groups page

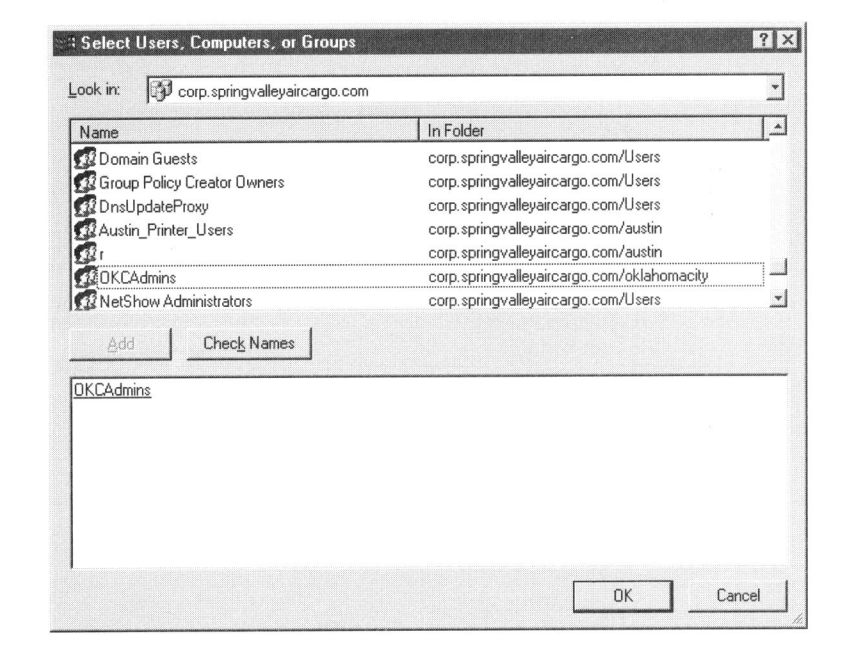

94 Chapter 2: Analyzing the Existing and Planned Business Models

FIGURE 2-9

Users or Groups page

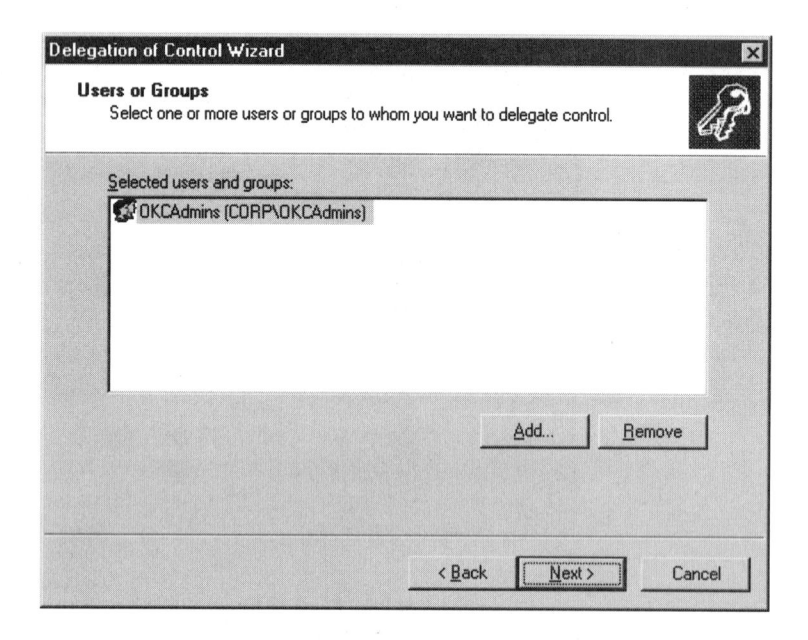

FIGURE 2-10

Tasks to Delegate page

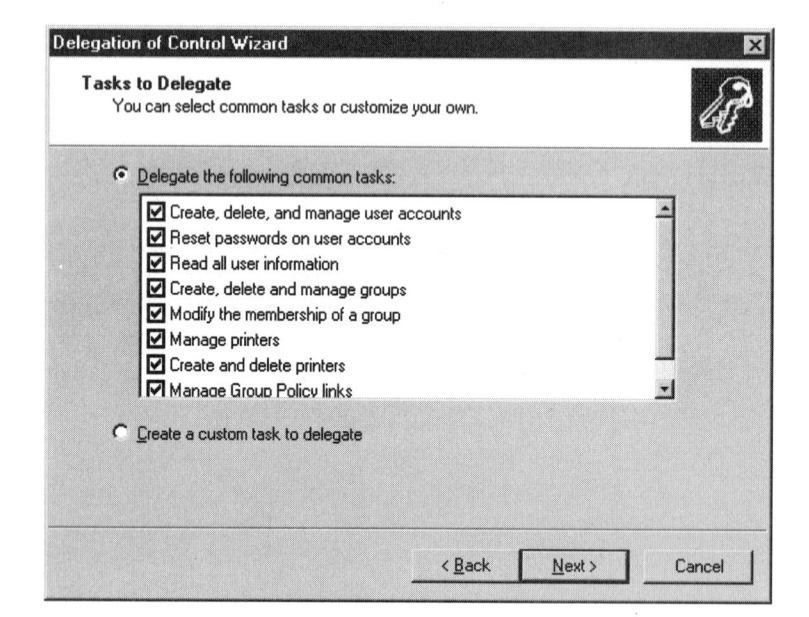

FIGURE 2-11

Completing the Delegation of Control Wizard

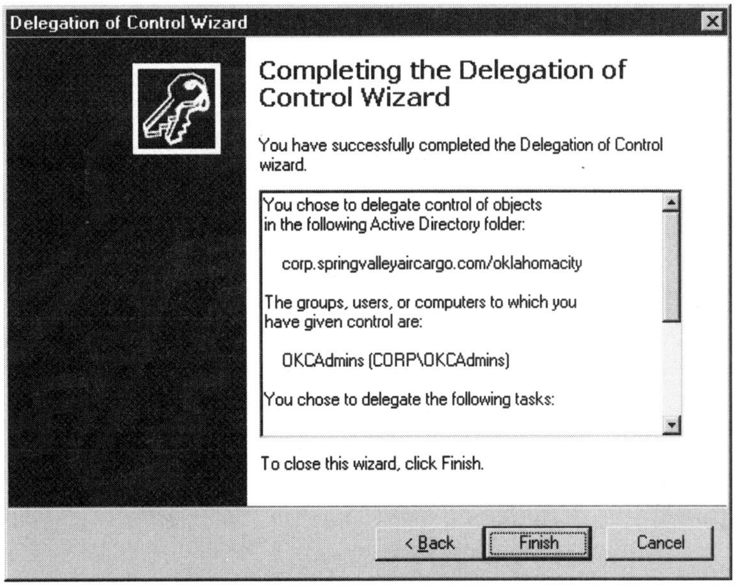
Delegation of Control Wizard
Completing the Delegation of Control Wizard
You have successfully completed the Delegation of Control wizard.
You chose to delegate control of objects in the following Active Directory folder:
corp.springvalleyaircargo.com/oklahomacity
The groups, users, or computers to which you have given control are:
OKCAdmins (CORP\OKCAdmins)
You chose to delegate the following tasks:
To close this wizard, click Finish.
< Back
Finish
Cancel

We didn't create the organizational unit. The preceding steps are the correct steps to take for delegating control once an organizational unit exists. However, a required object is the group OKCAdmins, and the question states that the OKCAdmins group already existed. This is an important point to note here, that in the certification exam it is critical to read the question thoroughly and know exactly what the question is asking for.

3
Analyzing Business Requirements

CERTIFICATION OBJECTIVES

3.01	Analyze the Existing and Planned Business Models and Organizational Structures
3.02	Analyze Factors That Influence Company Strategies
3.03	Analyze the Structure of IT Management
✓	Two-Minute Drill
Q&A	Self Test

As a company, the last thing you want is a reputation for allowing insecure network access. Without strong attention to security, internal users, partners, vendors, and customers will lose confidence in your company's computer system. Worse yet, hackers could attack your network and wreak havoc on your business systems. Lack of confidence will cost your business plenty, but it could be worse if your company's weak security structure is exploited; this could potentially lead to disastrous results.

This certification exam will test your skills in analyzing the business requirements for security and designing a security solution to meet those requirements. Planning and implementing appropriate security is critical whether your company is relatively small, supporting few users and physical locations, or quite large with several users performing various tasks in multiple physical locations. To begin, you need to formulate a plan, and be sure to document and create policies. Evaluate your existing network, your existing and planned business model. Determine what your company's needs are by looking at details and identifying user access requirements for various resources. Review the organizational structure in terms of management and company layout. Identify outside parties such as vendors, partners, customers, and potential mergers or acquisitions that will need to be considered when assessing your requirements.

Next, determine what kind of physical attributes you will need to address. Define the physical structure of your network. Identify any susceptibilities to security breaches from the inside of your organization. Additionally, look for potential weaknesses in your network that could make it vulnerable to outside attack.

Determine how and to what extent you want to monitor each event and whether you can afford to scale back the amount of auditing. Determine your authentication model. Migrating from Windows NT 4.0 or another operating system can entail additional planning and logistical issues. For instance, you will need to take into account a number of changes that have been added to Windows 2000's security regarding authentication. And lastly, deciding what type of encryption to use will be an important decision, as your data's integrity will depend on it. You need to review all of the laws that revolve around encryption and determine whether or not they affect your organization.

CERTIFICATION OBJECTIVE 3.01

Analyze the Existing and Planned Business Models and Organizational Structures

The first step in the process of determining your security is to take a close look at the existing and planned business models. Analyzing a business model should include looking at the current and planned geographic scope of the company, the organization of the company including the number of business units within the company, the amount of autonomy each business unit has, the management model, and the established company processes. Your job as a systems engineer will be to build a computing model that supports the state of the company today and allows the company to achieve its future goals.

Geographical Scope

Begin reviewing your company's model in terms of geographic scope by examining its parts. Try to categorize your company as a local, regional, national, or international firm. Remember to consider subsidiaries, branch offices, and any planned acquisitions or partnerships that will require common network or computing infrastructure. You may also choose to use a layered approach. For example, you might classify branch offices as local, regional offices as regional, the U.S. headquarters as national, and the entire company as an international firm. This may help you determine where to deal with various performance, legal, and security issues.

Companies that are classified as local tend to have all of their operations located in a single facility or on a single campus. Think of a local company as a company with a small number of local area networks (LANs).

A regional company has a number of locations all within close proximity of each other. Close proximity is somewhat subjective. Regional companies may have multiple offices within a state or within multiple neighboring states. For instance, a local hospital may have various clinics spread throughout a city or state. A small regional operation might have its networks connected through a metropolitan area network (MAN), but most are connected through wide area networks (WANs).

A national company can be thought of as an expansion of the regional network. Expanding on the previous example, a national network of hospitals could have networked systems connected through WANs all across the country. National companies operate throughout the whole of a country instead of just a part of the country. They are usually much larger than regional companies.

An international company crosses national borders. International companies are often referred to as multinational conglomerates. Networks for international companies are often very large and very complex, consisting of multiple interconnected WANs. Factors to consider when planning to meet business requirements include the security available on the communication lines in various countries and the encryption export laws.

Management Model

One of the key components of a management model is autonomy. Autonomy determines where decisions are made and resources are controlled. If a company has multiple locations or business units, those locations or business units will probably have some discretion when making decisions that involve business processes and resources. A unit with a lot of discretion and decision-making power has a lot of autonomy.

The terms *centralized* and *decentralized* are often used to describe the level of autonomy a unit has. A centralized organization gives very little autonomy to units within the organization. Most decisions are made at the corporate offices, and units are expected to abide by those decisions. The military is a good example of a centralized organization. Centralized organizations are often said to be command-and-control style organizations.

At the other end of the spectrum are decentralized organizations. In these organizations, units within the company have most of the decision-making authority. The parent company may exist only to provide common infrastructure needs for the units. Companies are often organized in this way to improve both their flexibility and their response to changing market conditions. Holding companies and cartels like OPEC are good examples of decentralized organizations.

The level of centralization, or autonomy, within a company often has great implications on how IT (Information Technology) services such as networking are designed and delivered. In a decentralized network, the lack of a core or strong backbone is often an identifying mark. Multiple sites and departments manage their own network systems. The majority of network administration is done locally by IT departments who cater to individual sites.

Data collection and maintenance services are also affected by the level of autonomy within an organization. In a decentralized organization, data is often maintained in a number of locations and replicated to a central site for reporting. A centralized organization is more likely to have fewer, but larger, databases that are maintained by the corporate IT group.

It is important not to overlook the needs of your business when it comes to the amount of autonomy in your company model. Remember to assess the needs of any partners who may access your network. For example, perhaps you have a business partner or a subsidiary sharing a database with your company. The database is located on a server within your domain—how do they access it? Is your company's network integrity at risk by allowing outsiders access?

The following are the pros and cons of centralized and decentralized IT organizations:

- An organization with a decentralized IT department does not need to rely on an entity outside of its location to deliver IT services. However, having local IT service means that local support will be an added expense.

- A company with a centralized IT department is in a better position to define and enforce common standards throughout a computing environment, but is less flexible and slower to respond to user needs.

Company Processes

Part of analyzing business requirements is learning more about your company's process. You need to understand how information flows through your network. It may help to review a typical (and atypical) service or product life cycle for your company. Try to identify what resources are used when. Try to identify who does what when, and what information is required for each step in the process. Finally, look for areas where security could be improved without hampering the process.

exam
Watch

Be sure you understand what factors are included when a company forecasts the effects on the business' security when changing to Windows 2000.

When analyzing your current and planned business requirements you should consider several factors. Among these are company priorities, projected growth, growth strategy, relevant laws and regulations, and the company's tolerance for risk. Consider the preceding items when reviewing your company's management model, your company's organization, any vendor and partner relationships, customer relationships, and acquisition plans. You will need a basic understanding, or even dedicated help from experts in these areas, to define security standards for your organization.

Company Organization

The amount of hierarchy in an organization has a number of implications when designing security for Windows 2000. A company can be described as being hierarchical or flat. If you look at an organizational chart and there are many levels of management between the lowest level on the chart and the CEO of the company, then the company is probably hierarchical in nature. If there are relatively few layers of management between the lowest level and the CEO, the company is a flat organization. The hierarchy in network and security management models often closely resembles the hierarchy in a company's management model.

In a Windows 2000 environment, hierarchical networks are constructed from the following elements:

- **Domain** All items within a domain are defined by the same security boundaries, including policies and relationships with other domains.
- **Tree** A set of domains that are interrelated. At the top is the *parent* or *root* domain. Domains connected to the root on the tree are referred to as *child domains*.
- **Forest** Multiple trees with trusts between them are referred to as *forests*. Forests are often offered as solutions for companies involved in mergers—rather than joining one domain into the other, they establish a bi-directional trust relationship that allows network exchanges to occur while minimizing administration.

Maintaining a hierarchical network is usually a more convenient solution for administrative and security reasons. Most notably, you are able (but are not required) to share policies and groups. You are in a better position to distribute network administration responsibilities, and your network can mimic your company's structure with more accuracy.

Sometimes however, the need for autonomy within various branches of the organization calls for a flattening of some parts of the network. It may be necessary to flatten the network and security model when a certain domain is overly restricted by some of the security or policy settings. Occasionally, certain domains need to work independently from the rest of the organization. A good solution to this problem is to set up a domain as an independent tree within the forest. This is accomplished by manipulating the trust policies on the new tree domain.

Becoming familiar with your current operating system structure is another critical step in the planning process. Migrating from Windows 4.0, or another version of Windows, or migrating from a system other than Windows such as Novell or UNIX will create more planning needs. Whichever system it is, you will need to have a sound understanding of the current security structure and how your business works within its parameters.

Vendor Relationships

Outside vendors who need access to your network to perform various functions open a prickly issue. As more businesses expand their networks, many are finding that outsourcing work optimizes the management of the enterprise. The following sections describe a few of the most popular types of vendor-related outsourcing.

EDI

Electronic data interchange (EDI) is the computer-to-computer electronic exchange of business documents using standard formats that are widely recognized both nationally and internationally. The use of standardized data formats allows organizations to exchange common business documents without having to customize their hardware or software system for each organization they do business with.

EDI typically is done over proprietary virtual private networks (VPNs) as transactions that are sent in a batch with other transactions. An EDI transaction has a data map heading that tells what the different fields in the transaction are so that the receiver can identify the sender's document. Each transaction type, such as an invoice, a purchase order, or whatever, is agreed to in a set of protocols created by industry groups.

There is a move underfoot to replace EDI transactions with transactions created with XML (Extensible Markup Language) tags over the Internet. This method, as exemplified by Microsoft's BizTalk or XML Interchange Server product, would seek to do away with expensive VPN traffic. A large number of XML standards have been or are being created at the moment by various industries.

ASPs

Application service providers (ASPs) are quickly changing the way businesses operate over networks. An ASP provides software programs or applications to clients or businesses over the Internet. The client or business rents the application from the ASP for a per-user, per-transaction, or per-month fee. The increasing availability of broadband, high-speed Internet access is one of the factors in the success of the ASP delivery model. By using an ASP, the customer does not have to come up with the investment necessary for the hardware, operating systems, databases, licenses, IT staff or third-party support, and ongoing overhead.

ASPs provide several online applications. Businesses large and small may use an ASP to access special-purpose software as an alternative to installing it in-house.

Businesses may choose to use an ASP for several reasons, including:

- Improved ability to access best-of-breed programs.
- To avoid the full cost of ownership.
- To avoid the problems of supporting an in-house system.
- To avoid the constant threat of obsolescence or the need to upgrade in-house solutions.
- To experience the comfort of knowing their data is secure and being backed up and maintained professionally.

Clearly the benefits of ASPs are plentiful; however, you still will need to assess security requirements prior to making changes and additions to your organization, including:

- Look for guarantees that your ASP is going to honor its commitment to keeping your site secure.
- Learn about the industry reputation of the ASP that your organization is considering.
- Find out what other customers say about the ASP's quality and security.

Full Service Providers

The strategy for Full Service Provider (FSP) business solutions for growing enterprises is to free companies from the headaches of managing back-end infrastructure so they can focus on their core business. FSPs provide storage and networking equipment, software, bandwidth allotment, and round-the-clock technical support, with help from blue-chip suppliers.

FSPs offer multilayer suites of help that are sandwiched between a company's application and the data center. The service is a packaged solution of hardware, software, and hosting facilities. As an extra safety measure, the service providers guarantee 100 percent uptime with 24x7 checking on the security, backup, and hosting of the Web site.

The benefits are that a company's sites and networking needs roll out much faster, with an experienced team running the site 24x7 and scalable software that quickly adds capacity. The only thing customers still need to do is build their own Web sites.

FSPs position themselves as neither application service providers nor a data center, but something in between. The typical ASP will host your software and then go to market with its own sales team and professional services. FSPs can manage the operations of your hosted service and allow your existing sales and professional services team to sell the service directly.

In exchange for its services, a monthly pay-as-you-go recurring charge based on the site's traffic is assessed.

The fees are expected to be in the tens of thousands of dollars, but price structures will vary with the needs of each client. Because of their typical guarantee of 100 percent uptime, FSPs stand to forfeit some of their fees if they do not deliver.

The quality and security of FSPs and ASPs should be scrutinized prior to implementation.

Access to Private Networks

Virtual Private Networks (VPNs) provide companies with secure, encrypted Internet connectivity for intranet, extranet, and remote access. VPNs give mobile workers and remote office sites access to the same robust IP (Internet Protocol) applications they use when connected to their corporate LAN, and allow applications such as e-commerce. Integrating security management into a VPN is critical and is typically accomplished by using a combination of server-based security parameters and a firewall. Windows 2000 has an enhanced digital certificate system to provide added security for VPNs.

SCENARIO & SOLUTION

How can hiring an FSP benefit my company's security?	Security can be boosted when a professional team builds and manages your infrastructure.
In what way does using an ASP make my company less vulnerable to security hazards?	Because ASPs have a dedicated staff of experts focusing on security, your company's safety is a primary concern of theirs.
In what way does it make my company more vulnerable?	Because your data is moving over the Internet, there is always the added risk of it being intercepted in transit.

Consultants

The country is sprouting millions of professionals who are deciding to work independently. They work as Web designers, programmers, strategy consultants, public relations specialists, writers, and administrators. They describe themselves as consultants, freelancers, moonlighters, or hired guns. These professionals are typically single-person or a few person outfits that can be hired by the hour, the day, the week, and so on. Independent contractors are usually hired by small to mid-sized firms in need of expertise. It is advisable to check the references of all consultants prior to hiring them—be sure to ask questions about security and reliability.

There is a second group of more formal consultants that is devoted to business and technology consulting. These consultants combine services such as strategy and change management with technology offerings to provide immense value for clients. Large consulting groups are capable of handling major and minor tasks, and charge a daily rate. Typically, a major consulting firm has established a reputation with the public and has multiple references; nevertheless, security should be made an issue and a clear set of protocols should be established to prevent a security breach.

Partner Relationships

Strategic partnerships enable business access to best-of-breed services from various facets of the business structure. Partners should always work together when creating solutions. If your organization is not directly communicating with your partner when making decisions, you risk several problems, including:

- Duplication of efforts
- Misinformation errors

- System conflicts
- Security breaches

If your organization is currently involved in partnerships, you need to look at the nature of these agreements; determine what the partner needs to know and what you need to know from the partner; determine how they can get that information; and determine whether the method with which you are exchanging information is both optimal and secure. If it is not optimal but it is secure, ask if that is worth it. On the other hand, if your method of information exchange is optimal but lacks security, you need to weigh the risks versus the rewards of your system and act accordingly.

Next you should ask how your plan could be adapted to expansion. Find out if there are any expansions or modifications coming up the pike that you will need to address. Determine whether your current system will still work if changes are made. A proactive method of handling such issues is always best.

Customer Relationships

Factors to consider in determining how relationships with your customers can influence your company strategy include:

- Determining user needs on your network and how much access they will require.
- Knowing the nature of the tasks that will be performed on your network.
- Determining whether other domains will have a "trust" relationship with your domain.
- Knowing the topology that will be used for access to the network.

By understanding the particular needs of your customers, you will have a firm grip on the current state of your relationships and be able to make proper decisions in the planning process for how to deal with your customers in a cost-effective and business-effective manner.

Acquisition Plans

Consolidation mergers and acquisitions can help a company in many ways. Businesses today are filled with competition that frequently results in gobbling up of value-added services and products through mergers and acquisitions. It's quicker than starting from scratch, delivers an immediate return on investment, and for those grappling with scarce IT staff resources, it offers an easier way to capture new employees. A company can expand services, boost staff, and build its strategy very quickly to keep pace with the Internet-speed economy. The cost if you lose your critical staff, security, and organization's reputation because you didn't integrate them properly can far outweigh the costs of taking the time and the investment that is involved in creating a secure solution.

One of the main challenges in an acquisition or merger is security. At times, mergers and acquisitions are not the most popular decisions among employees. It is crucial to be aware and cautious of any potential sabotage that could occur during the transition period.

Another big factor is the integration of the two or more systems that need to interface once the merger is complete. Determining what disparity exists between the two systems must take place early. Once the similarities and differences have been identified, you must decide what methods of integration will be incorporated. Will both system domains remain intact or will they merge? Are the two companies running on the same operating system? If the answer is no then you will need to consider several issues.

When integrating a network, what authentication system will you use? Windows 2000 uses Kerberos v5 as its default but also can run NTLM (Windows NT 4.0's default). The following are some reasons for using NTLM over Kerberos:

- A Windows NT workstation cannot authenticate to a Windows 2000 server running Kerberos.
- An NT workstation on a Windows 2000 network needs to authenticate on a Windows NT 4.0 domain controller residing on the network.

As a network administrator you must be proactive in the event of a merger or an acquisition. Merging companies frequently fail to have a cohesive plan for integrating IT departments and there is a miscommunication of corporate goals up front.

Eliminating or Integrating Other IT Departments

In the course of an acquisition or a merger, your company may be able to achieve considerable cost savings by either eliminating or integrating other IT departments into a single entity. The process has both risks and benefits that need to be weighed.

The following are some reasons to eliminate an IT department from your network:

- Economic benefits
- Security benefits
- A shift in technology makes a department redundant or obsolete
- A more qualified IT department can absorb duties of another IT department
- Resource limitations including staff and equipment

The risks that you run can be summarized as follows:

- Potential loss of data
- Customer disruption
- Costly projects required to merge IT functions
- Loss of essential personnel due to employee dissatisfaction
- System disruptions due to incompatible server and application platforms

Defining *Security Standards*

The process of defining your organizations' security standards should be a group process that involves as many decision makers as possible. You need to understand your company's goals and plans, both current and future, for this process. Document all standards as they are established and make sure that all those who will be affected receive copies so they are always up to date on organization policy.

CERTIFICATION OBJECTIVE 3.02

Analyze Factors That Influence Company Strategies

Identifying key factors in your company that influence the way strategy is developed is key in any successful business.

Company Priorities

Understanding your company's current business priorities is a starting point for determining what your future plans should include. Assessing your existing priorities will allow you to evaluate what works and what needs improvement. If your company is currently spread out with multiple policies at multiple locations, your job will certainly be more challenging.

Projected Growth and Growth Strategy

When assessing your company's growth it is helpful to look at past patterns and compare them to future goals. By being proactive and creating an outline for a growth strategy, you will be ahead of the game. Rather than having to react as new challenges greet your organization, you will have a concise and procedural plan in place.

Relevant Laws and Regulations

Current law imposes strict controls on the export of 128-bit encryption, putting any U.S. company that wants to conduct business globally in a tough position. Encryption affects businesses, particularly American businesses, heavily. IT staff and business executives must pay attention to government debates over export controls on 128-bit encryption or they may find their strategic plans for everything from globalization to electronic commerce put on hold.

At present, the strongest encryption available in Windows 2000 is a 128-bit key with the triple Data Encryption Standard (DES) encryption algorithm. It is quite strong, so strong in fact that the U.S. government will not allow it to be used outside of North America without a license.

exam
⚠atch

To keep encryption technology out of the hands of criminals, current law imposes strict controls on the export of 128-bit encryption, which is the most secure encryption currently on the market and the only encryption offering a reasonable assurance that it won't be broken.

Because those restrictions apply only to the export of encryption technology, businesses that operate globally—with overseas offices, owners, subsidiaries, customers, and partners—are immediately affected. Such companies can't encrypt their electronic communications using American 128-bit encryption without getting an export license;

FROM THE CLASSROOM

The Security Market

The two most frequently addressed professions when discussing security are the financial services industry and the healthcare industry. Both are in the midst of significant changes resulting in modifications, additions, and elimination of regulations and laws. Both also have a lot at stake when it comes to security, and many are often overwhelmed when asked to develop a security strategy for their organization.

The lines between banks, brokerages, and insurance companies are quickly blurring. Additionally, financial services formerly offered only by large institutions are now the domain of new, sometimes smaller, firms. The Internet has emerged as the great equalizer among these institutions.

Internet-based solutions allow customers more access to their financial information, but they also present new security and privacy challenges for financial services firms. How do we protect confidential customer information stored in our computer systems? How do we provide our customers with an enhanced level of service by allowing them to access their personal information and conduct transactions online?

The healthcare industry is undergoing dramatic changes with the emergence of integrated delivery systems, the transition towards electronic patient records, the shift towards consumer-driven healthcare due to the Internet, the growing emphasis on information technology, and potentially the most significant—the change in the regulatory environment.

Healthcare organizations will soon need to comply with government regulations mandated by the Health Information Portability and Accountability Act (HIPAA, 1996). As required by HIPAA, the Department of Health and Human Services released its proposed rule for Security and Electronic Signatures, which provides the guidelines for security compliance. Final rules on this standard are expected sometime during the first half of 2000, and healthcare companies will have only two years in which to demonstrate compliance (three years for small health plans).

Security has come to the forefront of concerns for both healthcare and financial industries. Having the knowledge to help financial or healthcare firms answer tough security questions will make you an indispensable member of your business team. Goals for a security specialist in healthcare should include striving to reduce costs, protect patient privacy, and secure confidential medical information. Likewise, a financial industry security specialist should always consider costs, protect the information of both the business as well as clients, and ensure secure transactions of all varieties.

—*Steve Jutunen*

they would need that technology at both ends of the communication, thereby necessitating export.

In the grand scheme of things, the number of affected companies is relatively small, and those that most need encryption, such as banks, can usually get a license. However, the time and effort involved can be extensive.

As more companies jump into electronic commerce on a global scale, the impact of encryption controls will be broader. New bills addressing various facets of the electronic security and privacy issue have been debated heavily over the past several years and many more are in the queue. With the stakes rising, the confrontation between the government and the business community over the issue of encryption export is far from over. As a network administrator, you will need to assess what, if any, encryption laws affect your company processes. If your processes are affected, you will need to plan accordingly to comply with the law.

on the job

You are an administrator in an international company and need to have remote access to machines on your network outside of North America to schedule system backups and to outinely check hard disk availability. You have not received a license to use 128-bit encryption. What are your alternatives?

- **No encryption** The least secure way to transfer data. You should avoid this option unless you don't mind outsiders being able to see your information.

- **Basic encryption** Uses a 40-bit Microsoft Point-to-Point Encryption (MPPE) key. This is a good option for servers working as VPN servers. The PPTP protocol is also available at this level. Security is bumped up to a 56-bit key if the L2TP protocol is used.

- **Strong encryption** Uses a 56-bit DES key. There are 72 quadrillion possible combinations—this is to say that strong encryption is fairly safe!

It is critical in situations such as this to weigh all your options when considering the proper encryption solution.

Company Tolerance for Risk

Determine the kind of information that your company works with and the costs that will be assessed if there is a breach in your security. If your business deals with relatively low-risk data such as temperature readings from small towns in Kansas, your tolerance for risk may not be so crucial. However, if your business is an

EXERCISE 3-1

Building a TCO Model for Your Security Strategy

In building a TCO model for your security strategy, it's essential to determine the separate costs associated with each of the following categories:

- **Equipment Costs**   Include firewalls, special software, and additional space used as a result of added equipment.
- **Setup Costs**   Include additional cabling, furnishings, staff time, steering committee time, documentation, physical labor, and time for setup.
- **Operating Costs**   Include costs of IS time for administration, connectivity services, depreciation expenses, costs associated with failure, training, service contracts, and upgrades.
- **Five-year cycle costs**   Doing this will allow better insight for the real Return on Investment (ROI)—when spreading out the costs versus the benefits over a longer amount of time you get a better perspective of the value.
- **Average monthly expenses**   This is one of the critical elements in establishing the long-term feasibility of the strategy.

Other options to consider include the security options that are available "out-of-the-box" in Windows 2000. You have already paid for them so you might as well use them. After determining which parts you will use, run a second evaluation of your network and determine where you are still weak. At this point it may be determined that you will need to install further precautions such as firewalls or other third-party software. It is also important to consider the comprehensive and long-term value of the computing solution and how it will service all of your organization's needs.

international bank, you will need to invest quite a bit more time and energy in establishing your security plan because the risk tolerance cannot get much lower.

Total Cost of Operations

As budgets become tighter, and the reliance on personal computers and IT as a whole becomes more prevalent in the workplace, many organizations are paying attention to the total cost of ownership (TCO) for systems and applications. The whole idea of TCO analysis, as first described and used by the Gartner Group, is to expose the hidden costs of a product over its projected life cycle. The TCO of Windows 2000 is not just the cost of the software—it's the cost of the hardware upgrades required to make a company's system capable of running Windows 2000. It's also the cost of the training required to get a company's IT staff ready to install and manage Windows 2000, the labor cost of the installation of the software, and the productivity cost as every user begins the process of getting used to the new product. Although cost is unmistakably a critical component of any IT investment, your company's integrity is obviously no less important. Hence the dilemma, spend more on IT that guarantees good security, or cut back on security spending to help meet the bottom line. Obviously there is a lot of middle ground that will likely become the place where your solution ends up.

Microsoft is meeting these needs through the ongoing Microsoft Windows Client Strategy. This strategy will deliver to customers a complete range of client solutions that address the core problems facing them today: how to reduce TCO and increase the return on investment. Microsoft will do this by providing solutions that take advantage of the Windows operating system as it exists today and as it evolves in the future, with special emphasis on options and functionality that address customer needs for maximizing their computing investments.

CERTIFICATION OBJECTIVE 3.03

Analyze the Structure of IT Management

By looking at your company's IT management structure you will be able to determine what sorts of factors your company should be concerned with when assessing your current network and planning future changes to it.

Administration

The two most common types of administration are centralized and decentralized, as described in the next two sections.

Centralized

As in previous versions of Windows NT, the domain is the starting point in a Windows 2000 network. Domains are a tidy way of organizing items connected to your network. A Windows 2000 domain can store over 10 million objects (where objects are defined as PCs, people, printers, and peripherals). Chances are most companies will never *have* to add additional domains; capacity for 10 million objects will generally be adequate to meet the needs of even the largest organizations.

Decentralized

Logic tells us that it would not be very effective if each department or project operated their own water, electrical, or sewer systems, so why would it be effective for them to operate their own networks?

A decentralized administration system offers more leverage to the individual sites because typically they are administered locally. However, with that freedom comes consequence. Organizations who have disparity within their networks can run into an array of difficulties including communication problems, data transfer interruptions, and, most importantly, security breaches. Although it is often difficult to have a completely centralized system, as an administrator you will want to keep at least a common set of security standards in place across the organization.

Outsourcing

Most businesses are initially adverse to the idea of outsourcing work. However, as companies find themselves bogged down in their business—be it selling, manufacturing, servicing, or what have you—companies are seeing the benefits of leaving IT jobs to experts.

Table 3-1 provides the benefits and drawbacks of outsourcing at a glance.

TABLE 3-1 The Benefits and Drawbacks of Outsourcing	Benefits	Drawbacks
	Can lower the initial cost of implementing and avoid staffing difficulties.	Many traditional networks are ill suited for outsourcing.
	If you hire properly, your outsourced initiatives will be left to experts.	Increased access to your business files requires added attention to protecting confidentiality, security, and competition issues.
	Allows your business to focus on its products and services rather than spending time attempting to deploy business solutions.	Outsourced help will not have the same local presence that onsite employees enjoy—this could result in dissatisfied users in need of special attention at their disposal.

By giving thought to the benefits and drawbacks you will be more informed when determining what kind of access to give outside users. As a general rule, however, you should always give outsiders (and insiders) the minimal amount of access possible while still enabling them to perform their job functions.

Decision-Making Process

A company's very survival requires it to use information technology to create competitive advantages as well as operational efficiencies. Consequently, IT staffers should be integrally involved in spearheading company business objectives regarding network security. As in all scenarios of business, a hierarchy will exist in the decision-making process, but having business-savvy IT staff involved in the process is a huge plus. If your organization does not already have staff capable of meshing business strategy and IT, then developing one should be stressed.

Organizations are increasingly taking on business decisions in addition to the traditional technology decisions that have defined their position. Driven by Internet advances, globalization, and corporate downsizing, progressive companies within the technology industry—and even a few outside it—are hiring individuals who can connect various business units to IT know-how.

Trends driving the reliance on technical staff in tech-savvy organizations include the need to control costs while promoting a global presence and the need to keep up with developments in technology. As organizations become more geographically dispersed in order to compete globally, technical infrastructure grows increasingly complex, forcing a greater commitment of IT resources. But simultaneously, the pressure to streamline operations demands that companies keep a careful eye on those soaring IT costs. The most successful companies today have a business-school approach to managing their units.

Businesses stand to gain on all fronts from the emergence of strong technical staff that understand their business objectives. Within the organization, a company will be able to move products to market more efficiently by allowing staff to connect the business units to IT resources.

Change-Management Process

Much like the preceding case with decision making, having savvy staff on hand to manage the business, as well as the IT operations, will make changes within the organization go more smoothly.

EXERCISE 3-2

Develop a Decision Tree

In the following exercise you will make a sample decision tree based on a fictitious idea to begin auditing all e-mail messages that go outside of the company. When you have finished reading, try to create a similar scenario that may occur in your company and map out the steps to best solve the problem.

1. The company's CEO reads a newspaper article describing lost employee hours due to personal e-mail.
2. The CEO calls a meeting to discuss the idea of auditing.
3. The CEO assigns various members of the decision-making party to research various topics that will need to be addressed, including:
   - Legal considerations
   - Logistical concerns
   - Determining the best method for conducting audits
   - Formation of a committee to draft the policy
4. The assigned staff conducts research and a committee is formed.
5. Legal considerations are addressed and the company learns that a notice to employees is not required but decides that it would be a nice courtesy to inform employees prior to beginning audits. (Note: the company was required to do legal checks in all states where they had offices due to differences in laws from state to state.)
6. A notice is drafted and distributed to the staff.
7. The committee drafts a formal auditing policy and submits it to the appropriate group for approval.
8. The committee learns that a number of software titles are available to perform auditing tasks on e-mail.
9. The committee reviews features and determines which title best suits their current and future needs.
10. The committee assigns the auditing project to the IT department.
11. The IT department determines who among them will be responsible for the task and who will be available as a secondary resource.

> 12. The committee gets approval for the audit policy and writes a summary of the procedure and submits it to the CEO for final approval.
> 13. The CEO approves and gives the green light for implementation.
> 14. The IT department implements auditing.

Security Risks

For those of you who are responsible for securing critical systems, and who fight the constraints of time and resources daily, there is one essential weapon you need to have in your arsenal: information. There are many security products on the market, and many vendors selling various solutions, but those products and vendors can't help you if you don't understand what they actually do, and how they actually help you. The single best way to avoid over-hyped solutions or problems is to understand what works, what doesn't, and why.

Internal

Much to the surprise of most organizations, most security breaches originate internally rather than from the outside world. Disgruntled employees, employees with too much free time, and employees with limited computer proficiencies can often be your worst enemy.

on the job

An employee, much to his dismay, was informed that he will be transferred from his comfortable job in southern California to a remote part of northern Canada. He is told to finish his reports by the end of the week and plan for the move next Monday.

He plans, but not what his manager had planned. He intends to quit with a bang—it is your job to be sure that it is not you who winds up getting that job transfer!

You should have a policy in place that states that the IT department is notified of any job change plans prior to the formal notification of the employee. That way the IT department can take proactive measures to ensure a safe and secure transition for all employees.

TABLE 3-2 Business Drawbacks and Security Risks with External Access

Type of Connection	Potential Business and Security Drawbacks
Dial-up	Slow transaction speed.
Digital subscriber line (DSL)	If you have file and print sharing turned on, you are vulnerable.
Cable	Similar risks to DSL.
Fiber Optic	Security is good but the cost of construction is high.

External

Contractors and other outsiders pose an obvious threat to your network security. You should always require anyone accessing your network to sign security agreements and any other agreements that may be prudent, such as a non-disclosure agreement if the outsider will have access to company secrets.

You should also consider what kind of external access is available on your network. Table 3-2 outlines some security risks with external access.

CERTIFICATION SUMMARY

The security of information in computer systems and networks has proven to be an extremely challenging problem. The administration of systems that enforce a consistently high level of security is difficult even in those cases when the system's functions and interfaces are limited, highly controlled, and change slowly. For businesses that are connected to networks and that also need to meet complex and rapidly changing functional requirements, the difficulty of achieving a high level of security skyrockets as the number of users and tasks increases.

Today's networks require that those systems be capable of protecting their sensitive information, and of operating reliably in the face of malicious attempts to disrupt them. As an administrator your job is to prevent disruption while steering users in a secure direction on the network, protecting your organization from within and from without.

Given the set of features and functions built into Microsoft products and the range of potentially threatening environments in which those products are used, the users and administrators of Microsoft products bear a significant responsibility for the security of the products and the information that they process. Because you cannot ensure that every product will resist every conceivable threat, you should document your plans to thwart all of the expected threats to each aspect of your network, the security that your users should expect you to provide, and what you expect from them in return. You should also document the user and administrator actions that are required to achieve the level of security that the network is capable of providing.

Recognizing that security is a matter of great concern to your business process, a commitment to pursuing an aggressive program of research and development aimed at continuous improvement in the security of your organization is crucial.

✓ TWO-MINUTE DRILL

Analyze the Existing and Planned Business Models and Organizational Structures

- ❑ Management models for networks are generally defined by whether they are centralized (on the same domain) or decentralized (that is, they are loosely connected or separate from other branches).
- ❑ You should have a firm understanding of your company's organization methods—is there a standard protocol for documenting, processing, and executing company directives or is there no structured method?
- ❑ Hierarchical company networks are broken into three main elements: domains, trees, and forests.
- ❑ Vendors can offer your business several interesting alternatives to doing work in-house. Some of the most notable are EDI, ASPs, and FSPs.
- ❑ VPNs are an emerging way for companies to harness the power of the Internet for use as a medium for data transfer between different physical locations on the same network.
- ❑ 128-bit encryption is the strongest encryption available, but you need to obtain a waiver from the government to use it outside of North America.
- ❑ You should always use at least 40-bit encryption for your data when it is traveling over the Internet.

Analyze Factors That Influence Company Strategies

- ❑ Understanding your company's tolerance for risk will help you decide what type of encryption to use.
- ❑ The Total Cost of Ownership (TCO) is an elaborate method used to understand the true value of your company's system.
- ❑ When developing future plans for security, you should factor in your company's future plans and what level of risk they carry if the data is insecure.

Analyze the Structure of IT Management

❑ Outsourcing is a potentially useful way of getting expert help on issues that affect your business.

❑ Outsourcing can be dangerous if you do not take the time to look at who you are hiring and make sure they are both up to the job and trustworthy.

❑ All parties involved should understand a company's decision-making process. If there is confusion over how a decision is made, the process can take much longer than necessary.

❑ Recognize that your most serious security risks can happen internally. Make sure that your staff is clear on what they have rights to and what is off limits.

❑ Having employees sign security agreements is a good way to enforce security policies in an organization.

SELF TEST

The following questions will help you measure your understanding of the material presented in this chapter. Read all of the choices carefully, as there may be more than one correct answer. Choose all correct answers for each question.

Analyze the Existing and Planned Business Models and Organizational Structures

1. A centralized management model is always a better solution for a large enterprise.

    A. False, a centralized management model should only be used in smaller enterprises because too many factors complicate a large enterprise and microscopic administration is necessary.

    B. True, a centralized management model simplifies the administration of a network and should therefore be used at all times.

    C. False, while in most cases a centralized model is preferable, there are instances that call for a decentralized method in order to cater to the needs of an individual site.

    D. False, whenever possible you should decentralize your network.

2. Your company has recently acquired another company. Both are running Windows 2000. You are required to choose the optimal way to utilize the two networks using a cost-effective and time-effective approach that disrupts users in both locations as little as possible. What should you do?

    A. Force the newly acquired company to join your existing company's domain.

    B. Create a trust relationship between domains that enables them to work together as known partners in a trust.

    C. Allow the two units to run autonomous networks and send data in packets when necessary.

    D. Build a new network that incorporates both networks.

3. A bank that has 14 offices in Boston is also part of a larger banking system that has offices in Los Angeles, New York, Chicago, Denver, and Atlanta. The conglomerates have several offices spread throughout the world. From a geographical perspective, what factors does a Boston administrator need to think about when determining security for the network?

    A. Regional issues

    B. National issues

    C. International issues

    D. All of the above

4. When determining what type of network your company should run, what factors should be weighed when questioning the value of a hierarchical network versus a flat one? (Choose all that apply.)

   A. The complexity and number of domains, trees, and forests that will be created if a hierarchical network is chosen.
   B. The number of networked devices that will reside on any given domain.
   C. The processor capacity of your network servers.
   D. The types of operating systems that will be on the network.

5. How is data transferred when using an ASP?

   A. Through a VPN
   B. Over the Internet
   C. Via radio or infrared
   D. Both A and B are correct

6. What purpose does an FSP fill for a business?

   A. It frees company staff from managing front-end infrastructure so they can focus on other aspects of their business.
   B. FSPs offer a single-layer suite to help companies consolidate their applications and data into one unit.
   C. It offers organizations a scalable network management and hosting system with 24 x 7 support.
   D. Most FSPs will charge a large one-time fee for their service.

7. What reason is not accurate when considering why my company should consider installing a VPN?

   A. Using a VPN can extend the boundaries of your LAN to anywhere an Internet access point is available.
   B. Using your LAN over a VPN is just as secure as using your LAN onsite.
   C. Any IP application can run over a VPN.
   D. Windows 2000 has enhanced the digital certificate system to provide added security for VPNs.

Analyze Factors That Influence Company Strategies

8. What is the best type of consultant to help with an enterprise-level installation of a major network upgrade?

   A. A private or independent contractor
   B. A consulting firm
   C. General phone support from the vendor
   D. Online support from the vendor

9. When hiring a consultant what should I look for? (Choose all that apply.)

   A. A proven track record for maintaining security
   B. References
   C. A mission statement
   D. A warranty

10. What is not a risk of poor or insecure communications with partners?

    A. Duplication of efforts
    B. System conflicts
    C. Data sharing
    D. Security breaches

11. What is not a reason why so many mergers are occurring in today's IT market?

    A. It is quicker to acquire a firm than to start one from scratch.
    B. With an acquisition also comes a staff of IT talent.
    C. Companies often lose a lot of staff when a merger takes place.
    D. A company can expand services and build markets faster with more resources.

Analyze the Structure of IT Management

12. What kinds of business decisions revolve around authentications? (Choose all that apply.)
    A. Whether to use *Kerberos v5* or *NTLM*.
    B. The number of network resources.
    C. The scope of available IP numbers.
    D. The OS versions running on your clients.

13. What laws regarding encryption do I need to be concerned with if I have an international company? (Choose all that apply.)
    A. The number of international offices I have connected to my company's network.
    B. The speed of the data transfers.
    C. The type of encryption I am using for data transfers.
    D. The countries to which I am transferring data.

14. If I have a VPN and want to implement simple encryption, what should I use?
    A. No encryption is necessary if you are using a VPN.
    B. Point–to-Point encryption.
    C. Strong encryption.
    D. You cannot use encryption on a VPN.

15. Why is TCO a major factor in business strategy?
    A. TCO reveals the annual total cost of a network.
    B. CEOs and other executive staff can refer to TCO data for a general understanding of the network architecture.
    C. TCO helps you understand and expose hidden costs in products and services during their life cycles.
    D. IT administrators always use TCO data when making security decisions.

16. Where do most IT-related security breaches originate?
    A. In "hacker rooms" on the Internet
    B. From outside attackers who probe the Internet for vulnerable sites
    C. From internal employees
    D. From old-fashioned thieves who steal hardcopy documents

17. Which of the following factors are business factors that I should consider when choosing a connectivity medium? (Choose all that apply.)

    A. Speed; in business, time is money and if your connection is slow then it is lost work time.
    B. Some connection media leave your system vulnerable to hackers if files are left open on the desktop.
    C. Many media require special modems, many of which are expensive.
    D. Local printing slows things down by adding additional connection options.

LAB QUESTION

Adding on to the work you did in creating an outline of your organization's existing and planned network, list in order the steps involved in this design process.

SELF TEST ANSWERS

Analyze the Existing and Planned Business Models and Organizational Structures

1. ☑ **C is correct.** You should always strive to have a centralized system for administration but you may not always be able to. Reasons to prohibit centralization include geographical limitations, management differences, lack of staff, demand for autonomy, and availability of bandwidth.

   ☒ **A is incorrect;** centralized management systems are not necessarily limited to smaller-sized companies. Several large organizations have successfully accomplished building and managing efficient centralized networks. Remember, however, that the more networked devices and users attached, the more complex your network becomes and should be closely monitored and documented to ensure peak performance and optimal security. **B is incorrect;** centralized management does not universally simplify the administration process for networks. There are several cases in which a centralized system does in fact have benefits, but there is no rule of thumb in this case. **D is incorrect;** decentralizing a network is often thought of as working backwards. There are of course several cases in which a decentralized network is useful for catering to special security needs or allowing more autonomy for a sect of users in an organization. However, whenever possible you want your network to have maximum function—this usually means having as much of your network centralized as you can manage.

2. ☑ **B.** The most cost-effective and time-effective approach to this problem is through the creation of a trust relationship between the two domains. By choosing this solution, your administrative tasks will be kept to a minimum and your likelihood of disrupting users will be lower than by choosing alternative methods.

   ☒ **A is incorrect** because while containing both companies in one domain may be more administratively effective, it is not a time-effective method of incorporating the new network. The amount of work involved in merging one domain into another is quite sizable. You will run the risk of interrupting users' tasks if you attempt to merge the domains because the complexity involved increases as the size of the network grows. **C is incorrect;** the idea of sending data in packets when necessary is an incredibly inefficient way to handle your problem. The amount of labor involved in setting up a system to accomplish this task would be better spent building a more permanent solution. **D is incorrect;** building a new network is an expensive, disruptive, and time-consuming process. Unless both networks are heavily outdated, you should always try to salvage an existing network and build upon it.

3. ☑ **D.** When determining what security issues you need to be concerned with, the first thing you need to do is examine the entire scope of your enterprise. You should begin regionally, then expand nationally and internationally when appropriate. In many cases, your company will institute a policy that assigns individuals to certain sectors of a network. This could result in making an individual exclusively accountable for only part of a network. However, unless there is an explicit policy showing this, you should never assume that jurisdiction of your security ends with your location. Today it is just as easy for someone on the other side of the world to break into your network as it is for someone down the street to do so.

4. ☑ **A and B.** An overly complex structure can lend itself to several problems in a networked environment. An organization should strive to take a sensible approach when designing its network so that it does not suffer from illogical or poor optimization. Building and managing a large hierarchical network is work and requires a great deal of planning for it to work properly. However, if done well, a smartly-developed hierarchical network will serve its users and end up being far less work than a flat network environment. Additionally, when developing a network you must be aware of how many devices will be attached to it.
☒ Answers **C** and **D** need not be weighed factors when considering a hierarchical network versus a flat one.

5. ☑ **D.** VPNs use the Internet to transfer data to and from locations within a network. Using PPTP or L2TP, which are supported in Windows 2000, a secure connection to a LAN can be remotely established. The ASP can easily establish such a connection once access to your network has been granted. Local access to private networks is becoming more common; using the Internet to gain this access is growing in popularity. Integration of security features in Windows 2000 is making remote connectivity more reliable and functional.
☒ **C** is incorrect; radio and infrared frequencies are not known to be reliable or efficient enough for an ASP to rely on them to provide application data to a client.

6. ☑ **C.** FSPs are built for growing enterprises to manage their infrastructure needs and support those needs full-time. Scalability is a big selling point in favor of FSPs. Organizations growing quickly can reap the benefits by sidestepping the mass complications that come with growth. Handing off the work to an FSP can be a major headache saver.
☒ **A** is incorrect; FSPs focus their services on the back-end infrastructure of a company, allowing the groups who hire them to focus their efforts on the front end. This way, companies who are in any business other than back-end network support can greatly benefit from a FSP—they get to work on what they know rather than try to learn about the infrastructure of tools that they don't know. **B** is incorrect; FSPs use a multi-layer approach to building a

company suite that stacks company applications on top of their data. The service is a package of hardware, software, and hosting. **D** is incorrect; the bulk of FSPs will charge a monthly fee based on the amount of services your organization is using.

7. ☑ **B.** Although it is safer now than it has ever been to access a LAN over a VPN, it is still running over the Internet, which makes it a less safe alternative to operating locally.
☒ **A** is incorrect; VPNs do extend the reach of your LAN to anywhere Internet access is available. **C** is incorrect; just as it is true for computers directly tied to your LAN, all VPN computers can access your IP-based applications. **D** is incorrect; the new enhancements to Windows 2000 digital certificate system extend the security of a VPN further than ever before.

Analyze Factors That Influence Company Strategies

8. ☑ **B.** When you are involved in a major project and consultants are deemed necessary, it is generally best to go with a reputable firm. On the whole, a large consulting firm will be very expensive, but keep in mind that they probably got to where they are by offering quality.
☒ **A** is not the best answer. Private contractors can often be good solutions too but you must do more homework when hiring them because typically there is less of a reputation to rely upon. **C** and **D** are incorrect. In a major upgrade you will likely need more than what is available from online and phone vendor support.

9. ☑ **A, B,** and **D** are correct; your organization cannot afford to have any breaches in its security. Being sure that your company hires someone who understands this is critical. Without this, your company runs a serious risk of having aspects of its network left unprotected. If your consultant does not have many references to provide then you should use caution—if the contractor is just starting out in his or her career then ask for educational references, anything to provide your organization with some evidence that the person is credible. Alarms should go off if there is reluctance on the consultant's part when asked to provide references. A warranty or some sort of guarantee that the contractor will back up what they do indicates confidence in their work. No one likes to do the same job twice and having a warranty usually gives them incentive to do the job right the first time; everybody wins.
☒ **C** is incorrect; while a mission statement is a great way to focus oneself, it has very little to do with how you should hire a contractor.

10. ☑ **C.** The point of a partnership is to allow data sharing.
☒ **A** partnership does not mean that you want to share everything about your company. That is why answers **A, B,** and **C** are important reminders of some of the risks involved for organizations that are involved in partnerships.

11. ☑ **C.** Holding onto staff is a huge challenge for many large and small companies involved in mergers. Often staff feels betrayed, lost in the shuffle, and forgotten about during mergers. As a result they frequently jump ship during or shortly after a merger. Many companies offer perks to keep talent around such as stock options and extended vacation time.
    ☒ **A**, **B**, and **D** are incorrect; however, all three are valid points and should be understood by anyone in IT during a merger or acquisition.

Analyze the Structure of IT Management

12. ☑ **A** and **D.** Kerberos v5 is Windows 2000's new authentication protocol. Kerberos runs as the default but NTLM is also available. NTLM is the authentication system that came in Windows NT 4.0. (Note: at the time of writing there are rumors that Microsoft plans to include a Kerberos patch in the next service pack for Windows NT 4.0—check Microsoft's Web site for updates.)
    ☒ **B** is incorrect because the number of network resources is incidental in determining the type of authentication system to choose. **C** is incorrect; the scope of IP numbers available on a network system is important when determining remote access but it has no bearing on the outcome of a local authentication system.

13. ☑ **C** and **D.** According to current U.S. laws, no one is allowed to use more than "Strong" encryption outside North America unless the government grants a special export license. Strong encryption is defined in Windows 2000 as a 56-bit DES key. The strongest encryption available in Windows 2000 is 128 bit. Obtaining a license is a lengthy process in which the applicant must prove to the government that there is a specific need to have the encryption. If caught using 128-bit encryption for international export without a permit, a company can expect to face heavy fines and possible prosecution.
    ☒ **A** is incorrect; the number of international offices that are connected to your office will interest your telecommunications company but is not a direct legal concern for your organization. **B** is incorrect; data transfer speed is not a legal hurdle for your company, but it is something you will need to consider when determining what the nature of your data transfers will entail.

14. ☑ **B.** Point-to-Point encryption, also called Basic encryption in Windows 2000, uses a 40-bit encryption key that is standard for most Internet sites.
    ☒ **A** is not correct. You should always use at least 40-bit encryption, especially for organization data. You would not want, for instance, to be sending personnel data over your VPN only to have it intercepted on the Internet—losing not only your work but also the information that most likely is not something you want to share with the world. **C** is

incorrect; unless you are sending highly sensitive material that you cannot have anyone see, strong encryption is overkill. Most VPNs are designed to allow LAN access with a decent amount of speed. Remember, the higher the encryption, the slower your access. **D** is incorrect; as stated previously, encryption is available for VPNs.

15. ☑ **C.** The main reason for TCO analysis is to expose the hidden costs of a product over its life cycle. TCO is not limited to Windows 2000 software. TCO is an all-encompassing view of the network that includes the costs of hardware, training, labor, and installations and maintenance.
☒ **A** is incorrect because TCO is not limited to annual costs. **B** is incorrect; although CEOs and other executive staff in an organization look at TCO data, it is not used to understand the network architecture in any direct way. **D** is incorrect; reviewing TCO data does not always result in security decisions. Although it is recommended that TCO data be utilized when discussing security policy, there is no direct correlation between a sound security model and TCO.

16. ☑ **C.** Many people are surprised to learn that the most frequent place for security breaches to begin is from within. Users on your network have more access than anyone else, spend more time on your network, and have more interest than most. It only stands to reason that you are most vulnerable from this population.
☒ **A** is incorrect; although hacker rooms or organized hacker groups manage to gain a lot of media attention and they should be taken seriously, the frequency of their attacks is much lower than internal attacks. **B** is incorrect; people who surf the Internet probing for vulnerable networks are a serious threat, but again, the frequency with which they attack is far less than internal breaches. **D** is incorrect; on the whole, more security breaches occur by traditional methods such as theft. However, IT-related breaches occur over the organizations' network.

17. ☑ **A and C.** With more availability of bandwidth options than ever before, organizations can choose from screaming fast to crawling slow and everywhere in between.
☒ **B** is incorrect because it is a misleading answer. If your network has file and print sharing turned on, your network will be more vulnerable to hackers when using DSL, cable, and dial-up access. However, simply having folders open on the desktop should not cause any major security hazards in you system. **D** is incorrect because printing speed is not related to connectivity unless you are printing at a remote site and your bandwidth is low.

LAB ANSWER

The steps to assessing and outlining your organization's existing and planned network are as follows:

1. Define the geographical scope.

2. Outline the nature of your existing relationships with clients and vendors. Note any potentially significant security issues that should be attended to.

3. Determine your organization's current and future uses for third-party vendor services such as EDI, ASPs, and FSPs.

4. Identify whether your company uses or has any future use for a VPN. If so, then determine the level of security that will be needed and whether any laws or regulations need to be considered.

5. Evaluate and verify that your organization's encryption is sufficient.

6. Verify the credibility of all outside vendors and be sure that any necessary documentation regarding security agreements has been signed and is on file.

7. Be sure that all users have signed a security agreement and are kept informed of any new security policies that are established as your network matures.

MCSE
MICROSOFT CERTIFIED SYSTEMS ENGINEER

4

Analyzing End-User Computing Requirements

CERTIFICATION OBJECTIVES

4.01	Analyze Business and Security Requirements for the End User
4.02	Analyze the Current Physical Model and Information Security Model
✓	Two-Minute Drill
Q&A	Self Test

Network security planning is a complex task involving many facets of the organization and the network infrastructure. Different members of an organization have unique perspectives on security planning and implementation. In this chapter, we'll examine three common business perspectives—executive, administrative, and technical—and learn how each viewpoint contributes to an integrated security solution. We'll briefly review four common user categories and discuss the security considerations for each group. We'll also look at physical and information security models and how Microsoft Windows 2000 provides tools for improved security for internal, external, local, and remote users.

CERTIFICATION OBJECTIVE 4.01

Analyze Business and Security Requirements for the End User

This chapter focuses on the business and security requirements for end users. Most of the material discussed here is covered in more technical detail throughout this book. In this segment, we'll limit our technical discussions to overviews, except when data is not covered elsewhere in the book.

Planning network security involves three primary groups. Executives are responsible for the overall success of the business and are concerned with security as it relates to business and industry issues. Administrators, such as Information Technology (IT) managers and network administrators, are concerned with overall network security planning, including network architecture, domain planning, and group policies. The Technical group is responsible for implementing network plans, including things such as group policies, routing protocols, and network monitoring. We'll look at each group and discuss their part in network security planning and implementation.

End users can be classified into four network user communities, each with distinct computing and access needs: Everyone, Staff, Users, and Partners. Each of these is discussed in this chapter.

Finally in this section, we'll review user applications and discuss what must be taken into consideration when setting up security for user applications.

Business Classes

Planning network security essentially involves three primary stakeholders: executive, administrative, and technical. Each community participates in planning and implementation at different levels and with different concerns. It is critical to involve each group in security planning to ensure that a thorough security model is implemented.

Executive

The executive group can contain upper management, division heads, or others who run business units, teams, or sections. They are involved with high-level strategic planning for the business. Typically, they look at the business, the industry, the economy, and the myriad of external factors that could potentially impact the organization, and develop strategies for both short- and long-term management. This high-level strategy, as it relates to the IT function, can involve the following factors:

Company Structure   Centralized or decentralized. They might ask questions such as: How should we organize our company, what are the costs associated with this, how will this impact our network infrastructure, how will this impact security?

Business Partnerships   Vendors, contractors, strategic partners. The questions asked here are: Who are our trusted partners, what data do they need to work more efficiently with us, what are the security risks, and what are the competitive implications of granting or denying access?

Product or Services   Defining and producing company products or services. The executive group will review how the product or service fits in the industry, who the competitors are, and how to provide these products and services to their market. Some of the questions they'll ask are: Will an Internet presence increase sales or name recognition, do we have competitors who are using technology to reach the market, how can we improve our efficiency and perhaps increase productivity or profitability through using technology, what are our competitive advantages and how do we protect them?

Financial   Financial health, revenue, costs, profitability, shareholder accountability. Executives are held accountable for the financial health of the organization. Therefore, they are concerned with lowering costs, improving productivity, increasing sales, and broadening their markets. They'll ask: How can technology improve the company's profitability, what are the costs and benefits of implementing new technology solutions, what are the financial risks of making more information publicly available via the Internet, what are the security risks and how can they be mitigated?

Once the executive group has decided upon the overall strategy for the company, the tactical planning and implementation are generally delegated to the administrative and technical groups.

Administrative

We often associate an administrative group with administrative assistants, secretaries, or general users. However, in this context, the administrative group is one that develops and oversees the implementation of the organization's overall network plans. As such, this group typically includes such members as the IT manager, network administrators, and others involved with the specifics of network planning. They are responsible for developing tangible plans for implementing the strategies developed by the executives of the company. They are held accountable for the success of technology implementations.

The key administrative roles are to design and oversee the implementation of security plans that support the security, availability, and performance of the network for users. These plans can include the following:

Overall IT Planning   The administrative group develops the overall strategic and tactical plans for the firm's IT department. These plans incorporate the elements discussed later in this chapter and provide a comprehensive roadmap for the organization's IT department to follow during the planning and implementation phase of any IT project.

Domain Structure   With Windows 2000, the organization of the domain structure has changed. With Windows NT 4.0 (and earlier), organizing users of a large company required multiple domains. In Windows 2000, the use of forests, domains, sites, and organizational units (OUs) expands the flexibility and scalability of the network. Each of these elements is discussed throughout this book and will not be addressed in detail in this chapter. However, the administrative group is involved with defining the optimal structure for the organization. The group must also take into consideration changes to the company that are planned, anticipated, or likely, such as a merger, acquisition, expansion, or move.

Topology of LAN/WAN   The administrative function within an organization develops a high-level plan for evaluating and implementing the network topology. The plan must factor in all the standard topology considerations such as speed, bandwidth, and physical connectivity. Additional factors such as cost, time to implementation, and scalability may be used to determine the best configuration for the firm today and in the future. Once these plans are finalized, the technology group will implement the details, such as procuring and installing the physical equipment (e.g., servers, bridges, routers, and hubs), and creating the domain structure and managing user accounts.

Internal and External Security and Access Policies As companies continue to leverage the expanding array of mobile and wireless technologies being developed and deployed worldwide, the need for comprehensive access policies and procedures becomes mission critical. Increasingly, company employees are on the move—traveling to customer and vendor sites, dialing in from home to check e-mail, or working from remote locations. In each case, access to corporate data is required and critical to successful operations. At each access point, there is significant potential for security degradation. Therefore, it is critical that the administrative group clearly delineates the access needs for company and partner users, and defines the security policies to be implemented.

The administrative group is responsible for creating network and security plans that meet the high-level needs of the executive group's strategies. They design and specify network structure, security technologies, and access methods. Next, we'll look at the group responsible for implementing, managing, and maintaining these plans.

Technical

The technical group can contain anyone on the IT staff, technical vendors and consultants, or users who assist the IT staff (such as clearing out a print spooler). However, in this context, the technical group typically contains members of the IT staff. As such, they are tasked with implementing the details of the plans developed by the executive and administrative groups. They manage the entire network infrastructure, including data centers, servers, hubs, routers, and telecommunications equipment. They manage user accounts, group policies, and other tasks related to maintaining a secure and fully operational network environment.

This group is responsible for the day-to-day operations of the network, for the security of the network, and the data traveling on that network. They are primarily concerned with tasks such as the following:

Creating Forests, Domains, Sites, and Organizational Units The design, creation, and implementation of these elements are the basic components of network security. The technical group is primarily responsible for implementing these elements in accordance with the strategic (executive) and tactical (administrative) plans developed for the company. It is important to remember, with regard to the user and network security, that these are the building blocks of a secure network. Sound planning and implementing of the overall network structure ensure it can be securely administered and managed by the technical group.

Implementing Windows 2000 Security Features   Windows 2000 provides a number of security enhancements. With Internet access and mobile access increasing exponentially, Microsoft has implemented security improvements to many areas of the Windows operating system and to remote access in particular. From Windows 2000 Data Center Server to Windows 2000 Professional, security has been incorporated at every level of the operating system. Some of the security features discussed throughout this book include user rights, policies and permissions, certificates, passwords, smart cards, NTFS, Encrypting File System (EFS), Layer 2 Tunneling Protocol (L2TP) with IP Security (IPSec), Secure Sockets Layer (SSL), Transport Layer Security (TLS), and virtual private networks (VPN). Each is discussed in this chapter and throughout this book. Windows 2000 provides many different levels of security for both local and remote access. The technical group is responsible for the implementation of these security features.

Working with End Users   The technical group is responsible for working with all end users to assist with using network resources. Users may need assistance working with the policies and procedures developed by the technical group. Users may require IT assistance with password guidelines, file system management, securing and working with mobile devices, using applications, and remote access. The technical group is charged with ensuring that the user has access to necessary resources, while making sure that corporate resources and data are as secure as possible at all times.

User Communities

Within an organization, access to resources is granted based on users' accounts or by group memberships. Group membership determines the extent of user rights within the network. There are four basic types of users, and all user accounts will fall into one or more of these categories. By understanding the nature of each, you can design a security solution that will meet the needs of the users and provide the highest security.

- **Everyone** This category can include all people accessing your network from any location, including staff, users, and partners. This could include users accessing the network internally and externally, from local and remote locations. These users cannot easily be identified and are generally considered anonymous users. Users accessing your Web site would be included in the Everyone group.

- **Staff** This group can include all people who work for your organization. They can be easily identified using standardized methods such as employee badges or card keys, and are assigned usernames on your corporate network. Typically, they use company e-mail, distributed applications, and Web sites (internal and external). They may be in local or remote locations, and may access resources via the local area network (LAN) or remote access methods.

- **Users** This group can include those who use applications to accomplish a variety of business functions. For instance, you may have a Human Resources (HR) users group that includes everyone who accesses a companywide Human Resources application. You may also have a Human Resources Managers users group, which would be a subset of the HR users group. Users are often organized into OUs for ease of administration in Windows 2000.

- **Partners** This set can include people from any organization or location who have a unique relationship with your company. They are required to follow standardized procedures so network security can be established and maintained. They often use network resources that have been externalized for the purpose of providing secure access to company information that you do not want to be generally available to the public. This collection of resources is called an extranet, and is provided to facilitate business transactions between your firm and an external, trusted partner firm.

Now that you have learned about the different business perspectives and user classes, Table 4-1 is a quick reference for questions relating to business and user classes.

TABLE 4-1

Business and User Reference

Choosing which partners need access to corporate resources	Executive
Develop competitive plan for using the Web	Executive
Provide access to branches located in five cities in the U.S.	Administrative
Plan extranet for trusted partners	Administrative
Create organizational units	Technical
Monitor network and Web site access	Technical
Work at remote branch	Staff
Work from home	Staff
Accounting department staff	User
Shipping and Receiving department staff	User
Access to public information on company Web site	Everyone
Anonymous access to FTP files on Web site	Everyone

User Location

Designing a security plan for a network requires secure access at local and remote locations. Users today travel more and have broader access to remote computing capabilities than ever before. With the explosive growth of Internet technologies over the past several years, more and more users are connecting remotely to both Internet and network resources. In this section, we'll discuss how the user's location impacts security planning, and what tools are available to the network administrator for maintaining the highest level of security possible. We'll see that users can be local or remote. They can be a part of your company's staff (Everyone, Staff, Users), or they can be external (Everyone, Partner). We'll look at local and remote access as it relates to these various user groups, and discuss the security considerations that must be reviewed for a comprehensive security solution.

Local

Local network users access the network from the premises of the company. The computers they work on are physically attached to the LAN via network cabling (such as Ethernet connections) or are communicating with your LAN via wireless technologies (infrared, for example). Local users are typically members of your company's staff or contractors who have been granted permission to access the network locally. The general public or members of trusted partners are not local users. Local security issues concern physical access to equipment, logical access to data (discussed in detail in the next section of this chapter), implementing group policies to manage user and group access, and ensuring users can access the data as needed. Among the security considerations when planning for local users are the following:

- Setting up and administering user accounts, groups, policies, and permissions
- Securing Windows 2000-based computers, files, folders, and network print resources
- Securing non-Windows 2000-based computers, files, folders, and network print resources

Remote

Companies can improve productivity by using Windows 2000 Routing and Remote Access Service (RRAS) to provide employees with remote access to resources on the internal network and help maximize speed and security. Windows 2000 also provides the ability to create a virtual private network (VPN) using Internet connections as a means of connecting from a remote location to corporate network resources.

Remote access encompasses a number of different methods of accessing company network resources. Remote access refers to both mobile users accessing network resources outside of the physical office via direct dial-up connections or via Internet VPN connections, and branch or remote office users accessing corporate resources via another network (wide area network, or WAN). Public users of information on your Web site and partner users accessing the extranet are remote users as well, but are more accurately considered to be external users. As such, the security concerns are different and will be discussed separately.

Enabling remote access introduces security issues primarily related to unauthorized access and intercepted data. Remote users must be authenticated, and the connections they use must be secure. Remote users' business concerns are having access to data when needed, connecting to the corporate network in a reliable manner, and keeping all data transmissions secure. The methods that can be employed for remote users in Windows 2000 are direct dial-up to a RRAS and VPNs.

Secure dial-up networking requires the use of connection protocols (Point-to-Point, PPP) and authentication protocols (MS-CHAP, among many others). Table 4-2 outlines the various dial-up clients and which authentication protocols are supported in Windows 2000.

TABLE 4-2   Supported Dial-Up Protocols

Dial-Up Client	Supported Windows 2000 PPP Features	Unsupported Windows 2000 PPP Features
Windows 2000	Multilink, Bandwidth Allocation Protocol (BAP), Microsoft Challenge Handshake Authentication Protocol (MS-CHAP), Challenge Handshake Authentication Protocol (CHAP), Shiva Password Authentication Protocol (SPAP), Password Authentication Protocol (PAP), Microsoft Challenge Handshake Authentication Protocol 2 (MS-CHAP v2), and Extensible Authentication Protocol (EAP)	
Windows NT 4.0	Multilink, MS-CHAP, CHAP, SPAP, PAP, and MS-CHAP v2 (with Windows NT 4.0 Service Pack 4 and later)	BAP and EAP
Windows NT 3.5*x*	MS-CHAP, CHAP, SPAP, and PAP	Multilink, BAP, MS-CHAP v2, and EAP
Windows 98	Multilink, MS-CHAP, CHAP, SPAP, PAP, and MS-CHAP v2 (with Windows 98 Service Pack 1 and later)	BAP and EAP
Windows 95	MS-CHAP, CHAP, SPAP, and PAP (with the Windows Dial-Up Networking 1.3 Performance and Security Upgrade for Windows 95)	MS-CHAP v2, Multilink, BAP, and EAP

Microsoft Windows 2000 supports a number of remote access Point-to-Point features. These features will not be discussed in-depth in this section, but will be explained fully in subsequent chapters.

A Routing and Remote Access Service (RRAS) running on Windows 2000 does not support the Serial Line Internet Protocol (SLIP) remote access protocol. SLIP clients cannot connect to a RRAS running Windows 2000. SLIP was supported in Windows NT 4.0 (and earlier).

Direct Dial-Up Connectivity   Direct dial-up connectivity is assigned on a per-user basis. Users to be granted dial-up permissions should be placed in a specific user group for ease of administration. There are a number of options for configuring

Analyze Business and Security Requirements for the End User

dial-up permissions. The User Properties Dial-in tab controls certain features of dial-up connections. Other options can only be controlled through Remote Access Policies and through Routing and Remote Access Service. These options are discussed in greater detail later in this book.

EXERCISE 4-1

Dial up permissions

1. In Windows 2000 Server, click Start and then Programs. Select Administrative Tools.
2. Select Active Directory Users and Computers.
3. Click Users and select a user from the right side. Right-click that user and select Properties from the context menu.
4. Click the Dial-in tab from the User Properties dialog box to access dial in permissions for this user.

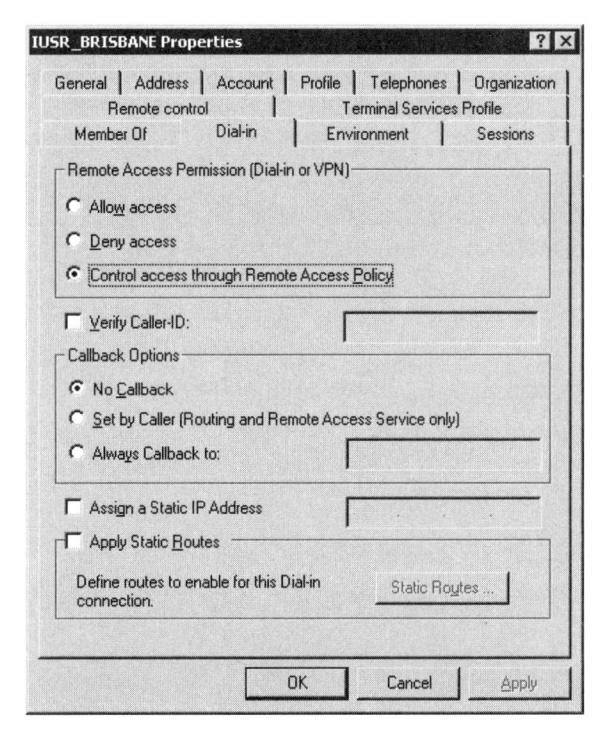

> 5. Notice that you must specifically allow or deny permission to dial in. Also notice that you can set dial-in permissions through Remote Access Policy.
> 6. Check Allow access.
> 7. Set callback options as desired (no callback is the default). Assign static IP address or static routes, if desired. Click OK to complete assigning dial-in permissions for user.

Next we'll review some of the dial-in features: callback, DNIS, ANI/CLI, and third party hosts that are enabled through remote access server settings.

Callback The callback feature causes your RRAS to disconnect from an incoming user connection and call the user back. Callback provides several advantages, including the ability for a company to use least-cost-routing for telephone calls going out to various destinations, thus saving on long distance telephone charges. Required callback also enhances network security because it ensures that only users at specified locations can access the server. By dropping the call and initiating an outgoing call, unauthorized personnel will be denied access.

To use the callback feature, a network administrator must configure it in the Dial-up Preferences menu option in the User's account. Users who are part of a group, such as sales representatives, should be placed in a Sales Reps Users group and remote access should be granted to the group. This ensures that rights are not granted to individual users, a situation difficult to maintain as a company grows and creates undue security risks.

To access the server, a user dials the specified access number, and the remote access server determines whether the username and password are correct. If they are, the server disconnects and returns the call.

Use callback when the telephone system does not support caller ID. If your telephone system supports caller ID, you can restrict the telephone number that the dial-up client must use when dialing the remote access server.

on the job

If the user is always at the same number (home, remote office), you can implement the callback option. Do not use the callback feature for users who travel to different locations.

DNIS Authorization   Dialed Number Identification Service (DNIS) authorization S can be used when you provide multiple phone lines for your dial-up users and you want to apply remote access policies based on the number dialed. You can assign different remote access policies to specific classes of users (executives, sales/marketing, or partners, for example) as a method of controlling and monitoring remote access.

ANI/CLI Authorization   Automatic Number Identification/Calling Line Identification can be used to authorize a dial-up connection when the dial-up user does not support secure authentication methods. There is no risk of the username and password being intercepted, because this information is not transmitted. ANI/CLI uses the dial-up user's telephone number to authenticate the user's connection.

Third-Party Security Host   You may consider using a third-party security host when you want to augment the security provided by a RRAS. A security host device sits between the dial-up modem and the remote access server. The host requires a dial-up user to have a security card to provide authentication by using an access code. The code changes with each connection, preventing an unauthorized user from intercepting and reusing a given code.

Virtual Private Networks   Virtual private networks (VPNs) enable users to securely connect to the corporate network via the Internet through a connection to their local Internet Service Provider (ISP). This reduces connection-time charges and may provide greater availability if the user travels and has an ISP with local numbers throughout the United States or country in which he or she is traveling.

Prior to Windows 2000, a somewhat secure method of communicating via VPN was using the Point-to-Point Tunneling Protocol (PPTP). Windows 2000 supports PPTP, but has the added capability of establishing a very secure connection using Layer 2 Tunneling Protocol (L2TP) in conjunction with Internet Protocol Security (IPSec). Using both L2TP and IPSec, a secure tunnel connection through the remote user's ISP to the corporate network can be established. Once this secure tunnel is constructed, the remote user can send and receive data secure from intrusion. L2TP is used to build the tunnel through which data travels, and IPSec secures the data itself.

IPSec is designed to encrypt data transmitted between two computers, protecting it from unauthorized modification and interpretation. Setting up IPSec without using L2TP requires specific knowledge and understanding of how the two computers will trust one another and secure their communications. In Windows 2000, IPSec is supported in L2TP; therefore, specific knowledge of how the computers will communicate is handled via the L2TP protocol.

Public

Public network users are those who connect anonymously to the company's Internet resources. The benefit is that resources are widely available. Exposing network resources to the public via the Internet, however, introduces significant risk that must be considered. Most companies today provide an external Web site that provides data to the general public as anonymous users. Ensuring the Web site is secure can involve techniques such as disabling all Server services not in use, disabling unused TCP/IP ports, and physically attaching the Web server on the outside of the firewall. The risks involved with public access involve attempts at unauthorized access and overloading the computers to disrupt service. These attacks, called Denial of Service (DoS) attacks, are discussed at the end of this chapter. Windows 2000 has many features that are directly related to hosting and securing a corporate Web site, such as Internet Authentication Service (IAS).

Trusted Partner

In today's business model, companies are forming alliances and partnerships as a means of expanding their scope or expertise quickly and efficiently. As a result, it is becoming more common for companies to rely on partner organizations, which are trusted organizations requiring special access to network resources. Depending on the nature of the partnership, you may need to share trade secrets or other confidential information with trusted partners, but protect that data from all others. Integrating partner organizations into your network involves creating and managing your extended network, or your extranet.

Timeliness and reliability of the extranet are of particular importance to partners. The relationship between your firm and the partner firm may be heavily dependent upon the data that is exchanged via the extranet. Delays and loss of data can be very costly for both firms.

For some organizations, internal business units may form different partnerships. The needs of each business unit and its external partners may vary. It is not uncommon to have different access and data needs among the business partners a firm may have. Therefore, the key elements to extending your corporate network resources to business partners are reliability, scalability, flexibility, and security.

Partner organizations require authentication and authorization just as all other users do. You must provide secure methods of connection, and you must protect data and applications that are exposed to the partner organization. Managing partner access can be accomplished by three methods. First, partners can be placed in OUs for ease of administration. Creating an OU for each partner organization can assist in maintaining high levels of security, while providing needed access. If you and your partner's networks are both Windows 2000 based, you can create a one-way trust relationship to the partner network by creating an explicit trust. This will enable secure communications via the Windows-based trust relationships. Finally, you can use third-party certificates to ensure partner users' authenticity. Certificates provide authentication from a mutually trusted third-party organization. These certificates verify the identity and authenticity of the partner organization in all transactions they perform on your network.

User Applications

The primary reason users access a network is to work with applications that perform specific functions related to their business or job function. Therefore, it is critical to assess the application needs of the users within the organization to ensure that security measures cover the risks and enable users to work productively with network resources.

Application Requirements

Users may want to access secured company applications when they are away from their offices. Some of these applications are relatively simple, such as calendars, company benefits registration, or a word-processing program. Others are more complex, such as financial systems and line-of-business applications. These applications must be secured to ensure that only authorized, authenticated users gain access to the data.

Active Directory can be used to control dissemination of software throughout the organization to ensure that only specified users can install and use a program. Use the security descriptors (Access Control Entries, or ACEs) on the Group Policy object for control over who receives the software. You'll read more about Group Policies in Chapter 10.

Often, an application is needed across the enterprise; for example, all Warehouse managers need to access the Inventory application. However, it's not uncommon to find different computers throughout an organization. From 486s to Pentiums to iMACs, organizations today generally have a wide range of computer equipment. This can cause a problem when trying to deploy an application that has specific hardware and software requirements. One method of addressing this issue is to use Windows 2000 Terminal Services.

Terminal Services is a technology that allows users to work with Windows-based applications that are hosted by a remote Windows 2000-based server. All data and application processing occurs on the server, and the results are transmitted to the client. Data transmitted via Terminal Services is somewhat unique. While it is not inherently encrypted, the data transmitted is screen refresh information. This information is extremely difficult to capture because the data bursts are so small (typically less than 20k), and because the data is only meaningful to the computer receiving the data (screen refresh data). However, additional security is available.

A core component of Terminal Services is the use of Remote Desktop Protocol (RDP) that runs over TCP/IP. It is a Unicode-compatible protocol that can be modified for different needs, including localization, automatic disconnection, and remote configuration. It supports three levels of encryption. Therefore, Terminal Services using RDP over TCP/IP is a very secure method of transmitting information from client machine to server.

When an application need to be deployed across a wide range of computers, Terminal Services provides a cost-effective and easy-to-manage solution.

Access to Terminal Services can be controlled through User Properties. Figure 4-1 shows a domain user's Terminal Services Profile options in Windows 2000.

Additional options regarding Terminal Services can be configured for the user in the domain user's Sessions tab, as shown in Figure 4-2. Session information is used to control the connection options for Terminal Services sessions, such as how to manage active and idle sessions, when to disconnect, and how to allow reconnection.

Application Roles

Determining how applications are used within your organization is an important component of securing your network. Applications can be used on the LAN or across the Internet. They can be categorized into distributed business applications such as word processing, spreadsheets, payroll, document management, and Human Resource management, and communication applications such as e-mail and groupware (e.g., Microsoft Outlook, Lotus Notes). In addition, applications can be installed on local machines, accessed from a server, or accessed via the Internet using Terminal Services.

Analyze Business and Security Requirements for the End User **151**

FIGURE 4-1

Domain user's Terminal Services Profile configuration

FIGURE 4-2

Domain user's Sessions configuration

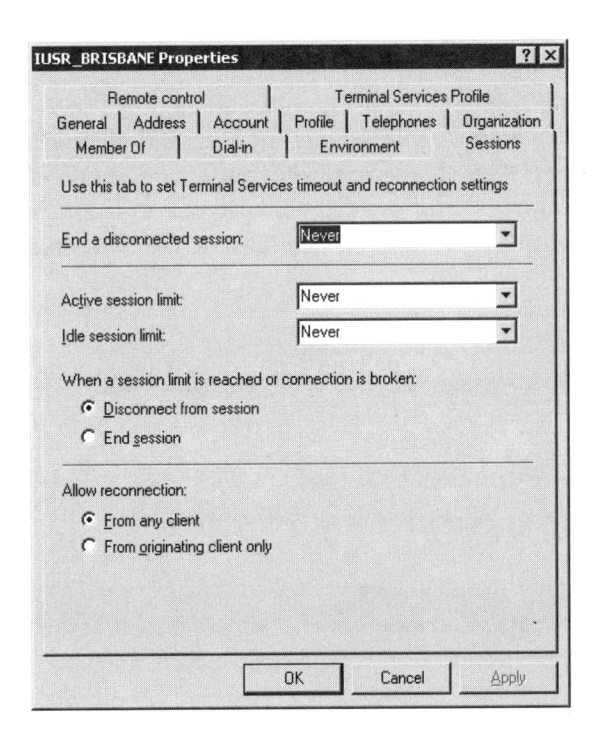

SCENARIO & SOLUTION

If Users Have…	Consider Using…
High-speed, reliable network connection	Distributed applications
486 computers, Macintosh computers	Terminal Services application (3rd party software is required for operation systems that are not Windows-based)
Special applications in Finance group	Group related applications by category in Add/Remove Programs
No access to the Internet	Distributed application or local install

Software applications can be grouped by category to make it easier to manage applications on the network. Knowing which groups use an application helps to determine how to categorize the software. Categories can be established so that users can find them more easily in Add/Remove Programs in Control Panel. For example, you could group all sales applications, all financial applications, and all warehouse applications.

on the job

To determine if an application should be deployed locally, via the network, or via Terminal Services, review your firm's computer equipment. Local installs should generally be reserved for stand-alone computers; network installs should be for distributed and communication applications; and Terminal Services should be used when users have access to the Internet and have a variety of hardware, or when centralized administration of the application is critical.

CERTIFICATION OBJECTIVE 4.02

Analyze the Current Physical Model and Information Security Model

Sound security design must consider both the physical security and the logical security of the network. The physical security involves the buildings, rooms, and computers that house and store the network components and data. Logical security is comprised of protecting the integrity and availability of the data itself. In this section, we'll examine both the physical and logical security considerations required for strong, secure network operations.

Physical Security

Internal attacks on computer networks are far more common than external attacks for two very simple reasons: Users have been granted some level of access to network resources and are likely to be more familiar with the network structure. Therefore, it is important to consider both internal and external threats when planning the physical and logical security of the network.

The administrative and technical groups are responsible for securing the physical systems and devices, protecting them from theft and illegal access. Any computer, whether it's a network server, a desktop, or a mobile device, needs to be physically secure. Physical access to a computer virtually guarantees access to the data on the computer. While security measures such as logon restrictions, strict password requirements, and restricted network permissions all play a vital role in securing the network, physical security is the foundation for all other layers of network security. If a person has access to a computer, he or she can work to overcome most network security measures.

Restricting or controlling access to the facility, the data centers, and users' desktops comprise the three primary levels of physical security. Each plays an important role in ensuring the overall security of the network.

Facilities

Controlling access to the business facility is the first line of defense in security planning. Many organizations today require card key access to buildings, others require employees to show identification, and some require guests to sign in or to be escorted by security personnel. The level of security for the facility depends on a number of factors, including the nature, location, and size of the business.

Some organizations are very well known and are likely to attract attention. This includes companies in the news, firms involved in political situations, or organizations working in controversial or highly competitive businesses. Clearly, extra measures must be taken to ensure that only employees or trusted partners gain access to the facility, and that their access is monitored appropriately. This may include entering and leaving the building, and access to restricted areas within the facility.

If a company is located in a busy, metropolitan area, it may require additional measures to avoid security breaches due to high-volume traffic. Companies located in multi-tenant high-rise office buildings should consider restricted access through card keys and other devices. Offices in remote locations are vulnerable to unauthorized access as well.

Large organizations also require additional physical security measures, as it is often impossible for security or administrative staff to know all company employees and authorized vendors or partners. Companies may also employ vendors and contractors who may require limited access. Identification badges, worn visibly, assist in securing the facility and restricting access only to personnel with proper identification.

In general, gaining access to the facility should require positive identification, whether through using keys, card keys, or badges. Consider the physical location of the office and the various security risks when determining the proper level of access security needed. Restricted building access is the most fundamental security measure an organization can take.

Data Centers (Servers)

Data centers are the heart of most companies. Within the data centers are the servers and backup devices that store and manage billions of bits of data that are vital to the ongoing operations of the organization. Physically securing the data centers is paramount. We'll review security considerations for each of the following:

- Data center access
- Server access
- Hubs, routers, and cabling
- Backup devices

Access to the data center should be very restrictive, since physical access to equipment is the most common method of obtaining unauthorized use of the machine. Many network tasks, including server management, can be accomplished from a computer other than the server. This reduces the need to access the server equipment. Maintaining an access list and enforcing strict access policies will minimize the potential hazards. Combination door locks, access cards, or employee identification badges can be used to restrict physical access.

Once inside the data center, there are many potential areas for security breaches. Clearly, restricting access to the room itself is the most critical. However, servers can be placed in racks or cabinets that can be locked. Some cabinets have panels that allow you to lock the CD-ROM and diskette drives, and the power and reset switches.

This prevents unauthorized access to the server itself. Ensuring that power cables cannot be intentionally or unintentionally unplugged is also important.

You can use the server's CMOS settings to disable the CD-ROM or diskette at boot-up. The CMOS settings can be password protected. You should not require a password for boot-up, however. Computers that are set to reboot after a critical failure will pause while waiting for the input of a password, which defeats the auto-reboot feature.

Hubs and routers carry and direct all network traffic for an organization. Critical hubs and routers should be located in the data center and, like servers, can be secured in locking cabinets. The most likely security risks to hubs and routers are intentional or unintentional halting of the device (power off, reboot), and tapping into network traffic. Today, protocol analyzers can be as small as a pocket calculator and capture gigabytes of data. If you require extreme security to guard against unauthorized network data capture, ensure that hubs and routers are in data centers, network cabling is either fiber optic or routed through walls and ceilings (not exposed), and that unused cabling and hubs are removed from open areas.

on the Job

Ensure that all vendors who are authorized to work on equipment, including printers, cabling, routers, hubs, and telecommunications equipment, wear visible identification badges. This will prevent unauthorized personnel (internal or external) from accessing network resources from inside the facility.

Backups provide a copy of the company's data. Backups are the last line of defense against data loss due to technical malfunctions, physical loss of data, or natural disasters. Backup devices today are typically tape drives that hold one or more tapes, although the backup medium may change as technology advances. The key point is that backup devices should be secured in the data center. Multiple sets should be made, and one set of tapes (or storage media) should be stored offsite in the event of theft or damage in the building or server area. Tape backups should be scheduled regularly, and access to completed tapes should be restricted to authorized personnel. You can also password protect the tape so that if a tape is stolen, it will require breaking the password.

The ability to back up and restore data can be tightly controlled. Backups can be either full (the entire system) or incremental (backing up just changes made since last full backup). In either case, the data must be kept secure. Therefore, it is recommended that network administrators use the following policies to safeguard backup data:

- Back up entire volumes to safeguard against entire disk unit failure.

- Back up directory services to prevent the loss of user account and security information.
- Create a backup log to make it easier to locate specific data and to facilitate data restores.
- Keep three copies of backup media to ensure against media failure and loss; store one copy offsite in a secure and properly controlled environment.
- Perform trial restorations to verify that files are being backed up properly. A trial restoration can also uncover hardware failures that do not show up under normal circumstances.
- Limit restore privileges to network administrators to limit exposure to systemwide information.
- Password protect backup media to prevent data from being restored on another machine where a person may have administrative access.
- Do not allow the same users to have both backup and restore privileges to prevent abuse of privileges; keep backup and restore privileges separate except for network administrators.

Microsoft Windows 2000 also introduced the ability to use smart cards as the strongest form of account authentication. Smart cards can be considered on systems requiring heightened security. They can be used on servers storing sensitive data, and on individual computers and workstations that require extra security. These cards contain a microprocessor and memory that store the user's private key, logon information, and public key certificate. The user inserts the card into a smart card reader attached to the computer. The user then types in his or her Personal Identification Number (PIN) when requested to complete the authentication process.

The combination of physical device and PIN is more difficult to attack because of the additional layer of information needed to authenticate the user. After a small number of unsuccessful PIN entries occur consecutively, a smart card will lock, making dictionary-type attacks virtually impossible.

A PIN does not have to be limited to a series of numeric characters; you can require that a PIN contain alphanumeric characters for added security.

User Workspace (Workstations)

Users today work on desktop computers, laptop computers, and mobile devices. While controlling access to the building or area is essential, there is still the risk of laptops or mobile devices being removed from the user's workspace. Perhaps more importantly, however, is the unrestricted access to devices connected to the network that the user's workspace provides. To protect the computers in the user's workspace, a network administrator should consider implementing the following security measures:

- Restricted access
- Strong passwords
- Single operating system
- Smart cards or other hardware security devices

Restricted Access As stated earlier, the best security is physically restricting access to work areas where computers are present. However, this is impractical in many companies. Therefore, ensuring that anyone accessing these areas is at least authorized to be in the building will reduce security risks.

Restricting user logon hours can also help prevent unauthorized use of computers, especially during hours when fewer people may be around, such as graveyard shifts and weekends. User's logon hours can be set to restrict access and, if desired, to forcibly disconnect the user from the network when the logon hours conclude. Figure 4-3, from a domain user's properties, shows the logon hours configuration.

You can forcibly disconnect the user when logon hours expire. This is done through Group Policy settings. This will cause the user to loose all current network connections and log the user off (see Figure 4-4).

FIGURE 4-3

Domain user's Logon Hours configuration screen

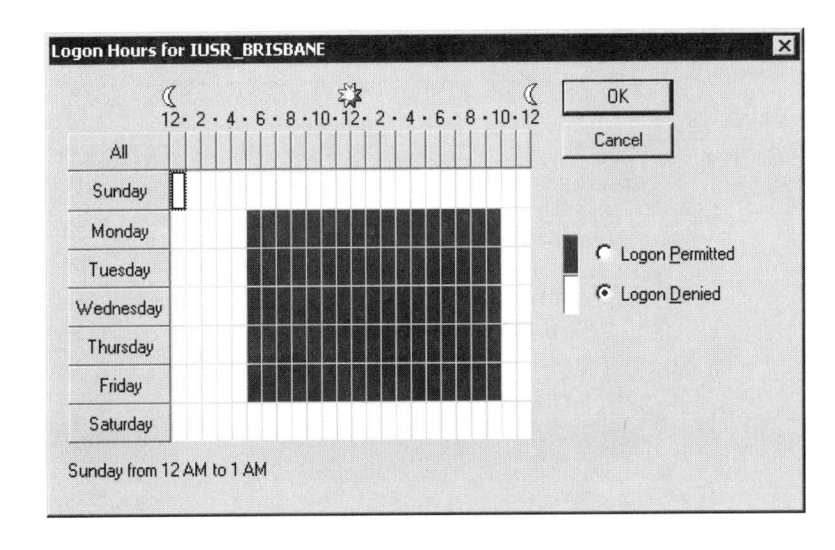

158 Chapter 4: Analyzing End-User Computing Requirements

FIGURE 4-4

Group Policy Security Options to forcibly disconnect users

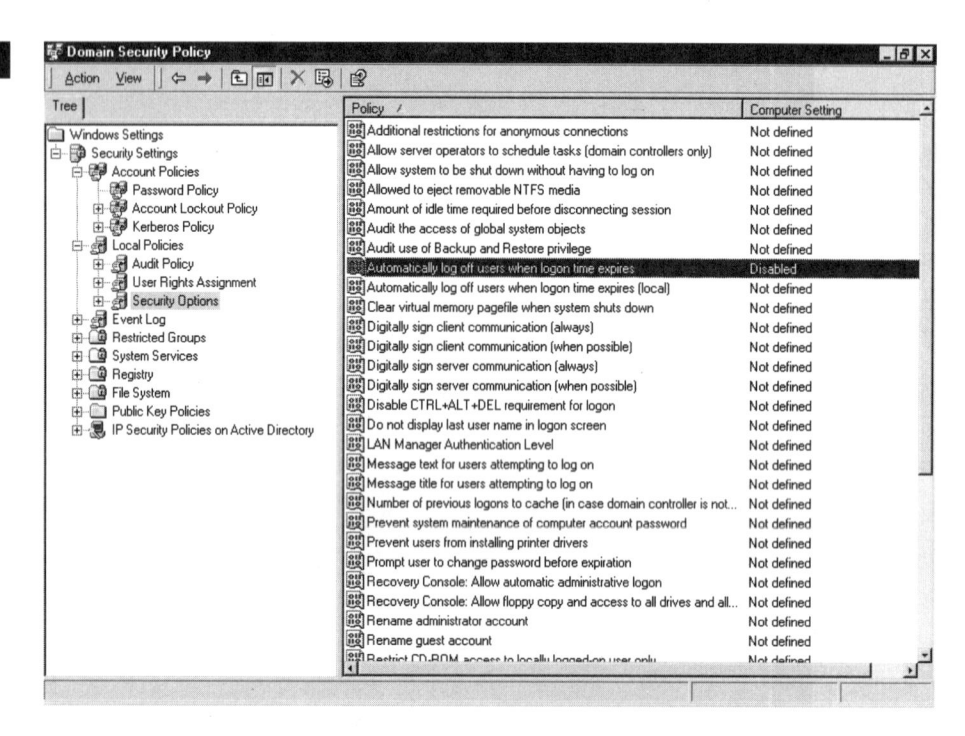

Policy	Computer Setting
Additional restrictions for anonymous connections	Not defined
Allow server operators to schedule tasks (domain controllers only)	Not defined
Allow system to be shut down without having to log on	Not defined
Allowed to eject removable NTFS media	Not defined
Amount of idle time required before disconnecting session	Not defined
Audit the access of global system objects	Not defined
Audit use of Backup and Restore privilege	Not defined
Automatically log off users when logon time expires	Disabled
Automatically log off users when logon time expires (local)	Not defined
Clear virtual memory pagefile when system shuts down	Not defined
Digitally sign client communication (always)	Not defined
Digitally sign client communication (when possible)	Not defined
Digitally sign server communication (always)	Not defined
Digitally sign server communication (when possible)	Not defined
Disable CTRL+ALT+DEL requirement for logon	Not defined
Do not display last user name in logon screen	Not defined
LAN Manager Authentication Level	Not defined
Message text for users attempting to log on	Not defined
Message title for users attempting to log on	Not defined
Number of previous logons to cache (in case domain controller is not...	Not defined
Prevent system maintenance of computer account password	Not defined
Prevent users from installing printer drivers	Not defined
Prompt user to change password before expiration	Not defined
Recovery Console: Allow automatic administrative logon	Not defined
Recovery Console: Allow floppy copy and access to all drives and all...	Not defined
Rename administrator account	Not defined
Rename guest account	Not defined
Restrict CD-ROM access to locally logged-on user only	Not defined

exam
⑭atch

The default setting for logon hours does not forcibly disconnect the user from the network. It will allow a user to remain logged on indefinitely, but prevents users from establishing any new connections on the network. Give serious consideration to whether you need to forcibly disconnect users from the network. While the benefit is increased security, the risk is impairing the user's ability to complete work, thus having a negative impact on productivity.

In addition, user logon rights can be further restricted. The following list shows the logon rights that can be assigned to a user. These rights can be managed with the User Rights policy.

- Access This Computer from Network
- Log On Locally
- Log On as a Batch Job
- Log On as a Service
- Deny Access to This Computer from the Network

- Deny Logon as a Batch Job
- Deny Logon as a Service
- Deny Local Logon

Strong Passwords   Strong passwords are key to end-user security. Enforcing the sophisticated password policies present in the Windows 2000 operating system will dramatically reduce the chance of hackers gaining access through password breaches. We'll discuss password strategies in more detail when we discuss data protection later in the chapter.

Single Operating System   Installing and running a single operating system on user computers will prevent rebooting into an unsecured operating system. For example, Windows 95 allows users to boot into DOS. This enables someone trying to bypass network security and access local information. By installing a single, secure operating system, network administrators can reduce the risk of unauthorized access through physically rebooting the system. Windows 2000 Professional is designed for use on the desktop and provides the enhanced security features that comprise the Windows 2000 operating system.

Smart Cards or Other Hardware Devices   Smart cards or other hardware-based security devices can prevent unauthorized use. By requiring users to use a smart card and PIN to access the computer, an added layer of security is introduced. As previously discussed, smart cards contain user's certificates and makes it difficult for an unauthorized user to circumvent security.

Finally, some companies secure keyboards and mice, making computer access more difficult. Computers in vulnerable areas of the facility can be physically locked to the desk to prevent the computer from being moved without proper authority. This is especially helpful with laptops and other mobile devices that are easily picked up and moved. In addition, computer cases can be locked to prevent physical access to the hard disk itself. Finally, devices can be installed to lock and disable the floppy drive and CD-ROM drive, preventing the installation or removal of data from the system.

Physical security has several layers and many different approaches. Developing a physical security plan provides the most secure setting based on the risks, costs, and needs of your business, while minimizing the impact on the end user. Securing the building, the servers, and the end-user computers are the three core components for strong physical security.

Data Protection

Most security breaches occur on poorly planned networks rather than on well-planned networks being intentionally attacked. Users placed in the wrong groups or being given the wrong permissions make networks vulnerable to intentional and unintentional data loss. In this section, we'll discuss data protection on the network in general, and, specifically, on local hard drives and on servers. Finally, we'll discuss methods of protecting data when connecting remotely to a network, whether as a mobile user or via a remote branch location of the company.

Properly managing user permissions is a fundamental method of keeping the network secure against unauthorized users. Once users are assigned to groups and groups have been assigned permissions, Windows 2000 uses several features to authenticate the user during the logon process.

User groups and group policies are covered in depth later in this book. However, a simple rule to remember is this: Always place users in groups and assign permissions to groups. Avoid granting permissions to individual users; it makes secure administration difficult and creates security holes.

Network Logon Authentication

Users are authenticated in one of three ways: NTLM, Kerberos, and certificates. In previous versions of Windows NT, NT LAN Manager (NTLM) was the protocol used for authentication. In Windows 2000, the NTLM authentication protocol is used by Windows 2000 clients to connect to servers running previous versions of Windows NT.

The primary authentication protocol for the Windows 2000 domain is Kerberos authentication. Kerberos credentials consist of the domain name and username (which could be in the form of Internet-friendly names, such as LisaM@yourcompany.com), and the Kerberos-style encrypted password.

The third and most secure authentication method uses certificates. Certificates can be issued by the Windows 2000 Certificate Authority (CA) or by a third-party Certificate Authority. Active Directory is used to publish public-key certificates for users, and standard directory access protocols are used to locate them. Private keys and certificates issued to end users are kept in secure storage, either on the local system or on a smart card.

Local Hard Drives

As mentioned earlier, securing or restricting access to the facility or the workspace is the first line of defense. The second line of defense is protecting the data on local hard drives. Data can be protected in several ways:

Require Users to Store Data Files on Network Servers End users typically do not do an adequate job of backing up their data. Therefore, rather than leaving the data on local hard drives exposed to loss (through theft or mechanical failure), critical data files can be stored on the network. Since network computers are routinely backed up, user data is protected. Using network data storage can be set up through user and group policies and enforced at logon. While a user can always choose to save a file locally, providing a home directory on a network server helps ensure routine backups of user data files.

Use the NTFS File System Users' local hard drives can be formatted using FAT or NTFS, depending on which Windows operating system they are running. Installing Windows NT or Windows 2000 enables the formatting of partitions and disks using the NTFS file system format. The NTFS file system allows users to control access to files, even if an unauthorized user gains access to the local machine. By restricting access to files and folders, users can ensure that data is secure against unauthorized users.

Use the Windows 2000 Encrypting File System (EFS) The Microsoft Windows 2000 operating system provides encrypting file system (EFS) technology that enhances the security of drives using the NTFS v5 format. While NTFS prevents unauthorized users from gaining access to files and folders, data can still be compromised. If the hard disk is removed and placed in a computer on which the unauthorized user has administrative privileges, he or she can gain access to the data on the drive.

EFS provides the encryption technology to store files securely. EFS addresses security concerns regarding third-party tools available today that can allow retrieval of files from an NTSF volume without an access check. The EFS encryption uses public key-based technology and runs as an integrated system service, which makes it easier to manage and more difficult to compromise.

Users should encrypt folders, rather than specific files, since files stored in a folder using EFS encryption are, by default, encrypted. Therefore, users should encrypt the My Documents folder if this is where they save most of their files. For increased security, users should also encrypt their Temp folder so that temporary files created by programs are automatically encrypted as well.

Remember that files transmitted over the network are not encrypted during the transfer. Other protocols, such as SSL/PCT or IPSec, must be used to encrypt the data over the wire. These protocols are discussed in depth later in this book.

> **exam**
> **⒲atch**
>
> *EFS encrypted files can only be opened by the user who encrypted it (except in a special circumstance in which a recovery agent can open the file). Encrypted files cannot be shared; therefore, EFS is NOT an option for files shared by users. Also, encrypting files on remote servers is not recommended. The Trust for Delegation check box must be selected in the server object in Active Directory, which may render the server vulnerable to impersonation attacks. Also, encrypted files sent over a network are unencrypted, unless an encryption protocol such as IPSec is used.*

Require All Users to Use Strong Password Formats   Password policies in Windows 2000 provide a number of options for requiring strong passwords. Strong passwords are passwords that are difficult to guess or compute because they are complex. Password policies are enforced at the domain level.

CertCam 4-2

EXERCISE 4-2

Setting Password Policy

1. In Windows 2000 Server, click Start, then click Programs, select Administrative Tools.
2. Select Domain Security Policy.
3. Click on the + to the left of Security Settings to expand the tree.
4. Click on the + to the left of Account Policies to expand the tree.
5. Click on Password Policy. On the right side of the screen, the password policy options are displayed.

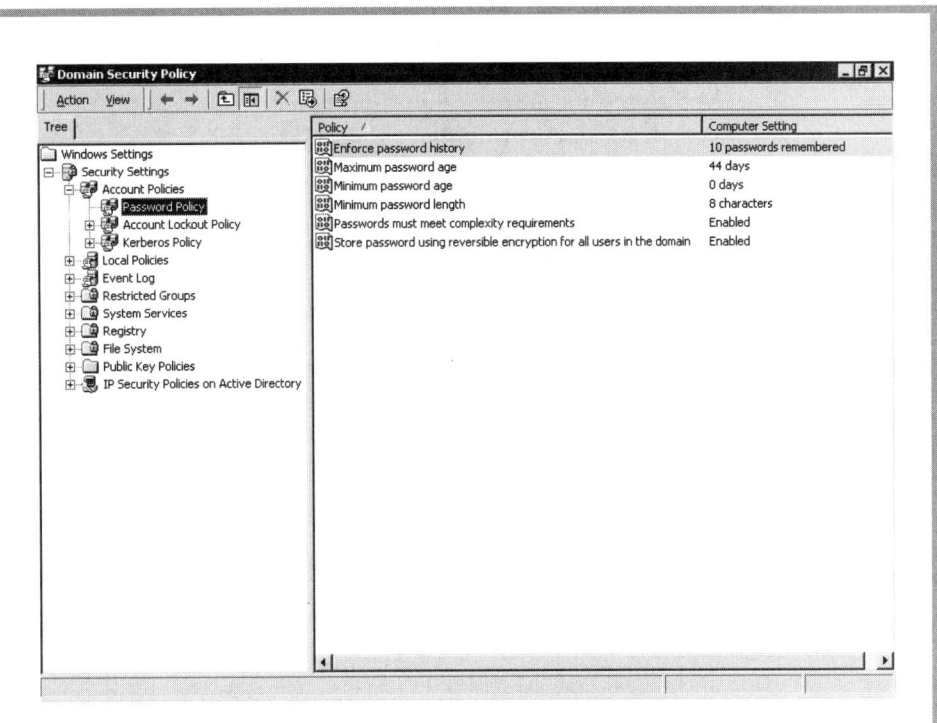

Analyze the Current Physical Model and Information Security Model

6. To change any password policy, double click on the password policy on the right side of the screen to display a dialog box that will allow you to change parameters related to that policy. Double-click Enforce password history. Change the setting to 10 passwords remembered. Click OK to close the dialog.

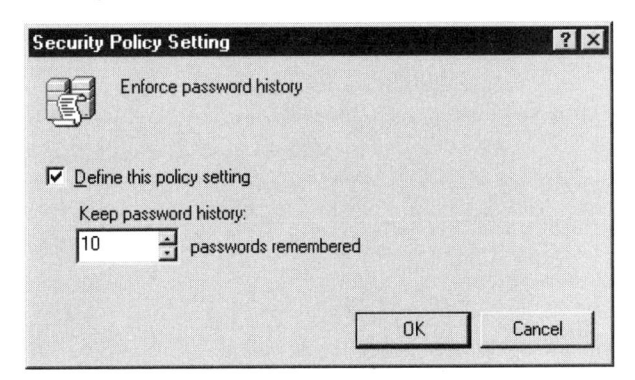

7. Close the Domain Security Policy window.

The elements of a strong password policy are outlined in Table 4-3.

One significant risk for using complex, strong password policies is that users will tend to write down their passwords in unsecured locations. It's not uncommon to find passwords written on scraps of paper on or around the computer. Require strong passwords, but keep security policies from having the opposite effect.

TABLE 4-3 Strong Password Components

Password Element	Benefit and Risk
Length greater than eight characters.	The number of possible combinations of characters is 8^7, or 2,097,152 combinations. This significantly reduces the chances of a lucky guess.
Require upper- and lowercase, numbers, and symbols.	This prevents simple dictionary cracking programs from working. Dictionary cracking programs run words from a dictionary through the system in an attempt to discover passwords.
Password uniqueness (cannot use password similar to previous ones).	Users often choose Monday1, and when forced to change their password will choose Monday2—it's easy to remember. However, it makes it easy to crack a password. Requiring uniqueness so that the new password cannot contain too many similarities to the expired password is recommended.
Password cannot contain user ID.	Related to requiring a unique password, passwords should not contain the user's first or last name or any part of the user's network username.
Passwords cannot repeat.	Users also tend to want to reuse passwords. Setting the system to save previous passwords prevents repeated patterns.
Password must change at first logon.	When a new user account is set up, the administrator can (and should) require the password to be reset immediately.

Use Password-Protected Screen Savers By requiring the use of password-protected screen savers, unauthorized users cannot gain access to the system without rebooting. Rebooting the system then requires authentication to access network resources. If the system is using NTFS and EFS, unauthorized users will be limited to physically removing the device from the premises in order to gain access to the data.

Lock the Computer By pressing CTRL-ALT-DEL and clicking Lock Computer, you can prevent unauthorized users from gaining access to your computer. Only you and members of the Administrators group on your computer can unlock it. You can also set up a screen saver so that whenever the computer is idle for more than a specified length of time, the screen saver starts and the computer automatically locks.

on the Job

To unlock the computer, press CTRL-ALT-DEL, type your password, then click OK. Also, if computers are shared by users (for instance, those working on different shifts), ensure that users do not lock their computers at the end of their shift.

Security Templates Security templates allow you to restrict access to three of the five Registry hives: HKEY_CLASSES_ROOT, HKEY_USERS, and HKEY_LOCAL_MACHINE. You cannot set permissions for Hkey_Current_Config or Hkey_Current_User.

Two of the default security templates restrict who can access the registry. The securews (secure workstation) template removes the Authenticated User group from the Power Users built-in group, but does not change the Discretionary Access Control List (DACL) of the Registry. The highsecws (high security workstation) template locks down the Registry by using DACLs. The use of security templates is discussed in greater detail later in this book.

Servers

Servers are essentially the lifeblood of the network in most organizations today. There are many considerations when planning to secure servers. The most common elements are discussed here.

Limit Access to Servers While it may seem like an obvious statement, limiting the physical and logical access to company servers is the first line of security. Carefully consider and plan how to administrate your servers, adding users to administrative groups or creating groups with certain administrative privileges on an as-needed basis. Enforce restrictive policies with regard to server access.

As mentioned earlier, smart cards add a layer of authentication that may be needed for access to sensitive data or servers.

Limit Use of Administrator Accounts Using accounts with administrative privileges rather than the default Administrator accounts when logging on to a server can also help prevent unauthorized access. Always log off the account before leaving to ensure strong server security.

Do Not Log On as Administrator for Routine Tasks Avoid running your computer as an administrator. Running Windows 2000 as an administrator makes the system vulnerable to attacks and security risks. Even visiting an Internet site while logged on as an administrator can be damaging. An unfamiliar Internet site may have code that can be downloaded to the system and executed. These are commonly known as Trojan Horses. If you are logged on with administrator privileges, a Trojan Horse can reformat your hard drive, delete your files, or create a new user account with administrative access.

Instead of logging on an administrator to do network tasks, use the *runas* command from a command prompt or *Run as...* from Windows Explorer. The runas command allows an application to be launched with administrative privileges without having to log on as an administrator. The benefit is that when the command or application has completed, that session terminates and no logoff is required. Therefore, leaving a server or computer unattended does not create the security breach that leaving an administrator account logged on would create.

Auditing Auditing allows you to monitor the use (and misuse) of the network and take appropriate action as needed. Auditing creates log files that you should review on a regular basis to ensure that network access has not been compromised. Table 4-4 lists audit events you can log, and the specific threat these audit events monitor.

Setting your servers to audit too many events will degrade system performance. Large audit files must be reviewed, and identifying relevant data will become quite difficult. Choosing to audit failure of events often provides more meaningful data, though you will have to choose audit events that meet the needs of your organization.

TABLE 4-4 Audit Events

Audit Event	Potential Threat
Failure audit for logon/logoff	Random password hack
Success audit for logon/logoff	Stolen password break-in
Success audit for user rights, user and group management, security change policies, restart, shutdown, and system events	Misuse of privileges
Success and failure audit for file-access printers and object-access events	Improper access to printers
Success and failure write access auditing for programs (.EXE and .DLL extensions)	Virus outbreak

Remote Users

Data protection for remote users is more difficult simply because the users are outside the company's secure computing environment. In this section, we'll discuss the two remote user groups: mobile users and remote site users. In all cases, using Active Directory User Account options provides the network administrator with a number of advanced security options. Assigning users to the proper groups, assigning permissions to groups appropriately, and enforcing logon requirements (logon hours, password requirements, etc.) are the most basic steps to securing any user account, be it local or remote. We'll cover the similarities and differences in protecting data for mobile users versus remote site users. We'll also discuss various data transmission risks for both mobile and remote users, and we'll look at the tools that Windows 2000 provides to secure data transmission.

Mobile Users   There are three risks for mobile users: loss of equipment, loss of data through equipment failure (hard disk crash), and interception of data being transmitted. We'll discuss each of these risks and the associated methods of mitigating each risk in this segment.

Protecting mobile user equipment from loss is difficult. Laptops, Palmtops, Pocket PCs, or other Personal Digital Assistants (PDAs) can easily be picked up and carried off at airports, car rental counters, and unfortunately, even at the user's desk. Keeping track of equipment serial numbers and providing locking devices on desks are about the only feasible methods of protection against actual loss of equipment.

Physical data protection for mobile users is also a difficult task. Encouraging users to make regular backups of their data when they are connected to either a local backup device or the corporate network will protect them in the event of disk failure. Creating home directories for users can encourage users to store critical files on network servers rather than on local hard drives. This has both positive and negative consequences. The upside is that corporate servers are regularly backed up; therefore, data loss should be minimal. The downside is that a user may not have data available on his or her hard drive when needed. Connecting to the corporate network to get a critical data file may be time consuming or overly burdensome for the mobile user. Encouraging users to store files locally and back them up to servers when connected to the network can be a good intermediate solution.

If the equipment is stolen, using the NTFS file system and the EFS will protect the data on the mobile device. Even if the device is stolen, the data cannot be easily recovered. As we discussed earlier, EFS encrypts files so that only the user can decrypt them (except in a special circumstance in which a recovery agent can open the file). The cautions are that EFS should not be used for shared files, should not be used on a network server, and that data files are transmitted unencrypted (unless a data encryption protocol such as IPSec is used). However, for physical data protection on a mobile device, NTFS combined with EFS is excellent protection against confidential data being compromised.

Encouraging users to secure their device with password-protected screen savers, or using CTRL-ALT-DEL to lock the device when not in use, will provide another line of defense against unauthorized use of the mobile device when the device is used at a branch or company location.

Branch Site Users A large company will often have several different site locations that all need to communicate with each other. There are several different methods of connecting the various sites. In this section, we will limit our discussion to the differences between remote users and branch site users, and discuss the Windows 2000 tools available to protect data transmission in both cases.

Users at branch locations of a company are also remote users. However, they often connect to corporate resources via a LAN at the branch site that connects to the main company location. Unlike mobile users, they typically are not connecting directly, via RRAS or VPN, to the corporate network. In cases where they do connect in that manner, they are considered remote users.

Branch users must take the same precautions as local users with regard to protecting both the computers and the data. In addition, the communication between branches must be secure. Both remote users and branch locations must ensure that the data transmitted via public lines is secure from intentional or unintentional tampering.

Remote Connections   As discussed previously, remote users can connect via dial up or VPN. In both cases, secure data transmission protocols are used to ensure the data in not tampered with. Data encryption can be employed in two ways: link encryption and end-to-end encryption. Link encryption encrypts the data only between two routers. Windows 2000 provides Microsoft Point-to-Point Encryption (MPPE), which is used in conjunction with MS-CHAP or EAP-TLS. If contained in North America, data transmissions can use 128-bit encryption. MPPE is used when IPSec is not available.

Windows 2000 also provides for end-to-end encryption using L2TP with IPSec. This encrypts data from the source to its final destination. For end-to-end data encryption, use L2TP combined with IPSec. The level of security used for the duration of the connection is dependent upon the L2TP security configuration. The three choices are no encryption, optional encryption, or required encryption.

Trusted Partners

Trusted partners are organizations with whom your company has a special relationship. As such, they may require access to your company's network resources. They typically access your network in much the same manner as a branch site. We have already discussed how to manage trusted partner user accounts and authentication. With regard to secure data transmission, trusted partners will require the same types of logon authentication and security as remote users. Thus, they can be granted dial-up permissions, they can gain access using VPN, or they can access secure Web sites using the Secure Sockets Layer (SSL) protocol. Using VPN with L2TP and IPSec provides end-to-end data security via tunneling and data encryption. A distinguishing characteristic of partners, however, is that they might always communicate with your company from a specific location and through a predefined link. Therefore, you can configure your proxy server to allow the extranet link from only that network address.

FROM THE CLASSROOM

Connection and Data Encryption Protocols

Students often get confused by the myriad of different protocols available. Windows 2000 provides even more choices for connection and data encryption protocols. The questions that many students ask are related to the differences between these protocols. While it is not necessary for you to understand the underlying structure of the protocols for the MCP exams, having a slightly deeper understanding of the protocols helps when trying to answer MCP exam questions, as well as when you're trying to apply your knowledge on the job.

Secure remote communications are generated by using three protocols: a tunneling protocol, an authentication protocol, and a data encryption protocol. The tunneling protocols available in Windows 2000 are PPTP and L2TP. L2TP is an enhanced version of PPTP, and is a new feature included in Windows 2000.

The authentication protocols include EAP, MS-CHAP, CHAP, SPAP, and PAP. These protocols are used during the creation of the PPTP-based VPN connection to authenticate the session.

Finally, there are two methods of encryption available. MPPE provides only link encryption, meaning that data is encrypted between two routers, for instance. When using MPPE, you can use either EAP-TLS or MS-CHAP. The second method of encryption is an end-to-end solution that uses IPSec to encrypt IP traffic from end to end after the tunnel is established.

Students sometimes find all these protocols confusing and, at times, overwhelming. It is important to understand the different types of protocols used to secure data in Windows 2000. In the classroom, we review the connection, authentication, and encryption protocols regularly so students understand the classifications and applications of these protocols. This is critical not only to successfully passing the MCP certification exam, but more importantly, to designing and maintaining a highly secure network environment.

—*Susan Snedaker, MCSE, MCP+I, MCT, MBA*

Public Users

Public users access corporate resources via Internet Web sites. Data generally is transmitted using the Hypertext Transport Protocol (HTTP), which is not secure. Secure communications can be accomplished by using Secure Sockets Layer (SSL) versions 2.0 or 3.0 and with Private Communications Technology (PCT) version 1.0 encryption.

SCENARIO & SOLUTION

Users travel frequently to branch sites	NTFS, EFS on laptops, dial-in or VPN connections
Users travel frequently to user sites	NTFS, EFS on laptops, dial-in or VPN connections
Five branch offices in the U.S.	VPN connection using 128-bit encryption for all data
Twenty branch offices worldwide	VPN connection using 56-bit encryption for all data
Users share files	NTFS
Users keep files locally	NTFS, EFS

Security Risks

As previously mentioned, while hackers and external security breaches receive a lot of press, the fact is that more damage will be done by people inside the organization than by people outside the organization. Nonetheless, both internal and external security measures must be implemented to ensure the security of the entire network.

Networks vary in size and type depending on their function within the organization. How users connect to the network depends upon where they are located. Internal users are physically located within the corporate network infrastructure. External users are remote from the corporate network infrastructure, and require RRAS or VPN. We'll discuss internal and external users, the most common security risks associated with both, and some of the tools available to maintain security on your network.

Internal

Regardless of how good your security plans are, your network is generally just one or two passwords away from being accessed by unauthorized personnel. Internal security risks primarily come from authorized users trying to gain access to restricted data. We've already discussed the importance of the physical and logical protection of facilities, data centers, and workstations. These are all components of managing internal security risks. In addition, using some of the methods previously described in this chapter will help thwart unauthorized access. To review, these can include:

- Strong passwords
- Locking workstations

- Restricting logon hours
- Using smart cards or certificates

External

Internal security breaches are far more common than external ones. Internal employees gaining access to personnel records or payroll data can cause significant loss of confidence in the organization or even do damage to data. Yet, external security breaches can be far more devastating to an organization. External gathering of confidential data or access to trade secrets could potentially destroy a business. Therefore, strong security must be maintained when exposing your corporate network and resources outside the organization.

The potential threats from outside of your organization come from the following:

Password Cracking Unauthorized attempts to break a password are called password cracking. It can be done in several different ways. The easiest way is through guessing the password, which is why the use of strong password policies is suggested. Another method of gaining passwords is through social engineering—people posing as authorities, such as network administrators, in an attempt to get legitimate users to divulge their logon information. Finally, there are sophisticated password cracking programs available that automate the guessing process. From simple dictionary programs that use every word in a dictionary as a potential password, to more sophisticated programs that will try every possible letter combination (often called brute force), hackers continue to hone their skills in an effort to break passwords.

In addition to strong passwords, which require passwords that look like 36$9!HSMrsrt&, you can use the additional security feature called account lockout. Once a number of unsuccessful attempts have been made to log on, the account becomes locked. The network administrator can choose to lock out the account for an interval of time (15 minutes, 1 hour, etc.) or until unlocked by a network administrator. Although it increases administrative work to unlock accounts, using a time interval to unlock the account could potentially provide an opportunity for an unauthorized user to attempt to gain access after the lockout interval has expired.

Trojan Horses A Trojan Horse is a piece of software that appears to do something useful, but actually performs hidden, usually damaging, action on the user's computer. For example, a Trojan Horse might appear to be a game program that actually deliberately erases files on the computer's hard drive. Another common method of delivering Trojan Horses is via e-mail. The message may indicate that the attached program is a software upgrade from a well-known vendor, such as Microsoft. Reputable software companies, like Microsoft, do not send updates to their software via e-mail. You may receive a notice that updates are available, but you will not receive software updates in this manner.

Users should be cautioned against downloading or running any program that is unknown to them. Many software vendors are now obtaining digital signatures to authenticate the code. It ensures that the code is from the source specified and that it has not been tampered with.

As a network administrator, one of the most critical defenses against this is to avoid doing nonadministrator tasks while logged on as an administrator. For instance, if you're working on a document in a word-processing program, then go out to the Internet to find some reference material, you should not be logged on as an administrator. Trojan Horses may attach themselves to your account information and use the administrator privileges to harm the network. Therefore, always do routine tasks logged on as a normal user. When administrative works needs to be done, either use the runas command, as discussed earlier, or log on an administrator and then remember to log off.

Viruses Viruses are computer programs designed to cause errors, malfunctions, or destruction of data on computers. They are similar to Trojan Horses except that a virus often attempts to run undiscovered, while a Trojan Horse may appear to be harmless when it is, in fact, extremely destructive. Viruses also tend to replicate themselves; therefore, spreading very fast.

on the job

A recent study of viruses indicated that it used to take several days for a virus to spread to networks around the world. A recent attack took only five hours to circumnavigate the world's networks. This underscores the need to work to prevent viruses from spreading to your company's network by using preventive measures described here.

Viruses come in many forms and are constantly changing as newer, more sophisticated programs are written to circumvent known security screening. The most fundamental security against viruses is to ensure that all computers on the network are using virus-scanning software. This can be enforced at logon, and policies can be created to ensure that each time the computer is booted or logged on to, virus software is run.

Creating policies and teaching users how to avoid viruses is the second line of defense. All diskettes should be scanned when inserted into a computer. Files received via e-mail or the Internet should be scanned. Users should never open files they do not recognize, or e-mail attachments from people they do not know.

Denial of Service   A Denial of Service (DoS) is an attack designed to disrupt or disable service. There have been numerous, well-publicized attacks on large companies in the past several years. This can cause such disruption of service that these attacks are being characterized as cyber-terrorism. These attacks block regular access by intentionally flooding the network with more information than it can process. This crowds out other services and prevents them from functioning properly. DoS attacks can cause loss of service to regular users by slowing or stopping internal intranets, and by preventing access to distributed applications. Generally, DoS attacks also can intentionally or unintentionally cause a loss of revenue for the company.

SCENARIO & SOLUTION

Dictionary attacks	Generally external	Prevented with account lockout, strong passwords
Social engineering	Generally external aimed at internal	Prevented with strong passwords, certificates, or smart cards for extra security; enable auditing to monitor
Denial of Service	External	Prevented by using DMZ and load-balancing; enable auditing to monitor
Unauthorized use of resources	Internal	Prevented by logon restrictions, proper use of permissions for users and groups; enable auditing to monitor

The best method of securing a network against unauthorized access or DoS attacks is to use a Demilitarized Zone (DMZ), or screened subnet. This creates a buffer zone that separates your network from the public. Distributing Internet interfaces provides both load balancing for the site and some protection against DoS attacks. The firewall has an additional network adapter that directs traffic to the DMZ based on a set of addresses assigned to that area. Within the DMZ, you can ensure that servers do not have access to the company's network or resources. Thus, if someone is able to breach security, the attacker cannot move through the DMZ and onto your corporate network.

CERTIFICATION SUMMARY

In this chapter, we looked at how to analyze the business and security requirements of end users, and how to assess the physical and information security models available in Windows 2000.

There are three primary business perspectives: executive, administrative, and technical. We learned that executives look at strategic business issues, administrators look at tactical planning issues, and technicians implement strategic and tactical plans related to the network infrastructure. We reviewed end-user communities: Everyone (all users), Staff (company employees), Users (classified by business function), and Partners (trusted, external users). We saw how each has unique computing needs, and how accessing the network differs among these groups.

Users can be internal or external, and they can be local or remote. These categories have some overlap, but as we saw, each has distinct criteria to define it. Internal users are those who are physically connected to the LAN. External users are those connected via remote connections, either through direct dial up, VPN connections, or the Web. Local users are usually internal users. They connect to network resources using LAN connections such as Ethernet connections. Remote users, on the other hand, can be employees of the company (internal) or trusted partners (external). They connect through direct dial up, through VPN connections, or access data via the Web. They can connect directly or via a remote site's LAN connection to the corporate network.

We also looked at physical security and the importance of securing the facility, the data center (servers), and user workstations. We discussed the various tools Windows 2000 provides to protect user data. From authenticating users during logon to ensure they have permission to access data to NTFS, EFS, and auditing, we have learned how unauthorized users can be prevented from accessing or viewing data.

We reviewed the concerns regarding remote data access. Using authentication, data encryption, and connection protocols, Windows 2000 enables secure transmission of data between routers (link) or from end to end. We also discussed how data can be secured for the public when being viewed over a Web site (SSL), and how trusted partners can gain secure access to corporate resources, ensuring that the data is transmitted in secure ways.

Finally, we reviewed the security risks that are internal and external to an organization. We discussed the importance of planning and proper administration of user and group policies. We saw that many threats come from inside an organization. We also discussed external threats, including Trojan Horses and viruses, and discussed setting up policies to ensure that users do not intentionally or unintentionally disrupt the network by introducing problems from external sources.

✓ TWO-MINUTE DRILL

Analyze Business and Security Requirements for the End User

- ❑ Executives view the business at the highest level, including competitors and the industry.
- ❑ Administrators view the business in terms of designing the network (domains, topology) and security policies.
- ❑ Technicians implement the plans and policies, and administer and manage the day-to-day network operations.
- ❑ User communities include Everyone (anonymous access), Staff (employees), Users (grouped by function), and Partners (members of other companies).
- ❑ Local users connect to the network via the LAN and are physically present at the company's facility.
- ❑ Remote users are outside the facility and can connect via RRAS services (direct dial up) or VPN (via an ISP through the Internet).
- ❑ Public users access information via corporate Internet Web sites.
- ❑ Trusted partners access data either locally or remotely, similar to company employees.
- ❑ Applications can be classified by user group to ease installation and administration.
- ❑ Applications can be made available via Windows 2000 Terminal Services, which provides ease of installation and administration, and bandwidth-efficient computing for end users on a variety of hardware platforms.

Analyze the Current Physical Model and Information Security Model

- ❑ Physical security must involve the facility, the data center (servers), and user workstations.
- ❑ Data can be protected by authenticating users at logon, NTFS file permissions, and EFS encryption methods.
- ❑ Security risks are both internal and external to the organization. Internal threats typically involve authorized users attempting to gain unauthorized access to data on the network.
- ❑ External threats include intentional and unintentional attacks. Trojan Horses and viruses are the most common external threats.

SELF TEST

The following questions will help you measure your understanding of the material presented in this chapter. Read all of the choices carefully, as there may be more than one correct answer. Choose all correct answers for each question.

Analyze Business and Security Requirements for the End User

1. Your company has three divisions: Sales, Finance, and Operations. The vice president of Sales has determined that your firm needs to provide real-time access to InfoGroup, a company that provides market research databases on sales history. InfoGroup is located in four major cities, including the one your company is in. They have 14 associates who will be accessing this data. What solution do you recommend? (Choose all that apply.)

   A. Put all the data on the Web site and update the site each day.
   B. Provide the 14 associates with a username and password, and allow them to dial in to your RRAS server to gain access to data.
   C. Provide access via VPN connection to gain access to data.
   D. Post the data to a secure FTP location and allow associates anonymous FTP access.

2. Which protocol in Windows 2000 allows for end-to-end encryption?

   A. Kerberos v5
   B. MS-CHAP
   C. TCP/IP
   D. IPSec

3. Which statement(s) about EFS is true? (Choose all that apply.)

   A. EFS encrypts only files that are transmitted across a local network.
   B. EFS encrypts files and folders, and must be used in conjunction with NTFS.
   C. EFS provides end-to-end encryption of files.
   D. EFS should not be used on files that are shared.

4. Which protocols can be used in virtual private network (VPN) connections? (Choose all that apply.)

   A. Point-to-Point Tunneling Protocol (PPTP)
   B. Layer 2 Tunneling Protocol (L2TP)
   C. IPSec (Internet Protocol Security)
   D. Kerberos v5

5. Which two technologies should be used to provide additional security for laptops?
   A. NTLM
   B. EFS
   C. Digital signatures
   D. 3DES
   E. IPSec

6. Your network security has been breached several times by authorized users gaining unauthorized access to data on the network. The president of your company calls a meeting of the IT group to discuss security concerns. The president believes that not only are the internal security breaches unacceptable, but he has reason to believe that a group of hackers located in Colorado is planning to attack your network. What solutions can you suggest? (Choose the best set of solutions.)
   A. 1a) Review user and group policies to ensure that user rights are appropriate.

      2a) Set auditing to monitor the following activities: 1) success and failure for object access, 2) success and failure for account logon events, 3) success and failure of directory service access.

      3a) Ensure that each user has strict logon/logoff hours, and choose to forcibly disconnect users when logon hours expire.
   B. 1b) Review user and group policies to ensure that user rights are appropriate.

      2b) Set auditing to monitor the following activities: 1) success and failure for object access, 2) success and failure for account logon events, 3) success and failure for account management.

      3b) Disable all server services not in use on computers connected to the Internet.
   C. 1c) Review user and group policies to ensure user rights are appropriate.

      2c) Set auditing to monitor all event failures.

      3c) Disable Remote Access Server and require users to use VPN only.

      4c) Require user authentication for all logons.

7. What is the Run As command used for?
   A. To allow an administrator to run an administrative program while logged on as a normal user.
   B. To allow one user to log on as another user to gain access to an application on a different domain.
   C. To allow the program to be run as an application in Terminal Services when specified in the program's Properties.
   D. To allow an administrator to log on as a normal user from remote workstations.

8. What technologies should be implemented to provide the highest level of security for communications between Company A's network and their trusted partner, Company B's network?

   A. PPTP
   B. L2TP over IPSec
   C. Basic authentication with SSL
   D. SSL, digital certificates, and ANI/CLI

9. When configuring dial-up access for different remote users groups, what is the best strategy to employ for a user group whose members are constantly traveling to different locations and whose access must be tracked?

   A. Enable the callback feature to save on long-distance phone charges.
   B. Configure the user's dial-up properties to use SSL.
   C. Enable ANI/CLI authorization.
   D. Enable DNIS authorization.

Analyze the Current Physical Model and Information Security Model

10. Your marketing department has staff who travel to three remote locations throughout North America. The data they work with is highly competitive information and must remain secure. Their laptops are Pentium III-based P500 or P600s with 64MB of RAM and internal 56K modems. What solutions would you recommend to ensure all data is maintained at the highest possible level of security?

    A. Install Windows 2000 Professional, use file compression on the FAT partition, and encrypt the users' My Documents folder using EFS; use 128-bit encryption via a VPN connection.
    B. Install Windows 2000 Professional, format the entire hard drive to use NTFS, encrypt folders with sensitive data using EFS, and access the network using VPN using SSL.
    C. Install Windows 2000 Professional, format the entire hard drive to use NTFS, encrypt folders (including My Documents and Temp) containing sensitive documents, access the network via VPN implementing L2TP with IPSec, choose 128-bit encryption.
    D. Install Windows 2000 Professional, format the entire hard drive to use NTFS, do NOT encrypt files that will be shared across the network, use VPN using SLIP and MS-CHAP, choose 40-bit encryption since remote users are not contained within the United States.

11. Which best describes the relationship between L2TP and IPSec?
    A. L2TP is the tunneling protocol used to create a secure point-to-point connection. IPSec is the IETF standard for data transmission interception methods.
    B. L2TP is the tunneling protocol used to create a secure point-to-point connection. IPSec is used in conjunction with L2TP to encrypt the data transmitted across an L2TP connection.
    C. L2TP is the tunneling protocol used when users dial directly in to a RRAS server. IPSec is the authentication protocol used.
    D. L2TP is the tunneling protocol used when users dial directly in to a RRAS server. IPSec provides certificates of authority to authenticate remote users.

12. Your firm wants to access resumes from potential candidates via your Web site. You want to ensure that the resumes remain secure, and that access to these resumes is only allowed by managers in the HR group. How should you set this up?
    A. On your Web site, provide a form that users can fill out. Store the results of that form on the Web server, and grant HR users group permission to access that folder.
    B. On your Web site, provide a form that users can fill out. Enable L2TP so all data sent to and from the candidate are secure. Provide access rights to the HR managers group only.
    C. On your Web site, provide an e-mail address. Ask potential candidates to e-mail their resumes. Set up a distribution list on your e-mail server to distribute the e-mail to all members of the HR group.
    D. On your Web site, provide a form that users can fill out. Enable Secure Sockets Layer, so all data sent to and from the candidate are secure. Assign permissions to the HR managers group to access the results file.

13. Your firm has experienced a number of access violations on users' desktop computers lately. Your manager has asked you to look into the problem. What would you do to both assess and address the problem?
    A. Ask users to log off their computers at night and lock them. Implement auditing to determine the nature of the access violations. Ask the cleaning crew if they've noticed any unauthorized users in the office late at night.
    B. Check to ensure that you require users to use strong passwords. Implement auditing to determine the time of day the access violations occurred. Check with HR to see if any users with extensive permissions have been fired recently.
    C. Ask users to log off their computers at night and lock them. Implement auditing to monitor any attempts at access violation. Check card key access permissions to both the building and the server room.

D. Check to ensure that you required users to use strong passwords. Change all user passwords and require them to be changed at next logon. Check card key access permissions to both the building and the server room.

14. A Denial of Service (DoS) attack is defined as:
    A. A virus that gets downloaded from the Internet onto your network.
    B. A flood of data aimed at your server intended to overload the processing capabilities.
    C. A message you receive when you attempt to dial in to a network without a legitimate user account.
    D. The result of an account lockout caused by too many failed attempts to reach a Web site that is busy.

15. Your network was recently hit hard by a new virus going around. You've installed a network version of the latest virus-scanning software. What else can you do to ensure the network is free from virus attacks?
    A. Enable auditing for success and failure for file-access and object-access events.
    B. Enable auditing for success and failure of write access for programs.
    C. Enable auditing for user rights and system events.
    D. Enable auditing for all success and failure events.

16. What are the three recommended ways to manage trusted partner access to your corporate network?
    A. Create a separate domain for the partner organization, create a one-way trust relationship, and require the use of strong passwords.
    B. Create a separate domain within the organizational unit, create a one-way explicit trust relationship between the networks (both must be Windows 2000-based networks), and require the use of EFS file encryption.
    C. Create an organizational unit for each partner organization, create a one-way explicit trust relationship between networks (both must be Windows 2000-based networks), and require the use of third-party certificates for user authentication.
    D. Create an organizational unit for each user in the partner organization, create a two-way explicit trust (so users on both networks can communicate with one another), and install a Certificate Authority on your network.

LAB QUESTION

You are the network administrator for an Internet startup firm, LM2. LM2 wants you to devise a solution so that nationwide sales representatives of LM2 can gain access to the financial application required to do their jobs. Currently, these sales reps are running different financial applications on their individual desktops and laptops. This same application is used by the Finance group at LM2 headquarters. They access the application via the LAN. Additionally, the sales reps need to send their weekly sales data to the vice president of Sales at LM2 headquarters. These are typically large Excel spreadsheets that average 50K per file. A sales rep may have to send two to four of these per week, depending on various business factors.

The president of the company has specifically told you that she expects this application deployment to be seamless. She has a meeting with the Board of Directors in 90 days, and this application must be up and running by then. The CIO mentioned to you in the hallway yesterday that he expected you to use the latest technologies and to ensure that the financial data transmitted by the sales reps is absolutely secure. He also mentioned that he really didn't want to see a large financial expenditure to get this done, since the company was in its last fiscal quarter of the year and is over budget on a number of items.

What solution would you recommend for deploying this financial application? Support your recommendation with specific data.

SELF TEST ANSWERS

Analyze Business and Security Requirements for the End User

1. ☑ **B, C.** The associates could be placed in a group that contains only users from InfoGroup. Their access could be managed through this group. You could also allow VPN connections and enable either link encryption or end-to-end encryption.
   ☒ **A** is incorrect. In this case, Web site access is unrestricted, and the data would be available to anyone visiting the Web site. Updating the site daily would require tremendous administrative time to keep current. **D** is incorrect. Anonymous access does not provide any level of security or authentication. The data needs to be real time. Creating files and posting to an FTP location would not provide real-time data.

2. ☑ **D.** IPSec is the protocol that provides for data encryption across the network wire, whether local or remote.
   ☒ **A** is incorrect. Kerberos v5 is the protocol used to authenticate users at logon, which replaces NTLM, used in Windows NT 4.0 and earlier. **B** is incorrect. MS-CHAP is a dial-up authentication method. **C** is incorrect. TCP/IP is a transmission protocol, but does not provide for encryption.

3. ☑ **B, D.** EFS allows files and folders to be encrypted. Users must have NTFS file system installed prior to using EFS. EFS files are encrypted and only the owner can decrypt them. Files that are shared with others should not be encrypted using EFS.
   ☑ **A** is incorrect. Encrypted files that are transmitted are unencrypted during transmission unless an encryption protocol is used. **C** is incorrect. End-to-end encryption is provided by IPSec, not by EFS.

4. ☑ **A, B, C.** PPTP was originally used in prior versions of Windows NT and is still supported in Windows 2000. L2TP was added as a method of providing enhanced security for remote communications. IPSec is used in combination with L2TP to provide a secure remote data transmission solution.
   ☒ **D** is incorrect. Kerberos v5 is used to authenticate users at logon.

5. ☑ **B, E.** EFS provides additional data security for data. Even if the hard disk is stolen, EFS provides encryption that is very difficult to bypass. IPSec provides secure remote access from client to gateway over the Internet using the Layer Two Tunneling Protocol (L2TP) secured by IPSec.
   ☒ **A** is incorrect. NTLM is used to authenticate users during logon when non-Windows 2000 servers are used. **C** is incorrect. Digital signatures are used to authenticate software integrity. **D** is also incorrect. 3DES is a security level associated with IPSec.

6. ☑ **B.** Reviewing user and group policies will help ensure users are granted appropriate permissions on the network. Auditing the success and failure of object access, account logon events, and account management will assist in monitoring inappropriate access and attempts to bypass or alter permissions. Finally, disabling all server services not in use on external servers will reduce the risk of someone gaining access through these services.

☒ **A** is incorrect. Monitoring the success and failure of directory access service will not provide data regarding unauthorized data access. Using logon hour restrictions may assist with limiting users on the local system, but does not address the external security risks. **C** is incorrect. Monitoring all failed events will create a large log file that may degrade system performance and make it difficult to discern relevant data. Both RRAS and VPN provide secure methods of communicating externally, so disabling RRAS does not address the external security concern. In Windows 2000, Kerberos v5 is used to authenticate each user logon. This is a security feature inherent in Windows 2000.

7. ☑ **A.** The security risk of doing routine tasks while logged on as an administrator is high. The Run As command allows the administrator to run a particular program as an administrator without logging on to an administrative account.

☒ **B** is incorrect. One user cannot log on as another user. The Run As command has nothing to do with running an application in a different domain. An administrator may need administrative rights to perform the Run As command in a different domain, but that is true even if the administrator is not using the Run As command. **C** is incorrect. An application is not set up to run via Terminal Services by using the Run As command in the Properties tab. An application must be deployed using Terminal Services. **D** is incorrect. An administrator should have a normal user logon that can be used to log on to any computer to which he or she has access.

8. ☑ **B.** L2TP over IPSec is the enhanced method of providing point-to-point tunneling in Windows 2000. L2TP creates the secure tunnel, and IPSec provides data encryption.

☒ **A** is incorrect. PPTP is provided in Windows 2000, but does not provide data encryption. **C** is incorrect. Basic authentication with SSL is used for secure connections to Internet Web sites. **D** is incorrect. SSL is used for secure Web connections. Digital certificates are used to authenticate people or software via the Internet. ANI/CLI is automatic number identification used in dial-up connections when the dial-up connection does not support secure authentication methods.

9. ☑ **D.** DNIS authorization can be used when you provide multiple phone lines for your dial-up users and you want to apply remote access policies based on the phone number dialed.

☒ **A** is incorrect. Enabling callback will save on long-distance charges, but users must be at a predetermined phone number to use the callback feature. **B** is incorrect. SSL is a secure protocol used to transmit data over the Internet. When users are dialing in to a RRAS server, SSL is not used. **C** is also incorrect. ANI/CLI is used to authenticate users based on the phone number used to dial in. If users are constantly at different locations, they cannot be authenticated using this method.

Analyze the Current Physical Model and Information Security Model

10. ☑ **C.** Installing Windows 2000 Professional will enable you to use the enhanced features of the Windows 2000 operating system. Formatting the drive to use the NTFS file system will enable the user to control access to files and folders. Once NTFS has been implemented, EFS can be used to encrypt files on the local hard drive. It is recommended that folders be encrypted, since files within those folders will inherit the encryption. Ensuring that the My Documents and Temp folders are encrypted will provide security on the two most commonly used folders for user documents. Accessing a remote network using a VPN connection using L2TP tunneling protocol and IPSec data encryption protocol over the network connection will provide the highest possible security.

    ☒ **A** is incorrect. File compression does not secure files. FAT is not a secure formatting method. Files stored on partitions or disks formatted using FAT cannot use EFS. Since all remote users are within North America, you can use 128-bit encryption, but that will not secure data on the remote users' laptops. **B** is incorrect. VPN does not use SSL to communicate. **D** is incorrect. You can encrypt files on the remote users' hard drive, since encrypted files are transmitted without encryption. You cannot use SLIP with Windows 2000 RRAS. MS-CHAP is an authentication protocol that can be used to authenticate users, but does not protect data. 128-bit encryption is limited to use within North America (United States and Canada), not just within the United States.

11. ☑ **B.** L2TP is a tunneling protocol (PPTP) used in Windows 2000. IPSec is the protocol used to encrypt data transmitted through the secure tunnel connection.

    ☒ **A** is incorrect. IPSec is not an IETF standard for data transmission interception. **C** is incorrect. L2TP is not used with users who dial directly in to a RRAS server. IPSec is not an authentication protocol. **D** is incorrect. L2TP is not used for direct dial-up access. IPSec provides data encryption; it is not an certificate authority and does not authenticate users.

12. ☑ **D.** Enabling SSL provides for secure data interchange via the Internet. Allowing only members of the HR managers group to access the file will provide the requisite security.

    ☒ **A** is incorrect. Without using some form of secure communications (in this case, SSL), the data will not be secure. All HR users may not be members of the HR management group, thus providing access to unauthorized users. **B** is incorrect. L2TP is a tunneling protocol used when establishing VPN connections. Providing permissions to the HR managers group will properly restrict access to candidates' resumes. **C** is also incorrect. E-mail communications are not inherently secure. A distribution to all HR members would give access to all HR users rather than just HR managers.

13. ☑ **C.** Logging off computers and using CTRL+ALT+DEL to lock them is one method of securing the desktop computer. Implementing auditing will alert you to future attempts at security violations, including the computer used, time of day, and other details of the attempt. Ensuring that a card key (or other identification) is required to enter the building and the server areas will provide additional, first-line security against internal attacks.
    ☒ **A** is incorrect. Auditing should be implemented, but it cannot tell you about a problem that occurred prior to initiating the audit. The cleaning crew is not responsible for the security of your network, nor will they necessarily recognize authorized users. **B** is incorrect. Strong passwords are certainly part of a secure network. However, auditing will not tell you what happened in the past. Your network security should include a process to remove users from the system when they are no longer employed by the company. **D** is incorrect; while strong passwords are certainly part of a secure network and ensuring that a card key (or other identification) is required to enter the building and the server areas will provide additional, first-line security against internal attacks, changing all users' passwords and requiring them to be changed at the next logon isn't the best solution.

14. ☑ **B.** A Denial of Service attack floods the server with requests to process data for the purpose of denying service to legitimate users.
    ☒ **A** is incorrect. A virus can be downloaded onto the network, but is not a DoS. **C** is incorrect. Depending on how you attempt to connect to a computer without a legitimate user account, the call may simply be dropped, or you may be prompted for your username and password. You will not receive a Denial of Service message in this circumstance. **D** is also incorrect. An account that is locked out due to too many failed logon attempts will notify the user that the account is locked out. It will not generate a Denial of Service message.

15. ☑ **B.** Auditing the success and failure of write access for programs will monitor changes to .EXE and .DLL files.
    ☒ **A** is incorrect. Auditing for success and failure for file and object access will help determine if users have improper access to printers or other files. **C** is incorrect. Auditing user rights and system events will help you determine if legitimate users are abusing their privileges. **D** is also incorrect. Enabling auditing for all events will degrade system performance and will create a log file too large to be easily reviewed.

16. ☑ **C.** Place each partner in an organizational unit for ease of administration. If both firms are running Windows 2000-based networks, a one-way trust can be implemented. Finally, requiring the use of third-party certificates will ensure the authentication of remote partner access.

☒ **A** is incorrect. It is not necessary to create a domain for your partner organization. Strong passwords are not enough to ensure remote access authentication, though they can be used as part of an overall strategy. **B** is incorrect. You cannot create a domain within an organizational unit. Also, EFS will secure data on local drives, but is not involved in remote user authentication. **D** is incorrect. You do not create organizational units for individual users. You do not want to create a two-way trust with a partner organization; communication between domains is bi-directional, even with one-way trusts. Finally, a Certificate Authority can be installed on your network, but you should require third-party certificates for all external partners so your organization is not burdened with maintaining and administering all certificates.

LAB ANSWER

Deploy the application using Terminal Services.

Put all remote sales reps in a Sales group. Allow dial-in access for all sales reps in this group.

Have sales reps use the financial application via Terminal Services, and use VPN (using L2TP with IPSec for end-to-end encryption) for their dial-in access.

Have all sales reps using laptops install Windows 2000 Professional, and use NTFS and EFS to encrypt critical data. For all desktop users with adequate hardware requirements, install Windows 2000 Professional and use NTFS and EFS as well.

For all files to be sent to the VP of Sales, save files in an encrypted folder (My Documents), and transmit via VPN to network share for access by VP.

All internal members of the Finance group can access the financial application via the Terminal Services or via a network installation, depending on intranet and Internet access at headquarters.

MCSE
MICROSOFT CERTIFIED SYSTEMS ENGINEER

5

Analyzing Technical Requirements

CERTIFICATION OBJECTIVES

5.01 Evaluate the Company's Existing and Planned Technical Environment

5.02 Analyze the Impact of the Security Design on the Existing and Planned Technical Environment

✓ Two-Minute Drill

Q&A Self Test

This chapter provides information and techniques for analyzing the technical requirements for an enterprise network design, focusing particularly on the security aspects you need to plan for. Analyzing your organization's technical goals can help you confidently recommend technologies that will perform to your group's expectations: the pillars in building high-level security for protecting your organization's data.

The objectives of this chapter are to address typical technical goals including company size, user distribution, resource distribution, site connectivity details, bandwidth, performance, data accessing methods, network roles and responsibilities, availability, performance, security, manageability, usability, adaptability, and affordability.

This chapter can help sort out the important issues from the trivial ones, allowing you to maximize your company's resources when evaluating technical requirements.

CERTIFICATION OBJECTIVE 5.01

Evaluate the Company's Existing and Planned Technical Environment

In this section, we will look at the methods used to evaluate your organization's existing and planned technical environment. Many of the current trends being utilized in networks will be reviewed and analyzed. You can expect to learn about ways to look at your company's qualities and how to assess them in light of many topics, including the size of your organization; the roles and responsibilities that you and others within the company have; and optimal and not so optimal techniques for distributing equipment, capital, and personnel in your enterprise. You will learn about performing an analysis of the performance of hardware, software, and other tools used in your network; techniques for assessing geographical disparity in your network; resource management techniques; and a review of some of the key laws and regulations that every company operating a network should be aware of.

Company Size

Your company's size makes an enormous impact on the way you carry out a technical requirements analysis. Generally, smaller companies will not have as elaborate networks; therefore, their requirements will be less than those of a large company running several networks in tandem, at multiple sites, hosting multiple users.

However, sometimes size does not tell the whole story when discussing network complexity. For instance, a small company may deal in a business that carries tremendous security risks. For this reason, some small companies will have to have highly detailed plans that are often equally or even more involved than some larger networks that may not deal with such mission critical information.

exam
Watch

The size of your company is only one of several factors in determining the level of security necessary for your network.

There are many ways to measure the size of a company as traditional models of connected employees may not apply in some instances. In an era where network services are abstracted into distributed computing architectures such as the Internet, there are many companies that have a small number of employees, but a very large number of connected users. Examples of this are Internet companies like Internet Service Providers (ISPs), Application Service Providers (ASPs), Storage Service Providers (SSPs), and other service providers. We are seeing examples of organizations that contain few employees, fewer still IT staff, and very large numbers of users. The number of users contained in your Active Directory is one reasonable measure of your enterprises' true size.

The key method you can use to protect any organization's IT assets is to institute rigorous security policies, as you will see subsequently in this chapter. Windows 2000 Server provides methods for establishing group policies that let you logically provide levels of access to system resources. The more users you must accommodate, the more important it is to have intelligently designed groups and access rights.

One of the main benefits of Windows 2000 Server's Active Directory is that it not only lets you create domains but organizational units (OUs) as well. In a hierarchical tree structure of a typical well-designed Windows 2000 security scheme, the architecture of domains is flattened compared to Windows NT Server. Obviously, this requires a large amount of account migration, which can be complex and troublesome. However, from a security standpoint, you achieve a considerable benefit when you create organizational units. The benefit of using OUs is that you can assign security for an organizational unit to a departmental administrator, thus pushing decisions about network resources down to the people most responsible for their assignment. The flip-side is that with an OU scheme, mistakes that are made for resource access in one OU aren't applied elsewhere.

It is equally important to understand how much the network will expand in the next year and in the next two years. As a rule, it is prudent to analyze goals for growth in the next five years also, but as we are all aware, a five-year plan in technology is not easily predicted. Nevertheless, in certain technologies such as telecommunication circuitry where the lifespan is frequently between 7 and 10 years as opposed to the typical three-year cycle in most other categories, some consideration is good. If you anticipate a certain growth, you can often design a network architecture in your schema that will accommodate that growth pattern.

When analyzing your organization's scalability goals, be aware of the impediments to scalability inherent in networking technologies.

Selecting technologies that can meet organizational scalability goals is a complex process with significant ramifications if not done correctly. For example, improperly selecting a hardware or software can potentially cause problems as the number of users increases.

Becoming informed about the scalability of local area network (LAN) and wide area network (WAN) technologies and internetworking devices is a critical part of analyzing your technical resources. Remember that top-down network design is a progression that takes time and thought; no one solution will fit all networks. Your design is as unique as your company and should receive thorough consideration. And as a rule, scalability goals and solutions are revisited during many phases of the network design process.

User Distribution

Your technical requirements will be greatly influenced by the way people access your network. For instance, if your company has a small number of connected users, with one or just a few sites, your task will be less difficult than if there are many sites. As the number of sites grows, so too will the level of sophistication surrounding how you deal with user distribution. The primary technical consideration here is that in order to achieve adequate performance in a distributed enterprise, you may be forced to replicate the Active Directory security database between domain controllers. Such replication introduces potential synchronization problems where changes in your security database may not be propagated quickly enough to plug a security hole. As an example, consider a situation where a user is deleted from the system at one site, but is still able to log into the system and access resources somewhere else. There really isn't any cure for this situation other than knowing the parameters involved: for example, how long it takes for the system to update and what kinds of security rules must be in place to accommodate this.

From a technical standpoint, user distribution focuses on a group of issues. To begin with, a company with a high number of users at a particular site will need an adequate number of support staff to meet the demands of those users. Likewise, if a smaller site exists, a fewer number of support staff shall be required. Many companies have policies in place that offer a ratio of support staff to users. If your company has such a policy then it should serve as a reference for determining your support-to-users ratio—if the policy is accurate then there should be a limited amount of bottleneck issues regarding technical support. On the other hand, if IT issues are piling up, or in the unlikely event that your support department is over-staffed, then perhaps it is time to reassess the policy to better fit your company's needs.

If no policy exists, then it is time to write one. Like all things in technology, policies evolve. Setting the groundwork for user distribution and support for those users can start off in inexact terms—you will become aware of any inaccuracies in your policy quickly if there is a problem, and revision can be completed at that time.

Resource Distribution

When conducting a resource distribution analysis, you should be concerned with your company's resources on the whole. This includes human resources, capital equipment, applications, knowledge workers, and network landscape. One method for securing access to resources is to isolate particular resources inside of a resource domain. This technique is akin to the system architecture employed in many sites using Windows NT 4 Server technology.

The number of employees in your company will help you make decisions about how to handle your resource distribution. Obviously, the balance of resources should sway toward those who will most frequently use them. But some cases will be different. Exceptions to this rule include areas where the staff that support the resources are not in close physical proximity to the users. More and more frequently cases of this are arising—for instance, many Wall Street firms have enormous IT departments that serve the offices of not only the company's Wall Street headquarters, but also the hundreds of satellite branches spread throughout the country and the world. Provided that the company can receive a fast bandwidth pipe into each office, it does not necessarily need to have the IT office onsite, and it likely makes much more financial sense to have the IT department offsite rather than consuming expensive office space on Wall Street!

In effect, as more speed is introduced through connection channels, the resource problem will likely evolve from a question about the proximity of resources to a question of whether to purchase and operate resources in-house or to outsource them—more on the outsourcing issue in the Resource Ownership section.

The issue of human resources is another strategic decision that must be considered carefully. Most estimates forecast a huge disparity between the technical jobs available and the number of qualified candidates available to fill those jobs—in short there is a tremendous shortage of talent. Although hearing this may initially make IT professionals smile knowing that their employment status is secure for the coming century, eventually, if not already, it will catch up to companies struggling to support their enterprises and cause serious hassles including major backlogging of yet to be completed work.

Companies need to be proactive about having an adequate number of staff on hand to support their enterprise. At times, this may mean bringing in contractors, or outsourcing portions or entire pieces of the company enterprise.

Assess Available Connectivity Between the Geographic Location of Work Sites and Remote Sites

Building a scalable network is critical for allowing quick growth in a network capable of supporting users both locally, at satellite locations, and remote users. For many enterprise networks, scalability is a primary goal. Large companies are adding users, applications, additional sites, and external network connections at a rapid rate. The network design that your company develops should be able to adapt to increases in network usage and scope.

Your overall plan for securing network traffic across sites should focus on two main factors: implementing secure channels and implementing secure traffic. Windows 2000 offers you technology that allows for both types of approaches. If you want to establish a secure channel, consider Virtual Private Networking (VPN) technology. Dial-in traffic, used through Routing and Remote Access Service (RRAS), can also be secured through features like dial back. The second factor for securing traffic involves either encrypting the traffic (done as part of VPN, or separately), or the use of authenticating agents such as Public Key Infrastructure (PKI) certificate servers.

When designing a network, you should try to avoid incorporating any elements that would make it hard to implement new technologies in the future. For instance, make sure that your investments in hardware, software, and connection media are compatible with your current equipment and can be upgraded to future innovations. Examples of software problems can be found in incompatibility issues. For instance, several programs, particularly databases, are developed to handle a limited amount of users and files; if the limits of the program are over-stretched, then the repercussions can be disastrous as your company risks program failure, loss of data integrity, or data loss.

Many companies often make the error of purchasing new equipment that is incompatible with their existing equipment—this can lead to an expensive and frustrating resolution, and if left unresolved can lead to multiple problems including legal violations, technical difficulties, and security hazards. A good network design can adapt to new technologies and changes. Changes can come in the form of new protocols, new business practices, new fiscal goals, new legislation, and a myriad of other possibilities. For example, some states have enacted environmental laws that require a reduction in the number of employees driving to work. To meet the legal requirement to reduce automobile emissions, companies need their remote-access designs to be flexible enough to adapt to increasing numbers of employees working at home.

A flexible network design is also able to adapt to changing traffic patterns and quality of service (QoS) requirements. In today's workplace, new applications allow companies to compete better by communicating more effectively. Technologies such as Voice over IP (VoIP), videoconferencing, computer-telephony integration, and collaborative systems improve the way a company functions. However, more demand is put on the infrastructure as these and other tools emerge in network environments. For companies to take advantage of these new tools, they must deploy QoS-based networks. This kind of multimedia needs the constant bandwidth that most current networks do not provide. Therefore, if your company intends to implement QoS, a great deal of planning and research should go into the necessary additions and changes that will need to take place on your network architecture in the foreseeable future. The review should encompass all aspects of your network, hardware, software, and connectivity.

On the Internet and in other networks, QoS guarantees in advance what network resources can or cannot be distributed to each connection. In addition to monitoring capacities, QoS suggests the ability to improve and, to some extent, facilitate measuring transmission rates, error rates, and other characteristics. One major benefit of QoS is the continuous transmission of high-bandwidth video and multimedia information.

One other aspect of adaptability is how quickly internetworking devices must adapt to problems and to upgrades. The bar of sophistication with regard to device connectivity has recently been raised, leaving administrators with the task of creating reliable methods for implementing these technologies in their enterprises.

Assess the Net Available Bandwidth

The available connectivity choices for companies are improving quickly. The time in which dial-up access was the best and most affordable method to connect between two sites is past, and now smaller companies can receive inexpensive and fast connectivity through digital subscriber line (DSL) or cable access. Larger enterprises may take advantage of more costly but more capable connections such as Frame-Relay, fiber optics, or T1/T3 lines. Following is a review of the available connections with a description and a discussion of their bandwidth.

In considering each of these connectivity options, keep in mind that they have different degrees of risk associated with them. A T1 line will come with some protection at your ISP, a DSL line has less, and a cable modem probably has the least secure connection. You should assume that all connections are at risk, and install hardware and software firewalls at each connected site. At the very minimum, install a software package that will keep out all but the very determined or expert hackers. Monitoring software can tell you a lot about what traffic is coming into your sites, where the traffic is coming from, and what risks you might have as a result.

DSL speeds run up to 1.5 Mbps at this time. Faster DSL speeds are under development. The maximum speed will depend on such factors as the distance between your DSL modem and the location of the central office and the condition of your line.

Cable modems work by connecting your PC to a local cable TV line, and receive data at about 1.5 Mbps. This data rate far exceeds that of the prevalent 28.8 and 56 Kbps telephone modems, and the 128 Kbps top rate of the Integrated Services

Digital Network (ISDN) lines. A cable modem can be added to or integrated with a set-top box that provides your TV set with channels for Internet access. In most cases, cable modems are furnished as part of the cable access service and are not purchased directly and installed by the subscriber. Keep in mind that should you decide to implement enterprise services using cable modem, this technology is shared by many subscribers on the same pipe and, consequently, represents something of a security risk.

ISDN lines are medium speed lines, operating at speeds from 64 Kbps to 128 Kbps. ISDN provides access and virtual always-on access through bi-directional, on-demand calling. ISDN lines are expensive compared to cable and DSL, but are appropriate for businesses with low use, medium performance needs, particularly in areas where DSL and cable services are unavailable.

Frame Relay provides fast connectivity for networks based on dedicated leased line connections. Because the lines are leased, the management is also outsourced, which allows for less work onsite. T1 lines provide proven performance at speeds from 128 Kbps to 1.536 Mbps. T1 has long set the standard for reliability and performance.

In Table 5-1, the left column shows the type of connection and the right shows the top speed of the connection.

A note about cable modems: Some vendors claim the upper limit of a cable modem is 52 Mbps, but this is misleading. Although it is possible to reach 52 Mbps, this speed is only available to an Internet Service Provider (ISP)—not currently to an individual PC. The reason for this is that the majority of today's PCs are limited to an internal design that can accommodate no more than 10 Mbps (although the

TABLE 5-1

Connection Types and Speeds

Type of Connection	Top Speed
Dial-up	56K
ISDN	64K–128K
DSL	1.5 Mbps
Cable	512 Kbps to 52 Mbps
T1	128 Kbps to 1.536 Mbps
Frame Relay	56 Kbps to 1.544 Mbps
Fiber Optic	Up to 2.5 Mbps

PCI bus itself carries data at a faster speed). The 52 Mbps cable channel is subdivided among individual users. Obviously, the faster the channel, the fewer channels an ISP will require and the lower the cost to support an individual user.

Analyze Performance Requirements

Understanding the performance requirements for your enterprise is a fundamental part of analyzing your company's technical requirements. Performance is particularly important when your company operates applications that require a high level of speed, memory, or a combination of both. The memory requirements for Windows 2000 are much greater than for Windows NT 4.0. For a Windows 2000 Server, the minimum required is 64MB just to install it, and Professional requires at least 32MB. If your enterprise plans to purchase new servers when making the transition to Windows 2000 then a standard between 256–512MB should be the range you go with. On the same note, most industry professionals advise a minimum of 128MB for Windows 2000 Professional machines. These numbers may sound high and costly but there are a few key reasons to justify them.

The likelihood of a server maintaining the same role throughout its lifespan is relatively rare—most servers wear several hats through their cycle of service. To this end, you will likely shift the amount of work put on the server at any given time. Domain controllers will need more memory to support services such as Active Directory, but on the other hand, a simple print server or file server will need far less memory. In either case, it is better to have too much than not enough, which leads us to another reason for expanding memory at the onset of purchase.

A homogeneous network is a happy network. As an administrator, the last thing you want is to be forced to remember what type of configuration you have in each machine whenever a new fix is needed. It is much more convenient to be able to transfer any given server to a new set of duties and be free of worrying about what kind of configuration exists in it.

Other performance considerations are in processor speed. There was a time when a low-end chip could do the job for most applications. However, that time is gone and anyone working on a project that involves graphics or heavy number crunching has felt the sting of having to drudge through the progression of a slow processor. As a rule, your company should purchase the fastest chips that it can afford. Because new chips arrive on the market approximately every three months and the average speed increase per release is 33 MHz (although lately, the speed is increasing to 100MHz), you can think that each 33 MHz improvement that you purchase is like adding three months to the lifespan of that computer. Usually, there is only a marginal difference between prices on these processors, and an added three months is more often than not well worth the investment.

Other performance requirements to consider include your bandwidth issue and how your company uses bandwidth in its business process. For example, many low-end companies use their connectivity for simple issues such as e-mail and occasional Internet access. However, more high-end companies are beginning to use their connections for a wide array of applications such as VoIP, teleconferencing, ASPs, and Full Service Providers (FSPs). VoIP is accomplished by converging voice and data networks into one, thereby allowing toll-bypass and huge savings on capital equipment. However, if the company does not have an ample supply of bandwidth, then the voice connection will be choppy and difficult to decipher—the same potential problem exists for teleconferencing.

Even companies that use their connectivity for basic e-mail and Web access need to be aware of performance issues. Companies that pool their access over a single server are in effect sharing the bandwidth available to all users who are accessing it. If several users are downloading large amounts of information simultaneously, the speed can become cripplingly slow. DSL lines often share phone and Internet access—if a user or users are accessing the DSL line while the phone is being used for a voice or fax transaction then the bandwidth will be reduced.

In conclusion, when performance is a priority (and it always is) a few rules can help your company stay on top of the issue. Monitoring potential bottlenecks and implementing proactive policies can help companies meet the needs of their staff, improve administrative tasks, and reduce costs by eliminating future expenses and labor costs involved with improvements and upgrades.

Analyze the Method of Accessing Data and Systems

Determining the optimal way for users to access data from the network has lasting effects on the performance of your network. Security permissions will frequently play an influential role in the method in which users access or do not access data and systems within your company's network or the networks of partners or others. When developing new or analyzing existing methods for accessing data and systems, you should resolve who needs to access specific data. For instance, it is likely that the engineering department will have a set of files and folders that they find mission critical. Likewise, the support staff will find that an entirely different set of files pertain to their work.

Another aspect to look at when determining data and systems access is departmental proximity to their related materials. For instance, off-site workers will have the most difficult time accessing networked data because they are not locally connected to the network. However, when departments are located in offices that are separate from the server that hosts their data, the issue becomes slightly more complex. Whenever possible it is best to offer users a local connection to their data. However, sometimes for various reasons this is not possible, and it is advisable to install a method of connectivity to make the process as painless as possible.

Analyze Network Roles and Responsibilities

As you know, networks are set up to allow users, administrators, and everyone in between access to a determined amount of stored information. It is the network administrator who determines who gets access to what. In the following sections we will discuss the expectations for various players in the exchange of networked information. In addition, suggestions for methods of analyzing existing and planned networks to assure optimal management are offered.

Administrative

As the controlling members of your network, administrators have the power to make or break the success of an organization's network. As in past versions of Windows, in Windows 2000, administrators are granted the highest level of security in server, application, data, and peripheral access.

User

The roles and responsibilities of your company's users are typically quite limited from an IT administration point of view. In fact, administrators should strive to allow users to have only enough leverage within the network to accomplish their work—and not a bit more. This wish is usually for the benefit of both the administrator and the users. A good part of the time, when a problem on the network arises it is because users had too much leverage and they got themselves into trouble—a vast majority of security breaches occur for this very reason. Therefore, for the good of the whole network, administrators should set policies on the network that allow users to navigate painlessly to the areas that they need to get to. However, they should never be allowed to access anything that they do not need—even if what they are accessing is seemingly harmless, bigger unforeseen problems could be hiding around the corner.

At some companies, employees can access Web servers to arrange business travel, search online phone directories, order equipment, and attend distance-learning training classes. The Web servers are centrally located and are either linked to an ISP from the server or in the case of some smaller organizations, they access the ISP directly from the desktop. Lately there has also been an increase in the number of users in companies with a desire to communicate with their company network while offsite—this is done through the implementation of *extranets*. An extranet is a private network that uses the Internet protocols and the public telecommunication system to securely collaborate with other networks for working with remote users, customers, vendors, and strategic alliances.

exam
Watch

When planning to implement an extranet, you should document it in your list of technical goals so you can design a topology and select bandwidth appropriately.

SCENARIO & SOLUTION

How can I optimize my company network?	Whenever possible, connect separated departmental LANs into the corporate network.
What indicators should be monitored to prevent network slowing?	Watch for LAN and WAN bottlenecks—problems are frequently caused by large increases in network traffic—and make appropriate modifications to prevent this.
How can I improve satellite office network speed?	Add new sites to support field offices and telecommuters.
How can I improve communications between satellite offices and headquarters?	Prioritize connectivity between satellite field offices or telecommuters and the corporate network.
What other general networking roles should be evaluated?	Perform appropriate measures to support communication with customers, vendors and resellers, and other business partners.

Service

In this section we refer to *service* as the method in which you offer service to your company's users, not in the traditional understanding that is used for Windows administrators. A service policy for your network is critical. The actual types and levels of service that should be offered to your users in the network will determine how your users work with the system. If only a limited or deficient amount of service is made available, your users will become dissatisfied with your network's operations.

Resource Ownership

We are entering an era, of which Windows 2000 Server will be part, when resources can be protected with various hardware and biometric devices. Microsoft has an Application Programming Interface (API) that lets developers integrate devices such as fingerprint access to computers. Over the lifespan of this operating system, you will see more and more servers and desktops come with integrated security features. Those features serve as a first layer of secure access to resources.

We will divide this section into two concepts—the macro and the micro. In the macro section we will discuss the idea of resource ownership of capital equipment, support, and other physical assets that are often but not always owned by the organization that uses them. For instance, the overwhelming majority of companies with networks today house their own servers, PCs, and peripherals. However, as companies grow, more and more frequently they outsource all or some of their resource ownership and management.

Groups entering into the resource ownership section are Full Service Providers (FSPs) and ASPs. ASPs will be discussed further in the Application section of this chapter. FSPs, as their name implies, are soup-to-nuts providers of everything that a network could need, encompassing all the software, hardware, and operations infrastructure necessary to provide a scalable, secure foundation for a company's network. Most FSPs target clients with enormous enterprises or .com industries and offer their services through a subscription. The premise of their offerings is that most businesses spend a good deal of time, money, and capital worrying about and building internal networks. FSPs allow these companies to avoid the hassle of working on their network problems and instead focus their efforts on whatever business they are in—letting the FSP take care of the networking issues. Most companies offering full service have several tiers of intensity. In other words, some clients may only want their servers and client workstations to be administered at a given site, whereas, other clients may want their whole network to be run at an enterprise level, including Web hosting, LAN and WAN upkeep, e-commerce maintenance, and a variety of other services. Generally speaking, if a client can think of it, there are FSPs out there who will do it for them. Of course this all comes at a price and it is up to the company contracting the service to decide at what point it becomes worthwhile to take advantage of this service.

Another breed of help can be found in traditional System Integrators (SI). SIs have been in existence since the early days of organizations converging to networked environments. Many of these groups function like FSPs in that they handle the majority of the technical expertise in establishing a company's network and other technical resources. The underlying difference between a traditional SI and an FSP is the notion that eventually the company hiring the SI will take over the management of the network, whereas the FSP assumes responsibility throughout the duration of the network. In short, the goal of the SI is to set up a reliable network that the company can run internally after it has been properly tailored to fit its specific needs.

Currently, a majority of organizations choose to handle the bulk of their own technical requirements in-house. This means that all servers, client workstations, peripherals, applications, storage, monitoring, capacity planning, geographic redundancy, and operating centers are controlled by staff employed by the organization or through contractors who work with the organization either periodically or on a retainer basis.

The microcosmic view of ownership concerns a different aspect of network building. Earlier we discussed the topic of administrator and user responsibilities and discussed methods for handling each. Here we will look at how to handle specific resources within your network. For instance, it is likely that the most important issue regarding network resources that concerns administrators and users is the method by which your organization decides to handle permissions to resources.

In Windows 2000, all files, directories, and resources have various levels of permissions assigned to them. Generally, ownership is granted to administrators to have full control rights to whatever resources they choose. It is the job of the administrator to determine whether to allow other users on the network to access resources. You can find the name of the owner of any file or folder through the Properties window by clicking Advanced and selecting the Owner tab, as shown in Figure 5-1.

A separate level of permissions can be assigned to each user for a particular folder or file. To make permission assignment easier on administrators, it can be done at the group level, thereby avoiding the laborious task of adding each name individually.

Resource ownership is a complex issue that should receive a good deal of consideration by every company.

FIGURE 5-1

The Owner tab displays the owner of a file

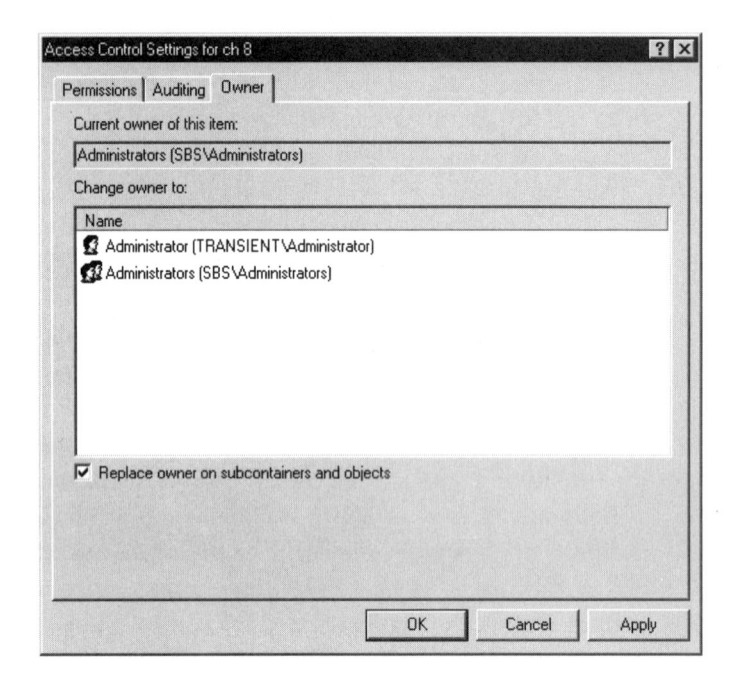

Application

Companies handle their application technical requirements by periodically upgrading to improve in meeting the needs of the enterprise or to alleviate bugs and other inconvenient anomalies that are found in dated software packages. Some companies have contracts or special agreements with software vendors who make company-specific applications, others develop their own applications in-house, while still others have their needs met with off-the-shelf, store-bought software.

Recently, companies billing themselves as ASPs are hosting their clients' software packages online. This eliminates any need for users to manually update, reprogram, or back up their data; the ASP does all of this for them. ASPs assume the responsibility of resource ownership of the servers and software that the client company uses. Companies taking advantage of this service are charged plenty for it;

however, the costs from the service are often made up in reduced costs in less onsite support staff and fewer capital purchases.

International Laws

As discussed in Chapter 3, United States law imposes strict controls on the export of 128-bit encryption, putting any U.S. company that wants to conduct business globally in a tough position. Encryption affects businesses, particularly American businesses, heavily. IT staff and business executives must pay attention to government debates over export controls on 128-bit encryption or they may find their strategic plans for everything from globalization to electronic commerce put on hold.

Table 5-2 describes the various levels of encryption.

FROM THE CLASSROOM

A Note on International Encryption Policy

When dealing with privacy issues, your company, particularly if it has an international presence, must seriously think about their encryption policy.

Strong encryption is a heated subject of debate not only in the United States, but in other countries as well, such as Argentina, Australia, Austria, Belgium, Bulgaria, Canada, Czech Republic, Denmark, Finland, France, Germany, Greece, Hungary, Ireland, Italy, Japan, Luxembourg, Netherlands, New Zealand, Norway, Poland, Portugal, Republic of Korea, Romania, Russian Federation, Slovak Republic, Spain, Sweden, Switzerland, Turkey, Ukraine, and the United Kingdom. Each of these countries have established laws and regulations regarding cryptography.

If your company has offices in any foreign countries, it is imperative that you be fully informed and educated on the laws of that area.

—*Steve Jutunen*

TABLE 5-2

Encryption Levels

Type of Encryption	What It Does
No encryption	The least secure way to transfer data—you should avoid this option unless you don't mind outsiders being able to see your information.
Basic	Uses a 40-bit Microsoft Point-to-Point Encryption (MPPE) key. This is a good option for servers working as virtual private network (VPN) servers. The PPTP protocol is also available at this level. Security is bumped up to 56-bit key if the L2TP protocol is used.
Strong	Uses a 56-bit Data Encryption Standard (DES) key. There are 72 quadrillion possible combinations—this makes strong encryption the safest legal option in the U.S.

EXERCISE 5-1

CertCam 5-1

Choosing an Appropriate Level of Cryptography

Using the preceding information, determine the type of encryption that you think would be most responsible. The following considerations will help you with this task:

1. Review any relevant laws and regulations that may affect your data transfer cryptography.

2. Once you are clear on acceptable and unacceptable cryptography rules, determine the level of sensitivity and risk that your data contains.

3. Outline where your data is transferred to and from (that is, intra-office, over a VPN to satellite offices, over the Internet, and so on).

4. Map out all locations that your data is transferred to and from your data transfer cryptography.

As always, document each step to provide a resource for others to follow.

on the Job

You work for an international company who has offices in major cities spanning the globe. You are given the assignment of installing firewalls and encryption software in the offices of several locations as a method to bolster security between offices that are interconnected using various topologies. Prior to leaving, be sure to investigate the laws of each location that you plan to visit for the obvious rules regarding the importation of equipment, and any taxes, licenses, or other bureaucratic procedures that need to be addressed. Additionally, learn if there are any laws that prohibit or limit the level of encryption that can be installed. This precaution may save you and your company a great deal of hassles, fines, or potential criminal prosecution—in short, a proactive style is well worth the time you could save if you press your luck!

An emerging method of data storage for technology is digital versatile disc (DVD). Although DVDs have made the biggest headlines in commercial markets where they are used for movie viewing, they are also a popular storage medium for certain data types. However, it should be noted that with DVDs, location makes a difference: As part of the Copyright Protection scheme used for DVDs, the DVD Consortium has set up six worldwide regions. Each region has codes set by the disk manufacturers that allow playback of some or all of the content. Microsoft plans deployment of software specific to the regional standards as required by the DVD Consortium and as part of the decryption license. Knowledge of this law could be important if your company purchases equipment or actual DVDs, because the location of purchase may conflict with the location of use and your company could potentially be violating regional laws without knowing it.

Software piracy is any occurrence in which an original computer program is copied without authorization from the author or publishing company. Laws and regulations exist in most countries condemning the practice of software piracy. For instance, piracy of software in the United States is punishable by statutory damages of up to $100,000 for each work infringed and may result in a felony conviction. Penalties for felony convictions include fines of up to $250,000 and imprisonment for up to five years.

exam Watch

Companies should make a practice of archiving all software licenses and be sure to follow the instructions regarding copying software to hard drives and floppy disks or CD-ROMs.

CERTIFICATION OBJECTIVE 5.02

Analyze the Impact of the Security Design on the Existing and Planned Technical Environment

In the previous section we outlined the areas to consider when analyzing technical resources. Now, we will apply those areas to the development of a security plan and look at how a security design affects your network's operations. Developing security policies in your company will have a multi-tiered impact on the various departments in your company. To meet the needs of all of the different IT departments, your company will require different policies. For instance, engineering, services, support, application development, and security auditing groups will require various levels of security that may or may not intertwine. In most cases, the groups mentioned will require at least some special privileges over traditional users.

In the following section we will discuss some of the issues that affect users and what elements should be analyzed to ensure that your security design and your technical environment gel together smoothly.

Assess Existing Systems and Applications

As a rule, an annual or set periodic review of existing systems and applications should take place within your organization. This is especially important for companies with the potential for security risks. Most notable among the applications that should be periodically assessed are virus detection tools, firewall software and hardware, and upgraded devices and applications.

Virus detection software is an indispensable element to any organization's system. New and potentially devastating viruses are written and dispensed into the networked world every day—many of them have been sophisticated enough to bring down some of the largest companies with seemingly impenetrable protection against malicious viruses. However, most virus software in existence scans only for code that has already been identified as malicious. Therefore, if at the time of purchase a virus had not been identified, that does not mean that it does not exist. It can potentially wreak havoc on your network three months later when it is introduced to your system.

Luckily, most anti-virus software companies offer online updates for their software. Engineers work constantly to identify the viruses that are sent into the world. When a virus is identified by an anti-virus company, the company adds it to their list of culprits. If the owner of the software downloads the update containing the identifying information about a new virus, the computer in which the update resides is safe from that virus. If any of the identified viruses should ever end up on that machine, the scanning software will pick it out and quarantine or delete the virus before it can inflict harm on the machine. In short, it is critical to update your company's computers virus patterns as often as possible.

A firewall is a set of related programs that is located at a network gateway server. When combined, they protect the resources of a private network from users on other networks. The term also applies to the applications used to operate the hardware. An enterprise with an intranet that allows its workers access to the Internet should have a firewall installed at each gateway server to prevent outsiders from accessing its own private data resources and for controlling what outside resources its own users can access. A firewall, working closely with a router, filters all network packets to determine whether to forward them toward their destination.

A number of firewall screening methods exist. A simple one is to screen requests to make sure they come from a previously identified domain name or IP address.

Frequently, mobile users working in a variety of capabilities need to access the network. It would seem that in such cases a firewall would become a hazard or at least cripple the user from gaining access. However, developers thought of this potential issue and have developed a system to allow remote access to the private network by the use of secure logon procedures and authentication certificates (further discussion of authentication certificates can be found in Chapter 8, "Designing a Windows 2000 Security Solution").

A number of companies make firewall products. Features include logging and reporting, triggering automatic alarms at the given thresholds of attack, and a graphical user interface for controlling the firewall. However, as crafty as the developers of these systems are, there is a devious minority working to crack the inner workings of this software. Therefore, periodic updates, fixes, and upgrades are necessary—check with your firewall vendor for methods of availability and frequency of distribution.

Identify Existing and Planned Upgrades and Rollouts

To keep pace with rapidly advancing technology and to meet the expanding needs for Internet access, companies must plan for continual upgrades to their networks, as well as perform routine scheduled maintenance on the entire system. Some interruptions to service are unavoidable when performing these tasks. However, whenever possible, management must schedule maintenance and upgrades during windows of time that will cause minimal service disruption. In today's 24x7 economy, this becomes a daunting task and management needs to make a thoughtful effort to minimize disruption.

Any software upgrade comes with a certain security risk; hardware upgrades have lower risks but are also not risk free. Given the pace of version upgrades, it should be part of your IT strategy to evaluate Service Packs and version upgrades early in their development cycles. Service packs often have as their main features improved security, but it is also not uncommon in a minority of cases for a service pack to degrade the security of your installation. Unfortunately, there is no hard and fast rule about what software and hardware combinations you should install and rollout. The best strategy is to institute a mechanism for monitoring vendor sites like Microsoft's for critical upgrades or for information about security issues. There are also many magazines, newsletters, and even services you can buy from vendors that follow ongoing security issues and advise you on how to best address them.

Analyze Technical Support Structure

Different groups of users will have different needs from technical support. Therefore, it is crucial for the parties involved in the development of a technical support structure to appropriately cater to the needs of each department in the organization. For instance, if your company staffs various groups with different and specialized levels of technical savvy, such as an application development staff, the method of delivering support to these people will assuredly be different from a group that specializes in engineering.

Your technical support staff can play a key roll in either improving your network security, or creating security problems. In analyzing your support structure, there should be an overall administrator in place and a defined policy manual in place with people in the support structure given areas of responsibility to administer.

Analyze Existing and Planned Network and Systems Management

When looking at your existing management, it is always important to watch for areas in which security creates an impact on your enterprise—this can be either a beneficial impact or a negative impact. Beneficial impacts should be identified to see if any qualities exist within them that could potentially be replicated elsewhere within the system. Likewise, it is critical for administrative staff to identify negative impacts that security precautions create. For instance, the added need to remember passwords, carry smart cards, or other inconveniences can create hassles that users do not want to deal with.

EXERCISE 5-2

Developing a Network Plan

Suppose your company is quickly growing and you are put in charge of developing a plan to keep your network on par with the rest of the company growth.

Use the following list of questions to analyze your organization's plans for expansion:

- How many more sites will be added in the next year? The next two years?
- How extensive will the networks be at each new site?
- How many more users will access the corporate network in the next year? The next two years?
- How many more servers (or hosts) will be added to the network in the next year? The next two years?

Approaching this problem is best done with a set of questions that, when answered, will enable you to determine the goals.

The goal for effective management of network and systems security should be a double-edged sword. On one side the managers should strive to find the most effective security possible. However, this should be done with thoughtful consideration to the amount of risk that is carried by each element of the network. In some cases, the strongest security possible is far from necessary. Sometimes the sensitivity of the data is low, and high-level security is overkill. Nevertheless, there are times when security is more important than anything; it is the lifeline of your company's success. In such cases security must override convenience or expense.

On the other side of this conundrum are the users and how various levels of security affect them. Security can often become a hazard for users attempting to navigate their way through a tightly maintained network. The goal here should be to reduce difficulty as much as possible. The goal of optimal network management is to make it easy for users to navigate while keeping security as tight as possible. Sometimes there must be a little give and take to make this happen.

on the job

A small enterprise with highly sensitive data was having trouble with the security of its information because the information was being distributed on printed copies to unauthorized personnel and customers. To deal with the problem, the administrative staff considered eliminating printing entirely at the company. Although this would solve the security problem, implementing such restrictions on printing privileges would make working more difficult for some users. Management decided to establish policies allowing only members of certain groups to print.

However, this alone was not enough because group members did not always log off the network when finished working. Consequently, others without privileges came on during the same session and printed freely.

When this problem was identified, the administrative staff decided to begin monitoring who printed what, and at what time. This report would be sent to all supervisors and management staff for review each week. A notice was sent out to all users informing them of the new policy. The problems with unauthorized printing vanished and users began logging off the network to close their sessions.

As a hidden bonus, the reduced number of logged in sessions resulted in a faster overall network due to reduced traffic.

CERTIFICATION SUMMARY

Analyzing the technical structure of your company is a big task. Analyzing the existing structure and future goals of the enterprise can help you confidently recommend and identify solutions for your environment. This chapter discussed the strategies needed for establishing some good practices for your company to introduce to your network management practice.

By reviewing and analyzing each part of your company's technical landscape, you will be better able to accurately plan and meet goals. The goals of a thorough review should include addressing company size, user distribution, resource distribution, site connectivity details, bandwidth, performance, data accessing methods, network roles and responsibilities, availability, performance, security, manageability, usability, adaptability, and affordability.

This chapter aimed to help classify the key elements of understanding and analyzing technical requirements for your network. By approaching your network in a planned and understood manner, your chances of identifying problems and finding resolutions are dramatically increased.

✓ TWO-MINUTE DRILL

Evaluate the Company's Existing and Planned Technical Environment

- ❑ The size of your company is only one of several factors in determining the level of security necessary for your network.
- ❑ Sometimes the size of a company does not tell the whole story when discussing network complexity.
- ❑ When analyzing your organization's scalability goals, be aware of the impediments to scalability inherent in networking technologies.
- ❑ Most estimates forecast a huge disparity between technical jobs available and the number of qualified candidates available to fill those jobs. In short, there is a tremendous shortage of talent that is expected to continue into the next decade.
- ❑ Building a scalable network is critical for allowing quick growth in a network capable of supporting users locally, at satellite locations, and remote users.
- ❑ As an administrator, a homogeneous network is of great assistance to you for accomplishing your work. Convenience is raised when you can transfer any given server to a new set of duties without having to guess its configuration.
- ❑ Many companies are beginning to use their connections for a wide array of applications such as Voice over IP (VoIP), teleconferencing, ASPs, and FSPs.
- ❑ Whenever possible, connect separated departmental LANs into the corporate network.

Analyze the Impact of the Security Design on the Existing and Planned Technical Environment

- ❑ Prioritize connectivity between satellite field offices or telecommuters and the corporate network; analyze the impact of your connections on the propagation of security information throughout your enterprise.

- ❑ If only a limited or deficient amount of service is made available, your users will become dissatisfied with your network's operations.
- ❑ Software piracy is any occurrence in which an original computer program is copied without authorization from the author or publishing company.
- ❑ It is critical to update your company's computers virus patterns as often as possible.
- ❑ Whenever possible, management must schedule maintenance and upgrades during windows of time that will cause minimal service disruption.
- ❑ In some cases the strongest security possible is far from necessary. Sometimes the sensitivity of the data is low, and high-level security is overkill.

SELF TEST

The following questions will help you measure your understanding of the material presented in this chapter. Read all of the choices carefully, as there may be more than one correct answer. Choose all correct answers for each question.

Evaluate the Company's Existing and Planned Technical Environment

1. What qualities should be considered when evaluating your company's technical environment? (Choose all that apply.)
    A. The size of the organization.
    B. The various roles and responsibilities of administrators and users.
    C. The costs of equipment and labor.
    D. All the above.

2. How much leverage should users have on the network?
    A. Enough to accomplish only their job functions.
    B. Enough to accomplish their job functions plus an extra amount to provide them with enough information to learn more about the network.
    C. They should always have the maximum amount of power in case they need to perform an advanced function.
    D. Their amount of leverage should depend on how well they are trusted in the organization.

3. What factors influence user distribution? (Choose all that apply.)
    A. Effective policy placement.
    B. Company size.
    C. Inconsistent bandwidth availability.
    D. Site size.

4. What are the benefits of writing policies for defining standards within your enterprise?
    A. To assist in identifying inconsistencies within your network structure.
    B. To offer assistance in the development and design of your network hardware.
    C. To assist in determining the number of staff that will be needed per task.
    D. To help set rules for a variety of issues that affect your network.

5. Is the availability of onsite resources always the ideal solution for an enterprise?
    A. Yes, given the option, there is no substitute for onsite resources.
    B. Yes, onsite resources are faster and cheaper than alternatives.
    C. No, utilizing offsite resources is a cheaper and faster solution.
    D. No, sometimes offsite solutions are a better avenue for a company to take.

6. What pragmatic options can be exercised when IT personnel resources are scarce? (Choose all that apply.)
    A. Hire more staff.
    B. Outsource to a consultant or service provider.
    C. Reduce the level of services.
    D. Lessen the number of jobs that your network performs.

7. What is an ideal connection choice for a small business seeking a higher bandwidth than a traditional dial-up connection, but looking to save money? (Choose all that apply.)
    A. Cable
    B. DSL
    C. Fiber Optic
    D. T1

8. Why is it advantageous to have a homogeneous set of equipment for your network?
    A. Homogeneity increases security by avoiding translations between different networking protocols on different machines.
    B. Homogeneity eases management by assuring that all workstations are configured identically.
    C. Homogeneity reduces costs by avoiding hardware replication; for example, different machines can share a single storage server.
    D. Homogeneity allows you to minimize management by decreasing network load.

9. What goals should be met when implementing an extranet? (Choose all that apply.)
    A. Increase the ability for partnered companies to communicate with each other.
    B. Allow offsite workers to safely access the company network.
    C. To allow an increased limit on bandwidth.
    D. To assist in the development of network design.

10. What options do companies have when they choose to outsource resource management?
    A. FSPs
    B. ASPs
    C. Systems Integrators
    D. Independent contractors
    E. All of the above

11. What is the difference between an ASP and an FSP?
    A. An ASP will handle all data input and transactions, whereas an FSP only does transactions.
    B. An ASP will host an application or a package of applications for a company who subscribes to that service, whereas an FSP will host, manage, and maintain a subscriber's network.
    C. An ASP is a snake, whereas an FSP is a nonsensical word.
    D. An FSP can handle a much higher amount of throughput compared to an ASP.

Analyze the Impact of the Security Design on the Existing and Planned Technical Environment

12. Which choice represents the highest level of encryption seen *within* the U.S.?
    A. Encryption is not allowed in the U.S.
    B. 40-bit
    C. 56-bit
    D. 128-bit

13. What does updating virus patterns mean?
    A. Identifying viruses.
    B. Falling victim to a virus.
    C. Writing a virus.
    D. Downloading identifying information on the most recently detected viruses.

14. Where should a firewall typically be placed in a network?
    A. Anywhere on the domain.
    B. On either the PDC or BDC.

C. At the gateway server.

D. It should be integrated into the telecom system.

15. What is not a benefit to assigning ownership and permissions to files and folders?

    A. Improved security.
    B. Limited user access to private information.
    C. Restricted administrative power over users.
    D. Enable granular differences among various users and groups.

16. Why are periodic updates, fixes, and upgrades necessary for firewalls?

    A. Because as good as firewall companies are—hackers are always better.
    B. Because on average a firewall only lasts 12 months before it is obsolete.
    C. Because intruders are constantly trying to figure out ways to penetrate firewalls, and periodically they are successful.
    D. Firewalls are a relatively unimportant aspect of security and upgrades are only important if your company deals with financial or other extremely high-risk information.

17. When reviewing technical requirements, why is it beneficial for a company to purchase plenty of memory and fast processors at the original time of purchase? (Choose all that apply.)

    A. An overabundance of memory is vastly preferable to an underabundance.
    B. Fast processors are less prone to security hazards.
    C. It is more cost effective.
    D. On average, each additional 33 MHz adds three months to the lifespan of a PC's processor.

18. What other potential benefit does not come from expanding bandwidth in an organization?

    A. Toll bypass through voice over IP (VoIP).
    B. Teleconferencing.
    C. Bolstered security through improved data transmission speed.
    D. Private lines improve security.

LAB QUESTIONS

Part of a good technical analysis is discovering new ways to improve and build upon your existing network. Taking from what you have learned in this chapter, try to apply some of the key concepts to analyzing your network by answering the following questions.

1. When looking at scalability, what areas should I focus my attention towards?

2. If there is a noticeable deficiency in the service available to some users in the network and an overabundance for others, how do I approach fixing the problem?

3. Prior to making modifications to my geographical network structure or adding a significant number of users to the network, what should I do first?

4. When troubleshooting a slow network, what is my main objective?

5. When upgrading my network to Windows 2000, what, if any, concerns should I have about my current application suites?

6. In an effort to add value to my company's network investment, what elements can I suggest be investigated?

SELF TEST ANSWERS

Evaluate the Company's Existing and Planned Technical Environment

1. ☑ **D.** The size of the organization, whether big or small, will play a major role in determining how your organization handles evaluating and developing technical environment strategies. The types and roles of personnel in your company are also important factors when evaluating. And as always, looking at the bottom line is crucial in the decision making process. It is important to mention that in technology especially, initial costs are typically high, but payoff can come quickly when efficient choices and sound decisions are made.

2. ☑ **A.** In order to maintain a high level of confidence in your network's security structure, it is crucial to tighten as many potential loopholes as possible. By disabling portions of the network that users do not need, you are making it less likely for a user to prod into an area of the network where they should not be, either knowingly or by mistake.
   ☒ **B, C, and D** are incorrect. Giving users extra slack to wander around the network is a dangerous idea and should not be practiced. Allowing even a little room to roam can be potentially disastrous depending on what exactly is accessible. Although some users may be initially miffed at the idea that they are not trusted to access certain areas, they will undoubtedly get used to the idea that they do not need the areas that are closed to them.

3. ☑ **D and C.** The size of the site will have a heavy impact on the level of sophistication surrounding your network and on how your distribution matures. Bandwidth availability is a crucial matter in networks that have several remote sites connected. In such cases, the distribution of resources can become much more flexible as groups are able to be less dependant on local resources.
   ☒ **A and B** are incorrect. Effective policy placement will not have a direct effect on your company's user distribution. Although the overall size of your company will have an impact on many things, it does not necessarily directly affect your user distribution.

4. ☑ **D.** Policies are an evolving set of documentation meant to assist management in identifying the best ways to streamline company processes. As the duration of policies expands, managers will be able to adjust them to maximize their efficacy.
   ☒ **A, B, and C** are incorrect. In identifying inconsistencies within the network structure, managers need to look at a wide variety of issues including performance, data access, user and resource distribution, and so on. Policies do play a part in this as well, but it is not their main purpose. The development and design of network hardware is relatively untouched by policymaking, as it deals with the capital expenditures and structure development rather than the method of using and handling the structure.

Determining the number of staff to use for a network is a problem that usually evolves with the growth of the network. Although it is good practice to have a set policy in place to give a general ratio of how many support staff to general staff are to be employed, this is the result of policymaking, not a direct benefit.

5. ☑ **D.** There are cases in which an offsite solution is a more pragmatic solution for a company to introduce for their networking issues. Example companies include those in remote areas who do not have the resources available to operate a network in-house. Some offices in high-rent metropolitan areas may need a strong level of technological backing, but for financial reasons it makes more sense to house the equipment elsewhere and run a fast connection to the office. Additional reasons include resource pooling between companies and a higher level of expertise from offsite contractors.
☒ **A, B,** and **C** are incorrect. As illustrated, an onsite solution is not always the best answer for a company because other factors may make alternative solutions more attractive or practical. Although it is usually true that onsite solutions are faster and cheaper than offsite ones, there are exceptions to this rule. On the same note, it is rarely the case, although it does happen, that an offsite solution is cheaper as answer **C** suggests.

6. ☑ **A** and **B.** Companies should be proactive in keeping their IT staff filled with qualified personnel. This is often easier said than done. Due to tremendous worker shortages in the technology sector, the ability to find, hire, and keep competent staff is difficult. Often the best alternative to having company personnel is to hire qualified contractors. Contractors come in all shapes and sizes, offering virtually any service imaginable to meet your IT needs—all of this of course comes at a price. Determining the level of value added versus the costs is important and at times a difficult task.
☒ **C** and **D** are incorrect. Reducing the level of service should be a last ditch effort for your IT team. Simplifying your network by cutting its job performance should not be done unless every other option has been exhausted—with one caveat to that. Trimming fat from your network is always a welcomed addition. Do not think that the number of network tasks indicates the effectiveness of a network. Often times it is a hindrance to have an overabundance of jobs working.

7. ☑ **A** and **B.** Both cable and DSL offer inexpensive solutions for reasonably fast connection bandwidth. As an added convenience, both cable and DSL offer full-time connectivity—eliminating the annoyance of dialing in to an ISP each time a session is started.
☒ **C** and **D** are incorrect. Fiber optic and T1 connections are very expensive and are not an ideal solution for a small business, as they are targeted to service major companies with large data transfers.

8. ☑ **B.** Homogeneity eases management. When all your machines are identical, an administrator can simply sit down at a machine and begin to work without having to figure out the particular configuration of the machine.
☒ **A** is incorrect because networking protocols are themselves the medium for communications between different machines. For example, many different machines can use TCP/IP, allowing them to communicate with one another easily. The protocol is standardized; inside one machine, the universal protocol and the machine communicate through *drivers*. Translation is not necessary once you have a protocol set up. **C** is incorrect because hardware replication will occur even in a homogenized space. **D** is incorrect because homogeneity is irrelevant to network load. Network load is a function of traffic on the network, which is entirely independent of the sorts of machines that are plugged into the network.

9. ☑ **A and B.** The primary goal of an extranet is safe, secure communication using Internet protocols and the public telecommunication system to securely collaborate with other networks for working with remote users, customers, vendors, and any other partners.
☒ **C and D** are incorrect. Bandwidth is not increased by the implementation of an extranet. And although the development in network design is a consideration when developing an extranet, it has little to do with the goals of implementation.

10. ☑ **E.** For outsourcing one or a group of applications, ASPs will provide the hosting service needed. ASPs offer in-house and custom-built applications for companies who would rather leave the day-to-day management to someone else. FSPs take the ASP approach a step further by offering hosting of not just applications but entire network services. Both ASPs and FSPs offer high levels of security to their clients and guarantee a nearly flawless reliability record—or they will compensate the company for any downtime.
Systems Integrators (SI) have long been the old reliable option for outsourcing network and resource management. Generally speaking, SI s are known to deliver a quality product or service at a hefty price to their customer. Independent contractors are similar to SI groups and are typically smaller, but often less established and therefore less expensive.

11. ☑ **B.** An ASP focuses its business on hosting applications for clients. The ASP hosts, maintains, upgrades, and debugs the application for the customer when needed. FSPs go a step further and provide more to their clients including full network hosting, service, maintenance, and assume responsibility for potential problems if they should arise in the network.
☒ **A, C, and D** are incorrect. FSPs are responsible for a wide variety of tasks and can be scaled to be more or less responsible depending on the desire of the client. However, there is no evidence to show that a FSP is more capable of handling more throughput than an ASP—such a comparison is too difficult to assess in general terms.

226 Chapter 5: Analyzing Technical Requirements

Analyze the Impact of the Security Design on the Existing and Planned Technical Environment

12. ☑ **D.** Although the exportation of data with 128-bit encryption is illegal in the U.S., it is considered perfectly legal to operate with this level of security as long as it does not go outside of the North American continent. When going outside of North America, data can be sent with nothing greater than 56-bit cryptography—still a very strong method.
    ☒ **A** is incorrect because not only allowed but an absolute *must*. **B** and **C** are the wrong encryption levels.

13. ☑ **D.** Engineers work constantly to identify and create fixes or quarantines for existing viruses. Anti-virus software owners can download updates that include newly identified viruses from sites provided by the software manufacturer.
    ☒ **A**, **B**, and **C** are incorrect. Identifying viruses is the process accomplished by anti-virus software; however, to accomplish this as thoroughly as possible, the latest updates must be installed.

14. ☑ **C.** To prevent outsiders from accessing private company data resources and to control what outside resources that internal company users have access to, a firewall should be typically placed at each gateway server on the network. Additional firewalls may be required within your organization depending on the sucurity requirements of various departments.
    ☒ **A**, **B**, and **D** are incorrect. Careless placement of a firewall leaves part or all of your network vulnerable to potentially harmful probing, both internally and externally.

15. ☑ **C.** Assigning ownership and permissions is a right that administrators have on files and folders, not a restriction.
    ☒ **A**, **B**, and **D** are incorrect. Improved security, the ability to limit user access to private information, and the potential to create granular levels of security within the network are all qualities of assigning ownership and permissions.

16. ☑ **C.** Several firewall makers have developed virtually impenetrable security boxes that make vulnerability to a hacker an extremely unlikely chance. However, although the level of sophistication remains high, there is a scheming and highly skilled group that continues to work at cracking both the hardware and software found in firewalls.
    ☒ **A**, **B**, and **D** are incorrect. Hackers, while good at defeating security, are not uniformly better than the makers of firewalls. In fact, many ex-hackers are now working for security firms who make the algorithms that comprise the security of a firewall. Firewalls do not have a general shelf life; depending on the type you buy, it can last for several years just like a regular PC. Many people are surprised to learn that everyone is vulnerable to hackers, ranging from home PCs to major companies. Firewall protection is a sound solution for anyone with sensitive data that is accessible from the Internet.

17. ☑ **A, C, and D.** Rarely is there a case where a user or an administrator complains that his or her PC or server has an overabundance of memory. Buying all equipment at the same time is an efficient method of purchasing. Many vendors offer bulk rate discounts for large quantity purchases and later installation time and labor costs are avoided. And lastly, it is accurate to assume that each 33 MHz adds three months to each computer's lifespan.
    ☒ **B** is incorrect and processor speed does not make a system less susceptible to security hazards.

18. ☑ **C.** Security is not improved simply by increasing the speed at which it transmits.
    ☒ **A, B, and D** are incorrect. VoIP and teleconferencing are both excellent ways to boost your network data, and voice budgets by converging the two. Private lines can improve security by preventing wire-tapping schemes. Fiber optic lines, for instance, will automatically detect any disruption along the line and notify both the customer and the provider immediately if there is a suspicion of line tampering.

LAB ANSWERS

1. Improvements that can be made to your company's strategy for dealing with size and resource issues.

2. Assess efficacy of roles and responsibility distribution.

3. Determine the need for system upgrades or replacements.

4. To identify system bottlenecks.

5. Determine if there is any need for application upgrades or replacements.

6. Identify potential improvements that can be made to your company's network through the use of existing resources (for example, VoIP, teleconferencing, and so on).

6

Designing a Security Baseline for a Windows 2000 Network

CERTIFICATION OBJECTIVES

6.01	Domain Controllers
6.02	Operations Masters
6.03	Servers
6.04	Group Policy Scenarios
✓	Two-Minute Drill
Q&A	Self Test

In this chapter we are going to cover in detail what domain controllers (DCs) do in Windows 2000. We will also cover Microsoft's new multi-master model and how it handles conflicts. We will also discuss the parts of Windows 2000 networking that have remained single master and what those operations are. Finally, we will cover Group Policy scenarios under Windows 2000 and, in particular, desktop systems, laptop systems, and kiosk configurations.

CERTIFICATION OBJECTIVE 6.01

Domain Controllers

In Microsoft networking, from the days of LAN Manager 2.0 to Windows 2000 we have dealt with the shared security unit called the domain. Although the "model" of the domain has changed, we have always had a server role called the domain controller. We have had primary domain controller (PDC), backup domain controllers (BDCs), and member server, which were typically reserved for application servers for better performance, for some time now.

on the job

The member server role didn't come about to the Windows NT operating system until version 3.5. In Windows NT 3.1 all servers were a domain controller, with one being the PDC and all others being BDCs. It is not ideal to make domain controllers application servers.

Now in Exercise 6-1, we will take an installed Windows 2000 Server, which is not affiliated with any domains, and make it into the first domain controller of a new forest and domain.

EXERCISE 6-1

Making a Windows 2000 Server into the First Domain Controller of a New Forest and Domain

1. Once Windows 2000 is running (as only a server role), click Start, and then Run.

2. Type **dcpromo.exe**. This will initialize the conversion of this server to a domain controller and allow us to create a new forest and domain.

3. Once you run **dcpromo**, you will see the following screen, welcoming you to the Active Directory Installation Wizard. Click Next to continue the installation.

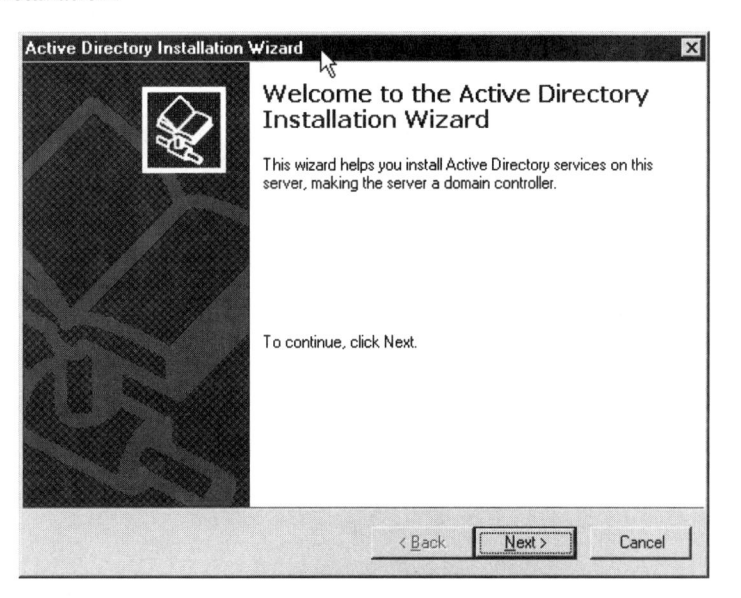

4. Next we must choose the domain controller type that we are setting up. For our exercise we are creating a new forest and tree, so we will select Domain Controller for a New Domain.

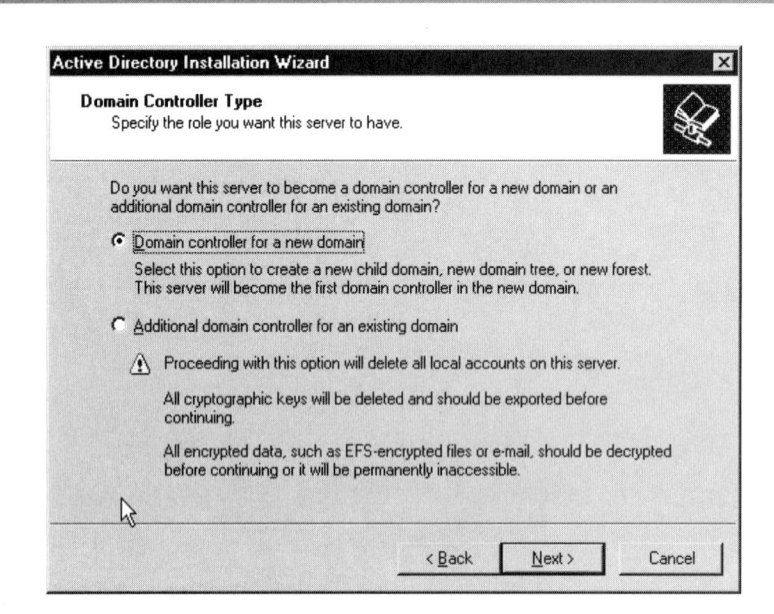

[Screenshot: Active Directory Installation Wizard — Domain Controller Type, with "Domain controller for a new domain" selected.]

5. Next we choose Create a New Domain Tree.

[Screenshot: Active Directory Installation Wizard — Create Tree or Child Domain, with "Create a new domain tree" selected.]

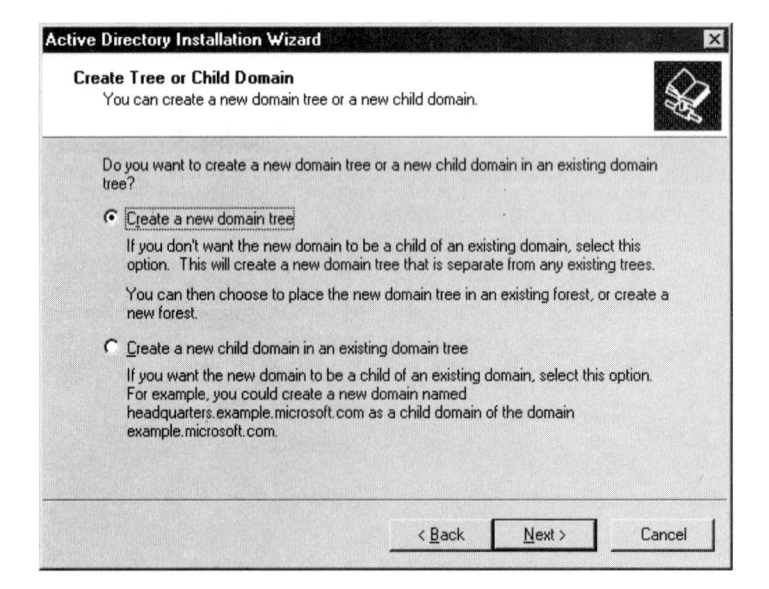

6. Now we must tell Active Directory our domain name, in this case our Domain Name Service (DNS) name. Here you do *not* include the host name, just the overall domain name. In this scenario we chose *corporate.com*.

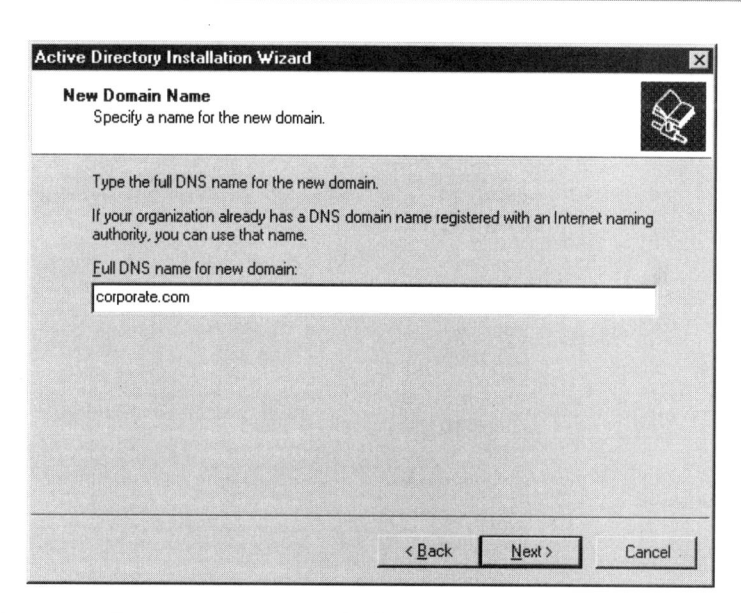

7. In the screen shown next, we are asked to enter the domain name for those clients that will be "legacy" based and be reliant on NetBIOS name resolution for network authentication. This is proof that Windows 2000 Server does start off in mixed mode.

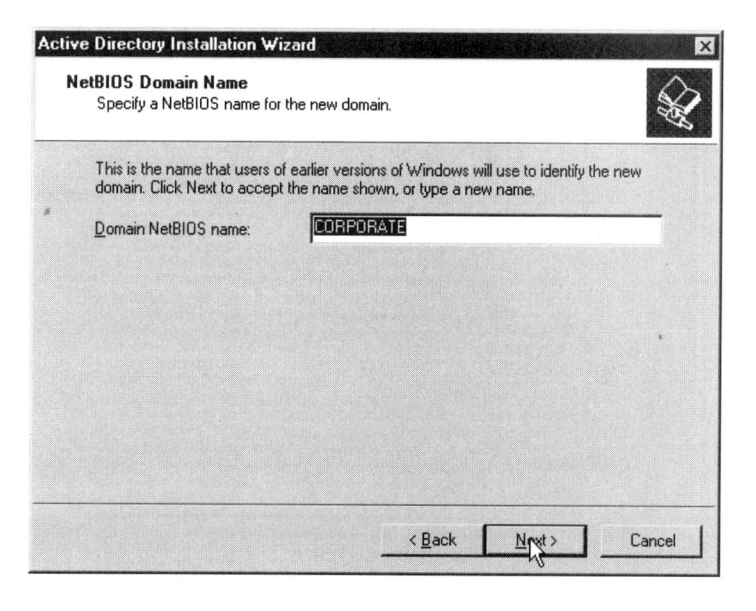

8. We now select where we would prefer Windows 2000 to set the database file and the Active Directory log, as shown next. For our example we will choose the defaults.

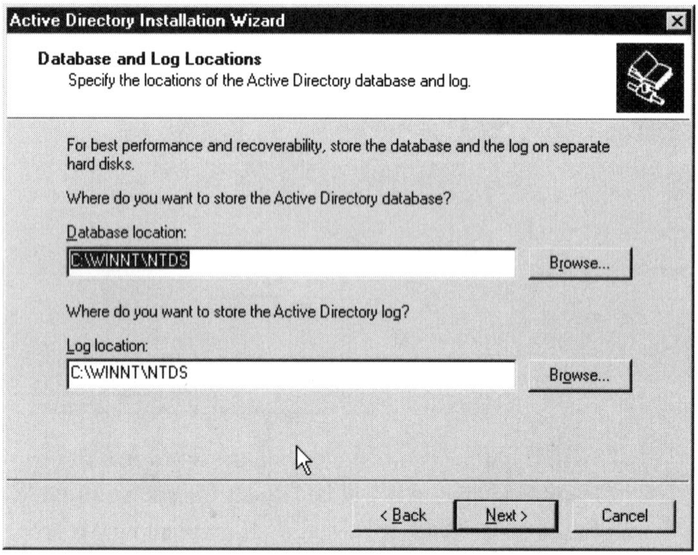
Active Directory Installation Wizard
Database and Log Locations
Specify the locations of the Active Directory database and log.
For best performance and recoverability, store the database and the log on separate hard disks.
Where do you want to store the Active Directory database?
Database location:
C:\WINNT\NTDS
Browse...
Where do you want to store the Active Directory log?
Log location:
C:\WINNT\NTDS
Browse...
< Back
Next >
Cancel

9. Now we must choose where the SYSVOL folder will reside. Remember that for a server to be a domain controller in Windows 2000's Active Directory, it must have a SYSVOL folder, and to do so that system must be running NTFS version 5.0. This is very important if you are testing this on a multiboot system. Obviously, in a production environment you would most likely never have a dual-boot scenario and so this wouldn't be a concern during installation.

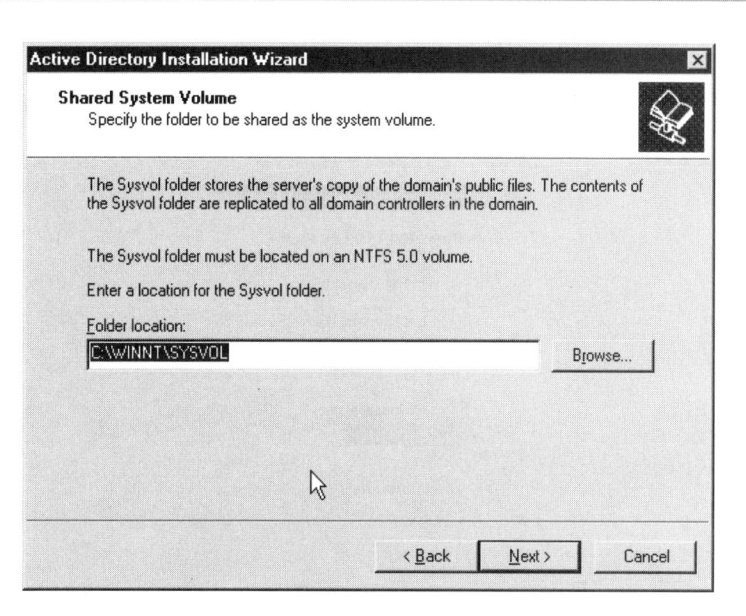

> [Screenshot: Active Directory Installation Wizard — Shared System Volume. Specify the folder to be shared as the system volume. The Sysvol folder stores the server's copy of the domain's public files. The contents of the Sysvol folder are replicated to all domain controllers in the domain. The Sysvol folder must be located on an NTFS 5.0 volume. Enter a location for the Sysvol folder. Folder location: C:\WINNT\SYSVOL. Buttons: < Back, Next >, Cancel.]

10. If DNS has *not* been installed previously on this system, then before continuing you will get the warning shown in the following illustration. Do not worry, for DCPROMO will allow you to install DNS while at the same time implementing Active Directory. Select Yes, Install and Configure DNS on This Computer (Recommended), after you have clicked OK on this warning dialog box.

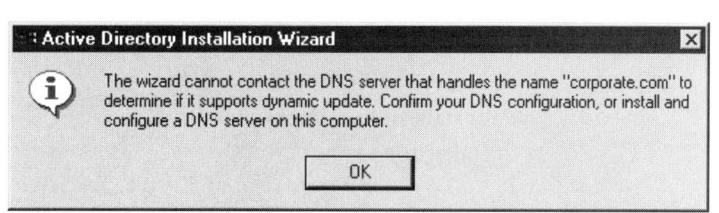

> [Screenshot: Active Directory Installation Wizard dialog — "The wizard cannot contact the DNS server that handles the name "corporate.com" to determine if it supports dynamic update. Confirm your DNS configuration, or install and configure a DNS server on this computer." Button: OK.]

11. Next we are going to choose to be compatible with pre-Windows 2000 systems. In the beginning, most Windows 2000 deployments will require this because many migrations will be from Windows NT to Windows 2000.

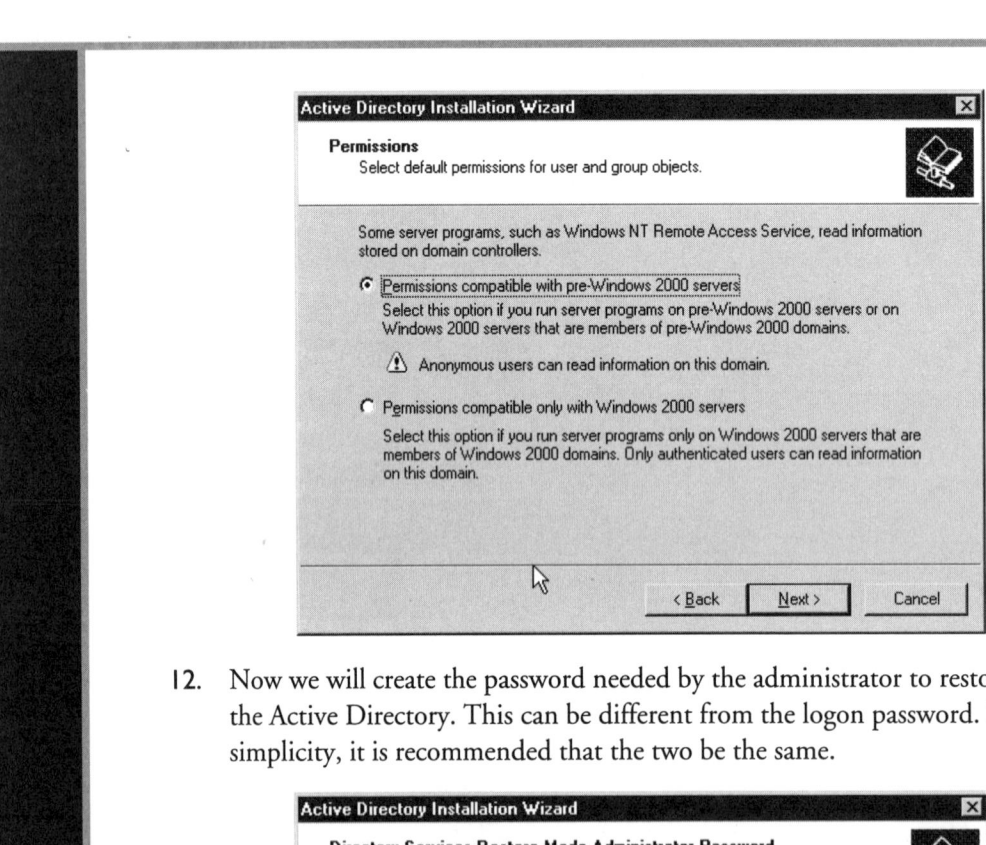

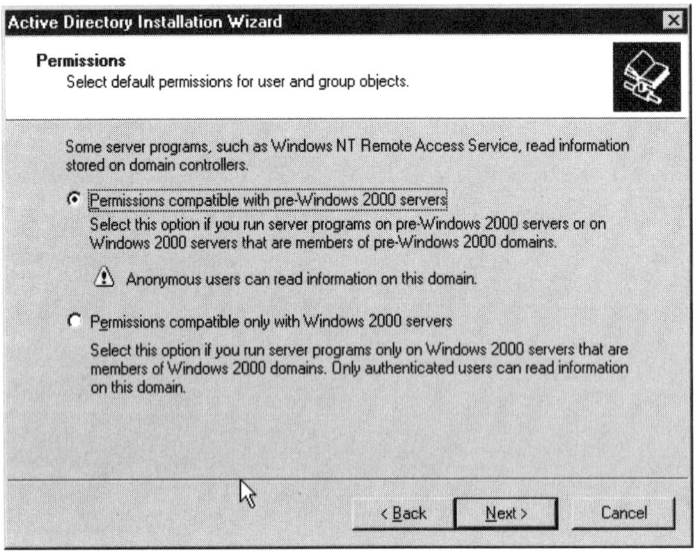
Active Directory Installation Wizard
Permissions
Select default permissions for user and group objects.
Some server programs, such as Windows NT Remote Access Service, read information stored on domain controllers.
Permissions compatible with pre-Windows 2000 servers
Select this option if you run server programs on pre-Windows 2000 servers or on Windows 2000 servers that are members of pre-Windows 2000 domains.
Anonymous users can read information on this domain.
Permissions compatible only with Windows 2000 servers
Select this option if you run server programs only on Windows 2000 servers that are members of Windows 2000 domains. Only authenticated users can read information on this domain.
< Back
Next >
Cancel

12. Now we will create the password needed by the administrator to restore the Active Directory. This can be different from the logon password. For simplicity, it is recommended that the two be the same.

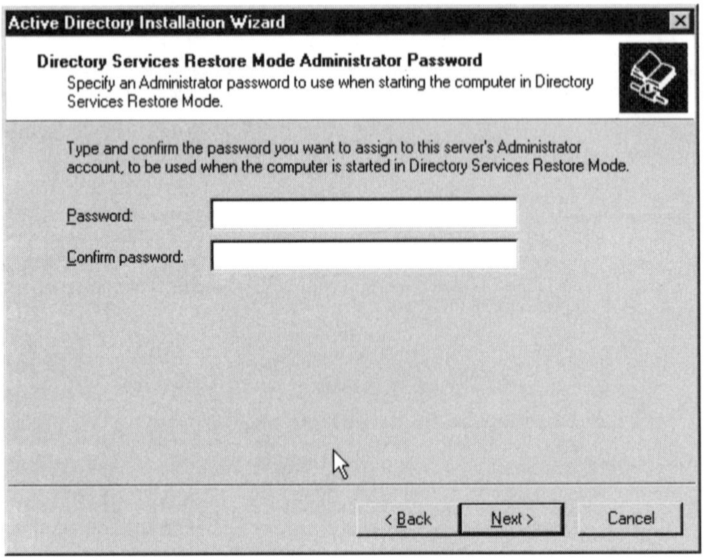
Active Directory Installation Wizard
Directory Services Restore Mode Administrator Password
Specify an Administrator password to use when starting the computer in Directory Services Restore Mode.
Type and confirm the password you want to assign to this server's Administrator account, to be used when the computer is started in Directory Services Restore Mode.
Password:
Confirm password:
< Back
Next >
Cancel

13. Now you will see a summary page of all the choices we made during the Active Directory Installation Wizard (DCPROMO.EXE) run. It is highly recommended that you check through this instead of just clicking Next to get done. If there is something that isn't correct, you can click the Back button and change the value of whatever attribute you need before implementing.

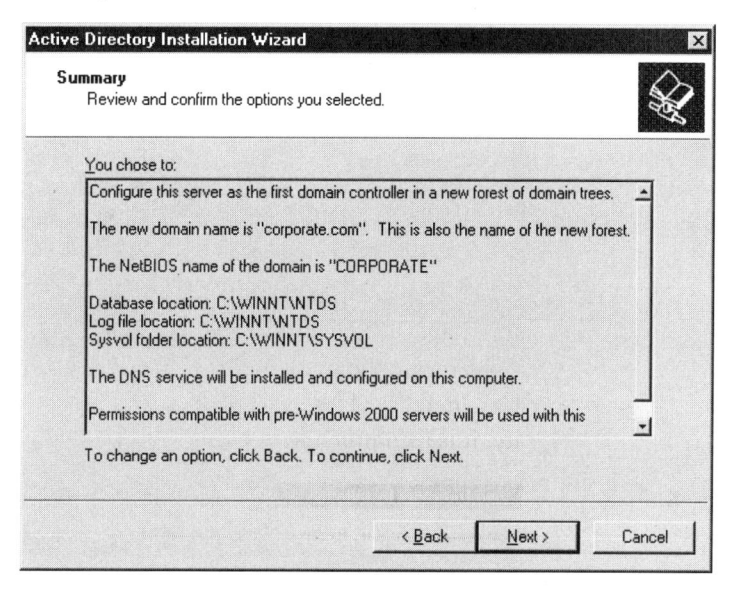

14. Once you have confirmed your choices and click Next, the implementation of Active Directory begins. If you realize at this point you made a mistake during the dcpromo process, then you will need to wait for the installation to finish, and then remove Active Directory and re-install it. So, it is *very* important to be sure about your values while running the AD wizard.

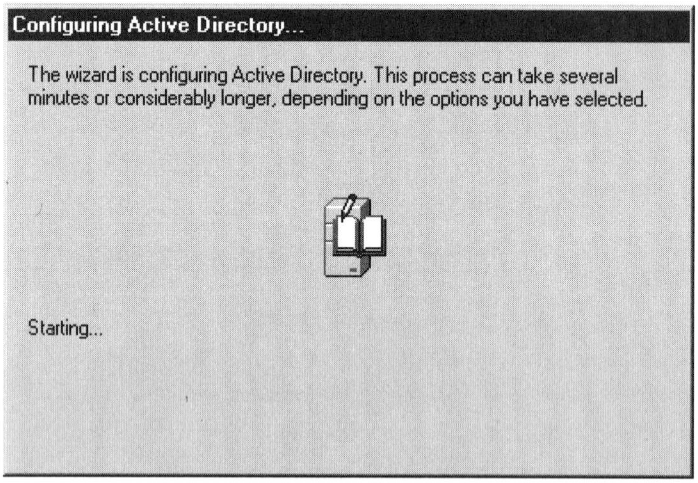
Configuring Active Directory...
The wizard is configuring Active Directory. This process can take several minutes or considerably longer, depending on the options you have selected.
Starting...

15. Now that Active Directory has been installed, you will be asked to allow Windows to re-start the system. Choose Yes and the first domain controller is complete. By being the first domain controller, it currently holds five roles that, when other domain controllers are added, can be disbursed. These roles are called *flexible service master operators* and are covered in more detail later in this chapter.

Active Directory Installation Wizard
Completing the Active Directory Installation Wizard
Active Directory is now installed on this computer for the domain "corporate.com".
This domain controller is assigned to the site "Default-First-Site-Name". Sites are managed with the Active Directory Sites and Services administrative tool.
To close this wizard, click Finish.
< Back
Finish
Cancel

> **exam**
> **⌚atch**
>
> *Remember that DNS, which supports SRV records, must exist for Active Directory to work. Also, for a system to be a domain controller in Active Directory it must have a SYSVOL folder, which must sit on an NTFS 5.0 partition. If not, then it is not a domain controller, but it can be promoted to one.*

With Windows 2000, each domain controller is considered equal to the next, or a "peer." With the arrival of Windows 2000, the use of a multi-master operations model was incorporated, except for a few roles that have to be defined on individual servers in order to avoid problems for certain functions during replication. In Active Directory, a *multi-master update* occurs with any domain controller to which you can connect. If the domain controller becomes disconnected from the network, updates are replicated throughout the forest as well as to that controller once network connectivity is restored. If two conflicting updates are made simultaneously, each set of updates is replicated. Even in the presence of conflicting updates, all domain controllers eventually converge to the same value. This process is called *conflict resolution* and is discussed later in this chapter.

In general, it is better to prevent conflicts than to resolve them after the fact, even with a reliable conflict resolution process. When domain controllers have conflicting versions of the directory schema, often, using the normal conflict resolution methods used by Active Directory can resolve the situation. Since the schema is updated infrequently and consistency of the schema is critical, conflict *prevention* is the best option. For example, suppose that an attribute of some object is changed on domain controller X. Then, before the change on domain controller X has replicated, the same attribute of the same object is changed on domain controller Y by another administrator. At this point, Active Directory must ensure that when replication has occurred, all replicas agree on the value of the updated attribute.

Active Directory ensures agreement by attaching a unique *stamp* to each replicated attribute value during an originating update. This stamp travels with the value as the value replicates. If the stamp of the value that was replicated is larger than the stamp of the current value, the current value (including the stamp) is replaced; otherwise, the current value (including the stamp) is left alone.

Stamps are primarily made up of three components:

- **Version**   Number or value that is incremented for each original write. Now with an original write, the updated attribute has a higher version number than the original attribute. Therefore, the attribute is changed and replicated throughout the domain.
- **Originating Time**   The time of the originating write.
- **Originating DSA (Domain Service Agent)**   Is a globally unique identifier (GUID) that identifies the domain controller that performed the originating write.

exam
Watch

The GUID is a reference point used in Active Directory and DNS to locate a domain controller primarily for the purposes of replication. This GUID is automatically generated for each domain controller, and is unique when created; therefore, it will not be duplicated.

CERTIFICATION OBJECTIVE 6.02

Operations Masters

With Windows 2000 the implementation of multi-master operations came about to the Microsoft networking world. This allowed all domain controllers in a single domain to contain a read and write replica of the domain objects and allowed modifications to these objects from any domain controller. In general, no server is to be more important than any other; they are all peers. This is true to some extent, but there are some exceptions within Windows 2000. These roles are referred to as operations masters, flexible single master operators, or FSMOs (pronounced *fizmo*), all referring to the same thing. This is done because some functions must remain single master based to avoid conflicts altogether on certain updates. We will examine each of the FSMO roles in detail. The FSMOs are schema master, RID master, PDC emulator, domain naming master, and infrastructure master.

exam
Watch

Windows NT used the single master role in that all updates with regard to the domain had to be made to the PDC.

As mentioned, Active Directory performs schema updates in a single master fashion to prevent conflicts. Only one domain controller in the entire forest, the domain controller holding the schema master role, accepts updates to schema objects. An administrator can shift the schema master role from one domain controller to another as the need arises, but at any moment only one domain controller holds the schema master role.

The schema master role is one example of a flexible single-master operation role, also called an operations master role or a FSMO role. Other operations master roles are a part of Microsoft Windows 2000 Server; each role controls another specific set of directory changes. For each role, *only* the domain controller holding that role can make the associated directory changes.

In small Active Directory deployments with a single domain controller, operations master roles are not a consideration. But if you are responsible for the operational health of an Active Directory deployment with more than one domain controller, you need to understand the following:

- Which domain controllers need to hold operations master roles?
- What functionality is lost when a domain controller holding an operations master role is unavailable?
- When a domain controller holding an operations master role is unavailable for an extended period, how do you respond to restore service?

In Windows 2000, and especially in Active Directory, certain operations are critical and should not be performed at the same time on different domain controllers. Active Directory ensures that these types of operations are performed in a single-master fashion. By single-master we mean that only one domain controller at a time can perform that particular operation.

A domain controller for any domain within a forest can hold a per-forest role for that forest. Only a domain controller for a specific domain can hold a per-domain role for that domain. So, a single domain controller can hold up to five operations master roles, including one of each role. Therefore, in the preceding example, the 11 roles might be held by as few as three domain controllers, or as many as 11.

When you create the first Microsoft Windows 2000 domain controller in a forest, the Active Directory Installation Wizard assigns all five roles to it. When you create the first Windows 2000 domain controller for a new domain in an *existing* forest, the Active Directory Installation Wizard assigns the three per-domain roles to it. In a mixed-mode domain environment (one that contains a mixture of Windows 2000, Microsoft Windows NT version 4.0, and Windows NT version 3.51 domain controllers), only the Windows 2000 domain controllers can hold operations master roles.

There are different types of operations that must exist. We will discuss the specifics of these operations. In Active Directory there are two forest-wide operations masters that must exist: Schema Master and Domain Naming Master. Next we'll look at the three domain-wide operations masters: RID Master, PDC Emulator, and Infrastructure Master.

Schema Master (One per Forest)

In Active Directory, the schema contains definitions for the universe of objects that can be stored in the directory, and it enforces the rules that govern both the structure and the content of the directory. The schema consists of a set of classes, attributes, and syntaxes that represent an instance of one or more classes in the schema. The schema specifies the relationships between classes of objects. Every object stored in the directory is an instance of one or more classes in the schema. *Print Queue*, *User*, and *Computer* are examples of classes in Active Directory. For example, if the schema contains a class called *User*, the user accounts Theresa and Albert are two objects in the directory that are instances of the class *User*. The object Theresa could contain an optional attribute defined for this class called *phoneNumber*. This attribute for the object Theresa of the class *User* might have the value of 704-336-5123.

Administrators and applications can extend the schema by adding new attributes and classes or by modifying existing ones, as shown in Figure 6-1. Schema definitions are required by applications that need to create or modify objects in Active Directory. Applications that are "directory-enabled" are programmed to recognize the attributes and syntaxes that are required to interact with the directory. The only domain controller that can perform updates to the directory schema is the schema operations master. Schema updates replicate from the schema master to all other domain controllers for the directory. Schema updates involve modifying the definition of what types of objects can be created in Active Directory.

Domain Naming Master (One per Forest)

The Domain Naming Master is the only domain controller in the forest that can add or remove existing domains from the directory. It can add or remove cross-

FIGURE 6-1

View of Active Directory schema attributes

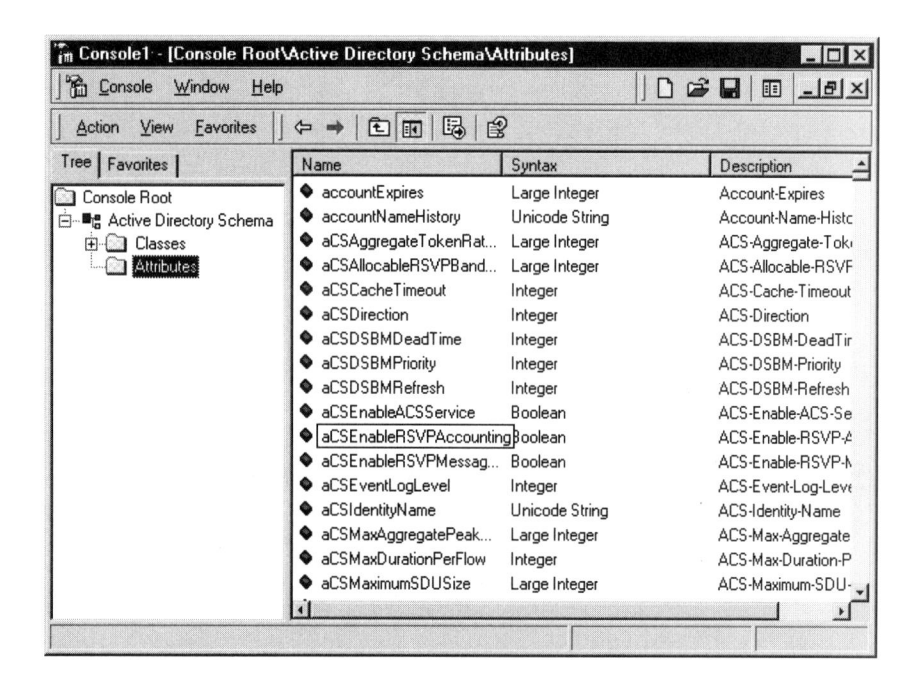

references to external directory services as well. The domain controller that has the Domain Naming Master role is the only domain controller that can do the following:

- Add new domains to the forest.
- Remove existing domains from the forest.
- Add or remove cross-reference objects to external directories.

By connecting to the domain controller holding the Domain Naming Master role, you can add (or remove) a domain to (or from) the forest. If the Domain Naming Master is unavailable, you cannot add or remove domains. If, for some reason, you prefer that another domain controller hold the Domain Naming Master role, you can transfer it to another domain controller.

To add a domain to a forest, use one of the following methods:

- The Active Directory Installation Wizard (DCPROMO). While creating the first domain controller of the domain, the wizard contacts the Domain Naming Master by means of Remote Procedure Call (RPC) in order to create the domain. (Note that you must have sufficient access permissions to create the domain.) If the Domain Naming Master is unavailable, a message similar to the following appears:

```
Active Directory Installation Failed
The operation has failed because <reason for failure>
To perform the requested operation, the Directory Service needs to
contact the domain naming master (server fp1.charlotte.com). The
attempt to contact it failed.

The error was: "The specified server cannot perform the requested
operation."
```

In this example, fp1.charlotte.com is the Domain Naming Master.

- The Pre-create subcommand is under the Domain Management option in the Ntdsutil command-line tool, followed by the Active Directory Installation Wizard. You can connect to the Domain Naming Master using the Ntdsutil tool to create a cross-reference object that names the new domain. The cross-reference object is found in the Partitions container of the Configuration directory partition. After the cross-reference object is replicated throughout the forest, you can run the Active Directory Installation Wizard to create the new domain using the newly created domain name. When you pre-create the cross-reference object, the Active Directory Installation Wizard does not require a connection to the Domain Naming Master to create the first domain controller of the domain. You must have sufficient access permissions to create a domain.

If the Domain Naming Master is unavailable when the Ntdsutil tool attempts to connect to it, a message similar to that shown in Figure 6-2 appears, with any user input shown in bold type.

Relative ID Master (RID) (One per Domain)

The RID master FSMO role holder is the single DC responsible for processing RID Pool requests from all DCs within a given domain. It is also responsible for removing an object from its domain and putting it in another domain during an object move. When a DC creates a security principal object such as a user or group, it attaches a unique security identifier (SID) to the object. This SID consists of a domain SID (the same for all SIDs created in a domain), and a relative ID (RID) that is unique for each security principal SID created in a domain. The following is an example of an SID and what each part represents:

FIGURE 6-2

Running Ntdsutil when the Domain Naming Master is offline

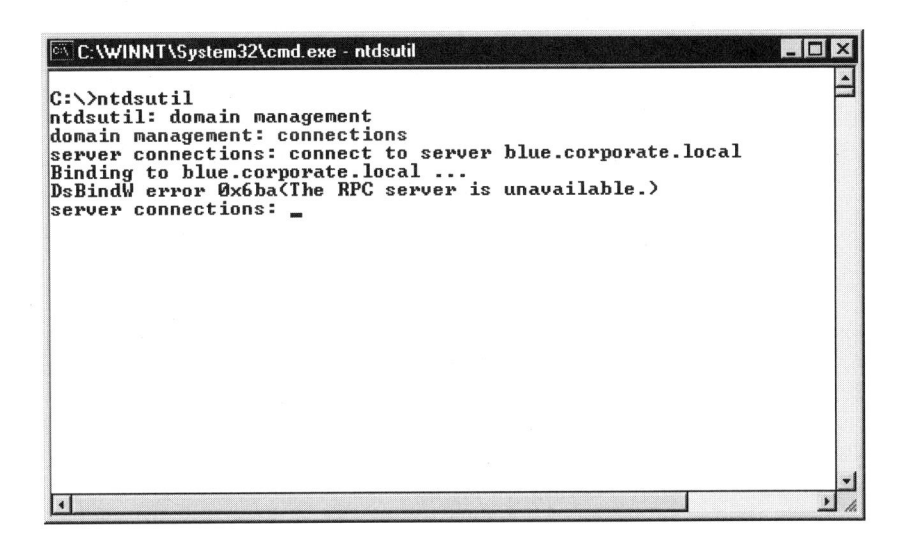

```
C:\>ntdsutil
ntdsutil: domain management
domain management: connections
server connections: connect to server blue.corporate.local
Binding to blue.corporate.local ...
DsBindW error 0x6ba(The RPC server is unavailable.)
server connections: _
```

S-1-5-24-1003446284-1157218903-809002120-512

The breakdown is as follows:

- **Revision level, 1** Indicates the version of the SID structure used in a certain SID. All SIDs that are created in Windows NT or Windows 2000 are revision one.
- **Identifier authority, 5** Identifies the highest level of authority that can issue SIDs for this particular type.
- **Domain identifier, 21-1003446284-1157218903-809002120** Identifies the domain.
- **Relative identifier (RID), 512 (Domain Administrators group)** Identifies a particular account or group relative to a domain.

Each Windows 2000 DC in a domain is allocated a pool of RIDs that it is allowed to assign to the security principals it creates. When a DC's allocated RID pool falls below a threshold, that DC issues a request for additional RIDs to the domain's RID master. The domain RID master responds to the request by retrieving RIDs from the domain's unallocated RID pool and assigns them to the pool of the requesting DC. There is one RID master per domain in a directory.

You can create a new security principal object (user, group, or computer) on *any* domain controller. However, as stated before, after creating several hundred security principal objects, a domain controller must communicate by means of RPC with the domain controller holding the domain's RID master role before creating the next security principal object. It needs to receive a new pool of RIDs from the RID master. Then, another several hundred security principal objects can be created, and when this set of objects has been created, the process of contacting the RID master repeats. If a domain controller's RID pool is empty, and the RID master is unavailable, you cannot create new security principal objects on that domain controller.

When using the Active Directory Users and Computers snap-in to create new objects, a message similar to the following displays when the domain controller's RID pool is empty and the domain's RID master is unavailable:

```
Active Directory Service
The object Kevin Russell could not be created.
The problem encountered was:
The directory service has exhausted the pool of relative
identifiers.
```

In this example, a new User object called Kevin Russell could not be created because the RID master has exhausted its pool of RIDs.

To move objects from one domain (the source domain) to another (the destination domain) using the MOVETREE.EXE command-line tool, you *must* connect to the RID master. If the RID master is unavailable, objects cannot be moved to other domains.

If you attempt to move an object from one domain to another using the MOVETREE.EXE tool and you specify a source domain controller that is not the RID master, you will see an unspecific "Movetree failed" error message.

Primary Domain Controller (PDC) Emulator (One per Domain)

From LAN Manager 2.0 all the way to Windows NT 4.0, every domain contained a primary domain controller. The functions of the primary domain controller included:

- Processing password changes from both users and computers.
- Replicating updates to backup domain controllers.

- Running the Domain Master Browser.
- Being the link for any and all trusts with other domains.

Windows 2000 operates with Windows NT 3.51 and Windows NT 4.0 workstations, member servers, and domain controllers. Therefore, one domain controller in a Windows 2000 system, the one holding the primary domain controller emulator role, can and should serve as primary domain controller for compatibility with older systems.

As we've stated, Active Directory uses multi-master replication for most directory updates. This means that unavailability of the primary domain controller emulator does not have the same impact as unavailability of the primary domain controller in Windows NT. If the primary domain controller emulator is unavailable, you lose the services mentioned earlier. Symptoms include:

- When a user of a Windows NT Workstation 3.51-based computer, or a user of a computer running Windows NT Workstation 4.0, Windows 95, or Windows 98 without the Active Directory client installed, attempts a password change, the user sees a message similar to the following: "Unable to change password on this account. Please contact your system administrator."

- In a mixed-mode domain, the event logs of Windows NT 3.51 or Windows NT 4.0 backup domain controllers contain entries showing failed replication attempts.

- In a mixed-mode domain, trying to start User Manager on a Windows NT 3.51 or Windows NT 4.0 backup domain controller results in a "domain unavailable" error message. If User Manager is already running, you will see an "RPC server unavailable" message. Attempting to create an account using the net user /add command results in a "could not find domain controller for this domain" message. When you run Server Manager, you will see a message similar to the following: "Cannot find the primary domain controller for *domain name*. You may administer this domain, but certain domain-wide operations will be disabled."

exam
Watch

There is no, nor are there plans for, an Active Directory agent for Windows NT 4.0.

As systems are upgraded, either to Windows 2000 or for Windows 95/98 by installing the Active Directory client, they cease to rely on the primary domain controller and instead behave in the following manner:

- Clients do not make password changes at the primary domain controller emulator. Instead, clients update passwords at any domain controller in the domain.

- When all backup domain controllers in a domain are upgraded to Windows 2000, the primary domain controller emulator does not receive any Windows NT 3.51 or Windows NT 4.0 replication requests.

- Clients use Active Directory to locate network resources. They do not require the Windows NT Computer Browser service.

Even after all systems are upgraded to Windows 2000, the domain controller holding the PDC emulator role still performs the following functions:

- Password changes performed by other domain controllers in the domain are sent to the primary domain controller emulator.

- When an authentication fails with an invalid password at other domain controllers in the domain, the authentication request is retried at the primary domain controller emulator before failing. If a recent password update has reached the primary domain controller emulator, the retried authentication request should succeed.

- When an authentication succeeds on an account for which the most recent authentication attempt at the domain controller failed, the domain controller communicates this fact ("zero lockout count") to the primary domain controller emulator.

Infrastructure Master (One per Domain)

Suppose you add a user to a group in the same domain using Active Directory Users and Computers. While still connected to the same domain controller, you can open up the group to examine its members and see the user you just added. If you then rename the user object (that is, change its *cn* attribute) and display the group membership, you will instantly see the user's new name in the list of group members.

When the user and the group are in different domains, there is a time lag between when you rename a user object and when a group containing that user displays the user's new name. (In Active Directory Users and Computers, selecting the Members tab of the group's property page shows the user's old name in the Name column.) This time lag is inevitable in a distributed system where sites function independently.

The domain controller holding the infrastructure master role for the group's domain is responsible for updating the *cross-domain group-to-user reference* to reflect the user's new name. The infrastructure master updates these references locally and uses replication to bring all other replicas of the domain up to date. If the infrastructure master is unavailable, these updates are delayed. In Figure 6-3 you see that by using ntdsutil with the roles switch, there are many ways to change FSMO operators.

In Exercise 6-2, we will walk through the steps needed to off-load a PDC emulator role to another domain controller.

FIGURE 6-3

Ntdsutil roles help screen

```
C:\WINNT\System32\cmd.exe - ntdsutil roles

C:\>
C:\>ntdsutil roles
ntdsutil: roles
fsmo maintenance: help
 ?                                  - Print this help information
 Connections                        - Connect to a specific domain controller
 Help                               - Print this help information
 Quit                               - Return to the prior menu
 Seize domain naming master         - Overwrite domain role on connected server
 Seize infrastructure master        - Overwrite infrastructure role on connected serv
er
 Seize PDC                          - Overwrite PDC role on connected server
 Seize RID master                   - Overwrite RID role on connected server
 Seize schema master                - Overwrite schema role on connected server
 Select operation target            - Select sites, servers, domains, roles and Namin
g Contexts
 Transfer domain naming master      - Make connected server the domain naming master
 Transfer infrastructure master     - Make connected server the infrastructure maste
r
 Transfer PDC                       - Make connected server the PDC
 Transfer RID master                - Make connected server the RID master
 Transfer schema master             - Make connected server the schema master

fsmo maintenance: _
```

EXERCISE 6-2

Off-loading a PDC Emulator Role to a Domain Controller

1. Click Start | Programs | Administrative Tools | Active Directory Domains and Trusts.

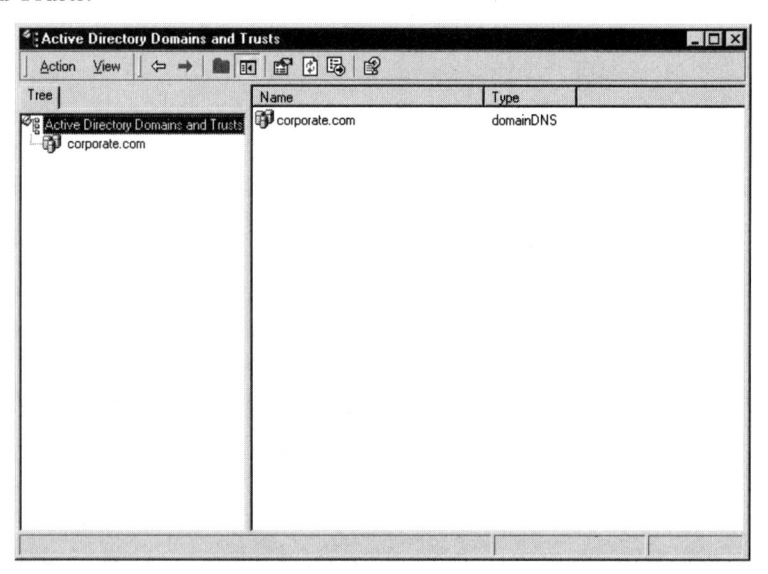

2. Right-click the top of the left pane window where it reads Active Directory Domains and Trusts, then choose Connect to Domain Controller as shown here.

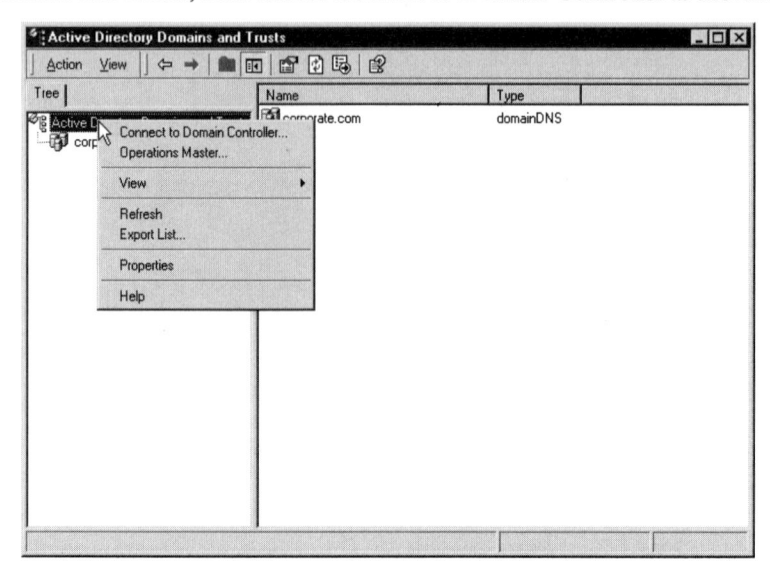

3. After selecting the DC you want to transfer to (shown in the first illustration that follows) and then selecting Operations Master from the shortcut menu shown in the second illustration following, change the operations master. Then click Change. Select Close on the screen shown in the third illustration following and it is done. In this scenario we were looking at changing the domain naming operations, but it would be similar for any of the other master operators.

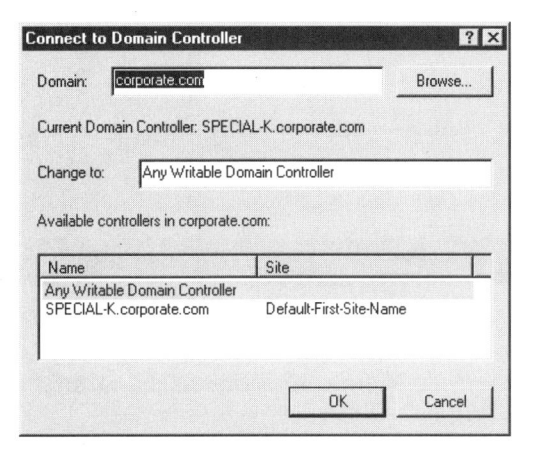

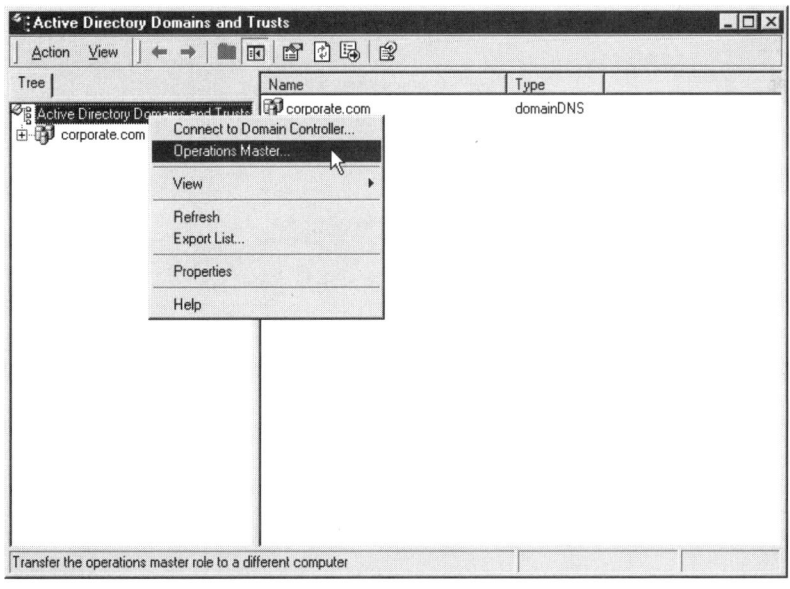

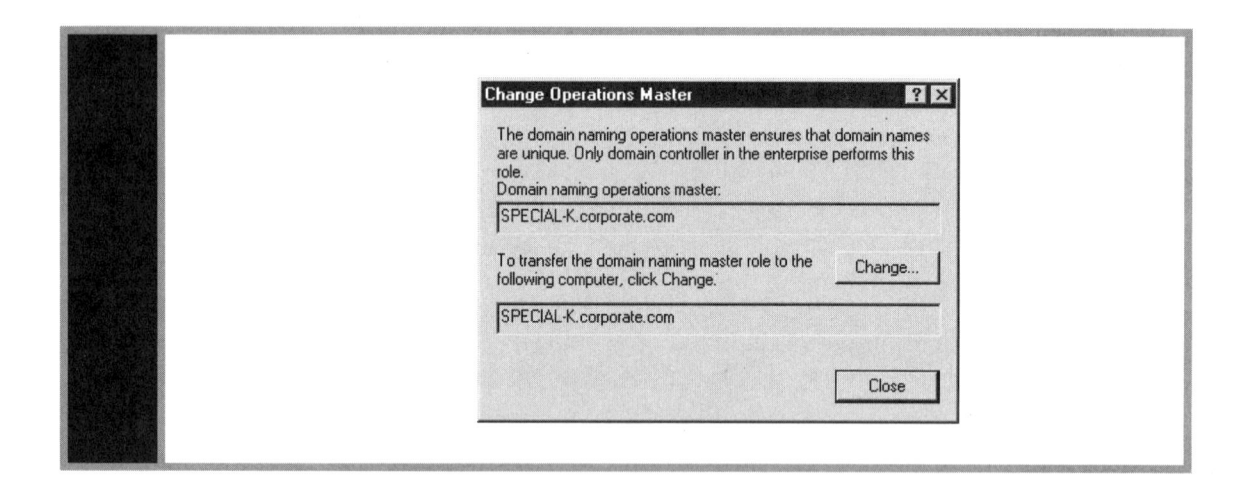

Change Operations Master

The domain naming operations master ensures that domain names are unique. Only domain controller in the enterprise performs this role.

Domain naming operations master:
SPECIAL-K.corporate.com

To transfer the domain naming master role to the following computer, click Change.

SPECIAL-K.corporate.com

[Change...] [Close]

---

on the Job *Operations masters can be changed for two operations across domains: schema master and Domain Naming Master (one per forest). To do this, you would first go through Active Directory, with the Active Directory and Domain Trusts utility, then change domains. Afterwards, select the appropriate domain controller and continue the transfer just as you did earlier.*

exam Watch *Windows NT replicated changes at the object level. In other words, if the password on user TAlcala has been changed under Windows NT, the entire TAlcala object would then be replicated. With Windows 2000 only the password for TAlcala is replicated. Windows 2000 replicates at the attribute level, which provides better use of system resources and network bandwidth.*

CERTIFICATION OBJECTIVE 6.03

Servers

As with Windows NT, Windows 2000 servers can be utilized in many different ways. In most LAN's today, you will see servers used in the following ways: File and Print Servers, Application Servers, and dial-in/RAS Servers. In the last five years, most IT departments have chosen to separate these services on different physical systems for better performance. The main reason for this is to allow the server to dedicate its processing power on a specific function. We will look at what variables are most important when optimizing these systems.

Memory

It is important to consider two main types of memory when you analyze server performance: Random Access Memory (RAM) and cache. The more you have of each, typically, the better the performance. Also, consider other factors such as the size and location of the paging file. For example, it is generally recommended to move the paging file from the system partition to another position for performance. However, doing this will eliminate the Crash-dump utility, which may not be wise.

Processor

The type of system processor, as well as the number of processors, affects the overall performance of the system. For example, now that Microsoft has dropped support for the Compaq Alpha, processor types from the Intel / Intel compatible line must be considered. Obviously, Windows 2000 supports symmetric multiprocessing (SMP), so that if a system has multiple applications running concurrently, or applications that are multithreaded, the overall processor power is shared.

Disk Subsystem

There are several factors that affect disk subsystem performance. Each of these factors should be taken into consideration during analysis and optimization.

Type and Number of Controllers

The controller type and the number of controllers affect the overall system responsiveness when responding to information requests being read from or written to disk drives. Installing multiple disk controllers can result in higher throughput. Note the approximate throughput of the following controllers:

- IDE controllers have a throughput of about 2.5MB per second.
- Standard SCSI controllers have a throughput of about 3MB per second.
- SCSI-2 controllers have a throughput of about 5MB per second.
- Fast SCSI-2 controllers have a throughput of about 10MB per second.
- PCI controller cards can transfer data at up to 40MB per second.

Busmaster Controllers

Busmaster controllers have an on-board processor that handles all interrupts until data is ready to be passed to the CPU for processing. This helps the processor to avoid interruptions for data.

Caching

Caching helps improve disk responsiveness as data is cached on the controller and does not require RAM or internal cache.

Controllers That Support RAID

Controllers that support hardware-level RAID (Redundant Array of Inexpensive Disks) can offer better performance than software implemented RAID. Implementing striping or striping with parity and disk mirroring can improve disk performance.

The Type of Work Being Performed

If the applications are disk-bound (many read and write requests), implementing the fastest disk subsystem provides the best performance. For single processor systems, implementing a Fast SCSI-2 as the minimum controller base is generally recommended.

The Type of Drives Implemented

Disk performance is generally measured in disk access time. It is not uncommon to find hard disk drives with access speed in the low teens or lower. It is good practice to implement drives that complement the rest of the architecture, such as the controller. Also, choose a manufacturer that supplies the fastest drive available in each of its systems.

Network Subsystem

Network performance and capacity may be affected by a number of factors. Consider each factor in its unique environment to determine whether or not it has an impact on network capacity and server performance.

Network Adapter Type

Implement a high bandwidth card (such as a 32-bit bus mastering card) and avoid programmed input/output (PIO) adapters, as they use the CPU to move data from the network adapter to RAM. Note the example transfer speeds of the following adapters:

- 8-bit network adapters transfer up to 400 kilobytes per second (KBps).
- 16-bit adapters transfer up to 800 KBps.
- 32-bit adapters transfer up to 1.2 megabytes per second (MBps).

Multiple Network Adapters

Installing multiple network adapters is beneficial in a server environment because it allows the server to process network requests over multiple adapters simultaneously. If your network uses multiple protocols, consider placing each protocol on a different adapter. It is not uncommon to have all server-based traffic on a single adapter, for example, while performing host access using SNA on a different adapter.

Number of Users

Consider not only the number of users concurrently accessing a server, but also the number of inactive connections since monitoring each connection requires processing time on the server.

Routers, Bridges, and Other Physical Network Components

Routers, bridges, and other physical network components affect performance of the network, as do data communications facilities.

Protocols in Use

Most protocols provide similar performance, so consider the amount of traffic generated to perform a given function. Reducing the number of protocols installed can increase performance.

Additional Network Services in Use

Services add memory and processor overhead on the system. These services could include any of the following:

- WINS
- DNS
- RAS
- SFM (Services for Macintosh)

Applications in Use

Applications naturally add memory and processor overhead on systems. Some examples of these applications are:

- SQL Server
- Exchange Server
- Systems Management Server (SMS)
- SNA Server

Directory Services (Domain Model and Structure)

The following factors may affect network capacity and performance:

- **Number of users** Consider not only the number of users and objects in the domain, but also the number of simultaneous logon requests validated by the domain controller or controllers.

- **Number of Domain Controllers** The more domain controllers in a domain, the more replication traffic is generated to assure all controllers are synchronized.

---

exam
Watch

Windows NT replicated changes at the object level. In other words, if the password on user TAlcala has been changed under NT, the entire TAlcala object is replicated. With Windows 2000, only the password for TAlcala is replicated, which is a better use of system resources and network bandwidth.

Application Servers

Application servers are accessed differently than a file and print server. While a file and print server is traditionally accessed with fewer numbers of requests (with each request a fairly large size on average), an application server is usually accessed with smaller, more frequent requests from the client computer. In addition, the application server has the overhead of actually running an application using memory and processor resources just like workstations.

When monitoring application servers, such as in a Microsoft SQL Server client/server environment, more processor and memory use occurs than in the file and print server environment. Disk and network resources are also used consistently in this environment.

Memory Implications

Memory is used for the server portion of the client/server application. Make sure to add sufficient RAM to support operating system and application needs. The amount of RAM required depends upon the particular system hardware and software configuration and needs.

Processor Implications

Applications run on the server side of the client/server; as a result, the processor is used to run the threads of the application. If a large number of users access this application from client components, upgrading or adding an additional processor may improve performance. If an application is processor-bound, use the most powerful processor available.

Computers that are capable of symmetric multiprocessing (SMP) allow use of multiple, though less powerful, processors instead of a single more powerful processor. Also, a mid-range processor may be used if fewer applications are used. Remember that when the processor becomes the bottleneck, additional processors can be added.

Disk Subsystem Implications

Client/server applications typically access large amounts of data; therefore, the demands on the disk subsystem are significant. Consider the disk controller and type of drive investments carefully.

Network Subsystem Implications

Client/server applications transfer many requests over the network for data access. These requests are often queries or commands that do not involve transferring large data files over the network as in a file and print server environment. It is very important to get the data into and out of the server as quickly as possible.

File and Print Servers

A file and print server is usually accessed by users for data retrieval and document storage, and is occasionally used for loading application software over the network. It is also used for managing print jobs to printers disbursed throughout the LAN. Memory and processor use are typically the greatest impact on a file and print server. The disk and network subsystems are important also, though memory and processor have the greatest potential for being overused on a file and print server.

When monitoring a file and print server for security issues and performance, be prepared to see numerous user connections, but also keep in mind that many of those connections may be inactive. Consider adjusting the auto-disconnect setting for each file and print server environment, especially if you are monitoring the server for performance.

Memory Implications

Memory is used for caching of opened files in a file and print server environment. Having enough RAM to allow for sufficient caching helps to improve performance when files are opened and continually accessed from the server.

Processor Implications

The processor is used for each network connection on the network; this means that all network connection traffic involves the processor. Having bus mastering network adapters and disk controllers helps to alleviate processing from the CPU, allowing more time for responding to data requests.

Disk Subsystem Implications

The disk subsystem is the primary server resource that users access. It will have a large effect on the overall perception of system performance, and ultimately, its capacity. The fastest and most efficient disk subsystem will provide the best overall performance improvement.

Network Subsystem Implications

A number of factors will affect the network subsystem (see the list in the Network Subsystem section). It will not matter how fast the disk subsystem is, how many processors are available, or how much RAM is installed in the server; if the network adapter card in the server is too slow, it cannot effectively perform transfers of data from physical network medium to RAM.

RAS Servers

RAS Servers are gateways to internal networks, usually via asynchronous communication but also supports other methods of connectivity such as ISDN, X.25, and so on. RAS (Remote Access Server) has been around since the days of LAN Manager. It is a remote node solution to accessing networks remotely. For small firms, it is not unusual to have only two modems supported. Windows 2000 RAS will support up to 256 simultaneous RAS connections. To do this, you would definitely need to add more serial ports to the system. This can be accomplished by installing and configuring multi-serial management devices such as a Digiboard or an Equinox board; there are others on the market also but these two tend to be the most popular. It is important to consider how to size up a RAS server. What implications will it have on memory, processing, disk I/O, and networking hardware?

Memory Implications

Just like any other system in Windows 2000, the greater the amount of memory, the better the performance. Consider what the maximum number of simultaneous users that will be supported on one server. Many administrators tend to use 2 to 4MB's of RAM per user as a rule of thumb for RAS (Terminal Server services will average around 8 to 12MB's per user). The more RAM, obviously, the less paging that will take place on the system and hence the better the performance. A single system that will support a maximum of 100 heavy users may need to be configured with approximately 200 to 400MB of RAM. Depending on the type of services and traffic being sent through the RAS server this parameter may need to be adjusted.

Processor Implications

Although not as important as it is in application servers, an undersized processor can cause problems for any server, including one running RAS. Although the system may not need more than one processor, it should have adequate speed for handling requests of the system. Once again depending on the services being handled by this server, a second processor may improve performance to some extent but probably not drastically. Look for a maximum increase of around 20 percent, depending on the supporting hardware.

Disk Subsystem Implications

The disk subsystem can have a huge impact on RAS server performance. Especially in the case where lack of RAM exists and paging increases. Making use of intelligent SCSI controllers can alleviate this pain, especially those that make use of Bus Mastering technology, whereas the controller can fetch data in and out of memory directly. Since a RAS server is most likely a passthrough box, this may not be as big an issue, unless the server is operating in other roles also along with being a RAS Server.

Network Subsystem Implications

The network subsystem, mainly the NIC (network interface card) must be able to handle a potential great deal of traffic going to and from the system. In most cases, this one NIC is the doorway for all remote users to resources within the network. For situations where a large number of users must be supported, an administrator will typically setup more than one RAS server to serve the remote users.

CERTIFICATION OBJECTIVE 6.04

Group Policy Scenarios

Windows 2000 introduces several new ways to manage computers and users in your environment. When you use Windows 2000 Server with Windows 2000 Professional, you can use Group Policy to control how a workstation functions and acts. Administrators can use Group Policy to specify options for managed desktop configurations for groups of computers and users. For exam 70-220, you will be asked detailed questions regarding the following scenarios:

- Desktop computers
- Laptop computers
- Kiosks

In the following exercise, we will go through the steps needed to install the files for Group Policy scenarios. The following steps apply to all the scenarios supported by Windows 2000.

Installing the Scenarios

When you install the Group Policy scenarios, Group Policy objects (GPOs) are installed on your domain controller. The Group Policy objects contain the appropriate Group Policy settings for each scenario. When you install Group Policy objects on a domain controller and then link one or more GPOs to a container, such as a site, a domain, or an organizational unit (OU), the settings apply to workstations and users associated with those containers.

Note that these scenarios are intended to be starting points from which you can develop settings that are tailored to your environment.

The procedures to install the scenarios are as follows:

- Install the scenario files to your local workstation.
- Install the GPOs on the domain controller.
- Create the organizational units (OUs) to link to the scenarios.
- Create user and computer accounts for each scenario.
- Define environment-specific settings.
- Customize settings for your environment.

Step 1: Install the Scenario Files to a Local Workstation

To install the scenario files to local workstations, you must be on a workstation connected to the domain controller where you want to install the scenarios. Run the Group Policy SCENARIOS.MSI file, which starts the Group Policy Scenarios Setup Wizard.

When you run the Group Policy Scenarios Setup Wizard, you have the option to install the Complete Setup or the Custom Setup. It is recommended that you choose the Complete Setup. Table 6-1 lists the files that the wizard installs, describes their function, and specifies the location where they are installed.

At this point, you can use the Remove option in the Group Policy Scenarios Setup Wizard to delete all the scenario source files (including the documentation) from the hard disk.

Step 2: Install the Scenario GPOs on the Domain Controller

After you run the Group Policy Scenarios Setup Wizard on a computer in the domain where you want to install the scenarios, you can install the Group Policy objects (GPOs) on the domain controller. *Note that you must have the appropriate permissions to install the scenarios on the domain controller.*

TABLE 6-1 Files Installed by the Setup Wizard (Group Policy SCENARIOS.MSI)

File	Location	Definition
LOADPOL.BAT	%ProgramFiles%\Group Policy Scenarios	Installs scenario GPOs
SAVEPOL.BAT	%ProgramFiles%\Group Policy Scenarios	Allows changes for scenario GPOs to be saved
SED.EXE	%ProgramFiles%\Group Policy Scenarios	Support file used by both LOADPOL.BAT and SAVEPOL.BAT
NLTEST.EXE	%ProgramFiles%\Group Policy Scenarios	Support file used by both LOADPOL.BAT and SAVEPOL.BAT
GPBACKUP.BAT	%ProgramFiles%\Group Policy Scenarios	Support file used by both LOADPOL.BAT and SAVEPOL.BAT
DSPROP.VBS	%ProgramFiles%\Group Policy Scenarios	Support file used by both LOADPOL.BAT and SAVEPOL.BAT
EDITLDIF.VBS	%ProgramFiles%\Group Policy Scenarios	Support file used by both LOADPOL.BAT and SAVEPOL.BAT
SCENARIONAME.XLS	%ProgramFiles%\Group Policy Scenarios\Docs	Spreadsheet that lists the Group Policy settings for each scenario

Read through all the installation steps before you start the installation process. After you run the LOADPOL.BAT file, you can no longer remove the GPOs from the domain controller by using the Remove option; you must remove the GPOs manually.

To install the GPOs on the domain controller, run the LOADPOL.BAT file, which you can find in the same directory as the installed .MSI package (by default, that directory is %ProgramFiles%\Group Policy Scenarios). This batch file creates 12 GPOs (a *user* and *computer* object for each of the six scenarios). The GPO names have the following format:

- <*ScenarioName*> computer settings
- <*ScenarioName*> user settings

ScenarioName stands for the name of the actual scenario, such as a Kiosk. This batch file installs these GPOs on to the domain controller of the computer that you are currently logged on to.

Step 3: Create the OUs to Link to the Scenarios

Create the organization unit (OU) structure you want to use for the scenarios. For testing, you might want to create a separate OU for each scenario.

Using the Active Directory Users and Computers snap-in, open the Properties dialog box for each OU and on the Group Policy tab, create links to the relevant GPOs. Click the Add button and then click the All tab to view the installed GPOs.

Computers and users in those OUs are now affected by the linked scenario Group Policy settings.

exam
  ⓦatch

When the Group Policy objects (GPOs) for these scenarios are applied to the affected clients, they rename the local built-in Administrator and Guest accounts to %Admin!!! and %Guest!!!; however, the passwords remain unchanged.

Renaming is done to create an extra barrier to potential network intruders. Renaming these well-known accounts forces the intruder to learn both the account name and the password to gain access to the network.

After the GPOs are applied, you must use the new account name to log on to the workstation as local administrator. Be sure to rename the accounts to ones that are difficult to guess and unique to your environment.

Step 4: Create User and Computer Accounts for Each Scenario

The user and computer objects need to be placed in the newly created OUs and customized for the specific scenario. For example, you might need to create a home directory or specify the profile path. Later in this chapter are specific instructions for each scenario. For more information, refer to the "User Account Setup" section of the scenario you want to install.

Step 5: Define Environment-Specific Settings

In each scenario, several Group Policy settings need to be customized for the environment where they are installed. Use the Group Policy snap-in to access the settings that are listed in Table 6-2.

TABLE 6-2 Environment-Specific Settings for Group Policy Scenarios

Group Policy Setting	Location	Defines
Internet Explorer and connection settings	\user configuration \windows settings \internet explorer maintenance \connection	Client connection settings for Internet Explorer
Software settings	\computer\configuration \software settings and \user configuration \software settings	Whether applications are defined or published
Scripts	\computer configuration\windows settings\scripts and \user configuration \windows settings \scripts	Where scripts are defined for the startup/shutdown of the machine or the logon/logoff of the user
Folder Redirection	\user configuration \windows settings \folder redirection	Will redirect contents in My Documents folder and Application Data folder

Step 6: Customize Optional Settings

You can customize other Group Policy settings, such as the ones described in the "Optional Settings" section of each scenario. Table 6-3 shows several group policy scenarios.

Desktop Computers

A workstation that uses the Desktop scenario has the following characteristics:

- Is the least managed of all of the scenarios.
- Holds settings that make the desktop easier to use.
- Holds settings that should reduce help desk costs and user downtime.
- Allows users to install available applications.
- Allows users to customize applications and the desktop.

This scenario is the least restrictive scenario. These Group Policy settings manage:

- Potentially harmful configuration settings, such as the ability to add or disable hardware devices.
- System or user environment settings, such as the location of the My Documents folder or the name of your Web home page. The Low TCO Desktop scenario ensures that workstations allow users to change most settings that affect them and prevents users from making harmful system changes. Hence, using this scenario can reduce unnecessary support calls.

TABLE 6-3 Group Policy Scenarios

Policy Scenario	Number of Users	User Data Saved	Can User Customize?	Applications Assigned	Published Applications
Desktop	Numerous	Yes	Nearly all settings	3 or more	Yes
Laptop	1	Yes	Some	3 or more	Yes
Kiosks	1	No	No	1	No

> ## FROM THE CLASSROOM
>
> ### Running Batch Files
>
> If you want to run the LOADPOL.BAT or SAVEPOL.BAT files more than once, you must first delete the destination files and directories to which the batch files write. For LOADPOL.BAT, you must delete the scenario GPOs in the directory. For SAVEPOL.BAT, delete the local copy of the GPO template directories. Both batch files fail if the destination already exists. This prevents you from accidentally overwriting existing GPOs in Active Directory or deleting data that exists in the local directories. For example, when using LOADPOL.BAT, if the GPO directories in the SYSVOL directory exist, or in the case of SAVEPOL.BAT, if the local directories exist, the batch files fail.
>
> To run LOADPOL.BAT a second time, remove the installed scenario GPOs from the domain. You do not need to remove all the scenario GPOs; any that remain are not overwritten and those that have been deleted are recreated from the installation defaults. You might receive error messages about not being able to recreate any scenario GPOs that have not been deleted, and you can safely ignore these messages.
>
> To run SAVEPOL.BAT a second time, delete the globally unique identifier (GUID) subfolders from the %Program Files%\Group Policy Scenarios\Policies folder.
>
> —*Gene Whitley, MCSE, CNE, CCA*

User Account Setup for Low TCO Desktop

The user account is a domain account; it needs no special privileges and is a member of the Domain Users group only.

User Data Settings

Set up the users' home directories on a network server as follows:

```
UserID
    CachedData_____shared as UserIDCached$
        My Documents
        AppData

    UncachedData_____shared as UserIDUncached$
        Profile
```

1. Replace *UserID* with the user's account name. The names of the shares and directories are not significant and can be renamed to suit local naming conventions.
2. Configure the UserIDCached$ share for automatic caching.
3. Configure the UserIDUncached$ share for no caching.

Do not create the network folder in advance. For example, if you plan to redirect the My Documents folder to \\Server1\Docs\%Username%, do not create the %Username% folder in advance. If the folder exists in advance and the current user is not the owner of the folder and its contents, the redirection process fails. For more information about folder redirection, see the information in Table 6-2.

If you must create the folder in advance, ensure that the user is the owner of the folder and its contents. To set ownership, use the SUBINACL.EXE file, which is available on the *Microsoft Windows 2000 Resource Kit* companion CD.

User Account Settings

Set the user profile path to *HomeServer.dom**UserID*Uncached$\Profile. Replace *HomeServer.dom* with the fully qualified name of the user's home server.

Laptop Computers

A laptop computer that uses the Laptop scenario has the following characteristics:

- Can be used by users who are away from the office most of the time and who log on by using low-speed, dial-up links but who also occasionally log on to high-speed network links.
- Can be used by users who are away from the office only occasionally and who log on by using Routing and Remote Access Service (RRAS) or remote network links.
- Allows users continuous access to data and user settings whether the computer is connected to or disconnected from the network.
- Allows users to log on to a laptop and a desktop computer simultaneously.
- Allows users to disconnect from the network without logging off or shutting down.

Laptop Settings

Laptop users are often expected to do much of their own computer support because onsite support is not readily available. For this reason, they usually have more privileges than equivalent users on a desktop computer (for example, they can install printers).

Laptop users, however, must be restricted from making system changes that might damage or disable their systems. For example, restrict laptop users from altering certain Internet Explorer settings, modifying the Start menu, and adding unapproved hardware devices. Although these users might need access to some of the Microsoft Management Console (MMC) administration snap-ins, make available only a restricted set.

Application installation (particularly for road warriors) is more likely to be initiated by the user than pushed by the administrator because of the unpredictability of when the user can connect to a high-speed network. For users who regularly visit the office, administratively published applications can be installed during the visit. Users who are in an office might infrequently need special privileges to allow them to install applications from CD ROM. You can allow this privilege by enabling Always Install with Elevated Privileges, which is in the Group Policy snap-in under \User (and Computer) Configuration\Administrative Templates\Windows Components\Windows Installer.

Laptop users can connect to and disconnect from remote access connections as defined under Network and Dial-up Connections. These are the minimum settings required for this scenario, but you can expand them as mentioned in the optional settings.

User Account Setup for Laptop

The Laptop user account is a domain account; it needs no special privileges and is a member of the Domain Users group only.

User Data Settings

Set up the users' home directories on a network server as follows:

```
UserID
    CachedData_____shared as UserIDCached$
        My Documents
        AppData
    UncachedData_____shared as UserIDUncached$
        Profile
        Network Documents    (optional)
```

1. Replace *UserID* with the user's account name. The names of the shares and directories are not significant and can be renamed to suit local naming conventions.
2. Configure the *UserID*Cached$ share for automatic caching.
3. Configure the *UserID*Uncached$ share for no caching.
4. On the local computer, create a folder to store any documents that do not require backup or synchronization with a file server copy:

    C:\Local Documents.

5. Create shortcuts to the Network Documents (this shortcut is optional) and Local Documents folders in the My Documents folder.

User Account Settings

Set the user profile path to *HomeServer.dom**UserID*Uncached$\Profile. Replace *HomeServer.dom* with the fully qualified name of the user's home server.

Security Configuration for Laptop

The security configuration is almost identical to the Low TCO Desktop scenario. It is based on the Secure Workstation (SECUREWS.INF) template with the following differences:

- Administrator and guest accounts are renamed.
- Logon message is enabled.
- More restrictive access controls are applied to the root directory (Everyone—Read).

Some laptop users who are away from the office for long periods of time might be expected to be part-time administrators. In such cases, make these users members of the local Power Users group. This allows them to write to parts of the file system and gives them a number of extra privileges, such as creating shares, doing backup and restore, and setting the system time.

In some cases, you might need to give these laptop users local administrator privileges, although this should be done with caution because a local administrator has the ability to circumvent Group Policy settings put in place by the domain administrator.

Kiosks

A workstation that uses the Kiosk scenario has the following characteristics:

- Is a public workstation.
- Runs only one application.
- Uses only one logon account.
- Runs unattended.
- Users are unknown to the owner of the kiosk.
- Users don't have to interactively log on, so there is no creation of numerous user accounts.
- Considered very secure.
- Easy to operate.
- Users mostly are not allowed to make changes from the default settings.
- No data is saved to the local drives.
- Machine is on all the time.

You can use the Kiosk scenario in a public environment where the computer is dedicated to running one application. For example, a kiosk could be located at an airport to allow passengers to check in and to allow visitors to view flight departure and arrival times.

The kiosk computer uses a single logon account and its users are anonymous to the kiosk owner. Because the computer is unattended, it is highly secure. The user interface is simple to operate, with little or no logon procedure. The user is restricted from changing user and system settings. The system may automatically reset to a default state at the start of each session. User sessions are usually anonymous, but the user can log on to an application-specific account, such as to a Web server application through Internet Explorer.

The kiosk user cannot save or write data directly to the hard disk. You can use a disk quota to prevent temporary files from filling the disk and a scheduled cleanup script to remove temporary files older than a specified number of days.

How the Kiosk Works

In a kiosk setting, the workstation is continuously logged on to one account. When the computer starts, the system automatically logs on by using the kiosk user account credentials, and the kiosk application starts automatically. The Start menu or icons do not display on the desktop. Users cannot customize the computer or save any data. Applications cannot be added or removed and the user cannot start any other applications or access the file system.

The dedicated application could be a Line Of Business (LOB) application, an application hosted in Internet Explorer, or another application, such as one available in Microsoft® Office for Windows. The default application should not be Windows Explorer or any other shell-like application. Windows Explorer allows more access to the computer than is appropriate for a kiosk computer. Be sure the command prompt is disabled and Windows Explorer cannot be accessed.

LOB applications should not contain "backdoors" that allow users to circumvent system policies. For example, they should not allow users access to the command prompt or to applications that allow access to the file system. Ideally, you should only use applications that adhere to Window 2000 Logo guidelines and that check for Group Policy settings before giving users access to prohibited features. You also need to check older applications and make unavailable any features that allow users to bypass administrative policy.

This scenario uses the AutoLogon feature to automatically log on with a domain user account. As a result, kiosk users do not know the user account name or password. Users are not allowed to change the password and screensavers are not password protected.

exam
Watch *The registry entries Run and RunOnce are disabled in the Kiosk scenario.*

User Account Setup for Kiosk

Unless the kiosk computer is a stand-alone computer, the user account usually is a domain account. The user account has no special privileges and is a member of the Domain Users group only.

User Data Settings

There is no requirement for a home directory or a roaming user profile directory.

User Account Settings

Enable the following settings:

- Password Never Expires.
- User Cannot Change Password.

Security Configuration for Kiosk

The security policies for the Kiosk scenario are based on the high-security template. Some of the security settings are as follows:

- Disables all guest account and anonymous access.
- Uses file system access control lists (ACLs) to prohibit changes to files or folders outside of the user's profile folder.
- Sets Registry ACLs to restrict access to the computer Registry hive, which prohibits changes to settings and limits Read access.
- Enables restrictive password and account lockout policy settings for the local accounts.
- Enables extensive security logging and system auditing.
- Renames the local administrator and guest accounts.
- Enables most of the C2 certification security options.
- Contains more restrictive access controls in the root directory (Everyone—Read).

Implementing the Low TCO Desktop Scenario

The Low TCO scenario is implemented as two different Group Policy objects:

- **Low TCO Desktop Computer Settings** Contain settings for Internet Explorer, Windows Installer, and System settings. Can also contain assigned applications.
- **Low TCO Desktop User Settings** Contain settings that restrict Internet Explorer and remaining user settings. Can also contain published applications.

CERTIFICATION SUMMARY

In this chapter we discussed in detail what a domain controller's role is in Windows 2000. We also covered Microsoft's new multi-master model and how it handles conflicts. We discussed parts of Windows 2000 networking that have remained single master and what those operations are. Finally, we covered Group Policy scenarios under Windows 2000 including Desktop systems, Laptop systems, and Kiosk configurations. At this point you should be confident in your understanding of these concepts. Re-read any sections that you are uncertain of in preparation of the Self Test section to follow, as it will test your working knowledge of these concepts.

✓ TWO-MINUTE DRILL

Domain Controllers

- **DCPROMO.EXE** Executable that runs the Active Directory Installation Wizard.
- **Domain controllers** Each holds a read/write copy of the Active Directory database (NTDS.DIT).
- **SYSVOL** Folder found on every Windows 2000 domain controller where domain replication takes place. SYSVOL can only exist on NTFS 5.0 partitions.

Operations Masters

- **FSMO** Flexible Single Master Operators.
- **RID master** Domain controller in charge of allocating pools of RIDs to domain controllers in common domains (every Windows 2000 has one).
- **Schema master** Domain controller that holds a writeable copy of the schema. The only server where modifications, additions, or deletions can occur for the schema throughout the forest.
- **PDC emulator** Domain controller primarily used for backward compatibility with Windows NT 3.51 and 4.0 Servers for their domain object updates.
- **Domain Naming Master** The only domain controller in the forest that can add or remove existing domains from the directory.
- **Infrastructure master** Domain controller responsible for updating cross-domain group-to-user references.

Servers

- **File and Print Servers** Typically a server with a large amount of drive space and sufficient amount of RAM in handling I/O requests from users of the network.
- **Application Servers** Often a member server that is dedicated entirely to running an application that is used throughout the network including Microsoft Exchange.
- **RAS Servers** Servers configured to allow access to an internal network via modem, ISDN, X.25, or other remote connection.

Group Policy Scenarios

- **Group Policy scenario** A method of controlling computer settings and managing user access rights using templates already created.
- **Desktop computer** Also known as TCO (Total Cost of Ownership) Desktop scenario, is the least managed, holds settings that make the desktop easier to use, and allows users to install available applications.
- **Laptop scenario** Can be used by users who are away from the central office most of the time, and who usually log on using asynchronous means, but also are capable of logging on to corporate network at normal speeds when located at the office.
- **Kiosk scenario** Typically a public workstation that runs only one application, uses one user logon account, and runs unattended. Considered very secure for many reasons such as the fact that no data is saved to the local drive.

SELF TEST

The following questions will help you measure your understanding of the material presented in this chapter. Read all of the choices carefully, as there may be more than one correct answer. Choose all correct answers for each question.

Domain Controllers

1. All domain controllers in Windows 2000 have at least this present.
    A. NetBEUI
    B. WINS client setup
    C. SYSVOL
    D. DHCP

2. The GUID is a _____.
    A. Reference point used in Active Directory and DNS to locate a domain controller primarily for the purposes of replication.
    B. Generally Unusual Identification
    C. Stamp
    D. User SID

3. The only client that cannot operate with Active Directory in native mode is _____.
    A. Windows 95
    B. Windows 98
    C. Windows 2000 Professional
    D. Windows NT Workstation

4. The IT manager has decided to turn one of the member servers in the domain into a global catalog server. What must be done to this system before it can be a GC?
    A. Must run DCPROMO.EXE and set up DNS on the server.
    B. Must run DCPROMO.EXE and promote the server to a domain controller.
    C. Must run SETUP.EXE and promote the server to a domain controller.
    D. Nothing, member servers can house the global catalog.

5. In Windows 2000 Server, why is it that an administrator with the appropriate rights can add and delete objects within the directory from any domain controller on the network?
   A. Because all domain controllers have a copy of the domain's SAM (security account management database).
   B. Because all domain controllers hold a read/write replica of Active Directory (NTDS.DIT).
   C. They can't because all changes must be made on the PDC (primary domain controller).
   D. They can't because each domain controller has its own SAM that it manages and these objects cannot be shared amongst other domain controllers, even if they are in the same domain.

6. Your network is made up of two domains working under one tree. Domain controllers for both domains are dispersed throughout the WAN. You create a user principal called Vwhitley in domain one and add it to groups that span both domains. After creating the account, you are informed that you have misspelled the user's name. It should be Pwhitley instead of Vwhitley. After making the change on a domain controller in domain one, you notice in domain two that the group memberships still point to the old incorrect username. Why could this be happening?
   A. The trust between domains one and two has been broken.
   B. Because this is an inter-domain change, there is a lag time before the infrastructure master in domain one updates its counterpart in domain two. This is normal.
   C. The network is down.
   D. The domain controllers in each domain are running different protocol stacks.

Operations Masters

7. The _____ is responsible for updating cross-domain group-to-user references.
   A. PDC Emulator
   B. Infrastructure Master
   C. RID Master
   D. Schema Master

8. FSMO is an acronym for _____.
   A. Flexible Single Master Operator
   B. Fast Systems Master Operator
   C. Flexible Single Master Organization
   D. Nothing at all

9. You are administering your newly formed Active Directory. You try to create a new user but can't. After attempting to create the user object you receive the following error:

   Active Directory Service

   The object *user* could not be created.

   The problem encountered was:

   The directory service has exhausted the pool of relative identifiers.

   What could be causing this?

   A. The Schema Master is offline.
   B. The RID Master is no longer online, and the pool of RIDs distributed earlier are gone.
   C. DHCP is not working right.
   D. You are running Windows 2000 in Native Mode

10. What command line tool can you use to create a cross-reference object that names a new domain?

    A. NTDSUTIL.EXE
    B. DCPROMO.EXE
    C. DSMIGRATE.EXE
    D. MOVETREE.EXE

Servers

11. You have received a new server with the following hardware specifications:
    - 512MB of RAM
    - 30GB of drive space
    - RAID Controller
    - Singe 550 MHz processor
    - 64 Port multi-serial adapter
    - PCI Network Interface Card (NIC)

What would typically be the best role for this server after examining the hardware?

A. Application Server
B. File/Print Server
C. RAS Server
D. DNS Server

Group Policy Scenarios

12. _____ are intended to be starting points from which an administrator can develop settings that are tailored for specific situations and environments.

    A. Access control lists (ACL)
    B. Access control entries (ACE)
    C. RAS Servers
    D. Group Policy scenarios

13. On your network you have installed Group Policy objects on a domain controller. You have linked each of the scenarios to a few of the domains in your company's forest. Who or what will these scenarios effect?

    A. They will apply to every user and workstation that is associated with the domains that have had the Group Policy scenarios implemented.
    B. Only the domain controller on which they were installed.
    C. All systems and users throughout the forest.
    D. None of the above.

14. _____ is the spreadsheet that lists the group policy settings for each scenario.

    A. AD.XLS
    B. GPO.xls
    C. Scenariosession.xls
    D. Scenarioname.xls

15. You need to install the Group Policy scenarios on a domain controller. Which Windows installer file do you execute to do this?

    A. SCENARIOSA.MSI

    B. Scenarios.msi

    C. Situations.msi

    D. Setupscenarios.msi

16. You set up Group Policy scenario objects and applied them to your clients. You notice that both the built-in Administrator and Guest accounts have been changed to %Admin!!! and %Guest!!!, respectively. What issues will you have with the passwords for these accounts?

    A. None.

    B. The passwords will change to *password*.

    C. The old passwords will be eliminated and no others will be added.

    D. The passwords will be changed to *%Admin!!!* and *%Guest!!!* respectively.

17. When using the Kiosk Group Policy scenario, each user logs on using _____.

    A. Nothing, the machine is always logged on using a single user account that the user is unaware of.

    B. Their own personal account.

    C. The administrator account.

    D. The guest account.

LAB QUESTION

In this lab question, we will create a design that will meet the requirements of our customer. Here is the situation:

- Currently, the client is set up with two different physical sites connected by two routers with a maximum of 256Kbps available bandwidth.
- The main site uses IP addresses in the range 10.1.1.1–10.1.1.200. The IP address scheme that is being used between the routers is 11.1.1.1 for the main site's router, and 11.1.1.2 for the second site's router interface to the WAN. The network serves 800 users. There are 700 at the main site and 100 at the second site. Inside the second site the IP address scheme is 12.1.l.200, and all are set with class C type subnetting.

- At this moment all servers run Windows NT Server 4.0.
- Currently, the PDC and all BDCs are located centrally at the main site.

Users at the second site are complaining about the time it takes to get authenticated on the network; once logged on, they are fine. They have just one member server serving their site as a file and print server. The network is serving Windows 2000 Professional workstations, Windows NT 4.0 workstations, and Windows 98 systems.

The first part of your assignment is to draw out the customer's current network configuration with the information you have been provided. Afterwards, you are to design a new Windows 2000 network running in mixed mode addressing the customer's issues. You must install Active Directory in the new network. In your design you must address the slowness of users at the second site authenticating on the domain. You must also upgrade all Windows NT 4.0 Servers to Windows 2000 Server. After doing so, you need to distribute the single master operations as evenly as possible. Many of the users at the second site use laptops and have requested remote dial-in access; the director of IT has also asked that you include specifications for this in your design.

Complete your diagrams and submit them to the corporation's director of IT and answer the multiple-choice question at the end of the lab. Your solution may differ from the one presented in this book. The main thing is to meet the criteria with a solution. Figure 6-4 shows the configuration of the current Windows NT network. Table 6-4 shows hardware settings for the current Windows NT network.

TABLE 6-4 Hardware Settings for Current Windows NT Network

Server Function	Processor(s)	RAM	Drivespace
PDC	1 Pentium Pro 200MHz	128MB	6GB
BDC/DHCP/WINS Server	2 Pentium III 300MHz	256MB	20GB
Member File/Print Server for Main Site	1 Pentium III 300MHz	256MB	80GB
Member File/Print Server for Second Site	1 Pentium III 300MHz	128MB	12GB

282 Chapter 6: Designing a Security Baseline for a Windows 2000 Network

FIGURE 6-4 Current Windows NT network

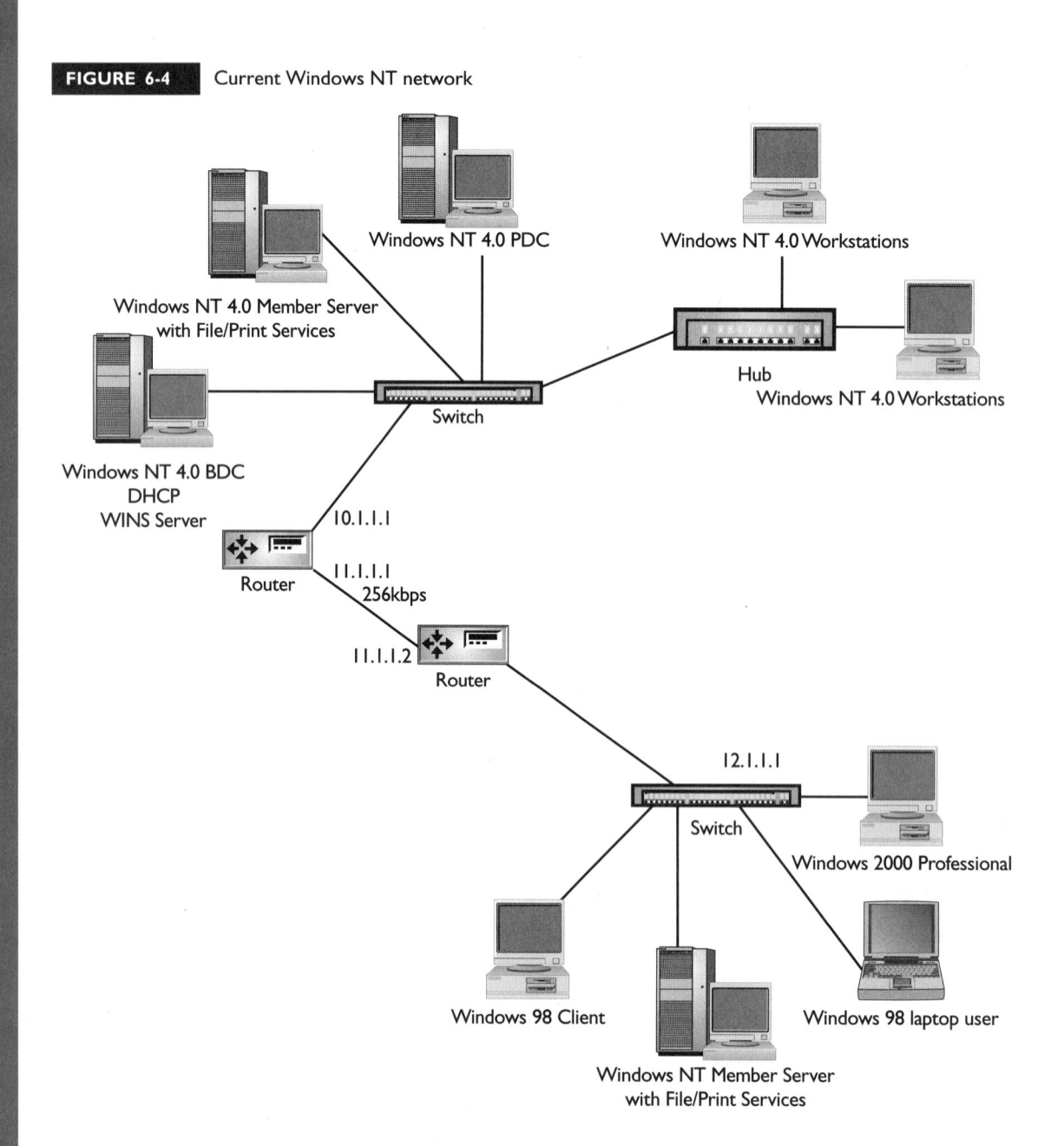

SELF TEST ANSWERS

1. ☑ **C.** All domain controllers under Windows 2000 have a SYSVOL folder on them, which is used in domain replication.
   ☒ **A** is incorrect because NetBEUI, which is a protocol, is not needed for any services under Windows 2000. It is only used (but not required) to communicate to legacy-based Microsoft networking products such as LAN Manager. **B** is incorrect because for Active Directory to even be installed, a server running DNS, which supports SRV records, must be running. NetBIOS name resolution is not required for Windows 2000 systems to communicate with one another. **D** is incorrect because DHCP is completely independent of domains. It simply distributes IP addresses on request by systems on the network.

2. ☑ **A.** GUID, which stands for globally unique identifier, is used by Active Directory and DNS to locate domain controllers for the purpose of replication.
   ☒ **B** is incorrect because GUID does not stand for Generally Unusual Identification. **C** is incorrect because a stamp is used by Active Directory for each replicated attribute value during an update. **D** is incorrect because it refers to the uniqueness of the user object, not a machine.

3. ☑ **D.** There is no redirector currently for Windows NT; therefore, once 2000 is in native mode, support for Windows NT is gone.
   ☒ **A, B,** and **C** are incorrect because each of these systems can operate in a Windows 2000 native mode environment, either straight out of the box or by adding a redirector written by Microsoft.

4. ☑ **B.** Because a global catalog server must run on a DC, you first must run DCPROMO.EXE and promote the member server to a domain controller.
   ☒ **A, C,** and **D** are incorrect because of the reason given in the preceding explanation.

5. ☑ **B.** All DCs (domain controllers) within the same domain hold read/write replicas of the Active Directory (NTDS.DIT). Windows 2000 server with Active Directory supports a peer-level operations scheme when it comes to managing objects in AD.
   ☒ **A** is incorrect because the SAM no longer exists in Active Directory. **C** is incorrect because except in a few cases, Windows 2000 uses a peer-level operations scheme, thus allowing changes to be made from any DC (domain controller). **D** is incorrect because there is no SAM, and the model described is legacy-based from the pre-LAN Manager 2.x days where every server was its own island.

284 Chapter 6: Designing a Security Baseline for a Windows 2000 Network

6. ☑ B. There is usually a lag time for cross-domain group-to-user references to be updated.
☒ A is incorrect because with both domains being in the same tree, there is an implicit trust between them. C is incorrect because if the network were down you would not have been able to query one of the DCs in domain two to know that the user principal had not been changed in that domain. D is incorrect because you must use TCP/IP to make use of Active Directory. Although other stacks are supported in Windows 2000, only TCP/IP will work with AD.

Operations Masters

7. ☑ B. The infrastructure master is the domain controller that is responsible for updating cross-domain group-to-user references.
☒ A is incorrect because the PDC Emulator is an operator whose primary role is that of communicating to Windows NT 4.0 BDCs and keeping them updated on changes in the domain. C is incorrect because the RID Master is responsible for distributing pools of RIDs to Windows 2000 domain controllers. D is incorrect because the Schema Master is in charge of holding the read/write version of the schema, which, if modified either by administrators or applications, then replicates the new schema updates to all Windows 2000 domain controllers throughout the network.

8. ☑ A. FSMO (pronounced *fizmo*) is an acronym for Flexible Single Master Operator.
☒ B and C are incorrect because they don't exist or mean anything in regards to Windows 2000 or Active Directory. D is incorrect because FSMO does stand for something in Windows 2000.

9. ☑ B. If the pool of RIDs for a domain controller are gone and the server cannot communicate to the RID Master then no object can be added to the Active Directory.
☒ A is incorrect. Although very important when modifications are being made to the schema, this operator has no role in distributing RIDs to domain controllers. C is incorrect because DHCP is used to distribute TCP/IP addresses on a network, not RIDs. D is incorrect because regardless of whether Windows 2000 is running in mixed mode or native mode, RIDs must be assigned to all objects in the directory.

10. ☑ A. NTDSUTIL is a command prompt utility that can be used to create a cross reference object that names a domain.
☒ B is incorrect because DCPROMO is a GUI-based wizard. C is incorrect because DSMIGRATE is used to migrate objects from other directory services (such as NDS) into Active Directory. D is incorrect because MOVETREE is used to move objects from one domain to another.

Servers

11. ☑ **C.** With the hardware specified, the best role for this new server would be as a RAS Server. The use of a 64 port multi-serial adapter signifies that this box has been configured for communications.
   ☒ With only 30GB of drive space, it is doubtful that this would be a file and print server, so answers **A** and **B** would not be correct. Also, with the system having only one processor, these may not be the best configuration settings for an application server, depending on the number of users. **D** is incorrect because although DNS could run on this system with no problems, its *best* role would not be that of a DNS server.

Group Policy Scenarios

12. ☑ **D.** Group Policy scenarios are objects that contain the appropriate settings for a certain situation or environment. Examples are the Kiosk, Laptop, and Desktop scenarios.
    ☒ **A** and **B** are incorrect because access control lists and access control entries deal with allowing access or denial to a certain resource such as a file or a printer. **C** is incorrect because a RAS Server is used as a means of allowing remote users access to the network.

13. ☑ **A.** They will apply to workstations and users associated with those domains. Remember, Group Policies apply to domains, sites, and OUs, not group names.
    ☒ **B** is incorrect because by being an object of Active Directory, Group Policy scenario objects are replicated to all domain controllers. **C** is incorrect because it is clearly stated in the problem that these objects are only implemented in a few of the domains within the forest. **D** is incorrect because of choice **A**.

14. ☑ **D.** SCENARIONAME.XLS is the file that lists the Group Policy settings for each scenario.
    ☒ **A**, **B**, and **C** are incorrect because they don't exist.

15. ☑ **B.** SCENARIOS.MSI executes the Group Policy scenarios wizard.
    ☒ **A**, **C**, and **D** are incorrect because they do not exist.

16. ☑ **A.** Nothing will happen; the passwords will remain the same.
    ☒ **B**, **C**, and **D** are incorrect because of the fact that nothing changes with the passwords, only the names of the local accounts change.

17. ☑ **A.** The user doesn't have to log on; the kiosk scenario is continuously logged on with an account that the administrator created. The user is unaware of the account.
    ☒ **B**, **C**, and **D** are incorrect because the kiosk scenario uses an account created by an administrator with appropriate rights. Administrator would provide too much access, the users do not have their own accounts for the system, and guest account by default is disabled.

LAB ANSWER

Again, this is a possible solution for the Lab Question as it meets all requirements and provides a viable solution. Figure 6-5 shows a possible solution for the lab exercise. Table 6-5 shows possible hardware configurations for the presented solution.

Now answer this question: What server should you upgrade first from Windows NT 4.0 to Windows 2000?

A. PDC

B. All member servers

C. All BDCs

D. Anywhere you want

A is correct. It is best to upgrade the original PDC from the Windows NT 4.0 network first, because of the fact that the first Windows 2000 Server domain controller holds all five FSMO operations—especially because of the PDC emulator service. This is also why answers **B**, **C**, and **D** are incorrect.

TABLE 6-5 Possible Hardware Configurations for the Presented Solution

Server Function	Processor(s)	RAM	Drivespace
DC/ PDC Emulator/ RID Master / DHCP Server	2 Pentium III at 500MHz or higher	1GB	10GB
DC/ Global Catalog/ DNS	2 Pentium III at 500MHz or higher	1GB	40GB
2 Win 2000 Member Servers / File and Print Servers at main site	2 Pentium III at 500MHz or higher in each	2GB each	200GB each
DC / Infrastructure Master / Domain Naming Master	2 Pentium III at 500MHz or higher	512MB	20GB
*DC / RAS Server / WINS Server / File and Print Server at second site	2 Pentium III at 500MHz	2GB	50GB

*It is usually recommended to implement some sort of multi-serial port management hardware. Such products from Equinox and Digi are very popular in the industry.

FIGURE 6-5 Possible solution for lab exercise

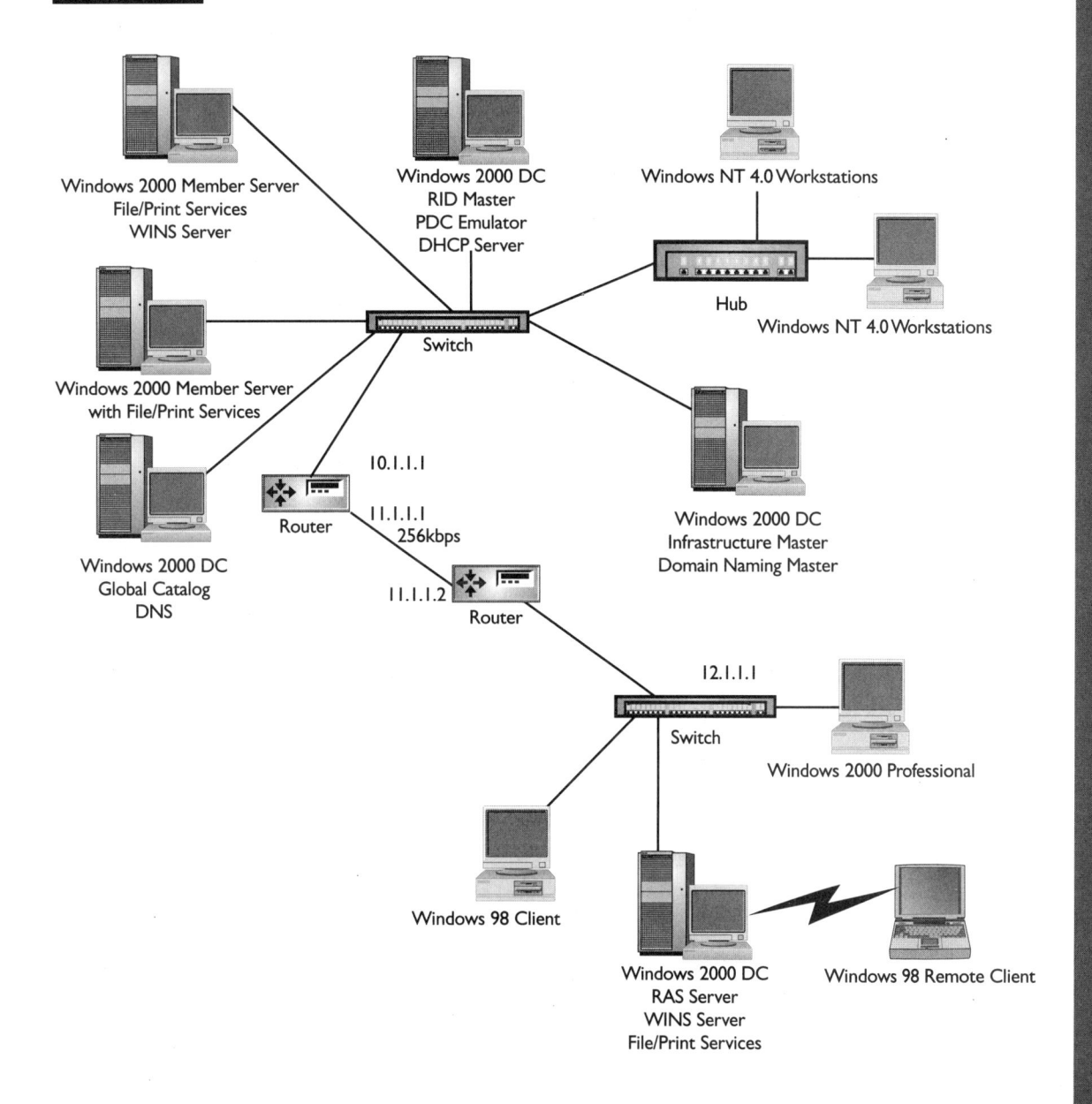

MCSE
MICROSOFT CERTIFIED SYSTEMS ENGINEER

7

Analyzing Security Requirements

CERTIFICATION OBJECTIVES

7.01	Identify the Required Level of Security for Each Resource
7.02	Active Directory Concepts
7.03	Active Directory Planning Considerations
7.04	Securing the Active Directory
✓	Two-Minute Drill
Q&A	Self Test

In this chapter, our focus is analyzing security requirements. We'll begin by discussing the required level of security for various resources in a domain, including printers, files, and shares. We'll also examine the security required for accessing resources from the Internet and through direct dial-up access.

Once we've looked at the security levels required for network resources, we'll discuss how security for these resources is maintained in Windows 2000. Active Directory is the basis for all security enforcement within the Windows 2000 operating system.

We'll begin with an overview of Active Directory, its components, and the relationship between those components. Next, we'll look at Active Directory planning and how the various components contribute to overall network security. Finally, we'll discuss securing Active Directory to ensure that your network maintains the level of security needed for your organization.

CERTIFICATION OBJECTIVE 7.01

Identify the Required Level of Security for Each Resource

Determining the level of security for each resource is part of network security planning. This process is called defining a baseline. As such, you must assess the needs of your users and the threats to your network and your infrastructure to determine baseline security needs. The baseline security needs are defined as the minimum security that the network needs. Remember that more security is not always better—as in the case of password policies that are so complex users write their passwords on a notepad next to their computer. The security measures must be commensurate with the risks to the network and the needs of the users.

Printers, files, shares, Internet, and direct dial-up access all have exposure to security breaches. Table 7-1 identifies the common security risks, the element exposed, and the Windows 2000-based solution.

TABLE 7-1   Risk Types

Risk	Element	Solution
Data interception	Printer, file, share, Internet, and dial-up access	Secure printers, encrypt data
Manipulation	File, share, Internet, dial-up access	NTFS, EFS, L2TP with IPSec, VPN
Masquerade, impostors	Printer, file, share, Internet, dial-up access	Kerberos authentication, smart cards, certificates
Replay attack (user information captured and used again to gain access)	Printer, file, share, Internet, dial-up access	Kerberos authentication, smart cards, certificates
Identity interception	Printer, file, share, Internet, dial-up access	Strong passwords, smart cards
Social engineering (impostors get users to divulge log-on credentials)	Printer, file, share, Internet, dial-up access	Educate users about company policies and procedures
Denial of service	Internet	Firewall and other Internet security methods

exam ⓦatch — *You are likely to run into questions regarding various security risks for an organization. Understanding and remembering these basic risk categories will help you in scenario-based questions on the MCP exam.*

Printers

The primary risk to network printers is unauthorized access—either users printing materials they shouldn't or users printing on a printer that has a special purpose. For instance, you may want to limit access to a high-speed color printer to the graphics department staff. The two primary risks here are:

- Unauthorized users printing material to which they should not have access
- Unauthorized use of the printer

Files

Files contain data that can be sensitive, confidential, or simply needed in day-to-day operations. Other than attacks caused to disrupt service such as Denial of Service, Trojan horse, or virus attacks, most attacks to a network are designed to gain access to data. Therefore, it is critical to assess the security risk to network files.

Part of this planning process should include assessing the nature of your company, the industry you work in, the location of your resources, the technology used by your company, and the reputation of your company. For instance, if you work for a firm that manufactures a chip used in a patented, highly competitive electronic device, your data may be very valuable to your competitors, or your firm may simply be in the news enough to attract notice. If your firm is a design firm, perhaps a competitor would like an early look at a new product that you have on the drawing board or have just announced in a press release. These are just a few examples of reasons unauthorized users may attempt access to sensitive data. The most common risks to files are:

- Unauthorized access of files
- Unauthorized manipulation of files—moving, deleting, modifying, encrypting
- Viruses—corruption, deletion, unauthorized replication or forwarding
- Macro language viruses, which are specific to an application that uses macro language programming and cause unexpected behavior including deletion or modification of data
- Trojan horses—corruption, deletion, destruction of data

Shares

The same risks that apply to files also apply to folders. Unauthorized access to shares can cause destruction, loss, or manipulation of data. In addition, there is a risk that an attacker could "walk" through your network tree if shares are not adequately protected. The common risks here are:

- Unauthorized access to shares and files
- Unauthorized manipulation of data within shares, such as moving, deleting, modifying, encrypting

Identify the Required Level of Security for Each Resource

- Viruses—corruption, deletion, unauthorized replication or forwarding of data within shares
- Trojan horses—corruption, deletion, destruction of data
- Using share access to move up or down the directory tree structure

Internet Access

Perhaps the most widely discussed risks today come from the Internet. As use of the Internet has grown, risks associated with the Internet have grown. These risks come in the form of attacks to Web sites as well as intrusion into a corporate network through the Internet. Attacks can be intentional and aimed directly at your company, such as a Denial of Service (DoS) attack that floods the Internet-based server with so many requests that it becomes overloaded and cannot process legitimate requests. Attacks can also be more general and aimed at the public rather than a specific company. Recent virus attacks such as the Melissa virus and the Love Bug virus were not targeting any particular group or company, but spread quickly to any vulnerable target.

The typical attacks, both targeted and general, are discussed in the following list.

- **Denial of Service** Loss of service to normal users, overload of server, loss of data or revenue
- **Malicious mobile code** Auto-executing code such as ActiveX control or Java applet loaded from the Internet
- **Trojan horses** Program downloaded for a benign purpose that has destructive capabilities
- **Viruses** Corruption, deletion, or unauthorized replication or forwarding caused by files sent through Internet e-mail or other Internet means
- **Web site corruption** Data on a Web site can be modified or deleted causing loss of service and loss of revenue
- **Unauthorized access to network** Risk of attack from the Internet through any computer attached to the Internet; network security can be compromised including confidential information, financial data, and trade secrets

on the Job *Use best practices to avoid virus and Trojan horse attacks. Never go out to the Internet logged on as a network administrator. Also, educate users to download software that is known to them or that contains a digital signature. Never open e-mail attachments that you are not expecting, from someone you don't know, or that appear to be suspicious.*

Dial-in Access

The risks associated with dial-in access are similar to internal risks. As we've discussed throughout this book, more attacks occur from inside an organization than from outside. Nonetheless, providing dial-in access to users exposes your network to outside attacks. From users attempting to access resources remotely for which they do not have adequate permissions to unauthorized users attempting to gain access to network resources through remote access, network security planning must recognize these external threats and address them in a manner that maintains high levels of security while allowing legitimate users access to network resources when they are away from the office.

- **Unauthorized access** Through identity interception, masquerading, replay attack, data interception, or social engineering attack.

- **Unauthorized manipulation of data** If unauthorized access is gained, data can be modified or deleted, and confidential information can be compromised including financial data or trade secrets.

As you can see, identifying the specific security risks to these resources within your organization is the basis for developing a security plan that will ensure the integrity of the network without causing undue hardship for users. A network so tightly secured that even authorized users have trouble gaining access to resources will cause as much of a problem as unauthorized access will. Loss of productivity, loss of revenue, and loss of customers can occur when security is too tight, preventing authorized users from gaining legitimate access to resources. Loss of productivity, revenue, and customers can also occur when security is too lax and unauthorized activities occur on the network. It becomes clear that an effective security plan must find the balance between the two.

EXERCISE 7-1

Evaluating the Security of Network Resources

You are a network administrator who has been tasked with evaluating the security of your network resources. You've been asked to provide a brief outline of the risks that your network has at the present time. The following information is the current data about your network.

- The company has one location and 10 sales people who travel nationally.
- All employees have dial-in access through Routing and Remote Access Service (RRAS).
- The company just launched a Web site for e-commerce.

Based on this information, let's walk through the steps that you would follow to evaluate the security risk for each element.

1. Identify internal and external risks:
   - *Internal* Very low internal risks. User logon authentication required, but data does not appear to need to be encrypted on the local area network (LAN). All users should have virus protection software installed and should not download unknown files from the Internet.
   - *External* Fairly high risks. Traveling employees' laptops could be lost or stolen and data could be intercepted. Web site for e-commerce vulnerable to DoS type attacks and attacks to gain access to the network.

2. Identify sources of risk:
   - *Internal* Internet downloads, e-mail
   - *External* Lost or stolen laptops (data loss), Web attacks

3. Identify ways to mitigate risk for each source:
   - *Internal* User authentication, virus software, user education, network auditing to monitor virus attacks, attempts at unauthorized use, dial-in access
   - *External* Laptops can be formatted with NTFS; files can be encrypted with Encrypting File System (EFS). All communication between remote users and headquarters should use authentication and encryption. A Web site should have a firewall and a DeMilitarized Zone (DMZ) zone, shares should be evaluated for risk, unused services and ports on Web servers should be disabled, and Web activity should be monitored for evidence of DoS type attacks.

SCENARIO & SOLUTION

Corporate laptops are stolen (Data interception security risk)	NTFS, EFS
New employees unfamiliar with company or computers (Social engineering, virus, or Trojan horse attack security risk)	Educate users regarding IT and company policies
Company announced IPO involving e-commerce (Web site DoS attacks security risk)	Load balancing, DMZ, firewall
New branch site coming online (Data interception, manipulation, impostors security risk)	Secure VPN connections, encrypt data

CERTIFICATION OBJECTIVE 7.02

Active Directory Concepts

In this section, we'll look at the components of Active Directory in order to understand concepts related to securing the network. Active Directory is a new feature in Windows 2000 and provides the framework for the logical security for the domain. In this section, we'll look at the components in Active Directory and learn how each one plays a role in maintaining a secure environment.

Active Directory supports network security in three ways:

- Defines security boundaries using domains
- Supports security settings using organizational units, user and Group Policies
- Provides delegation of administration

Active Directory, a directory service, is the backbone of the distributed security services in Windows 2000. Active Directory (AD) contains information about users, computers, printers, files, folders, applications, connections, and all other network resources. Each of these resources is defined as an object. Each object can have many attributes depending on the class to which the object belongs. For instance, the user object defines an individual user. Because the object belongs to the user class, it must have certain attributes such as name, unique ID, and perhaps location. Each object has attributes that are either required or optional. For instance, the user object *must* have a name and a unique ID, but it might also have address, telephone number, and social security attributes associated with it as optional attributes.

In Windows 2000, authentication for domain users is based on user accounts contained within Active Directory. The user object has certain characteristics, among them permissions associated with that user. When the user logs on, the logon information is compared to the AD information. Once identity is verified, the user obtains a unique security ID that contains all their group membership and domain rights.

Examples of common objects are printers, computers, users, files, shares, or connections. Each object is stored with a list of access control entries (ACE) that together comprise the object's access control list (ACL). This list is sometimes referred to as a discretionary access control list, or DACL. You will find these terms used interchangeably. When a user requests a network resource, the ACL is compared with the user's security ID to determine if the user has adequate permissions to perform the task requested.

As a user requests access to network resources, their unique identifier is compared with the attributes of the object they want to access. If their identifier allows the appropriate level of privileges, the user is granted access to the object. Access can include creating, modifying, writing, reading, moving, or deleting files, for instance.

This is the method AD uses for managing security on the network. Let's look at some of the components of AD to better understand how AD forms the framework for security in Windows 2000.

Directory Service

A directory service is a network service that provides information on how to locate resources. By providing a consistent method of naming and locating resources, directory services make these resources available to users and applications. Directory services enable the user to locate resources without having to navigate the complex structure of the network environment. In Windows 2000, Active Directory provides the directory service functionality.

Later in this chapter, we'll discuss replication of directory services to understand how this information is distributed across the network and how it is kept up-to-date.

Schema

Schema is the term used to describe the organization of a database structure. AD's schema contains the definitions of the objects that can be stored in AD, including computers, users, printers, files, and applications, to name a few.

The AD schema contains two types of definitions: classes and attributes. Object classes are described as a set of required and optional attributes. Attributes are the values that the object can or must have. For instance, when you create a new user, you are creating a new instance of the user class as a user object. The attributes, specified by the class definition, include name, login ID, location, and so on.

The schema maintains the organization of the data in Active Directory and ensures that all objects comply with required attribute information, based on their class. Using the earlier example, you could not create a new user object without supplying a name, which is a required attribute of the user object.

The schema is a directory partition of the Active Directory. It therefore can have attributes assigned to it like just like other objects, including security attributes. The directory partition is a unit of replication. We'll discuss replication later in this chapter.

Global Catalog

The global catalog has two distinct purposes: to manage user logon in a native, multi-domain model and to provide directory information on the location of any object in the forest, regardless of the exact location of the data.

A global catalog is a domain controller that stores three directory partitions: domain directory partition, schema directory partition, and configuration directory partition. It also contains partial information from all other domain directory partitions within the forest. This information is stored in a single database, NTDS.DIT on that server.

The global catalog stores information that is needed to determine the location of any object in the directory and is created automatically by the AD replication system.

on the Job

As noted in Chapter 4, physical security of the servers is critical. There are utilities commonly available on the Internet that allow for raw access of the NTDS.DIT file when booting in DSRepair mode. Accessing this file provides global knowledge of network resources that could be used to disable the network.

The global catalog is required for network logon. If no local global catalog is present, a global catalog on a remote site can be used for logon authentication. If no global catalog is available at all, a user will be logged on using cached information. This process is similar to the logon process in Windows NT 4.0 where a primary domain controller (PDC) or a backup domain controller (BDC) was required for logon authentication and when none was online, the user was authenticated using cached information.

Trust Relationships

Trust relationships are relationships between computer domains that dictate how resources may be accessed by members of the other domain. Trusts can be one-way, non-transitive, or two-way transitive. In Windows 2000, trusts are two-way transitive trusts by default. However, there are five types of trust relationships.

A one-way trust means that domain A trusts B, but B does not trust A. Non-transitive means that it does not pass through. Therefore, if domain A trusts B, and domain B trusts C, a non-transitive relationship means that A does not automatically trust C. This type of trust is useful when a business partner needs access to resources in a particular domain.

A two-way transitive relationship is established in two directions. Domain A trusts B, and B trusts A. Transitive trusts minimize the number of trusts in a domain; for example, if domain A trusts B, and B trusts C, then A implicitly trusts C. This is the default trust relationship between domains in native mode (all Windows 2000 domain controllers).

Although there are only two types of trusts that can be established within Windows 2000, there are five types of trust relationships that can be established. These are delineated in Table 7-2.

TABLE 7-2
Trust Relationships in Windows 2000

Type of Trust	Parameters
Tree-Root Trust	Established when you add a new tree to a forest. It can be set up only between the roots of two trees in the same forest, and it is a transitive, two-way trust.
Parent-Child Trust	Established when you create a new domain in a tree. It can be set up only between two domains in the same tree and namespace, the parent domain is always trusted by the child domain, and it is a transitive, two-way trust.

TABLE 7-2	Type of Trust	Parameters
Trust Relationships in Windows 2000 (continued)	Shortcut Trust	Established manually to improve logon efficiency by shortening the trust path. Also called a cross-link trust. It can be set up between any two domains in the same forest, must be set up manually in both directions, and must be transitive.
	External Trust	Established manually between Windows 2000 domains in different forests or in a mixed setting between a Windows 2000 domain and a Windows NT domain. It is one way, can be set up manually in both directions to establish a two-way trust, and is non-transitive.
	Non-Windows Kerberos Realm Trust	Established between a non-Windows Kerberos Realm (similar to a domain) and a Windows 2000 domain. Allows for cross-platform interoperability and security services based on Kerberos v5. It can only use Kerberos v5 authentication. It is one-way by default. A two-way relationship can be established manually. It is non-transitive by default. The trust direction is from the non-Windows realm to the Windows 2000 domain.

Trust relationships are used to provide resource access to users in other domains. As such, they are a core component of overall domain security.

Namespace

Namespace refers to the Domain Name System (DNS) name of a domain. In Windows 2000, the namespace is the domain name. The namespace is hierarchical and the name of the child domain is placed to the left of the DNS name. For instance, if your namespace is A.com and you create a separate sales domain called Sales, its namespace would be Sales.A.com. If you created a child domain under the parent sales domain called Europe, its namespace would be Europe.Sales.A.com.

Sites

Active Directory is organized in both physical and logical structures. The logical structure is used to organize network resources. These are called organizational units (OUs) and are discussed in the next section. The physical structure is used to configure and manage network traffic. In Active Directory, the physical structure has two components: domain controllers and sites.

Domain controllers are used to control information and network traffic within a domain. A domain can have one or more domain controllers. Domain controllers can also play one or more specific roles within the domain. Some of the roles are global catalog server or operations master. A domain controller can own one or more of these roles: Schema Master, Domain Naming Master, RID Master, PDC Emulator, and Infrastructure Master.

A site is defined as one or more IP subnets connected by a high-speed link. Defining sites as subnets connected by high-speed links allows you to optimize user access and replication traffic on the network. Sites correlate to the physical structure of your network. Typically, a company will have one or more locations. These locations may be connected by a very high-speed link such as a T1 backbone, as in the case of a company with a multi-building campus. In other cases, these locations may be connected by a slower wide area network (WAN) connection, as in the case of regional branch offices. Determining how your company's physical infrastructure is configured will give you a baseline for forming sites in Active Directory.

Client computers are assigned to sites based on their IP address. Each site can be one or more subnets. Each subnet will have a range of IP addresses used to define that subnet, and each client computer will belong to one of those subnets based on its IP address.

on the job

Sites may or may not contain domain controllers. If a domain controller is not present in a site, user authentication must be obtained from a remote domain controller. This may slow down user logon if the connection to the remote domain controller is slow or unreliable.

When you create the first domain controller in Windows 2000, the Active Directory Installation wizard will automatically create the first site. It is called Default-First-Site-Name, which you can change to any name desired. The domain controller is assigned to this site as are any subsequent domains added. The initial site, Default-First-Site-Name, contains all IP subnets by default. Later, you can change the configuration to better map to your organizational needs.

> **exam**
> **⍟atch**
>
> *Unless you specifically create a new site, all domain controllers created will be placed in the default site, Default-First-Site-Name. On exam questions, if you see Default-First-Site-Name, remember that this is the default configuration that contains all domain controllers and all IP subnets, unless otherwise specified.*

EXERCISE 7-2

Default-First-Site and New Sites

1. In Windows 2000 Server, click Start | Programs | Administrative Tools | Active Directory Sites and Services.

2. Click the + sign next to Sites to expand the tree. The tree should include the Default-First-Site-Name site, unless you have already modified this.

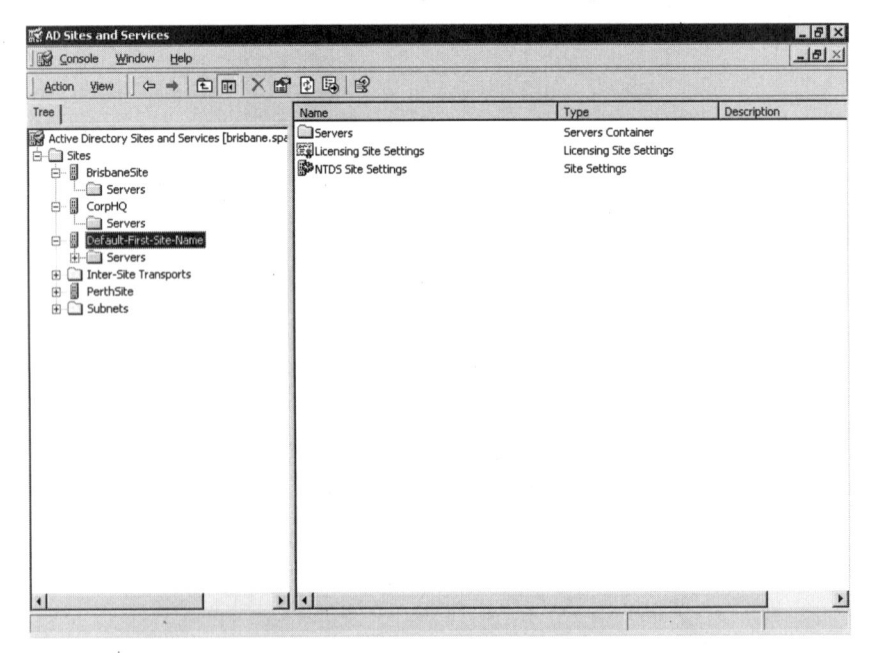

3. Right-click Sites, and select New Site from the context menu.

4. In the New Object—Site dialog box, type a name for your new site (choose any name that is descriptive of the site such as *FoothillsOfficeSite* or *ClevelandCampusSite*, for example. Site names cannot contain spaces).

Active Directory Concepts

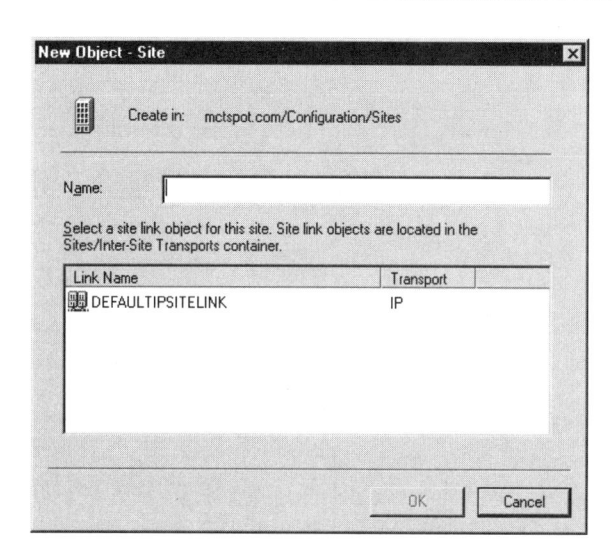

5. Click a site link, then click OK. (DEFAULTIPSITELINK is the default link and can be selected if no other link is available.) You will see a dialog box similar to the one shown here.

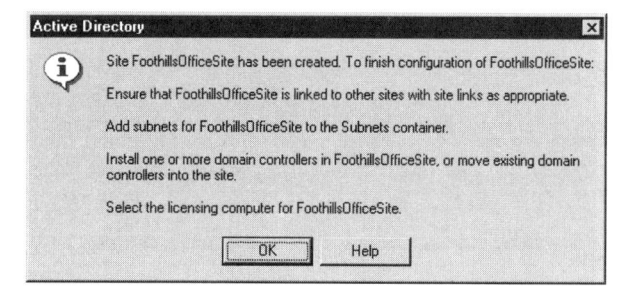

Create a new site link:

6. With Active Directory Sites and Services still open, click the + to the left of Sites to expand the tree.
7. Click the + to the left of Inter-Site Transports to expand that tree.
8. Right-click IP, then click New Site Link.
9. Type a name for the new site link that is a logical representation of the link. For instance, Boston-Cleveland.

10. Click two or more sites to include in this link, as shown in the first illustration that follows, and click Add. The sites will be linked, and the site link will appear as shown in the second illustration.

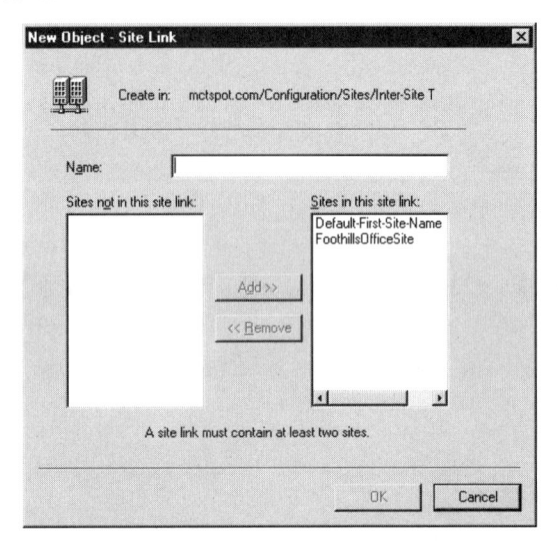

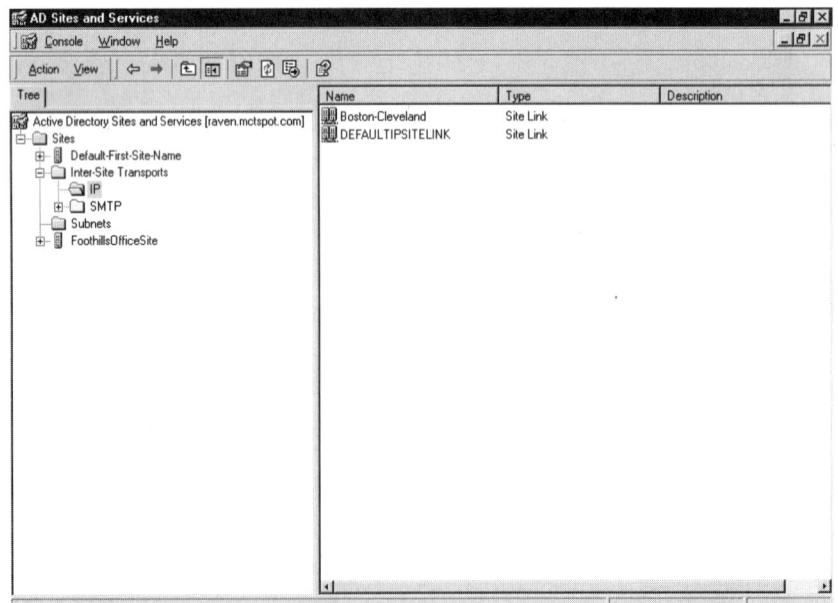

11. Click OK to exit.

Organizational Units

Organizational units (OU) are the logical groupings of network resources providing ease of administration and a consistent manner of delegating authority for network security. OUs are container objects within Active Directory that can be used to organize objects in a domain. OUs can contain user accounts, groups, computers, printers, or even other OUs. Generally, OUs are organized in a way that reflects the logical organization of your company. Department or geographical boundaries might be used to define OUs. Each domain can implement its own OU without impacting other domains. For instance, if your company has three locations and each location is a site, you could create three OUs to reflect the resources at each site. Alternately, you could create OUs based on roles within the company such as creating an OU for Human Resources, an OU for Engineering, and an OU for Sales. In this case, the OUs would include users from all three sites. The Human Resources OU would contain users from sites 1, 2, and 3. Defining OUs eases network administration and often reflects the structure of the company's IT infrastructure. Because network administration tasks are delegated through the use of OUs, defining OUs that mirror your organization makes sense.

Delegation of administration is considered to be one of the most important features of Active Directory. Delegation reduces a domain administrator's need to manage down to the most granular detail of the domain. You can grant specific permission for the OU and the objects in the OU such as computers, users, or printers. Delegation is an important aspect of security management in Windows 2000. Delegation is discussed in more detail later, as well as in Chapter 10.

Replication

All objects in a forest are contained in the Active Directory. The directory tree is divided up and hosted on different domain controllers throughout the forest. Changes are propagated and tracked among domain controllers. This process is known as replication.

A full copy of the directory is called a full replica. It contains all the information for all attributes for all objects in the forest. It contains three directory partitions: domain, schema, and configuration. A full replica of the domain partition is stored on all domain controllers in that domain. A partial replica contains a subset of the attributes of all directory partition objects. Partial replicas are stored only on global catalog servers. A domain controller stores only copies of objects that actually pertain to that domain and copies of the schema and configuration objects for the forest of which the domain is a member.

Changes to the objects in AD must be tracked throughout the domain. Replication is used to propagate changes to ensure that all replicas remain up-to-date. There are four methods of replication: multi-master, store-and-forward, pull, and state-based. Windows 2000 uses state-based replication.

- **Multi-master**   Changes can be made to the directory on any domain controller within a forest. Replication topology defines the system used to determine which domain controller replicates to other domain controllers. This minimizes network replication traffic yet ensures that directory information is kept up-to-date.

- **Store-and-forward**   This method of replication is designed for use over slower WAN links. The directory updates first to nearby domain controllers and then updates to domain controllers farther away. When an update is sent to a remote server, that server replicates to servers nearby. Thus, replication traffic on the network is minimized.

- **Pull**   A server can request an updated replica. The request specifies the information that is needed based on changes it has already received. The receiving server essentially brings itself up-to-date. An alternate method is push replication. This occurs when the source replica pushes the information out to the receiving replica without being queried. Push replication is less reliable than pull replication because the source has no way of accurately assessing the data that the receiving replica has. Therefore, pull replication is more reliable.

- **State-based**   Active Directory uses state-based replication. In state-based replication, each master applies updates to its replica and does not maintain a change log file. Instead, it manages the replica by the current state of the data within the replica. The state of the replica is defined as the current state of all objects within the replica. This state information is used to resolve conflicts and to avoid sending an entire replica during replication. Each server stores information about how up-to-date it is with respect to all other replicas and thus manages its own current state. It therefore performs fewer database updates, which minimizes network replication traffic, and it is very reliable.

Replication is crucial to a secure environment because changes, such as removing file permissions for a particular user group, must be spread quickly and reliably throughout the domain.

Group Policies

Active Directory contains Group Policy objects. These objects can be used to manage computers and users as groups. This eases administration and allows for managing the domain in a secure and organized manner. You can assign rights and permissions to groups of users or computers at once. For instance, you could use a Group Policy to provide the finance group with access to the a line-of-business application and assign security levels to this group. Using Group Policies, you can define user and computer environments so that the configuration provides the needed services for the user, minimizes administration of the accounts, and ensures consistent application of security policies.

You can define a security configuration within a Group Policy object. Security is then applied to the members of the group as part of the security enforcement at logon. Windows 2000 provides several security templates that can be used as-is or can be modified based on your unique requirements. The three preconfigured templates are compatible, secure, and high secure.

- **Compatible**   Template used to allow users to run older programs. Programs that are not certified to run on Windows 2000 will require the compatible template. However, this is not a secure environment.

- **Secure**   Template used to secure areas of the operating system that are not secured by default.

- **High secure**   Template used to increase security settings. It requires all network communication to be digitally signed and encrypted. This may prevent Windows 2000 computers from communicating with other computers running older operating systems. However, this provides the highest level of security.

on the Job

Using the high secure template could degrade system performance because it requires all network communication to be digitally signed and encrypted. Encrypting data on an internal network takes both processor time and bandwidth which may degrade performance to an unacceptable degree.

Windows 2000 comes with three predefined security groups that are used in Active Directory Services.

- **Domain local groups**   Used to give access rights to file systems or printers located on any computer in the domain and where broad access rights are appropriate.

- **Global groups** Used for combining users who have common job functions. Typically, membership in these groups will change frequently.
- **Universal groups** Used in large, multi-domain settings where there are groups in each domain that need similar access rights. Typically, you would add global groups to universal groups. This helps reduce replication of changes that would occur if you were to make frequent changes to the universal group membership directly. One restriction of universal groups is that your network must be running in native mode—all Windows 2000-based domain controllers. There is no need for universal groups in a single domain model.

exam 🕅 *a t c h*

Place users into global groups, then place global groups into local groups. On the MCP exam, this method is considered to be a best practice, even though you can assign permissions directly to individual users. Also, computer local groups are local to a computer and not recognized anywhere else—don't be fooled by this group when answering questions on the MCP exam.

Group Policy provides a streamlined method of assigning and managing security configurations in a consistent and logical manner across the domain. As such, it is a core component of a secure network solution.

SCENARIO & SOLUTION

Branch locations in Boston, Atlanta, and Phoenix. Slow WAN connection between branches.	Create three sites or use three domains. Use sites if administration is centralized, use domains if each branch manages their own network independently.
Manages user logon in Windows 2000 native mode.	Global catalog service on domain controller.
Connection to partner network required.	One-way, non-transitive trust to external domain. Could be external trust (Windows-based) or non-Windows Kerberos Realm trust (non-Windows based cross-platform).
One group manages all printers company-wide.	Create printer OU.
Each master updates its replica and does not maintain a change log file.	State-based replication used in Windows 2000.
Need to give permissions to similar groups in different domains.	Universal groups.

FROM THE CLASSROOM

Learning the Details of Windows 2000

Windows 2000 contains many new features. Familiarity with Windows NT 4.0 certainly helps students by providing a solid foundation in some of the fundamentals such as TCP/IP, routing, DNS, name resolution, authentication, and so on. In any course of study of Microsoft technologies (or any technology, for that matter), I always encourage my students to dig a bit deeper into the details. Although passing the MCP exam may not require specific knowledge of where a protocol fits in the OSI model or the exact format of a packet, knowing these kinds of details enhances your overall understanding of the material and provides a broader foundation for working on these technologies.

In the classroom, I encourage students to study one particular topic in-depth and report on it to the class. This is not a formal study or presentation, but an opportunity for each student to study and learn about some of the details of Windows 2000. For instance, how does RPC (remote procedure call) work? What is it used for? What layer of the OSI model does it work in? What is it used for in Windows 2000? What could go wrong with RPC? What would the symptoms be? Where would you look to find the problem? What steps could be taken to resolve it? What would be the implications of this kind of fix? By having each student focus on one particular aspect of the material, the entire class gains a greater depth of knowledge. You'd be surprised how many times knowing some minute detail of the material comes in handy; both on the job and in the exams.

Following are some of the resources I encourage my students to use—both to provide background information on the topics covered in the course, and as auxiliary materials to use when they're on the job. I encourage each of you to find your favorite list of Windows 2000 resources, to use as a reference during your studies and as on-going sources of information when you're on the job. Staying up-to-date is relatively easy with the wealth of resources at your disposal.

- **This book**
- **Microsoft Windows 2000 Resource kit**   Provides over 7200 pages of reference material on every aspect of Windows 2000
- **Microsoft Technet**   Located at www.microsoft.com/technet, this site has resources on every aspect of Microsoft products, including the Knowledge Base (KB) that provides current information on bugs, problems, and fixes to Microsoft products.
- **Windows 2000 magazine**   One of many Windows NT/2000 resources that provides tips, tricks, how-tos, and discussions on a variety of Windows NT/2000 related topics.

FROM THE CLASSROOM

- **Web sites** There are too many to list here, and they do change from time to time. However, you can find a lot of very useful links by reading through material on Microsoft's Technet site. One word of caution here: not every Web site is run by experts. Make sure that you verify information that you find on Web sites with another source. If two or more sources concur, you've probably got good information. Finally, if you want to test a trick, a tip, or a procedure that comes from one of these sites, try it in a test lab. The last thing you need is to take your network down when trying to tune it up!

—*Susan Snedaker, MCSE, MCP+I, MCT, MBA*

CERTIFICATION OBJECTIVE 7.03

Active Directory Planning Considerations

In this section, we'll learn about the planning considerations for the components of Active Directory. We'll look at how namespace conventions impact planning. We'll take a look at sites, site links, and replication, and learn what needs to be kept in mind to design an efficient and secure network. Finally in this section, we'll cover organizational units and Group Policies and learn how security can be optimized through these components of Windows 2000.

Namespace

As discussed previously, a domain is identified by its DNS name. DNS is used to locate the domain controllers within a domain. The name resolution is hierarchical. Thus, if you had a domain called DNS.com, a child of that domain might have the name Sales.DNS.com indicating that Sales is a child of DNS in the forest hierarchy. Another example is shown in Figure 7-1.

Planning your domain will have an impact on several factors: directories in the domain, replication of the directories in the domain, and traffic related to clients in the domain.

FIGURE 7-1 Domain hierarchy

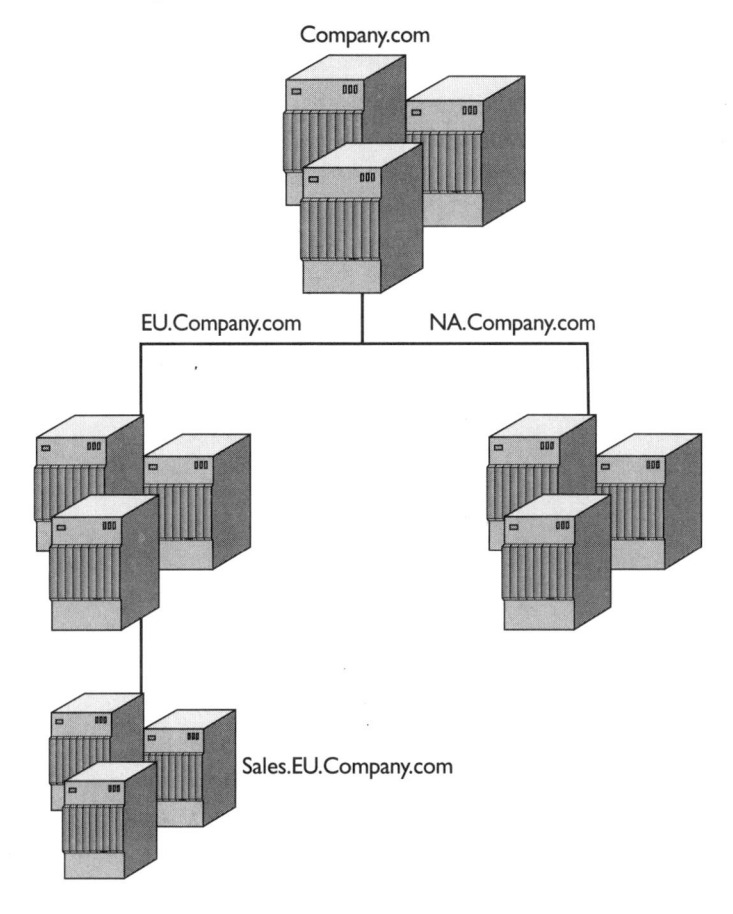

Windows 2000 is designed to operate in a single-domain mode. When planning, you may want to consider multiple domains in these situations:

- *If you have existing Windows NT domains that you want to preserve*
- *For administrative purposes*   If a domain has unique security requirements, you may want to consider keeping it as a separate domain. For instance, if you have an R&D group that requires significantly higher security, these resources could be placed in a separate domain. Divisions of companies sometimes require separate domains because they have different requirements, such as security restrictions, or they are administrated by separate departments or organizations.

- *To physically partition* Physical partitions allow for reduced domain replication traffic on networks. For instance, in a company with several branches, if users in your company always log on at their location, replicating headquarter information to each remote branch may not make sense. In this case, using multiple domains reduces unneeded replication traffic.

A well-designed namespace will make overall domain administration much easier because it provides a logical method of identifying and location resources.

> **exam**
> **Watch**
>
> *These are the only three scenarios likely to appear on the exam. Windows 2000 supports very large, single-domain environments that Windows NT did not. If faced with the choice between a single domain and a multi-domain model and you're unsure of the answer, select single domain unless one of the preceding three scenarios has been presented.*

Sites

Active Directory site topology is the physical representation of your network. Site topology is defined on a per-forest basis. Site topology is used to route queries (to locate resources) and replication traffic more efficiently.

A LAN or set of LANs with high-speed connections is considered a site. A site link is a slow or unreliable link that connects two sites. A WAN would be considered a site link. Any link that is slower than the speed of the LAN is considered to be a slow link.

Planning sites is relatively simple because a site is a LAN or set of LANs and is based in the physical topology of your network. Therefore, the physical structure of your company should be the starting point for site planning. Using three steps for planning your sites will ensure that your site topology works properly.

1. Define sites and site links based on the physical layout of your network.
2. Place servers in those sites based on network and user needs.
3. Define how changes after deployment would impact users and develop processes that can be used to implement change, if needed.

Site-Based Replication

The Knowledge Consistency Checker (KCC) is built into Windows 2000. It is used to create and maintain replication connections between domain controllers. The KCC will automatically create replication connections based on the site topology. There are two types of site replication: intra-site and inter-site.

Intra-Site Replication   Intra-site replication has these characteristics:

- Data is not compressed.
- Replication partners notify each other of changes to data and of the need to replicate.
- Replication partners poll each other periodically to determine the need to replicate.
- Replication uses the Remote Procedure Call (RPC) protocol.
- Replication connections can be created between any two domain controllers in the same site.
- KCC creates multiple replication connections to minimize the lag between replication.

Inter-Site Replication   Inter-site replication has these characteristics:

- Data is compressed because it is traveling over a slower link, and there is reduced required bandwidth.
- Replication partners do not notify each other of changes or the need to replicate data.
- Replication partners poll each other at specified intervals during scheduled periods.
- Replication uses RPC over TCP/IP or Simple Mail Transfer Protocol (SMTP) because it is traveling over a WAN link.
- Replication connections are created between bridgehead servers.
- One domain controller per site is designated at the bridgehead server by the KCC to handle all inter-site replication for that site.
- The KCC will automatically create connections between bridgehead servers based on least-cost routing.

In Active Directory, one server is designated as the bridgehead server to perform site-to-site replication. Bridgehead servers are designated automatically by the KCC or they can be manually assigned.

exam
⒲atch

Remember that RPC is always used for intra-site replication. Also remember that TCP/IP is used for inter-site replication unless the site supports only SMTP. In a scenario-based question, it might state that the site can only access Internet e-mail, which would indicate it supports SMTP.

Global Catalog-based Replication

As discussed earlier, the global catalog contains three partitions: domain directory, schema directory, and configuration directory. Site information (sites, site links, and subnets) is stored in the configuration directory partition and is replicated as part of AD replication.

Some planning considerations are:

- Create sites based on LANs or sets of LANs connected by high-speed backbone.

- Create a site for each location that does not have direct connectivity to the rest of your network and is reachable only by SMTP mail (e-mail connection).

- Determine which sites will have domain controllers. If a site will not have a domain controller, merge it with another site. Sites without domain controllers must send user logon authentication traffic across the WAN.

- For each site, record the set of IP subnets that comprise the site. Site names are used by DNS, so make sure that site names comply with DNS naming conventions—use only alphanumeric characters or the hyphen in names.

- The client will attempt to communicate with domain controllers first. If a site does not have a domain controller, it should be connected to a site with a domain controller using a fairly fast connection. Consider merging these two sites into one.

- Any time two networks are separate by links that are heavily used during certain periods of the day, you should divide those networks into separate sites.

- If your entire network is comprised of high-speed, reliable connections, consider the entire network one site.

Site Links

Sites are connected by site links. Name the site links in a manner that reflects the connectivity of that site link. Remember that site links are transitive. If site A is connected to B and B is connected to C, site A, by default, is connected to site C. This information is used by the KCC when replicating data.

There are four aspects to site links that affect replication that must be considered when planning your links.

- **Replication schedule**   Replication polling happens only during scheduled periods. The default schedule allows polling to happen throughout a seven-day period.

- **Replication interval**   Replication polling happens at specified intervals, during the scheduled period. The default polling interval in Windows 2000 is 180 minutes, or three hours.

- **Replication transport**   Remember that intra-site replication always uses RPC over TCP/IP. However, site links refer specifically to inter-site replication. Inter-site replication uses RPC over TCP/IP except in cases in which sites cannot communicate using TCP/IP. In these cases, SMTP is used for inter-site replication.

- **Link cost**   KCC uses link cost as a part of determining replication. Link cost is a relative value given to the cost of the link to reflect available bandwidth or cost of bandwidth.

on the Job

Remember two things here. Link cost is the relative cost; the values can range from 1 to 32,767 (default is 100). Therefore, assess your current links (or planned links) and ensure that you begin with costs somewhere in the mid-range. Additionally, remember to use the same guidelines for each site link—consistency of your definition will help ensure efficient use of resources during replication. For instance, you may want to give all T1 connections a cost of 100 and all 56K dial-up connections a cost of 1000.

EXERCISE 7-3

Site Link and Replication Configuration

In this exercise, we'll configure the site link you created in the last exercise.

1. In Windows 2000 Server, click Start | Programs | Administrative Tools | Active Directory Sites and Services.
2. Click the + to the left of Sites to expand the tree.
3. With Sites expanded, click the + to the left of Inter-Site Transports to expand the tree.
4. Click IP.
5. Right-click the site link you just created, and select Properties from the context menu.
6. The site link has three property sheets: General, Object, and Security. Select the General tab.

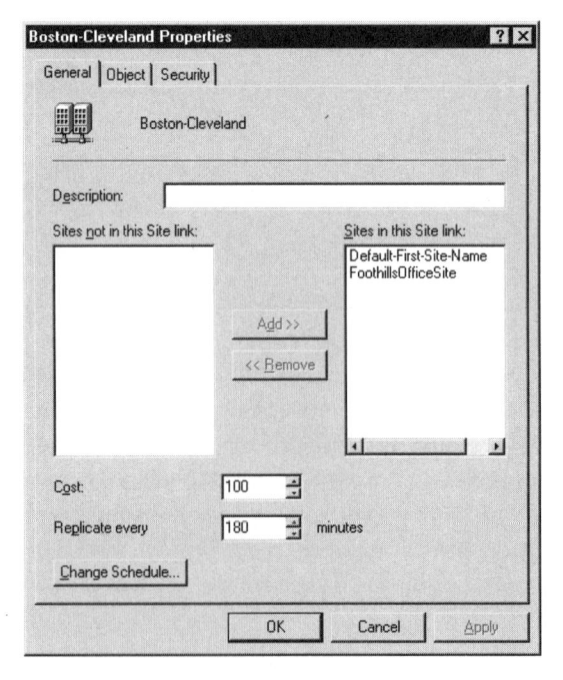

7. Notice the default values for Cost (100) and replication interval found in the Replicate Every box (180 minutes).

8. Click the Change Schedule button to display the replication schedule dialog box.
9. As shown in the next illustration, select a replication schedule or leave the default values.

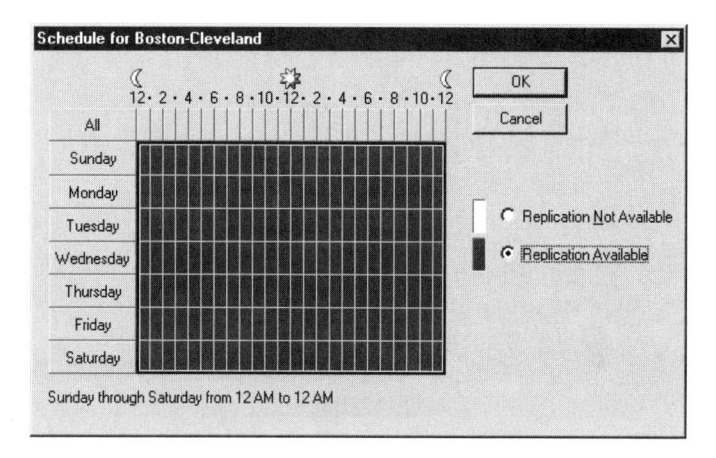

10. Click OK to accept changes to the Replication Schedule.
11. Click OK to accept changes to the site link configuration.

Organizations Units

Unlike sites, organizational units are logical groupings. Organizational units can contain users, computers, printers, or other organizational units. OUs are used for delegation of administration.

Planning organization units should be based on the roles within an organization. For instance, all warehouse computers, users, and printers could be placed in an OU. All network administrators or all external sales representatives could be placed in an OU. There are three ways to delegate administration through OUs: by physical location, by business unit, or by role.

OUs organized by physical location could be OUs such as North America, South America, and Europe, or Seattle, Denver, Atlanta, and Boston. If your company has several campuses in one city, it could be East Campus, West Campus, River Campus, and Hill Campus.

OUs organized by business unit could include all objects (computers, users, printers) belonging to Human Resources, Marketing, Engineering, and so on.

OUs can also be organized by role. For instance, administration of all printers could be delegated to a group of administrators. They would manage and administrate everything related to printers for your organization.

The steps for planning an OU structure are as follows:

1. Create OUs to delegate administration.
2. Create OUs to hide objects.
3. Create OUs for Group Policy.
4. Understand the impact of changing OU structures after deployment.

These steps should be followed in the order given. There is only one way to delegate administration, but several ways to create Group Policy. Therefore, deciding how to delegate administration should be the basis for all OU planning.

In previous versions of Windows NT, the only delegation of administration that could be done was through built-in local groups. These built-in groups have predefined permissions and capabilities. They were not flexible and could not be modified. Windows 2000 provides far more flexibility. As such, it is critical to create a well-defined plan before implementing OUs.

exam
Watch

You're likely to encounter a number of scenarios on the MCP exam that pertain to OUs. Make sure you fully understand OUs and how they relate to sites, domains, and network infrastructure.

Group Policies

Sound Group Policy planning can greatly ease the administrative work once a network is implemented. The following are some guidelines for planning Group Policies. More detailed information regarding Group Policies will be covered in Chapter 10.

1. Minimize the number of Group Policy objects that apply to users and computers.

- Group Policy objects are downloaded to a computer during startup and to a user at logon.
- Avoid creating unintended security conflicts.

2. Identify which Group Policy settings you want to change from their default values.
3. Identify and describe the impact of changing the settings for the Group Policy.
4. Determine if there are any special security requirements and identify how Group Policy should be configured to meet those needs.

Group Policy planning should incorporate the same planning principles that have been discussed throughout this book. Identifying the needs of the organization, identifying the risks to data and network security, and implementing Group Policies to mitigate those risks are the three major steps. It is critical to remember that sometimes less is more, especially in the case of Group Policies. Too many Group Policies or too many customized Group Policies can make administration more complex and create unexpected security holes through conflicting policy enforcement at logon.

There are nine Group Policy security settings:

- Account Policies
- Local Policies
- Event Log
- Restricted Groups
- Systems Services
- Registry
- File System
- Public Key Policies
- Internet Protocol Security Policies on Active Directory

SCENARIO & SOLUTION

What are the two main network traffic considerations for sites?	User logon and replication
What are the two main considerations for domain planning?	Administrative control, unique requirements
If a replication connection breaks due to hardware failure, what must you do?	Nothing, the KCC will create a new connection object.
Your company has four domains. How many sites must you create?	Sites are physical groupings, and domains are logical groupings. There is no necessary correlation.
Your company has four departments and six locations. How many OUs should you create?	The decision should be based on how network functions are managed. If managed by role, create four OUs; if managed by location, create six OUs.
Legal department users should not have access to Control Panel on any computer they work on.	Place users in a user group. Use Group Policy settings to enforce computer settings at logon.

CERTIFICATION OBJECTIVE 7.04

Securing the Active Directory

In this section, we'll learn about how to secure the network and the components of Active Directory. As we've learned, Active Directory is the foundation for controlling security on the network. Thus, we'll review several methods of managing security through Active Directory including how permissions and ownership are managed, and how delegation can be used within the Active Directory structure.

Permissions Inheritance

As we have discussed, all objects in Active Directory have an access control list (ACL) comprised of access control entries (ACE). Access control information is written to the object's security descriptor when the object is created.

After an object is created, its security information can be changed by the owner or by a user who has the owner's permission to change it. Changes can also come from changes to the security descriptor of the parent object.

Some objects can contain other objects. For instance, a folder can contain many files as well as other folders. A file, in this case, would be a child object of the parent object, folder.

Permissions can be explicit, inherited, or inheritable. Each is discussed later. It is important to understand how permissions are set to maintain a secure environment. Permissions can be acquired through inheritance and are called *inherited permissions*. Permissions that are directly placed on an object are called *explicit permissions*.

One of the most powerful features in Windows 2000 is the automatic propagation of inheritable permissions. In Windows NT, permissions were only inherited at the time the object was created. In Windows 2000, permissions automatically propagate. This means that if changes are made to permissions at the top-most level of the tree, these changes to the DACL are propagated to the subfolders and files (child objects) automatically.

Permissions on a parent object that apply to the child objects are called inheritable permissions. There are two check boxes in this dialog box that determine how permissions will propagate.

- Allow inheritable permissions from parent to propagate to this object
- Reset permissions on all child objects and enable propagation of inheritable permissions

Allow Inheritable Permissions from Parent to Propagate to This Object

Selecting the Allow Inheritable Permissions from Parent to Propagate to This Object check box causes the inheritable permissions of the parent object to be inherited by the child object. Removing the check mark from this box causes the child object to have only its own default permissions, depending on the type of object.

Inherited permissions cannot be changed by the owner of a child object. Changes can be made only by the owner (or those authorized by the owner) of the parent object. The owner of the child object can only choose to inherit or not inherit permissions from the parent but cannot modify the inheritable permissions in any way.

The owner of a child object can also add explicit permissions to the object's DACL. For instance, you may want to add the Marketing Group with Full Control, even though they are not specified in the parent object's permissions.

Explicit permissions are listed before inherited permissions on the assumption that explicit permissions are modifiers of the inherited permissions. Permissions are processed in the order in which they are listed in the ACL.

Reset Permissions on All Child Objects and Enable Propagation of Inheritable Permissions

The owner of a parent object can choose to override the explicit permissions of the child objects. In this case, a check mark is placed in the box next to this option. When this option is selected, automatic propagation removes the explicit permissions of the child objects. It also sets the option to Allow Inheritable Permissions from Parent to Propagate to This Object on all child objects.

This is a powerful tool for securing the network. For instance, suppose at the time of creation, an NTFS folder contained the permissions Full Control for the Everyone Group. Let's also suppose that several folders (child folders) under that (parent) folder were created. At the time of creation, in Windows NT, those child folders would inherit the same permissions—Full Control for Everyone. Let's also suppose that information is confidential and should not be seen by anyone outside the Payroll department. In Windows NT, the permissions would have to be changed for each child folder within the parent. In Windows 2000, you can remove the Everyone Group from the permissions for the parent folder and those changes are automatically propagated to each child folder. Securing network resources can now be automatically applied by changes at the root or parent level rather than having to go through each child object to ensure the resources are secure.

on the job

To view the permissions for an Active Directory object, you must enable the advanced features.

View the Permissions for an Active Directory Object

1. From Windows 2000 Server, click Start | Programs | Administrative Tools.
2. Select Active Directory Users and Computers.
3. Select an object such as a computer or user. Right-click the object and select Properties.
4. Notice that you do *not* have a Securities tab, as you can see in the following illustration.

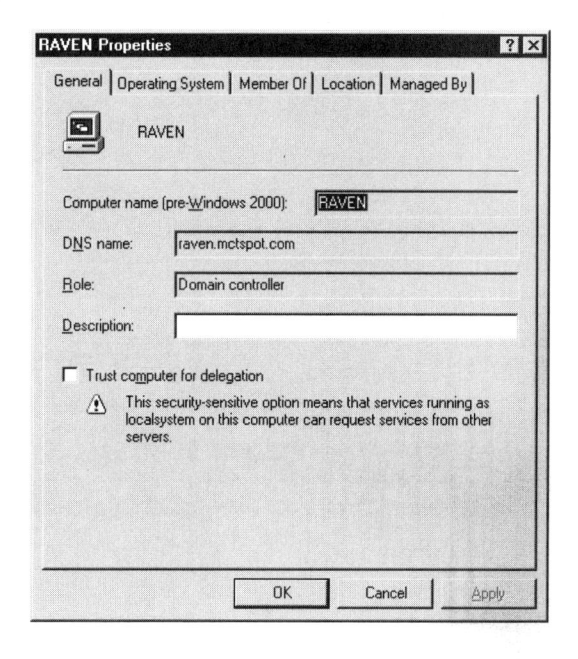

5. In Active Directory Users and Computers, click the View menu and select Advanced Features, as shown here.

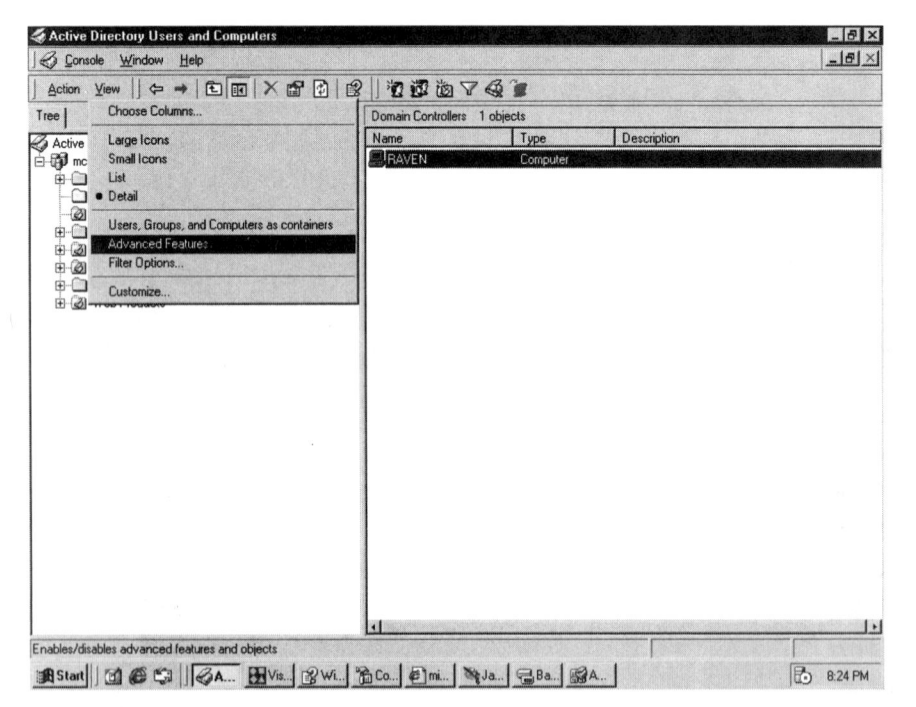

6. Select the same object as before and right-click. Select Properties from the context menu.

7. Notice that you now have a Security tab. Click the Security tab to display permissions for this object.

Securing the Active Directory **325**

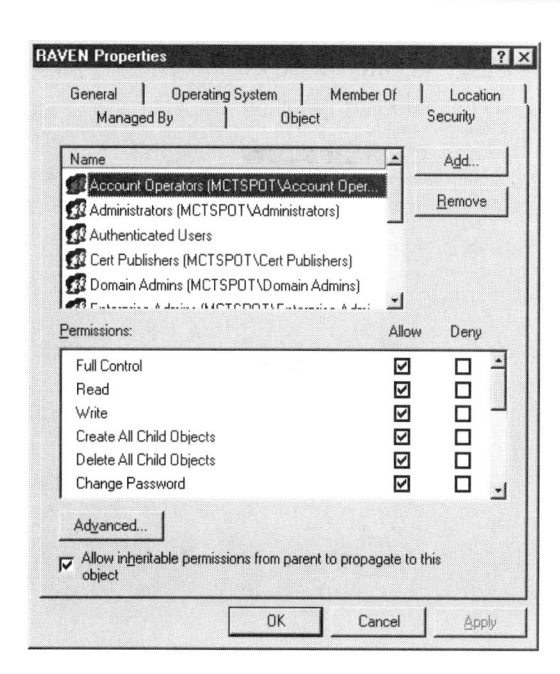

8. Click the Advanced button to view or modify the access control list for the object.

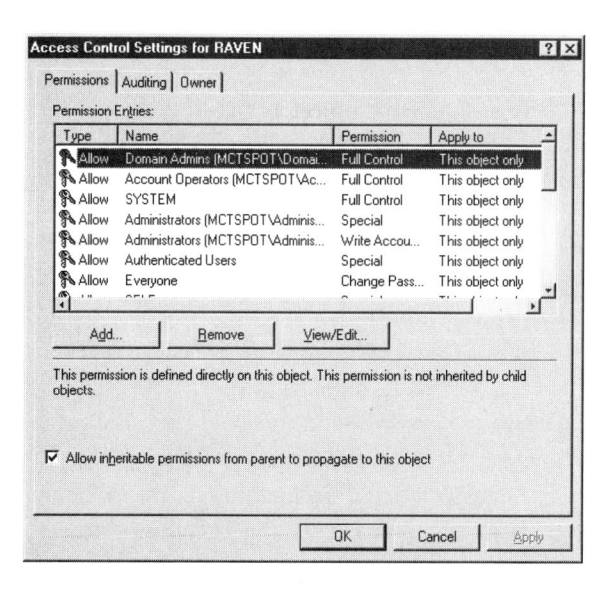

You must select Advanced Features as an added measure of safety. In Windows 2000, you can define permissions to a very granular level of detail. In many cases, default permissions are adequate. In order to change those default permissions, Windows 2000 requires you to enable Advanced Features so you do not inadvertently change permissions on an object.

Permissions are combined if there is a conflict between user and group permissions. There is one exception to this rule. If you deny access to an object for a user or group, that permission will override any other permissions granted related to that object. A user can be a member of a group that has permissions to access a particular object. You can specifically deny that user the right to access that object, even though that user is a member of a group that does have access. In this way, you can specifically deny permissions, when it is appropriate to do so.

Object Ownership

The creator of an object is, by default, the owner. If you create a file on a network share, you are the owner of that file and can set the security for that file. You can decide that Marketing should have Read Only access to the file and that Engineering should have No Access.

The owner of an object can also grant permission for others to Change Permissions. This permission can be withdrawn by the owner and essentially gives another user complete control over that object.

The owner information is stored with the object. For all objects created, the individual's security identifier (SID) is assigned to the owner field. There is one notable exception to this: objects created by one administrator are owned by the group, not the individual. If an object is owned by the administrators group, all members of that group have the inherent right to change permissions for that object. As discussed previously in this book, it is important not to log on to a system as an administrator to do routine tasks. This creates a security risk, but as you can see, it also may have other unintended results. When logged on as administrator, the objects you create are owned by the group by default. This is built into the system and cannot be changed.

Object owners can be changed in two circumstances: if the owner gives another permission to do so and if a member of the administrator group takes ownership. Just as in previous versions of Windows NT, the object owner can give someone (or a group) the Take Ownership permission. In Windows 2000, the permission is called the Modify Owner permission, but it has the same effect.

By default, the Administrators group has the Take Ownership of Files or Other Objects permission. This permission can be granted to other groups, if desired. This enables members of that group to take ownership of a file or folder without the owner's permission.

When a user takes ownership of an object, his or her SID is placed in the Owner field of the object's security descriptor. In the Access Control Settings Owner tab, you can view and modify ownership of an object, if you have adequate permissions to do so. In addition, there is a Replace Owner on All Subcontainers and Objects check box. This allows the user to take ownership of all subfolders and files at once. This is another default permission of the administrator group. Regular users only have this permission if it has been explicitly granted to them. They must have the Take Ownership permission for the parent object and the Take Ownership permission for all child objects as well.

One interesting feature is that there is no option for giving ownership to another user or group. This is to prevent someone from doing something to a file or folder then covering their tracks by assigning ownership to another.

Finally, you can track the Take Ownership events in the system through auditing. In the Access Control Settings for an object, selecting the Auditing tab will allow you to audit all activities related to taking ownership of the parent and child objects.

on the job

Make sure that every object has one user with Full Control permission. This can be a member of the administrator group or it can be the owner. Failure to have one user with Full Control could make the object inaccessible, even to an administrator.

Delegating Administrative Control

Windows 2000 provides the ability to delegate administrative control through the use of organizational units (OUs). Through OUs, the administration of the network can be delegated for efficiency while still maintaining a high level of security. Delegation is achieved through organizational units, per-attribute access control, and access control inheritance.

Delegation should begin with two steps: create top level OUs and delegate full control. Typically this control is limited to the administrator group and allows them to create objects, fix errors, and create additional domain controllers. You can create separate OUs for each unit that needs to be administrated separately, create a local group that represents the highest administrative level for that unit, and assign membership to that group. Members of that group are the new OU administrators.

Permissions are inherited by child objects, so permissions set for the OU by the administrators creating the OU would set the highest permissions allowed by the administrators of the OU. For instance, if you created an Engineering OU, you could set the permissions for the administrators of that OU to create, delete, and modify users and computers for that OU only. Those permissions would propagate to the child objects within that OU by default. However, the administrators of the Engineering OU would not have permissions to create, delete, or modify users in the Sales OU.

The Delegation of Control Wizard is used to grant standardized permissions at the OU level. The Delegation of Control Wizard has four standard options, each accessible in separate screens of the wizard:

- Users or Groups
- Tasks to Delegate
- Active Directory Object Type
- Permissions

In the Tasks to Delegate option, you can access a common list of tasks or you can choose to customize tasks. When you select customize, the Delegation of Control Wizard presents Active Directory Object Types and Permissions.

Securing the Active Directory **329**

EXERCISE 7-5

CertCam 7-5

Using the Delegation of Control Wizard

1. In Windows 2000 Server, click Start | Programs | Administrative Tools | Active Directory Users and Computers.
2. Select the OU for which you want to delegate control and right-click that OU. In this case we are delegating control of the Engineering OU.
3. Select Delegate Control from the context menu.

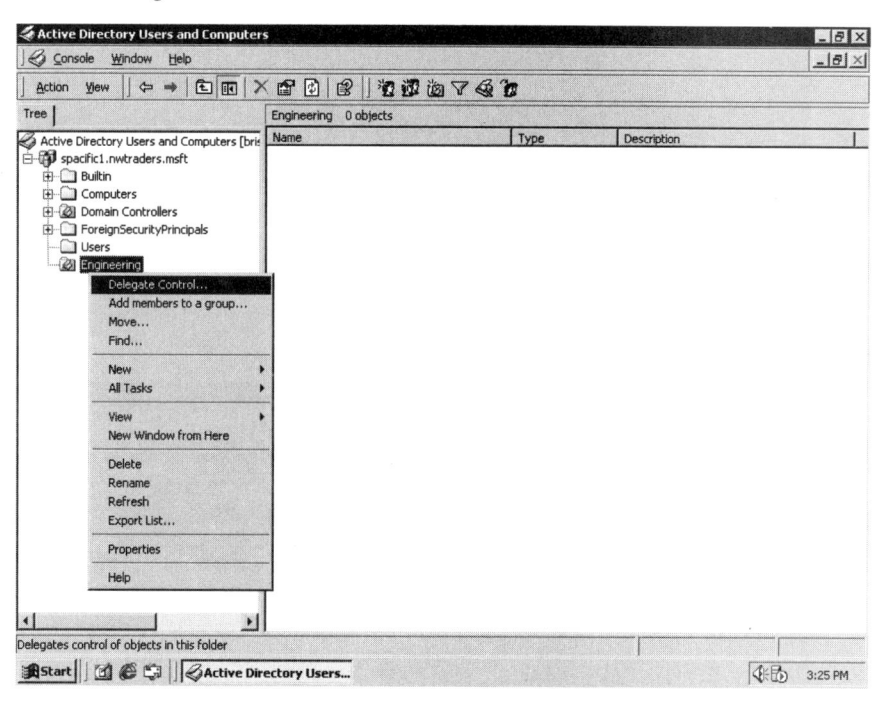

4. The Delegation of Control Wizard will start. Click Next.

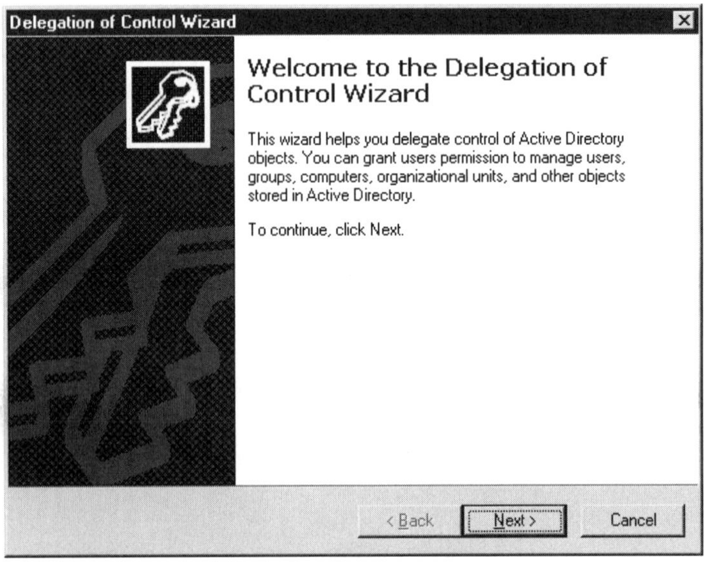
Delegation of Control Wizard
Welcome to the Delegation of Control Wizard
This wizard helps you delegate control of Active Directory objects. You can grant users permission to manage users, groups, computers, organizational units, and other objects stored in Active Directory.
To continue, click Next.
< Back
Next >
Cancel

5. Click the Add button to add users or groups.

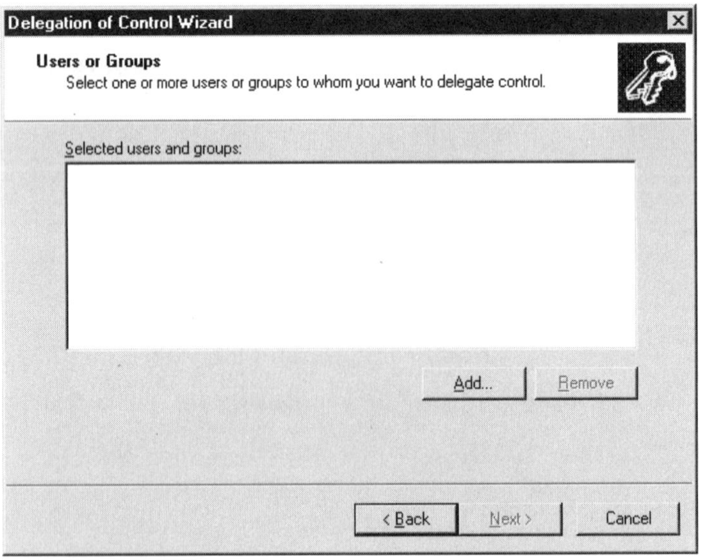
Delegation of Control Wizard
Users or Groups
Select one or more users or groups to whom you want to delegate control.
Selected users and groups:
Add...
Remove
< Back
Next >
Cancel

6. Once you've added users or groups, click OK to continue, as shown in the following illustration.

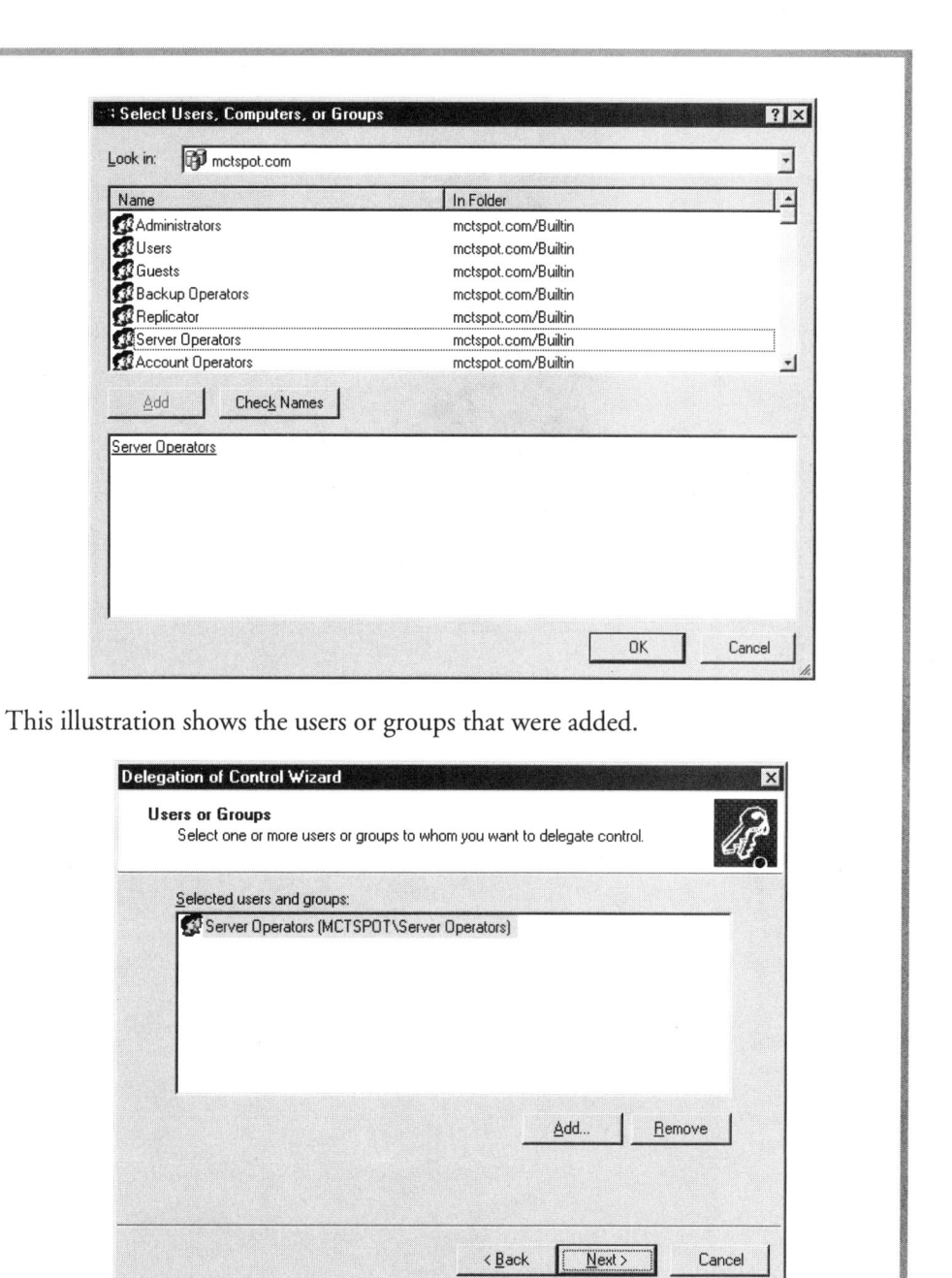

This illustration shows the users or groups that were added.

7. You can select from six predefined tasks or you can select the radio button to create a custom task to delegate. Click Next to continue.

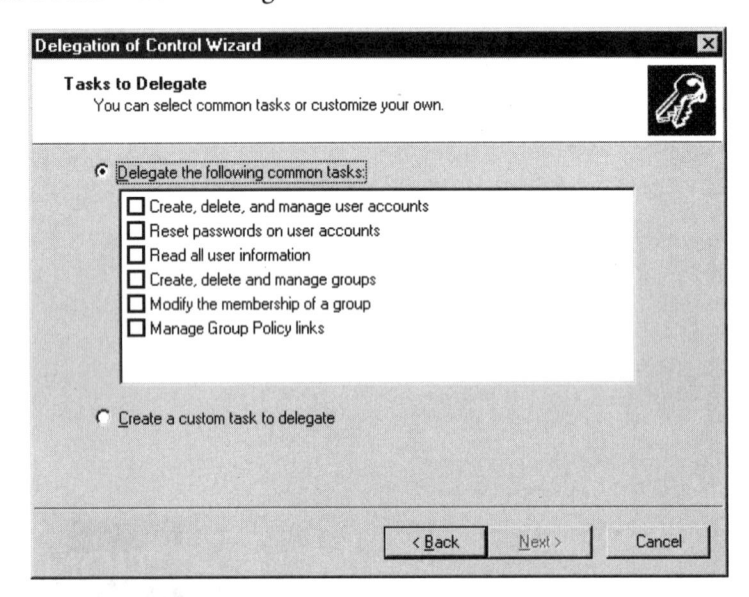

8. Click Finish to close the Delegation of Control Wizard.

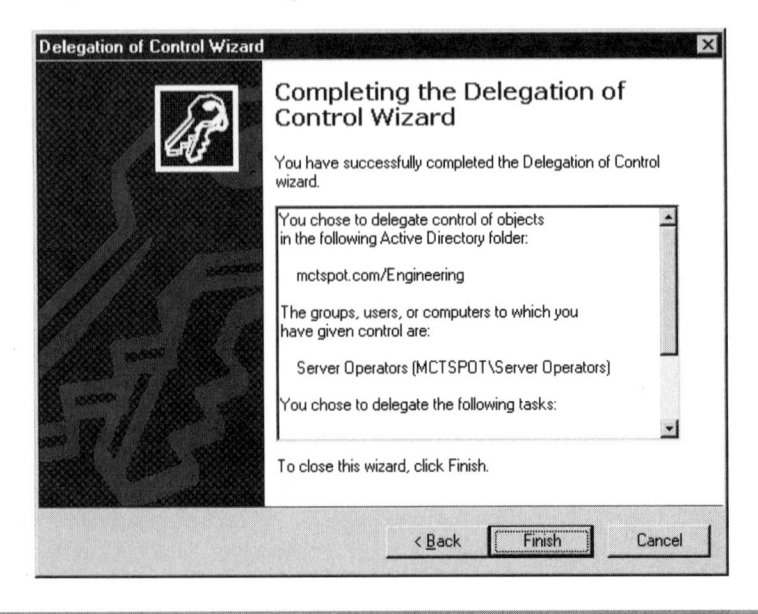

on the job — *You can use the Delegation of Control Wizard to grant permissions at the OU level. To grant more specialized permissions, you must access the object itself.*

Customized Administrative Control

Delegation can be standard or customized. Standard delegation can be managed through the use of the Delegation of Control Wizard that allows administrators to set permissions at the OU level. More specialized permissions can be granted, if needed. To access customized settings, you must enable Advanced Features in the View menu in Active Directory Users and Computers. With Advanced Features enabled, you can now access the Securities tab in the Properties dialog box for any object selected. Permissions can be customized in this way.

Customizing permissions should be performed at a group level. Customizing permissions on individual users or other objects can create an administrative complexity as well as creating unintended security holes.

SCENARIO & SOLUTION

A user cannot find an object on the network.	The user may not have the Read permission for that object.
A user cannot access a network printer, even though the user is a member of the Power Printing group that has access to the printer.	The user may have been specifically denied permission to use the printer.
A member of the administrator group created a file on the network. Who is the owner?	By default, the entire administrative group is the owner of any object created by a member of the administrator group (while logged on as administrator).
What are the permissions on a parent object that apply to the child object?	Inheritable permissions.
Explicit permissions were placed on a child object but now seem to be missing.	The owner of the parent object is selected. Reset permissions on all child objects and enable propagation of inheritable permissions.

CERTIFICATION SUMMARY

Network security is based upon managing access to a wide variety of resources including users, computers, files, folders, and printers. Understanding the security requirements for these network resources and defining a baseline security model helps the network planning process. By applying appropriate restrictions on network resources, the administrator can accomplish two key goals: securing the network from unauthorized use and providing access to resources for users.

Active Directory plays a vital role in network security. As we've seen, Active Directory is involved with security in two primary ways. First, all user authentication information is stored in Active Directory. The AD authenticates users on the network and is the first stop on the security path for a user. Second, AD stores information about the access control list (ACL) for each object in the domain including users, computers, printers, files, folders, and connections. Each object has attributes and these attributes are stored along with the object in AD. This provides directory services for the domain as well as security for the objects in the domain.

Delegation of authority is one of the new features of Windows 2000 and is implemented through the use of organizational units (OU) within Active Directory. The ability to delegate, along with the use of Group Policies, provides for a consistent method of planning and maintaining network security across the domain.

Active Directory is key to a secure network environment and understanding how to properly plan and manage the security features inherent in AD will ensure your network remains secure.

✓ TWO-MINUTE DRILL

Identify the Required Level of Security for Each Resource
- ❑ Unauthorized access can occur through masquerading, impostors, or identity interception.
- ❑ A Denial of Service attack overloads the computer causing normal users to be denied service.
- ❑ Trojan horses and viruses attack data on networks but typically can be avoided by educating users and employing virus-scanning software.
- ❑ Shares that are not secure can expose your entire network to an intruder.

Active Directory Concepts
- ❑ Active Directory is used to authenticate domain users based on user account information.
- ❑ Each object in Active Directory has a discretionary access control list (DACL), sometimes called an access control list (ACL), that is comprised of access control entries (ACE).
- ❑ The global catalog authenticates users during logon in a native, multi-domain model.
- ❑ Trust relationships can be one-way, non-transitive, or two-way, transitive.
- ❑ In a native Windows 2000-based environment, all trusts are two-way, transitive by default.
- ❑ There are five trust relationships: tree-root, parent-child, shortcut, external, and non-Windows Kerberos Realm.
- ❑ Sites are local area networks (LANs) or LANs connected by high-speed links.
- ❑ Organizational units (OU) are logical groupings used for delegation of administration.
- ❑ Replication is the process of keeping the Active Directory information current in all domain controllers.
- ❑ Group Policy objects can be used to manage users and computers in groups.
- ❑ Universal groups are only used in large, multi-domain environments.

Active Directory Planning Considerations

- Windows 2000 is designed to run in a single domain environment, regardless of the size of the organization.
- Multiple domains should be considered when you have existing Windows NT domains you want to preserve, when you want to administer resources separately, or when you want to partition your network to reduce network traffic.
- Sites are used for replication by the Windows 2000 Knowledge Consistency Checker (KCC).
- Intra-site replication uses RPC over TCP/IP as the replication method. Inter-site replication uses RPC or SMTP if two systems or sites cannot communicate using TCP/IP.
- Site links are used for replication and have four components: schedule, interval, transport, and cost.
- Group Policy security templates provide standard security settings, but they can be modified.

Securing the Active Directory

- Permissions can be inherited, inheritable, or explicit.
- Inheritable permissions pass from the parent to the child object.
- Inherited permissions are permissions on a child object that were inherited from the parent object.
- Explicit permissions are permissions that are placed on the object in addition to inherited permissions.
- Permissions propagate according to settings. Typically, permissions propagate to the child objects.
- Objects created by users in the administrative group, when logged on as administrators, are owned by the group. This feature cannot be changed.
- An administrator can take ownership of an object.
- Delegation of permissions is done through delegating control of OUs.
- The Delegation of Control Wizard allows for standard delegation to OUs.
- Customized delegation can be done through modifying the permissions on the particular objects.

SELF TEST

The following questions will help you measure your understanding of the material presented in this chapter. Read all of the choices carefully, as there may be more than one correct answer. Choose all correct answers for each question.

Identify the Required Level of Security for Each Resource

1. A person named Jamie is in the break room talking with Chris and Adam. He mentions that he's a new network administrator hired to evaluate network security. He asks Chris and Adam for their logon names and passwords so he can do some undetected "sniffing" in order to see if he can break the security precautions on the network. What type of risk is this?

    A. Impressor
    B. Social engineering
    C. Influencer
    D. Credential replication

2. Which is *not* a security risk associated with the Internet?

    A. Denial of Service
    B. Malicious signature
    C. Trojan horses
    D. Viruses

3. Users at your company travel frequently. The data they carry is very sensitive data. What steps should you take to ensure that the data remains secure? (Choose the best solution.)

    A. Have all users back up their data to a network share nightly. Enforce strong passwords and educate users about virus protection. Install virus software on all user computers and ensure all removable media is scanned prior to use.
    B. Ensure that all shares are disabled, copy shared files to a secure network location, and encrypt all files using EFS on FAT32 partitions.
    C. Have users convert to NTFS and use EFS to encrypt all secure files on user computers. Enable secure communication protocols through remote access settings.
    D. Have users convert to NTFS and use EFS to encrypt all secure files on user computers, and have users enable Kerberos v5 authentication protocol.

4. Macro viruses are associated with what?
   A. E-mail attachments
   B. Application files
   C. ActiveX or Java applets
   D. Printers

Active Directory Concepts

5. Which are *not* security aspects of Active Directory? (Choose all that apply.)
   A. Defining security boundaries using domains
   B. Supporting security settings using organizational units, and user and group policies
   C. Providing protocol authentication
   D. Providing delegation of administration
   E. Supporting native Windows 2000 non-Kerberos authentication

6. What are the three directory partitions of the global catalog?
   A. Domain directory partition, schema directory partition, and configuration directory partition
   B. Domain directory partition, configuration directory partition, and replication directory partition
   C. Schema directory partition, configuration directory partition, and replication directory partition
   D. DNS directory partition, DHCP directory partition, and schema directory partition
   E. DNS directory partition, DHCP directory partition, and IP directory partition

7. Which of the following statements describes the user authentication process in Windows 2000?
   A. A PDC or a BDC is required for logon in a native Windows 2000 network. If the PDC is not available, logon credentials are replicated from the BDC to the client machine and the user is logged on using cached credentials.
   B. The KCC is required for network logon. If no KCC is available, the Kerberos v5 protocol is used to authenticate the user from cached information.

C. The global catalog is required for network logon. If no local global catalog is present, a global catalog on a remote site can be used for logon authentication. If no global catalog is available at all, a user will be logged on using cached information.

D. The Active Directory schema is used for authentication using the Kerberos v5 protocol. In a mixed environment, the schema uses either Kerberos v5 or NTLM, depending on which protocol responds to the KCC.

8. Delegation of administration is accomplished through which Windows 2000 component?

   A. Organizational units
   B. Site links
   C. Object permissions
   D. Access Configuration Entries

9. Which is the default method of replication in Windows 2000?

   A. Multimaster
   B. Store-and-forward
   C. Store-and-hold
   D. Push
   E. Pull
   F. Push-Pull Timed Interval
   G. State-based
   H. Master Replication Protocol

Active Directory Planning Considerations

10. Your company has 14 branch locations and five core groups: Human Resources (HR), Marketing/Sales (MS), Engineering, Manufacturing, and Corporate. Based on this information, what factors would you use in planning your organizational units?

    A. The 14 branch locations would become the OUs for the domain. Each branch administrator would be given control over their OU and they would create sites for each of the five core groups.

    B. The five core groups would become the OUs for the domain. Each of the 14 branch locations would have to create local OUs that reflect the overall corporate OU structure.

340 Chapter 7: Analyzing Security Requirements

    C. The five core groups would become the OUs for the domain. All resources from each group would be placed in its respective OU and administration of each OU would be delegated to ease administration.

    D. The 14 branch locations would become sites. Each site can contain unlimited OUs as long as each OU has a contiguous namespace within the forest. The five core groups would be assigned through Group Policy objects in Active Directory.

11. Which protocol is used for site replication? (Choose all that apply.)

    A. SMTP
    B. RDP
    C. TCP/IP
    D. RPC
    E. IPSec

12. Your company is changing rapidly. Every weekday for the past month, you've been asked to add or remove users from different departments. You have three local buildings connected by a high-speed backbone. You have two international offices connected by a slower, dedicated WAN connection. If your site link replication interval was set to 7200, what are some likely network behaviors you would expect to see?

    A. Users at local offices would have trouble logging on because the slow WAN link replication would degrade system performance.

    B. Users at remote offices may have trouble logging on because the replication interval is so long. A security risk could be created because users who are no longer valid would still be authorized until the next replication cycle. Local users would experience no difference in network performance.

    C. Users at local offices would notice decreased local logon authentication performance, but once on the network they would experience normal performance. Remote users would have no trouble logging on but would notice decreased system performance on the network.

    D. The users at both local and remote locations would experience decreased system performance. SMTP would be used for the remote office and therefore the replication would be slower and less secure than if using TCP/IP. Security would be compromised as a result.

13. What is the impact of creating multiple Group Policies that apply to a particular user or computer?

    A. User logon could be very slow and user permissions may not be configured as desired.

    B. User logon could be very slow, but user permissions will be correctly applied.

C. User logon will be normal, but user permissions may not be configured as desired.

D. User logon will be normal and user permissions will be configured as desired.

Securing the Active Directory

14. What is the impact on a child object of selecting the Reset Permissions on All Child Objects and Enable Propagation of Inheritable Permissions check box? (Choose all that apply.)

    A. Explicit permissions on the object will be overwritten.
    B. Inherited permissions on the object will be overwritten.
    C. Inheritable permissions on the object will be reset.
    D. Implicit permissions on the object will be overwritten.

15. The View | Advanced Features function in Active Directory Users and Computers allows you to do which of the following?

    A. View the Advanced Features of a site link connection.
    B. View the Advanced Features of the domain configuration.
    C. View the Advanced Features of the replication interval for a link object.
    D. View the Advances Features of the Security settings for a user or computer object.

16. Lisa is logged on to her computer as a regular user. However, Lisa is also a network administrator. She uses the runas command to run a procedure as a network administrator without logging off her normal user account. In this procedure, Lisa creates a new file object. By default, who is the owner of the object?

    A. Lisa / Normal User
    B. Lisa / Network Admin
    C. Normal user group
    D. Network Admin group

17. Which is a default permission of the network administrator group by default? (Choose all that apply.)

    A. Ability to take ownership of any object.
    B. Ability to assign ownership to another user of any object.
    C. Ability to replace the owner on all subcontainers and objects.
    D. Ability to modify ownership of an object in Access Control Settings.

LAB QUESTION

You are a Windows 2000 security architect hired by Raven Recruiting, a national IT recruitment firm, to analyze security and provide a security plan for their network that is migrating to Windows 2000.

Personnel and Locations

Raven Recruiting employs approximately 2500 people at 200 branch offices within eight different regions. Each branch office employs 5–20 people and has one branch manager and one IT staff member. Within each region, there is one regional manager. Company headquarters is located in Indianapolis, Indiana. Headquarters staff number approximately 150 and includes accounting, payroll, HR, and IT employees. In addition, there are two sites that process payroll only: San Diego, California and Austin, Texas. Between one and five sales department personnel may exist at onsite customer locations.

Existing WAN Environment

Indianapolis is connected to all other locations by a fractional T1 (128 Kbps). Each outlying location exists as a single IP subnet with one router. All locations employ TCP/IP as the transport/network protocol. Servers are configured with static IP addresses, and all clients are assigned their IP configuration using Dynamic Host Configuration Protocol (DHCP). There is no WAN connection, other than the Internet, between onsite customer locations and company headquarters.

Existing Network Resources

Indianapolis houses 28 Windows NT 4.0 and 4 UNIX servers with the following roles:

- 1 certificate server
- 2 file/print servers
- 25 terminal servers
- 1 IIS server running Outlook Web Access (OWA) (OWA1)
- 2 domain controllers (DC1 and DC2)
- 3 Exchange 5.5 servers
- 4 UNIX servers running Oracle
- 1 RAS server (RAS1)

Accounting, payroll, sales, and HR use Windows 98 as their client, whereas IT uses Windows NT 4.0 Workstation. All sales personnel use laptop computers. Each branch office has one computer with a modem that is used to dial in to headquarters and connect to a Terminal Server. Applicants access OWA1 to apply for jobs by posting resumes to a Recruiting public folder. All branch offices, including branch IT personnel, require secure access to the Recruiting public folder. Off-site employees connect to OWA1 to access their e-mail and submit time reports. San Diego and Austin access the UNIX servers at corporate headquarters to submit payroll information. All branch managers and HR personnel have access to a shared HR folder on a file/print server located at corporate headquarters for retrieving and updating confidential HR information. Sales personnel routinely send e-mail communication through the Internet to employees and customers, including weekly work schedules.

Goals

- Upgrade all computers (except OWA1) to Windows 2000 and create one Active Directory tree.
- There should be no change to the WAN.
- Easily accommodate future growth.
- Require secure communication to HR folder, Oracle database, and Terminal Servers.

As part of your security analysis, you need to answer the following questions:

1. What is the primary security requirement for Raven Recruiting?

2. Identify the different groups of users that need access to the network by location and the method by which they gain access. Which of these methods requires secure communication? Which requires authentication?

3. Which permissions should you grant for the HR folder? Groups to include are Network Administrators, HR Users, and Branch Managers. Standard NTFS permissions include Full Control, Read, Read and Write, and No Access.

344   Chapter 7:   Analyzing Security Requirements

SELF TEST ANSWERS

Identify the Required Level of Security for Each Resource

1. ☑ **B.** An attempt to gain logon information or other security information from legitimate users through conversation or other seemingly innocent means is called social engineering.
   ☒ **A** is not correct. An impostor, not an impressor, is one who poses as a user on the network. Although this person is pretending to be someone he is not, there is a more precise term for this type of attack. **C** is not correct. Although a person attempting social engineering may have to be quite influential to gain the desired information, this is not a category of risk. **D** is not correct. Unauthorized users may attempt to capture user credential and re-use them (replay attack), but this is not called credential replication. In addition, what Jamie attempted to do is considered social engineering because he was attempting to gain legitimate user information though social means.

2. ☑ **B.** The attack type, known as *malicious mobile code*, is auto-executing code such as Active X control or Java applet loaded from the Internet. It is not known as a malicious signature.
   ☒ **A** is not correct. A Denial of Service attack is an attack associated with Web sites that causes loss of service to normal users, overloads servers, and can cause loss of data and revenue. **C** is not correct. A Trojan horse attack can occur when a user downloads a program from the Internet for a benign purpose. A Trojan horse will appear to be benign and may have very destructive capabilities. **D** is not correct. Viruses can be downloaded as part of a file from the Internet or can be attached to e-mail. E-mail can be internal to your company or can be external and travel through the Internet.

3. ☑ **C.** Users who travel typically use laptops to access the corporate network. Installing the NTFS file system and encrypting sensitive data using EFS will protect the files. Using secure communication protocols (depending on method of remote access) will secure the data transmissions as well.
   ☒ **A** is not the best solution. Although these precautions are good measures, they do not ensure the safety of sensitive information in user files, especially when accessing the network remotely. **B** is not correct. Disabling shares does not significantly heighten security on user computers, unless permissions on those shares are excessive. More importantly, EFS can only be used on NTFS, not FAT or FAT32 file systems. **D** is not correct. Using NTFS and EFS is correct, but users cannot enable Kerberos v5 authentication. This is the default method of user authentication in Windows 2000 and is not enabled or disabled by users.

4. ☑ **B.** Applications that use macro language code, such as Microsoft Word, can have viruses that use the macro code language to cause problems to files associate with that application.
☒ **A** is not correct. Viruses are often sent as e-mail attachments. Although macro viruses are often delivered as part of the e-mail attachment, it is the attachment (application file) that contains the virus, not the e-mail message itself. **C** is not correct. ActiveX or Java applets can be downloaded and cause problems, though these are not considered macro viruses. To protect against rogue applets, ensure the component is digitally signed or from a known, secure source. **D** is not correct. Printers are not associated with viruses.

Active Directory Concepts

5. ☑ **C and E.** Active Directory does not provide protocol authentication. In a native Windows 2000, all users authentication uses Kerberos v5 authentication.
☒ **A** is not correct. Defining security boundaries using domains is one aspect of Active Directory. **B** is not correct. Active Directory does support security settings using organizational units, and user and group policies. **D** is not correct. Through organizational units, Active Directory provides the ability to delegate network administration.

6. ☑ **A.** The three partitions are domain directory partition, schema directory partition, and configuration directory partition.
☒ **B** through **E** are not correct. There are no replication directory partitions, DNS directory partitions, DHCP directory partitions, or IP directory partitions in Windows 2000.

7. ☑ **C.** The global catalog is required for network logon. If one is not available, either locally or remotely, the user's cached credentials will be used.
☒ **A** is not correct. The primary domain controller (PDC) and backup domain controller (BDC) are controllers used in down-level Windows NT domains. In Windows 2000, PDCs and BDCs are replaced by multi-master domain controllers. **B** is not correct. The KCC, or Knowledge Consistency Checker, is used for site replication of Active Directory information. In a native Windows 2000 environment, Kerberos v5 is always used for authentication and is not connected to KCC activities. **D** is not correct. The schema describes the organization of the Active Directory. It manages all objects and their attributes. It is not directly involved with user logon authentication.

8. ☑ **A.** Organizational units (OU) are used to delegate authority for network administration in Windows 2000.
   ☒ **B** is not correct. Site links are used to define the replication path for Active Directory information. **C** is not correct. Object permissions are used to determine which users (or other objects) have access to that object. When administration is delegated, the group to whom administration was delegated may have permission to change permissions for various objects. **D** is not correct. Each object in Active Directory has an access control list that is comprised of access control entries. These are not used for delegating administration.

9. ☑ **G.** Windows 2000 uses state-based replication in native mode. In this type of replication, the state of the Active Directory information is used by each domain controller to determine how current its own information is. This type of replication does not keep a change control log.
   ☒ **A** is not correct. Multimaster is a replication method but is not the default method used in Windows 2000. **B** is not correct. Store-and-forward is a replication method but is not the default method used in Windows 2000. **C** is not correct. There is no Store-and-hold replication method. **D** is not correct. Push replication is a replication method but is not the default method used in Windows 2000. **E** is not correct. Pull replication is a replication method but is not the default method used in Windows 2000. **F** is not correct. Push-Pull Timed Interval is not a replication method. **H** is not correct. There is no Master Replication Protocol. Replication occurs using either Remote Procedure Call for intra-site replication or RPC over TCP/IP or SMTP for inter-site replication.

Active Directory Planning Considerations

10. ☑ **C.** The core groups would become the OUs. All users, computers, and other network resources connected to a core group would be placed in the respective OU.
    ☒ **A** is not correct. Locations reflect the physical structure of the company. OUs are used to reflect the logical structure of the company. In addition, an administrator would not create sites within a branch for groups. Sites are created for physical networks connected by high-speed links. **B** is not correct. The five core groups would become the OUs for the domain, but each branch does not need to copy this configuration, as this applies to the entire company structure. **D** is not correct. The 14 branches may become sites if each is connected with slower WAN links. Each site can contain unlimited OUs, but OUs should reflect the organization of the entire company, not just each particular site. Finally, contiguous namespace has to do with domains, not with OUs.

Self Test Answers **347**

11. ☑ **A, C,** and **D.** SMTP is Simple Mail Transport Protocol and can be used for inter-site replication if TCP/IP is not available. Typically, sites that can send and receive e-mail through the Internet are capable of inter-site replication using SMTP. TCP/IP is the transport protocol used with RPC for intra-site replication as well as for inter-site replication. Remote Procedure Call protocol is used with TCP/IP for intra-site replication.
☒ **B** is not correct. RDP is remote desktop protocol used with Terminal Services. **E** is not correct. IPSec is used with L2TP to encrypt data on a network.

12. ☑ **B.** A replication interval of 7200 minutes, or five days, would cause new users to not have access to the network until the changes were replicated. Old users who may have been removed or had permissions changed would still have access until replication occurred. Therefore, users at the remote sites may have trouble logging on and there is a security risk because old users have not yet been removed. Unless your network users groups (and permissions) are fairly static, you would not want to set replication interval for such a long period of time. Local users will experience no difference because the replication interval for intra-site replication was not specified.
☒ **A** is not correct. The local LANs are connected by a high-speed link. Therefore, they would be considered one site. Intra-site replication would be performed differently than inter-site replication. The question refers to site link replication, the inter-site replication that will occur between the main offices and the international locations. Local users would not have trouble logging on. The slow WAN link would not necessarily degrade system performance. Typically, in these situations, the replication is scheduled for "off" hours when network traffic is low so that the replication process does not take network bandwidth away from users and applications. **C** is not correct. Users at local offices would not notice decreased local logon authentication performance. Remote users would have trouble logging on, due to permissions not being updated regularly. If a user could gain access to the network, they would not experience decreased system performance. **D** is not correct. The users at both local and remote locations would not experience decreased system performance. System performance should not be impacted by a long replication interval. There was no mention as to whether or not the remote sites could use TCP/IP. SMTP is used only when TCP/IP cannot be used.

13. ☑ **A.** Group Policies are applied at the time of logon. If multiple Group Policies are applied, it could slow down the user logon and authentication process. If multiple Group Policies are applied, their permissions may be in conflict and may cause a user to have permissions that were not as intended.
☒ **B** is not correct. User logon will likely be slower but permissions may not be applied as desired, due to conflicts in various Group Policy settings. **C** is not correct. User logon is likely to be slower. Permissions are likely to have unintended settings due to conflicts in Group Policy settings. **D** is not correct. User logon is likely to be slower and permissions are likely to contain conflicts.

Securing the Active Directory

14. ☑ **A and B.** Explicit permissions are set on an object after inherited permissions are set. Selecting the reset permissions check box will overwrite and reset all explicit permissions. Inherited permissions are passed from the parent object to the child object. Choosing to reset permissions and enable propagation of inheritable permissions means that permissions will be copied from the parent to the child. This results in the child object's inherited permissions being reset.

    ☒ **C** is not correct. Inheritable permissions are permissions on the parent object that may be passed on to child objects. Selecting the reset permissions check box will not impact inheritable permissions. **D** is not correct. Implicit permissions is not a legitimate permissions category in Windows 2000.

15. ☑ **D.** In Active Directory Users and Computers, clicking the View menu and selecting Advanced Features enables you to view the Security tab on the object's property sheet. This allows you to view and modify security settings for the object.

    ☒ **A, B,** and **C** are not correct.

16. ☑ **D.** When a member of the network administrators group creates an object, that object is owned by the group, by default. Even though Lisa may be logged on as a normal user, when she uses the runas command, she is logged on as a network administrator for that procedure. Because the file was created during that procedure, the object is owned by the network administrator group by default.

    ☒ **A, B,** and **C** are not correct.

17. ☑ **A, C,** and **D.** Answer **A** is a default permission of the network administrator group. This permission is helpful if a user has ownership of a file or folder and leaves the company. The file or folder is not left inaccessible. Answer **C** is correct. By default, members of the network administrators group can select a check box that enables them to replace the owner on all subcontainers and objects. Answer **D** is correct. To modify the ownership of an object, the Access Control List Owner setting can be changed. However, you cannot give ownership, you can only take ownership, if you have adequate permissions to do so. The network administrators group, by default, has Full Control and permission to take ownership of any object in the network.

    ☒ **B** is not correct. In Windows 2000, you cannot assign ownership of an object. This prevents users from modifying files and then giving ownership to someone else without their explicit knowledge and permission. The only way someone else could get ownership is if they are given explicit permission to change ownership by the object owner *and* they choose to take ownership.

LAB ANSWERS

1. The primary security requirement for Raven Recruiting is secure communication.

2. The different users that need access to the corporate network include applicants (public), employees at onsite customer locations (remote sales personnel), internal employees at corporate headquarters, and internal employees at branch offices. Table 7-3 illustrates the methods by which they currently gain access and the Windows 2000 technologies that could be used to authenticate and secure access.

3. The HR folder contains confidential data and is accessed only by HR, the Branch Managers, and IT. In addition to reliable authentication, communication to the HR folder must be secure. HR and Branch Managers require read and write access to this confidential data so that they can both retrieve and update information, whereas IT should have full control.

TABLE 7-3 Raven Recruiting Network Access Methods

User	Access Method	Windows 2000 Security Technologies That Might Be Applied
Applicants	Internet access to OWA1	Secure Sockets Layer (SSL) for encryption of data; authentication not required
Employees at onsite customer locations	Internet access to OWA1 Internet (to communicate with employees and customers send personal schedules through e-mail)	Encrypted authentication with SSL Digital certificates for encrypting e-mail data and providing digital signatures
Internal employees at corporate headquarters	LAN	Kerberos authentication with IPSec for encryption of all LAN traffic
Internal employees at branch offices	Dial-up RAS LAN/WAN	MS-CHAP authentication with Remote Data Protocol (RDP) for secure Terminal Server connections Kerberos authentication with IPSec for encryption of all LAN traffic

8
Designing a Windows 2000 Security Solution

CERTIFICATION OBJECTIVES

8.01	Design the Placement and Inheritance of Security Policies
8.02	Design an Authentication Strategy
8.03	Design a Public Key Infrastructure
8.04	Design Windows 2000 Network Services Security
✓	Two-Minute Drill
Q&A	Self Test

352 Chapter 8: Designing a Windows 2000 Security Solution

Security risks vary from location to location, covering variances in size and data sensitivity. Some organizations do not deal with particularly important data whereas others contain mission critical information that carries with it the future of the company. Many companies are responsible for supporting only a handful of users and physical locations that deal with relatively trivial information, and therefore may not pay as close attention to security. Meanwhile, other organizations budget hundreds of thousands and even millions of dollars to ward off security threats. Whatever your company is like, having a firm network security knowledge base will assist you in determining your organization's security strategy.

This certification exam will test your ability to analyze your networks' requirements for sound security. Understanding the major aspects of security will prevent many mistakes from occurring in your security strategy development. Moreover, a strong knowledge base developed during planning will greatly increase the success of implementation.

CERTIFICATION OBJECTIVE 8.01

Design the Placement and Inheritance of Security Policies

Organizations vary in size and complexity. Small networks exist with only a few computers, users, and other objects for the Active Directory (AD). On the flip side, there are some organizations with thousands of entries in their AD. With size comes complexity. Deciding where to begin is the first part of the challenge. Determining where to put security policies is a difficult challenge; many of the choices you make in the early stages of placement will be difficult to take back down the road.

The next step is to determine the method to best and most efficiently pass down your policies from one computer to the next on your network. Are there extenuating circumstances that disallow you to enjoy a seamless downward streaming of your policies or is everyone on your network going to have the same permissions? The notion of inherited security policies is both a convenience and a challenge.

Sites

Networks can generally be broken into two categories; local area networks (LANs) and wide area networks (WANs). Each physical location in a LAN or WAN is considered a site.

As an organization expands, it will probably divide into multiple sites. Organizations vary in their geographical scope from regional, to national, to international. WANs are established to allow multiple sites of an organization to communicate with each other. However, it frequently is neither financially rewarding nor time efficient to have one WAN controlling an entire organization. Financially, organizations must consider the fact that network line fees are quite sizable, especially if your communications company charges are based upon frequency and duration. From a management perspective, even if connected on the most sophisticated broadband lines, your company will suffer major lost work time if left waiting for information to transfer to and from a network server to a client or other server at a different site.

Most organizations are approaching the problem of WANs by dividing their networks into smaller parts along the general guidelines of sites, domains, and organizational units. By breaking a network into smaller pieces, your organization will benefit from increased network efficiency by performing many tasks locally. By creating this solution, your organization can avoid the slow process of authentication over the WAN; it can now be done locally. However, if you are going to allow your users to authenticate locally you will first need to make a set of changes to your domain structure.

Domains

Domains harbor all objects on a network, where objects are defined as users, computers, printers, and anything else that can attach to the network. Windows 2000 networks can be based on one domain or several.

There are a number of ways to break up a domain, including geographically and by discipline or department. For example, a company with offices spread over several continents would likely benefit from having multiple domains in place—the alternative is to force everyone, regardless of location, to log in to the same domain. If that domain is located in New York and there is an office in Tokyo, the Tokyo users are required to log in to a New York server each time they begin. This can eat up a ton of resources. This organization should consider setting up a separate domain in Tokyo. Dividing domains by department is another pragmatic way of issuing rights—this way, domains function as security boundaries. For example, the accounting department could have their own domain while the personnel department has their own—if neither department has reason to gain access to the other department's information, keeping them on the same domain is an added security risk.

Generally, objects within a domain share a common set of rules regarding security, groups, and permissions.

Organizational Units

By grouping subnet computers into the same site, a Windows 2000 network can direct the computer to the nearest domain controller. Generally, it is good practice to have a domain controller at each site. The immediate cost of maintenance is outweighed by the convenience and financial reward of having a local controller; this simplifies the management process and increases network transaction speed.

Say that your organization has an international presence with offices spread out over North and South America, Europe, Africa, and Asia. Your company has several divisions—many that are interrelated, and others that are independent. Some of the offices in your organization house several disparate divisions. From a security perspective there would be no reason to allow, for example, the accounting department access to the maintenance department's files, or vice versa.

Each organization must decide the optimal way to handle the structure of their domain. Because each organization is different, there is no one-size-fits-all method for breaking down a domain structure. However, all domain structure decisions will have lasting effects; if your early decisions are incorrect, your organization will suffer.

As we have pointed out, the main decision to make when determining your organizational unit structure involves determining whether to break down your company based on physical locations or based on sites. Alternatively, you could break down your company based on department or discipline. Of course, doing both physical location and departmental division is becoming more popular especially with larger companies that break down a company by site and department. This results in the creation of several domains, but offers a great deal of leverage where administration is concerned.

Design an Encrypting File System (EFS) Strategy

Cryptography is the process of encrypting data to prevent unauthorized parties from viewing or modifying it. It is used for a broad range of files ranging from e-mail messages and documents to online transactions and purchases. Here are some common questions people have on cryptography:

EFS works at the file level to protect data from outside access. If an unencrypted file is copied and pasted into an encrypted folder, it becomes encrypted automatically. If the unencrypted file is placed into an encrypted folder using drag and drop, the file is not automatically encrypted. Only the person who originally encrypted the files is allowed to access these files, with the exception of recovery agents. Protection with EFS spans over a network regardless of location of the data as long as it resides somewhere on the network. This is particularly useful for users who travel and use a notebook computer—if their PC is lost or stolen and they have organization data that should be kept internal, they have little to worry about as long as they used EFS to encrypt those files. The same is true for a group of users who share a computer; if data is not available to all who access a particular PC, EFS should be used to secure data.

SCENARIO & SOLUTION

What does cryptography entail?	Cryptography is comprised of two processes—encryption and decryption.
What is encryption?	The process of scrambling data so that it becomes unreadable—the sender of dta typically does this.
What is decryption?	The process of putting encrypted data back into readable form—the recipient of the data typically does this.

EXERCISE 8-1

Encrypting a Folder Using EFS

The following exercise will show you how to encrypt a folder utilizing Windows 2000's new EFS.

1. Choose the folder or file that you want to encrypt.
2. Right-click the chosen item and pick Properties from the list of options.
3. Click the Advanced button.
4. Select the check box labeled Encrypt Contents to Secure Data and then click OK.

5. A warning will appear that allows you to both confirm the encryption and determine the scope of the encryption, as shown in Figure 8-1. (Note that the default setting selects both the file and the parent folder. If you are saving the file in a folder containing documents that other users access, you will need to change the selection to Encrypt the File Only.)

When designing an organization's strategy to define company policy for EFS, be aware of the ramifications of allowing users to utilize EFS. Determine what level of access users will have to the EFS capabilities of Windows 2000. Keep in mind, however, that if you over-empower your users, the risk of encrypting files that should not be encrypted increases. On the other hand, if you do not give enough encryption capability to users, they will be forced to leave important files unencrypted.

EFS boosts the security found in the NT File System (NTFS) encryption, making it more secure and offering much faster encryptions and decryptions of files that are EFS enabled. Unlike a typical public key decryption procedure, the decryption in EFS occurs automatically; users can access files they've encrypted with EFS like they would access any other file or folder.

An author of a document who uses EFS is the only person who will ever be able to open the document, with the exception of recovery agents

EFS is used strictly to encrypt file and folder data. System files as well as compressed files cannot be encrypted.

CERTIFICATION OBJECTIVE 8.02

Design an Authentication Strategy

Implementing a strong authentication strategy in your organization could be the most important aspect of your network's security. Authentication is the process of verifying

FIGURE 8-1

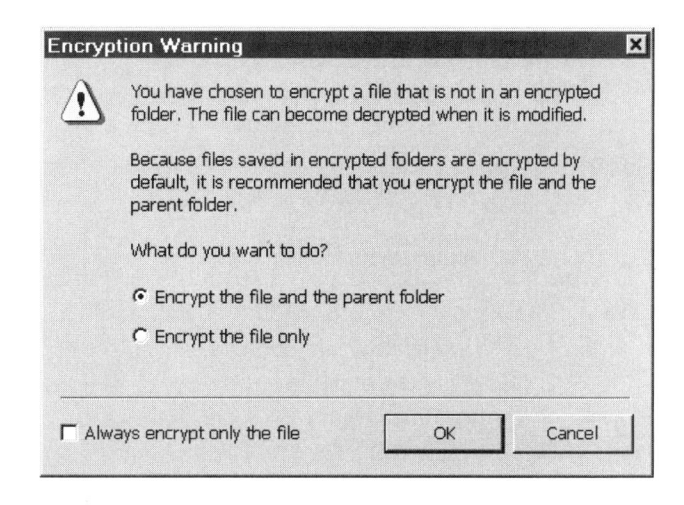

After selecting "Encrypt contents to secure data," the user is given a choice to either encrypt the file and the parent folder or just the file

the identity of anyone trying to use a network. By authenticating, the user is granted a set of rights that vary depending on his or her needs; needs are determined by the network administrator. If rights are assigned intelligently, the user can accomplish anything he or she needs with the rights he or she has been assigned. If rights are assigned carelessly, the user may have too little or too much access to the network, which could mean trouble later on. Next we outline some of the key items to consider when determining your organizations' authentication policy.

Select Authentication Methods

A network authenticator is a special packet that contains information that is unique to the sender or client—and incidentally, one of the most important aspects of network security. By authenticating a user you give that user rights within the network. When it is done properly, authenticating once will get the user through your network without any hitches—the user can go about his or her normal work and not be interrupted by needing to authenticate again for access to certain areas of the network with higher security.

Microsoft has greatly increased the number of methods for authentication in Windows 2000. Determining which methods to employ depends on the structure and needs of each organization. The following section will describe several of the options available. Some of the options are new, others have improved features from older varieties, and still others have been around for a long time and have not been changed for Windows 2000.

Certificate-based Authentication

Certificates meet a basic security need in Windows 2000. They authenticate Active Directory users—in other words, they verify whether the person who is logging on is that person or an impersonator.

An important note: certificates only work if they are used properly. While this may sound redundant or intuitive, there is subtle meaning behind it. For instance, a particular application or service such as e-mail might fail to query a certificate to verify whether a user is in fact who he says he is. This kind of problem is likely the fault of the administrator who failed to set up the certificates to work with e-mail services. Of course, your organization may not be worried about e-mail certificates; in that case you have nothing to worry about by not having a certificate-based authentication.

As Figure 8-2 illustrates, each certificate contains the following:

- Public key of the entity presenting the certificate.
- A start date and expiration date.
- Identifying information about the certificate's entity.

Windows 2000 also uses certificates to support smart card authentication. Smart cards carry private key data that associates the user of the card with an account in the Active Directory using a digital certificate. Further discussion of smart card usage in Windows 2000 will occur later in this chapter.

EFS, discussed earlier, also uses digital certificates. A certificate is used to encrypt the data, ensuring that if the files or folders are stolen from the drive or if the actual drive is stolen, then files and folders are not decrypted.

FIGURE 8-2

A certificate in Windows 2000

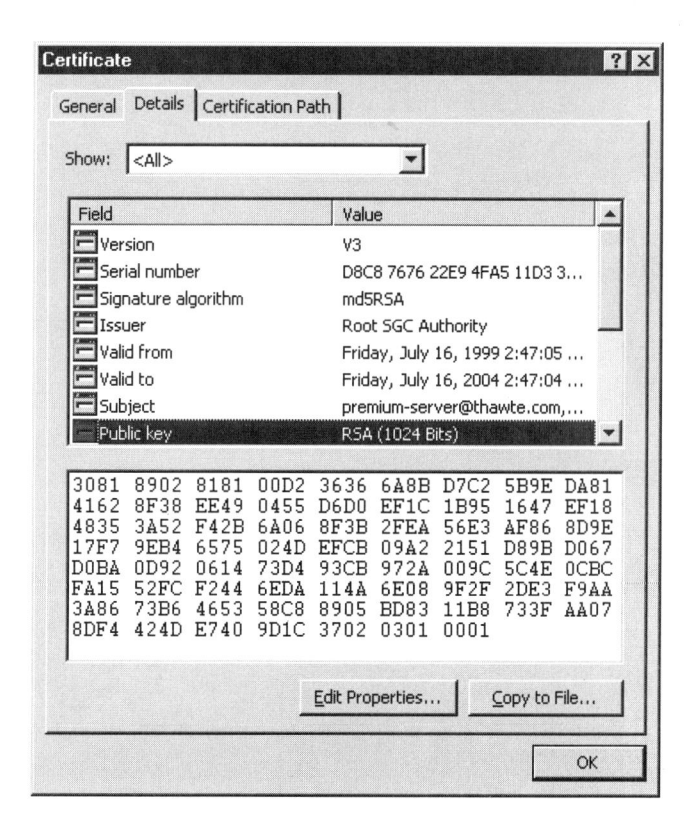

Kerberos Authentication

Microsoft introduces Kerberos in Windows 2000 as a new authentication protocol declaring tighter security and enhanced network efficiency. Kerberos is the standards-based authentication protocol in Windows 2000. Kerberos is a vast improvement when compared to NT LAN Manager (NTLM), the authentication protocol found in Windows NT 4.0. Improvements include a quicker execution time for the authentication process and a higher grade of security, largely due to a more robust authentication mechanism. Streamlining jobs and eliminating redundancy leave the user with a much faster session time and the traffic caused by using resources on your network is greatly reduced.

When a client logs in to the network, a contact with the Kerberos Distribution Center (KDC) is established. When the user needs to access a resource such as a printer for the first time, the KDC is contacted for a session ticket that enables access to the resource. Once this ticket has been granted, the user never needs to contact the KDC again for the duration of the network session (see Figure 8-3). In the section on NTLM, note the difference between the Kerberos procedure and NTLM's method—you will see a clear reason why Kerberos is so much faster and more organized.

Because Kerberos is not backward compatible with earlier versions of Windows, you cannot use it to manage authentication on any network computers other than those running Windows 2000.

FIGURE 8-3

NTLM requires that authentication be processed by the PCC or BDC for each request

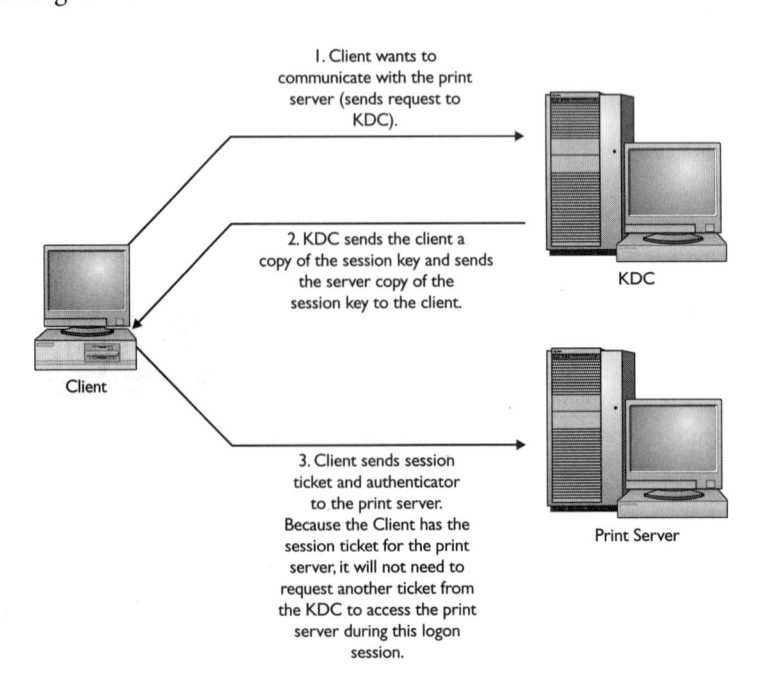

1. Client wants to communicate with the print server (sends request to KDC).
2. KDC sends the client a copy of the session key and sends the server copy of the session key to the client.
3. Client sends session ticket and authenticator to the print server. Because the Client has the session ticket for the print server, it will not need to request another ticket from the KDC to access the print server during this logon session.

FIGURE 8-4

NTLM Requires that authenitcation be processed by the PCC or BDC for each request

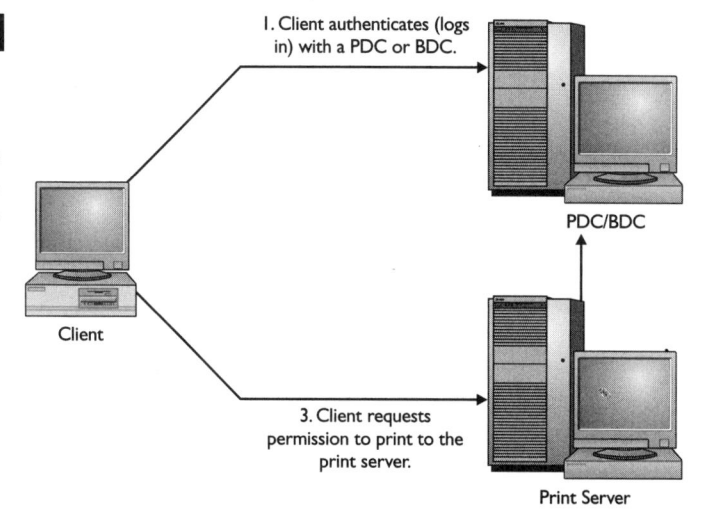

1. Client authenticates (logs in) with a PDC or BDC.

3. The print server checks with the PDC or BDC to authenticate whether the client has permission to utilize the resource. The print server will check with the PDC or BDC EVERY time the client requests permission to print.

3. Client requests permission to print to the print server.

Client

PDC/BDC

Print Server

When a workstation needs a network resource, such as a printer, it requests a ticket from the KDC. Once the workstation has the ticket, it can access the printer as many times as necessary without having to obtain another ticket from the KDC.

NTLM

NTLM was the default authentication system in Windows NT 4.0 and is backward compatible with Windows 2000 for networks that run earlier versions of the operating system (OS). In NTLM, the client contacts a primary domain controller (PDC) or a backup domain controller (BDC), as shown in Figure 8-4, to log on to a domain. Once logged in, if the client needs an additional resource such as a printer, it will contact the server that maintains the resource. The server will contact the domain controller that maintains the resource responsible for delivering the

SCENARIO & SOLUTION

If I have a network running both Windows NT 4.0 and Windows 2000, which authentication system is recommended?	Because Kerberos is not backward compatible with Windows NT 4.0 you will have to run NTLM.
Which authentication system is faster?	Kerberos
When accessing network resources, which authentication system requires a separate permission grant for each request?	NTLM

client's request and authenticate the user/client as a trusted subject. This process repeats every time the client reestablishes a session and needs a printer resource.

RADIUS

Remote Authentication Dial-In User Service (RADIUS) protocol greatly reduces problems with security and user account management in Remote Access Service (RAS). RADIUS lets Internet Service Provider (ISP) RAS servers forward user authentication requests to a corporate network through the Internet. The corporate network can use its existing user directory, such as a Windows NT directory service, to authenticate users for both ISP and corporate network access. RADIUS thus removes the requirement of maintaining a separate user database for the ISP and buying individual user accounts from the ISP.

With the recent rise in mobile users, virtual offices, and telecommuting, many Windows NT network managers have installed RAS servers with modem pools in their networks to provide dial-in service to remote users for accessing corporate network resources. As the number of remote users grows, so too does the addition of more modem pools and RAS servers.

Faced with a growing need for additional RAS support, administrators need to develop long-term solutions. One popular strategy is to outsource RAS to an ISP, whereby the ISP hosts and supports RAS for the outsourcing company.

Before going further, network managers need to address two areas of concern when outsourcing RAS: security and user account management. If RAS security is substandard, intruders can steal sensitive business data while the data is in transit over the Internet. Without centralized user account management, users need an extra account, in addition to their corporate network account, to dial up an ISP. Network managers have no control over the way an ISP manages its user accounts. However, ISPs that have many Points of Presence (POPs) and RAS servers need centralized user account databases for user authentication; the alternative is to maintain user accounts on every RAS server.

Windows 2000 and Windows NT 4.0 support network tunneling and RADIUS. Tunneling technologies are well known in today's Windows NT world. RADIUS, however, is relatively new in Windows NT.

Digest Authentication

Windows 2000 adds Digest Authentication (DA), based on Request for Comments (RFC) 2069, to Internet Information Services (IIS) to increase the security for

Internet users on the network. DA prompts a user of a browser for an ID and a password. The ID and password are protected in transit from the server to the browser by a hash—created from the user ID and password and coupled with the server's public ID. DA can only be used on servers running Windows 2000 since it is integrated into IIS 5.0; earlier versions of Windows NT are not capable of utilizing DA unless they use third-party Web server software.

Users must be using a browser with HTTP 1.1, as DA does not support earlier versions.

Smart Cards

A *smart card* is similar in size to a credit card. It is capable of storing information by using an integrated microprocessor chip located within it. Integration of smart cards into Windows 2000 is one of the most exciting pieces of security enhancement available. In order to use or develop smart card applications, you need a few things, namely: a smart card reader; software to communicate with the reader as well as software to communicate with the card that has been plugged into the reader; and, of course, smart cards.

The major security benefits that smart cards offer include:

- Smart cards assist in fraud reduction.
- Users have no way of knowing when they have lost their user ID and password because they are not physical objects, they are knowledge. With smart cards, if the object is lost then the user can report it and get a new one issued.
- If the card is lost it can be eliminated from the system, making it useless to anyone who tries to make unauthorized use of the card.

The following types of smart cards are available:

- **Memory cards** Containing select information such as identification numbers, PINs, and other security codes.
- **Processor cards** Containing an actual processor capable of performing low-level computations.
- **Electronic purse cards** Similar in concept to credit cards.
- **Security cards** Used for storing security data such as passwords, PINs, and other such security information.

FROM THE CLASSROOM

Smart Cards

Due to the newness of smart cards in the market, people frequently have some introductory questions about them. Following are a few of the most common questions and answers.

What is a smart card and how is it used?

A smart card is a card similar in size to a common credit card. The difference is that it has a chip embedded in it. By adding a chip to the card, it becomes a smart card with the power to serve many different uses. As an access-control device, smart cards protect personal and business data so that only the appropriate users are granted access. Another application provides users with the ability to make a purchase or exchange value. Smart cards provide data portability, security, and convenience. Smart cards help businesses evolve and expand their products and services in a changing global marketplace. Banks, telecommunications companies, computer software and hardware companies, and airlines all have the opportunity to tailor their card products and services to better differentiate their offerings and brands. The combination of applications available on smart cards also may help them to develop closer relationships with their customers.

How is a chip card different from a magnetic stripe card?

Commercial magnetic stripe cards are limited in their ability to carry information. A smart card is capable of a great deal more because it has relatively powerful processing capabilities that allow it to execute tasks such as data encryption.

My company is on a tight budget; what can I expect to pay for a card?

Chip cards range from $0.80 to $15 depending upon their capacity and quantities.

How secure and confidential are smart cards?

Smart cards actually offer more security and confidentiality than other financial information or transaction storage vehicles. A smart card is a safe place to store valuable information such as private keys, account numbers, passwords, or valuable personal information. It's also a secure place to perform processes that one doesn't want exposed to the world, for example, performing a public key or private key encryption.

Chip cards have the computational power to provide greater security, allowing verification of the cardholder. Entering a PIN is one method of verification. The benefit of the smart card is that you can verify the PIN securely, offline.

—*Steve Juntunen*

Design a Security Group Strategy

Windows 2000 Group Policy (GP) is an enhancement of system policies found in Windows NT 4.0. Group Policy objects (GPOs) are Active Directory-based objects that let you centrally configure your Windows 2000 clients and servers. This means that the GPO is the actual policy that you associate with a domain. In Windows NT 4.0, a single system policy file encompassed all functionality to ensure policy enforcement. However, in Windows NT 4.0 a policy's enforcement depends on the Registry settings of the user and computer.

Policy enforcement changes in Windows 2000 with the introduction of GPO. GP covers all of the same functions found in Windows NT 4.0 such as desktop lockdown, program and file access, and software identification, as shown in Figure 8-5. The administrator experience is considerably streamlined, offering an administrator the ability to make much broader strokes in setting up Group Policies.

FIGURE 8-5

The look and feel of the Group Policy management console is similar to that found in WIndows NT 4.0

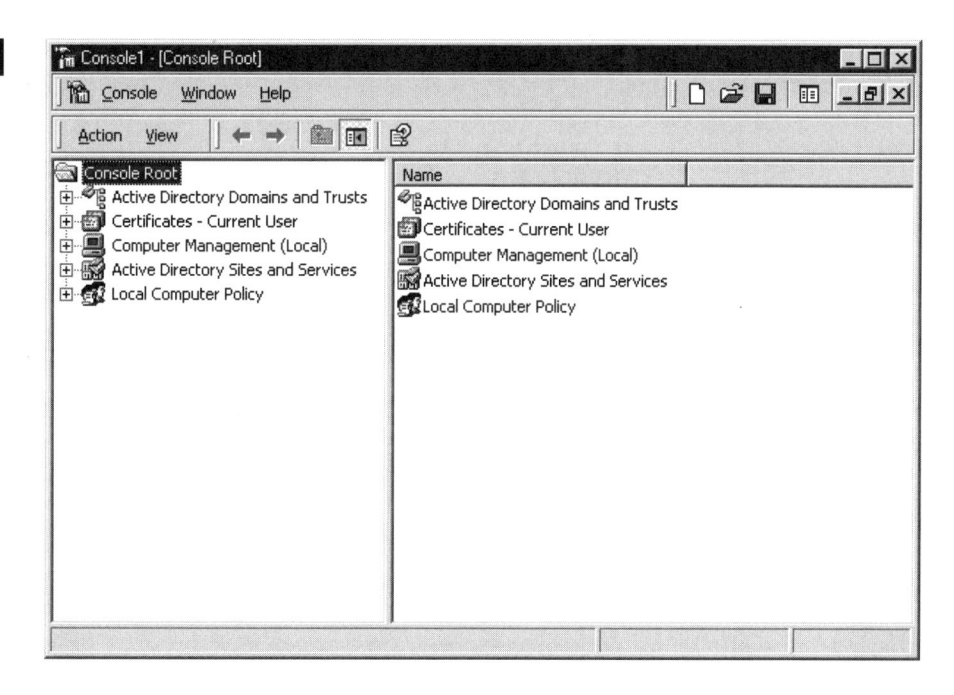

Windows 2000 GPO harnesses both files and any associated AD objects. This way, the administrator can set specific settings to:

- Establish cross-network security settings with precise granularity, covering network, domain, and computer.
- Direct folders to network locations rather than local computers.
- Set software installation rights and settings, including rights to assign and publish software.
- Make Registry policy edits.
- Set various scripts, such as logon/logoff, startup/shutdown, and browser functions.

GPs applied to objects in the AD follow an order of inheritance to manage the changes that result from the introduction of a new policy. The purpose of the order is to determine which policies will take effect. For instance, a policy that is placed higher on the chain of command, such as the organization's domain, will have a more profound effect on the organization than one placed in a small user's group at a single site. A policy put in place at the domain will propagate to all the members

CertCam 8-2

EXERCISE 8-2

A Defined Policy Conflict

Two policies have been defined at different locations for a computer and a conflict occurs. Answer the following:

- How will the two policies react?
- How can you determine which policy will take effect?

A conflict in policies will occur whenever the stance of two policies addressing the same topic is not the same. In such cases, the pecking order of determining the result goes from Local, Site, Domain, to OU (commonly called LSDOU), with the latter policies taking precedence over all policies applied earlier, unless actions have been taken to Block Inheritance. Even this can be overridden using No Override. By default, Local Group Policy objects are not applied to computers that are members of a domain.

of that domain—all the sites that are members of that domain, and all the local computers that are members of those sites. Likewise, an organizational unit (OU) policy will overrule a domain policy.

<table><tr><td>exam
⟨watch</td><td>*OU policies override domain and site policies, and domain policies override site policies. One caveat: if a user policy has been added to a profile, it will override any of the other policies if a conflict arises.*</td></tr></table>

The key to effective management of network services in Windows 2000 is the Microsoft Management Console (MMC), shown in Figure 8-6. Designing a Group Policy (GP) strategy becomes easier in Windows 2000 with the introduction of the MMC. MMC lets you manage all aspects of your network from one console. You can use a variety of MMC snap-in tools to manage most networking features. For instance, a MMC snap-in tool, Network Services Management, groups several network services tools within one console. MMC snap-ins are tools specifically geared toward configuration management of Windows 2000 network services, rather than tools for generically monitoring all the network devices in your infrastructure. With MMC all you need is the appropriate snap-in; if one does not exist for your task you can build one using the MMC creation kit.

FIGURE 8-6

The Microsoft Management Console allows networking management through the addition of snap-in tools

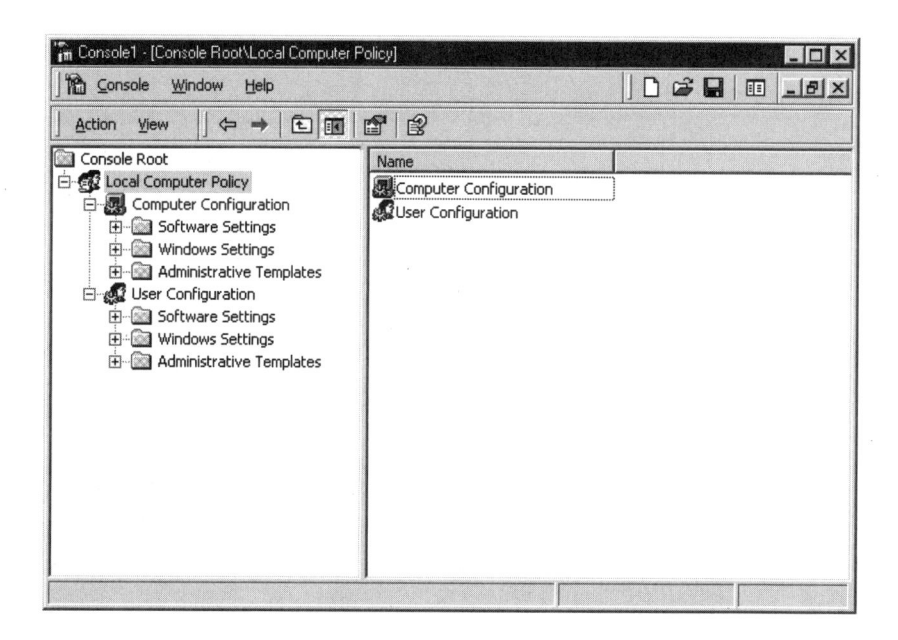

exam Watch *MMC snap-ins are preferred tools for managing and configuring network services in Windows 2000; however, these snap-ins do not necessarily replace more robust third-party network-management tools.*

MMC ships with BackOffice products such as Internet Information Server (IIS) 4.0, Microsoft Transaction Server (MTS), and Systems Network Architecture (SNA) Server. In Windows 2000, MMC provides an extensible container for management tools related to the operating system, BackOffice products, and third-party services.

The idea is to have one console to manage your whole environment. To manage GPOs with MMC you use the Group Policy Editor (GPE) snap-in seen in Figure 8-7, which is similar to POLEDIT.EXE in Windows NT 4.0.

Prior to using GPOs you need to set up an AD domain network. As mentioned, AD allows the administrator to create a centralized policy infrastructure that can be deployed to all Windows 2000 servers and clients. One security caution should be noted, on each Windows 2000 computer a local GPO exists that cannot be centrally administered. Having local GPOs allows local administration of a computer that your organization determines is not needed or not wanted in the AD. Choosing which computers to allow on your AD is as important as having an AD in the first place.

FIGURE 8-7

The Group Policy snap-in is a component of the MMC

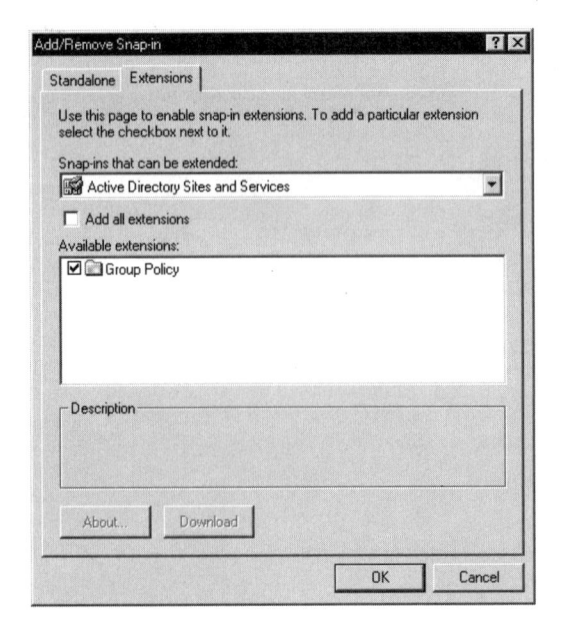

Computers that are going to be accessed by unknown parties should be kept out of your AD; set up a separate domain or workgroup and make any necessary adjustments to their GPOs in the local security settings, as shown in Figure 8-8.

CERTIFICATION OBJECTIVE 8.03

Design a Public Key Infrastructure

Windows 2000's Encrypting File System (EFS) uses a public key scheme to encrypt and decrypt data found in files and folders. Public key cryptography employs two keys for each encryption/decryption procedure. Public key/private key encryption is an asymmetric form of encryption; that is, one key is used to encrypt, and a different key is used to decrypt. One key is made freely available; this is referred to as the public key. The public key is used to encrypt files. The second key is referred to as the private key, which is used to decrypt. Only the recipient of an encrypted message

FIGURE 8-8

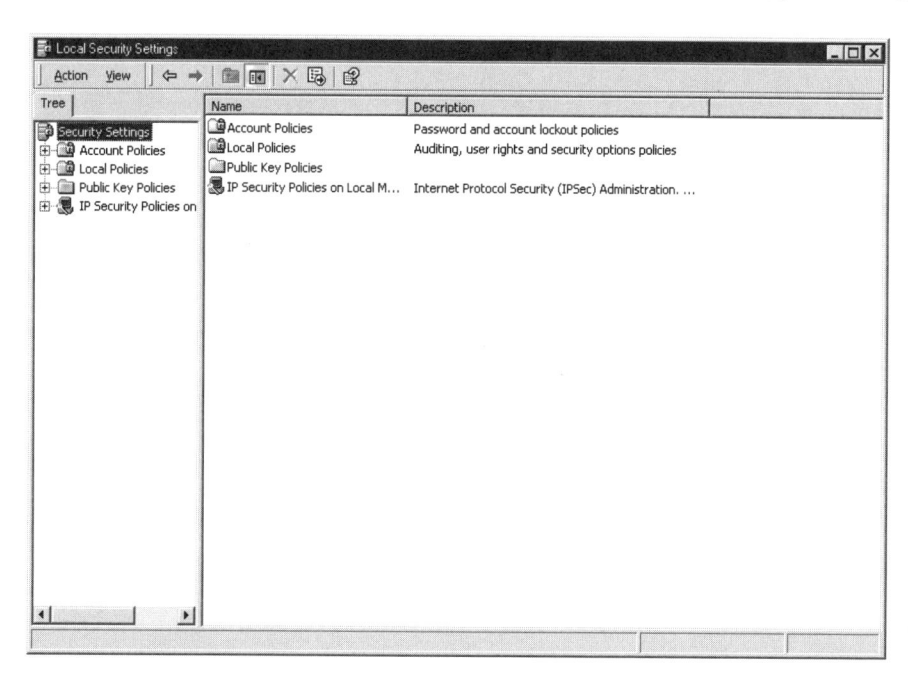

Adjusting local security settings is done in the Local Security Settings console

holds this key. The two keys work in tandem in message coding and decoding. The following is an example of the process.

on the Job — *John needs to send Sue an e-mail message intended only for her. On the network, John obtains Sue's public key and uses it to encrypt the message. The encryption process entails using a cryptographic algorithim, also known as a cipher, and a number called a key to scramble the plain text information into an encrypted result.*

Sue receives the document as an encrypted file—the encryption public key is her own. She can then use her private key to decrypt the document.

Design Certificate Authority (CA) Hierarchies

In public key infrastructure (PKI) exchanges, users like John have digital signatures to prove network identity, just as they have handwritten signatures to verify offline identity. They know they have the correct key to verify the signature because the certificate authority's main duty is to verify online identity. Think of the certificate authority (CA) as a network border patrol booth—each time entry or exit occurs, users must stop at the booth and show proper identification (like a passport) before proceeding. In online transactions, proper identification is synonymous to owning a digital certificate. To obtain a digital certificate a user securely generates a private key, and after verifying identity with the CA, the CA signs a private root key to the user's public key. Combining the user's public key and the signature of the CA gives the user a complete digital certificate.

Identify Certificate Services Roles

Microsoft Certificate Services (CS) offers administrators powerful policy and auditing tools. It does this by managing the issuance, renewal, and revocation of certificates, avoiding any reliance on external certificate authorities. Using CS, an organization has full control over the policies associated with the issuance, management, and revocation of certificates. Control over format and the contents of the certificates is also included. CS helps administrators by logging all transactions, enabling them to track, audit, and manage certificate requests. The CS default policy is preset to grant certificates to a trusted set of users based on a preset Windows 2000 user group of administrators, accounts, and servers. Sample policies are included with Certificate Services. Administrators should use caution when

Design a Public Key Infrastructure **371**

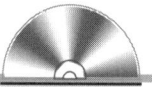

EXERCISE 8-3

CertCam 8-3

Using Certificate Authorities and Digital Certificates Together in a Transaction

This exercise covers CAs and digital certificates and how they work together in online transactions.

In this scenario John wants to grant Sue member access to his e-commerce site.

1. When Sue wants to access the site she must sign on with her private key, which was issued by a CA that we will refer to as Safe Inc.
2. Once on the site, Sue decides to make a purchase.
3. To accomplish this she sends both her order request and her digital signature to John's site.
4. He will use Sue's public key, which is stored in her certificate.
5. Upon receipt of this information, John needs to obtain the digital certificates of Sue and Safe Inc. to verify the signature.
6. Because Safe Inc. is the assignee of Sue's public key; John is able to validate her certificate by verifying Safe Inc.'s signature.
7. Next, John uses Sue's certificate to validate the signature on the order.
8. If everything checks out, Sue is verified.

accepting these defaults outright; sometimes they offer too much leverage for an organization and need tailoring to meet organizational needs.

Administrators can issue certificates in several standard formats. Table 8-1 lists some of the more popular formats and gives some background knowledge on each of them.

Manage Certificates

Although issuing certificates is easy, managing them effectively and securely is a bigger challenge. Certificate management includes many tasks. You need to determine the required client information, choose request-processing procedures, set validity periods, revoke certificates, manage certificate storage, and ensure server security.

Knowing the information that you require from clients when they request certificates depends on understanding your businesses security requirements. Generally, browser certificates have default application forms available in the CA for Type 1 and Type 2 certificates. For example, a customer making an Internet-based transaction might submit only minimal information such as a name or an e-mail address for certificates, so that they feel safe when they make purchases; a Type 1 certificate is most appropriate for such a task. A Type 2 certificate is typically more inquisitive of its user. For example, bank customers might have to submit more identifiable information, such as names, account numbers, personal identification numbers, and Social Security numbers.

TABLE 8-1 Certificate Formats

Standard	Definition
X.509	The X.509 standard defines what information can go into a certificate, and describes how to write it down (the data format). All X.509 certificates have the following data: signature, version, serial number, signature algorithm identifier, issuer name, validity period, subject name, and subject public key information.
PKCS	The Public Key Cryptography Standards are specifications designed to speed up the implementation of public-key cryptography. This standard describes syntax for a request for certification of a public key, a name, and possibly a set of attributes.
SSL (Secure Sockets Layer)	The SSL protocol runs above TCP/IP and below higher level protocols such as HyperText Transfer Protocol (HTTP) or Internet Message Access Protocol (IMAP). It uses TCP/IP on behalf of the higher level protocols, and in the process it allows an SSL-enabled server to authenticate itself to an SSL-enabled client, allows the client to authenticate itself to the server, and allows both machines to establish an encrypted connection.
SET (Secure Electronic Transaction)	SET provides a basic architecture for Internet commerce while remaining consistent with the traditional credit card payment infrastructure. The protocol is designed to let developers easily integrate it into the existing global financial backbone rather than layer a new set of protocols and applications over the existing transaction services.
S/MIME	S/MIME is a specification for secure electronic mail. S/MIME stands for Secure/Multipurpose Internet Mail Extensions and was designed to add security to e-mail messages in MIME format. The security services offered are authentication (using digital signatures) and privacy (using encryption).

Integrate with Third-Party CAs

The Web has opened great opportunities for doing business on the Internet. The business-to-business economy is fueling a greater need for companies to interoperate with others. This results in a variety of data exchanges that require an element of security to ensure a safe business climate. In every type of business conducted over the Web, whether it's e-commerce, information exchange, or data mining, all active participants must ensure the security and privacy of sensitive information transferred between Web servers and browsers.

Digital certificates contribute a major role in Web security. Digital certificates are electronic documents that computer systems use to identify and authenticate users participating in an application, such as Web browsing, e-mail, and file transfer. Traditional user logons and firewalls can't protect sensitive information when systems transfer it between Web servers and browsers. However, combined with other security technologies—encryption, digital signatures, and the Secure Sockets Layer (SSL) protocol—digital certificates can prevent data eavesdropping, tampering, and repudiation (denial of involvement) over the Web.

A certification authority is a trusted entity responsible for issuing digital certificates to individuals or systems based on verification of the applicants' identities. You can request certificates from a public CA. However, as companies demand more certificates for their Web servers and browsers from a third party, they are becoming more concerned about confidentiality, cost of ownership, quality of service, and other issues. To obtain third-party certificates, you must release confidential business information about employees, customers, suppliers, and partners. You must pay subscription fees of tens to hundreds of dollars per certificate per year; at $50 per certificate, a 1000-employee company spends $50,000 a year on certificates. If you use a third-party CA, you do not control the certificate process, such as generation, retrieval, and revocation of certificates, which can be a time-consuming process.

To address companies' concerns about the disadvantages of working with third-party CAs, groups are developing products that allow individual sites to be their own CA when using Windows 2000. With this software, you can be the CA and issue certificates for Web servers and browsers used by your company and customers.

Chapter 8: Designing a Windows 2000 Security Solution

CERTIFICATION OBJECTIVE 8.04

Design Windows 2000 Network Services Security

Appropriately protecting an organization's network services can be one of the most important undertakings because they are the pulse of most networks. Moreover, as new applications come to the marketplace the majority of them need to utilize the services found in Windows 2000. Having a service fail can cause a domino effect in your network operations.

In this section we review the main services used in Windows 2000 and point out the areas where security concerns arise. Understanding the vulnerabilities can assist in producing a solid strategy for combating potential threats in your network services.

DNS Security

Domain Name System (DNS) Servers are attractive targets for intruders. They have every IP address of every host on your network. This sort of information can be valuable to anyone who may want to probe your network. Security in DNS begins in the Active Directory (AD).

exam
Watch

By choosing to integrate DNS into Active Directory, you secure resource records using standard Windows 2000 AD object security. This also allows for automatic replication of DNS changes via Active Directory instead of using the conventional method of replication DNS zone files.

DNS Manager is a separate MMC snap-in tool. Microsoft has expanded the scope of DNS' responsibilities in Windows 2000, making it the primary name service for the OS. Because of this, the tools for administrating the DNS console have been tweaked to add convenience. Added is the ability to create new primary and secondary zones, static entry of resource records, and configuration of global options for the DNS service. Support for dynamic DNS (DDNS) and support for hosting DNS zone files within AD are also added. Dealing with primary and secondary servers is an issue of the past. Now primary domains forward changes in zone information to secondary domains. This results in greater organization through consolidation and easier security management.

RIS Security

Remote Installation Service (RIS) lets you place images of built systems onto a central server and then download those images to a computer with an empty hard disk. All the target computer needs is a network interface card (NIC) and a special boot disk to get the process rolling. RIS also lets you do a simple unattended installation over the network, which is a convenient way to put Windows 2000 Professional on a system without a CD-ROM or an already-copied i386 directory. Of course, you can make such installations easier with unattended installation scripts, which RIS also supports. Out of the box, RIS helps you install Windows 2000 Professional from the i386 directory or with a prebuilt image. As of this writing, users are able to install only Windows 2000 Professional; using RIS to install Windows NT Server or Windows 9*x* is not yet possible.

When using RIS, it is important to be sure that your security settings transfer completely. Pay close attention to your copied settings in the AD and the CA. When creating installation scripts, be certain to assess the rights that you will want to grant users; if there will be various access levels you will either need to create multiple installation scripts or tailor each computer after using RIS. Figure 8-9 shows some of the options that you can grant to users. As always, when deploying a remote setup, a lab test should be conducted first in a safe environment to assure that all proper pre-configured settings take to the RIS clients.

RIS allows the administrator to set up the security parameters of an installation, thereby determining the level of access that will be granted on the new computer.

SNMP Security

In Windows NT 4.0 and earlier versions of Windows, several network management tools rely on Simple Network Management Protocol (SNMP) agents to monitor the devices and provide information to the management console or server. However, few of these tools provide visibility above the Open Systems Interconnection (OSI) network layer of services; instead, they must rely on the individual vendors of those

FIGURE 8-9

Choice Options Properties window

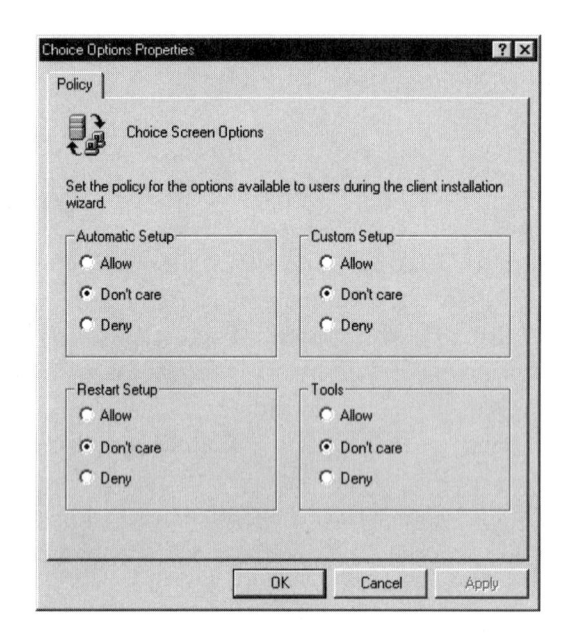

services to provide for management. Windows 2000 steps in to fill this network management role.

Windows 2000 has enhanced services to support and improve the functionality of the network's distributed infrastructure. Enhanced services include:

- Dynamic Host Configuration Protocol (DHCP) servers on your network must be authorized by Active Directory. This prevents unauthorized DHCP servers from causing problems on the network.

- Domain Name Server (DNS) is used to locate the nearest available domain controller each time a client logs into the domain. Each domain controller acts as a KDC so the nearest available domain controller becomes the preferred KDC of the client for the duration of the client's logon session. DNS and Kerberos work hand in hand to logon users.

- IP Security (IPSec) brings new standards for authentication, integrity, and encryption of network-layer traffic.

Windows 2000 tools provide a basic interface for configuration, management, and some monitoring of the network services provided. Windows 2000 network services tools should not be confused with some third-party network management tools that provide the robust enterprise-level monitoring, alerting, and reporting of network devices.

Terminal Services Security

Terminal Services offer a great amount of leverage and flexibility for administrators to administer a high number of client terminals without a lot of effort. You *can* use Terminal Services to replace your PCs and create a purely Windows-based terminal network. The Terminal Services model in which all of a company's business applications reside in one location and users access those applications through Windows-based terminals comes to many administrators' minds when they think of thin-client solutions. But thinking that a Terminal Services network can contain only Windows-based terminals seriously underestimates the OS's possibilities.

EXERCISE 8-4

Deciding to Run Terminal Services

Determine whether there is a need or an advantage to running Terminal Services in your organization. To help you decide, answer the following questions.

1. Does your organization run Microsoft Office-type applications on your network's PCs? If so, and you don't want to run them from the server, then Terminal Services is not a good solution for your organization.

2. Are your company's business-critical applications run from local hard disks or from a central server? If from a central server, then Terminal Services could be a good solution. With this in mind, administrators should make sure that terminal clients have only the rights needed to complete their tasks.

3. Are user-rights settings empowering users beyond their functional needs, creating a potential hazard because users interact directly with the server? If granted an overabundance of privileges, potential problems could arise ranging from accidental data deletion to a malicious attack on your servers.

CERTIFICATION SUMMARY

Developing a strong security plan in Windows 2000 takes planning, time, and testing. This chapter has discussed the strategies needed for establishing and inheriting security policies in a network. Beginning with the placement and inheritance of security policies, we learn that new features such as digital certificates found in the Active Directory will allow a whole new level of manipulation regardless of your network's size. Designing an authentication strategy explains the application of digital certificates, encryption, and EFS to your network. In the section on public key infrastructure, we reviewed how certificates are set up, used, and administered in the network. And we discussed the network services security in Windows 2000 where some potential security hazards are pointed out including DNS and SNMP. Lastly, we discussed Terminal Services security.

✓ TWO-MINUTE DRILL

Design the Placement and Inheritance of Security Policies

- ❑ Security administrators will be able to use digital certificates in Active Directory, and control administration with greater granularity because of the new directory services.
- ❑ The Active Directory (AD) can exist in small networks with only a few computers, users, and other objects or on larger networks with thousands of entries into their AD.
- ❑ Windows 2000 networks are commonly divided into smaller parts beginning with sites, then domains, and then organizational units.
- ❑ Domains work as security boundaries by blocking users without explicit access privileges from gaining access.
- ❑ Conflicting policies are resolved in a hierarchical model where sites are overruled by domains, and domains are overruled by OUs.

Design an Authentication Strategy

- ❑ Digital certificates are electronic documents that computer systems use to identify and authenticate users participating in an application, such as Web browsing, e-mail, and file transfer.
- ❑ Encryption is the process of scrambling data to make it unreadable to an unprivileged user. Decryption is the process of unscrambling the data to make it readable.
- ❑ EFS allows users to protect files and folders by encrypting them with a public/private key scheme that utilizes their user profile for convenience.

Design a Public Key Infrastructure

- ❑ Companies using certificates for their Web servers and browsers from a third-party vendor need to consider confidentiality, cost of ownership, and quality of service issues.

- A Certification Authority (CA) is a trusted entity responsible for issuing digital certificates to individuals or systems based on verification of applicants' identities.
- Using CS, an organization has full control over the policies associated with the issuance, management, and revocation of certificates.

Design Windows 2000 Network Services Security

- DNS servers have every IP address of every host on your network—this sort of information can be valuable to anyone who may want to intrude.
- Simple Network Management Protocol (SNMP) agents monitor devices and provide information to the management console or server.
- Remote Installation Service (RIS) lets you place images of built systems onto a central server and then download those images to a computer with an empty hard disk.
- The Terminal Services model is based on a company's business applications residing in one location and users accessing those applications through Windows-based terminals.

SELF TEST

The following questions will help you measure your understanding of the material presented in this chapter. Read all of the choices carefully, as there may be more than one correct answer. Choose all correct answers for each question.

Design the Placement and Inheritance of Security Policies

1. Complete the following sentence to make a true statement. EFS boosts the security found in NTFS, thereby:

    A. making it more secure and offering much faster encryptions and decryptions of files that are EFS enabled.

    B. making it less secure but offering much faster encryptions and decryptions of files that are EFS enabled.

    C. making it more secure while offering much slower but more careful encryptions and decryptions of files that are EFS enabled.

    D. making it more secure and offering much slower encryptions and decryptions of all files.

Design an Authentication Strategy

2. What function does RADIUS perform?

    A. Radius lets an ISP's RAS server forward user authentication requests to a corporate network through the Internet.

    B. Radius lets a VPN server forward user authentication requests to a VPN.

    C. Radius lets an ISP's RAS servers forward user authentication requests to a corporate network through the company intranet.

    D. Radius lets an ISP server forward user authentication requests to a corporate network through the Internet.

3. What type of platform is appropriate for Digest Authentication?

    A. RAS
    B. All BackOffice applications
    C. Windows 2000 running IIS
    D. XML

4. What is *not* necessary to use Smart Cards?

   A. A smart card reader

   B. A proprietary satellite

   C. Software to communicate with the reader and card

   D. Smart cards

5. What are the main objectives when managing certificates? (Choose all that apply.)

   A. Gaining required data on users.

   B. Establishing appropriate start and end dates for certificate validity.

   C. To provide guaranteed server security.

   D. All the above.

Design a Public Key Infrastructure

6. What type of certificate is best for online banking?

   A. Type 1

   B. Type 2

   C. A S/MIME

   D. PPTP

7. Why are DNS servers attractive targets for intruders?

   A. They have every IP address of every host on your network.

   B. They allow users to rename a server from a remote location.

   C. Most servers store their certificates in DNS.

   D. Servers can be renamed.

8. When authoring Web content for a company that uses Digest Authentication (DA) and IIS 5.0, what factors need to be considered? (Choose all that apply.)

   A. The version of HTTP.

   B. The number of users accessing the network.

   C. The type of operating system that the host server will be running.

   D. The daily traffic that will visit the site.

9. Why is Kerberos a faster, more time-efficient method of authentication?
   A. Kerberos is backward compatible with legacy OSs.
   B. The client contacts the server each time it requires an additional resource such as a printer.
   C. Once a KDC session is initiated, the user can have access to network resources for the duration of his or her session.
   D. Processor speeds have increased since NTLM and Kerberos is better designed to take advantage of the speed.

10. Where are all objects on a network grouped?
    A. In the Certification Authority (CA).
    B. In domains.
    C. In a Group Policy object (GPO).
    D. In a SQL database.

11. What is the Local Security Policy? (Choose all that apply.)
    A. The written policy of the security department regarding computer access.
    B. A Group Policy.
    C. A policy created during Windows 2000 installation.
    D. The most secure policy on a network.

12. How do security certificates work?
    A. Information is stored in the certificate that dynamically creates private key access.
    B. To unlock a file or folder, the user manually inserts a digital certificate.
    C. The CA holds public keys and the user holds the private key.
    D. They harness both files and any associated AD objects.

13. When using RIS on client computers what are the potential security hazards? (Choose all that apply.)
    A. Local security settings may override OU settings.
    B. Local security settings could be too rigid or too passive for the needs of an organization.
    C. User rights to the network may be inaccurately copied to the client.
    D. Windows 95 settings are not properly copied using RIS.

14. How do CAs work in Windows 2000?
    A. Trusted CA root certificates are stored by the organization in a certificate store. When the trusted server contacts another server storing its certificate, a trust confirmation occurs and a connection is established.
    B. Before a business partner runs a file of any type, it checks the certificate store to ensure verification of the file.
    C. Private keys stored on the server are used to verify a CA's authenticity.
    D. Users obtain CAs in Windows 2000 by requesting them from third-party vendors to ensure authenticity when making networked transactions.

Design Windows 2000 Network Services Security

15. What is the purpose of including Digest Authentication (DA) in your security plan?
    A. To do cross-authentication between Windows 2000 servers and servers running other OSs such as Windows NT 4.0.
    B. To keep a log of all Internet-based network authentications.
    C. To verify security in IIS and other BackOffice applications.
    D. To increase the security for Internet users on the network.

16. What must be set up prior to using GPO?
    A. Digest Authentication
    B. Active Directory
    C. Kerberos
    D. A RAS server.

LAB QUESTION

Creating a New Group Policy Object (GPO)

By default, creation of new Group Policy objects is limited to domain administrators, enterprise administrators, Group Policy administrators, and the operating system. To allow a non-administrator or group to be able to create GPOs, that user or group must be added to the Group Policy Administrators security group. When a member who is not an administrator of the Group Policy Administrators group creates a GPO, they become the creator/owner of that GPO and can edit the GPO in the future. Only those GPOs that the user creates or those explicitly delegated for use by members of the Group Policy Administrators group can be edited; full control of all the GPOs for the domain is not given to Group Policy Administrators.

Assuming that the user has the proper access level, what are the steps to follow to create a new GPO?

SELF TEST ANSWERS

Design the Placement and Inheritance of Security Policies

1. ☑ **A.** EFS allows for faster and more secure encryptions and decryptions of files that are EFS enabled.
   ☒ **B** is incorrect as it is not *less* secure but *more* secure. **C** is incorrect as it is not slower but rather faster encryption and decryption of files that are EFS enabled. **D** is incorrect as it should be files that are EFS enabled and not all files.

Design an Authentication Strategy

2. ☑ **A.** An existing user directory, such as an NT directory service, authenticates users for both ISP and corporate network access. RADIUS thus removes the requirement of maintaining a separate user database for the ISP and buying individual user accounts from the ISP.
   ☒ **B** is incorrect because RADIUS is not specifically tailored to work with VPNs. **C** is incorrect because RADIUS uses the Internet not an intranet. **D** is incorrect because RADIUS uses RAS.

3. ☑ **C.** Windows 2000 adds Digest Authentication (DA) to IIS to increase the security for Internet users on the network.
   ☒ **A** is incorrect. Digest Authentication does not use RAS. **B** is incorrect. Although BackOffice uses IIS, it is not a fundamental part of it. **D** is incorrect. XML is a markup language for the Web and is not related to DA.

4. ☑ **B.** Although it may be nice to own one's own satellite, it is not necessary to operate smart cards. Many third-party vendors will allow access to their satellites in order to provide dynamically changing personal identification numbers that are read by the smart card. This way, the user of a smart card can simply cancel the card if it is ever lost or stolen and the satellite will no longer send updated PINs to it.
   ☒ **A** is incorrect. You need a smart card reader to operate a smart card network authentication system. Many smart card devices in Windows 2000 support plug and play. **C** is incorrect. Like any other device or program, software is a necessary component to a smart card system. **D** is incorrect. Yes, you do need smart cards to operate a smart card authentication system.

5. ☑ **D.** Certificate management includes many tasks. You need to determine required client information, choose request-processing procedures, set validity periods, revoke certificates, manage certificate storage, and ensure server security.

Design a Public Key Infrastructure

6. ☑ **B.** Type 2 certificates achieve a high level of security that is obtained by gathering a lot of data on the user. In an online transaction it is likely that the user will be required to submit a name, PIN, Social Security number, and possibly more.
☒ **A** is incorrect. A Type 1 certificate does not demand a great deal of information for a certificate to be administered—often just a name and perhaps a password or PIN. **C** is incorrect. S/MIME is a specification used for secure electronic mail and is therefore not applicable to an online banking transaction. **D** is incorrect. Point-to-point Tunneling Protocol (PPTP) is best fitted for virtual private networks (VPN) and is not a practical solution for conventional online banking transactions.

7. ☑ **A.** Domain Name System (DNS) servers contain a list of IP addresses and their related server names.
☒ **B** is incorrect. The ability to rename a server is not given in DNS. **C** is incorrect. Certificates are stored in a certificate store on the server, not in DNS. **D** is incorrect. Servers are not renamed in DNS.

8. ☑ **A and C.** Users must be using a browser with HTTP 1.1, as DA does not support earlier versions. The type of operating system must also be considered since IIS 5.0 runs only on Windows 2000.
☒ **B and D** are incorrect. The number of users and the amount of daily network traffic have no influence on the success or failure of DA.

9. ☑ **C.** When a client logs in to the network a contact with the Kerberos Distribution Center (KDC) is established. When the user needs to access a resource such as a printer for the first time, the KDC is contacted for a session ticket that enables access to the resource. Once this ticket has been granted, the user never needs to contact the KDC again for the duration of the logon session.
☒ **A** is incorrect. Kerberos is not backward compatible. Therefore, if you are running a non-heterogeneous environment you should consider alternative options. **B** is incorrect. The qualities described in this answer are more closely related to NTLM, Windows NT 4.0's default authentication system. **D** is incorrect. Processor speed has no effect on making the choice between Kerberos and NTLM.

10. ☑ **B.** Users, printers, servers, and all other networked objects are grouped into domains. Sizes of domains vary and can be divided to ease manageability and increase flexibility.
☒ **A** is incorrect. The CA verifies the authenticity of a certificate sent by a trusted or not trusted party. **C** is incorrect. Network objects are not grouped in a GPO. **D** is incorrect.

Chapter 8: Designing a Windows 2000 Security Solution

Although it is possible to create a database that maintains information regarding your networked objects, it does not occur automatically, nor is it a particularly effective way to manage your objects.

11. ☑ **B and C.** LSPs are Group Policies set on a local machine during the installation process. The administrator can later change the settings in the LSP to fit the needs of the organization.
☒ **A** is incorrect. Although a written policy is useful it is not referred to as a LSP in Windows 2000. **D** is incorrect because the LSP is the first policy applied to a computer, and elements or all of that policy can be overridden by site, domain, or OU policies.

12. ☑ **C** is correct. Certificates authenticate Active Directory users by matching the public key, held in the certificate, to the private key, held by the user.
☒ **A** is incorrect. Information that is stored in certificates is static. **B** is incorrect because users do not interact with digital certificates. **D** is incorrect. Certificates do not use associated AD objects, GPOs do.

13. ☑ **B.** You should always have a firm understanding of your organization's established local settings. Generally you want to avoid hindering users from accomplishing their work by implementing limits; however, you should strive to lock down any elements of the computer that will not be needed by the users but could potentially cause a security problem.
☒ **A** is incorrect. Local security settings do not override OU settings. In fact the converse is correct. **C** is incorrect. RIS allows users to install unattended computer images over a network. As long as the result image allows the user to log in to the network there should not be any issues with user rights because they are dealt with at the network server, not at the client. **D** is incorrect because RIS does not work with Windows 95 or any OS's other than Windows 2000 Professional.

14. ☑ **A.** When a partner of yours trusts you, they will install a certificate of yours in their certificate store. That way, when you attempt to access a secured file of your trustee, they can confirm your identity by checking your certificate against the certificate they have stored.
☒ **B, C, and D** are all incorrect.

Design Windows 2000 Network Services Security

15. ☑ **D.** DA prompts the user of a browser for an ID and a password. The ID and password are protected in transit from the server to the browser by a hash—created from the user ID and password and coupled with the server's public ID.
☒ **A** is incorrect. DA is not used to provide cross-authentication for Windows 2000 and

other OSs. **B** is incorrect. DA does not work as a log—event viewer is used for this purpose. **C** is incorrect. Although DA is used for IIS security, it does not have anything to do with other BackOffice applications.

16. ☑ **B.** Active Directory allows the administrator to create a centralized policy infrastructure that can be deployed to all Windows 2000 servers and clients.
☒ **A** is incorrect. Digest Authentication is not directly related to GPOs and is not necessary for proper GPO functioning. **C** is incorrect. Kerberos is set up by default during setup. However, it is possible to use NTLM instead and therefore is not a requirement for GPOs. **D** is incorrect. RAS is not a necessary component to use GPOs.

LAB ANSWER

To create a new GPO, perform the following steps:

1. Choose the object to which you want to apply the Group Policy; for instance, choose a domain that exists on your network.
2. Right-click the site, domain, or OU that you want to apply a new GPO to and choose Properties.
3. Click the Group Policy tab.
4. Click the New button.
5. Type a name for the new Group Policy.
6. Click the Edit button and tailor your new policy to the specifications you want.

9
Understanding Policies

CERTIFICATION OBJECTIVES

9.01	Overview of Group Policy and the Microsoft Management Console
9.02	Applying Group Policy
9.03	Configuring Group Policy
9.04	Designing an Audit Policy
9.05	Security Templates
✓	Two-Minute Drill
Q&A	Self Test

In this chapter, you will see how Group Policy works to control and configure the security environment in Windows 2000. We'll start with a basic overview of Group Policy and how it is implemented in Windows 2000. This overview will provide a background for the next major topic, "Designing an Audit Policy." Finally, we will examine how to use security templates provided with Windows 2000 to configure security for an Active Directory object, or for a local machine.

CERTIFICATION OBJECTIVE 9.01

Overview of Group Policy and the Microsoft Management Console

Group Policy is a set of configuration options that can be applied to an Active Directory object to define the behavior of the object and its child objects. Group Policy can serve many purposes, from application and file deployment to global configuration of user profile settings and security deployment.

If you have extensive experience with Windows NT 4.0, you will discover that many of the administrative settings that were scattered throughout various administrative tools are now combined in one place and easily accessible in the Group Policy MMC (Microsoft Management Console). For example, the setting of audit policies, the assignment of user rights, and the management of account policies (governing user passwords) are now all accomplished through the Group Policy console.

You can use Group Policy to run scripts at specified times, to fine-tune security settings, and to control the user environment to whatever degree you desire. Group Policy gives an administrator the power to enhance productivity and security throughout the organization by completely managing the users' desktop environment.

The Group Policy MMC

Because Group Policy is such a powerful tool, it should be used only by designated Group Policy administrators. Microsoft has recognized this, and has taken steps to make it difficult for the uninitiated to use Group Policy. If you look for the Group Policy Editor in Windows 2000's Administrative Tools, you won't find it. Group Policy is managed through a custom MMC (which you must create and to which you add the Group Policy snap-in) that can be accessed from the command line, or from dialog boxes available in other tools such as Active Directory Users and Computers and Active Directory Sites and Services.

The Microsoft Management Console is a key feature in Windows 2000, and is designed to ease the burden of administration by providing a standardized interface for using administrative tools and utilities. The management applications that are contained in an MMC are called *snap-ins*, and custom MMCs hold the snap-ins required to perform specific tasks. Custom consoles can be saved as files with the .MSC file extension. Figure 9-1 shows the Group Policy Console for a domain controller.

Creating a custom MMC for administering Group Policy is easy. We will create a Group Policy console later in this chapter. First, let's look at some of the terminology that you must understand when discussing Group Policy. It's especially important to familiarize yourself with the following terms and their acronyms:

- Group Policy Object (GPO)
- Group Policy Container (GPC)
- Group Policy Template (GPT)

Group Policy Object

Policies are stored in a *Group Policy object (GPO)*. If you think of the Group Policy snap-in as the application that creates group policies, just as Microsoft Word is an

FIGURE 9-1

A custom Group Policy console

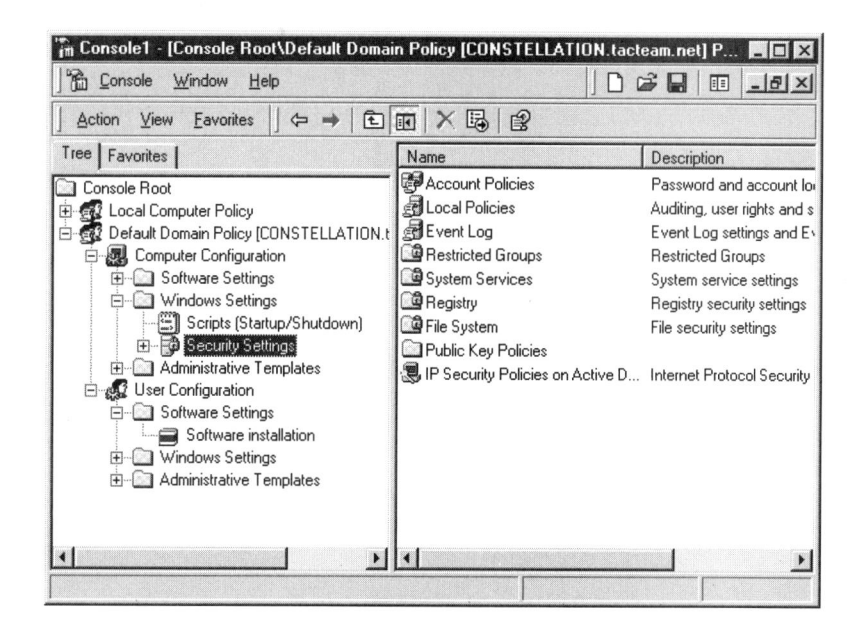

application that creates documents, the individual GPOs would be analogous to individual document files, each of which contains information separate and distinct from other documents.

Local versus Nonlocal GPOs

Group Policy objects can be either local or nonlocal, depending on the type of Windows 2000 computer where they are stored. Nonlocal policies are stored on domain controllers and are dependent on Active Directory. Nonlocal policies can be applied to a site, a domain, or an organizational unit (OU). Microsoft uses the acronym SDOU to refer to these together.

Local policies exist on all Windows 2000 computers. These computers store one local Group Policy object, which contains a subset of the settings available in a nonlocal GPO. When these computers belong to a Windows 2000 Active Directory domain environment, both local and nonlocal GPO settings will be applied. If there is a conflict, the local settings are overwritten by nonlocal settings. The local Group Policy object cannot be deleted.

Local Group Policy is the only way to apply Group Policy in a workgroup environment.

Group Policy Container

Nonlocal Group Policy objects consist of two parts, which are stored separately, the Group Policy container (GPC) and the Group Policy template (GPT). The information contained in GPC and GPT is synchronized through a common globally unique identifier (GUID).

The *Group Policy container* is a directory service object, which includes subobjects for Machine and User Group Policy information. The GPC contains the following data:

- **Version information** Used to ensure that the information is synchronized with Group Policy template information.
- **Status information** Indicates whether the Group Policy object is enabled or disabled for this site, domain, or organizational unit (SDOU).
- **List of components** Specifies which extensions to Group Policy have settings in the GPO.
- **The class store** Information for software installation; used when assigning or publishing applications.

Overview of Group Policy and the Microsoft Management Console

exam Watch

Remember that Windows 2000 non-domain controller computers have only one local GPO, and it is stored in %SYSTEMROOT%\System32\GroupPolicy. Group Policy containers are Active Directory objects, and apply only to nonlocal policies. ("SYSTEMROOT" refers to the directory into which Windows 2000 was installed, typically named WINNT.)

Group Policy Template

A Group Policy template (GPT) is a node structure consisting of the GPT folder and a set of subnodes, which together contain all the Group Policy configuration settings for that particular GPO. The GPT is located in the system volume folder on the Windows 2000 domain controllers. The folder name is the GUID of the GPO to which it applies, which is a hexadecimal number. The path would look like the following:

```
%systemroot%\Sysvol\sysvol\tacteam.net\Policies\{A432C8532-F089-22d4-78E4-00C8FEd00C43}
```

The subfolders in the GPT folder depend on what group policies are set.

SCENARIO & SOLUTION

What is the function of the \ADM subfolder?	It contains the .ADM files (administrative templates) associated with this GPT.
What is the function of the \USER subfolder? What about those sub-subfolders?	It contains the REGISTRY.POL file with the Registry settings applied to users. It also contains subfolders of its own: \USER\APPLICATIONS Contains .AAS files (Advertisement) used by the installation service. \USERS\FILES Contains files to be deployed to users. \USER\SCRIPTS Contains the scripts and associated files for *logon* an *logoff* scripting.
What is the function of the \MACHINE subfolder?	It contains the REGISTRY.POL file with the Registry settings applied to computers. (It also contains subfolders similar to those in the \USER subfolder, with the same functions except that they are applied to computers. For example: \MACHINE\SCRIPTS contains scripts and files for *startup* and *shutdown* scripting)

exam⍺tch

The REGISTRY.POL files in Windows 2000 are not compatible with the NTCONFIG.POL and CONFIG.POL files created by the System Policy Editor in Windows NT 4.0 or Windows 9x. System Policies created with System Policy Editor cannot be applied to Windows 2000 computers. However, you can use System Policy Editor to apply System Policy to down-level clients in a Windows 2000 Domain. You must use the Policy Editor specific to the client operating system receiving the System Policy.

EXERCISE 9-1

Deploying the Group Policy Editor Microsoft Management Console Snap-In

Log onto a Windows 2000 computer with administrative privileges.

1. Click Start | Run.

2. In the Open box, type **mmc** and click OK. This will open an empty MMC console, shown here.

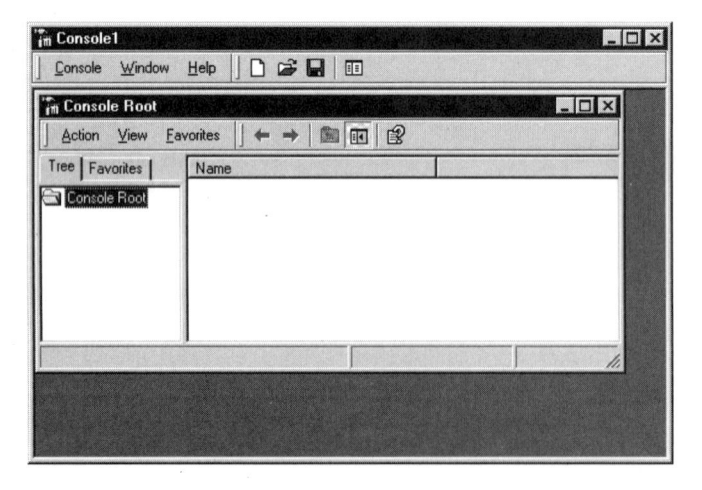

3. The next step is setting the mode for your new console. Saving a console in *User mode* means that those who use it cannot add or remove snap-ins or save the console. If you save it in *Author mode,* access will include full functionality, including the ability to modify the console. We will save our Group Policy console in Author mode; to do so, click the Console menu and choose Options.

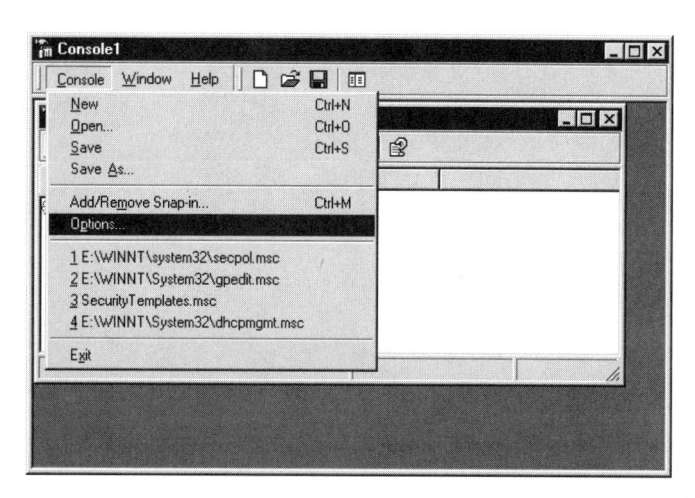

4. The Options dialog box (shown in the following illustration) will appear, allowing you to select the mode in which the console will be saved (or, if User Mode is chosen, further define the level of access). Choose Author Mode and click OK.

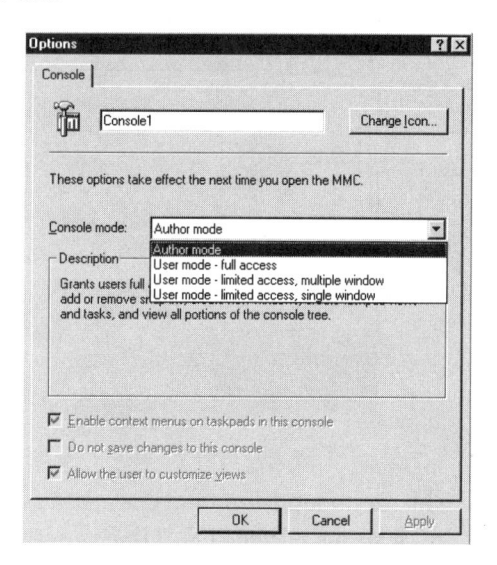

5. Now we will add the Group Policy snap-in to our console. Refer back to the illustration in step 3, and this time select Add/Remove Snap-in. The following dialog box will appear.

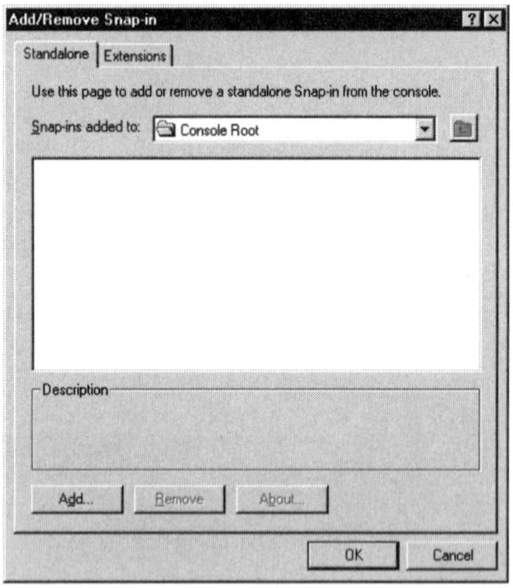
Add/Remove Snap-in
Standalone
Extensions
Use this page to add or remove a standalone Snap-in from the console.
Snap-ins added to:
Console Root
Description
Add...
Remove
About...
OK
Cancel

6. Click Add to select a snap-in to add to the console. You will have several choices, shown here.

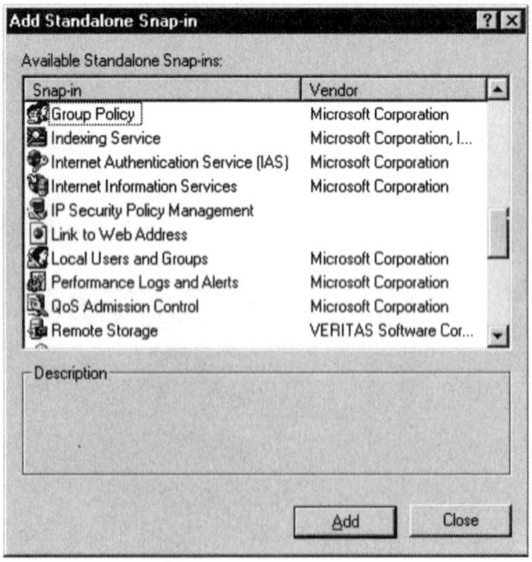
Add Standalone Snap-in
Available Standalone Snap-ins:
Snap-in
Vendor
Group Policy
Microsoft Corporation
Indexing Service
Microsoft Corporation, I...
Internet Authentication Service (IAS)
Microsoft Corporation
Internet Information Services
Microsoft Corporation
IP Security Policy Management
Link to Web Address
Local Users and Groups
Microsoft Corporation
Performance Logs and Alerts
Microsoft Corporation
QoS Admission Control
Microsoft Corporation
Remote Storage
VERITAS Software Cor...
Description
Add
Close

7. Highlight Group Policy and click Add to select the Group Policy Object (GPO). By default, the GPO that this snap-in will control is the Local Computer, as shown in the following illustration.

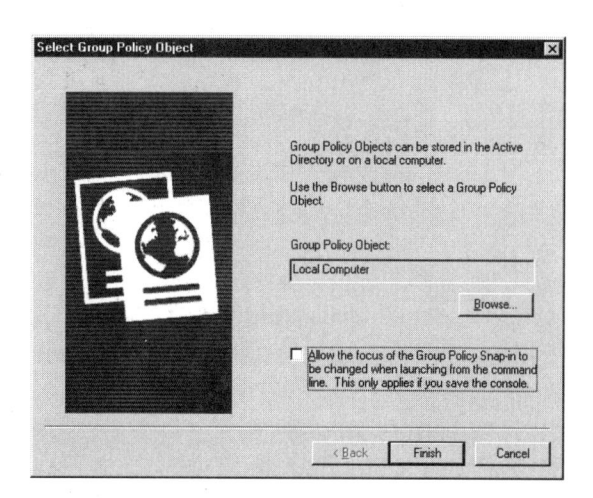

8. If you are logged on to a domain controller and wish to use the MMC to manage Group Policy for the domain, click Browse. You will see a dialog box similar to that shown here.

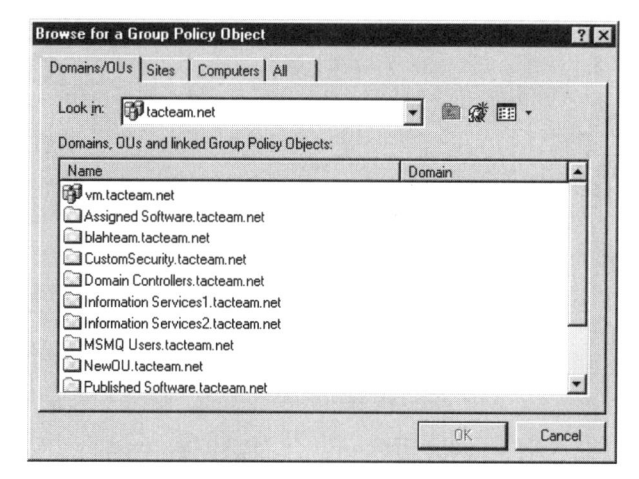

9. Select the GPO that you wish to manage with this Group Policy snap-in. For the purposes of this exercise, choose the Default Domain Policy.

10. Click OK and then click Finish at the next screen. You will now see the selected GPO in the console tree.

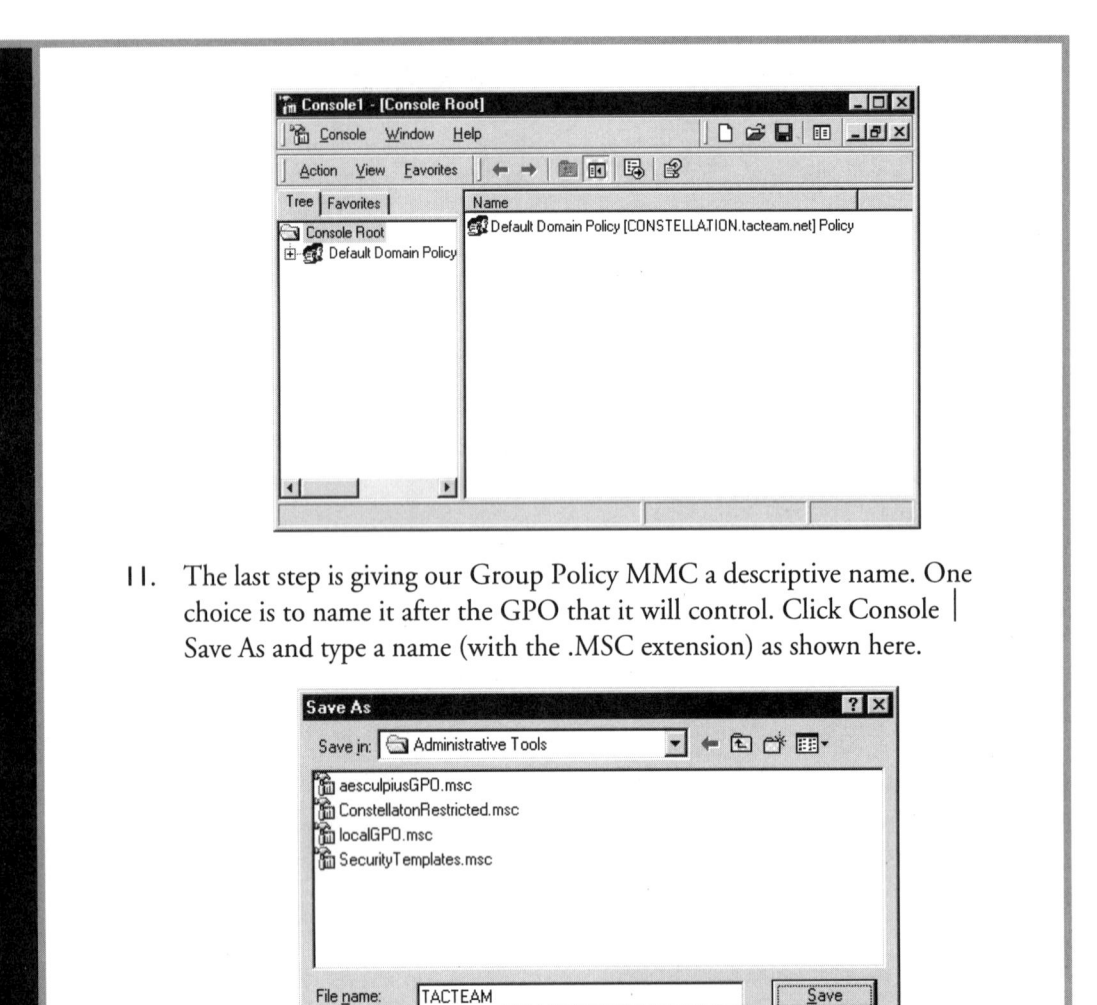

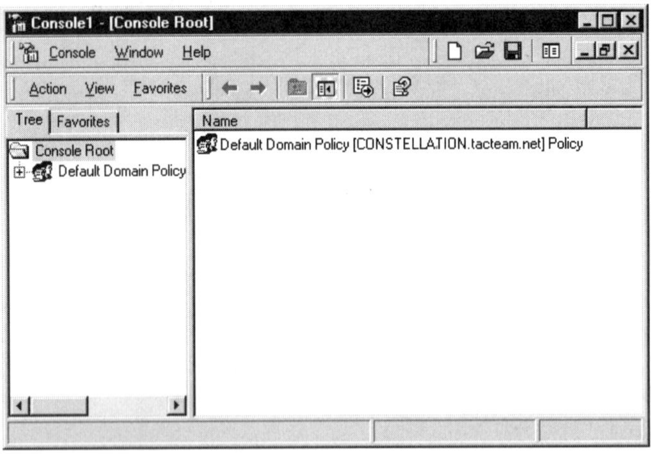
Console1 - [Console Root]
Console Window Help
Action View Favorites
Tree Favorites
Name
Console Root
Default Domain Policy
Default Domain Policy [CONSTELLATION.tacteam.net] Policy

11. The last step is giving our Group Policy MMC a descriptive name. One choice is to name it after the GPO that it will control. Click Console | Save As and type a name (with the .MSC extension) as shown here.

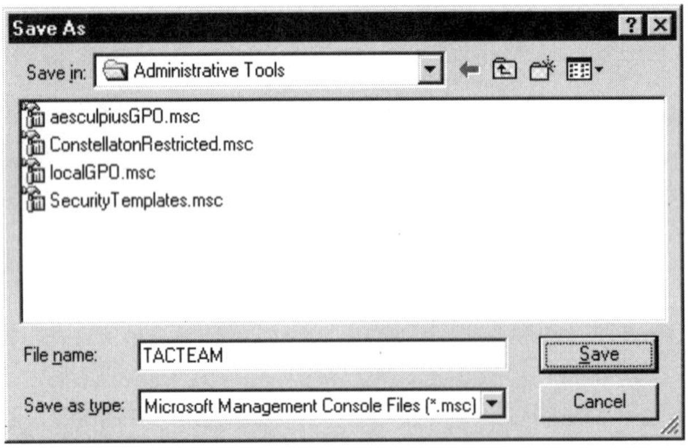
Save As
Save in: Administrative Tools
aesculpiusGPO.msc
ConstellatonRestricted.msc
localGPO.msc
SecurityTemplates.msc
File name: TACTEAM
Save
Save as type: Microsoft Management Console Files (*.msc)
Cancel

By default, the console file will be saved in the My Documents folder. You can create a shortcut on the desktop to make the console easier to access.

In the next section, you will learn how to use our console to apply Group Policies to users and computers in the domain.

CERTIFICATION OBJECTIVE 9.02

Applying Group Policy

Group policies are applied to two types of Active Directory objects: *users* and *computers*. *Security groups* can be used to filter policies, but the policies are not applied to groups directly.

Computer policies are applied at the time the machine boots into Windows 2000, and user policies are applied at the time that the user logs on.

Order in Which Policies Are Applied

Policies are applied in the following order:

1. The Computer Group Policy is applied. After the computer policies are applied, the user logs on, and the user policies are applied.
2. *Windows NT 4.0 style* policies are applied first.
3. *Local* Group Policy is applied.
4. *Site GPOs* are applied.
5. *Domain GPOs* are applied.
6. *OU GPOs* are applied, starting with the parent OU and proceeding through child OUs.

If there are multiple GPOs for a site, a domain, or an organizational unit, the administrator can specify the order of application using a prioritized list of GPOs.

The policy entries applied first are overwritten by those applied later when there are conflicts. If there is no conflict, the effective policy will be an accumulation of all applied policies. A good way to remember this is to think "*The last one there wins!*"

As you can see from the order for processing Group Policy, the local Group Policy object is the least influential of Windows 2000 Group Policies in an Active Directory environment because it is overwritten by nonlocal policies that are applied later.

exam
⍨atch

Windows 2000 clients do not process Windows NT 4.0 .POL files. However, you can turn on Windows NT 4.0 style settings in Group Policy. You are strongly discouraged from doing this because these settings can tattoo the Registry, and are applied when the user logs on, after the computer-specific Group Policy settings have been applied. This means that they can overwrite these after the user logs on. However, they are reset after the first Group Policy refresh. Avoid implementing Windows NT 4.0 style Group Policy settings.

Modifying Default Policy Application Behavior

Windows 2000 provides several ways to modify the default behavior when it comes to the application and the *inheritance* of Group Policies.

Policy Filtering   Group Policy can be filtered by *security group* membership. In Windows 2000, computers can belong to security groups. This is in contrast to how groups were configured in Windows NT 4.0, where only users and other groups could be members of a group. To define which computers and users a Group Policy object influences, administrators can use security groups.

exam
⍨atch

Remember that in Windows 2000 what you formerly knew as a "group" is now referred to as a "Security Group." Windows 2000 supports two types of groups, Security Groups and Distribution Groups.

For any Group Policy object, administrators can *filter* the Group Policy object's effect on computers that are members of specified security groups. To do so, use the standard access control list (ACL) editor. (To use the ACL editor, click a Group Policy object's property sheet, and then click Security. See Figure 9-2.)

If you do not want a particular Group Policy to apply to a security group, then you need to remove both the *Read* and the *Apply Group Policy* permissions for that group. In this way, you filter out the application of the Group Policy for that group. If I wanted to prevent the Default Domain Policy from being applied to the Domain Admins security group, I would highlight the correct group and remove the check mark from the Allow check box for Apply Group Policy and Read.

on the
❶ob

The policies in a GPO apply only to the users who have Read permission for that GPO. You can filter the scope of the GPO by creating security groups and assigning Read permissions to those groups (in other words, you can prevent the policy from applying to a particular group by denying the group Read permission to the GPO).

FIGURE 9-2

Using the ACL editor to modify the access control entry for a security group that contains computers

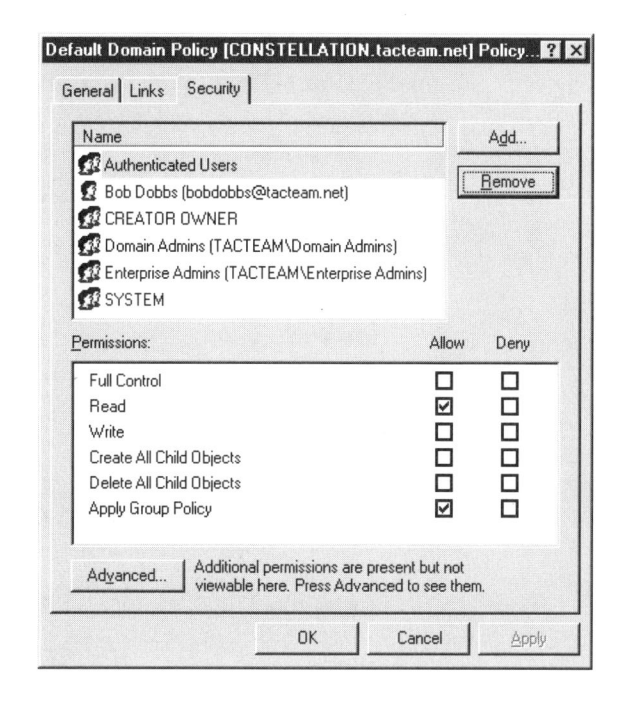

Blocking Policy Inheritance   As an administrator, you can block the inheritance of policies, which would, by default, be propagated from higher site, domain, or organizational unit levels.

To do this, you right-click the SDOU name in the Active Directory Users and Computers MMC, select Properties, and click the Group Policy tab (as shown in Figure 9-3).

Select the Block Policy Inheritance check box. If this option is selected for a child-level GPO, the child object will not inherit any policy from a parent-level GPO.

exam
 ⓦatch

You cannot block inheritance at the site level, because sites do not have any policy to inherit.

Enforcing the Higher-Level Policies with the "No Override" Option
You can force child containers to inherit policies from their higher-level container objects, so that the policies in the selected GPO *cannot* be overridden. To do this, refer back to Figure 9-3, and this time click the Options button. You will see the dialog box in Figure 9-4; select No Override.

404 Chapter 9: Understanding Policies

FIGURE 9-3

Blocking inheritance using the Group Policy tab of the Properties sheet for the tacteam.net domain

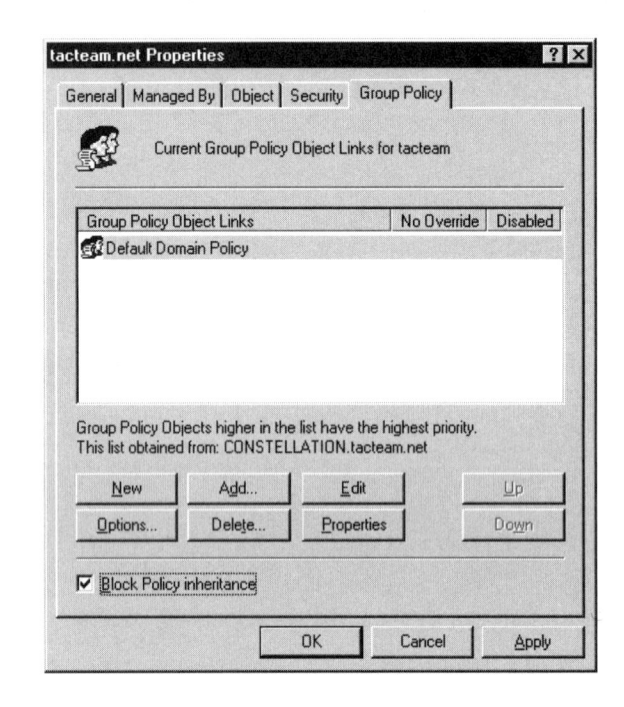

Disabling the Group Policy Object for a Specific SDOU If you do not want the selected GPO to be applied to a particular container object (site, domain, or organizational unit), you can select the Disabled check box shown in Figure 9-4 to accomplish that. You could also delete the link from the Group Policy object to the SDOU. The advantage of disabling the GPO is that you can easily re-enable it without having to remember what GPOs were linked to the SDOU.

FIGURE 9-4

Using No Override to prevent other GPOs from overriding this GPO's policy settings

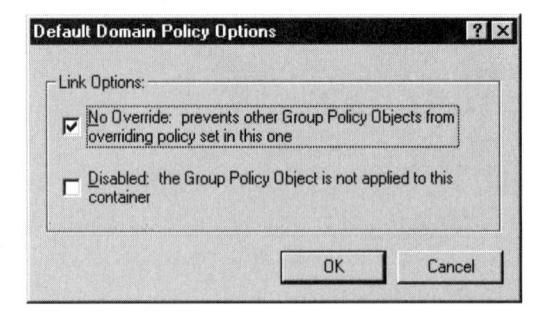

CERTIFICATION OBJECTIVE 9.03

Configuring Group Policy

The details of how to configure Group Policy are contained in Osborne/McGraw-Hill's *MCSE Windows 2000 Directory Services Administration Study Guide (Exam 70-217)*. We will look at an example of how to configure Group Policy by examining scripts.

Scripts

Group policies can be used to assign and run scripts at prescribed times, such as when a user logs on or when the computer is shut down. Scripts are stored in the Scripts subfolder in the GPT.

Scripts assigned to run at logon or logoff are stored in the \USER\SCRIPTS subfolder of the GPT, and those assigned to run when the computer starts up or shuts down are stored in the \MACHINE\SCRIPTS subfolder.

Guidelines for Implementing Group Policy

The following guidelines will help you to implement Group Policy in the most effective and efficient way:

- Use Group Policy rather than Windows NT 4.0 system style policy whenever possible. Windows NT style policies can create problems that are difficult to control and troubleshoot.

- Use the Block Policy Inheritance feature sparingly. Routine use of this feature makes it difficult to troubleshoot policy.

- Use the No Override feature sparingly. For the same reason, routine use of this feature makes it difficult to troubleshoot problems related to Group Policy.

- Minimize the number of Group Policy objects associated with users in domains or organizational units. The more Group Policy objects that are applied to a user, the longer it takes for the user to log on. If more than 1000 GPOs are applied to a user, then there will be a failure in Group Policy application.

- Filter policy based on security group membership. Users who do not have an access control entry (ACE) directing that a particular Group Policy object be

EXERCISE 9-2

Assigning a Script to Run at User Logon

To assign a user logon script, following these steps:

1. Open the Group Policy snap-in.
2. In the console tree, expand the User Configuration and Windows Settings nodes, and click the Scripts node.
3. In the details pane, click the Logon icon. You should see the Logon Properties dialog box as shown here.

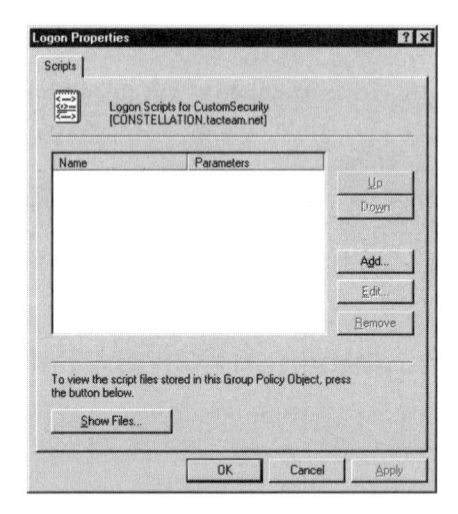

4. On the Logon Properties page, click Add. You will see the Add Script dialog box, as seen here.

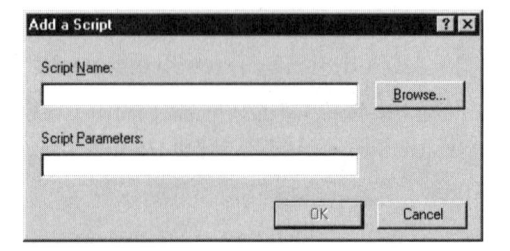

5. On the Add a Script dialog box, set the options you want to use, and then click OK:

    - **Script Name** Type the path to the script, or click Browse to search for the script file in the Netlogon share of the domain controller.

- **Script Parameters** Type any parameters you want to use as you would type them on the command line.

6. On the Logon Properties page, specify any options you want to use:

   - **Up Down** If you assign multiple scripts, the scripts are processed according to the order you specify. To move a script up in the list, click it and then click Up; to move it down, click Down.
   - **Add** Opens the Add a Script dialog box where you can specify any additional scripts to use.
   - **Edit** Opens the Edit Script dialog box where you can modify script information such as name and parameters.
   - **Remove** Removes the selected script from the Logon Scripts list.
   - **Show Files** Use to view the script files stored in the selected Group Policy.

applied to them can avoid the associated log-on delay, because the Group Policy object will not be processed for those users. You can also avoid having policy apply to administrators or other key personal by filtering Group Policy by security group. Filtering can be done only using membership in security groups.

- Override user-based Group Policy with computer-based Group Policy only when absolutely necessary (loopback). This should be done only if you need the desktop configuration to be the same regardless of what user logs on.
- Avoid using cross-domain Group Policy object assignments because the processing of Group Policy objects will take much longer.

CERTIFICATION OBJECTIVE 9.04

Designing an Audit Policy

In Windows 2000, as in Windows NT 4.0, the means by which you track security-related events is called *auditing*. It is important that your audit policy be carefully planned. Implementing the audit feature without first developing a strategy can create more problems than it solves. Auditing is not enabled by default and there is a good reason for that. Each organization's auditing needs will be different; in fact, the auditing strategy for the same organization may change according to current security priorities and vulnerabilities.

In this section, we will discuss the steps involved in developing a viable audit policy for your network. Before we look at the pros and cons of various strategies, we will briefly examine how Windows 2000 security auditing works.

Overview of Windows 2000 Security Auditing

When you enable auditing, you will select specific events to be audited. This means that when a certain action is performed or a certain resource is assessed, Windows 2000 will make an entry in the *security log*, accessed through the Event Viewer in Administrative Tools.

Viewing entries in the Event Viewer is very similar to performing the same task in Windows NT 4.0. However, enabling auditing is not. In Windows 2000, auditing is enabled and configured as a part of Group Policy, using the Group Policy MMC.

Events to be Audited

You will find audit policies for the Windows 2000 domain in the Default Domain Policy, at computer configuration\windows settings\security settings\local policies\audit policy, as shown in Figure 9-5.

As you can see in the right console pane, there are nine possible events that can be audited. You can enable auditing for any or all of these events.

Considerations in Selecting Events to be Audited

Although it might seem prudent to audit as many events as possible, there are several drawbacks to selecting an excessive number of events to be audited.

- The audit log will use large amounts of disk space.
- Auditing requires memory and processor usage, which can have a negative impact on computer performance.
- The log will contain unnecessary information, making it more difficult to find the information that *is* significant.

FIGURE 9-5

Locating the domain audit policies

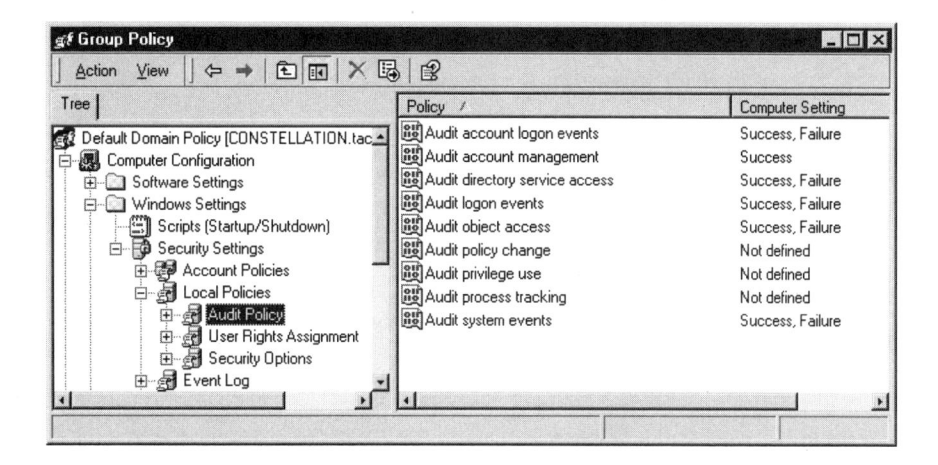

Because of this, it is important to select events carefully, after evaluating your security requirements and determining exactly which events need to be tracked.

Auditing Options

Once you have enabled one of the nine audit policies, you can choose from three options: to audit successes, failures, or both. In the next section, when we discuss planning the audit strategy, we will examine when and why you would use each option. No auditing of that event will take place unless at least one of the two check boxes is selected.

Viewing the Results of Auditing

When an audited event occurs (for example, a successful logon), it will be entered in the security log. The Event Viewer will provide you with information about the dates and times of these occurrences, as well as the account name used and the workstation from which the logon took place. See Figure 9-6 for a look at the properties of a successful logon event.

Planning your Auditing Strategy

Planning your audit strategy can be divided into four steps:

1. Deciding whether to audit security events.
2. Determining which events to audit.

3. Deciding whether to audit success, failure, or both.
4. Determining the disposition of the security event log.

Deciding Whether to Audit Security Events

Whether to implement auditing at all is the first step in planning an audit strategy. To make this decision, you need to assess the level of your organization's security needs: low, medium, or high. Only in an extremely low security environment, where all network data is or could be public record, might you consider no auditing at all.

In most corporate environments, there is at least some confidential data on the network, and some vulnerability to unauthorized access. Some administrators make the mistake of thinking there is no risk of intrusion if the network is not connected to the Internet or other outside networks. You must remember that the biggest security risks are often from inside the organization, and unless the physical security at all your locations is airtight, outsiders may still gain access from internal computers.

FIGURE 9-6

Information available for an audited event

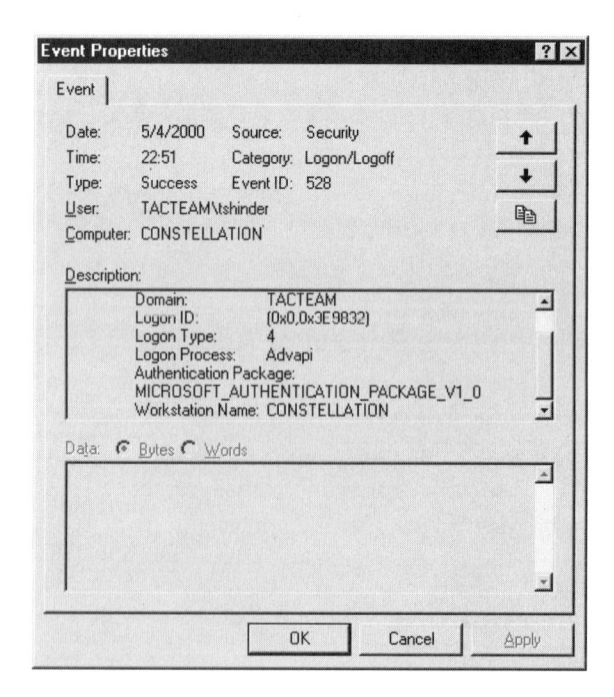

on the Job *If you believe your environment is physically secure, have you ever considered the janitorial staff that has freedom to roam through the building at night after everyone else is gone? How difficult would it be for someone, set on penetrating your network, to pose as a cleaning person and gain physical access to your workstations and servers?*

Determining Which Events to Audit

Once you've decided that you *will* audit security events, the next step is to determine which events to audit. This will vary based on the required security level and the areas in which your network is most vulnerable.

A low-to-medium security network may benefit from routinely auditing such events as failed attempts to logon, access to directory services, and access to objects. You will probably want to audit both failed and successful changes to user accounts and to audit policies themselves.

This is a prudent plan that is easy to implement and manage, and will not overburden the system's resources.

exam Watch *When you enable auditing of object access, you will not audit access to all objects—this would be a massive, and unnecessary, undertaking. Instead, audit access to specific objects of a confidential nature. For example, you might audit access to a shared folder that contains sensitive legal documents.*

In a high security environment, you will want to audit more extensively. Both successful and failed logons, object access, and policy changes should be audited, as well as account management events, directory service access, and perhaps use of user rights and process tracking.

exam Watch *Be aware when planning for auditing of object access that auditing entries are inherited by child objects from the parent object. To prevent this, you must clear the check box to Allow Inheritable Auditing Entries from Parent to Propagate to this Object on the Auditing tab for the object, which is accessed by right-clicking the object, selecting Properties, Security, and clicking the Advanced button.*

Deciding Whether to Audit Success, Failure, or Both

After determining which events to audit, you must decide whether to audit successful completion of the action or access to the resource, failed attempts to perform the action or access the resource, or both. Thus, for each audit event, you have three options: Success, Failure, or both.

For example, if you suspect that someone is trying to hack into the network by guessing passwords, you may wish to audit logon failures. Although an authorized user might mistype his or her password occasionally, a large number of failed logons indicates a possible security breach.

Determining the Disposition of the Security Event Log

The information provided by the security log can be sensitive in itself. Furthermore, it will be useful to you only if it is there when you need it.

Using the same Group Policy console for the default domain policy, you can set the maximum size for the security log, restrict guest access to the log, set a number of days to retain the security log, and determine the retention method to be used. Retention methods you can select from are:

- Overwrite events by days
- Overwrite events as needed
- Do not overwrite events (Clear log manually)

Don't forget to consider retention and access to the log as part of the overall planning of your audit strategy.

CERTIFICATION OBJECTIVE 9.05

Security Templates

Microsoft provides a full set of templates that conform to a number of common security scenarios. These security templates can be broken down into two general categories: default and incremental. The *default* or *basic* templates are applied by the operating system when a clean install has been performed. They are not applied if an upgrade installation has been done. However, they can be applied *after* the upgrade has been completed.

The *incremental* templates can be applied after the basic security templates have been applied. The four types of incremental templates are: *Compatible, Secure, Highly Secure,* and *Dedicated Domain Controller.* Table 9-1 describes the function of these provided templates.

You can save time and effort during an initial rollout by applying these templates to workstations, domain controllers, and member and stand-alone servers. Then as time allows, you can customize and fine tune security settings for local computers, organizational units, or an entire domain.

TABLE 9-1 The Default and Incremental Security Templates

Template Security Level	Description
Basic	These include the BASIC*.INF templates. Use these to correct configurations that you want to return to baseline. These Basic or *default* templates allow you to "roll-back" security to the original installation defaults.
Compatible	These are the COMPAT*.INF templates. By default, all users are power users on Windows 2000 Professional. If you do not want your users to have Power User rights, the Compatible configuration alters the default permissions for the users group so that legacy applications can run properly. Many non-Windows 2000 certified applications require that a user have an elevated level of permissions in order to run properly. If you choose to apply the Compatible templates, you loosen security so that you do not have to place ordinary users into the power users group to run non-Windows 2000 certified applications.
Secure	These are the SECURE*.INF templates. The Secure templates will increase the level of security applied to account policy, certain Registry keys, and auditing. Permissions to file system objects are not affected with this configuration.
Highly Secure	These include the HISEC*.INF templates. Highly Secure configurations add security to network communications. IPSec will be configured for these machines, and will be required for communications. Down-level clients will not be able to communicate with machines that have the Highly Secure templates applied to them.
Dedicated Domain Controller	These are the DEDICA*.INF templates. These templates optimize security for local users on domain controllers that do not run other server applications (which is the preferred configuration for domain controllers).

Configuring Security

You can manually configure security by making changes in the appropriate nodes in Group Policy. However, whether you edit your security configuration in "live" fashion, or through templates, you cannot define new security attributes. Only modification of *existing* Windows 2000 security elements is configurable. Microsoft or third parties will include extensions to the security attributes in the future.

You should configure security, and changes to an existing security configuration, using security templates. By using a security template, you can configure security settings in the template. After you have completed making the changes in the template, import that template's settings into the Group Policy for the domain or OU.

By using templates to configure security, you never have to worry about "lost" configuration settings. If you ever make manual changes to domain or OU policy, and you don't care for the results, you can always reapply the template.

When configuring a template for your security policy, you will focus attention on the following:

- Account Policies
- Local Policies
- Event Log
- Restricted Groups
- System Services
- Registry
- File System

Account Policies

Account policies define aspects of security relating primarily to passwords and Kerberos behavior. The password Policy contains entries related to password aging and password length. Account Lockout policy determines how many bad tries a person gets before the account is locked out. Kerberos policy applies only to domain controllers, because local logons do not use Kerberos. Kerberos entries include maximum lifetimes for various tickets, such as user tickets and user renewal.

You may remember where account policies were configured in Windows NT 4.0: User Manager for Domains.

Local Policies and Event Log

Local policies include the *Audit Policy, User Rights Assignment,* and *Security Options* nodes. Some Audit Policy selections include auditing logon events, use of user privileges, systems events, and object access. The User Rights Assignment node includes granting or denying user rights such as the right to add workstations to the domain, change the system time, log on locally, and access the computer from the network.

Perhaps the most significant differences from Windows NT 4.0 system policies are found in the Security Options node. Here you can make changes that could only be made through direct Registry edits in Windows NT 4.0. Examples of such Security Options include: clearing the pagefile when the system shuts down, message text during logon, number of previous logons kept in cache, and shut down system immediately if unable to log security audits. Figure 9-7 depicts some of the entries seen in the local policies node.

The improvements in local policy management are tremendous with the addition of the configurable objects available in the Security Options node.

Event Log

The Event Log node allows you to configure settings specifically for the Event Log, as seen in Figure 9-8.

FIGURE 9-7

Local Policies node in the basicdc security template

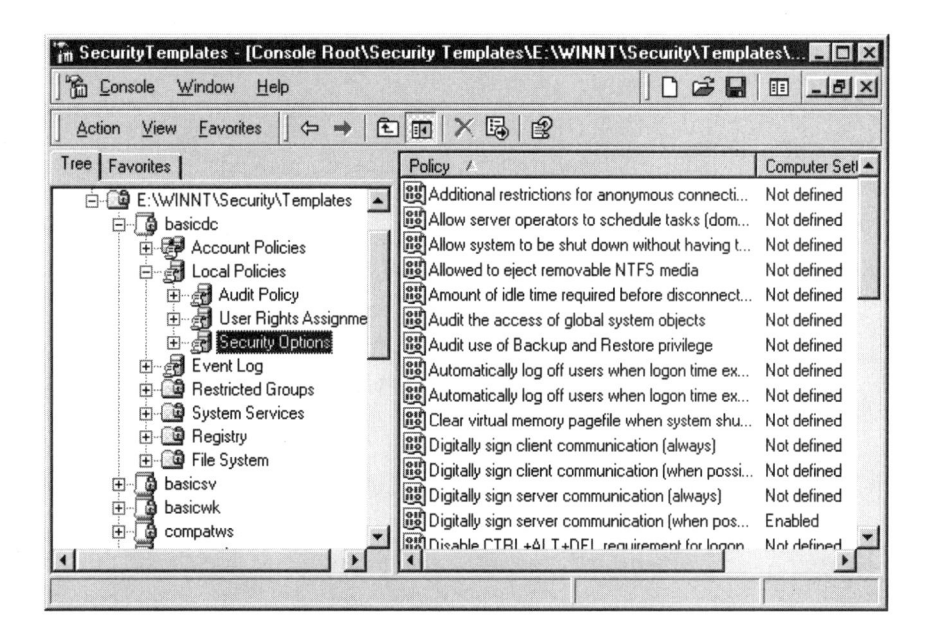

FIGURE 9-8

Settings for the Event Log in the basicdc security template

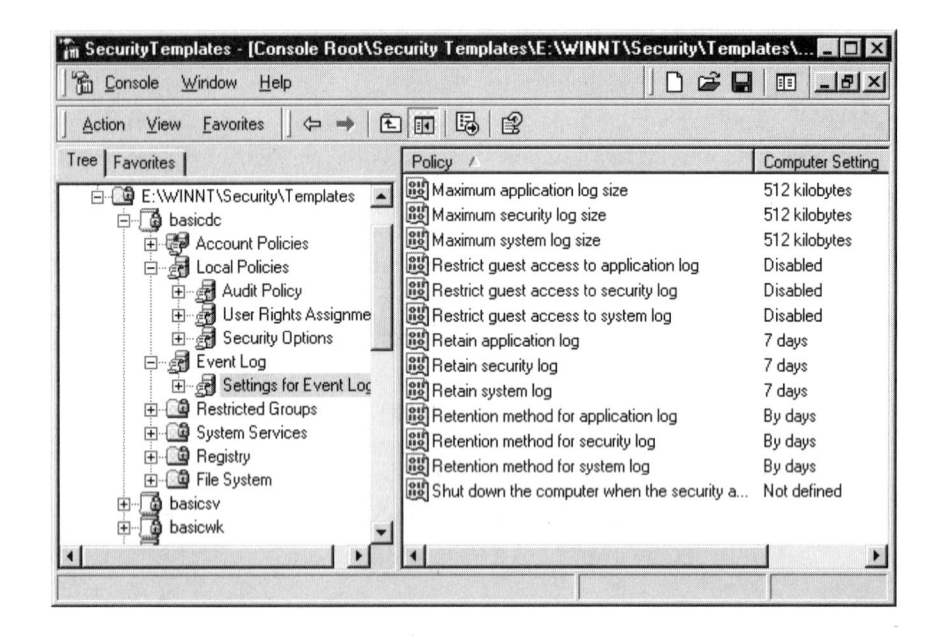

Policy	Computer Setting
Maximum application log size	512 kilobytes
Maximum security log size	512 kilobytes
Maximum system log size	512 kilobytes
Restrict guest access to application log	Disabled
Restrict guest access to security log	Disabled
Restrict guest access to system log	Disabled
Retain application log	7 days
Retain security log	7 days
Retain system log	7 days
Retention method for application log	By days
Retention method for security log	By days
Retention method for system log	By days
Shut down the computer when the security a...	Not defined

Event log configuration settings allow you to configure the length of time logs are retained and the size of the event logs. You can also configure the system to shut down if the security log becomes full.

Restricted Groups

The Restricted Groups node represents a new security option that was not available in Windows NT 4.0. You can predefine, through policy, members of a particular group.

For example, there are times when the administrator needs to temporarily add users to groups with a higher classification than the users typical group membership. This might be the case when an administrator goes on vacation and another member of the team is assigned full administrative rights.

However, often this "temporary" promotion ends up being a permanent one, and the user remains in the administrators group. Groups may also become permanent members of other groups, when you wished for only a temporary elevation of privileges. By defining Restricted Group membership rules, you can return group membership to that defined by security policy. Figure 9-9 shows the Restricted Groups node entries.

Users are added to restricted groups by double-clicking the group in the results pane and adding new members from there. You can also restrict what groups the

FIGURE 9-9

Restricted Groups and group members in the basicdc template

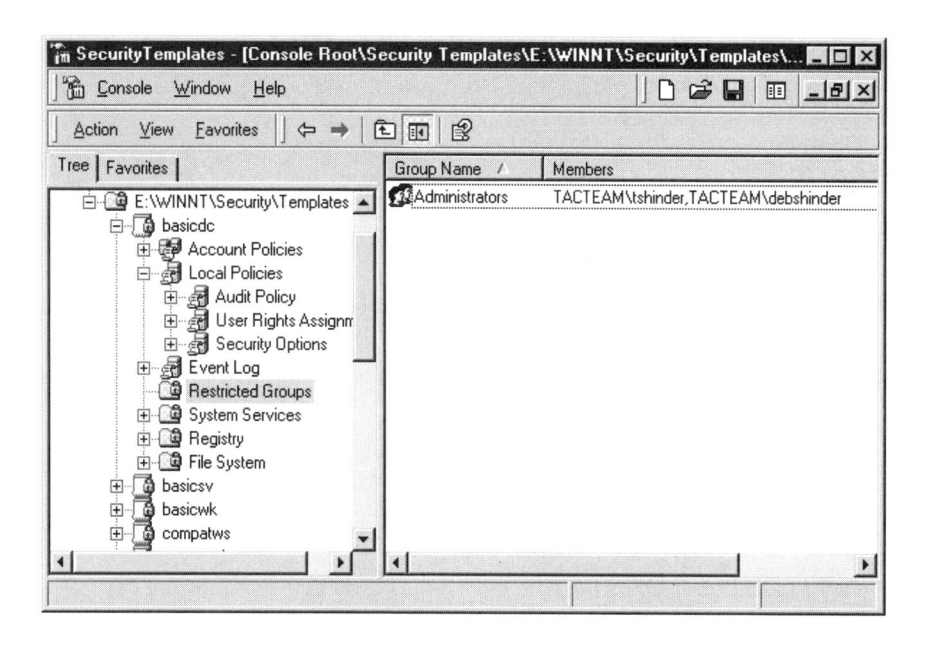

[Screenshot of Security Templates MMC console showing the basicdc template expanded with Account Policies, Local Policies (Audit Policy, User Rights Assignment, Security Options), Event Log, Restricted Groups (selected), System Services, Registry, and File System. Right pane shows Administrators group with members TACTEAM\tshinder, TACTEAM\debshinder.]

group itself can be a member of (a type of recursive checking), using the nested group capabilities now available in Windows 2000.

on the Job — **Although Restricted Groups seem like a virtual panacea, they suffer from the inability to control how long the temporary members of the group can stay in the restricted group. The temporary members will be dropped from group membership the next time Group Policy is refreshed.**

Registry Security

Registry keys can be protected by policy. You can define a security policy for a Registry key or a value in the database, and then customize the propagation of the setting through the Key Properties dialog box. Figure 9-10 shows an example of how to control propagation of security settings. Figure 9-11 shows what the Registry key pane looks like.

This approach is much easier and less error prone then controlling security of Registry entries through the Registry editor, where each machine must be configured individually or through scripting.

exam Watch — **You should not manually set security on Registry keys unless you have a compelling reason to do so. Incorrectly configuring security on the Registry could lead to a computer that does not function properly, or at all.**

FIGURE 9-10

Template Security Policy Setting

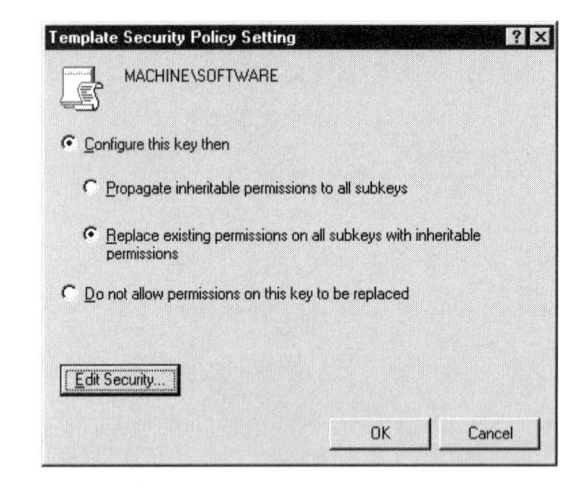

File System Security

The File System Security node allows you to configure NTFS permission for all local drives. It is not uncommon for a number of different administrators to "get into" the Explorer and "customize" the NTFS permissions on files and folders.

FIGURE 9-11

Registry Security Template objects

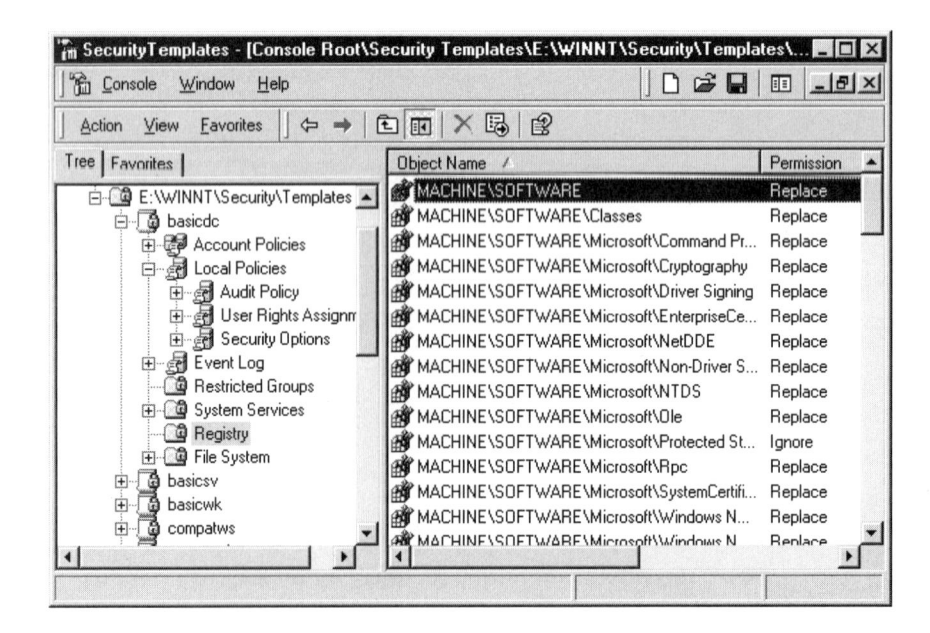

File and folder security should be part of a well thought out and implemented security plan. This security plan can be realized by setting File System Policy in the templates. You can then periodically audit the status of the file system to look for inconsistencies between the plan and the actual state of NTFS permissions in the local environment. Figure 9-12 shows some File System Security objects.

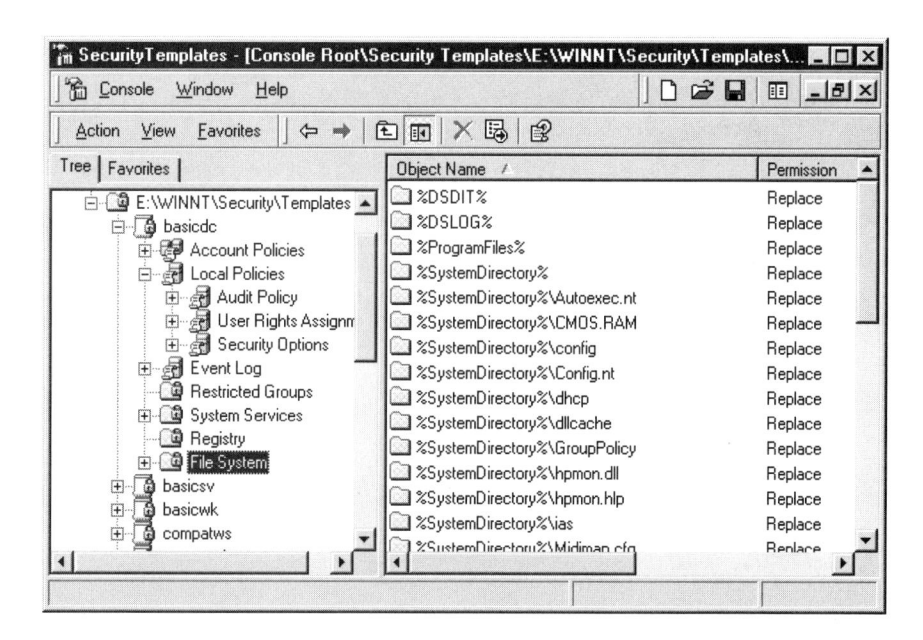

Note that in the template the volume letters are not pre-assigned. You can add local volume letters by right-clicking the File System node, and picking the volumes you want included in the template.

System Services Security

The System Services node allows you to control security and startup policy on all the services defined in the template. Controlling startup behavior of system services can save the administrator many headaches. Consider the situation of users starting up their own Remote Access Service (RAS) or Dynamic Host Configuration Protocol (DHCP) services haphazardly. This type of situation creates a large security risk for your network.

You can set restrictive networking services startup properties, and assign all computers that require certain services to an OU that does have the right to start up particular networking services.

Figure 9-13 shows some of the content of the Services node.

FIGURE 9-12

File System Security objects

FIGURE 9-13

The System Services node in the basicdc template

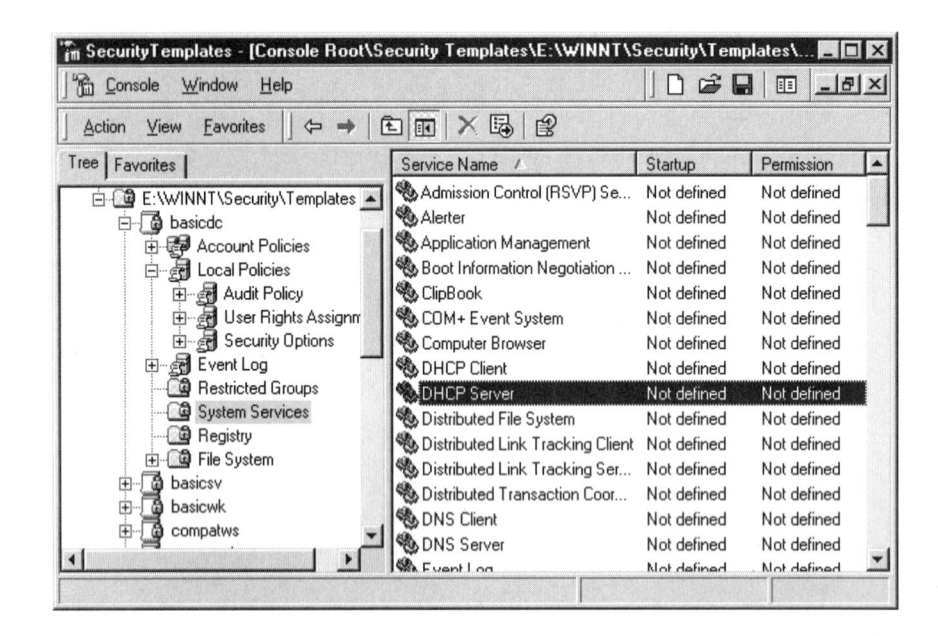

FROM THE CLASSROOM

Using Templates

I've found that the idea of using templates is a little confusing to students at times. The students often get the impression that the actual template is imported into the security configuration of Group Policy. However, a template just provides a method of choosing which settings you want to use. Think of the last time you went to the tattoo parlor to get a tattoo. The tattoo artist did not just start drawing on your arm. Rather, he first created a stencil or *template* and then applied that to your arm. Then he painted the outline of the tattoo on your arm through the template. The template provided the framework of the drawing to be made. In the same way, the security templates provide the framework for which you create the security settings that will be placed into the Group Policy.

—*Thomas W. Shinder, M.D., MCSE, MCT*

Security Templates

EXERCISE 9-3

CertCam 9-3

Creating and Configuring a Security Template

In this exercise, you will create a new security template and then make configuration changes to the template. Do not perform these steps on a live production network without the permission of your network administrator.

1. Log on as Administrator at a Domain Controller.
2. Click Start | Run | MMC. This opens an empty MMC console in which we will add the security templates snap-in.
3. Click the Console menu, and then click Add/Remove Snap-in. This takes you to the Add/Remove Snap-in dialog box.
4. Click the Add button. In the Add Standalone Snap-in dialog box, scroll down and click Security Templates, as pictured below. Click the Add button. Click the Close button on the Add Standalone Snap-in dialog box. Click the OK button on the Add/Remove Snap-in dialog box.

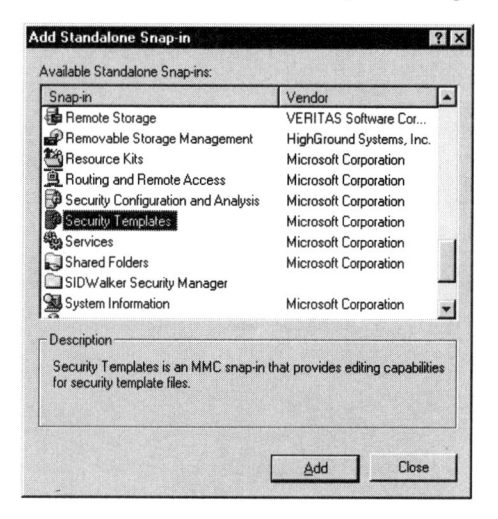

5. Expand the Security Templates node in the left pane, and expand the node just under that, which represents the path to the security templates folder.

You should see something like what is in the following illustration. Make note of the security templates that are included with Windows 2000.

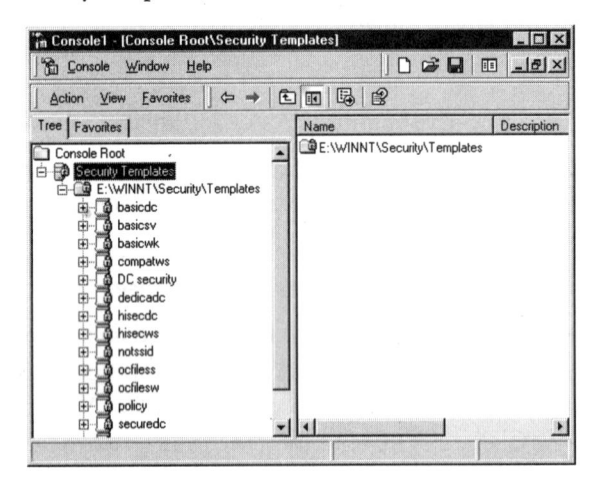

6. We do not want to make any changes to the predefined templates. The easiest way to create a new template is to copy an existing template that is close to what we want, and then make changes to the copy. To create the copy, right-click the basicwk template, seen in the left pane. Click Save As, and type **customwk** in the file name box. By default, the new template should be stored in the same location as the other security templates. Click Save. You should now see the template in the left pane, as seen here:

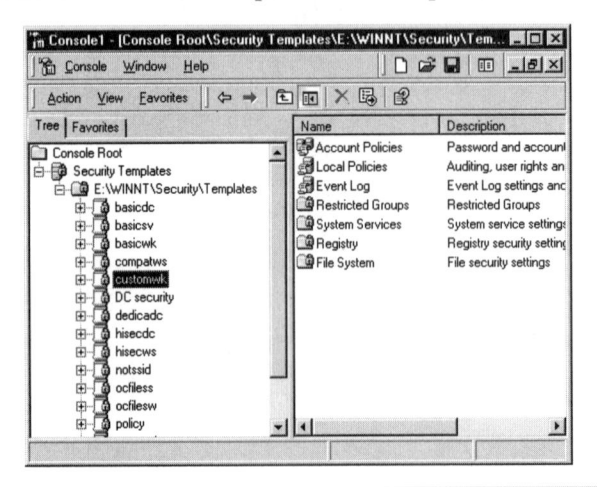

7. Expand the customwk node, and then expand the Account Policies node. Click the Password Policy node. In the right pane, you see several password policy options that you can configure. Double-click Passwords Must Meet Complexity Requirements. You will see what appears here:

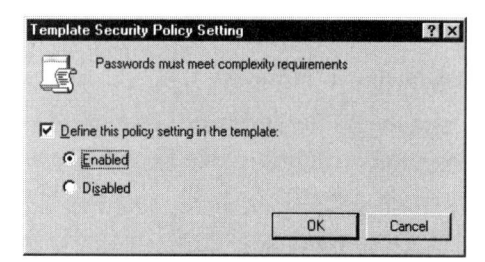

8. Select the check box for Define This Policy Setting in the Template. Then select the Enabled option button. Click OK. You should now see in the Computer Setting column that the status has changed to Enabled.

9. Now you must save the changes that you made to the template. Right-click customwk, and click Save. The changes you made to the template have been saved.

Creating and Applying New Security Templates

In order to take advantage of security templates, you need to know how to create your own customized templates and security settings. After completing your security configuration, you will need to apply these changes to your SDOU. We will examine how to create the new template, and then how to apply the template settings.

After creating custom templates, it is a good idea to back them up to a safe place. This will greatly speed up your disaster recovery measures should you ever find that you need to rebuild the server. You do not need to back up the default templates because they will be restored when you reinstall the operating system.

EXERCISE 9-4

Applying a Custom Template to OU Policy

In this exercise, you will create an organizational unit, and then apply the customwk template's security settings to that OU. Since this template was created based on the basicwk template, we certainly don't want to import its settings and apply them to the entire domain!

1. Log on as Administrator.
2. Open the Active Directory Users and Computers console. Click Start | Programs | Administrative Tools | Active Directory Users and Computers.
3. Right-click a domain name, and trace down to New and then trace over and click Organizational Unit.
4. In the New Object–Organizational Unit dialog box, type **CustomSecurity** in the Name text box. Click OK.
5. Right-click the CustomSecurity OU now seen in the left pane and click the Properties command. This opens the CustomSecurity Properties dialog box. Click the Group Policy tab.
6. There is no Group Policy object linked to the new OU. To create a new Group Policy to link to the OU, click the New button. Replace the default name of the Group Policy with the name **CustomSecurity** and press ENTER. We want to edit the CustomSecurity Group Policy, so click the Edit button.
7. Expand the Computer Configuration node, and then expand the Windows Settings node. Click the Security Settings node. (If you receive an error in the right pane that says "Windows cannot open the template file", you will need to close the Group Policy editor, and the Properties dialog box, and then reopen the Group Policy editor.) Right-click the Security Settings node and click Import Policy, as seen here:

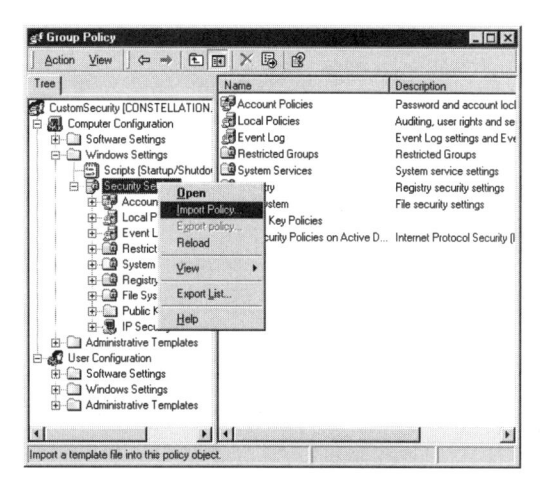

8. In the Import Policy From dialog box, select the CUSTOMWK.INF file and select the Clear This Database before Importing check box. Click Open.

9. The security settings have been imported into the CustomSecurity Group Policy object. Because we chose to clear the database, all previous security settings have been removed and replaced with the settings in our imported template. If the database had not been cleared, the settings would have been merged with those already existing in the GPO.

10. Click the Password Policy node in the left pane. You can see that our password security policy is now part of the security settings for this Group Policy object.

11. Close the Group Policy window, and click OK on the CustomSecurity Properties dialog box.

The Group Policy will be applied to members of the OU after the next policy refresh period is completed. You can also force Group Policy application using the secedit command with the /refreshpolicy switch.

CERTIFICATION SUMMARY

In this chapter, you learned what Group Policy is and reviewed some of the basic functionality of Group Policy. You learned that Group Policy can be implemented at many different levels, and that you can use Group Policy to achieve a level of control over your network and network clients that was not available in Windows NT 4.0.

We reviewed and examined auditing in Windows 2000. You saw that you must plan your auditing policies very carefully, or you may have significant problems with performance on the machine performing the auditing function. Auditing policies need to be customized for the level of security required in the environment in which they are designed.

Finally, we covered the security templates included with Windows 2000, and how you can create your own security templates. You saw how to create your own custom security configurations in a template, and then import those configuration settings into you own GPO for a domain, a site, or an organizational unit.

✓ TWO-MINUTE DRILL

Overview of Group Policy and the Microsoft Management Console

- ❑ Group Policy allows you to set configuration settings on machines in an OU, domain, or site.
- ❑ Group Policy is managed through a Microsoft Management Console, which can be customized according to the administrator's needs by adding *snap-ins*.
- ❑ Group Policy objects can be broken down into two major categories: local and nonlocal.
- ❑ A Group Policy object consists of a Group Policy template and a Group Policy container.
- ❑ Local Group Policy is the only way to apply Group Policy in a workgroup environment.

Applying Group Policy

- ❑ Group Policy is applied to computers and users.
- ❑ Learn the order in which Group Policy is applied: Computer policy, Windows NT 4.0 Style policy, Local policy, Site policy, Domain policy, and OU policy.
- ❑ The "Last one there wins!" subsequent policy application overwrites policy settings made previously.
- ❑ No Override prevents policy settings from being overwritten by other policy settings applied later in the application process.
- ❑ No Inheritance prevents group policy from being inherited from higher-level objects. No Override takes precedence over No Inheritance.
- ❑ Group Policy cannot be directly applied to groups. However, you can work around this problem by using policy filtering.
- ❑ You can disable a Group Policy link so that you do not have to delete it. This is very helpful during Group Policy troubleshooting.

Configuring Group Policy

- ❏ Use Group Policy rather than Windows NT 4.0 system style policy whenever possible.
- ❏ Use the Block Policy Inheritance feature sparingly and Use the No Override feature sparingly.
- ❏ Minimize the number of Group Policy objects associated with users in domains or organizational units.
- ❏ Filter policy based on security group membership.
- ❏ Override user-based Group Policy with computer-based Group Policy only when absolutely necessary.
- ❏ Avoid using cross-domain Group Policy object assignments.

Designing an Audit Policy

- ❏ Audit policy should be carefully planned, and the plan should include the level of auditing required for the security required of the networking environment.
- ❏ The results of the auditing process will appear in the Event Monitor in the Security Log.
- ❏ Auditing can have a large impact on processor utilization, disk access, and memory. Be judicious about the level of auditing you implement.
- ❏ Pay close attention to how the Security Log in the Event Viewer is handled. Important events can be overwritten if you have not configured it correctly.

Security Templates

- ❏ Security templates provided with the Windows 2000 operating system come in two types: Basic and Incremental.
- ❏ Basic templates are applied during the installation of the operating system. Incremental templates should be applied after the basic template settings have been implemented.

- Basic security template information is not applied on machines that have been upgraded, or on those that use the FAT file systems for the boot partition.
- The security templates allow you to configure security for the following nodes in Group Policy: Account policies, Local policies, Event Log, Restricted Groups, System Services, Registry, and File System.
- You cannot apply different Account Policies in a single domain. Account Policies set at the site or OU level will be ignored.
- Always apply new security policy through templates. In this way, you can easily revert to your previous policy by reapplying the template that was in use.
- There is no Undo button to allow you to undo the changes you make when you apply new security settings when importing templates.

430 Chapter 9: Understanding Policies

SELF TEST

The following questions will help you measure your understanding of the material presented in this chapter. Read all of the choices carefully, as there may be more than one correct answer. Choose all correct answers for each question.

Overview of Group Policy and the Microsoft Management Console

1. Group Policy is a set of configuration options that can be applied to which of the following? (Choose all that apply.)

    A. A site.
    B. A domain.
    C. An organizational unit.
    D. A Windows 3.1 computer.

2. Group Policy objects can be created or edited using which of the following tools? (Choose all that apply.)

    A. A custom MMC created by the user.
    B. From the Group Policy shortcut in the Administrative Tools menu.
    C. From the Active Directory Users and Computers shortcut on the Administrative Tools menu.
    D. From the Active Directory Sites and Services shortcut on the Administrative Tools menu.

3. You are the system administrator of a small office that has 10 Windows 2000 Professional computers and a single Windows 2000 Server computer. The Windows 2000 Server is not a domain controller and security is managed in a workgroup environment. You want to lock down the desktop and security configurations on the client workstations. How can you implement Group Policy to accomplish this task?

    A. Link a Group Policy to a site.
    B. Link a Group Policy to a domain.
    C. Link a Group Policy to the workgroup.
    D. Configure a Local Group Policy on each workstation.

4. Your company has recently upgraded its network and domain structure from Windows NT 4.0 to Windows 2000. You have created extensive System Policy settings using the Windows NT 4.0 System Policy editor, and have saved those settings to an NTCONFIG.POL file. How can you apply these settings to your Windows 2000 client machines?

A. Export the NTCONFIG.POL settings into a Group Policy template.

B. Import the NTCONFIG.POL settings directly into a Group Policy object.

C. Manually configure the desired settings in a Windows 2000 Group Policy object.

D. Place the NTCONFIG.POL file in the NETLOGON share of the PDC emulator.

Applying Group Policy

5. You want to apply a Group Policy to a group you have created, named Temps. However, when you try to assign the policy to the group, you find that you cannot do this. What might be causing the problem?

    A. You can apply Group Policy to built-in groups only.

    B. The Temp group name is reserved, and therefore you cannot apply Group Policy to it.

    C. You cannot apply Group Policy to groups.

    D. You must first create a distribution group named Temps before you can apply Group Policy.

6. Your organization has a single Windows 2000 domain and several organizational units that you use to manage Users and Computers through Group Policy. You want to enforce different password policies for the different OUs, but you find that after configuring the OUs with different policies, they are not applied. What is causing this problem?

    A. You must first refresh Group Policy so that it is applied to the OUs.

    B. You must set the refresh interval and offset so that they equal seven.

    C. You must first disable the default domain policy.

    D. You must create another Active Directory domain if you wish to implement a second password policy.

7. Which of the following is true of the \USER subfolder in the Group Policy template? (Choose all that apply.)

    A. It contains the REGISTRY.POL file with the Registry settings applied to users.

    B. It contains the .ADM files.

    C. It contains several subfolders.

    D. It contains the scripts and related files for startup and shutdown scripting.

8. You are configuring Group Policy, and you want to create a new site Group Policy. However, you receive a message that you do not have permission to create a new Group Policy. Why can you not create a new site Group Policy?

432 Chapter 9: Understanding Policies

    A. You are not a member of the Domain Admins Group.
    B. You are not a member of the Enterprise Admins Group.
    C. You are not a member of the Group Policy Admins Group.
    D. You are not a member of the Domain Users Group.

Configuring Group Policy

9. Which of the following recommendations will reduce the difficulty of troubleshooting Group Policy problems? (Choose all that apply.)

    A. Disabling Windows NT 4.0 Policy Settings.
    B. Using the No Override option sparingly.
    C. Using the Block Inheritance option sparingly.
    D. Using System Policy Editor to create policy for Windows 2000 domains.

10. Your organization uses Windows 2000 domains and organizational units. You also run several kiosk-like computers in the lobby of your building for public access. You would like to make sure that no matter who logs on to the machines in the kiosks, only the policy for the computer takes effect, regardless of which user logs on. How can you do this?

    A. Attach a loopback serial adapter to the kiosk machines.
    B. Enable loopback processing through the Administrative templates.
    C. Selectively disable User Policy settings in the Group Policy Object link.
    D. Set the Computer Policy settings to No Override in the Group Policy Object link.

11. What is the limit on the number of Group Policy objects that can be applied to a User Account before there is a failure in Group Policy?

    A. 1.
    B. 100.
    C. 1000.
    D. 10000.

Designing an Audit Policy

12. You have created an audit policy to audit all successful and unsuccessful access to files and folders on your server. After configuring the audit policy, you get complaints from users telling

you that it takes longer to access files from the network server than it used to take. What might be the problem in this situation? (Choose all that apply.)

A. Auditing all files on a server will consume an excessive amount of processor time.

B. Auditing all files on the server will require an excessive amount of disk access time.

C. Auditing all files will require excessive network traffic.

D. Auditing all files requires excessive time to study the Security Log.

13. You are the administrator for a small law firm that has 60 network clients and two Windows 2000 Server computers. One of the Windows 2000 Server computers is used for remote access, and the other is a Domain Controller, which doubles as a file server. The machine used as a remote access server also runs WINS, DHCP, and DNS Services. The law firm handles product liability cases made against large companies, with potential payoffs in the tens or hundreds of millions of dollars. Which of the following would you implement as part of your auditing solution? (Choose all that apply.)

A. Successful logons.

B. Unsuccessful logons.

C. Policy changes.

D. Object access.

14. You suspect that someone is trying to hack into the network using a brute force or dictionary attack. What single auditing function would you implement to ascertain which user account may have been compromised?

A. Successful log offs.

B. Server shutdown.

C. Unsuccessful log offs.

D. Unsuccessful logons.

15. You want to go into the Event Viewer and check your security log for audit activities from two months ago. When you open the Event Viewer and go into the Security Log, you find that those log entries are no longer available. Why might this be the case? (Choose all that apply.)

A. The maximum log file size was exceeded.

B. Overwrite Events as Needed was selected.

C. Overwrite Events Older than 7 Days was selected.

D. Do not Overwrite Events was selected.

Security Templates

16. You have made several configuration changes to the security policy on your local machine. However, you find that after configuring local security policy, your changes have not taken effect. You restart the computer hoping that your changes will work, but they still are not implemented. What might be the problem?

    A. You must refresh the local security policy with the secedit command.

    B. You need to reload the local security policy using the reload command.

    C. Higher-level policy is overwriting your settings.

    D. You cannot configure a local security policy.

17. You would like to reverse the changes you made to an organizational unit's Security Policy after you imported a security template's settings to the OU. How would you go about doing this?

    A. Use the undo button in the Group Policy editor.

    B. Export the changes you made to the Group Policy in the Group Policy editor.

    C. Import the basic template OU template.

    D. You cannot undo the changes directly.

LAB QUESTIONS

You are about to upgrade your Windows NT 4.0 domain to a Windows 2000 domain. You have a single Windows NT 4.0 Server computer acting as a PDC for 300 network clients. The PDC has three partitions on its 6.4GB hard disk, and all of the partitions are formatted with FAT16.

After the upgrade, you notice that the security that you thought would be applied to system objects on the Windows 2000 Domain Controller have not been applied. After researching the subject, you realize what the problem was, and you correct the problem.

After correcting the problem, you decide that you want the highest level of security possible on the Domain Controller. After performing some more research, you make the changes necessary to apply the highest level of security you can on the Domain Controller with basic tools supplied "out of the box" on the Windows 2000 Domain Controller.

1. Why wasn't security applied during the upgrade process?

2. After determining why security wasn't applied during the upgrade process, what did you do to provide a *basic* level of security to the Domain Controller?

3. After providing a basic level of security to the Domain Controller, what did you do next to create a high level of security?

SELF TEST ANSWERS

Overview of Group Policy and the Microsoft Management Console

1. ☑ **A, B, and C. A** is correct because you can apply Group Policy to a site. **B** is correct because you can link a Group Policy object to a domain. **C** is correct because you can link a Group Policy object to an organizational unit.
   ☒ **D** is incorrect because you cannot link a Group Policy object to a Windows 3.1 computer.

2. ☑ **A, C, and D. A** is correct because you can create your own custom Group Policy Console. When you create the console, you choose what the focus of the console will be. That focus can be for any Group Policies available to the console. **C** is correct because you can access Group Policy through Active Directory Users and Computers. **D** is correct because you can access Group Policy from Active Directory Sites and Services.
   ☒ **B** is incorrect because there is no shortcut to the Group Policy editor in the Start menu.

3. ☑ **D** is correct because in a workgroup environment, no Active Directory structures can be applied to the client computers. In a workgroup environment, you can still apply Group Policy by configuring the local Group Policy on each workstation in the workgroup.
   ☒ **A** is incorrect because you must install Active Directory to access Sites and Services. **B** is incorrect because you must install Active Directory to configure domain policy. **C** is incorrect because you cannot link a Group Policy object to a workgroup because workgroups are not part of the Active Directory structure.

4. ☑ **C** is correct because Windows NT 4.0 NTCONFIG.POL files have a structure that is different from Group Policy. Because of the basic incompatibility between the System Policy editor created files and Group Policy, you cannot import those settings created in the NTCONFIG.POL file into Group Policy. You will need to manually configure Group Policy with your desired configuration.
   ☒ **A** is incorrect because you cannot export NTCONFIG.POL settings into a Group Policy template. **B** is incorrect because you directly import NTCONFIG.POL settings into a Group Policy object. **D** is incorrect because Windows 2000 network clients do not use the NTCONFIG.POL file to receive policy.

Applying Group Policy

5. ☑ **C** is correct because you cannot link a Group Policy object to a security group. GPOs can only be links to sites, domains, and organizational units. This represents a major difference in how policy is applied when compared to Windows NT 4.0 System Policies. You can use filtering as a workaround for this problem.

436 Chapter 9: Understanding Policies

    ☒ A is incorrect because you cannot apply Group Policy to groups, whether they are built-in or not. B is incorrect because the Temp name is not reserved, and you still could not link the GPO to the group even after you created it. D is incorrect because distribution groups are not a factor in the problem of linking GPOs to groups.

6. ☑ D. Only one password policy can exist per domain. Domain controllers ignore password, lockout, and Kerberos policies defined at any other level.
    ☒ A is incorrect because even if you were to use the manual refresh command, it still would not apply a different password policy to OUs. B is incorrect because the refresh interval makes no difference. The default refresh interval for Group Policy is 90 minutes, with a default offset of 30 minutes. C is incorrect because even if you disable the default domain policy, it will not allow OUs to have their own password policies.

7. ☑ A and C. The \USER folder contains the REGISTRY.POL file with Registry settings applied to users, and has several subfolders, such as \USER\APPLICATIONS and \USER\SCRIPTS.
    ☒ B and D are incorrect. The .ADM files are contained in the \ADM subfolder, and the scripts for startup and shutdown (which apply to the computer, not the user) are contained in the \MACHINE\SCRIPTS subfolder.

8. ☑ B. You must be an Enterprise Admin in order to create a new Group Policy object.
    ☒ A, C, and D are incorrect because they are not Enterprise Administrators.

Configuring Group Policy

9. ☑ A, B, and C. A is correct because you avoid many problems by disabling Windows NT style policies. B is correct because you can reduce troubleshooting problems when you use the No Override options infrequently. C is correct because you can simplify troubleshooting Group Policy behavior by using the Block Inheritance attribute sparingly.
    ☒ D is incorrect because you cannot use the System Policy Editor to create policy for Windows 2000 network clients.

10. ☑ B. Normally, when a user logs on, policy linked to the user account will be applied, and if there are conflicts between user settings for the Computer Account and the User Account, then the User Account Policies overwrite the Computer Account linked policies. You can change this default behavior by enabling loopback processing. Loopback can be enabled to be in either a replace or a merge mode. In Replace Mode, the user policies defined in the Computer Accounts Group Policy objects replace the User Account's Group Policy Object settings. In Merge Mode, the Computer Account's User Settings are merged with the User Account's User settings, and if there is a conflict, the Computer Account's User Settings are applied.

☒ **A** is incorrect because a loopback serial adapter is used to troubleshoot serial port problems. **C** is incorrect because you cannot selectively disable User Policy settings in a Group Policy Object link. **D** is incorrect because you cannot selectively enforce No Override to parts of a Group Policy.

11. ☑ **C** is correct because if you apply more than 1000 policies to a particular user account, failure in Group Policy processing will take place.
☒ **A**, **B**, and **D** are incorrect because they specify the incorrect number of policies.

Designing an Audit Policy

12. ☑ **A** and **B**. When you audit all files for successful and unsuccessful access, you create excessive strain on the processor, memory, and disk subsystems of the server. This can have a profound negative effect on server performance. You should audit only specific files of interest, and for a short period of time, in order to reduce the negative impact such auditing behavior might exert.
☒ **C** is incorrect because auditing does not typically increase the amount of network traffic. Answer **D** is incorrect because, although it might take a lot of time on your part to sift through the Security Log, this is not a factor in why the users have noticed decreased performance.

13. ☑ **A**, **B**, **C**, and **D**. All of these choices should be implemented in a high-security environment. Although the law firm is relatively small, and only has two server computers, the nature of the cases that they deal with requires you to treat the environment as a high security network, because of the high risk of illegal break-in and data retrieval by unauthorized third parties. Object access auditing for all files that may represent proprietary information or information that may give an advantage to a courtroom opponent should always be auditing for successful and unsuccessful access. This will create a heavy burden on the server, and require large amounts of disk space. You should take these requirements into account and purchase as much RAM as possible, and as powerful a processor, or multiple processors, as possible. You may also consider placing the operating system on a hardware Redundant Array of Inexpensive Disks (RAID) so that you can implement disk striping. You will require hardware RAID, because the operating system and logs are written to the boot partition, and you cannot place the boot partition on a fault tolerant partition.

14. ☑ **D** is correct because when a hacker uses a brute force or dictionary attack, it is likely that he will suffer many failed logons before the correct character sequence is entered. If you audit unsuccessful logons, you will see that a specific account, or several user's accounts are reported to have unsuccessful logons, and perhaps at times of the day when those users would not be available to attempt a logon.

438 Chapter 9: Understanding Policies

☒ **A** is incorrect because a successful log off would give you no useful information regarding a dictionary attack. **B** is incorrect because a hacker attack of this type would not be characterized by a server shutdown. **C** is not correct because, like answer A, it would not provide helpful information when such a hacker attacker is taking place.

15. ☑ **A, B, C,** and **D.** All of these settings could lead to a situation where the log entries from two months ago would not be available, depending on when the log was last cleared.

Security Templates

16. ☑ **C.** The most likely cause of this problem is that the local policy settings are being overwritten by higher-level group policy settings. There may be a site, domain, or organizational unit policy that is overwriting the settings in the local Group Policy.

    ☒ **A** is incorrect because refreshing a local Group Policy will not allow those settings to not be overwritten. **B** is incorrect because even if you reload the local security policy, it will not overwrite the setting made at a higher level. **D** is incorrect because you can create a local security policy, and it is the only way to configure policy-based security in a workgroup environment.

17. ☑ **D.** There is no direct mechanism, such as an undo button, that will allow you to reverse the change. Before you enact any changes to a security policy, back up the present configuration by exporting the current settings to an .INF file. Then you can restore the system to its previous state by importing the .INF file into the database, and reapplying the changes.

    ☒ **A** is incorrect because there is no undo button that would allow you to reverse the changes made to Group Policy. **B** is incorrect because there is no facility that tracks the changes you made from the previous Group Policy. **C** is incorrect because there is no basic OU template.

LAB ANSWERS

1. When Windows 2000 is installed on an NTFS partition, the basic security template information will be included when setting up the security settings. In the case of a Domain Controller, the basicdc template would be applied to the Group Policy security settings.

   However, when a domain controller is upgraded from Windows NT 4.0 to Windows 2000, no security templates are applied. This is to prevent any customized security settings you may have already created on the Windows NT 4.0 Domain Controller from being overwritten by the template's security settings.

The present scenario presents an even more pressing problem. All the partitions are FAT16, which means that no security has been placed on the local files. The boot partition must be an NTFS partition to support local security settings.

2. To solve this problem *after* the upgrade is completed, you should use the *convert* command to convert the FAT16 partition to NTFS 5.0. After the boot partition has been upgraded to NTFS, you can apply NTFS permissions to secure the file system.

   At this point you should apply one of the basic security templates. The basic security templates should always be applied first if the machine has not yet had basic security applied. In this case, you would want to import the basicdc template into the machine's security settings in Group Policy.

3. In order to upgrade the level of security over that provided with the basic security template, you should then apply one of the incremental templates. Since we are seeking the highest possible security with one of the "out of the box" solutions, we would import the hisecdc template into the machine's security settings in Group Policy. At this point, you have upgraded the Windows NT 4.0 Primary Domain Controller and applied the highest level of security possible from the preconfigured templates.

10
Data Security

CERTIFICATION OBJECTIVES

10.01	Design a Delegation of Authority Strategy
10.02	Disaster Recovery
10.03	Design an Encrypting File System Strategy
✓	Two-Minute Drill
Q&A	Self Test

Chapter 10: Data Security

This chapter deals with three different components of an overall Windows 2000 security solution: delegation of authority strategy, disaster recovery strategy, and Encrypting File System (EFS) strategy.

In Windows 2000, the ability to delegate administrative tasks allows for a more flexible and scalable administrative model than in previous versions of Windows NT. In this chapter, we will explore issues with designing and implementing a delegation of authority strategy, as well as how to create an Active Directory structure to support delegation of authority. A general methodology is discussed for delegating authority within a domain, as well.

This chapter also focuses on critical data security issues, including disaster recovery and encryption. We will explore best practices for preparing for disaster recovery in Windows 2000, including backup and restore procedures, fault tolerance, and emergency repair procedures. In addition, we will explore Windows 2000 EFS by discovering how it offers protection against unauthorized access to sensitive data and what the best practices are for implementation and recovery.

CERTIFICATION OBJECTIVE 10.01

Design a Delegation of Authority Strategy

The administration model of Active Directory allows authorized users to perform administration in the Active Directory. A user can be authorized by a higher authority to perform a specified set of actions on a specified set of objects and object classes in some identified subtree of the directory. This is called delegated administration. Delegated administration allows very detailed control over who can do what and allows specific privileges to be granted without having to elevate privilege levels beyond what is needed.

In previous versions of Windows NT Server, you delegated administration using built-in local groups such as the Account Operators group, or by creating multiple domains and having distinct sets of domain administrators. For example, to delegate the management of a set of users, you created a new account domain. To delegate management of resource servers such as file or print servers, you created resource domains. In Windows 2000, it is possible to delegate administration within a domain using organizational units (*OUs*). An *OU* is a container that you use to organize objects within a domain into logical administrative subgroups. OUs are easier to create, delete, move, and modify than domains, and they are better suited to the delegation role.

Delegating administration in your organization has several benefits. Delegating specific rights enables you to minimize the number of users who must have high levels of access. Accidents or mistakes made by an administrator with restricted capability will have an impact only within their area of responsibility. Previously, in your organization it might have been necessary for groups other than IT to submit change requests to high-level administrators, who would make these changes on their behalf. With delegation of administration, you can push responsibility down to the individual groups in your organization and eliminate the overhead of sending requests to high-level administrative groups.

Access Control

In order to formulate and implement a coherent strategy for delegating administration, it is important to first understand how access to objects is controlled in Windows 2000.

Security Principals and Access Control Lists

Each domain database contains security principal objects, such as users, groups, and computers. Security principal objects are special in that they can be granted or denied access to the resources on a network, including Active Directory objects. Security principal objects must be authenticated by a domain controller for the domain in which the security principal objects are located. Authentication is done to prove the identity of the objects before access to a resource is allowed.

An access control list (ACL) is a list of access control entries (ACEs) stored with the object that it protects. In Windows 2000, an ACL is stored as a binary value called a Security Descriptor. Each ACE contains a security identifier (SID), which identifies the principal (user or group) to whom the ACE applies and information on what type of access (permission) the ACE grants or denies. Access control lists protect all objects in the Active Directory. ACLs determine who can see the object and what actions each user can perform on the object. The existence of an object is never revealed to a user who is not allowed to see it.

ACLs on directory objects contain ACEs that apply to the object as a whole and ACEs that apply to the individual attributes of the object. This allows an administrator to control not only which users can see an object, but what properties those users can see and modify. For example, all users might be granted read access to the name and telephone number attributes for all other users, but the ability to read security properties of users might be denied to everyone except members of a special security administrators group. Furthermore, individuals might be granted write access to personal attributes such as the telephone and mailing addresses on their own user objects.

Ownership

Every object (whether in the Active Directory or in an NTFS volume) has an owner. The owner controls how permissions are set on the object and to whom permissions are granted. When an object is created, the person creating the object automatically becomes its owner. Administrators will create and own most objects in Active Directory and on network servers (when installing programs on the server). Users will create and own data files in their home directories, and some data files on network servers.

Ownership can be transferred in the following ways:

- The current owner can grant the Take Ownership permission to other users, allowing those users to take ownership at any time.

- An administrator can take ownership of any object under his or her administrative control. For example, if an employee leaves the company suddenly, the administrator can take control of the employee's files.

Taking ownership of an object is a one-way process. The user who has *the take ownership* or *modify ownership* permission granted through the object's ACL can take ownership but not assign ownership. On NTFS objects, a user must implicitly have the *take ownership* permission to take ownership. On Active Directory objects, the permission required to take ownership is *modify owner*.

Inheritance

Inheritance lets a given ACE propagate from the container where it was applied to all children of the container. Inheritance can be combined with delegation to grant administrative rights to a whole subtree of the directory in a single operation. If any of the child objects are also containers, the ACEs are applied to the children of those containers as well. With inheritance, you can apply a delegated right to an entire subtree of OUs instead of a single OU. For example, a domain administrator can grant full control of a departmental OU to a department's IT administrator. The department's IT administrator will then have full control over all divisional OUs underneath the department OU. You can also block ACE inheritance on an object to prevent ACEs from a parent container from applying to that object or any child objects. Inheritable ACEs apply only within a domain and do not flow down to child domains.

Design Basics

An organizational unit (OU) is the container that you use to create an administrative structure within a domain. The following characteristics of OUs are important to consider when creating administrative structure in a domain.

- OUs can be nested. An OU can contain child OUs, enabling you to create a hierarchical tree structure inside a domain.

- OUs can be used to delegate administration and control access to directory objects. When you use a combination of OU nesting and access control lists, you can delegate the administration of objects in the directory in a very granular manner. For example, you could grant a group of Help desk technicians the right to reset passwords for a specific set of users, but not the right to create users or modify any other attribute of a user object.

- OUs are not security principals. You cannot make OUs members of security groups, nor can you grant users permission to a resource because they reside in a particular OU. Because OUs are used for delegation of administration, the parent OU of a user object indicates who manages the user object, but it does not indicate the resources that a user can access.

- Group Policy can be associated with an OU. Group Policy enables you to define desktop configurations for users and computers. You can associate Group Policy with sites, domains, and OUs. Defining Group Policy on an OU basis allows you to use different policies within the same domain.

- Users will not navigate the OU structure. It is not necessary to design an OU structure that will appeal to end users. Although it is possible for users to navigate the OU structure of a domain, it is not the most efficient way for a user to discover resources. The most efficient way to find resources in the directory is by querying the global catalog.

At first, you might think about creating an OU structure that mirrors your business organization and its various divisions, departments, and projects. It is possible to create such a structure, but it might prove difficult and expensive to manage. OUs are for delegating administration, so the structure you create is most likely a reflection of your administrative model. The administrative model of your organization might not map exactly to your business organization.

For example, consider the business-oriented structure shown in Figure 10-1. OUs have been created for the Web Products (Web Products OU), Publishing (Publishing OU), and Training Centers (Training Centers OU) divisions, where the users on the Web Products teams are in the Web Products OU, and so on.

Assume that the company in this example uses a centralized administration model. A single group of administrators manages all of the users across the company, regardless of business division. During the day-to-day operation of the company, many things can happen. If a person transfers between the Web Products and Publishing divisions, an administrator has to move that person's user account from the Web Products OU to the Publishing OU. If the number of transfers is high, this could amount to a significant amount of work for the administration group. What is actually being accomplished though?

For the same company, now consider an OU structure that consists of a single OU that contains all user accounts. If a user transfers between business divisions, no additional work to move the object is created for an administrator. Whenever

FIGURE 10-1

OU structure aligned with business structure

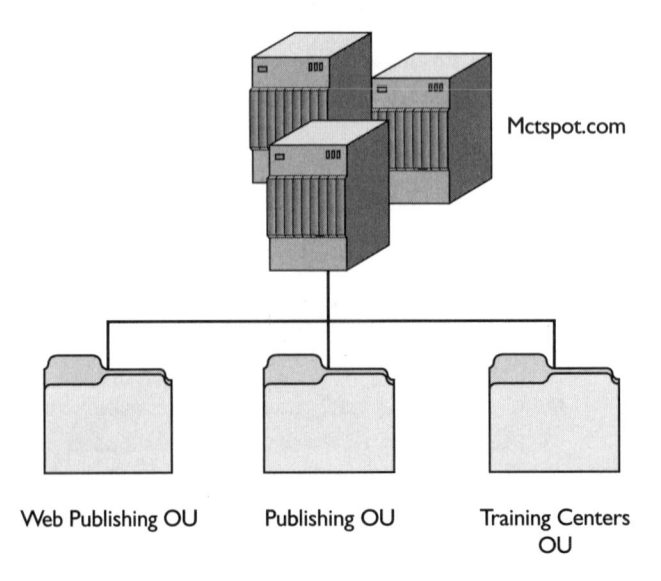

Mctspot.com

Web Publishing OU   Publishing OU   Training Centers OU

you create structure, make sure that it serves a meaningful purpose. Structure without justification will always create unnecessary work.

Security groups, unlike distribution groups, are used to control access to resources, such as objects within an OU or even the OU itself. Whereas security groups define groups of users based on common resource access, an OU hierarchy establishes the containment of resources so that the administrative workspace can be partitioned. For example, if a company employs full-time IT administrators at each geographic location, you might consider an upper-level OU structure based on geography. If the engineering department needs full access to a set of servers within the branch OU, then a child OU that contains the specified servers can be created and full control access can be granted on the child OU to the Engineering global security group. In this example, the local IT administrators are still in control of all branch resources ultimately, yet the engineering department manages a subset of the resources within the branch.

Alternatively, you might want to mirror your business structure in your OU structure to make it easy to generate lists of users based on business unit. Using OUs is just one way of doing this. Your business structure might more closely reflect the way resource access is granted to your users. For example, users on a particular project might be granted access to a specific set of file servers, or users in a particular division might be granted access to a particular Web site. Because resource access is granted using security groups, you might find that your business organizational structure is best represented in security group structures instead of OUs.

Creating OUs to Delegate Administration

In versions of Windows NT before Windows 2000, delegation of administration within a domain was limited to the use of built-in local groups, such as the Account Administrators group. These groups had predefined capabilities, and in some cases the capabilities did not fit the needs of a particular situation. As a result, there were situations in which administrators in an organization needed high levels of administrative access, such as Domain Administrators rights.

In Windows 2000, delegation of administration is more powerful and flexible. This flexibility is achieved through a combination of organizational units, per-attribute access control, and access control inheritance. Administration can be delegated arbitrarily by granting a set of users the ability to create specific classes of objects, or modify specific attributes on specific classes of objects. For example, your human resources department can be granted the ability to create user objects in a particular OU, but nowhere else. Helpdesk technicians can be granted the ability to reset the passwords of users in that OU, but not the ability to create users. Other directory administrators can be granted the ability to modify the address book attributes of a user object, but not be allowed to create users or reset passwords.

The steps to creating an OU structure plan for a domain are:

1. Create OUs to delegate administration.
2. Create OUs to hide objects.
3. Create OUs for Group Policy.
4. Understand the impact of changing OU structures after deployment.

It is important to follow the steps in the order presented. You will find that an OU structure designed purely for delegation of administration is shaped differently than an OU structure designed purely for Group Policy. Because there are multiple ways of applying Group Policy, but only one way to delegate administration, you should create OUs for delegation of administration first. In this chapter, we will explore creating an OU structure for delegation of administration only.

Your OU structure can become complex very quickly. Note the specific reason for creating an OU each time you add one to the plan. This will help you make sure that every OU has a purpose, and it will help the readers of your plan to understand the reasoning behind the structure.

When creating the OU plan for each domain, consult the following groups in your administrative organizations:

- Current domain administrators who are responsible for user accounts, security groups, and computer accounts.
- Current resource domain owners and administrators.

The OU structure that you create will depend entirely on how administration is delegated within your organization. Three ways by which you can delegate administration are:

- **Physical location**   For example, administration for objects in Asia can be handled by an autonomous set of administrators.
- **Business unit**   For example, administration of objects belonging to the Manufacturing division can be handled by an autonomous set of administrators.

- **Role or task** This division is according to the type of object being managed. For example, a set of administrators might be responsible only for computer account objects.

These three dimensions are frequently combined. For example, there can be an administrative group that is responsible for computer account objects in Tucson for the Training Centers business unit, as shown in Figure 10-2.

Whether or not the Tucson OU is the child of the Training Centers OU depends on whether the Training Centers administrators delegate authority to the Tucson administrators, or vice versa. It is also possible that the Tucson administrators are completely autonomous from the Training Centers administrators, in which case the two OUs would be peers.

FIGURE 10-2

Two-tiered structure

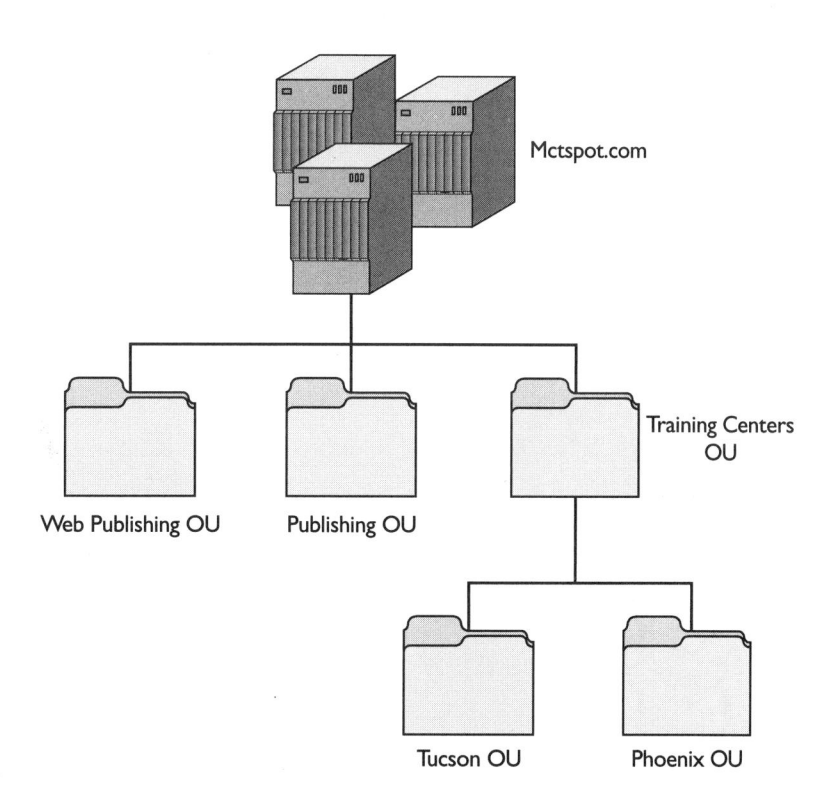

Delegation Methodology

Starting with the default structure inside a domain, create an OU structure using the following primary steps:

1. Create the top layers of OUs by delegating full control.
2. Create the bottom layers of OUs to delegate per-object class control.

To begin, only domain administrators have full control over all objects. Ideally, domain administrators should only be responsible for:

- Creating the initial OU structure.
- Repairing mistakes. Domain administrators not only have full control by default, they also have the right to take ownership of any object in the domain. Using this right, domain administrators can gain full control over any object in the domain, regardless of the permissions that have been set on the object.
- Creating additional domain controllers. Only members of the domain administrators group can create additional domain controllers for a domain.

Delegating Full Control

If you have units in your organization that need to be allowed to determine their own OU structure and their own administrative model, use the following steps:

1. Create an OU for each unit.
2. Create a local group for each unit representing the highest level administrators in that unit.
3. Assign the corresponding group full control over its OU.
4. If the unit is allowed to set its membership, place the unit's administrators group into the OU. If the unit is not allowed to set its own administrator membership, leave the group outside the OU.

Example of Delegating Full Control

The Training Centers unit of the Mctspot.com company is the result of a merger of two companies, where the Training Centers unit retained a fully autonomous IT group. In this situation, the Training Centers unit gets its own OU from the root of the domain. Because they are allowed to define the membership of their administrators group, the group is placed into the Training Centers OU. If the Training Centers unit itself had completely autonomous operations in Tucson and Phoenix, the Training Centers administrators might again create OUs and delegate full control. As shown in Figure 10-3, the Training Centers administrators have retained the ability to set the membership of the Tucson and Phoenix administrators groups.

FIGURE 10-3 Delegating full control

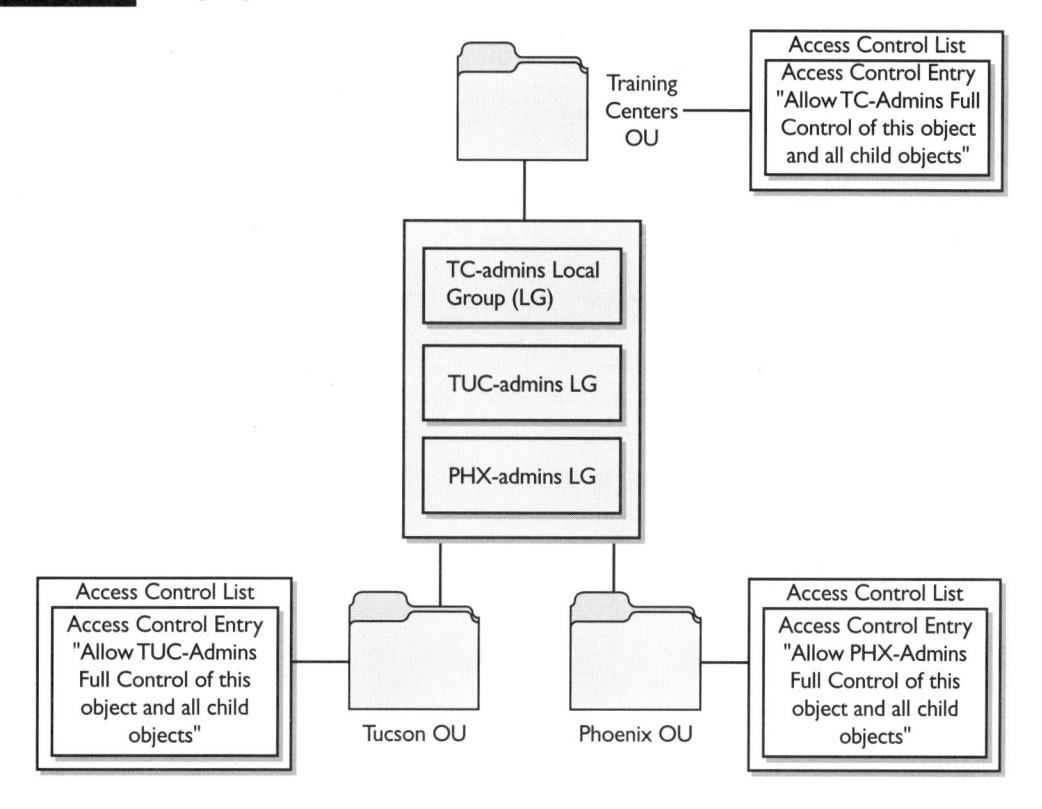

If you do not have any units in your organization that need full control, domain administrators will determine the remainder of the OU structure.

Delegating Per-Object Class Control

Groups with full control can decide if additional OUs are necessary to delegate more restrictive control. A simple way to do this is to consider each object class that will be created in the directory, and determine if management of that object class is delegated further in the organization. Although the schema defines many different kinds of object classes, it is only necessary to consider the object classes that your administrators will create in the Active Directory. At minimum, you should consider:

- User account objects
- Computer account objects
- Group objects
- Organizational unit objects

As you examine each object class, separately consider:

- Which groups should be granted full control over objects of a particular class? Groups with full control can create and delete objects of the specified class and modify any attribute on objects of the specified class.
- Which groups should be allowed to create objects of a particular class? By default, users have full control over objects that they create.
- Which groups should only be allowed to modify specific attributes of existing objects of a particular class?

In each case that you decide to delegate control, you will:

1. Create a local group that will be allowed to perform the specific function.
2. Grant that group the specific right on the highest OU possible.

exam
Watch

When reading the case studies on the Microsoft exam, diagram the current IT administrative structure of the organization. The current IT structure will be an important item when answering any questions dealing with the delegation of permissions to various OUs.

To move an object between two OUs, the administrator performing the move must have the ability to create the object in the destination container and to delete the object from the source container. For these reasons, you might want to create a separate group for administrators that can move objects, and grant them the necessary rights on a common parent OU.

The list of objects to be considered can grow as you deploy more Active Directory-aware applications. However, some applications will create objects in the directory that do not require hands-on management. For example, print servers running Windows 2000 automatically publish print queues in the directory. Because the print server takes care of the management of the print queue object, it is not necessary to delegate management to a special administrators group.

By modifying the ACL on the default Computers container, you can delegate the ability to create computer account objects to all users, with no administrative attention required. Computer accounts would be created when users join a computer to a domain in the default Computers container.

Example of Delegating Per-Object Class Control

The Tucson location for the Training Centers unit of the Mctspot.com company is home to two Windows NT 4.0 resource domains, Consulting and Training. Part of the Windows 2000 migration will involve consolidating those two domains into the Mctspot.com domain.

The Consulting and Training administrators use the domain today to:

- Create computer accounts for team members.
- Share file system space on Windows NT 4.0 backup domain controllers (BDCs), where access to the file system and shares are controlled by local group membership.

Using delegation of administration, it is simple to replace resource domains with OUs. In this case, groups are created to administer each kind of object, and they are granted full control in a project-specific OU. Project-specific OUs are necessary to prevent Consulting administrators from being able to manipulate Training objects, and vice versa. Figure 10-4 illustrates this concept.

FIGURE 10-4 Replacing resource domains

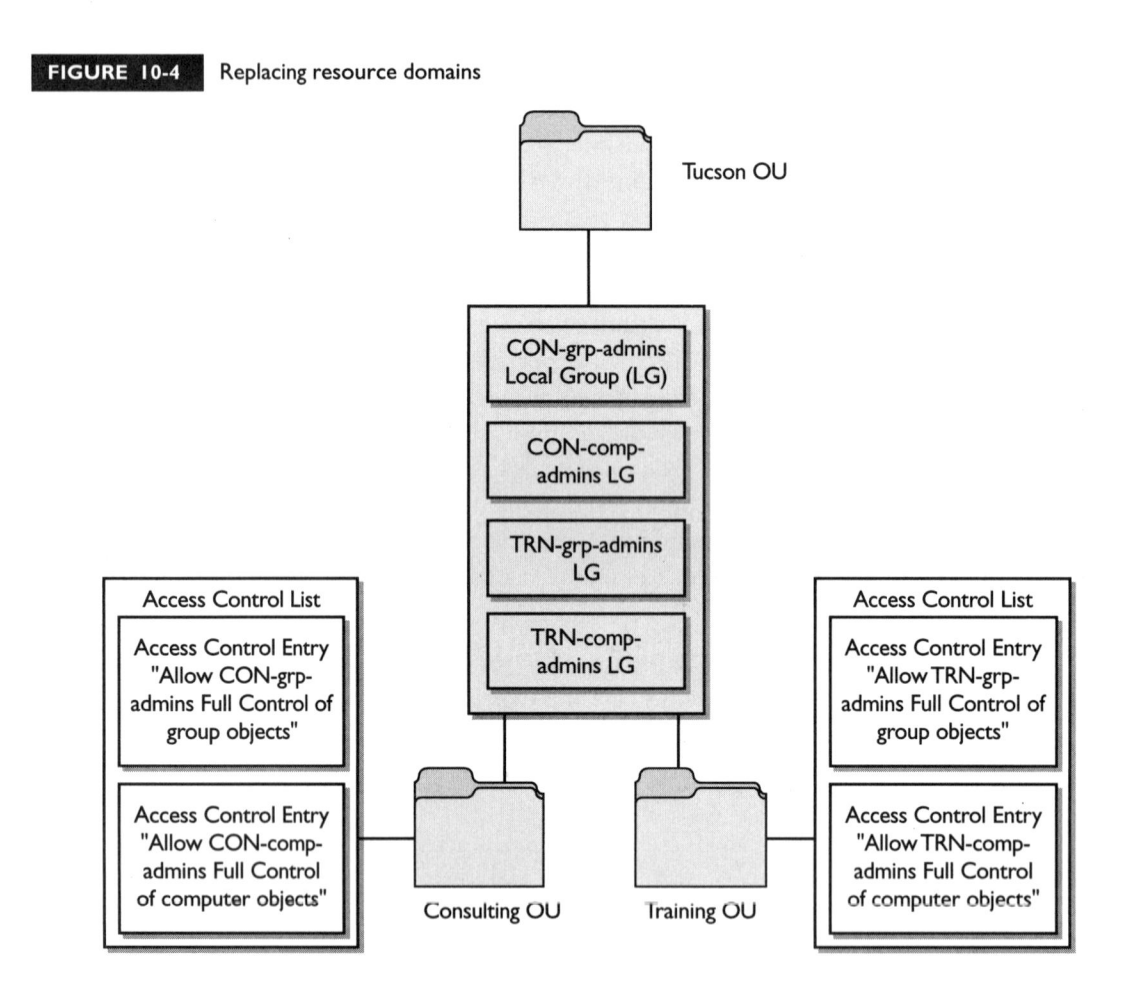

[Figure 10-4: Diagram showing Tucson OU containing CON-grp-admins Local Group (LG), CON-comp-admins LG, TRN-grp-admins LG, and TRN-comp-admins LG. Consulting OU has an Access Control List with ACEs "Allow CON-grp-admins Full Control of group objects" and "Allow CON-comp-admins Full Control of computer objects". Training OU has an Access Control List with ACEs "Allow TRN-grp-admins Full Control of group objects" and "Allow TRN-comp-admins Full Control of computer objects".]

Delegation Procedures

To delegate administration on an OU, you grant a group specific rights over an OU. To do this, you need to modify the access control list (ACL) of the OU. When an object is created in the directory, a default ACL is applied to it. The default ACL is described in the schema definition of the object class. The easiest way to add to the ACL of an OU is by using the Delegation of Control Wizard in the Microsoft Management Console (MMC) snap-in for Active Directory Users and Groups. The Delegation of Control Wizard functions by providing administrators with a set of dialog boxes designed to specify the following items:

- To whom the administrator wants to delegate authority.
- The objects to which these users should have authority.
- The permissions the designated users have over these objects.

The Delegation of Control Wizard dynamically creates ACEs on the target container object. The tasks can be selected from a pre-compiled list of commonly delegated tasks, or the administrator can choose to create a custom task to delegate. The Delegation of Control Wizard does not provide functionality to remove access control entries. If an administrator wants to reverse configuration settings created with Delegation of Control Wizard or perform advance editing, he or she must manually gain access to the Security tab on the Property page for the object.

When modifying the ACL of a container, it is highly recommended to always assign permissions to groups, not individual users. Managing the membership of a group is simpler than managing an ACL on an OU. When users change roles, it is much easier to discover and change their group memberships than to check the ACLs on every OU. Where possible, delegate to local groups instead of global or universal groups. Unlike global groups, local groups can have members from any trusted domain, making them better suited for granting resource permissions. Unlike universal groups, local group membership is not replicated to the global catalog, making local groups less resource intensive.

Exercise 10-1 illustrates how to use the Delegation of Control Wizard to delegate specific authority on a particular OU and how to view or modify ACEs on an OU.

on the job

To gain more experience using the Delegation of Control Wizard to delegate different types of authority, read the Step-by-Step Guide to Using the Delegation of Control Wizard on the Microsoft Web site at http://www.microsoft.com/technet/win2000/delestep.asp.

456 Chapter 10: Data Security

EXERCISE 10-1

Delegating Administration for an OU

In this exercise, you will use the Delegation of Control Wizard to delegate the management of user accounts in an organizational unit to a local group. You will then view the properties of the OU to see what ACE was added and what permissions were given. This exercise assumes you are running Windows 2000 Server that is set up as a domain controller and you have administrative access to the domain for practice purposes.

1. Click Start | Programs | Administrative Tools | Active Directory Users and Computers. Active Directory Users and Computers will appear, as shown here:

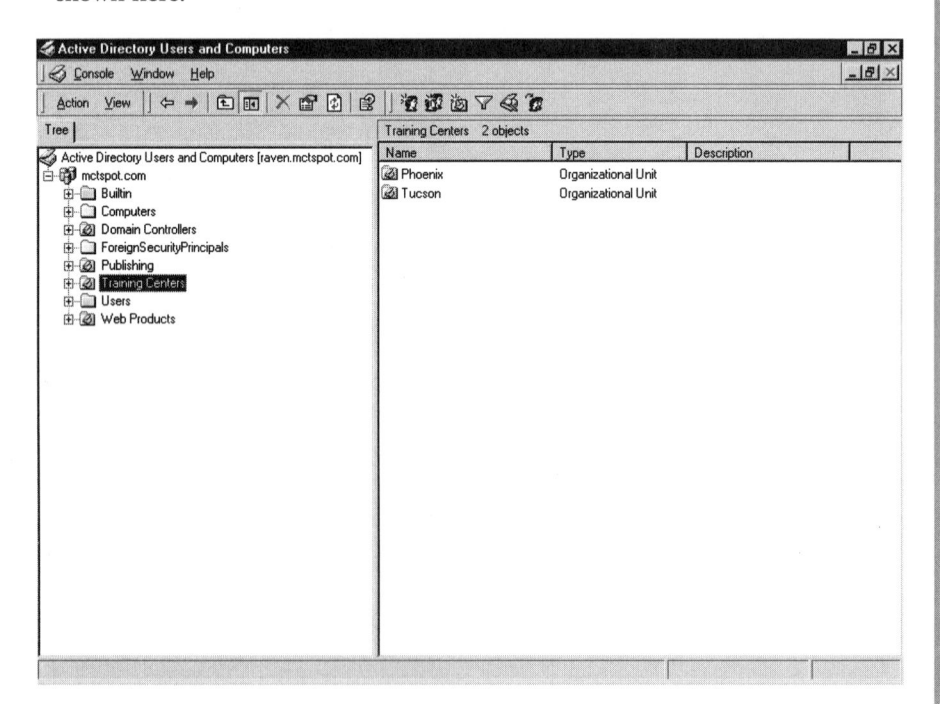

2. Right-click any organizational unit container, then select Delegate Control. The following illustration shows the dialog box that will appear.

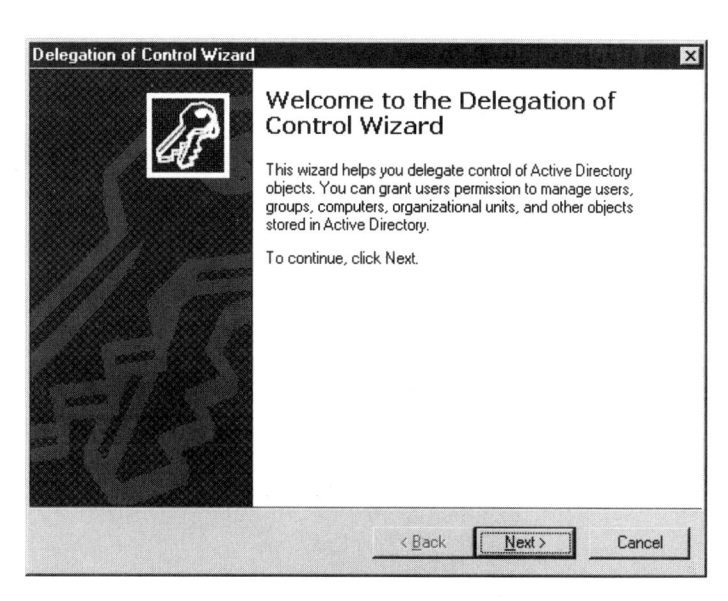

3. Click Next. In the next dialog box, you can add one or more groups or users to whom you want to delegate control. Click Add, select a domain local group that you wish to add from the domain database, then click Add. Click OK to return to the wizard, which should now look similar to this:

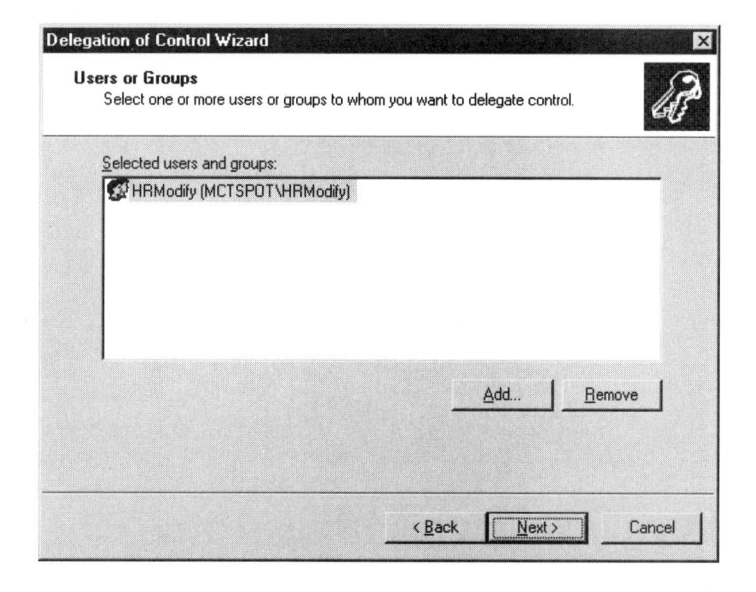

4. Click Next. In the next dialog box, select Create, Delete, and Manage User Accounts.

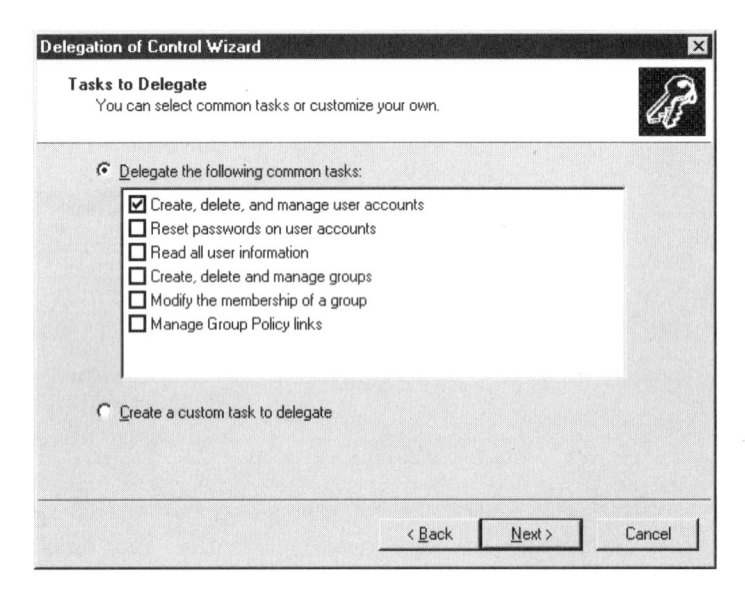

5. Click Next. A dialog box similar to this will appear displaying summary information of the ACEs that you are about to create for the OU.

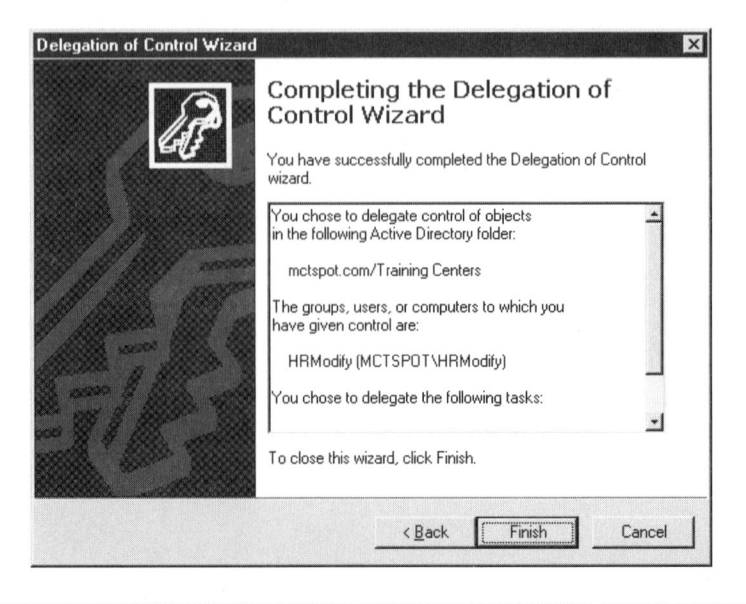

6. Click Finish. You should now be back at the Active Directory Users and Computers console. To see what specific ACEs the wizard added to the OU, click View from the task bar in Active Directory Users and Computers, then click Advanced Features. This will allow you to view the security properties of the OU.

7. Right-click the OU and select Properties. Select the Security tab.

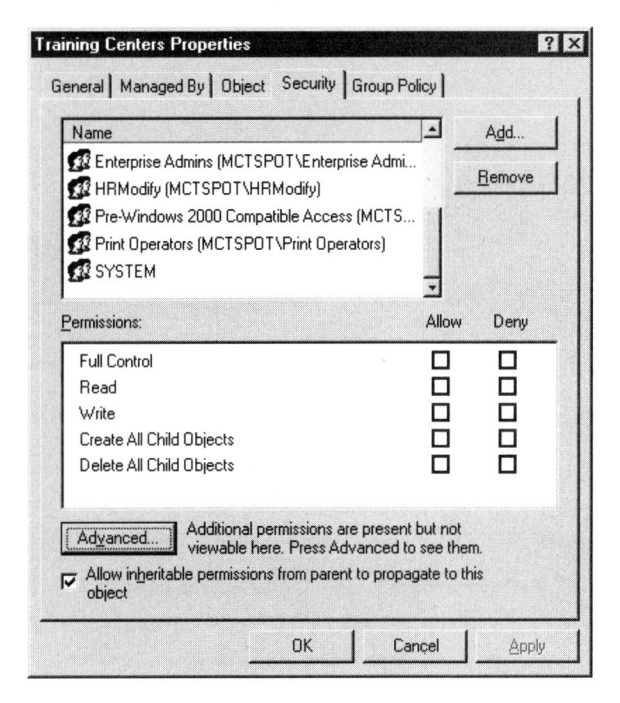

8. Click Advanced to view all of the access control entries for this OU, including entries specific to this object and all inheritable entries from the parent object. The following screen shows the HRModify group that was delegated control using the Delegation of Control Wizard earlier. You will see two entries that were added by the wizard for the HRModify group: Full

Control over all user objects in this OU and Create/Delete User Objects for this OU and all child objects.

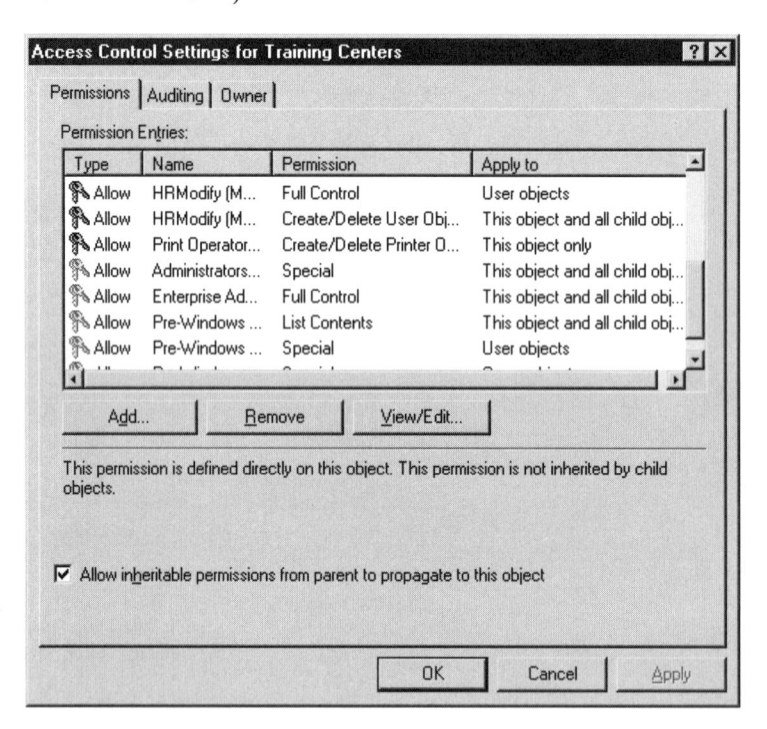

Access Control Settings for Training Centers

Permissions | Auditing | Owner

Permission Entries:

Type	Name	Permission	Apply to
Allow	HRModify (M...	Full Control	User objects
Allow	HRModify (M...	Create/Delete User Obj...	This object and all child obj...
Allow	Print Operator...	Create/Delete Printer O...	This object only
Allow	Administrators...	Special	This object and all child obj...
Allow	Enterprise Ad...	Full Control	This object and all child obj...
Allow	Pre-Windows ...	List Contents	This object and all child obj...
Allow	Pre-Windows ...	Special	User objects

Add... | Remove | View/Edit...

This permission is defined directly on this object. This permission is not inherited by child objects.

☑ Allow inheritable permissions from parent to propagate to this object

OK | Cancel | Apply

9. To see the individual permissions granted by a particular standard permission, click the permission entry and choose View/Edit. The Full Control standard permission grants every individual permission available for user objects. The second screen displayed shows the individual permissions granted by the Create/Delete User Objects standard permission for this object and all child objects.

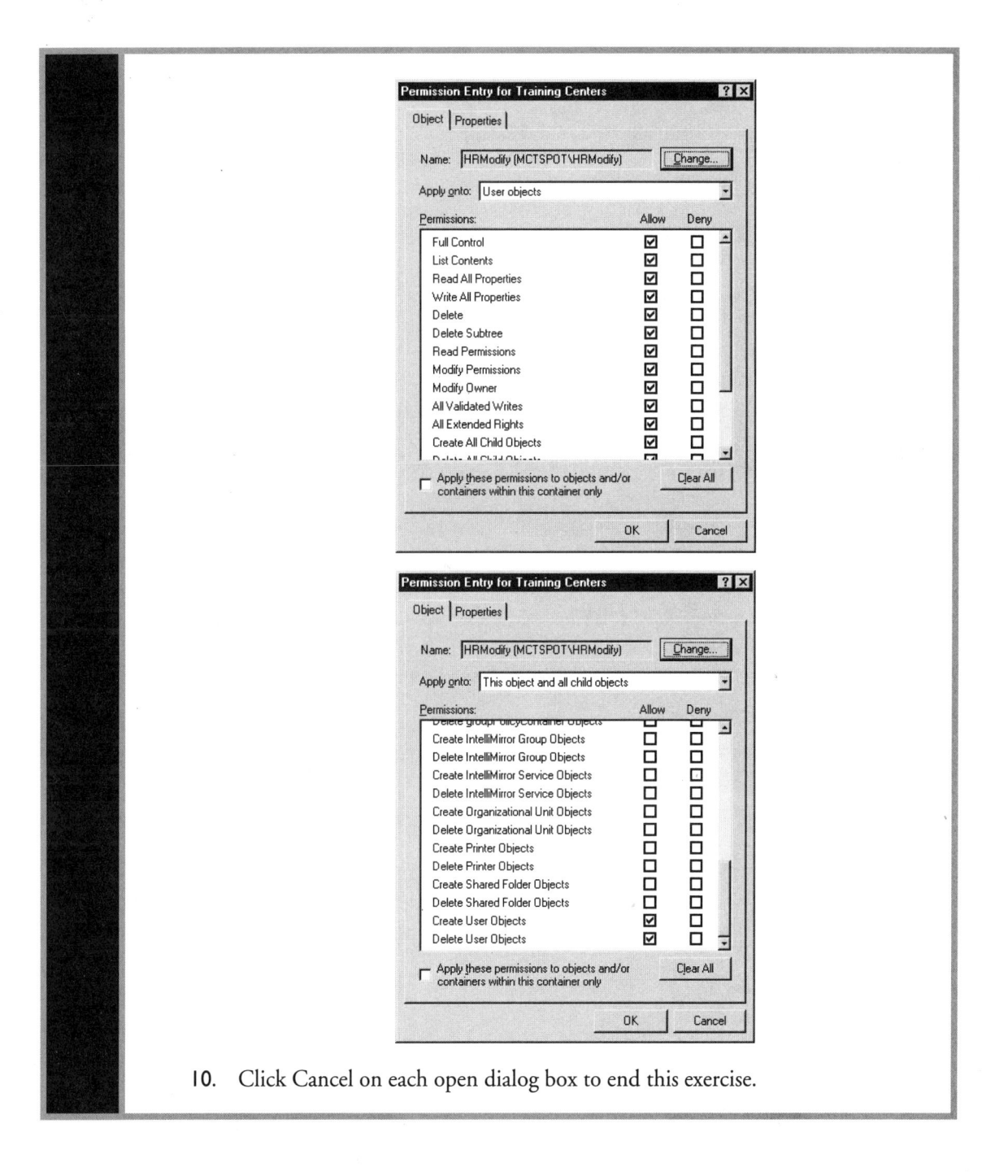

10. Click Cancel on each open dialog box to end this exercise.

FROM THE CLASSROOM

Other Delegation Methods

Although the use of the Delegation of Control Wizard within an appropriate OU structure provides the foundation for delegating administrative authority from the top down, there are several related methods in Windows 2000 for granting groups or individual users a prescribed degree of control over a set of objects. These related methods include the use of built-in security groups, delegating control of sites and services, and delegating control of Group Policy objects (GPOs).

- **Built-in security groups** All Windows 2000 installations have predefined security groups with special permissions and rights already assigned to each group. Built-in security groups can be viewed in the Active Directory Users and Computers console. From the View menu, select Advanced Features. The predefined security groups are in the Builtin and Users folders. To delegate control of a built-in security group, open the property sheet of the group, select the Security tab, and add the group's manager to the access control list and select the appropriate privileges.

- **Delegating control of sites and services** There is a Delegation of Control Wizard for use on specific sites and services. It operates in a similar manner to the wizard used in Active Directory Users and Computers. For example, you could delegate the right to create new remote access accounts within a site.

- **Delegating control of Group Policy objects** When delegating control of GPOs, you can assign management of Group Policy links for a site, domain, or organizational unit. Tasks that can be delegated include assigning, creating, or editing GPOs on a container. Delegating control of GPOs allows distributed administration of client configurations within a site, domain, or OU. You can delegate control of GPOs using the Delegation of Control Wizard in Active Directory Sites and Services or Active Directory Users and Computers, depending on the scope of administration.

—*Christopher Jeffry Rima, MCSE+I, MCT*

SCENARIO & SOLUTION

In a company with decentralized administration of IT resources, what standard permission should a domain administrator assign to child OU administrators for the child OU?	Full Control
When constructing an OU plan for your domain, what should you first use to develop the appropriate OU hierarchy?	First create an OU hierarchy based on delegation of administration.
What types of groups should be assigned when delegating control on an OU?	Domain local groups should be used, as they can contain groups from other trusted domains.
In a domain with four division OUs and one accounts OU, where should you delegate control to the Help Desk group so they are able to reset password?	To the accounts OU only.
If a branch office manager needs to be able to add and delete user accounts, what common delegated permission should you assign her using the Delegation of Control Wizard?	Assign her the delegated permission: Create, Delete, and Manage User Accounts.

CERTIFICATION OBJECTIVE 10.02

Disaster Recovery

Despite the best prevention methods, network hardware and software do fail occasionally and data can be lost or services can be rendered inoperable. In addition to a security plan, a recovery plan is required to be able to recover network resources and minimize the downtime of mission-critical network services in the event of failure. Network failure can result from one or more factors, including:

- Theft or sabotage
- Viruses
- Loss of power

- Natural disasters (fire, flood, earthquake, and so on)
- Failure of hard disks or hard disk subsystems
- Operating system crashes
- Accidental deletion or manipulation of files

In order to protect the network from such events, an administrator should develop a comprehensive disaster recovery plan that answers the following questions:

- What are the essential services and data that might need to be recovered?
- What is an acceptable time period for recovery of these services and data when failure occurs?
- What are the single points of failure in the network? In order to improve availability, which systems should provide fault tolerance?
- How often should backups be performed?
- Will you perform incremental or differential backups? When should full backups be performed?
- What backup hardware will you use?
- Should the backup process be automated or not?
- Will you perform backups online (while users are working) or offline?
- Who will have proper access and rights to back up and restore system data and user data?
- Where will you store the backups?
- How will you ensure that backups can be recovered in the event of failure?
- How long will you save the backups before reusing the medium?
- How will you protect data and system software against viruses? What are the possible access points in your network that might allow the introduction of viruses?

In this section, we will briefly review the importance of several disaster recovery mechanisms. Although a disaster recovery plan is usually developed separately from a security plan, it is important to understand the risks associated with network failure when planning a security solution for a network.

> **exam**
> **Watch**
>
> *Disaster recovery is not an explicit exam objective for Exam 70-220: Designing Security for a Microsoft Windows 2000 Network. Disaster recovery is discussed here to highlight some of the critical components recommended when planning an overall security framework.*

Fault Tolerant Volumes

Fault tolerance can be applied to any part of the network, including network cabling, network servers, services, and data. Fault tolerance is not a replacement for regular backups. Instead, fault tolerance provides a higher level of availability of network services and data in the event of failure. A network's level of fault tolerance is defined as the ability of the network to continue functioning if one or more physical components fail. Building fault tolerance into a network can be accomplished by including one or more of the following components:

- Dual disk controllers
- Fault-tolerant disk arrays; that is, RAID (Redundant Array of Inexpensive Disks)
- Fault-tolerant network topology (for example, star or star-bus)
- Uninterruptible power supplies (UPSs)
- Network load balancing
- Server clustering
- Distributed file system (Dfs)
- Redundant network interfaces (multihoming)
- Symmetric multiprocessing (SMP)

The most common point of failure in a network is its power supply. The three basic problems that can arise include (1) failure of the internal power supply on a network component such as a server, a switch, or a router, (2) voltage variations, and (3) loss of external power. Probably the two best fault tolerant mechanisms for protecting against power problems are (1) redundant power supplies, or alternatively, having spare power supplies on hand, and (2) implementing an appropriate UPS to protect against voltage variations and the temporary loss of external power. To protect against power outages that last more than one hour, an auxiliary generator might be required. Regardless of whether you implement a UPS or not, large fluctuations in voltage, such as those due to lightning strikes or other natural disasters, are rarely preventable without investing a larger sum of money in advanced surge protection devices.

Next to power failures, the most common failure is probably hard disk failure. Even though today's hard drives have a published mean time to failure (MTTF) upwards of 35 to 50 years, there is a much higher possibility that a drive will fail during it's initial use. Moreover, published MTTF values do not take into account degenerative or catastrophic failures due to power problems. For these reasons, a reliable, fault-tolerant RAID system is often necessary to protect against data loss when one or more disks fail.

RAID can be implemented by the disk controller (that is, hardware-level RAID) or by the operating system or a third-party software utility (that is, software-level RAID). When compared to the software RAID provided by Windows 2000, hardware-level RAID provides support for more RAID levels, can support hot-swap and hot-spare drives, and has better performance due to caching on the controller. In contrast, software-level RAID is almost always less expensive and easier to implement.

Table 10-1 shows common levels of RAID and their level of fault tolerance. Read and write performance is shown as compared to a single disk.

Windows 2000 Disk Management supports RAID levels 0, 1, and 5 only. In addition, Windows 2000 Disk Management requires a minimum of three disks to implement RAID-5, up to a maximum of 32 disks.

Even though RAID will increase your overall level of fault tolerance, there can still be a single point of failure with the disk controller unless multiple identical controllers are implemented. In the case of RAID-1, this is known as disk duplexing. Although controller failures are less likely to occur than disk failures, it is wise to be prepared.

Several factors determine which RAID level is the most appropriate, including budget, level of protection desired, and availability and performance requirements. The costs associated with hardware-level RAID are higher than software-level RAID, although hardware-level RAID provides better performance. RAID-1 is more expensive than RAID-5, although it provides better performance for write-intensive applications, such as databases, and causes no performance loss if a single disk fails. It is generally recommended to mirror your Windows 2000 system partition (that is, the boot drive) and implement RAID-5 for data and applications. RAID-5 strikes a good balance between fault tolerance and performance, keeping in mind that

TABLE 10-1 Common RAID Levels

Level	Number of Disks	Read Performance	Write Performance	Description
0	n*	fastest	fastest	Stripe set without parity. Not fault tolerant. Data is striped across multiple disks. Failure of single disk results in data loss.
1 (mirrored)	2n*	slightly faster	no loss/gain	Mirroring. Data is mirrored on a second disk. Failure of single disk causes no data loss and no loss in performance.
3	n+1	faster	slightly slower	Stripe set with byte-level parity. Data is striped across multiple disks at the byte level with parity information written to a single disk. Failure of single disk causes no data loss, yet will cause a significant performance loss.
4	n+1	faster	slightly slower	Stripe set with block-level parity. Data is striped across multiple disks with parity information written to a single disk. Failure of single disk causes no data loss, yet will cause a significant performance loss.
5	n+1*	faster	slightly slower	Stripe set with interleaved block-level parity. Data is striped across multiple disks with parity information distributed across all disks. Failure of single disk causes no data loss, yet will cause a significant performance loss.
10	2(n+1)	faster	faster	Mirrored stripe set. Data is striped across multiple disks, all of which have a mirror. Failure of a single disk causes no data loss or loss in performance. Failure of a second disk may result in data loss.

performance can suffer greatly if a single disk fails, depending on how write-intensive your applications are. If maximum fault tolerance and performance are required and cost is not an issue, hardware-level RAID-10 is the best solution.

468 Chapter 10: Data Security

> **on the job**
>
> *If you decide to use software mirroring on your system partition (that is, the boot drive), make sure you create a Windows 2000 fault-tolerant boot floppy disk and test it. By modifying the ARC (Advanced RISC Computing) pathname in the BOOT.INI file, you can instruct Windows 2000 to access the appropriate boot partition containing the operating system files (for example, C:\WINNT).*

Windows 2000 supports built-in software-level RAID. In order to configure software-level RAID in Windows 2000, click Start | Programs | Administrative Tools | Computer Management. Figure 10-5 shows the location of the Disk Management tool used to manage disks and the volumes they contain.

Windows 2000 requires that you convert your disks to dynamic disks in order to create striped, mirrored, or RAID-5 volumes. A *dynamic disk* is a disk that is managed by Windows 2000 Disk Management. Dynamic disks cannot contain partitions or logical drives and they are not accessible from other operating systems, such as MS-DOS. In order to create a striped, mirrored, or RAID-5 volume, you right-click an area of available space on one or more dynamic disks where you want to create the volume, select Create Volume, then answer the questions presented in

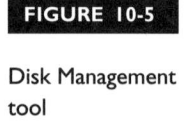

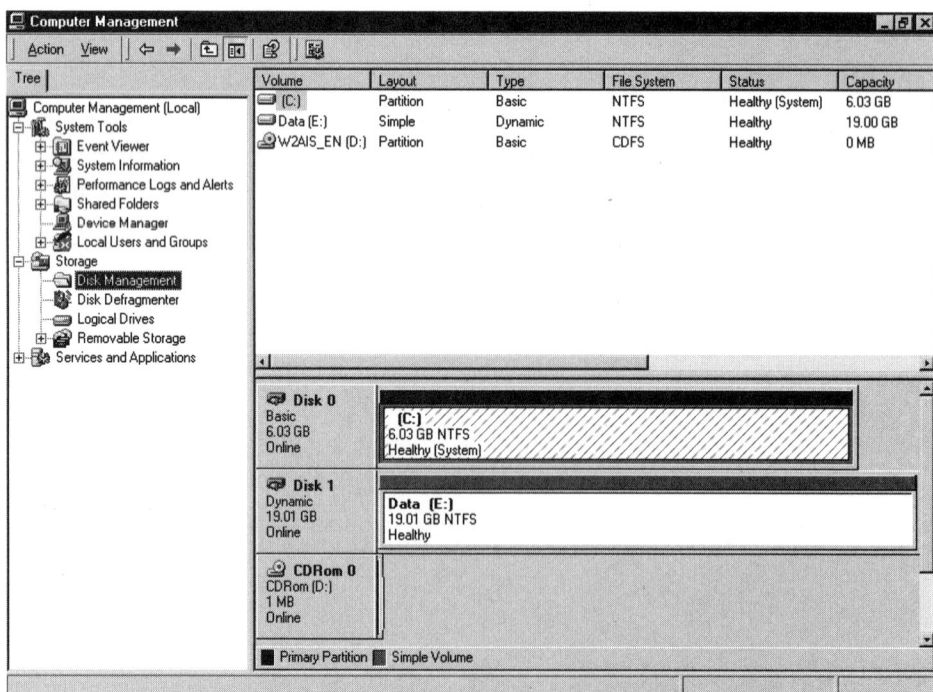

FIGURE 10-5

Disk Management tool

the Create Volume wizard. In order to create a dynamic volume, you must be logged on as the administrator or as a member of the Administrators group. In all cases when working within Disk Management, it is highly recommended that data first be backed up.

Backup Utility

Although UPS systems and fault-tolerant volumes provide a high-level of data protection and availability, there is no substitute for an effective backup strategy. Windows 2000 Server introduces a number of new or enhanced file system, data storage, and System State features, all of which need to be considered when planning a backup and restore strategy.

on the job

Backup products not aware of new Windows 2000 features, such as NTFS 5.0, System State data, or Remote Storage, could cause loss of data. Check with your backup vendor to ensure that all backup products are Windows 2000 compliant.

FIGURE 10-6 Windows 2000 backup and recovery tools

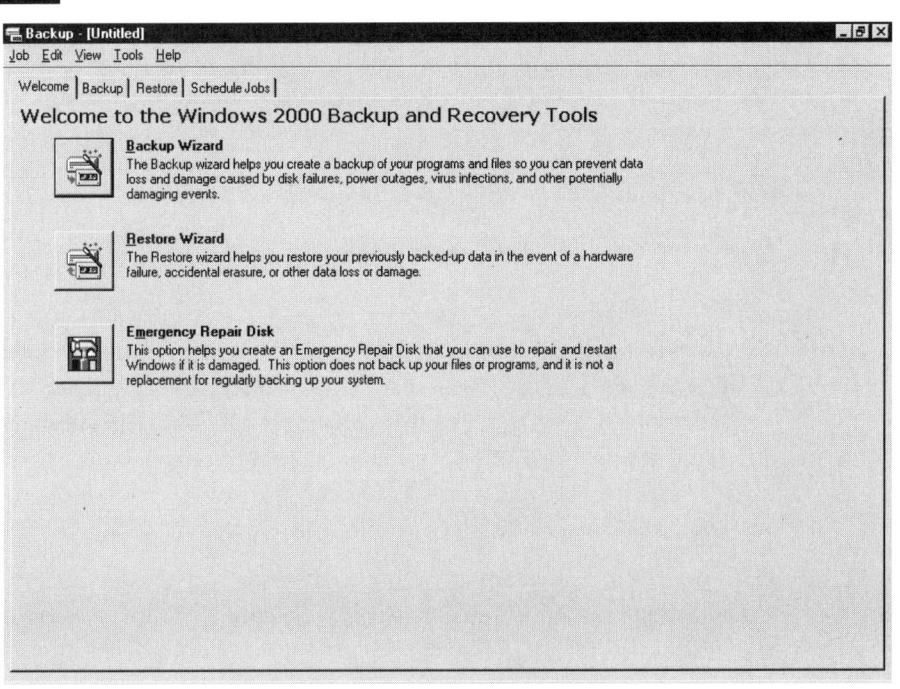

To assist with regular backups, Windows 2000 provides a totally new backup utility called Backup. Backup can be invoked from the command line using ntbackup or from Start | Programs | Accessories | System Tools | Backup. Backup offers three wizards, as shown in Figure 10-6.

Backup lets you perform the following tasks:

- Back up selected user files and folders located on your hard disk to a tape drive, a logical drive, a removable disk, or to a library of disks or tapes organized into a media pool.
- Back up your computer's System State, which are the files central to system operation. System State data includes the Registry, Active Directory, Sysvol (a replicated data store that includes the policies and scripts used by Active Directory), the COM+ database, and boot files.
- Restore backed-up files and folders to your hard disk or any other accessible disk.
- Schedule regular backups.
- Back up Remote Storage data and data stored on mounted drives.
- Create an Emergency Repair Disk (ERD), which helps repair system files if they become corrupted or are accidentally erased.

Before using the Backup utility, it is important to understand several items related to backing up and restoring data in Windows 2000.

- **Backing up and restoring system state data** System State data is backed up and restored as a set and cannot be broken down into individual components. In addition, System State data can only be backed up on the local computer.
- **Active Directory tombstone lifetime** The Active Directory tombstone lifetime is the length of time that deleted objects are maintained in Active Directory before they are permanently removed. The default is 60 days. Therefore, the age of the backup tape should not exceed this length of time, otherwise a restore will cause Active Directory to reject all of the data as out of date.
- **Backup and restore rights** Only members of the built-in Backup Operators group can back up and restore data, by default. In addition, users who have the Back Up Files and Directories and Restore Files and Directories rights

can also back up and restore data. Rights are granted to groups of users using Group Policy. Only members of the local Administrators group can back up and restore System State data, by default.

- **Protecting the Boot Configuration** The System State data and boot volume should be backed up after successfully installing Windows 2000. Current backups should be maintained if disk configuration changes. Windows requires the following hidden, system files to boot: BOOT.INI, NTLDR, BOOTSECT.DOS, NTDETECT.COM, and NTBOOTDD.SYS (if Windows is installed on a Small Computer System Interface (SCSI) disk).

- **File system constraints** The Backup utility can be used to back up or restore data on FAT16, FAT32, or NTFS volumes. Data that is backed up from a Windows 2000 NTFS version 5.0 volume and restored to a non-NTFS 5.0 volume will lose certain features. NTFS 5.0 features that will be lost include file permissions, encryption, disk quota information, mounted drive information, and Remote Storage information. In addition, file permissions should only be selectively restored if restoring to a computer in the same domain as that of the original owner's account.

- **Restoring replicated data** Replicated data, such as data replicated among domain controllers, can be restored three different ways:

  - **Non-authoritative restore** When data is restored non-authoritatively, more recent data from other domain controllers will replicate to the restored domain controller. This is the default restore method. Non-authoritative restores provide a starting point for replication of changed data to occur (that is, data that has been modified since the time of the backup). In the absence of a non-authoritative restore, all data will be replicated on a new domain controller.

  - **Authoritative restore** When an authoritative restore is performed on a domain controller, the restored data is considered authoritative in relation to its replication partners. In effect, the authoritative restore will roll back the data to the time of the backup. Authoritative restores are atypical and are used to restore data that may have been accidentally deleted from a replicated set of data, such as the accidental deletion of an OU from Active Directory. Special care must be taken when performing an authoritative restore, as data loss can occur when rolling back objects within a replicated data set.

- **Primary restore** Primary restores are done when all domain controllers have failed and you want to rebuild the domain from backup or when the domain controller being restored is the only domain controller in the domain. Primary restores should not be done on a domain controller if any other domain controllers are working within an active domain. Typically, you would use a primary restore for the first domain controller being restored, then a non-authoritative restore for each additional restored domain controller.

- **Information required to perform a restore** Certain information may be required when performing a restore. This information may be unavailable unless it is written down and secured prior to the occurrence of a disaster. This information includes:

  - **Disk configuration** Record the volumes and size of the disks in the system. In the case of a complete disk failure, all disk configurations must be restored to their original state prior to restoring System State or other data. You should also record the system directory; for example, C:\WINNT.

  - **Domain name** Record the domain name and be prepared to re-create a machine account within the domain, even if the name of the restored computer does not change.

  - **Local administrator password** This password is used to log on to the restored machine to establish a domain account for the machine and properly join the domain. Also, the local administrator account is required to restore the System State data on a domain controller.

  - **Computer name** Record the computer name so you can restore a machine with the same name and avoid having to change client configuration settings.

  - **IP addresses** Record the static IP address information, unless you are using Dynamic Host Configuration Protocol (DHCP).

  - **Video settings** If screen resolution and color depth are important, record these settings so that they can be properly set once a machine is restored.

Other than simple backup and restore of user or application data, it may be necessary to fully restore Windows 2000 Professional or Server should a catastrophic event occur, such as the inability to repair the boot process in a no-boot situation or when a hard disk failure occurs. In events such as these, the computer must be restored from the ground up, starting with hardware repair or replacement and a clean install of the operating system itself. The following steps describe the general process by which a Windows 2000 Professional or Server machine can be restored in the event of catastrophic failure.

1. Prepare the machine for a new installation by repairing or replacing any failed hardware, or, in the case of a new machine, by adding the appropriate disks. A local tape drive must be attached to the system for the restore.

2. Boot from the Windows 2000 installation CD used for the original installation on the failed machine. Install Windows 2000 as a stand-alone machine; that is, do not join a domain or install as a domain controller.

3. During the installation, specify the same configuration options used on the failed machine: for example, windows installation directory, computer name, and so on.

4. Using Disk Administrator, manually restore disk configurations as they were on the failed machine. Specifically, the same number of drives of equal or larger size must be restored to the same or larger size disks in the same locations.

5. Ensure that the tape drive and media are recognized by Windows 2000. You can use the Add/Remove Hardware wizard in Control Panel in Windows 2000 to troubleshoot or add devices.

6. Start Backup and load the appropriate catalog from the tape. Ensure that the Windows 2000 system directory of the failed machine is the same as the system directory of the restored machine. If not, you will have to reinstall the operating system to a directory with the same name prior to restoration. Failure to do so will cause the restore to fail.

7. Depending on the type of restore you are doing on a Windows 2000 Server domain controller, follow the appropriate steps in Table 10-2. If you are restoring Windows 2000 Professional or Server (non-domain controller), you would use the Backup utility Restore Wizard to restore the System State and appropriate system files normally.

Chapter 10: Data Security

8. If you are restoring a Windows 2000 Server, you may optionally need to restore and reconcile network services, such as the DHCP service, WINS server, Certificate server, Media Services server, Exchange Server, or SQL Server.

on the job

For more information on restoring and reconciling server services, as well as verifying Active Directory restoration, read the Windows 2000 Server Disaster Recovery Guidelines White Paper on the Microsoft Web site at http://www.microsoft.com/windows2000/library/operations/fileandprint/recovery.asp and the help files for the particular service.

TABLE 10-2 Restoring Active Directory on a Domain Controller

Type of Restore	When to Perform	Steps
Primary	On the first or only domain controller in the domain	1. Boot into Directory Services Restore Mode by pressing F8 during Windows 2000 startup. 2. Log on with the local Administrator account. 3. Once the computer is booted, you will see *Safe Mode* on all four corners of the desktop. Click OK when the dialog box warns you that you are in Safe Mode. 4. Start the Backup utility. On the Restore tab, expand File, expand the appropriate Media Created *date* at *time* entry, and then select the System State check box. Click Start Restore. 5. Select the Advanced option to access the Advanced Restore Options dialog box, then select the check box When Restoring Replicated Data Sets, Mark the Restored Data as the Primary Data for All Replicas. 6. Finish the restore by accepting the default options, then reboot.
Non-authoritative	When at least one other domain controller in the domain is available and functioning correctly. Must always be performed before an authoritative restore.	1. Boot into Directory Services Restore Mode by pressing F8 during Windows 2000 startup. 2. Log on with the local Administrator account. 3. Once the computer is booted, you will see *Safe Mode* on all four corners of the desktop. Click OK when the dialog box warns you that you are in Safe Mode. 4. Start the Backup utility and click the Restore Wizard. 5. Expand File, expand the appropriate Media Created *date* at *time* entry, and then select the System State check box. 6. Click the Advanced button to select any other options. 7. Click Finish. When you are prompted to reboot the computer, click No if you are going to perform an authoritative restore of Active Directory objects. Otherwise, click Yes.

TABLE 10-2 Restoring Active Directory on a Domain Controller *(continued)*

Type of Restore	When to Perform	Steps
Authoritative	When information has been accidentally deleted from a replicated data set—for example, Sysvol or Active Directory—and automatically replicated to other domain controllers.	1. Perform a non-authoritative restore of Active Directory and Sysvol (described earlier). 2. When prompted to restart the computer after the non-authoritative restore, select No. 3. Use Backup to restore the System State again to an alternate location. This will restore a copy of the Sysvol that you wish to make authoritative to an alternative location for later use. Again, select No to restart the computer after the restore is successful. 4. Use Ntdsutil to authoritatively restore Active Directory objects. The Ntdsutil command-line utility lets you mark Active Directory objects for authoritative restore. You can access help by typing **Ntdsutil /?** at the command prompt. 5. If you want to perform advanced Active Directory verification, you must remain in Safe Mode to do so. Otherwise, reboot the machine normally to allow the Active Directory and the original Sysvol to be published by Active Directory to all other domain controllers. 6. Wait several minutes to allow publication to occur, then copy the Sysvol restored to the alternate location over the existing one. Note: When authoritatively restoring Active Directory, you should also authoritatively restore Sysvol at the same time to ensure the two are always synchronized.

9. Complete the restoration of any additional user or application data that still needs to be restored to additional drives.

10. Verify that the network card is operational and the bindings are active. The network adapter driver or drivers may need to be reinstalled if there is no network connectivity.

11. Verify video settings, if applicable. The video adapter driver may need to be reinstalled if it is not recognized.

Emergency Repair

There are actually several methods that are used to repair a Windows 2000 machine that will not boot correctly. Boot problems can occur when system files become corrupted or accidentally erased, or when installed services or device drivers aren't working correctly. It is generally a safe idea to try one or more of the following recovery options before performing a full restore from a backup. The methods that exist to repair a system when a boot problem occurs include:

- **Safe Mode**   During Windows 2000 startup, press F8 when prompted to access Safe Mode.
- **Windows 2000 Recovery Console**   The Recovery Console is accessed during the text portion of Windows 2000 setup using the CD or boot floppies, by choosing the Repair option.
- **Emergency Repair Process**   The emergency repair process is also accessed by choosing Repair from the text-mode portion of Windows 2000 setup.

If you press F8 when starting Windows 2000, you are presented with the following options:

- Safe Mode
- Safe Mode with Networking
- Safe Mode with Command Prompt
- Enable Boot Logging
- Enable VGA Mode
- Last Known Good Configuration
- Directory Services Restore Mode (Windows 2000 domain controllers only)
- Debugging Mode
- Boot Normally

Safe Mode allows you to start Windows 2000 with a minimal set of drivers. Safe Mode generally allows you to bypass installed drivers that may be causing a boot problem, so that you can remove or reinstall an updated version within Windows 2000. The Last Known Good Configuration option works just like it did in Windows NT, allowing you to back out of a change you made prior to the reboot. For example, if you install a new hardware driver that now is causing the system to be unbootable or is causing a Windows 2000 error prior to the logon screen, and you haven't logged on yet, you can restart the system and choose Last

Known Good Configuration to recover a copy of the Registry that existed prior to you installing the driver. As with Windows NT, the Last Known Good Configuration option will not work if you successfully log on after the reboot. Neither Safe Mode nor Last Known Good Configuration will work if system or boot files have become damaged or deleted.

The Recovery Console is new in Windows 2000 and provides some great features when attempting to repair a failed boot. Using the Windows 2000 Recovery Console, you can obtain limited access to NTFS, FAT, and FAT32 volumes without starting the Windows graphical user interface (GUI). The Recovery Console requires administrator credentials and requires the SAM database be intact so that authentication can occur. Specifically, an administrator can:

- Use, copy, rename, or replace operating system files and folders.
- Enable or disable services or devices from starting when you next start Windows 2000.
- Repair the active system partition boot sector or the Master Boot Record (MBR) if they have become corrupted or if another operating system is installed after Windows 2000.
- Create and format partitions and drives.

on the job

For a list of commands and further instructions on how to access and use the Recovery Console in Windows 2000, read the Knowledge Base article Q229716, Description of the Windows 2000 Recovery Console, on the Microsoft Web site at http://support.microsoft.com/support/kb/articles/q229/7/16.asp.

The emergency repair process in Windows 2000 allows two choices, manual and fast repair. Manual repair provides the following choices:

- **Inspect Startup Environment** This option checks the ARC path in the BOOT.INI file for a path to the Windows 2000 boot partition and %SystemRoot% folder. It does this by using the SETUP.LOG file on the Emergency Repair disk and reading the values for the Windows 2000 installation directory. If the BOOT.INI file is missing or corrupt, a new one is created with a valid ARC path. If the BOOT.INI file is present, the ARC path is checked and updated if needed.

- **Verify Windows 2000 System Files** This option verifies that each Windows 2000 file required to boot is good and matches the file that was originally installed. The Windows 2000 files that are checked include NTLDR, NTDETECT.COM, ARCSETUP.EXE, and ARCLDR.EXE, among others. Verification is performed by using the SETUP.LOG file to compare cyclic redundancy check (CRC) values for each file. If files are missing or corrupt, you are prompted to replace or skip the file. If you choose to replace the file, you will need a Windows 2000 installation CD-ROM or OEM driver disk that contains the correct files.

- **Inspect Boot Sector** This option repairs the active system partition boot sector so that NTLDR is the bootstrap file. If the partition uses the FAT or FAT32 file system and contains a non-Windows boot sector, this repair option also creates a new BOOTSECT.DOS file to be used to dual-boot MS-DOS, Microsoft Windows 95, or Microsoft Windows 98, if these operating systems were previously available. If you also select the Inspect Startup Environment option and a new BOOTSECT.DOS file is created, "C:\="Microsoft Windows" is added to the BOOT.INI file.

It is important to note that the Windows 2000 Manual Repair option does not give you the choice to repair the Windows 2000 Registry files. However, the Fast Repair option does. The Fast Repair option performs all the repairs available in Manual Repair, but you are not prompted for choices. In addition, the Fast Repair option tries to load each Windows 2000 Registry file (SAM, SECURITY, SYSTEM, and SOFTWARE). If a Registry file cannot be loaded for any reason, a new copy will be made from the %SystemRoot%\Repair folder to the %SystemRoot%\System32\Config folder. Therefore, the Fast Repair option may revert parts of the operating system's Registry back to the time when Windows 2000 was first installed. If this occurs, you need to restore your last System State from backup or manually copy a more recent version of the Registry files from the %SystemRoot%\Repair\Regback folder to the %SystemRoot%\System32\Config folder by using the Recovery Console. The files that are located in the Regback folder are from the last time you created an Emergency Repair disk and chose the option to also back up the Registry files to the Repair folder.

The Windows 2000 Emergency Repair disk, like the Windows NT Emergency Repair disk, can be used to repair a boot problem, as noted earlier. However, the Windows 2000 Emergency Repair disk cannot store the Windows 2000 Registry because of its larger size. In fact, when you create a Windows 2000 Emergency Repair

Continuing Education
Course Comment Form
(Final Evaluation)

Course Title: _____

Course Number: _____ **Sec:** _____

Teacher: _____ **Date:** _____

Kindly share your comments with us now that your course is completed.

_____
_____
_____
_____
_____
_____
_____
_____
_____
_____
_____
_____
_____
_____
_____
_____
_____
_____
_____
_____
_____

disk, the only files that get copied to the disk are: SETUP.LOG, AUTOEXEC.NT, and CONFIG.NT. Only the SETUP.LOG is used if this floppy disk is present—to find the Windows 2000 installation point where the Repair folder exists—and neither the AUTOEXEC.NT nor CONFIG.NT file is ever replaced! Weird, huh? I thought so too. If you do not have an Emergency Repair disk and you would like to perform an Emergency Repair, you can ask the Emergency Repair process to try to locate Windows 2000 for you by choosing the L option. In fact, the Repair folder and its contents are much more important than the existence of an Emergency Repair disk in Windows 2000 when attempting to perform the repair process. Exercise 10-2 illustrates the process of creating an Emergency Repair disk in Windows 2000 using the Backup utility. RDISK.EXE is no longer available in Windows 2000 to create an Emergency Repair disk.

CertCam 10-2

EXERCISE 10-2

Creating a Windows 2000 Emergency Repair Disk

In this exercise, you will create an Emergency Repair disk that can be used to help restore system information in the event that system or boot files are missing or corrupt. In creating the Emergency Repair disk, the %SystemRoot%\Repair\Regback folder will be created with the most recent repair information.

1. Obtain a formatted, 3.5-inch floppy diskette.
2. In Windows 2000, click Start | Run, type **ntbackup**, and press ENTER.
3. The Backup utility will appear. Select Emergency Repair Disk from the Welcome tab. Select the check box Also Backup the Registry to the Repair Directory. Insert a blank, formatted floppy disk into drive A: and click OK.

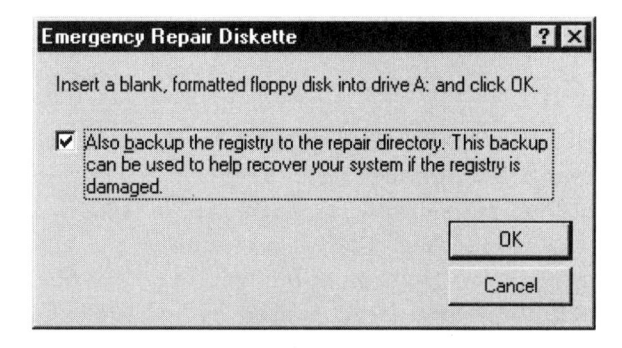

4. The Emergency Repair disk will be created and you will see the progress bar:

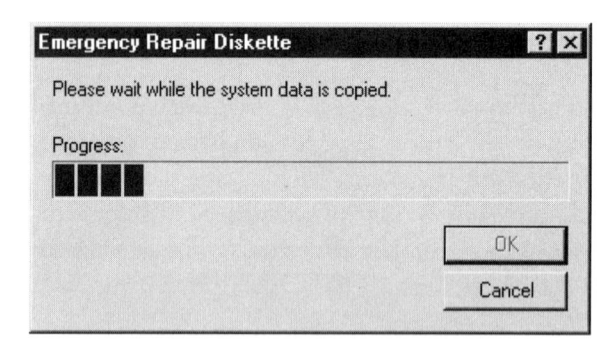

5. When the files are finished copying, you will see a dialog box showing successful completion:

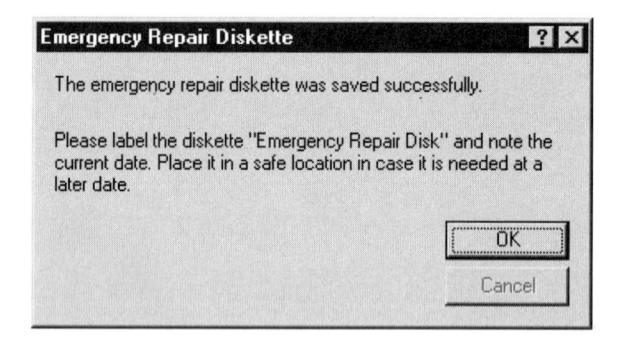

6. Click OK. Navigate to your %SystemRoot%\Repair\Regback folder on your hard drive. List the contents of the Regback folder, noting the different files that make up a large portion of the Registry.

on the job

For more information on the Emergency Repair process in Windows 2000, read the Knowledge Base article Q238359 on the Microsoft Web site at http://support.microsoft.com/support/kb/articles/q238/3/59.asp. A comprehensive set of information on the repair and recovery options in Windows 2000 can also be found on the Microsoft Web site at http://www.microsoft.com/technet/win2000/win2ksrv/manuals/srvgs/ sgsappa.asp.

SCENARIO & SOLUTION

Which Emergency Recovery option will validate the Registry files and can restore them from the Repair folder if they are damaged?	Fast Repair.
Which disaster recovery mechanism serves as an adequate substitution for regularly backing up System State and other critical data?	There is no adequate substitute for regular backups.
Which disaster recovery mechanisms can repair the active system partition boot sector, if it becomes corrupt?	Recovery Console or Emergency Repair process.
When attempting to restore Active Directory on a domain controller, how must you boot Windows 2000?	You must boot into Directory Services Restore Mode by pressing F8 first during startup.
Which restore mode should be used when restoring Active Directory to a new domain controller when other domain controllers already exist in the domain and no loss of data has occurred?	You should perform a non-authoritative restore from backup.

CERTIFICATION OBJECTIVE 10.03

Design an Encrypting File System Strategy

File encryption is new tool in Windows 2000 that allows a user to encrypt data directly on volumes that use the NTFS file system so that the data cannot be used or modified by any other user. By encrypting data stored on a disk, the user is able to protect both the confidentiality and the integrity of the data. File encryption is available in Windows 2000 through the Encrypting File System (EFS). Encrypting stored data should not be confused with encrypting data transmitted over the network. The encryption of data transmitted between two networked computers is implemented differently through the use of industry-standard protocols, such as Internet Protocol Security (IPSec), Secure Sockets Layer (SSL), and Transport Layer Security (TLS).

Prior to Windows 2000, the primary method used to prevent unauthorized access to local data using Windows NT was to store the data on an NTFS partition and use the access control list (ACL) of the folder or file to prevent unauthorized access. Although the use of ACLs works quite well while a user operates within Windows, it cannot prevent unauthorized access to data if the operating system is bypassed. If someone has physical access to a system, they can boot another operating system from a floppy or from the hard drive, if one is installed. While inside another operating system, a person could use a third-party tool to read the NTFS on-disk structures, thus bypassing Windows authentication and the NTFS ACL of an object. Third-party tools that run on MS-DOS or UNIX make bypassing the built-in security features of Windows rather easy. Although most modern personal computers allow the use of a boot password to prevent booting into another operating system, these passwords do not provide strong security nor are they in widespread use. Even if they are used, a malicious user with physical access to the computer can remove the hard drive and plug it into another computer where they have sufficient access.

Encryption of stored data is considered one component of an overall security plan and may or may not be required depending on the security requirements. Typical scenarios where data encryption is relevant include:

- **Stolen laptop** At the time of the writing of this book, the news was reporting a problem with stolen laptops at the State Department. Encrypting the data on the laptop could have thwarted this problem. Because of the size and portability of laptops, they are easy targets for thieves. Although the thief might simply be interested in reselling your laptop, they also have easy access to confidential data stored on the laptop's hard drive, even if this confidential data is stored on an NTFS volume.

- **Unrestricted access** Because desktop systems are often left unattended in unrestricted areas, it is rather easy for someone to sit down at a workstation while another person is logged on and quickly save data to a floppy drive or other portable device. Although Windows NT and 2000 allow a user to lock their workstation rather easily without having to log off, these precautions cannot be enforced.

- **Encryption services that require manual encryption and decryption** It is important that any encryption service provide real-time encryption and decryption when a user opens or saves a file. If a third-party encryption service requires the user to manually encrypt the file after use, or manually decrypt the file before use, then it discourages the user from encrypting files at all. In Windows 2000, the encryption and decryption of data are transparent to the user.

- **No data recovery**   If a third-party encryption or decryption service is used, it might not provide data recovery or it might provide data recovery using a password. Where password-based recovery is used, it creates a weak point of access. A thief can gain access to all the encrypted files using only a password. EFS uses public key cryptography, not passwords, to provide for emergency file recovery.

- **Application temporary files**   Many applications, including most Microsoft Office applications, create temporary, unencrypted copies of the encrypted file while a user is modifying the file. These temporary files, although typically deleted after modifications are made and the file is closed, can be left unencrypted on the disk, thus causing a security leak. Best practices, such as encrypting at the folder level, can ensure that temporary application files are also encrypted by EFS.

- **Application-level encryption**   If a third-party tool uses application-level encryption, then the user's encryption key may be stored in a paging file, an operating system file used to temporarily store application data on the hard drive while the application is in use. By mining a paging file for a user's encryption key, access to all data encrypted with the key can be accomplished. EFS in Windows 2000 is integrated with the operating system such that it prevents the leaking of key information to pagefiles.

- **Password-derived encryption keys**   Encryption keys derived from passwords are considered weak security. Dictionary attacks can breach this type of security if complex passwords are not enforced. EFS uses public-key cryptography, not user passwords, to provide strong encryption keys.

It is important to be aware of the limitations of EFS as a security solution. For instance, EFS is not used to (1) encrypt data travelling across the network, (2) authenticate users, (3) secure dial-in or VPN connections, or (4) encrypt data on non-Windows 2000 machines.

EFS Overview

EFS works as an integrated system service in Windows 2000 and complements existing access controls. EFS implements data encryption using a combination of symmetric key encryption and asymmetric (public key) encryption. When a file is encrypted, a randomly-generated symmetric key is created called the file encryption key (FEK). The FEK is used to both encrypt the plaintext file before it is stored on the disk and to decrypt the encrypted file. The FEK is then encrypted using the user's public key and stored in a header attached to the file known as the data decryption field (DDF). The FEK can only be extracted from the DDF using the user's private key, which is safely contained elsewhere. The public portion of a user's key pair used to encrypt the FEK in the DDF is obtained from the user's X.509 version 3 certificate. The enhanced key usage for these certificates must be *File Encryption*. When the user who created the file goes to open the encrypted file in the future, the user's private key is used to decrypt the FEK in the DDF. Then, the FEK is used to decrypt the encrypted file stream.

Although the user who originally encrypts a file typically is the one who decrypts the file by using his or her private key, circumstances may arise where the user's private key is unavailable and a second party must recover the file. You might need to recover a file if:

- A person leaves the company
- A person loses his or her private key
- A law enforcement agency makes a request

In order to provide for the recoverability of encrypted files in such cases, the FEK is also encrypted using one or more public keys from other users known as *recovery agents*. The public key for a recovery agent is obtained from the recovery agent X.509 version 3 certificate, which is also stored on the computer. The enhanced key usage for these certificates must be *File Recovery*. These additional encrypted FEKs are stored in additional headers of the encrypted file known as data recovery fields (DRFs). If multiple recovery agents are defined, a DRF will be created for each EFS recovery agent that exists. The domain administrator, using the Encrypted Data Recovery Agent (EDRA) policy for the computer, typically defines who the recovery agents will be for computers in the domain. EDRA policy is discussed later in this chapter.

Both the user's and the recovery agent's public keys are stored on the computer where encryption occurs in the form of X.509 version 3 certificates. The private portion of a user's key pair is stored safely elsewhere in smart cards or in the protected key store in Windows 2000. The user's private key is not stored in the Security Accounts Manager (SAM) database or in a folder somewhere, and is therefore not compromised by unauthorized access to the hard drive. Recovery agents also store the private portions of their keys safely elsewhere (on smart cards or other secure storage devices).

Figure 10-7 illustrates the encryption process for files. Although Figure 10-7 shows only one recovery agent, there can actually be several recovery agents with independent keys that cause the creation of several DRFs.

Figure 10-8 illustrates the decryption process. The FEK is used to decrypt file data reads on a block-by-block basis. Therefore, the entire file does not have to be decrypted because random access to a large file will only decrypt the specific blocks read from disk for that file.

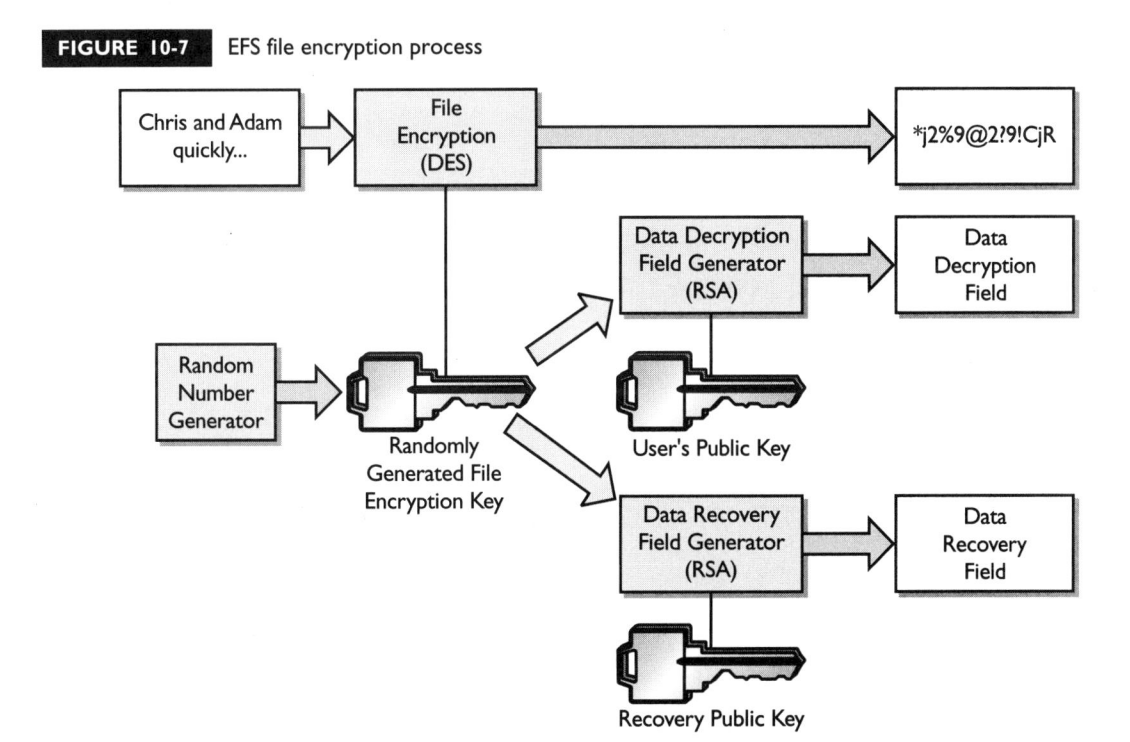

FIGURE 10-7   EFS file encryption process

FIGURE 10-8 EFS decryption process

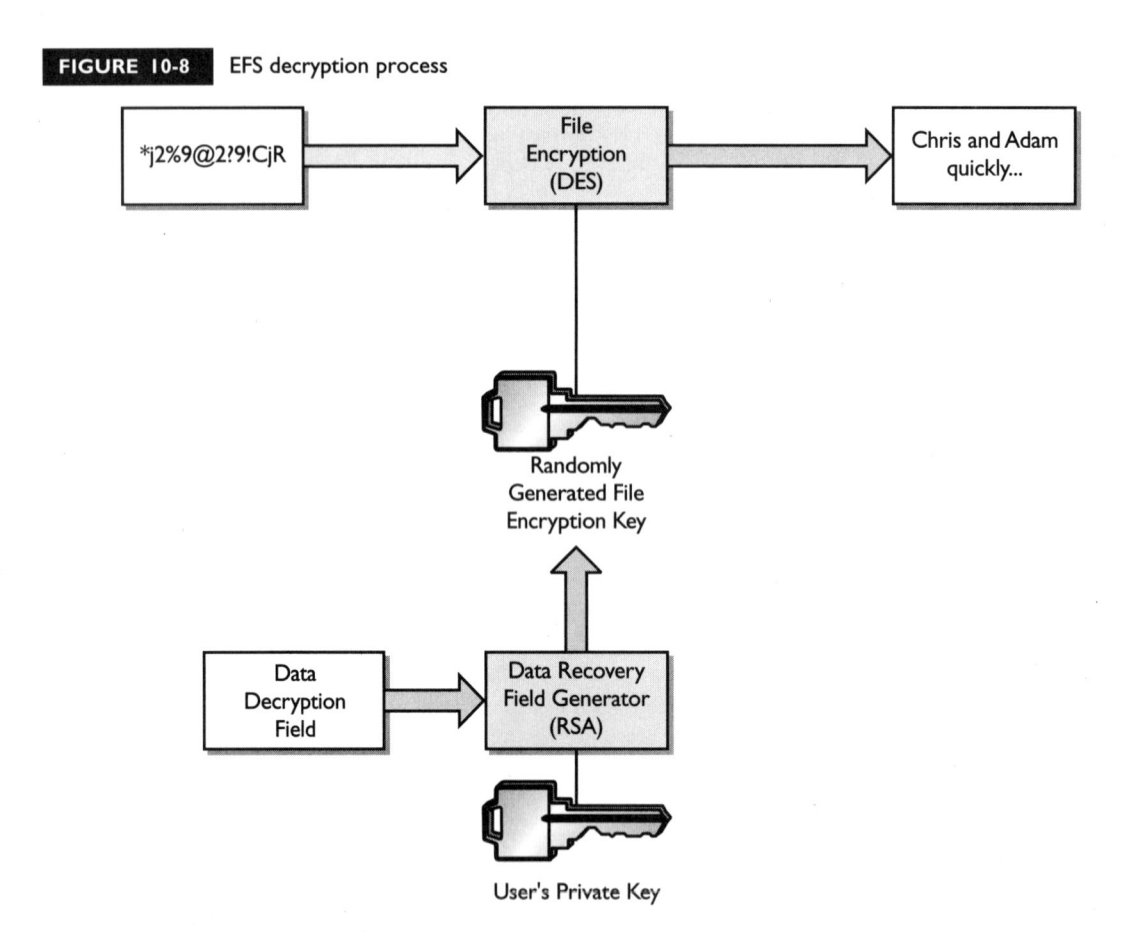

Figure 10-9 illustrates the file recovery process, which is similar to decryption except the recovery agent's private key is used to decrypt the FEK in the DRF.

Encryption and Decryption

Encryption and decryption occur transparently to the user once configured. In other words, a user does not need to manually encrypt or decrypt a file before or after use. EFS allows users to start encrypting files with no administrative effort. For example, when a user marks a folder or file for encryption using Windows Explorer, EFS automatically generates a public-key pair and has the pair certified by a certificate authority (CA). If a CA is not available to issue a certificate, EFS will

FIGURE 10-9 EFS file recovery process

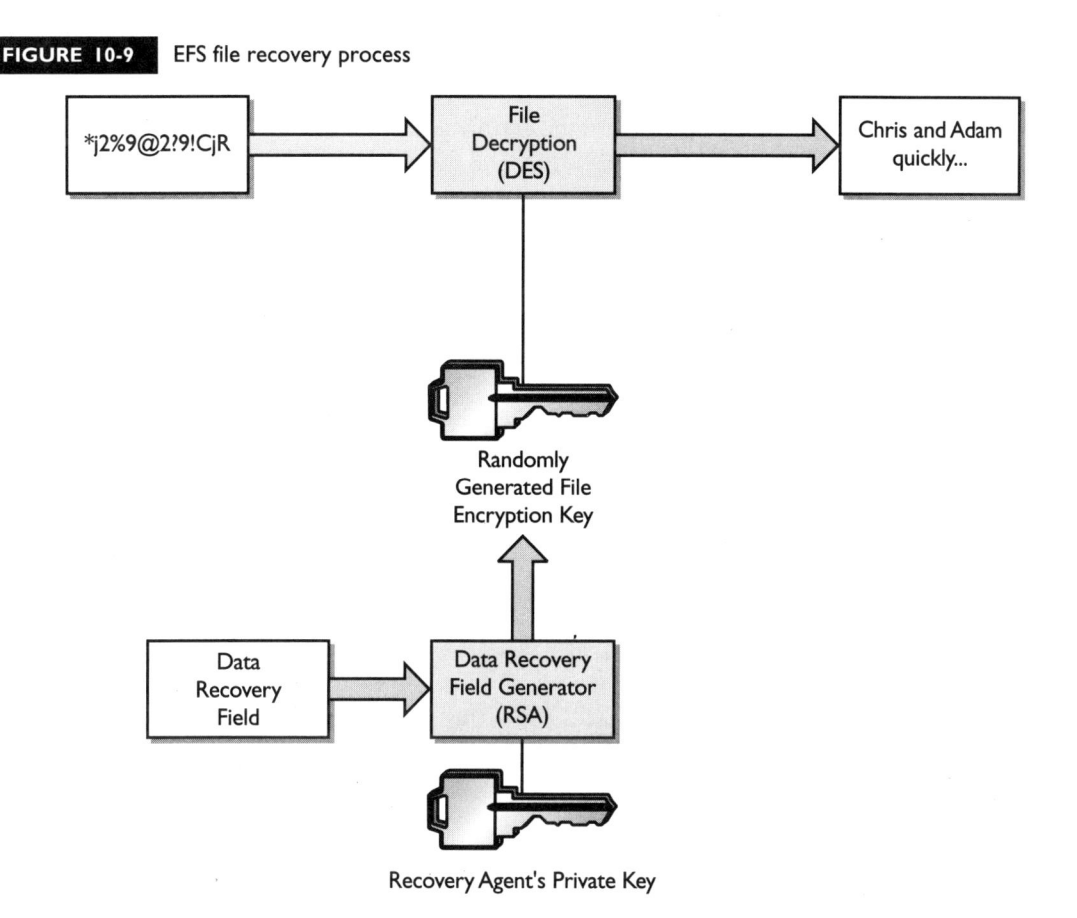

self-sign the certificate. When an encrypted file needs to be opened, EFS will automatically detect an encrypted file and locate a user's certificate and associated private key in the user's certificate and the private key store. If any other user attempts to open an encrypted file, they will receive an access denied error because the user will not possess the key to decrypt the DDF.

File encryption and decryption are supported on a per-file or per-folder basis. If a folder is marked for encryption, all files and subfolders created *after* the folder is marked will be automatically encrypted, by default. Because EFS only encrypts files, folders that are marked for encryption are not actually encrypted. Instead, marking a folder for encryption allows the propagation of the encryption attribute to all files and subfolders created underneath the folder. Windows Explorer provides

488 Chapter 10: Data Security

a graphical interface for encrypting and decrypting folders and files. Additionally, the *cipher* command-line utility provides the ability to encrypt and decrypt folders and files from a command prompt. In this section, we will discuss using Windows Explorer to encrypt and decrypt files and folders; cipher will be discussed in a later section.

Let's explore encrypting a folder from the Windows Explorer interface. Exercise 10-3 illustrates how to encrypt a folder on a local machine using Windows Explorer.

EXERCISE 10-3

Encrypting a Folder on a Local Machine

In this exercise, you will encrypt a folder on a local machine and learn how to detect whether a file or folder is encrypted.

1. Right-click the selected folder to bring up the *<folder name>* Properties dialog box. The folder must exist on an NTFS partition. The following window shows the properties dialog box for a folder.

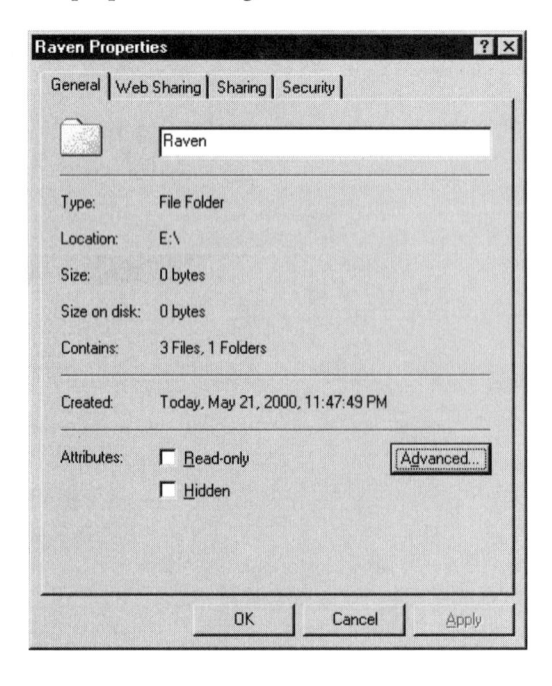

2. Click Advanced on the General tab. The following window shows the Advanced Attributes dialog box.

3. Select Encrypt Contents to Secure Data.

Advanced Attributes

Choose the settings you want for this folder
When you apply these changes you will be asked if you want the changes to affect all subfolders and files as well.

Archive and Index attributes
- [ ] Folder is ready for archiving
- [x] For fast searching, allow Indexing Service to index this folder

Compress or Encrypt attributes
- [ ] Compress contents to save disk space
- [x] Encrypt contents to secure data

[OK] [Cancel]

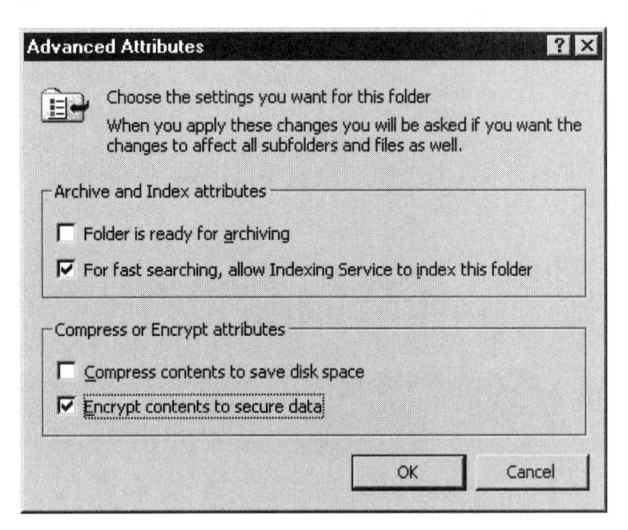

4. Click OK to close the Advanced Attributes dialog box. Then click OK or Apply at the folder properties dialog box. A dialog box, shown below, may prompt you to encrypt the folder only or all existing contents. The previous window does not appear if the folder is empty.

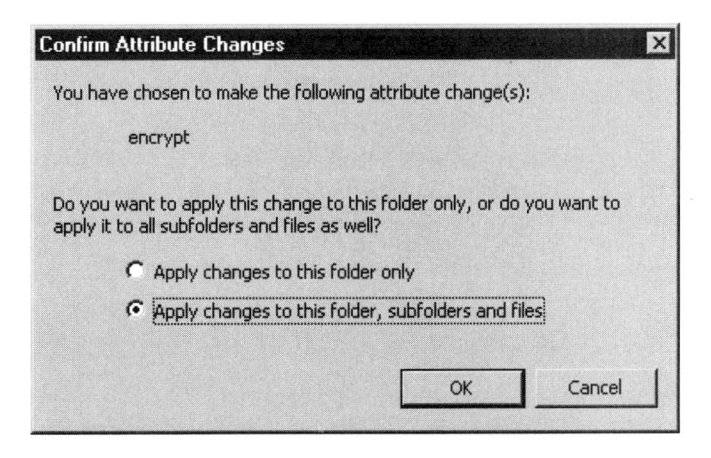

Confirm Attribute Changes

You have chosen to make the following attribute change(s):

encrypt

Do you want to apply this change to this folder only, or do you want to apply it to all subfolders and files as well?

○ Apply changes to this folder only
◉ Apply changes to this folder, subfolders and files

[OK] [Cancel]

If you choose Apply Changes to This Folder Only, no existing data within the folder will be encrypted. However, all files or subfolders created *after* the folder is encrypted will inherit the encryption attribute of the folder. If you choose Apply Changes to This Folder, Subfolders and Files, then all existing files and subfolders within the current folder will be encrypted as well.

5. Click OK on the Confirm Attribute Changes dialog box, if present. You can confirm that encryption occurred by verifying the state of the Encrypt Contents to Secure Data attribute check box. Alternatively, you can view the presence of the E attribute for the folder and its files within Windows Explorer. In order to view folder and file attributes, select View then Details from within Windows Explorer, then right-click anywhere on the field headings and select the Attributes option as shown here:

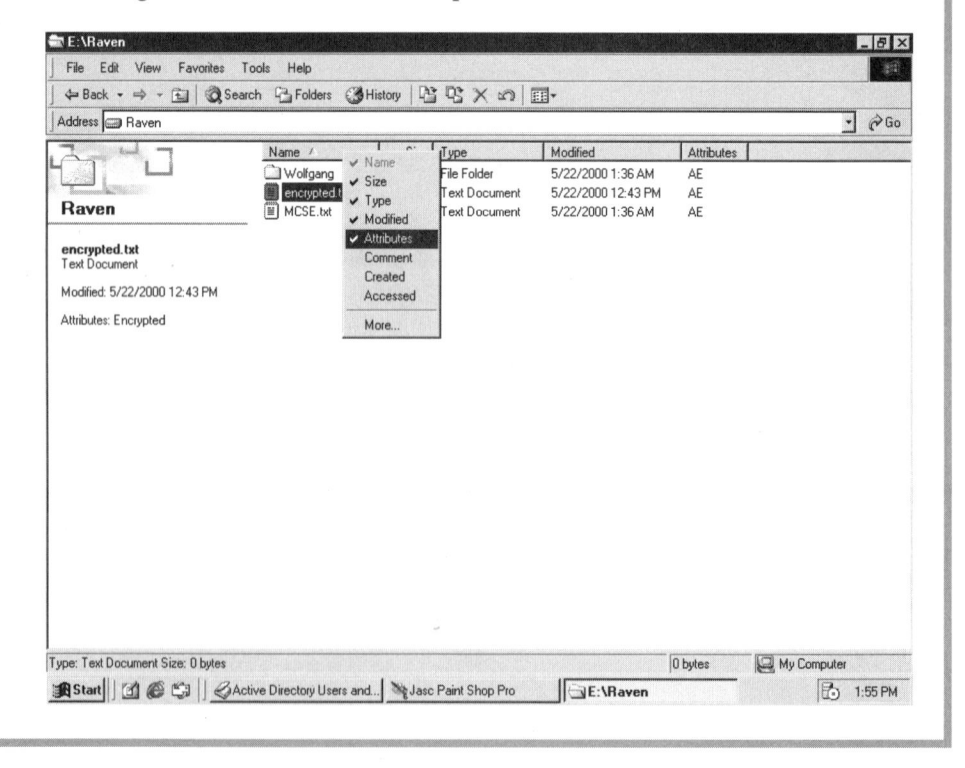

Encryption and decryption on individual files occur in a similar manner as demonstrated in the exercise. Although the encryption process is exposed for individual files, it is a better practice to encrypt folders where the file or files exist. By encrypting folders instead of individual files, applications that create temporary copies of encrypted files in plaintext cannot inadvertently leave files in plaintext after modifications have occurred. Encryption at the folder level ensures that all files created in the folder (including temporary files) are encrypted. Even though a folder is encrypted, the folder's list of files is not encrypted. Therefore, a user with appropriate permissions to the folder can still enumerate files as usual. Figure 10-10 shows the Encryption Warning dialog box that is received when an individual file is set for encryption within a folder that is not encrypted.

In order to decrypt a folder or an individual file, the process in the preceding exercise is reversed. For example, clearing the Encrypt Contents to Secure Data check box allows the user to decrypt the currently selected folder. It also allows the user to decrypt all files and subfolders in the folder, in addition to resetting the folder as unencrypted. Exercise 10-4 illustrates the process of decrypting a folder.

FIGURE 10-10

Encryption warning when encrypting a file within an unencrypted folder

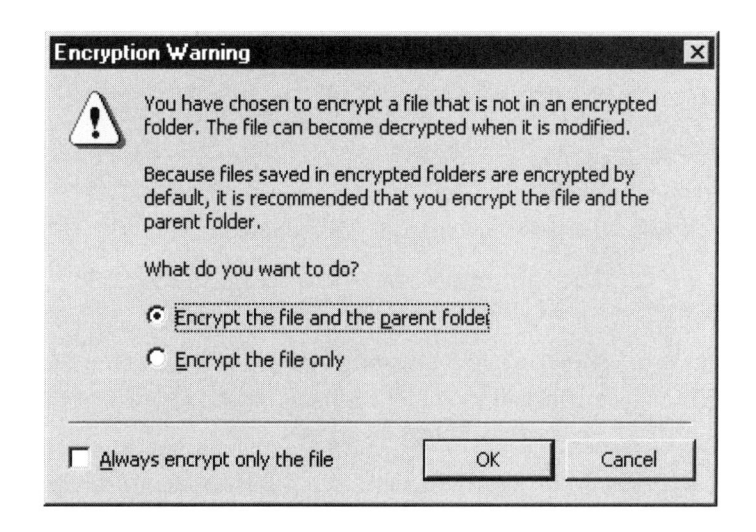

EXERCISE 10-4

Decrypting a Folder on a Local Machine

In this exercise, you will decrypt the folder that you encrypted in Exercise 10-3.

1. Right-click the selected folder to bring up the *<folder name>* Properties dialog box, as shown in the windows in Exercise 10-3, step 1. The folder must exist on an NTFS partition and already have the encryption attribute.

2. Click Advanced on the General tab. The Advanced Attributes dialog box appears as shown in step 3.

3. Click to clear the Encrypt Contents to Secure Data check box.

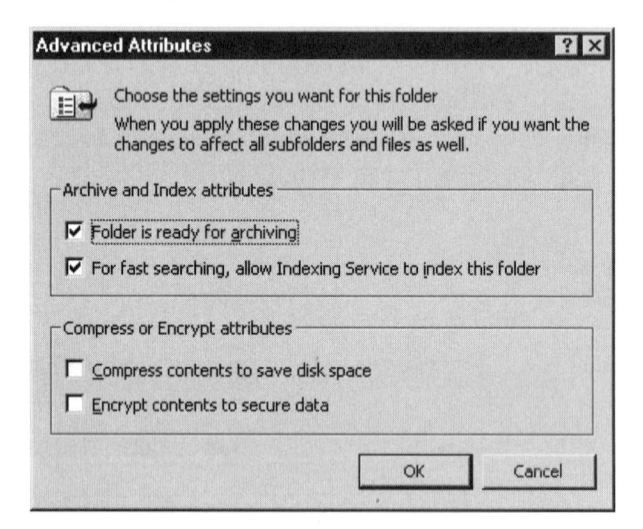

4. Click OK to close the dialog box.

5. Click OK to close the Advanced Attributes dialog box. Then click OK or Apply at the folder properties dialog box.

6. A dialog box may prompt you to remove the encryption attribute for the folder only or remove it for all existing content. This dialog box does not appear if the folder is empty.

> **Confirm Attribute Changes**
>
> You have chosen to make the following attribute change(s):
>
> decrypt
>
> Do you want to apply this change to this folder only, or do you want to apply it to all subfolders and files as well?
>
> ○ Apply changes to this folder only
> ◉ Apply changes to this folder, subfolders and files
>
> [OK] [Cancel]

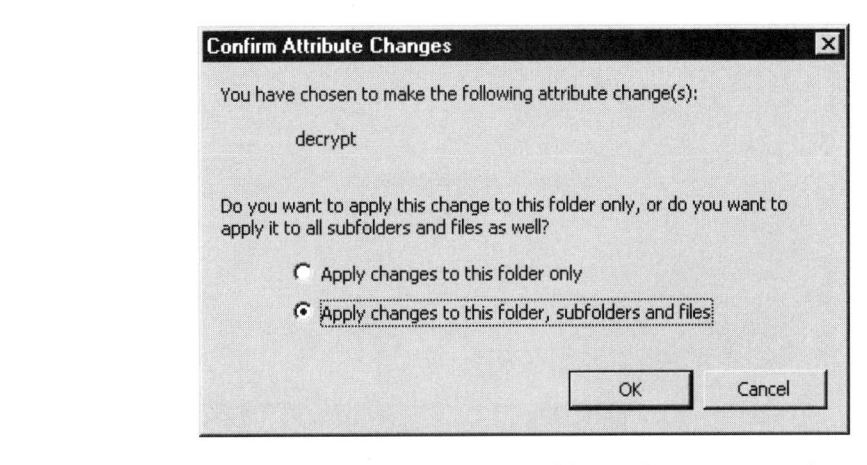

If you choose Apply Changes to This Folder Only, no existing data within the folder will be decrypted. However, all files or subfolders created *after* the folder is decrypted will not inherit the encryption attribute. If you choose Apply Changes to This Folder, Subfolders and Files, then all existing files and subfolders within the current folder will be decrypted as well.

7. Click OK on the Confirm Attribute Changes dialog box, if present. You can confirm that encryption occurred by verifying the state of the Encrypt Contents to Secure Data attribute check box.

EFS supports the encryption of files and folders on a remote server, as well. If the remote machine is configured as *trusted for delegation,* EFS will be able to use the key from the user's roaming profile so that that same key is used across systems. If the remote machine is not *trusted,* then a local profile is created on the machine, and the key is local to that machine and can be used on that machine only. Therefore, moving encrypted files from the server would require the user to move his or her keys also. Figure 10-11 shows the computer property dialog box where a server can be trusted for delegation by selecting the Trust Computer for Delegation check box on the General tab.

494 Chapter 10: Data Security

FIGURE 10-11

Computer property dialog box showing trust computer for delegation

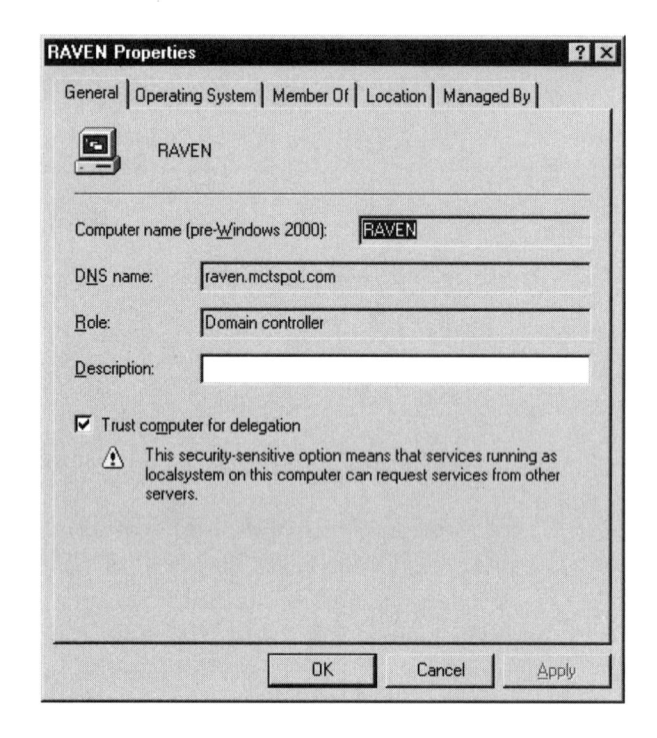

Exercise 10-5 illustrates how to encrypt a folder on a remote server. The folder in question must be on an NTFS version 5.0 volume or this exercise will not work.

EXERCISE 10-5

Encrypting a Folder on a Remote Server

In this exercise, you will connect to a remote server share using a mapped drive letter, then encrypt and decrypt a file.

1. Use the Tools menu in Windows Explorer to map a network share on the remote server to a local drive letter.
2. Once mapped, navigate to the folder on the remote server as in Exercise 10-3.
3. Follow the steps in Exercise 10-3 to encrypt the folder.

Although the sharing of encrypted folders is exposed to the user in Windows 2000, any users other than the user who encrypted the folder or a recovery agent will be denied access to the encrypted contents of the network share. Figure 10-12 shows a sample error received when another user attempts to open an encrypted file from a remote share where the user has appropriate permissions.

exam
Ⓦatch

A user should not encrypt shared files on the network that are used by more than one person. If a user encrypts shared data, then other users will be denied access even if they have appropriate permissions to the shared folder. In the event that file encryption is required to protect user data, you should encrypt only personal data individually.

Table 10-3 summarizes what happens to the encryption status when a user copies or moves a file or a folder.

In all cases, if a user with appropriate permissions attempts to copy or move an encrypted file to a non-Windows 2000 workstation across the network, they will receive an Error Copying (or Moving) File dialog box with access denied, as shown in Figure 10-13.

In all cases, if an encrypted file or folder is copied or moved to an NTFS 5 volume on the same system, the file will remain encrypted and will be identical to the original. However, if the copy or move is between remote NTFS 5 volumes, the file will be encrypted but may not be identical to the original. If no roaming profile exists on the remote server or the server is not *trusted for delegation,* then a new key will be used to create a new FEK. This occurs because the original FEK cannot be exported across the wire securely.

FIGURE 10-12

Error received when attempting to open an encrypted file from network

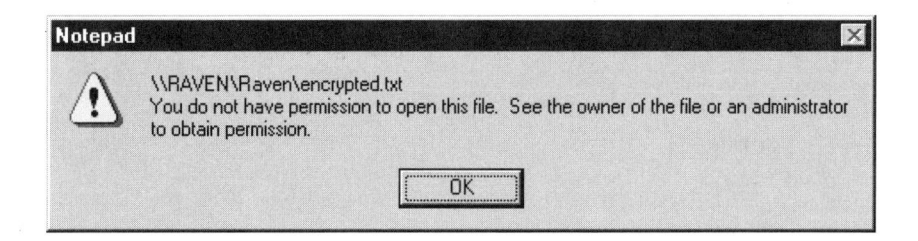

TABLE 10-3 Results when Copying or Moving an Encrypted File or Folder

Action	From	To	Result
copy or move encrypted file or folder	local NTFS 5 volume	local NTFS 5 volume	encryption remains
copy or move encrypted file or folder	local NTFS 5 volume	local non-NTFS 5 volume	file or folder is plaintext
copy or move encrypted file or folder	local NTFS 5 volume	share on remote NTFS 5 volume	encryption remains, but with new FEK if no roaming profile exists
copy or move encrypted file or folder	local NTFS 5 volume	share on remote non-NTFS 5 volume	file or folder is plaintext
copy or move encrypted file or folder	share on remote NTFS 5 volume	local NTFS 5 volume	encryption remains, but with new FEK if no roaming profile exists
copy or move encrypted file or folder	share on remote NTFS 5 volume	share on remote NTFS 5 volume	encryption remains
copy or move encrypted file or folder	share on remote NTFS 5 volume	local non-NTFS 5 volume	file or folder is plaintext
copy or move unencrypted file or folder	share on remote non-NTFS 5 volume	local encrypted folder on NTFS 5 volume	file is marked for encryption as if new
copy or move unencrypted file or folder	local non-NTFS 5 volume	local encrypted folder on NTFS 5 volume	file is marked for encryption as if new

FIGURE 10-13

Error message received when copying encrypted file to a non-Windows 2000 workstation

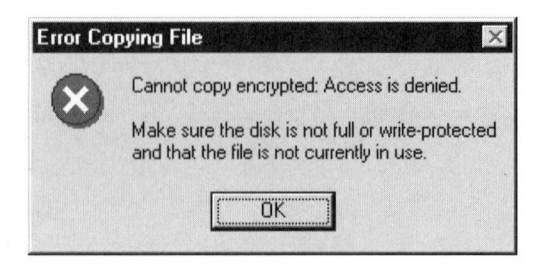

Let's explore what happens to an encrypted directory when it is copied between NTFS5 volumes on the same workstation. The same outcome would be observed if the folder were moved. In order to complete Exercise 10-6, you will need access to a Windows 2000 workstation with at least two NTFS volumes.

Although Windows 2000 Help claims that users must use the Cut and Paste commands when moving or copying encrypted files or folders, using drag-and-drop to move or copy will also cause the file or folder to retain its encryption status. It is also important to note that any user with appropriate permissions can delete an encrypted file, even if he or she is not the user who created it. Moreover, an encrypted file can be renamed (assuming the user has appropriate permissions) and the file will still retain the encryption.

Cipher Command

In addition to the graphical interface, Windows 2000 includes the cipher command-line tool for more robust encryption functionality for administrative operations. The cipher utility allows a user to encrypt and decrypt folders and files

---

EXERCISE 10-6

CertCam 10-6

Copying an Encrypted Folder Between Windows 2000 NTFS Volumes

In this exercise, you will see the results of copying an encrypted folder from one NTFS5 volume to another NTFS5 volume.

1. Create an empty folder on an NTFS volume and mark it as encrypted.
2. Select the folder in Windows Explorer, right-click, and select Copy.
3. Open the folder on another NTFS volume where you want to place the copy.
4. Right-click and select Paste.
5. You can confirm that the copied folder retained the encryption attribute by verifying the state of the Encrypt Contents to Secure Data attribute check box or by viewing the E attribute in the Details view in Windows Explorer.

from a command prompt, as well as view the encryption state for a file or a folder. Figure 10-14 illustrates the use of the cipher command without any parameters. Objects appear with a *U* if unencrypted or an *E* if encrypted.

In order to view the cipher command options, you type:

```
C:\>cipher /?
```

The cipher command supports the following options:

```
C:\>cipher /?
Displays or alters the encryption of directories [files] on NTFS partitions.
  CIPHER [/E | /D] [/S:dir] [/A] [/I] [/F] [/Q] [/H] [/K] [pathname [...]]
    /E        Encrypts the specified directories. Directories will be marked
              so that files added afterward will be encrypted.
    /D        Decrypts the specified directories. Directories will be marked
              so that files added afterward will not be encrypted.
    /S        Performs the specified operation on directories in the given
              directory and all subdirectories.
    /A        Operation for files as well as directories. The encrypted file
              could become decrypted when it is modified if the parent
              directory is not encrypted. It is recommended that you encrypt
              the file and the parent directory.
    /I        Continues performing the specified operation even after errors
              have occurred. By default, CIPHER stops when an error is
              encountered.
    /F        Forces the encryption operation on all specified objects, even
              those which are already encrypted. Already-encrypted objects
              are skipped by default.
    /Q        Reports only the most essential information.
    /H        Displays files with the hidden or system attributes. These
              files are omitted by default.
    /K        Creates new file encryption key for the user running CIPHER. If
              this option is chosen, all the other options will be ignored.
    pathname  Specifies a pattern, file, or directory.

Used without parameters, CIPHER displays the encryption state of
the current directory and any files it contains. You may use multiple
directory names and wildcards. You must put spaces between multiple
parameters.
```

FIGURE 10-14

Cipher command without any parameters

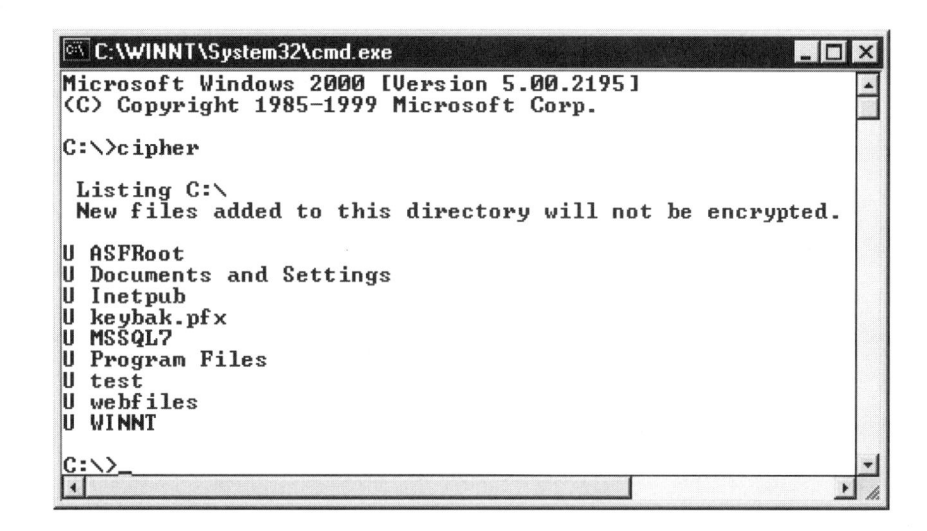

```
C:\WINNT\System32\cmd.exe
Microsoft Windows 2000 [Version 5.00.2195]
(C) Copyright 1985-1999 Microsoft Corp.

C:\>cipher

 Listing C:\
 New files added to this directory will not be encrypted.

U ASFRoot
U Documents and Settings
U Inetpub
U keybak.pfx
U MSSQL7
U Program Files
U test
U webfiles
U WINNT

C:\>_
```

Exercise 10-7 illustrates how to use the cipher command to encrypt the C:\My Documents folder. Exercise 10-7 assumes you have a folder named My Documents on the C:\ drive.

It is important to note that users cannot encrypt system, compressed, or Windows 2000 boot files. EFS is intended to encrypt and decrypt user data. System data, such as the Registry, system DLLs, and other files used by Windows 2000, must never become encrypted because the EFS driver and supporting components do not become active until Windows 2000 is running. Therefore, if any of the files used by Windows 2000 are encrypted, the system would become useless or you may not be able to boot the operating system. EFS provides a certain level of protection by not allowing users to encrypt files or folders that have the System attribute set. If a user attempts to encrypt a system file, they will receive a similar error to the one shown in Figure 10-15.

In addition, compression and encryption cannot both be in effect on a folder or file. For example, when attempting to compress an encrypted file or encrypt a compressed file, the user is not given the option to choose both the Compress Contents to Save Disk Space and the Encrypt Contents to Secure Data check boxes. These functions are mutually exclusive.

EXERCISE 10-7

Using the Cipher Command to Encrypt and Decrypt a Folder

In this exercise, you will encrypt and decrypt your C:\My Documents folder using the **cipher** command line utility.

1. Open a Windows 2000 command prompt.
2. Type at the C:\> prompt:

   ```
   cipher /e "my documents"
   ```

3. After pressing ENTER, you should receive the following:

   ```
   C:\>cipher /e "my documents"
       Encrypting directories in C:\
       my documents       [OK]
       1 directorie(s) within 1 directorie(s) were encrypted.
   ```

4. In order to encrypt the folder as well as all of its contents, type at the C:\> prompt:

   ```
   cipher /e /s:"my documents" /a
   ```

5. In order to decrypt the folder and all of its contents, type at the C:\>prompt:

   ```
   cipher /d /s:"my documents" /a
   ```

FIGURE 10-15

Error received when attempting to encrypt a system file

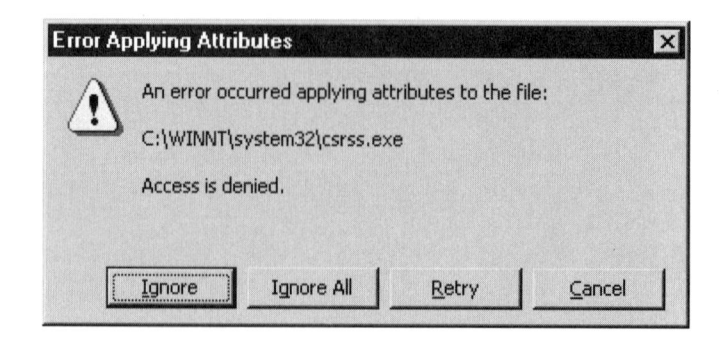

EFS Backup and Recovery Operations

EFS provides users the ability to transfer encrypted files across systems through standard backup and restore mechanisms. This allows the security of the file to remain intact even if the file is put on removable media or sent using e-mail. Remember, encrypted files copied across the network between separate Windows 2000 NTFS volumes are delivered unencrypted across the wire, and get new FEKs if the server is *trusted for delegation* and the user does not have a roaming profile on the server. Also, if an encrypted file is simply copied to removable media from within Windows 2000, the encryption will be lost. The preferred method of transferring an encrypted file in order to retain its original encryption settings is to:

1. Back up the encrypted file to removable media, such as a floppy disk formatted with FAT or backup tape, using a backup tool. The backup tool will preserve the encryption of the file on the hard disk.
2. Transfer the backed up file (a .BKF file if using the Windows 2000 Backup utility) to the other computer either using removable media or through an e-mail attachment.
3. Restore the backup file on the remote computer to a Windows 2000 NTFS volume. The restored file will keep its encryption intact.

It is important to note that encrypted files restored on a separate machine will still be inaccessible to users other than the person who encrypted the file or one of the designated recovery agents defined on the computer where the file was originally encrypted. In order to transfer an encrypted file to another user other than a recovery agent, you will need to decrypt the file first. Once the user copies the decrypted file to their workstation, they can encrypt it again using their public key.

Let's explore how to move an encrypted file between machines using the Windows 2000 Backup utility. It is important to note that this is also the preferred method used by a recovery agent to recover a file if the user is no longer with the company or loses his or her private key. Exercise 10-8 illustrates how to transport an encrypted folder using backup and restore procedures. Exercise 10-8 assumes you have access to two machines running Windows 2000 in the same domain.

Backing Up and Restoring an Encrypted Folder

In this exercise, you will back up an encrypted folder to another location on your hard drive, then restore it to see the effect of the restore procedure on the folder's encryption status.

1. Start the Windows 2000 Backup program by clicking Start | Programs | Accessories | System Tools | Backup. Select the Backup tab. If Backup is not installed, you can install this program by clicking Start | Settings | Control Panel | Add/Remove Programs.

2. Use the browser to locate and check the encrypted folder that you want to back up.

3. Select the backup file (for example, C:\backup.bkf) where you want to back up the entire folder.

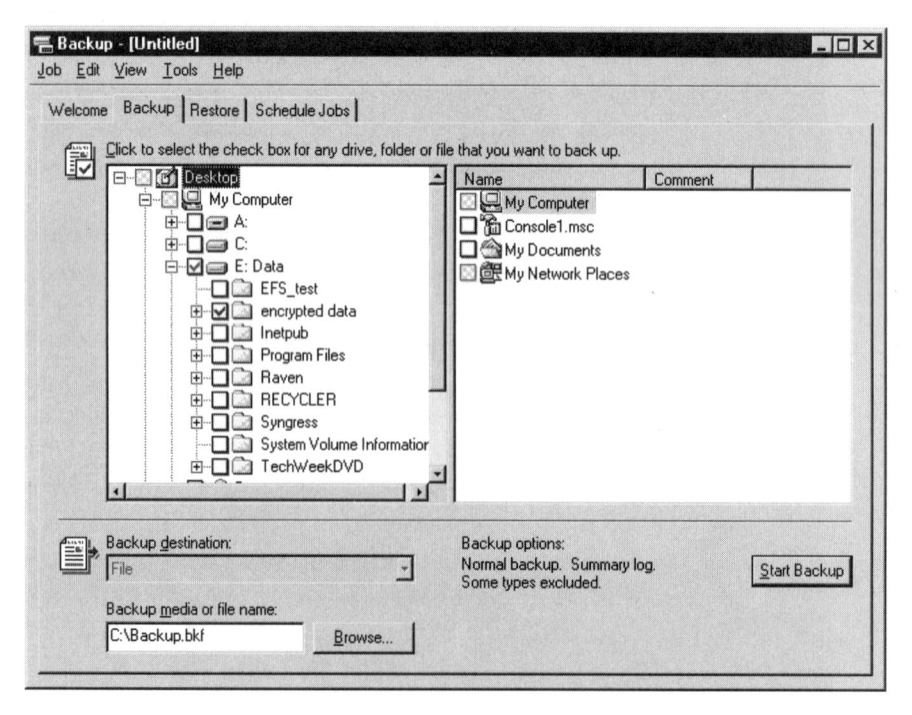

4. Click Start Backup.

5. Click Start Backup on the Backup Job Information dialog box to proceed with the backup.

6. The utility will then back up the entire encrypted folder to the backup file (for example, C:\backup.bkf). This file can be copied to removable media and will be secure because it will remain encrypted.

The last part of this exercise is to restore the backup file to an NTFS partition on a Windows 2000 workstation so that the encrypted folder, as well as the NTFS security settings, can be restored properly. For the purposes of this exercise, you can choose to restore the backup file on the same workstation. In real life, you could send the backup file to the recovery agent as an e-mail attachment or send it using "snail" mail and he or she would perform the remaining steps.

7. Start the Windows 2000 Backup utility as before. Select the Restore tab.

8. Right-click File and select Catalog File....

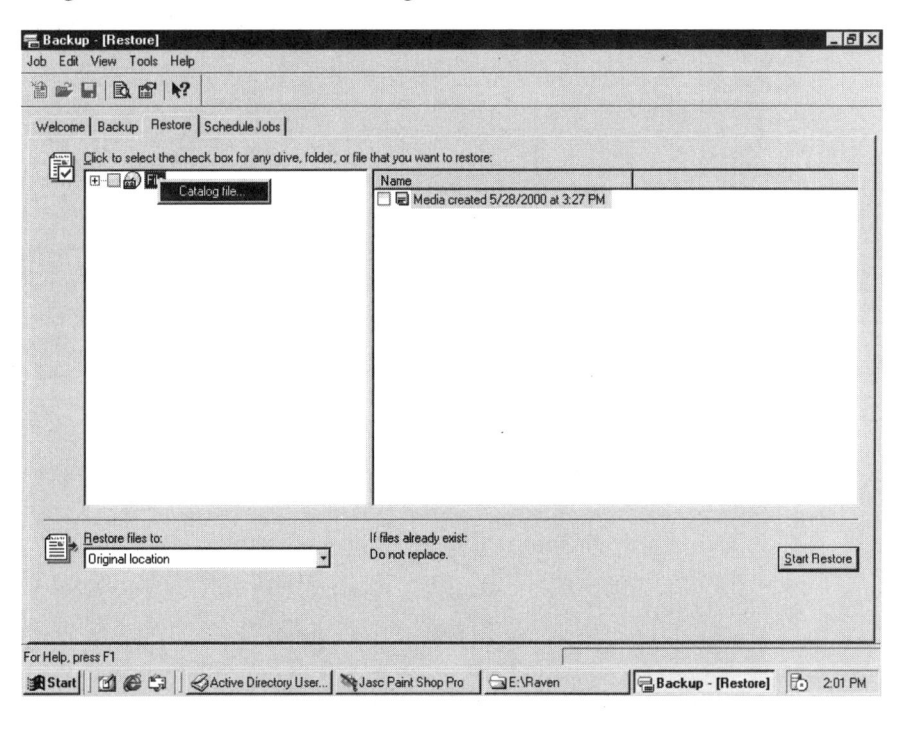

9. Type the path to the backup file (for example, C:\backup.bkf).
10. In the left pane, select the encrypted folder that needs to be restored. All data contained within the folder will be restored along with the folder itself.
11. Choose to restore files to Alternate Location. Type or browse to the folder on a Windows 2000 NTFS partition where you want the encrypted folder to be restored to. If you want to create a new folder to restore to, you can click Browse... and create a new folder first.

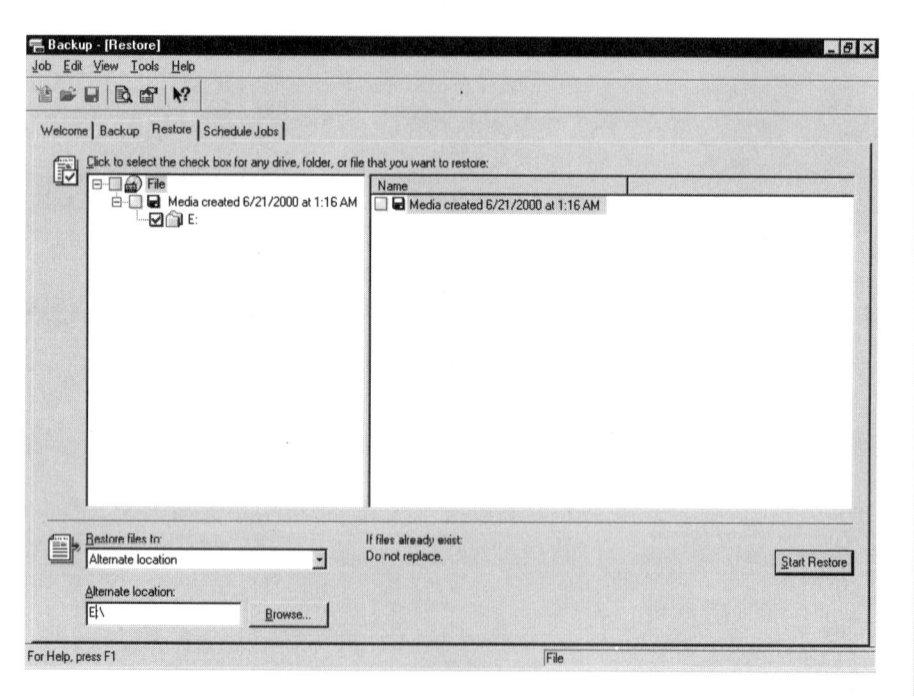

12. Click Start Restore.
13. Click OK on the Confirm Restore dialog box.
14. Click OK on the Enter Backup File Name dialog box.
15. The Restore Progress dialog box will show you the progress of the restore of the encrypted folder and its contents. To verify the restore happened successfully and that the encryption was retained, view the properties of the restored folder.

Design an Encrypting File System Strategy **505**

If this procedure were being performed to recover an encrypted file, the recovery agent would be able to decrypt the file through Windows Explorer or using the cipher command after it was restored on a secured machine where the recovery keys were kept. Once the folder had been decrypted, the recovery agent could use the Backup utility to back up the folder and return it back to the user to be restored in an unencrypted state. Alternatively, a recovery agent can go to the workstation where the encrypted file exists and load his or her recovery certificate and private key to perform the recovery on the local machine. This alternative method is not considered a best practice, however, as the recovery agent's private key is very sensitive and should not be left on an unsecured machine.

on the job

A best practice is to export the recovery agent's EFS private key, remove it from the computer, and store it in a safe place away from encrypted data. In the event that encrypted data needs to be recovered, the Recoverys Agent's EFS private key can be restored to a physically secure workstation. A description of the steps to back up and restore a recovery agent's EFS private key can be found in the following Microsoft Knowledge Base Articles: Q241201 (How to Backup Your EFS Private Key to Allow Data Recovery) and Q242296 (How to Restore an Encrypting File System Private Key for Encrypted Data Recovery).

EFS recovery policy is configured as part of the overall security policy for the system using Group Policy objects at the domain, organizational unit (OU), or computer level. If the workstation is not part of domain (that is, it is stand-alone), then EFS recovery policy can be configured locally. EFS recovery policy is implemented in the Encrypted Data Recovery Agents (EDRA) node of the of Public Key Policies area of the Group Policy snap-in. By integrating the EFS recovery policy within Windows 2000 Group Policy, the application of the recovery policy is handled by the Windows 2000 security subsystem. Therefore, enforcing, replicating, caching, and updating the recovery policy is handled automatically and enables users to use file encryption on an offline system, such as a laptop, using cached credentials. Figure 10-16 shows the location where recovery policy is configured within a default domain policy.

Encrypted Data Recovery Agents policy configuration

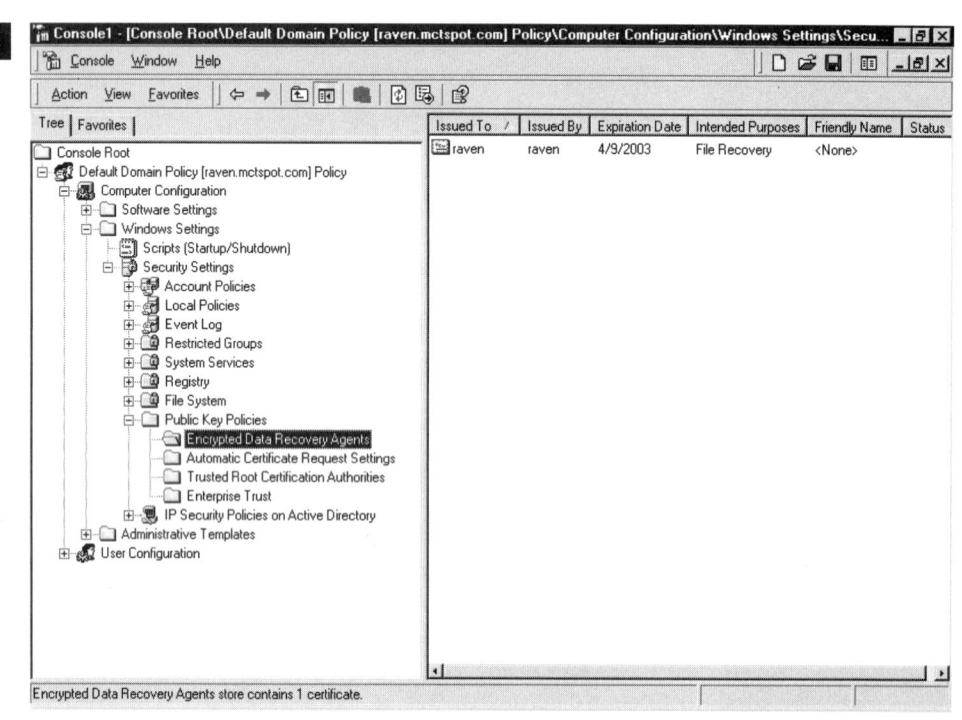

FIGURE 10-16

This interface allows a domain administrator to define one of three categories of recovery policy:

- No recovery policy
- Empty recovery policy
- Recovery policy with one or more X.509 version 3 certificates belonging to individuals identified as recovery agents for that scope of administration (domain, OU, or computer)

An administrator would set up *no policy* by right-clicking the Encrypted Data Recovery Agents node and selecting Delete Policy. Setting up *no policy* will allow the default local policy on computers to be used, in effect allowing local administrators to control the recovery of data on their individual workstations. An administrator can set up an *empty policy* by right-clicking the Encrypted Data Recovery Agents node and selecting Initialize Empty Policy. Setting up an *empty policy* will turn EFS off for all computers within the scope of the policy, thereby disabling a user's ability to encrypt files. In order to add an existing certificate or create a new certificate to add to the recovery policy, an administrator can right-click the Encrypted Data Recovery Agents node and choose Add or Create. In all cases, the Key Usage of any new or existing certificates must be *File Recovery.*

> **exam**
> **⊕atch**
>
> **The ability to encrypt files requires that a data recovery policy be set up at the domain, OU, or computer level, or even locally (for computers that are not part of a domain). Setting up an "empty" policy will turn EFS off, thereby disabling a user's ability to encrypt files on computers that fall within the scope of the policy.**

In a domain environment, the default recovery policy will include the domain administrator account, by default. In a stand-alone environment where there are no domains, such as a home office, the local administrator account is automatically configured as the default recovery agent. Recovery policy in the stand-alone environment is managed through the Local Computer Policy snap-in, much the same way as in Figure 10-16. To reduce the amount of administration, EFS automatically configures a self-signed certificate for the domain administrator and local administrator accounts if no certificate authority is available. Domain administrators can delegate recovery policy to security administrator accounts using Windows 2000 Directory Service delegation features. This provides better control and flexibility on who is authorized to recover encrypted data. An administrator can also use different Group Policy scopes to specify different recovery agents for different parts of the organization. For example, the recovery agents for Human Resources may be different than the recovery agents for other OUs.

EFS maintains policy enforcement by regenerating recovery information and regenerating user information every time an encrypted file is open. This ensures that frequently used files always contain current user and recovery information. If recovery policy changes, EFS will generate new recovery information for the file by comparing current policy against the existing file when it is opened. If a recovery policy exists with any invalid certificate, EFS will consider the whole policy invalid and turn encryption off for any new encryption. However, existing encrypted files can still be decrypted. All certificates, recovery or user, are checked for validity whenever encryption occurs. In order for a certificate to remain valid, it cannot be revoked, expired, have incorrect key usage, or exist in a CA chain with improper trust relationships. The only exception to this rule is self-signed certificates, which are generated if no CA exists and which remain valid as long as they have not expired. If a user certificate expires, EFS will renew a user's certificate automatically, either by using a configured CA or by generating a new, self-signed certificate.

EFS Security Considerations

In order to rely upon EFS to properly secure physical data from unauthorized use, it is important to analyze how EFS handles various threats to the security of encrypted files and the system on which they are housed. In this section, we will explore various threats and learn how EFS handles them.

- **Attempting to open another user's encrypted file** When any user attempts to open an encrypted file, EFS will attempt to locate the user's private key to decrypt the DDF in the header of the file. The user's private key will either come from the protected key store in Windows 2000 or from a smart card possessed by the currently logged-on user. If the user attempting to open the file does not possess the appropriate private key, the FEK cannot be obtained from the DDF and the user will receive an Access Denied error message.

- **Physical access to the disk** Someone with physical access to the disk may attempt to bypass the encryption technology by deleting the recovery portion of the encrypted file or using some sort of brute-force decryption on the bits. Attempting to decrypt the readable bits would require implementation of the EFS encryption scheme, which uses the DESX encryption algorithm and a strong 128-bit encryption key. In addition, EFS will attempt to re-create the recovery portions of the file each time it is opened, thereby thwarting any manipulation of the file headers.

- **Fatal failures during encryption or decryption operations** EFS ensures that failures during encryption or decryption do not cause data loss. EFS makes a plaintext backup while a file is being processed for encryption or decryption. The backup is deleted once the process has successfully finished. However, when the plaintext backup is deleted, the plaintext bits may still be left on the disk until NTFS needs those blocks for a new file. Therefore, it is best to initially create a new directory and copy, move, or save files to that directory.

- **Potential for the system to become unbootable** If certain files become encrypted that are necessary for the system to boot into Windows 2000, the system will be unbootable. Because EFS is not operational until the system is booted, boot files that are encrypted will not be able to be read during boot.

To thwart this type of problem, EFS will not allow the encryption of files or folders marked with the system attribute. Moreover, encryption of a root directory is not allowed.

- **Attempting to bypass or alter recovery policy** Because recovery policy is propagated by Windows 2000 Group Policy, the only way to bypass it is to remove the workstation from the network. If a local administrator attempts to define a different local EFS policy, domain policy will take precedence.

- **Attempting to remove recovery policy** Removing recovery policy will disable EFS.

- **Changes to recovery policy** If recovery information is intentionally manipulated by a rogue user or valid changes are made to recovery policy by administrators, EFS will recompute the recovery information on the encrypted file when it is opened. Encrypted files that have not been opened for a long time will have outdated recovery information attached to them. Therefore, it is very important that recovery certificates and private keys be archived indefinitely after recovery policy has changed.

- **Changes to user certificates and keys** If users lose or destroy their key information and are regenerated new keys, then a designated recovery agent for that computer will need to perform file recovery so the user can re-encrypt the file or files with his or her new key. Similar to recovery policy, user certificate or key changes are handled when an encrypted file is opened by EFS. If the key used to open the file is not current, EFS will recompute the DDF with the user's current key.

Recommended Best Practices

When using encryption, a user relies on the system to keep the encrypted data confidential. To this end, it is important to adhere to the following guidelines using EFS on any workstation.

1. Encrypt the local My Documents folder (%UserProfile%\My Documents) to ensure that Microsoft office documents will be encrypted.

2. Encrypt the Temp folder (%TEMP%) to ensure that temporary files saved to this location by applications are encrypted and to avoid leaks.

3. Always encrypt folders instead of individual files to ensure that files don't get decrypted by applications that write temporary file copies within the same directory.

4. Always generate private keys associated with recovery certificates on a secure computer, or export these keys and certificates to a .PFX file protected by a strong password, then remove the certificate and store the .PFX file on a floppy disk in a secure location, along with the password.

5. Data that is transferred across the network is not encrypted. To ensure the security and integrity of data transferred across the network, implement IPSec or TLS/SSL protocols.

6. Do not encrypt files that are shared on the network among several users. Personal files should be encrypted individually because the current design of EFS does not allow the sharing of files.

7. Do not copy or move encrypted files to removable media or non-NTFS version 5 volumes, as they will transfer unencrypted. Instead, use the Windows 2000 Backup utility to transfer encrypted files for secure storage and transmission.

SCENARIO & SOLUTION

Which Windows 2000 technology provides additional security for portable computers?	Encrypting File System
How should you encrypt personal and shared documents used by a department's personnel?	Encrypt only personal documents individually. Shared files cannot be encrypted if they are used by more than one person.
True or False: EFS can be used to encrypt data travelling over the network, as when copying an encrypted file to or from a network share.	False. Use IPSec or TLS/SSL to encrypt data travelling over a network.
How do you allow local workstation administrators to control recovery policy within a domain?	Set up "no policy" at the domain level.
How can you send a recovery agent an encrypted file to recover, if the user who encrypted the file leaves the company?	Use Windows 2000 Backup to back up the encrypted file, then send it to the recovery agent using e-mail. Alternatively, a recovery agent can install his or her private key on the local machine and recover the encrypted file, although this is not a best practice.

CERTIFICATION SUMMARY

In this chapter, we explored issues related to delegating control of administrative tasks, disaster recovery procedures, and protecting data through encryption.

When planning a delegation of authority strategy, it is important to first build an OU structure that reflects how IT tasks are handled by an organization, not necessarily how the business is structured. Once an OU structure is in place, it is generally wise to delegate administration on OUs down to the lowest level possible to distribute low-level tasks, such as user and group management, to local administrators. Delegation of authority is accomplished by modifying the ACL on an Active Directory object, such as an OU. A typical methodology used is for the domain administrator to enable full-control permissions for high-level OU administrators and allow high-level OU administrators to create child OUs for further delegation of administration. Use of the Delegation of Control Wizard can simplify assigning common tasks to lower level administrators.

It is important to plan and test a disaster recovery strategy while the network is functioning correctly. Disaster recovery becomes necessary on most networks, at some point. Mechanisms used to prevent and recover from disasters on Windows 2000 networks include fault tolerant disk arrays (RAID), uninterruptable power supplies (UPSs), frequently-updated virus protection software, and regular backups of System State and critical user and application data. Administrators should periodically test the restoration of backup sets to ensure that domain controllers and resources can be restored in case of fire, theft, and so on. Restoring Active Directory and other replicated data sets from backup can be done in one of three modes (primary, authoritative, or non-authoritative), depending on various circumstances.

EFS in Windows 2000 provides encryption of local and remote data storage so that unauthorized users are not able to read data, even if they have physical access to the machine or medium (as in the case of theft). EFS is typically recommended on laptops or other workstations, where physical security is not guaranteed and critical data must be secure from unauthorized persons. A user who encrypts data with EFS is the only person who can then view that data, unless it is recovered by a recovery agent. EFS is not a solution for encryption of network data or user authentication. EFS uses a combination of public and private key cryptography and X.509 version 3 certificates to protect data and allow for the transparent encryption and decryption of encrypted data when it is in use on a local machine or remote share. EFS recovery policy ensures that encrypted data can be recovered by administrators in the event that the user leaves the company or management needs access. EFS recovery policy, which is fully configurable by administrators, is integrated with Windows 2000 Security Policy and can be enforced through Group Policy to all computers in a domain.

✓ TWO-MINUTE DRILL

Design a Delegation of Authority Strategy

- ❑ A company's core domain/OU structure should reflect its delegation of authority strategy first and foremost, and not necessarily its business or organizational structure.

- ❑ A company with centralized IT administration means that domain administrators will typically be responsible for creating the entire OU structure and for most administrative tasks within an organization (such as user and group management).

- ❑ A company with decentralized IT administration translates into administrative tasks being delegated to the lowest-level OU possible.

- ❑ Administrators should delegate tasks within an OU to local security groups for ease of management.

- ❑ Delegation of authority is accomplished in Active Directory Users and Computers either by using the Delegation of Control Wizard to delegate common tasks within an object or by modifying the ACL on the Active Directory object (for example, an OU) through that object's Security properties.

- ❑ Common tasks that are often delegated to OU administrators at various levels within a domain include managing user accounts, managing groups, managing group membership, resetting user passwords, and managing Group Policy links.

Disaster Recovery

- ❑ Supported disaster recovery and prevention mechanisms in Windows 2000 include fault-tolerant disk arrays (RAID), UPS systems, virus protection software, regular backup procedures of system and user data, and the Emergency Repair process.

- ❑ Windows 2000 supports RAID levels 0, 1, and 5 on dynamic disks, which are disks that are fully managed by Windows 2000 Disk Administration.

- ❑ The ability to back up the System State in Windows 2000 allows for the restoration of Active Directory and other critical system files, should there be a disaster.

- Active Directory and other replicated data sets on domain controllers can be restored in one of three modes: primary, authoritative, and non-authoritative, depending on the state of the domain at the time of the restore and whether deleted or missing data needs to be recovered.
- Emergency Repair Disks are created using the Backup utility in Windows 2000 and not Rdisk, which is no longer available. The creation of an Emergency Repair Disk also backs up the Registry and system file information so that they can be restored in the event that a file or Registry problem causes Windows not to load properly.
- The Recovery Console in Windows 2000 allows a local administrator to access files on an NTFS, FAT, or FAT32 volume and also provides a new set of repair options when Windows 2000 will not load properly.

Design an Encrypting File System Strategy

- EFS allows users to encrypt all files within an NTFS directory using a strong public key-based cryptographic scheme.
- Individual file encryption is not recommended because of the unexpected behavior of applications in opening and saving files.
- Backup and restore of encrypted files is supported by EFS using a backup utility such as Windows 2000 Backup, thereby protecting file encryption during transport.
- EFS prevents the leaking of key information to page files and ensures that all copies of an encrypted file, even if moved, remain encrypted on Windows 2000 NTFS partitions.
- EFS does not provide encryption of network data if an encrypted file is copied or moved across the network.
- EFS supports encryption of remote files accessed through file shares, by using the same key and certificate if roaming profiles exist and the server is trusted for delegation, or by using local profiles and keys on the remote server.
- EFS Recovery Policy is integrated with Windows 2000 Security policy and is required in order to encrypt data. Administrators can delegate recovery policy to individuals with recovery authority, and different recovery policies may be configured for different parts of the organization.

SELF TEST

The following questions will help you measure your understanding of the material presented in this chapter. Read all of the choices carefully, as there may be more than one correct answer. Choose all correct answers for each question.

Design a Delegation of Authority Strategy

1. What administrative tool is used to assign special permissions to an OU?
   A. Active Directory Sites and Services
   B. Active Directory Users and Computers
   C. Windows Explorer
   D. Domain Security Policy

2. You have been hired to plan an Active Directory hierarchy for a small firm that is expanding into different areas of the country with new branch offices. The company has several divisions spread out geographically that require separate security boundaries. The company has a centralized IT department at corporate headquarters with day-to-day operations being handled by branch IT administrators. Which hierarchical structure would you recommend?
   A. The best strategy is a hybrid structure with the upper levels designed by project or group task and the lower layers designed by division.
   B. The best strategy is a hybrid structure with the upper levels designed by division and the lower layer designed by location.
   C. The best strategy is a hybrid structure with the upper levels designed by location and the lower layers designed by division.
   D. The best strategy is a design based on location only.

3. Which type of permission requires an administrator to create a custom task when using the Delegation of Control Wizard to delegate permissions on an OU?
   A. Full Control
   B. Manage Group Policy links
   C. Read all user information
   D. Reset passwords on user accounts

4. Which is a better solution than assigning permissions for a group of users at the task or attribute level (for example, allowing the group to change user permissions for subset of computers within an OU)?

   A. Organize the specific resources, such as a group of servers managed by Human Resources, in their own domain and provide the appropriate permissions for the group at the domain level.

   B. Create a separate site, place all the resources in the site, and assign the group appropriate permissions on the site.

   C. Create a separate OU that includes the appropriate resources and assign Full Control permission on the OU to the group.

   D. Create a separate OU that includes the appropriate resources and assign permissions for the specific task on the OU to the group.

5. You are a domain administrator and you want to create a small group of highly-trusted administrators called OwnHR that will be able to take ownership of any user or group account created within the company's Human Resources OU branch of the domain. Only domain administrators will have rights to modify OwnHR membership. The HR OU administrators already have Full Control over the HR OU and they have created several child OUs underneath the HR OU for further delegation of administrative tasks. What method would you use to accomplish your objective?

   A. Create a domain local group called OwnHR and assign this group the Modify Owner special permission on all users and group objects in the HR OU and all child OUs.

   B. Create a local group in the HR OU and assign this group the Modify Owner special permission on all user and group objects within the HR OU and all child OUs.

   C. Create a domain local group called OwnHR and assign this group the Modify Owner special permission on all users and group objects within the HR OU.

   D. Create a local group in the HR OU and assign this group the Modify Owner special permission on all user and group objects within the HR OU.

6. You are the new CIO for a small Web development company that has one office and approximately 40 employees. The company has five main clients that provide the majority of its revenue. The company employs graphic artists, programmers, and sales managers in cross-functional teams. In addition, a separate network technician is assigned for each client under that project's cost center. Each client contracts the company to provide Web hosting and

516 Chapter 10: Data Security

Web content services for e-commerce transactions. What OU hierarchy would you design before implementing Windows 2000?

A. Location-based OU hierarchy

B. Organizational OU hierarchy

C. Functional OU hierarchy

D. Functional, then organizational OU hierarchy

Disaster Recovery

7. Which Windows 2000 tool or tools can be used to manage fault-tolerant dynamic disks on a domain computer? (Choose all that apply.)

    A. Disk Administrator within the Computer Management console

    B. The Computers object within Active Directory Users and Computers console

    C. Device Manager

    D. Disk Management within the Computer Management console

8. Which fault-tolerant mechanism can be implemented to ensure availability if a single disk controller fails on a server?

    A. RAID 0

    B. Disk duplexing

    C. RAID 1 (disk mirroring)

    D. RAID 5 with a multi-channel controller

9. You have been tasked with providing a backup and recovery strategy for a company with one Windows 2000 domain that includes three domain controllers in various locations within the company. You want to plan for complete recovery in the event of a domain controller failing completely. What data should you back up?

    A. Back up the Windows NT boot files, the %SystemRoot%\Repair folder, the Registry, and any critical user and application data.

    B. Back up the Windows NT boot files, the %SystemRoot%\Repair folder, and the System State data.

    C. Back up the System State data, the system partition (for example, the C:\ drive), and any critical user and application data.

    D. Back up the Windows NT boot files, the %SystemRoot%\Repair folder, Sysvol, the Registry, and any critical user and application data.

10. Which emergency repair option will restore the Registry from the last time the Emergency Repair Disk was created, if the Registry is damaged or unreadable and a boot problem occurs as a result?

    A. Fast Repair
    B. Manual Repair
    C. Verify Windows 2000 system files
    D. Inspect startup environment

11. Which statement is false regarding the Recovery Console?

    A. The Recovery Console can only be accessed by the local administrator.
    B. The Recover Console provides a command that automatically verifies and restores deleted or corrupt system or boot files necessary to boot Windows 2000.
    C. The Recovery Console allows a troubleshooter limited access to any NTFS, FAT, or FAT32 volumes on the local machine.
    D. The Recovery Console allows a troubleshooter to repair a corrupted boot sector or a virus-infected master boot record (MBR).

Design an Encrypting File System Strategy

12. You wish to encrypt a set of sensitive documents on your laptop running Windows 2000 Workstation in order to protect them while travelling to a remote client site. All volumes are formatted with NTFS version 5.0. What is the easiest method to encrypt the necessary data prior to your departure?

    A. Place all the documents in a new folder, then encrypt the new folder by selecting the Apply Changes to This Folder Only option.
    B. Encrypt each document individually, then create a new folder and move the documents into the folder.
    C. Create a new folder, select the Encrypt Contents to Secure Data check box in the folder's property sheet, then move each of the documents into the new folder.
    D. The data cannot be encrypted using EFS on an NTFS version 5.0 volume.

13. When a user encrypts a folder using EFS and then copies it from an NTFS 5.0 volume on a user's desktop machine to a floppy disk, what happens to the copied folder?

    A. The folder and its content remains encrypted with the user's private key.
    B. The folder and its content remains encrypted, but a new FEK is generated for every file copied.

518 Chapter 10: Data Security

    C. The folder and its content are decrypted.

    D. An error is generated claiming the user doesn't have correct permissions, and the copy process fails.

14. If a domain administrator chooses to delete recovery policy at the domain level (thereby removing all recovery certificates from the policy), what is the effect of this action?

    A. Users will not be able to encrypt additional files on computers in the domain.

    B. Users will still be able to encrypt files on computers in the domain.

    C. Local administrators will need to add recovery agents to the recovery policy on the local computer before users will be able to encrypt additional files.

    D. All files on domain computers will automatically become decrypted and no future encryption will be able to occur.

15. What is the preferred method for recovering an encrypted file when the user who encrypted the file has lost his or her private key?

    A. E-mail the file as an attachment to a recovery agent, who will recover the file on his or her machine, then re-encrypt it and send it back using e-mail.

    B. Back up the encrypted file using the Backup utility. Then, e-mail the backup file as an attachment to a recovery agent. The recovery agent will log on to the recovery machine as the original user, decrypt the file, back up the decrypted file, then send it back to you.

    C. Back up the encrypted file using the Backup utility. Then e-mail the backup file as an attachment to a recovery agent who will restore the file on the machine where the recovery keys are kept. After restoring the file, the recovery agent will decrypt the file, back it up again, and return it to you.

    D. The recovery agent can export their private key and recovery certificate. After logging on to the user's computer, they can import their private key and recovery certificate on the user's machine. After importing their recovery key, they will decrypt the file, then log off.

16. Which is *not* a recommended best practice when implementing EFS?

    A. Export the recovery agent's private key and certificate to a .PFX file, protect it using a strong password, and secure that file on a floppy disk.

    B. Encrypt the My Documents folder.

    C. Encrypt the Temp folder (%TEMP%) to ensure temporary files created by applications remain encrypted.

    D. After removing a recovery agent from recovery policy, dispose of his or her private key and certificate by deleting it off the recovery machine to ensure that it cannot be used to decrypt any files encrypted under the old policy.

17. If no CA exists when a user first encrypts a folder, what is the result?

   A. EFS will generate a self-signed certificate and the user will use the self-signed certificate for encryption.
   B. An error appears because a CA must be available prior to encryption.
   C. EFS will prompt the user for an encryption password if no CA exists.
   D. EFS will encrypt the folder with the recovery agent's public key only.

LAB QUESTION

You are the network architect for Crowe Media Ltd., a medium-sized media consulting firm. Crowe Media Ltd. has 30 offices located throughout the United States. Corporate headquarters is located in Los Angeles with three regional headquarters located in New York City, Chicago, and Los Angeles. Each regional headquarters has its own IT staff that report to the corporate IT staff based in Los Angeles. Figure 10-17 shows the organizational chart for Crowe Media Ltd.

You have provided all of the network staff with a questionnaire and have met with each of the regional IT staffs. Table 10-4 lists the current IT duties and groups serviced.

FIGURE 10-17 Crowe Media Ltd. organizational chart

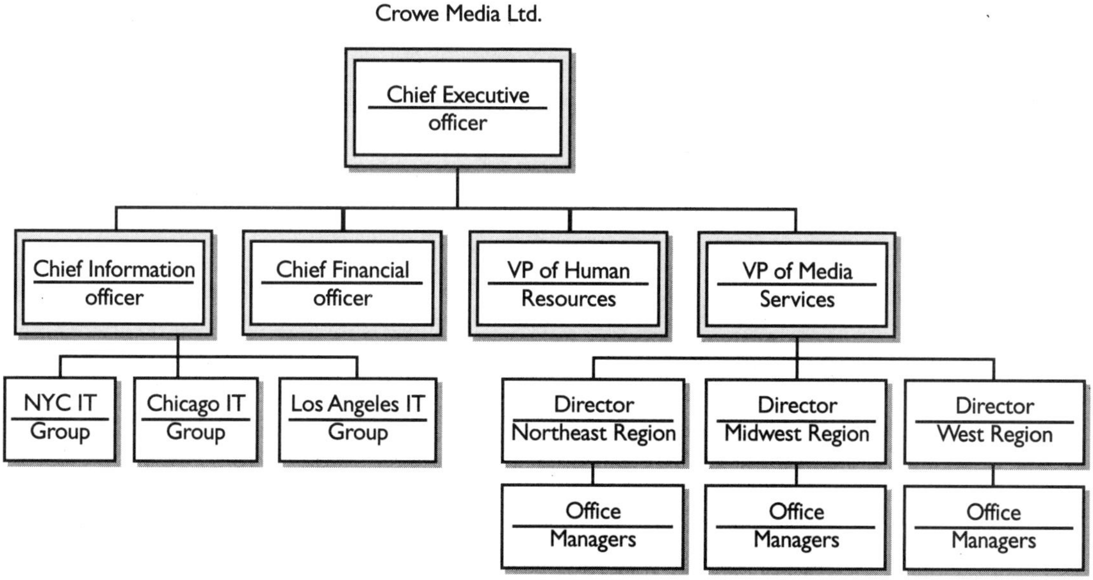

TABLE 10-4 Crowe Media Ltd. IT Administrative Responsibilities

Job Title	Duties Performed	Groups Serviced
Network Administrator	All network roles	All Crowe Media employees, desktops and servers
Help Desk	Account management, desktop support	All Crowe Media employees
Network Support Specialist	Server support, performance monitoring, network support, and account management	All servers and users in a region
Network Support Specialist	Server support, performance monitoring, network support, and account management	All servers and users at the corporate headquarters

Your job is to create an OU hierarchy to support the delegation of administrative authority for Crowe Media Ltd. Use corp.crowemedia.com as your root domain name. Do not add any other information to the diagram other than the OU structure. Explain the justification for your chosen design.

SELF TEST ANSWERS

Design a Delegation of Authority Strategy

1. ☑ **B.** Delegating control and changing permission on an OU in Active Directory is accomplished through Active Directory Users and Computers.
   ☒ Choices **A, C,** and **D** are incorrect because OU objects are not viewed in any of these tools.

2. ☑ **C** allows for additional geographic and divisional growth without having to change the upper layer of the hierarchy. When new branch offices come online, they can be added to the upper hierarchy. Divisional separation is attained through division OUs within each organization. If reorganization occurs, divisional OUs can move between upper-level location OUs rather easily.
   ☒ **A** is incorrect because the company does not have a strongly decentralized IT function by project, product, or customer. **B** is incorrect because the company does not have a distributed IT structure with distinct business units. **D** is insufficient because it does not provide for divisional boundaries among the different locations.

3. ☑ **A.** Full Control is not defined on one of the predefined lists of common tasks available when using the Delegation of Control Wizard to delegate control.
   ☒ **B, C,** and **D** are all included in the predefined list of common tasks.

4. ☑ **D.** It is generally better to segment the OU structure based on administrative needs and then modify OU attributes, instead of maintaining separate permissions on separate ACLs for various users within an OU.
   ☒ **A** is incorrect because domains are not created for the organization of resources, but rather for defining strong security boundaries within an organization. **B** is incorrect because sites are primarily created to manage replication traffic over WAN links. **C** is incorrect because the group is to be assigned a specific task and does not have the need to fully administer a set of resources.

5. ☑ **C.** The only way for the domain administrators to control membership to this group is to define the group in the Domain container. With Full Control permissions on the HR OU, the HR administrators will be able to modify this group's membership. In addition, you only need

522 Chapter 10: Data Security

to assign the Modify Owner special permission to the top-level HR OU, as all child OUs will inherit the permission of the parent automatically.

☒ A, B, and D are all incorrect for the preceding reasons.

6. ☑ C. A small company that has its IT administration organized around specific projects or clients is best served by a functional OU hierarchy. A function-based hierarchy considers only the business functions of the organization, without regard to geographical location, departmental, or divisional barriers. Choose this approach only if the IT function is not based on location or organization.

☒ A and B are incorrect because the company has only one location and employs cross-functional teams. D is incorrect because divisional security boundaries are unimportant in a small company like this.

Disaster Recovery

7. ☑ B and D. Management of disks and disk volumes is typically done through the Disk Management object in the Computer Management console. In addition, by right-clicking a computer in Active Directory Users and Computers and choosing Manage, you can launch the Computer Management console.

☒ A is incorrect because there is no tool called Disk Administrator in Windows 2000. C is incorrect because Device Manager is used to view and manage resource settings and drivers for installed hardware.

8. ☑ B. Disk duplexing, an extension of RAID level 1, not only mirrors a volume on a separate disk, but each disk is attached to its own controller card. This configuration allows access to the data in the volume if either one of the controllers or one of the disks in the mirror fails.

☒ A is incorrect because RAID 0 defines a stripe set volume, which is not fault tolerant. C is incorrect because RAID 1 does not define redundant controllers, only redundant disks. D is wrong because a multi-channel controller does not provide controller redundancy, only better performance when doing simultaneous reads and writes.

9. ☑ C. To fully restore a domain controller, you must successfully restore its System State (which includes the Active Directory, Registry, Sysvol, and other important system files). In addition, it is generally recommended to back up the C:\ drive along with the System State, as well as any critical user data stored on the domain controller.

☒ A and D are incorrect because they are missing the System State. B is incorrect because backing up the \Repair folder is not required when backing up the System State, and because backing up the entire C:\ drive is recommended over backing up just the boot files.

10. ☑ **A.** The Fast Repair option performs all the repairs available in the Manual Repair option, plus the Fast Repair option will copy missing or corrupted Registry files from the %SystemRoot%\Repair folder to the %SystemRoot%\System32\Config folder, assuming the \Repair folder can be accessed.
☒ **B** is incorrect because the manual repair option does not give you a choice to repair the Registry files. **C** is incorrect because this option will only verify that each system file in the Windows 2000 system or boot partition is readable and matches the files that were originally installed. **C** is typically used if a critical system or boot file is accidentally deleted or becomes corrupt. **D** is incorrect because this option only operates on the BOOT.INI file to ensure the ARC pathname, which specifies the path to the Windows 2000 boot partition and %SystemRoot% folder, is correct based on entries in the SETUP.LOG file. If the BOOT.INI file is missing or corrupt, it creates a new one using the %SystemRoot% location data obtained from the SETUP.LOG file.

11. ☑ **B.** The Recovery Console does not provide a command that will automatically verify and replace missing or corrupt system or boot files. This is accomplished by performing an emergency repair.
☒ **A, C,** and **D** are all true statements regarding the Recovery Console. The utilities for repairing a corrupted boot sector or a master boot record are Fixboot and Fixmbr, respectively.

Design an Encrypting File System Strategy

12. ☑ **C.** The easiest method is to mark a new folder for encryption, then any new documents moved to, copied to, or created within the folder will inherit the encryption attribute of the folder.
☒ **A** is incorrect because the Apply Changes to This Folder only option will not encrypt any files or folders currently in the folder, only those added afterwards. **B** is incorrect because encrypting files individually is too time-consuming. Additionally, any files or folder created inside a decrypted folder will not be encrypted. **D** is incorrect because EFS is only able to encrypt data on NTFS version 5.0 volumes.

524 Chapter 10: Data Security

13. ☑ **C.** When copying or moving a file or a folder to a non-NTFS 5.0 volume (such as a floppy disk that is formatted using FAT), the file or folder is decrypted. Only NTFS 5.0 volumes support encryption of stored data.
☒ **A** and **B** are incorrect because the floppy is a non-NTFS 5.0 volume. **D** is incorrect because copying encrypted files to local FAT partitions occurs without warning or errors of any kind.

14. ☑ **B.** If the domain recover policy is deleted (effectively establishing "no policy"), then users can continue encrypting files as before, except recovery policy will be enforced by the default recovery policy defined on the local computer. The default recovery policy on the local computer lists the local administrator as the sole recovery agent.
☒ **A** is incorrect because the default local recovery policy still exists. **C** is incorrect because the default local recovery policy becomes the new recovery policy. **D** is incorrect because all previously-encrypted files will remain encrypted with recovery information from the old domain recovery policy. As these files are modified, they will be re-encrypted with the local recovery policy information.

15. ☑ **C.** The preferred method for restoring an encrypted file or folder is to have the recovery agent recover the encrypted file on a designated, secure machine where the recovery key is kept. Although the recovery key can be exported, then imported on the machine where the encrypted file resides, it is not a best practice because leaving a private recovery key on an unsecured machine poses a security risk.
☒ **A** is incorrect because attempting to add the encrypted file as an e-mail attachment without first backing it up will result in an Access Denied error message. This is the same result as if someone other than the person who encrypted the file attempted to copy the encrypted file. **B** is incorrect because private keys are not associated with user accounts. Therefore, logging on as the user will not make the user's private key available. Private keys are kept in a secure key store on the machine where the file was encrypted or kept on a smart card, and if lost (for example, by a disk crash or loss of smart card), they cannot be regenerated elsewhere. **D** is not a preferred method because the recovery agent's private key is left on the unsecured machine.

16. ☑ **D.** If a recovery agent is removed from recovery policy, his or her private key and certificate should be archived indefinitely in the event any encrypted files with old recovery policy information go unchanged for long periods of time and need to be recovered at some future date. When encrypted files are modified, recovery policy information in the file header

is compared to current policy and updated based on any recovery policy changes that have occurred. Encrypted files that go unchanged for long periods of time will retain old policy information.

☒ **A** is a best practice, because recovery keys should be exported and stored in a secure location to assure that recovery information will not be inadvertently lost. **B** and **C** are also best practices, because applications often create temporary copies of encrypted files that can be inadvertently left in a decrypted state should the application not terminate properly.

17. ☑ **A.** If no CA exists, EFS will generate a self-signed certificate for the user. Self-signed certificates are valid as long as they have not expired.

☒ **B** is incorrect, as stated in the preceding explanation. **C** and **D** are incorrect because EFS requires a user to possess a X.509 version 3 certificate, with enhanced key usage as *File Encryption*.

LAB ANSWER

This scenario is typical for many companies looking to migrate to Windows 2000 and having to plan an OU structure to support IT administrative duties. The key pieces of information that you should draw from this scenario in order to plan an OU hierarchy are the following:

- Each region has its own IT staff and manages all users and computers within their region.
- Corporate headquarters has its own IT staff and manages all users and computers within their region.
- Basic duties are broken down into account, server, and desktop management.

The preferred solution for Crowe Media Ltd. is an initial design as shown in Figure 10-18.

You may have a variation of this design that meets the necessary requirements. In any case, the top-level OU hierarchy for this company, as shown, should be based on the four administrative IT groups for each of the three regions as well as corporate headquarters. The top-level OUs are containers that partition the IT resource space so that authority over objects can be distributed. The computers and users OUs underneath each top-level OU further partition the resource space so that the account management and server/desktop management can be delegated to different groups, such as the help desk and server support groups.

This OU hierarchy can be extended to include additional child OUs under the regional OUs if additional requirements dictate. For example, if mobile users are to have specific security policies

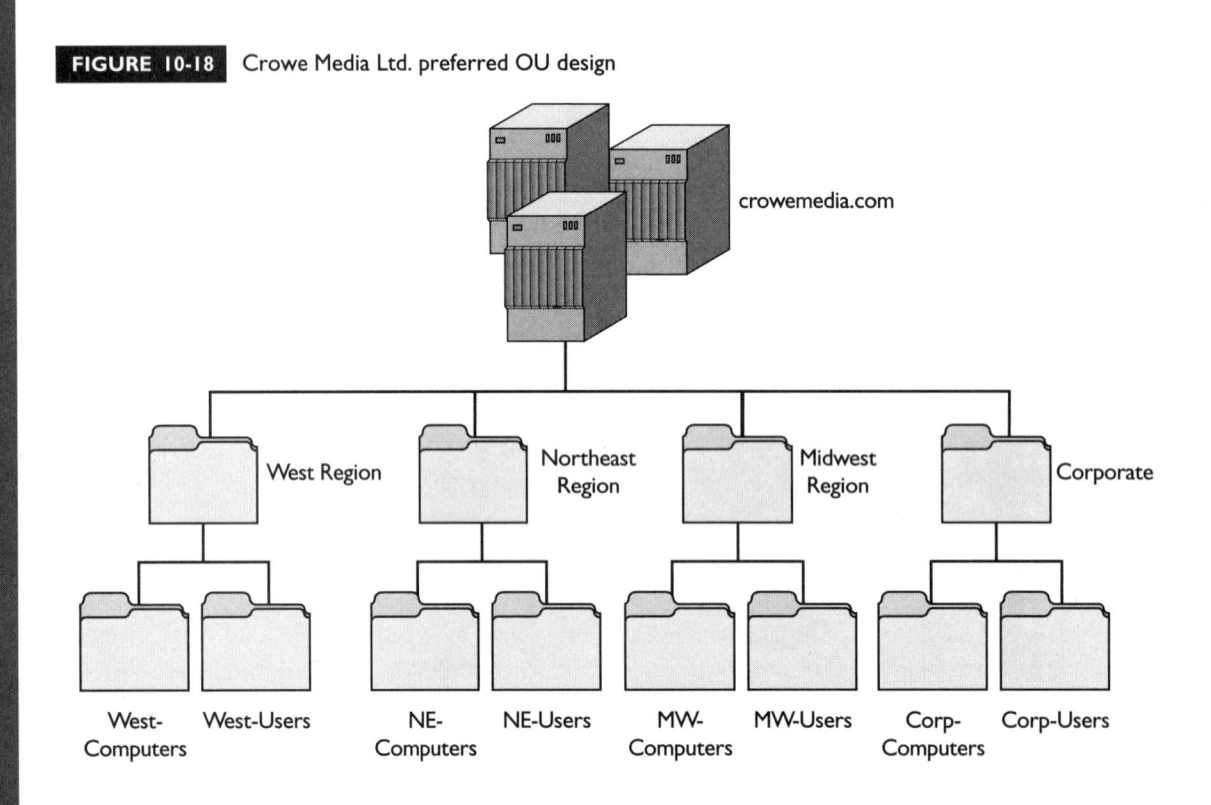

FIGURE 10-18 Crowe Media Ltd. preferred OU design

applied only to their laptops when they dial-in to the corporate network, then a mobile OU could be created under each regional OU for applying Group Policy. The hierarchy shown is resistant to organizational restructuring. For example, additional top-level OUs could be created if acquisitions or mergers take place. Moreover, if people move within the company, user accounts can be moved between regions fairly easily.

MCSE
MICROSOFT CERTIFIED SYSTEMS ENGINEER

11

Designing a Security Solution for Access Between Networks

CERTIFICATION OBJECTIVES

11.01	Provide Secure Access to Public Networks from a Private Network
11.02	Provide External Users with Secure Access to Private Network Resources
11.03	Provide Secure Access Between Private Networks
11.04	Design Windows 2000 Security for Remote Access Users
11.05	Design an SMB Signing Solution
11.06	Design an IPSec Solution
✓	Two-Minute Drill
Q&A	Self Test

Chapter 11: Designing a Security Solution for Access Between Networks

In this chapter, we will cover six different objectives for the exam. Half of the objectives will be providing access to users, whereas the last half will cover designing different aspects of network security within Microsoft Windows 2000. First we'll discuss providing secure access to public networks from a private one. This chapter will talk in detail about providing users of your private intranet access to the Internet, but doing it securely. The second objective we'll cover will be providing external users (either remote company employees or customers) secure access to private network resources, whether it is accessing e-mail or clients securely sending in orders for purchases. Another topic that will be discussed is providing secure access between private networks. This is becoming more and more popular as many companies wish to secure local area network traffic, especially around such functions as payroll, human resources, and other private information systems.

After covering the first three objectives, we'll focus on the designing aspects of the exam. We'll look at designing security for remote access users, then cover something that actually became available in Windows NT 4.0 Service Pack 3, which is Server Message Block (SMB) signing. We will finish by covering the topic of designing an Internet Protocol Security (IPSec) solution with Windows 2000.

CERTIFICATION OBJECTIVE 11.01

Provide Secure Access to Public Networks from a Private Network

Providing secure access to public networks, such as the Internet from a corporate private network, is becoming more and more of an issue. In this section, we'll cover what you can expect on the exam as it pertains to this issue and what options you have as an administrator with Microsoft Windows 2000. Many of the features that are seen in specialized products, such as firewalls, routers, proxy servers, and so on, are now services available under Windows 2000 Server and Advanced Server. By using a service such as Routing and Remote Access Service (RRAS), we can provide routing access to the Internet, among other things.

When using a Windows 2000 Server as a gateway to the Internet, the system must be a multi-homed machine running RRAS. The system can be set with two network interface cards (NICs) or just one NIC and one modem; either way it must be able to connect to two different networks. One NIC will connect to the internal network, while the second NIC or the modem will connect to the Internet. Windows 2000 gives you a couple of options for providing access to the Internet. You can use Internet Connection Sharing (ICS) or you can route and use Network Address Translation (NAT). A very big distinction between ICS and NAT is that ICS is a *feature* of the Network and Dial-Up tools, whereas NAT is an actual routing *protocol.*

exam
⚪ a t c h

For the record, NAT can receive public addresses from a Dynamic Host Configuration Protocol (DHCP) server provided by the ISP. This can be done by selecting the Automatically Assign IP Addresses by Using DHCP check box in the NAT properties sheet.

EXERCISE 11-1

Connecting RRAS to the Internet

We will set up RRAS to connect us to the Internet, turn on routing, and use NAT. For our example we will assume a static IP address given to us by the Internet Service Provider (ISP), which will probably be the most likely scenario you will face with this type of setup. We will be setting up RRAS to make use of a dial-up demand connection type.

1. When initially setting up RRAS, the service must be enabled for us to be able to set up the configuration. Just as the information pane states in the RRAS console, shown in the following illustration, click Action | Configure and Enable Routing and Remote Access.

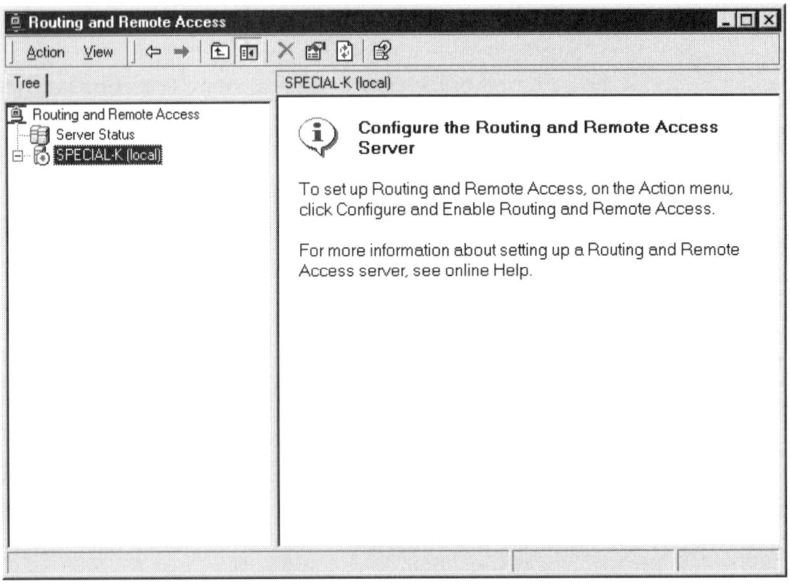
Routing and Remote Access
Action View
Tree
SPECIAL-K (local)
Routing and Remote Access
Server Status
SPECIAL-K (local)
Configure the Routing and Remote Access Server
To set up Routing and Remote Access, on the Action menu, click Configure and Enable Routing and Remote Access.
For more information about setting up a Routing and Remote Access server, see online Help.

2. The RRAS setup wizard will appear. At this point, we will click Next to continue with the configuration.

Routing and Remote Access Server Setup Wizard
Welcome to the Routing and Remote Access Server Setup Wizard
This wizard helps you set up your server so that you can connect to other networks and allow connections from remote clients.
To continue, click Next.
< Back
Next >
Cancel

3. Choose Internet Connection Server and then click Next.

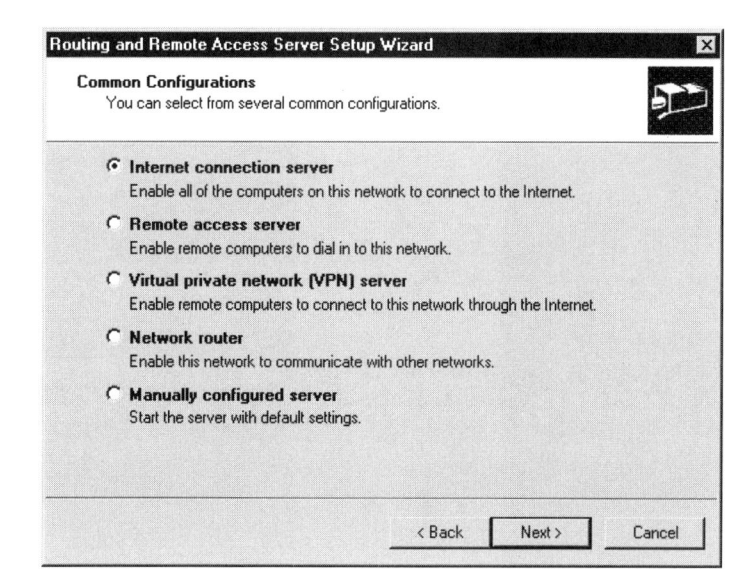

   Routing and Remote Access Server Setup Wizard

   Common Configurations
   You can select from several common configurations.

   - ⦿ **Internet connection server**
     Enable all of the computers on this network to connect to the Internet.
   - ○ **Remote access server**
     Enable remote computers to dial in to this network.
   - ○ **Virtual private network (VPN) server**
     Enable remote computers to connect to this network through the Internet.
   - ○ **Network router**
     Enable this network to communicate with other networks.
   - ○ **Manually configured server**
     Start the server with default settings.

   [< Back] [Next >] [Cancel]

4. We have the choice to select Internet Connection Sharing (ICS) or set up a router with NAT (see the following illustration). Microsoft suggests in situations for small networks such as those for the home or small offices to choose the ICS selection. For our example, we will select Set Up a Router with Network Address Translation (NAT) Routing Protocol. This is what you will most likely see when implementing RRAS for small and medium-sized networks, in addition to those that are very interested in requesting stronger network security.

Routing and Remote Access Server Setup Wizard

Internet Connection Server Setup
You can create a basic Internet connection with limited administrative control, or a more complex Internet connection with full administrative control.

Select a setup method based on the complexity of your network.

○ Set up Internet connection sharing (ICS)
  Select this option to connect a single network (for example, a small office or a home network) to the Internet.

⦿ Set up a router with the Network Address Translation (NAT) routing protocol
  Select this option when you have multiple network connections or when you need routing protocols or demand-dial connections.

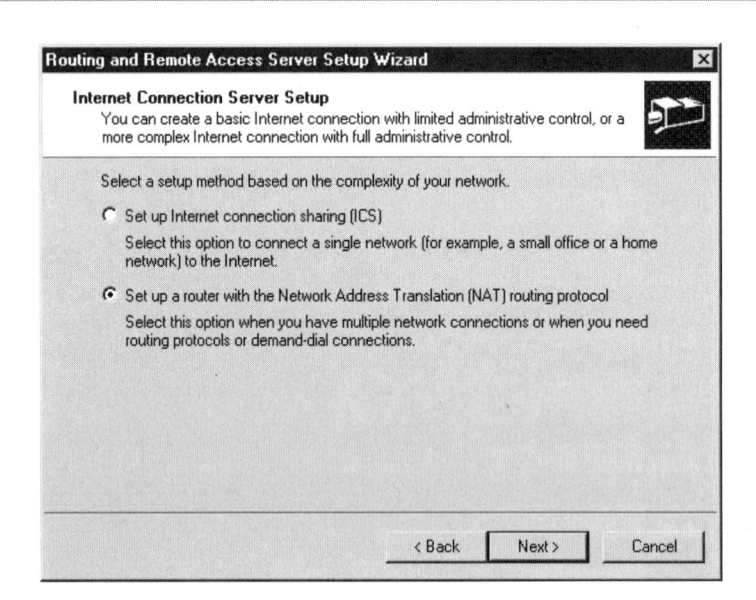

[< Back] [Next >] [Cancel]

Using NAT will allow you, the administrator, to share a single public IP address with your internal clients / nodes. Also, as previously mentioned, this provides a better level of security in that you are able to hide the IP addresses of your internal network.

Remember though, that in our scenario we are going to throw a small wrench into the works. Beware, MCSE exams love to hit you with things you would never expect and things you would rarely see, if ever. So let's take a look at one that you could see on the exam. For this example, our company is having some budget problems and can't afford a dedicated link. So we have to set up a demand-dial Internet connection. This will allow us to connect *only* when internal network users require access. Lucky for us, Windows 2000 RRAS is able to automate this process. Remember we said that the RRAS machine must be multi-homed; one NIC connected to the internal network, the other "connection" (NIC or modem) to the Internet. For us it will be a modem. To do this we must have the access phone number of the ISP and we must have a user ID and password to connect, just like you would if you were connecting through a dial-up at your home. Now we will click Next on the Internet Connection dialog box.

5. Select Next when the Applying Changes dialog appears:

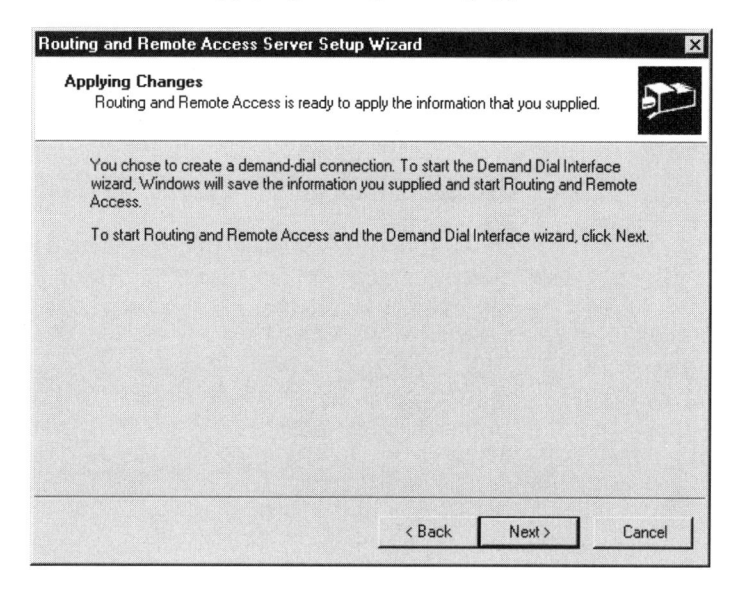

6. We now see the dialog box for setting up demand dial-up. Once again, choose Next.

7. Now we need to give the demand dial interface a descriptive name, preferably one that makes sense to us, the administrator, and anyone else who has to follow our work at some later time. In our example, we'll choose Internet-Demand Dial. The interface connecting to the Internet is a demand dial connection.

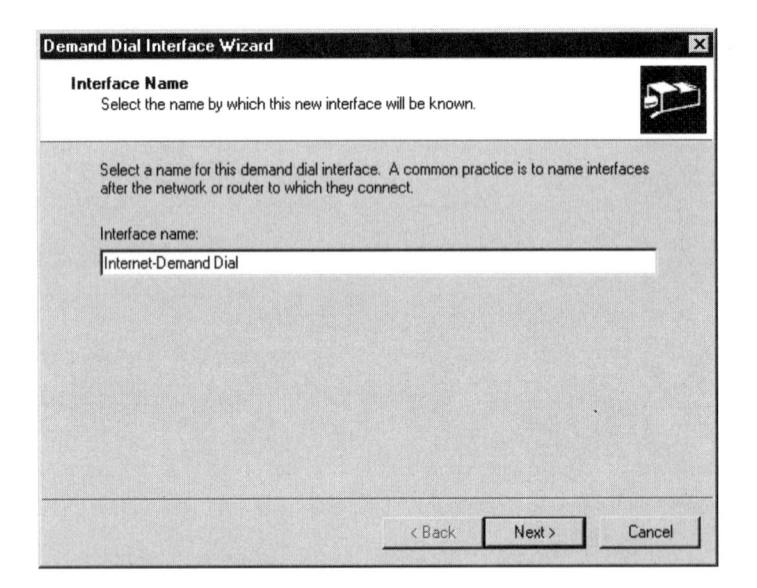

8. After naming the interface, we will select Next to select the appropriate connection type. We will choose Connect Using a Modem, ISDN Adapter, or Other Physical Device. We can also choose to use a virtual private network (VPN).

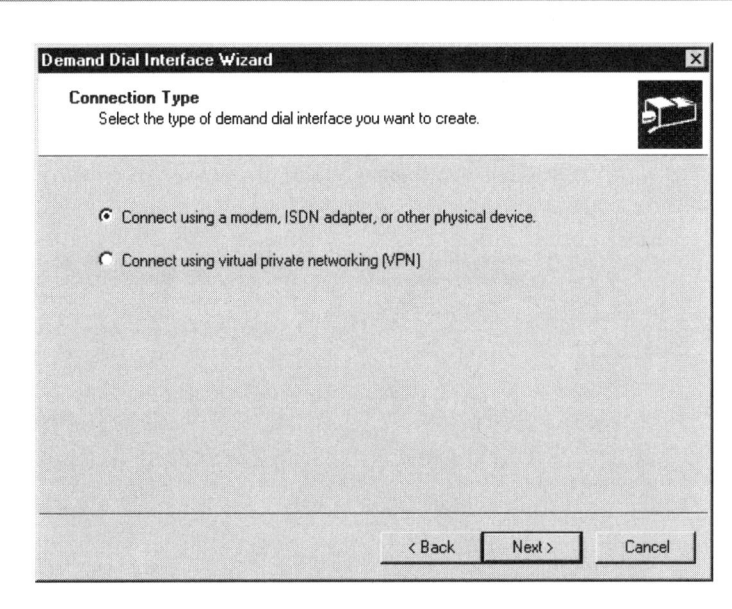

Provide Secure Access to Public Networks from a Private Network   **535**

9. Now we will select our device. Choose the modem you are using to connect to the Internet, as shown here:

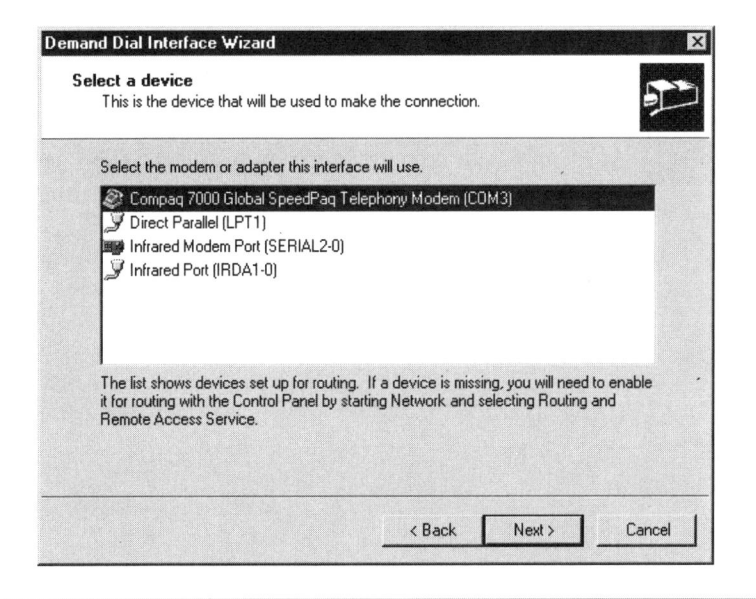

10. Now we will type the access phone number to our ISP. Of course, in our example, the Xs shown in the following illustration represent each digit of the phone number. Separating the numbers with dashes is *not* required; it's just easier to read. As you see, we may also type any alternate numbers that might be used to connect to our ISP.

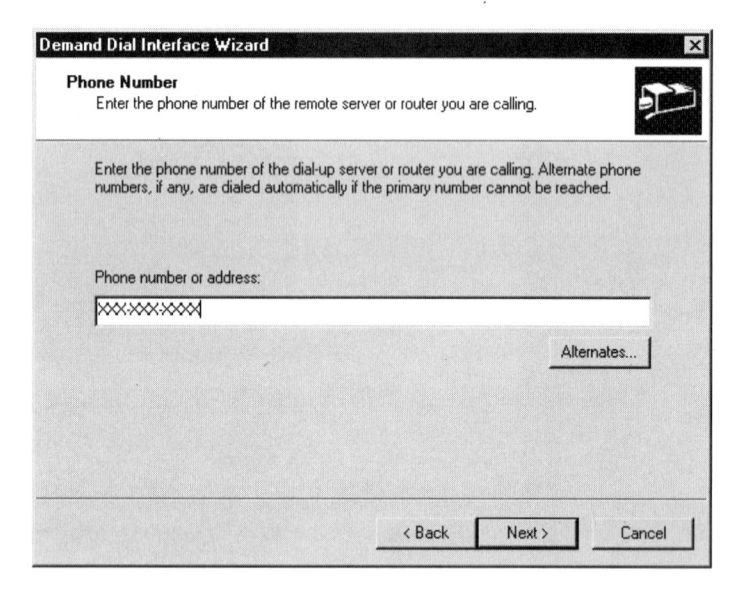

11. Our next task is to select the appropriate transports and security options for our connection. As you can see here, we will definitely choose to route IP packets because we are connecting to the Internet, but if we were routing to a different network that was running only IPX packets, then we could route them.

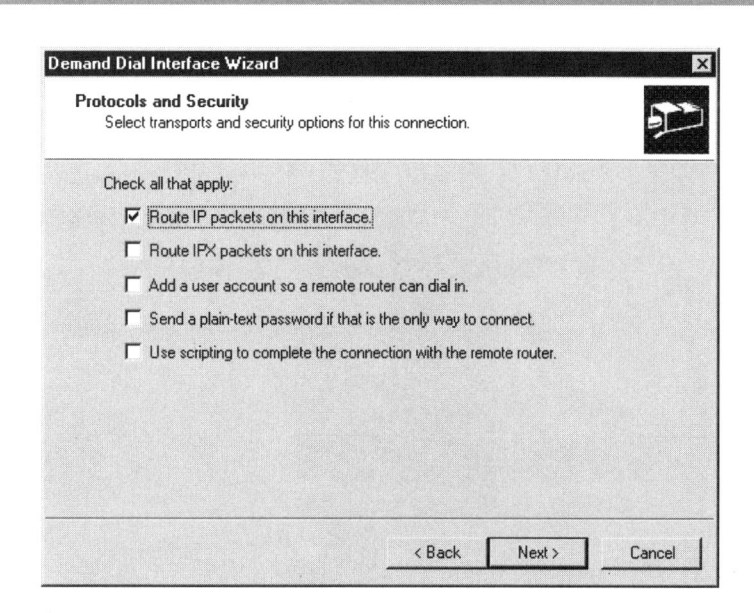

Provide Secure Access to Public Networks from a Private Network **537**

12. We now have to set up the connection to use the appropriate account that the ISP has provided us, along with the correct password. Once you have finished typing the credentials, select Next.

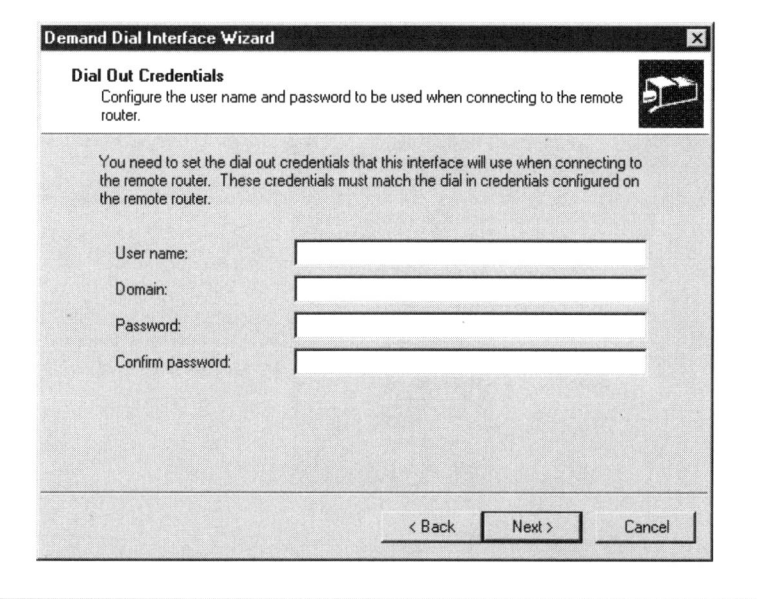

13. This brings us to the finish of the Demand Dial Interface Wizard. In situations in which you are connecting to an ISP that is not using a Windows 2000 server or requiring domain authentication, the Domain option should be left blank. Click Finish and the demand dial connection is completed.

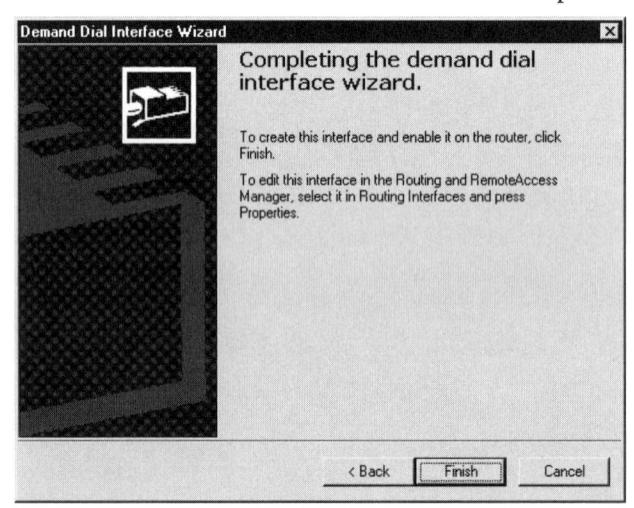

14. Next you will see the completion screen for RRAS. This dialog box will give you a summary of your setup and the interface on which NAT is installed.

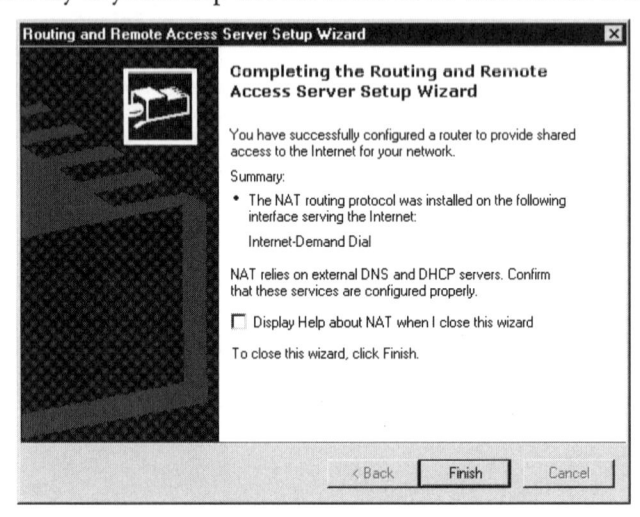

15. As you guessed, you aren't quite finished yet. As you see in the dialog box for the completion of RRAS, NAT relies on external Domain Name System (DNS) and DHCP servers. You must confirm that you have these settings correct. In our example, the connection to the Internet *must* have a static IP address. This is *only* for our example though. Remember from the earlier Exam Watch that NAT can be set to use DHCP to obtain public addresses.

CERTIFICATION OBJECTIVE 11.02

Provide External Users with Secure Access to Private Network Resources

In this part, we will go over all areas that are available to you in setting up secure access to private network resources for external users. Now, in a day and time when being able to access internal network resources is becoming more and more important, the ability to provide external users access to resources internally without leaving the door wide open is a necessity. By using technologies such as dial-up services and VPNs, Windows 2000 provides a complete remote access solution for many types of networks.

In Windows 2000, there are many different ways to provide remote access. The first is using Remote Access Service (RAS), commonly referred to in the Microsoft community as a RAS server. This service has been a part of the Microsoft networking packages since the days of LAN Manager, but it was enhanced with Windows 2000. Another way is something that became available with Windows NT Server 4.0 under Service Pack 3, and that is the use of virtual private networks. It is not unusual for a company to choose to deploy both RAS and VPN services at the same time, although many may choose either RAS or VPN. One is not dependent on the other. Finally, an administrator may choose to set up a stand-alone Certificate Authority (CA) server. Let's look at how each meets the needs of its users.

RAS, also referred to as a dial-up server, is able to meet most of the needs of a small remote access population. This is usually accomplished through the use of analog or Integrated Services Digital Network (ISDN) devices. The remote user population is able to dial in directly without acruing high long distance costs. If this is not possible, an administrator should consider switching to a VPN.

VPNs are great for lowering long distance bills for remote access to the corporate internal network. VPNs allow remote users to take advantage of connections they may already have with the Internet while also maintaining security. VPNs support whatever connection you have to the Internet; that is, no new hardware is required to implement a VPN. You can use modems, ISDN modems/routers, cable modems, or even digital subscriber line (DSL) connection devices.

Basic RAS Setup

To set up dial-up access for remote users to your internal network with Windows 2000, you must have at least one analog modem connected to a serial port on the server. Along with this you must have at least one analog phone line that is able to receive dial ups from remote users. This is fine as long as you don't exceed two, but what do you do if you need to expand your connectivity? Do you just buy a new server? Well you could, but most likely your IT director may balk over that. It's pretty simple actually; you can install multiport serial adapters. Two main products in this market are digiboards (Digi International) or equinox cards. Both do an exceptional job and are supported under Windows 2000 HCL (Hardware Compatibility List). These adapters allow you to install four, eight, 16, or more ports that can be used to configure modems. In Figure 11-1, you see the basic premise of a RAS connection.

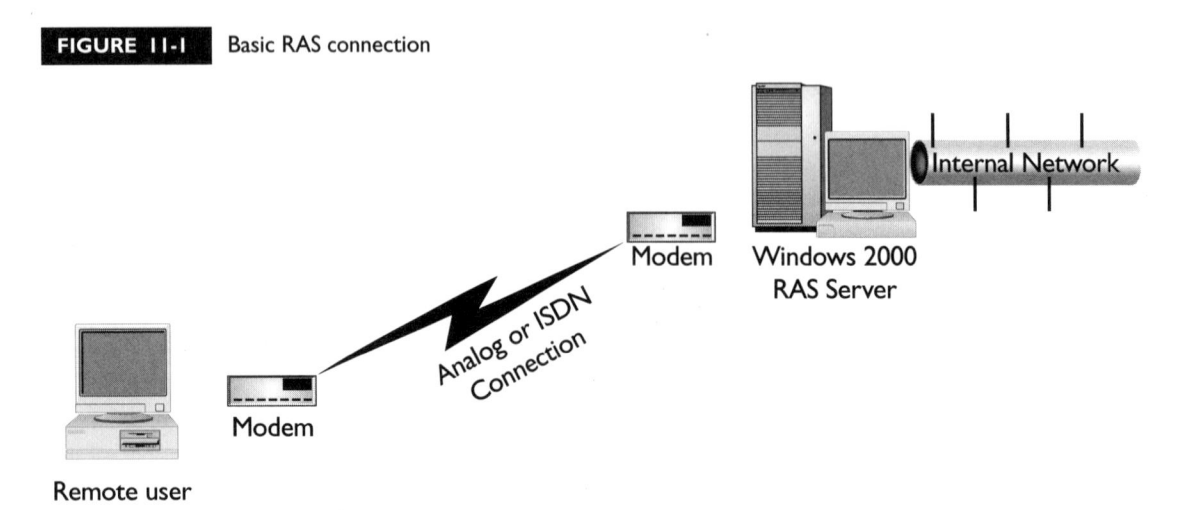

FIGURE 11-1 Basic RAS connection

Basic Setup of VPN

VPNs are another way of allowing remote users to gain access to internal networking resources, but they do so through the Internet (typically). VPNs will be discussed in greater detail later in this chapter but for now let's look at the basic premise. Typically, to allow clients to access your network using VPN, you have to set up a VPN server or gateway (usually these terms are synonymous). This is usually done by connecting one NIC, within the VPN server, to the internal corporate network. The other NIC is connected to the Internet. VPN clients will connect to the Internet using their local ISPs, then open a connection to the VPN server. The additional connection on the client side will appear as another dial-up connection but it calls a certain server name or Internet Protocol (IP) address to connect the pipe. This is discussed in greater detail later in this chapter. Figure 11-2 shows how this appears logically and physically. The line titled Virtual Network is how it appears to the end user. The connections shown above this line are actually what is taking place and where.

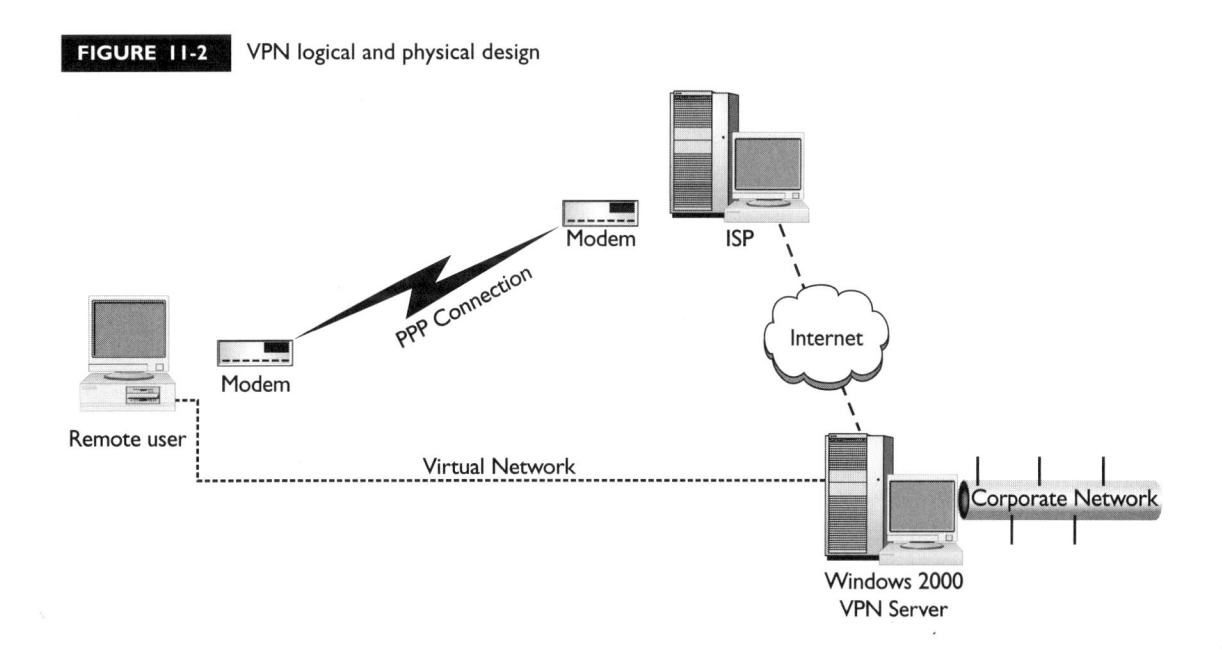

FIGURE 11-2 VPN logical and physical design

EXERCISE 11-2

Enabling Remote Access on a Internet Connection Server

Depending on your remote access needs, you can deploy dial-up and VPN services on the same machine or separate them onto dedicated servers. For this exercise, which performs a RAS and VPN setup, we will configure one Windows 2000 server as a combined dial-up Remote Access Server and VPN server; that way we cover both in one swoop.

The "Connecting Your Network to the Internet" guide configures a Windows 2000 server as an Internet connection server that provides access to the Internet and shares this connection with local area network clients. This Internet connection server can be enabled as a Remote Access Server by enabling and configuring RAS from the RRAS tool. The following illustration is a screenshot of the properties, which will confirm that the server is a Remote Access Server.

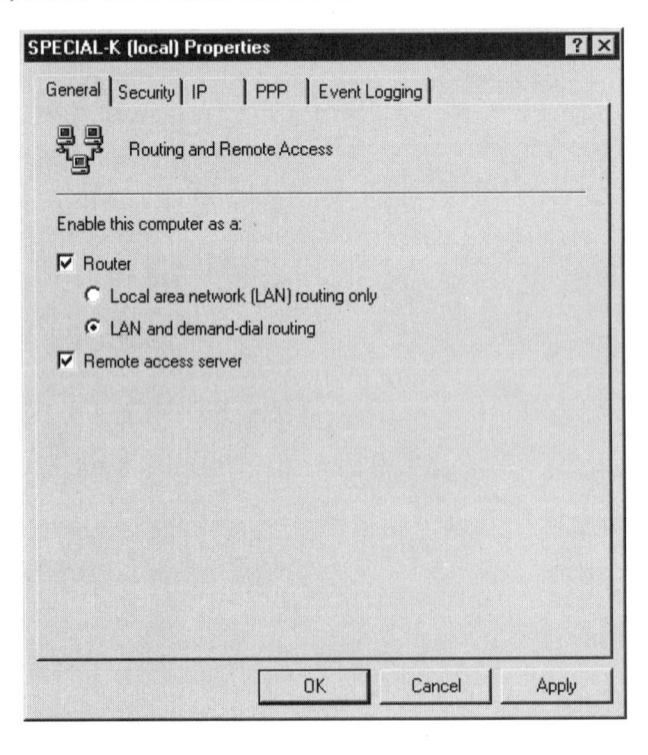

Now let's configure our machine into a RAS and VPN server. To do so we must perform the following steps.

1. Open the Routing and Remote Access tool from the Administrative Tools folder on the Start menu.
2. Right-click the server name and choose Configure and Enable Routing and Remote Access, just like we did in the first exercise earlier in the chapter.
3. After the Welcome screen, click Next.
4. We now come to the Common Configurations dialog box. Choose Remote Access Server. We choose this option because we are creating a server that supports both RAS and VPN.

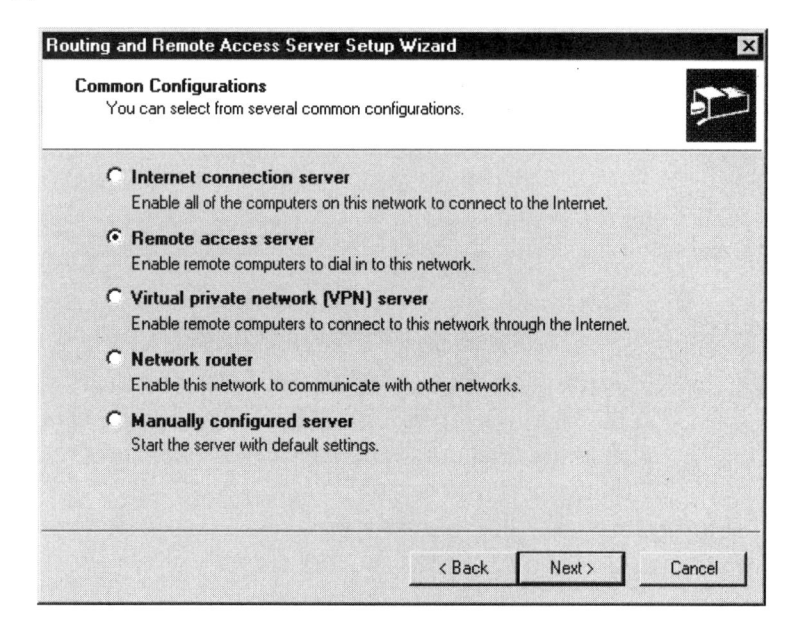

5. Next we see a list of networking protocols for remote clients. These are the protocols that remote clients will be allowed to use. For our example, our remote clients will only be allowed to use TCP/IP, as shown here:

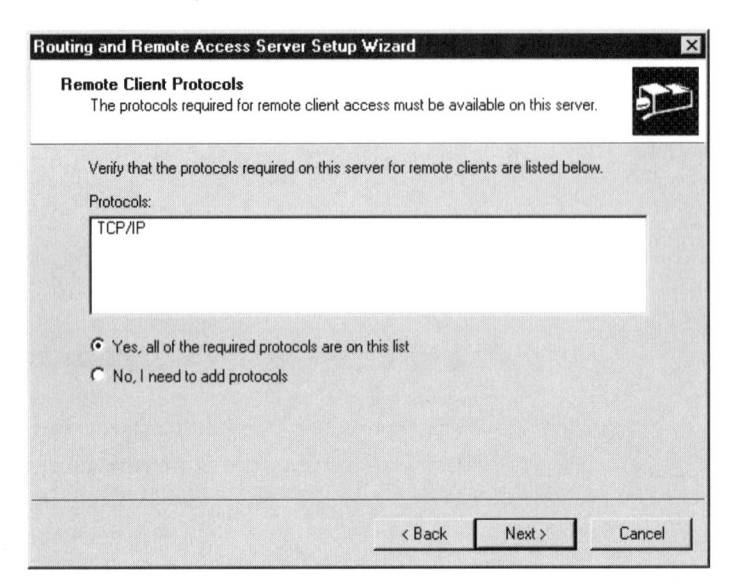

6. Now because the server is also going to be a VPN server, it will have two NICs. Choose the NIC pointing to your internal network, *not* the Internet.

7. Next is the IP address assignment for remote clients. You can use either DHCP if a server on your network is so configured or set up a pool of valid IP addresses for clients to use when they connect. A static pool of addresses is chosen, as shown here:

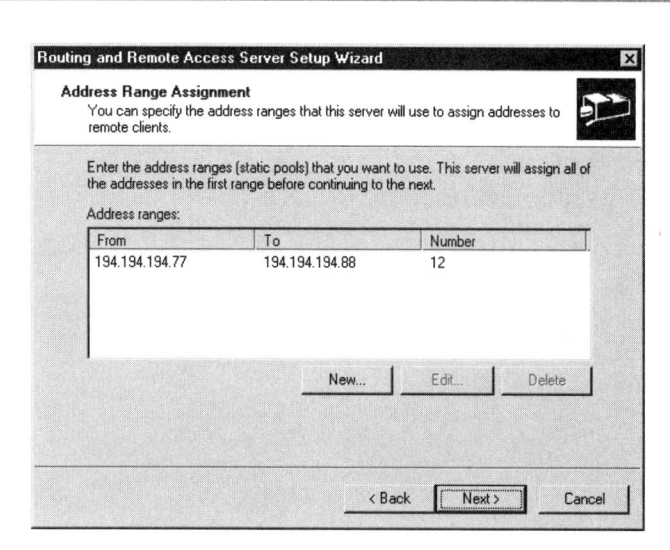

8. Our next choice is to select what authentication service to use. You are given the option of using RADIUS (Remote Authentication Dial-In User Service) or choosing not to use it, in which case Active Directory will handle the authentication. In this exercise we'll select not to use RADIUS. RADIUS is covered in more depth later in the chapter.

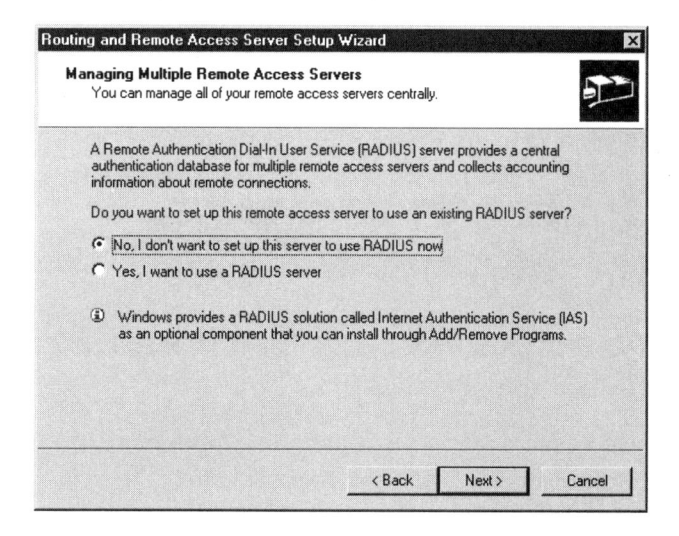

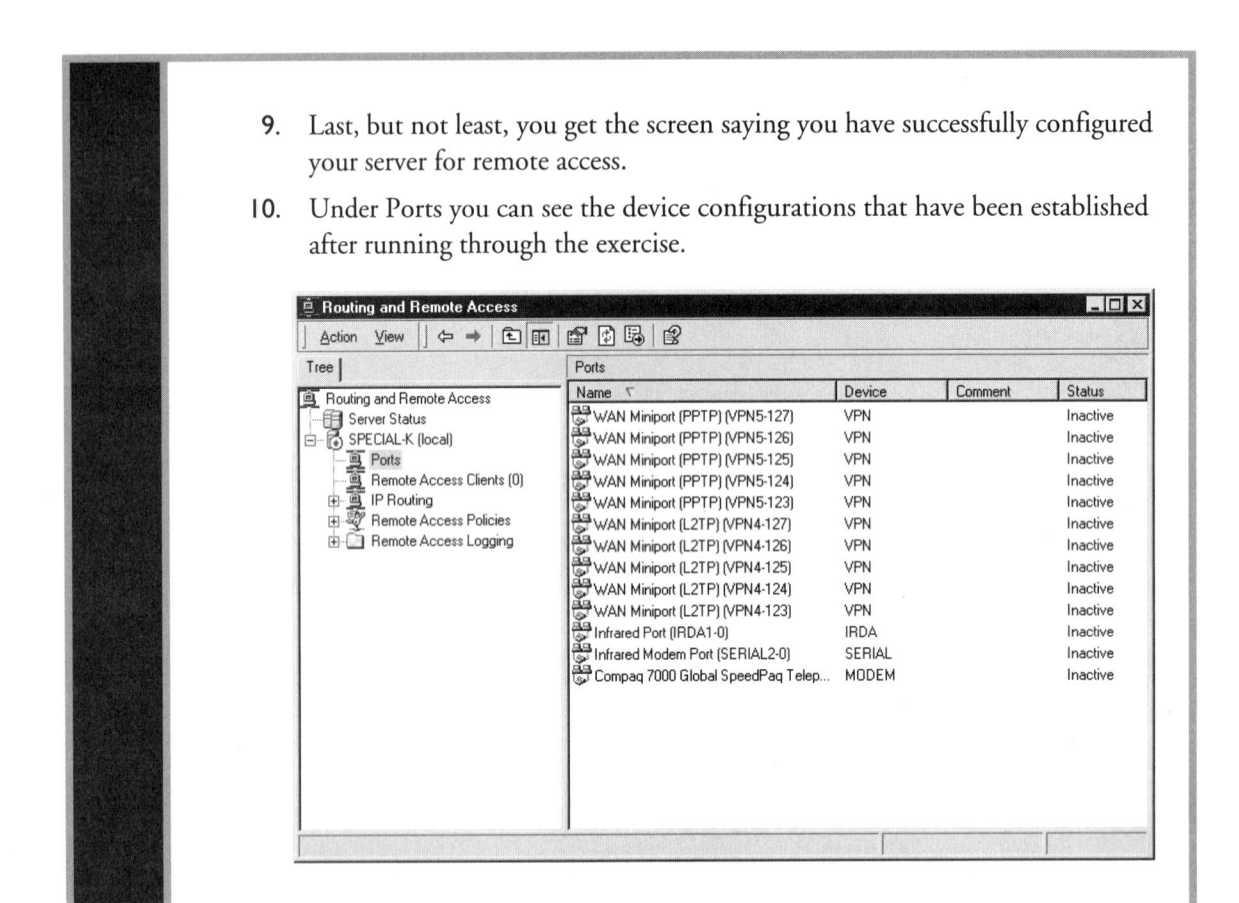

9. Last, but not least, you get the screen saying you have successfully configured your server for remote access.
10. Under Ports you can see the device configurations that have been established after running through the exercise.

CERTIFICATION OBJECTIVE 11.03

Provide Secure Access Between Private Networks

In providing secure access between private networks, we are trying to prevent information from being stolen from within the same organization or entity. Today, more and more information is being stolen from within a company's private network. Now with the use of IPSec, along with the Active Directory service, Windows 2000 administrators are able to maintain central control of policy-based security administration. Another way of providing secure access between private networks is through the use of Certificate Authority servers. CAs are a key component of any corporation's public key infrastructure (PKI). An administrator can create an enterprise CA server and build a CA hierarchy for the entire enterprise. This of course requires each packet to be digitally signed and authenticated. For more detailed information on PKIs and CA servers, please refer to Chapter 8 of this book.

Within a LAN

Within a local area network (LAN), administrators can create their own enterprise certificate authority server and expand it to a complete CA hierarchy. By creating an enterprise CA server, an administrator can control the digital certificates of an entire organization, a domain, or even a site.

Within a WAN

IPSec can be used to provide secure exchange across a wide area network (WAN). This is accomplished through a site-to-site VPN connection. By taking advantage of L2TP/IPSec, administrators are not locked into a specific vendor's product. With the use of router-to-router communication, IPSec can secure data traveling across a private site-to-site WAN.

Across a Public Network

For situations in which Windows 2000 must operate with third-party routers or gateways that do not support Layer 2 Tunneling Protocol (L2TP)/IPSec or Point-to-Point Tunneling Protocol (PPTP) with VPN tunneling, the option to use IPSec in tunnel mode to encapsulate IP packets and to optionally encrypt them is supported.

Creating an Enterprise Root CA

The enterprise CA is the root of a Windows 2000-based CA hierarchy. So when should you set up an enterprise CA? You should set up an enterprise CA if you will be issuing certificates to users and machines within your corporation. Normally for security purposes, the enterprise CA is configured to issue certificates only to subordinate CAs, but in Exercise 11-3, Creating an Enterprise Root CA, we will be issuing certificates to our users and machines from our enterprise CA.

So how do we know that this works? There are a couple ways. The first, which is the easiest, is to go out to a command prompt and type **net start**. All services that are running will be shown. Certificate Services should be one of those. You can also test this with Internet Explorer 5.0. Go to the following URL: http://<server name>/certsrv. You'll then go through a group of questions requesting a certificate.

EXERCISE 11-3

Creating an Enterprise Root CA

Before creating the enterprise CA, we must make sure the following exists:

1. Windows 2000 DNS is installed (required by Active Directory).
2. Active Directory (AD) is installed. The enterprise policy places information in the AD.
3. The enterprise administrator privileges are set on the DNS, AD, and the CA server.

Now, let's go through setting up an enterprise CA server. Remember you must have enterprise administrator rights.

1. Go to Control Panel.
2. Double-click Add/Remove Programs.
3. Select Add/Remove Windows Components to start the wizard.
4. Select the Certificate Services check box and click Next.
5. At this point we will be asked if we intend to use the Web components of the certificate services. For this exercise we'll leave the box unchecked.
6. Next you are prompted to specify the type of certification authority you want. We will be installing the Enterprise CA Server root. The reason for root is because this is the first CA server in the enterprise. If there was already a CA root, then we could select CA enterprise subordinate.

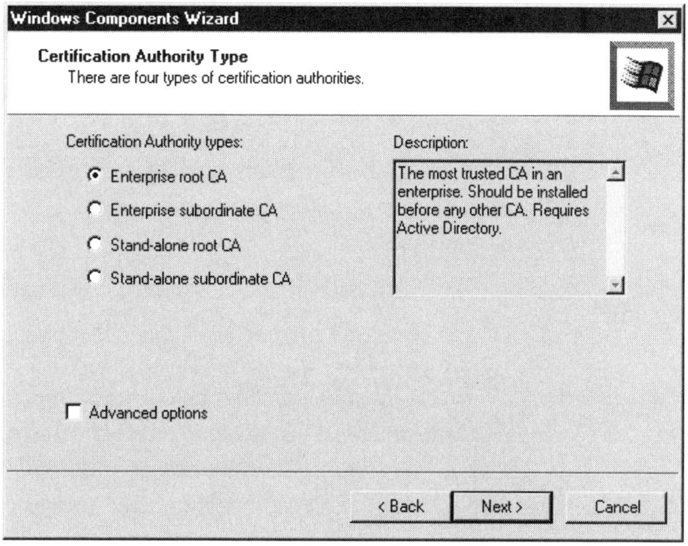

7. If you need to change the cryptography settings, then you would select Advanced Options. The following illustration shows the options you would get by selecting Advanced Options. For our exercise we will leave this at default.

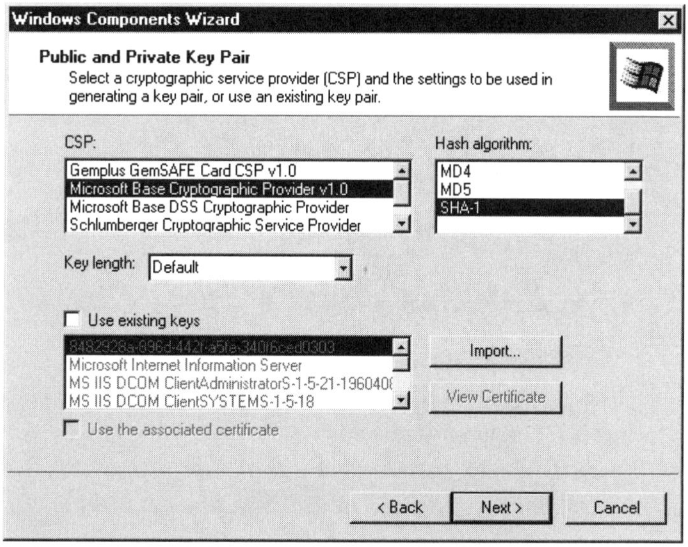

8. Now we are asked for some identification information. Not all of these fields must be completed. As a recommendation, include the CA Name, CA Description, and for the meantime leave the Valid For entry set at two years. Here is a little note on the Valid For entry. Each time a root certificate expires, an administrator has to update all trust relationships, and perform the administrative steps needed to move the CA to a new certificate. Select Next to continue.

9. You now will see a dialog box that defines the locations of the certificate database, the configuration information, and the location where the Certificate Revocation List is stored. At this point Microsoft recommends that you select the Shared Folder check box. You create this and point newly created subordinate CA servers here. In the real world, you should probably set this up even if you have only one enterprise CA server. Because we are setting up only one server, there is no need to select Shared Folder.

10. Note that if you are running Internet Information Services (IIS), you will be asked to shut it down. Select OK and the system will shut it down for you.

11. Next, setup will copy files from the Windows 2000 Server CD-ROM onto the system.

12. Once this is done, select Finish and the wizard is complete.

CERTIFICATION OBJECTIVE 11.04

Design Windows 2000 Security for Remote Access Users

With Windows 2000, authorization for remote access clients is granted based on the dial-in properties of a user account and remote access policies. Remote access policies are a set of conditions and connection settings that give network administrators more flexibility in authorizing connection attempts. The Windows 2000 Routing and Remote Access Service and Windows 2000 Internet Authentication Service

(IAS) both use remote access policies to determine whether to accept or reject connection attempts. With remote access policies, you can grant remote access by individual user account or through the configuration of specific remote access policies.

Managing by User Account

Managing remote access by user account is used in Windows NT version 3.5x and 4.0. With Windows 2000, if you wish to manage remote access on an individual per-user basis, set the remote access permission on those user accounts that are allowed to create remote access connections to Allow Access. Modify the profile properties of the default remote access policy called Allow Access if Dial-In Permission Is Enabled for the needed connection parameters.

Managing Access by Policy

The access by policy administrative model, according to Microsoft, is intended for Windows 2000 Remote Access Servers that are either stand-alone or members of a Windows 2000 native mode domain. For the following exercise, we will go through the steps needed to accomplish this task.

CertCam 11-4

EXERCISE 11-4

Managing Access by Policy

1. To manage remote access by policy, set the remote access permission on all user accounts to Control Access through Remote Access Policy (if in Native mode; if not go to Step 2).

2. Define the new remote access policies that allow or deny access based on your needs. If the remote access server computer is a member of a Windows NT 4.0 domain or a Windows 2000 mixed mode domain and you want to manage access by policy, set the remote access permission on all user accounts to Allow Access.

3. Remove the default policy called Allow Access if Dial-In Permission Is Enabled (if it is there; if not then continue) and create new policies that allow or deny access. A connection that does not match any configured remote access policy is denied, even if the remote access permission on the user account is set to Allow Access.

EXERCISE 11-5

Setting up RAS Rights with Policies in a Mixed Mode Domain

What we are going to do now is set up our mixed mode Windows 2000 domain to allow us to manage using policies and grant access based on group membership.

1. First thing we need to do is go into Active Directory Users and Computers and right-click the Users container.
2. Select New | Group.
3. Set the group name to **RAS Users**, and keep it as a global and security group.
4. Once this is done, go to each user you want to give dial-up access to and right-click the object and choose Properties.
5. Go to the Dial-In tab and select Allow Access, as shown here:

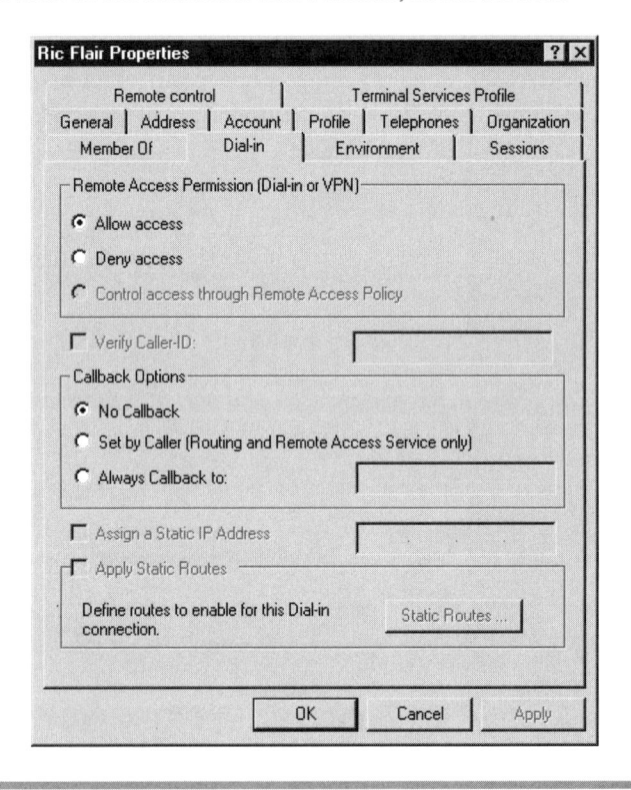

6. Next we will add our users to the group RAS Users. To do so, right-click the RAS Users group and select Properties. Go to the Members tab and add your users.

Now it is time to create the policy. At this point you might be asking why manage this through policies if all I had to do was grant dial-up access? There are a couple of reasons. First, using groups has always been the best route to providing access to services and resources when it comes to managing systems, whether it's Windows NT, NetWare, or Windows 2000. The second reason is because policies provide a plethora of options, whereas before in Windows NT, we really didn't have as many.

7. Now we turn our attention to RRAS. In RRAS, highlight the entry titled Remote Access Policies and right-click it. Select New Remote Access Policy.
8. Now give the policy a meaningful name. For example: **Policy for RAS Group Members**.
9. Click Add to specify the conditions.
10. Select NAS-Port-Type and click Add.
11. In the available types list choose Async (modem). Click Add and then click OK.
12. Now you will see a condition labeled NAS-Port-Type Matches Async.
13. We're not done. Click Add at the bottom of the screen.
14. Now just as we selected NAS-Port-Type, we will select Windows-Groups.
15. You will see a dialog box that will allow you to add groups, so from here we will click Add.
16. In the Select Groups dialog box, select the group RAS Users.
17. You'll then be told that RAS Users is in the condition matching your domain name. Click OK.

18. Now you see your conditions that must be matched. They should look similar to the ones shown here:

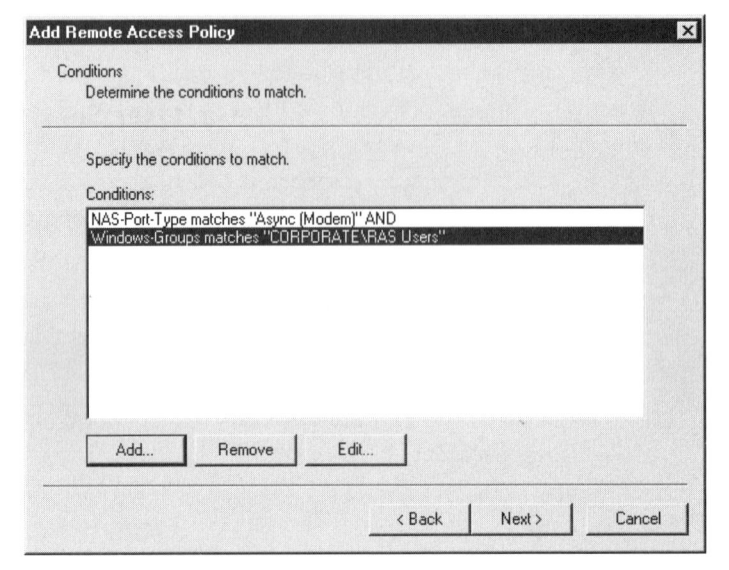

19. Click Next.
20. Select Grant Remote Access Permission.

Congratulations, you are done.

exam
⍥atch *In a mixed mode domain, if the user account is granted dial-in access, but has a policy that denies it, the policy takes precedence.*

Authentication Protocols

Now we will cover an area that is quite new to people in the Windows NT world overall, which is the authentication protocols that are used with Windows 2000. Some you will recognize from the days of LAN Manager or Windows NT 3.1. Others are new to most Windows NT and future Windows 2000 administrators. Let's take a look at them.

Extensible Authentication Protocol (EAP)
Extensible Authentication Protocol (EAP) is an infrastructure that allows the addition of arbitrary authentication methods such as certificates, one-time passwords, smart cards, and token cards. In Windows 2000 it also works with RADIUS and IAS, which are discussed in the next section.

Remote Authentication Dial-In User Services (RADIUS)
The Remote Authentication Dial-In User Services (RADIUS) protocol is a software-based security authentication method developed by the IETF (Internet Engineering Task Force). It sends authentication requests to a RADIUS server. Users' rights and configuration information are stored on the RADIUS server. Under Windows 2000, RADIUS is implemented as Internet Authentication Service (IAS). The use of RADIUS allows the remote access user authentication, authorization, and accounting data to be maintained in a central location, rather than on each network access server (NAS). Users connect to RADIUS-compliant NASs, such as Windows 2000–based computers, that are running the Routing and Remote Access Service, which in turn, forward authentication requests to the centralized IAS server.

Challenge Handshake Authentication Protocol (CHAP)
The Challenge Handshake Authentication Protocol verifies the identity of the peer, using a three-way handshake. The authenticator sends a challenge message to the peer. The peer returns the user name and an MD5 hash of the challenge, the session ID, and the client's password. The authenticator then checks this response, and if the values match, the authentication is acknowledged; if not, the connection is ended. CHAP provides protection against playback attack because the challenge value changes with every message. Because the password is never sent unencrypted over the network or link, it is considered very difficult to crack.

Microsoft Challenge Handshake Authentication Protocol (MS-CHAP)
The Microsoft Challenge Handshake Authentication Protocol is similar to CHAP but is considered more secure. As with CHAP, the authenticator sends a challenge to the peer. The peer must return the user name and an MD4 hash of the challenge string, the session ID, and the MD4-hashed password. This sort of design manipulates a hash of the MD4 hash of the password, and provides an additional level of security because it allows the authenticator to store hashed passwords instead of clear-text passwords.

Microsoft Challenge Handshake Authentication Protocol (MS-CHAPv2)

Microsoft Challenge Handshake Authentication Protocol (MS-CHAPv2) is the most updated version of MS-CHAP, and is available with the implementation of Windows 2000. It provides mutual authentication and asymmetric encryption keys.

Internet Protocol Security (IPSec)

Internet Protocol Security (IPSec) can provide many things, along with many methods. It can provide authenticity, data integrity, privacy, and anti-replay protection. Hence, we have an end-to-end security solution from client to server, server-to-server, and even client-to-client. By using L2TP and IPSec tunnels, or the pure IPSec tunnel mode, one is able to provide secure connections across private wide area networks or Internet-based networks. IPSec is an architecture, a protocol, and an Internet Key Exchange (IKE) protocol. For reference, an IKE is a fairly complex security negotiation between two computers, normally using PKI certificates for mutual authentication.

exam ⓦatch

IPSec tunnel mode is not designed to be used for virtual private network (VPN) remote access. IPSec's transport mode is. Windows 2000 uses IPSec transport mode for securing the data.

Layer 2 Tunneling Protocol (L2TP)

With L2TP being a combination of Point-to-Point Tunneling Protocol (PPTP) and Layer 2 Forwarding (L2F), the IETF mandated that one standard be created. L2TP encapsulates Point-to-Point Protocol (PPP) frames to be sent over IP, X.25, Frame Relay, or Asynchronous Transfer Mode (ATM) networks. When configured to use IP as a transport, L2TP can be used as a VPN tunneling protocol over the Internet. Through the use of PPP, L2TP has multi-protocol support such as IPX and AppleTalk. It is also an excellent solution for multi-vendor interoperability.

As of this writing, only L2TP over IP networks (L2TP/IPSec) is defined. L2TP frames are encapsulated as User Datagram Protocol (UDP port 1701) messages. It can be used as a tunneling protocol over the Internet or private intranets. As it pertains to Windows 2000, L2TP's encryption is provided by IPSec Encapsulating Security Payload (ESP).

exam ⓦatch

It is possible to create L2TP connections in Windows 2000 without being encrypted by IPSec.

SCENARIO & SOLUTION

Is it better to use RADIUS, or to use Active Directory to authenticate?	It depends on what you are doing. RADIUS was mainly added to improve Microsoft's standing with ISPs. Most corporate networks will do quite well by authenticating through Active Directory.
What is PKI?	It stands for public key infrastructure. PKI is not a product (at least, not yet). It is a set of tools used to accomplish a network built around using public keys and cryptology.

With the use of PPP, a wide range of authentication options apply, such as the use of CHAP, MS-CHAP, MS-CHAPv2, and EAP.

exam watch

Due to incompatibilities between IKE and network address translation (NAT), it is not possible to use L2TP/IPSec mode through a network address translator while taking advantage of automated key exchange.

The following is the path that tunneled data takes through the Windows 2000 networking architecture from a VPN client over a remote access VPN connection using a regular analog modem. A diagram is shown in Figure 11-3.

1. An IP datagram, IPX datagram, or NetBEUI frame is submitted by the appropriate protocol to the virtual interface that represents the VPN connection using NDIS (Network Driver Interface Specification).

2. NDIS submits a packet to NDISWAN, which optionally compresses and provides a PPP header consisting of only the PPP Protocol ID field.

3. NDISWAN submits the PPP frame to the L2TP protocol driver, which encapsulates the PPP frame with a L2TP header. In the L2TP header, the Tunnel ID and the Call ID are set to the appropriate value identifying the tunnel.

4. The L2TP protocol driver then submits the resulting packet to the TCP/IP protocol driver with information to send the L2TP packet as a UDP message from port 1701 to 1701 with the IP addresses of the VPN client and the VPN server.

558 Chapter 11: Designing a Security Solution for Access Between Networks

5. The TCP/IP protocol driver constructs an IP packet with the appropriate IP header and UDP header. IPSec then analyzes the IP packet and matches it with a current IPSec policy. Based on the settings in the policy, IPSec encapsulates and encrypts the UDP message portion of the IP packet using the appropriate ESP headers and trailers. The original IP header with the protocol field set to 50 is added to the front of the ESP packet. The IP driver then submits the resulting packet to the interface that represents the dial-up connection to the local ISP using NDIS.

6. NDIS submits the packet to NDISWAN.

7. NDISWAN provides PPP headers and trailers and submits the resulting PPP frame to the appropriate WAN miniport driver representing the dial-up hardware.

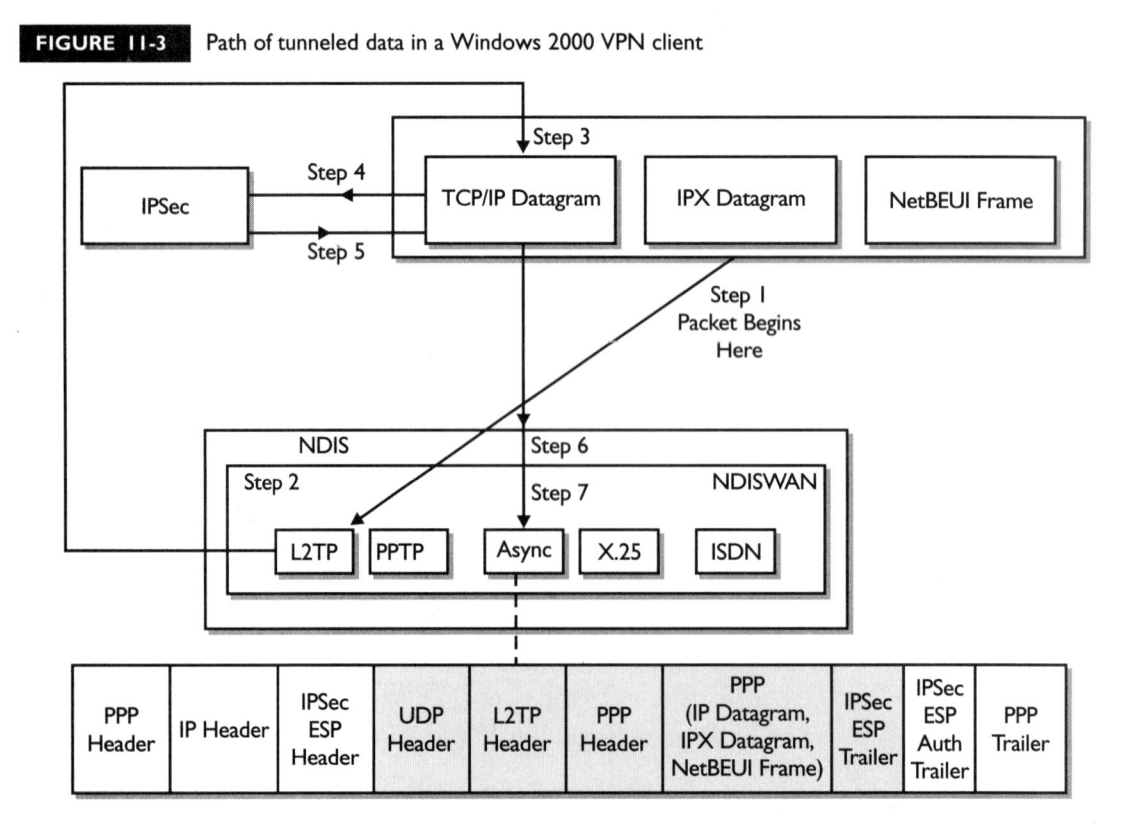

FIGURE 11-3 Path of tunneled data in a Windows 2000 VPN client

Point-to-Point Tunneling Protocol (PPTP)

PPTP is able to provide authenticated and encrypted communications between a client and a gateway or between two gateways, without requiring a PKI. It uses a TCP connection for tunnel maintenance and a Generic Routing Encapsulation (GRE) encapsulated PPP frames for tunneled data. Although it is easy and cheap to administer, PPTP can be passed through NAT, as opposed to L2TP/IPSec. This NAT capability eliminates the requirement that each PPTP endpoint have a registered IP address when used across the Internet.

> **exam**
> **Watch**
>
> *It is because of IKE (Internet Key Exchange) that L2TP has an incompatibility with NAT.*

Bandwidth Allocation Protocol (BAP)

Bandwidth Allocation Protocol (BAP) is a PPP control protocol that is used on a multiprocessing connection to dynamically add and remove links.

Bandwidth Allocation Control Protocol (BACP)

Bandwidth Allocation Control Protocol (BACP) is a PPP network control protocol that negotiates the election of a favored peer for a multiprocessing connection. If both ends of the connection issue a connection request at the same time, then the connection request of the favored peer is performed.

Inbound Connections

Inbound connections are those where access to the internal network or resources within the internal network are being accessed by users outside of it. These users could be dialing in using a modem and connecting directly to the internal network or they could make use of an existing public network, such as the Internet, to gain access to resources within. Either way, security must be in the forefront of any such implementation. In the following sections, we cover both virtual private networks and Routing and Remote Access Service—two services within Windows 2000 that are used for this very purpose.

Virtual Private Networks

One of the hottest technologies around for network administrators is the virtual private network (VPN). So what is a VPN? Most likely that question or some variance of it will be asked on the exam, so let's answer it. A virtual private network is the *extension* of a private network that encompasses links across *shared* or public networks such as the Internet. It enables you to send data between two computers in a manner that emulates the properties of a point-to-point private link, while doing so across a shared or public network. So is that all there is to it? Not quite; there is one more piece of the puzzle that fully defines a VPN. That piece is the *encryption* of the data being sent. The bottom line is that VPNs allow you to use public or shared networks to transport the packet, and they also emulate a private link in that the data is encrypted for confidentiality. Figure 11-4 shows the logical equivalent of a VPN.

exam
Watch

As mentioned earlier, it is possible to create a tunnel and send the data through it without encryption. But remember that this is not a VPN because the private data being sent across the shared or public network is in an unencrypted and easily readable form.

FIGURE 11-4

Logical view of a virtual private network

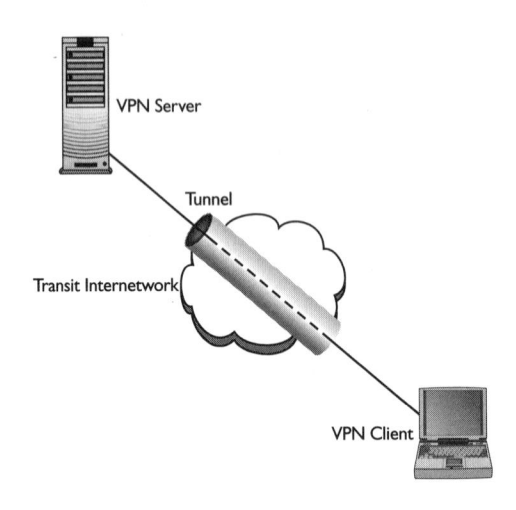

In Windows 2000, a VPN connection consists of the following components:

- **VPN server**   A computer that *accepts* VPN connections from VPN clients. It can provide a remote access VPN connection or a router-to-router VPN connection.
- **VPN client**   A computer that *initiates* a VPN connection to a VPN server. This client can be an individual computer that obtains a remote access VPN connection or a router that obtains a router-to-router VPN connection. This does *not* have to be a Microsoft VPN client. It can be any VPN client that supports either Point-to-Point Tunneling Protocol (PPTP) or Layer 2 Tunneling Protocol (L2TP) that uses IPSec.
- **Tunnel**   Where the data is encapsulated within the connection.
- **VPN connection**   The part of the connection where the data is encrypted.
- **Tunneling protocols**   Standards used for communicating that manage tunnels and encapsulate private data. Examples: PPTP and L2TP.
- **Transit internetwork**   The public or shared network used for crossing by the encapsulated data. With Windows 2000, the transit internetwork is *always* an IP intranetwork. This can be the Internet or a private IP-based intranet.

RRAS

Routing and Remote Access Service, code-named steelhead at the time, actually came about in Windows NT 3.51 Service Pack 2. Although now considered somewhat inadequate in today's world, it was a major step in the evolution of Windows NT (now 2000). But why combine routing with RAS? Microsoft's explanation is that combining the two services lies in the Point-to-Point Protocol (PPP). As we all know, it is commonly used to negotiate point-to-point connections for remote access clients. PPP provides the following:

- **Link parameter negotiation**   Agreement between the client and the server on the size of the packets as well as how they are framed.
- **Exchange of authentication credentials**   The process of logging on with the use of a username and password is a prime example.
- **Network layer protocol negotiation**   The act of negotiating and obtaining a valid IP address.

Combining routing with Remote Access Service allowed the use of the existing PPP client/server infrastructure that already was used by RAS in the past.

Outbound Connections

Connecting to and accessing private network resources through the Internet or some other public network is where VPNs take over. This allows the administrator to centrally maintain security from outbound connections while also allowing users to make use of local ISPs. This prevents the users from having to make long distance calls and racking up very large phone bills.

Connecting to a VPN

In connecting to a VPN, all that a user does is create a VPN session under Dial-Up Networking and click Make a New Connection. In the following exercise, we will cover the steps needed to set up the client piece.

CertCam 11-6

EXERCISE 11-6

Connecting to a VPN

1. After making a new connection as described in the preceding paragraph, the welcome screen appears. Click Next. The Network Connection Wizard will then ask you for the type of connection that you would like to create.

2. After this is done you will select the initial dial-up connection that you are to use to access the Internet. In this case, we are connecting to our local ISP, which we had already configured when setting up Internet access.

3. After this, the Network Connection Wizard asks us for the name or IP address of the system we want to connect to. This is our VPN server.

4. Next, we are asked if we want to make this connection available to all users or just for ourselves. For our example we are selecting *Only for Myself*. Other circumstances may arise in which it is necessary for others who use this machine to have access to the VPN connection.

5. We are finished with the setup and only have to name the connection. We've chosen to call it Mystic Corp. VPN. Your name can be whatever you want it to be as long as it makes sense to you and you know what it is.

Remote Access Policies

Back in the old Windows NT days, administrators authorized access based on a simple Grant Dial-In Permission to User option in User Manager for Domains or the Remote Access Admin utility. Callback options were also configured on a per-user basis. With Windows 2000, authorization is granted based on the dial-in properties of a user account *and* remote access policies. Remote access policies are a set of conditions and connection settings that give network administrators more flexibility in authorizing connection attempts. The Windows 2000 Routing and Remote Access Service and Windows 2000 Internet Authentication Service (IAS) both use remote access policies to determine whether to accept or reject connection attempts. In both cases, the remote access policies are stored locally.

With remote access policies, you can grant or deny authorization by the time of day, the day of the week, and by the Windows 2000 group to which the remote access user belongs. You can also decide by the type of connection being requested (RAS client or virtual private network connection).

on the job

It is important to note that with remote access policies, a connection is authorized only if the settings of the connection attempt match at least one of the remote access policies (subject to the conditions of the dial-in properties of the user account and the profile properties of the remote access policy). If the settings of the connection attempt do not match at least one of the remote access policies, the connection attempt is denied regardless of the dial-in properties of the user account.

User Dial-In Settings

With Windows 2000, the user account for a stand-alone or Active Directory–based server contains a set of dial-in properties that are used when allowing or denying a connection attempt made by a user. For a stand-alone server, you can set the dial-in properties on the Dial-In tab on the user account in Local Users and Groups. For an Active Directory–based server, you can set the dial-in properties on the Dial-In tab on the user account in Active Directory Users and Computers.

Remote access properties, whether they be for a VPN or dial-up, should by used by administrators to determine whether remote access is explicitly allowed, denied, or determined through remote access policies. If access is allowed, remote access policy conditions, user account properties, or profile properties can still deny the connection attempt.

on the Job *The Control Access through Remote Access Policy option is available only on user accounts in a Windows 2000 native-mode domain or for local accounts on remote access servers running stand-alone Windows 2000.*

By default, the Administrator and Guest accounts on a stand-alone remote access server or in a Windows 2000 native mode domain are set to Control Access through Remote Access Policy. Those for a Windows 2000 mixed mode domain are set to Deny Access. New accounts created on a stand-alone remote access server or in a Windows 2000 native mode domain are set to Control Access through Remote Access Policy. New accounts created in a Windows 2000 mixed mode domain are set to Deny Access.

Policies and Conditions

Remote access policy conditions are one or more attributes that are compared to the settings of the connection attempt. If there are multiple conditions, then all of the conditions must match the settings of the connection attempt in order for the connection attempt to match the policy.

Routing

In routing, we can use policies to be set to certain criteria; for instance, set "NAS-Port-Type" matches "Ethernet" to block TCP port 25. We could also have it block all protocols. The use of policies within Windows 2000 expands the capabilities of the Windows NT family of operating systems to a level never seen before.

Using Multiple Profiles

A remote access policy profile is a set of properties that are applied to a connection when the connection is authorized—either through the user account permission setting or the policy permission setting. Profiles are made up of the following:

- **Dial-In Constraints** Can be the day and the time that a connection is allowed. Other constraints are Idle Disconnect Time, Maximum Session Length, Dial-In Number, and Dial-In media (ISDN, modem, or VPN).

- **IP Properties** Specify whether a specific IP address for a connection can be requested by the client. An administrator can also use the IP properties tab to define remote access policy filtering.

- **Multilink** Enables multilink connections and determines the maximum number of ports that a multilink connection can use. Additionally, you can set Bandwidth Allocation Protocol (BAP) policies that determine BAP usage and when extra BAP lines are dropped.
- **Authentication** Sets the types of authentication that are allowed for a connection and allows an administrator to specify the EAP type that must be used. Additionally, you can configure the EAP type. By default, MS-CHAP and MS-CHAPv2 are enabled.
- **Encryption** Encryption properties can be set to the following:
    - **No Encryption** Allows a non-encrypted connection.
    - **Basic** For dial-up and PPTP-based VPN connections, Microsoft Point-to-Point Encryption (MPPE) with a 40-bit key is used. For L2TP over IPSec-based VPN connections, 56-bit Data Encryption Standard (DES) is used.
    - **Strong** With dial-up and PPTP-based VPN connections, MPPE with a 56-bit key is used. For L2TP over IPSec-based VPN connections, 56-bit DES encryption is used.
    - **Strongest** With dial-up and PPTP-based VPN connections, MPPE with a 128-bit key is used. For L2TP over IPSec-based VPN connections, triple DES (3DES) encryption is used. This option is only available on North American versions of Windows 2000.
- **Advanced** Advanced properties specify the series of RADIUS attributes that are sent back to the RADIUS client by the IAS server. RADIUS attributes are specific to performing RADIUS authentication and are ignored by the Remote Access Server. By default, Framed-Protocol is set to PPP and Service-Type is set to Framed.

CERTIFICATION OBJECTIVE 11.05

Design an SMB Signing Solution

Server Message Block (SMB) signing, also known as the Common Internet File System (CIFS), requires that every packet is signed for and every packet is to be verified using encryption. When implementing an SMB signing solution, administrators should anticipate a 10 percent to 15 percent degradation in server performance. SMB signing does not increase the amount of traffic on the network; instead, it adds more CPU cycles to the machines themselves. The sacrifice of performance is to protect against an old password eavesdropping technique called "pass the hash" or a "man in the middle" attack. SMB signing can only be done with Windows NT 4.0 Workstation clients that run Service Pack 3 or higher, Windows 2000 machines, and Windows 98 clients. This is *not* supported with Windows 95 clients.

In the following exercise, we will use a two-system setup along with a hub/switch (or crossover cable). Both systems will run Windows 2000. It doesn't matter if both run Professional, Server, or any combination. This exercise will work with all. For my setup, I will be using Professional on one station and Server on the other.

In designing our SMB signing solution, we must decide how stringent we want this policy to be. As you've seen throughout this book, nearly everything you configured in Windows NT through the Registry is now easily manageable and accessible through a tool.

EXERCISE 11-7

Implementing an SMB Signing Solution

For this exercise, we are going to require SMB signing and no reverting back for machines that do not support it. This is as tight as you can get it with SMB signing. The following steps will allow us to accomplish this:

1. We will open the local computer policy snap-in through the MMC, and go to computer configuration/windows settings/security settings/local policies/security options.

2. Once there we will go to the right pane in the window and select Digitally Sign Client Communication (Always). As you see in the following illustration, it is set to Not Defined (on Server) or Disabled (on Professional). We will change it to Enabled.

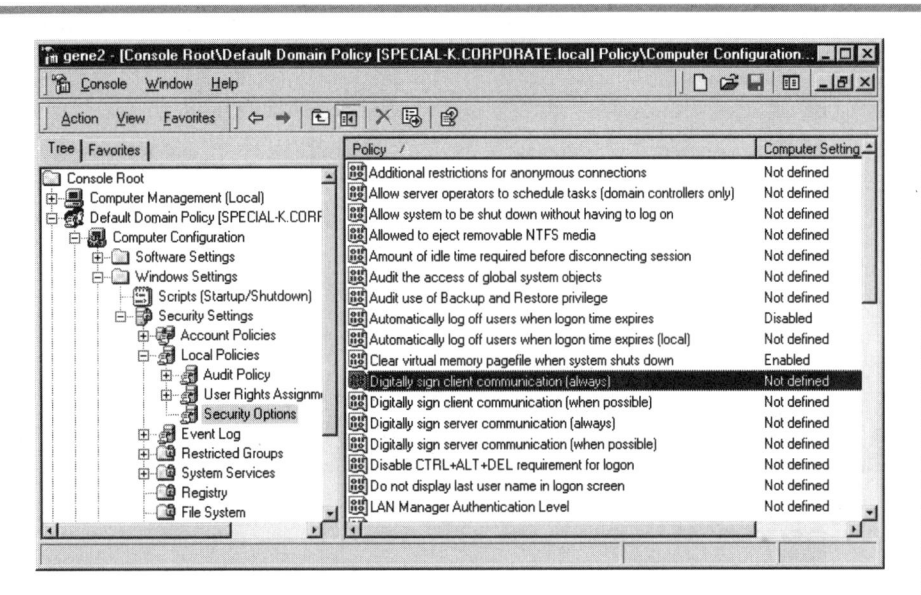

3. Right-click this setting and select Security.
4. You will now see a dialog box allowing you to enable this feature. Select the Define This Policy Setting check box, then select Enabled. 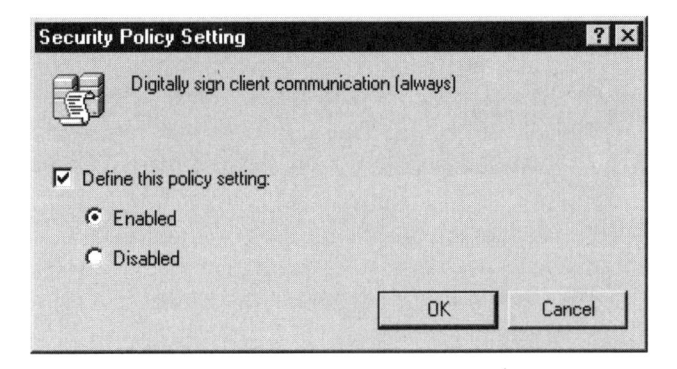
5. Next we will enable Digitally Sign Server Communication (Always), and perform the same steps that we took to enable the previous policy.
6. Perform these same steps on the second machine.
7. Once this is done, we have an SMB signing solution, where communication with the use of SMBs will require digital signatures. If a client is not set up to use SMB signing, they will not be able to communicate with the server and request access to resources.

SCENARIO & SOLUTION

What is SMB signing?	It is Microsoft's answer to a few attacks such as "pass the hash" and "man in the middle." It puts a digital signature on every SMB packet that is sent.
Are SMBs the same as CIFS?	Yes. Microsoft has only renamed the server messenger block to common internet file system. They are hoping more vendors begin using CIFS as a standard.

CERTIFICATION OBJECTIVE 11.06

Design an IPSec Solution

An IPSec solution within Windows 2000 incorporates the use of security, user, and domain policies. What this means is that with Windows 2000, an administrator can apply policies enterprise-wide (Group Policy) or down to a single user or workstation (locally) using Active Directory. It uses cryptography-based security to provide access control, connectionless integrity (UDP 500), data origin authentication, protection against replays, confidentiality, and limited traffic flow confidentiality. Creating an IPSec policy automatically assigns and distributes this to Windows 2000 members through the Group Policy. An automatic security negotiation and key management service is also provided using IKE (Internet Key Exchange), which in Windows 2000 is referred to as Security Association (SA). The implementation of IKE provides three authentication methods to establish trust between computers.

- **Public/Private key signature using certificates** Is compatible with several vendor systems such as Microsoft, Entrust, Verisign, and Netscape.
- **Kerberos v5.0 authentication** Provided by the Windows 2000 domain that serves as a Kerberos v 5.0 KDC (Key Distribution Center).
- **Passwords** Also known as *pre-shared authentication keys,* are strictly for establishing trusted connections between computers.

In designing an IPSec solution, an administrator or consultant will follow a four-step process, as follows:

1. Evaluate the information being sent over the intranet and the Internet.
2. Create numerous communication situations or scenarios.
3. Determine the levels of security required for each of the preceding scenarios.
4. Build the security policies through use of the Windows Security Manager.

IPSec setup involves describing the traffic characteristics on which to filter (source or destination IP address, protocol, and port), then specifying what service characteristics to apply to the traffic that matches the filters. Take an example where two machines are configured to use IPSec between them by being members of the same Windows 2000 domain and activating the lockdown policy. If the computers are *not* members of the same domain or a trusted domain, then trust must be configured using a password or pre-shared key in lockdown mode by:

1. Setting up a filter that specifies all traffic between the two hosts.
2. Choosing an authentication method. (Selecting pre-shared key, and entering a password.)
3. Selecting a negotiation policy. (*Lockdown* in this case, indicating that all traffic matching the filters must use IPSec.)
4. Specifying a connection type (LAN, dial-up, or all).

Figure 11-5 shows the flow of Windows 2000 IP Security. The security policies assigned to machine 1 and machine 2 by the network administrator will determine the level of security for the communication. This is picked up by the policy agent on each machine and passed to the Internet Security Architecture Key Management Protocol (ISAKMP/Oakley) service and then to the IPSec driver. The ISAKMP/Oakley service on each machine uses the negotiation policies associated with the assigned security policy to establish the key and a common negotiation method (referred to in the diagram as a security association). This is done as a short conversation over UDP port 500. This is where the Internet Key Exchange (IKE) takes place. The results of the policy negotiation between the two computers are passed to the IPSec driver, which uses the key to encrypt the data. Last but not least, the IPSec driver sends the encrypted data to machine 2. The

FIGURE 11-5

A Windows 2000 IPSec implementation

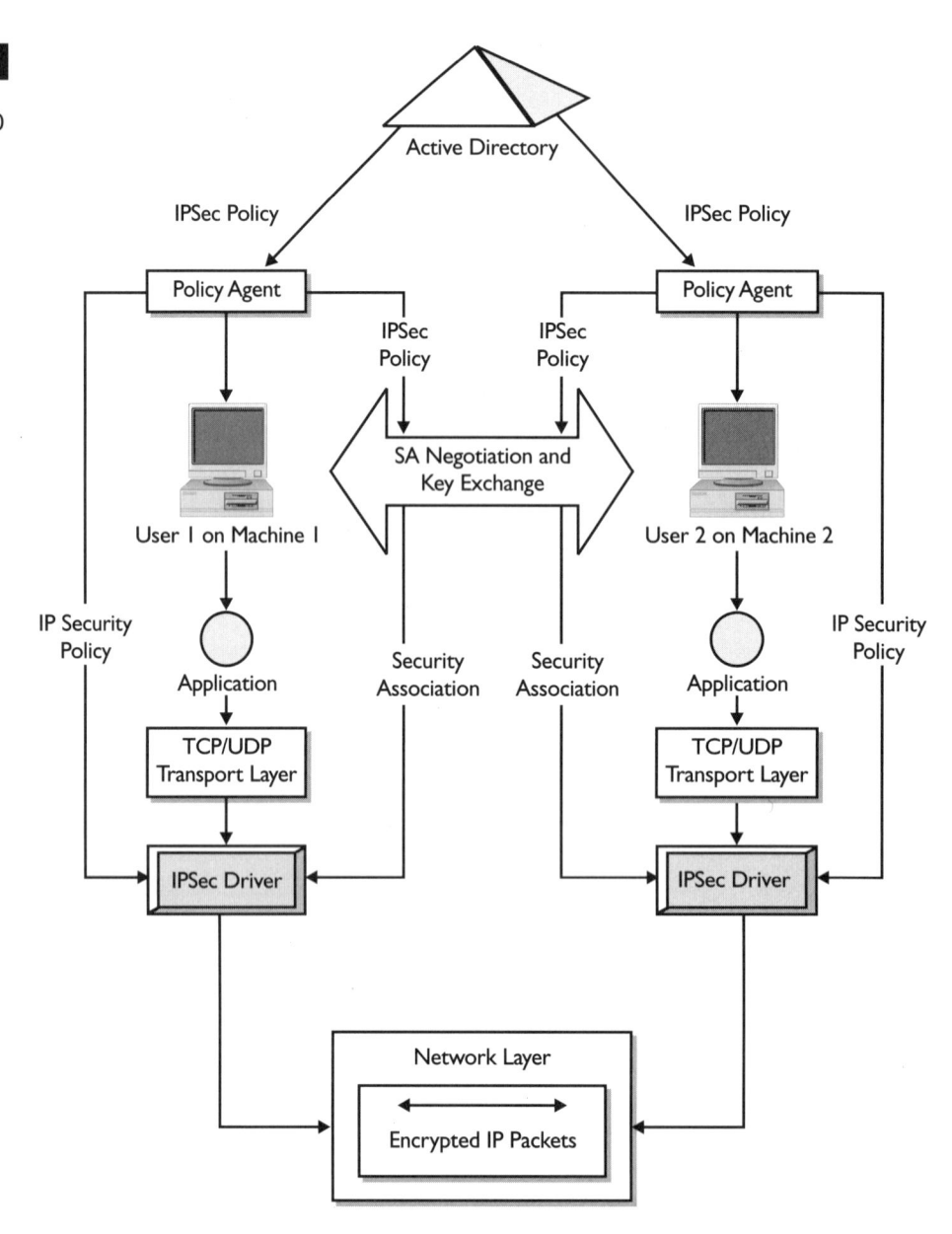

IPSec driver on machine 2 decrypts the data and passes it up to the receiving application waiting for its arrival. All of this will happen with something as insignificant as a simple PING.

Design an IPSec Solution **571**

on the job

In a scenario in which a machine is running Windows 2000 while configured for IPSec, and another is running Windows 9x (as well as earlier versions of Windows NT), the Windows 2000 machine will send the data without encryption unless otherwise specified in the IPSec policy. If this is set in the policy then the other computer must run Windows 2000.

Figure 11-6 is part of a network trace on this process. You see in the diagram the use of UDP 500, and ISAKMP as the protocol being used.

Evaluating Information

On all networks, information sent over the wire, whether it be internal or out to the Internet, is subject to interception, examination, and modification. So, when evaluating information, an administrator or a consultant must determine which kinds of information are most valuable and what communication scenarios are most vulnerable and where.

FIGURE 11-6

Network trace of IKE negotiation

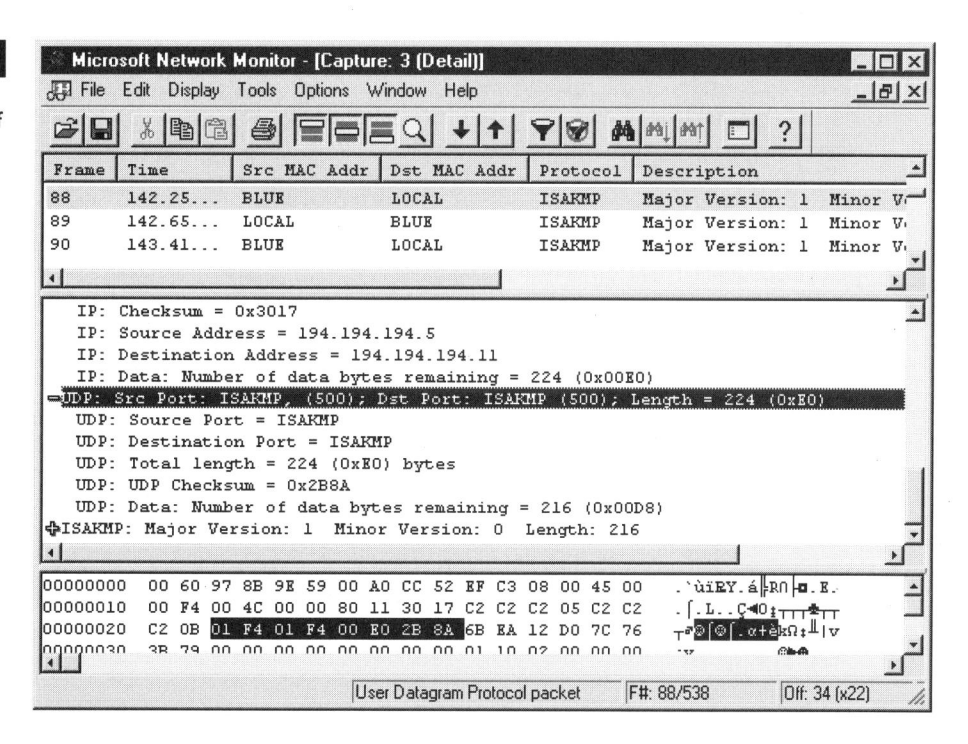

```
Microsoft Network Monitor - [Capture: 3 (Detail)]
File  Edit  Display  Tools  Options  Window  Help

Frame  Time       Src MAC Addr   Dst MAC Addr   Protocol   Description
88     142.25...  BLUE           LOCAL          ISAKMP     Major Version: 1  Minor V
89     142.65...  LOCAL          BLUE           ISAKMP     Major Version: 1  Minor V
90     143.41...  BLUE           LOCAL          ISAKMP     Major Version: 1  Minor V

  IP: Checksum = 0x3017
  IP: Source Address = 194.194.194.5
  IP: Destination Address = 194.194.194.11
  IP: Data: Number of data bytes remaining = 224 (0x00E0)
 UDP: Src Port: ISAKMP, (500); Dst Port: ISAKMP (500); Length = 224 (0xE0)
  UDP: Source Port = ISAKMP
  UDP: Destination Port = ISAKMP
  UDP: Total length = 224 (0xE0) bytes
  UDP: UDP Checksum = 0x2B8A
  UDP: Data: Number of data bytes remaining = 216 (0x00D8)
 ISAKMP: Major Version: 1  Minor Version: 0  Length: 216

00000000  00 60 97 8B 9E 59 00 A0 CC 52 EF C3 08 00 45 00
00000010  00 F4 00 4C 00 00 80 11 30 17 C2 C2 C2 05 C2 C2
00000020  C2 0B 01 F4 01 F4 00 E0 2B 8A 6B EA 12 D0 7C 76
00000030  3B 79 00 00 00 00 00 00 00 01 10 02 00 00 00

User Datagram Protocol packet    F#: 88/538    Off: 34 (x22)
```

Creating Scenarios

Most organizations will have certain patterns to their information flows. An administrator can determine these predictable patterns. For instance, a site in Charlotte may send purchase orders, sales forecasts, and other important information to the headquarters in Houston. Therefore, each of these communication scenarios can have different individual IP Security policies. Another example might be that an administrator believes all communications with the R&D department should be completely secure.

Determining Required Security Levels

Depending upon the sensitivity of the information and the relative vulnerability of the transmission carrier, the required security levels could change. In Windows 2000, using Security Manager lets an administrator easily set the appropriate level of security.

Secure Servers

IPSec for all unicast IP traffic is either *requested but optional*, or *requested and required*, as established by the administrator's configuration of the server. Using this model, clients need only a default policy for how to respond to security requests from servers. Once IPSec security associations (one in each direction) are established between the client and the server, they remain in effect for one hour after the last packet was sent between them. After that hour, the client cleans up the security associations and returns to the initial "respond only" state. If the client sends unsecured packets to the same server again, the server will re-establish IPSec. This is the easiest approach to take, and can be done safely as long as the first packets sent to the server by the application do not contain sensitive data, and as long as the server is permitted to receive unsecured, clear text packets from clients.

Lockdown Servers

If the server is directly accessible from the Internet, or if the first client packets contain sensitive data, then the client must receive an IPSec policy so that it requests IPSec for traffic when it attempts to send data to the server. Clients and servers can have specific rules for permitting, blocking, or securing only certain network packets (protocol or port specific). This approach is more difficult to configure and prone to error because it requires in-depth knowledge of the type of network traffic that an application sends and receives, and administrative coordination to be sure that all clients and servers have compatible policies.

Building Security Policies with Security Manager

Security Manager allows an administrator to set security settings and assign them to groups of computers or to a single computer. Policies are built and assigned using this utility.

Creating an IPSec Policy in Windows 2000

Now that we have an overall understanding of IPSec and the use of policies to enforce these standards, let's walk through one ourselves. In this section and in the following sections, our task is to create an IP Security policy that will allow communications to our server to be secured and encrypted.

To perform this, we need a minimum of two machines along with a hub or switch (cross-over cable is fine also). Our first machine will be running Windows 2000 Server and set up with Active Directory. This means we will also set up DNS and incorporate it with AD. On the second machine, we will install Windows 2000 Professional. The second machine will join the domain.

1. To create your own console, click Start | Run.
2. At the Open dialog box type **MMC**.
3. We suggest adding the following snap-ins for this console: Computer Management for the local machine, the Group Policy snap-in, and the Computer Management for your workstation machine. Once this is all set up, we can move on to creating our IPSec policy. You should have something similar to Figure 11-7.

on the job

With the introduction of the MMC in such products as IIS 4.0, the evolution of this tool has progressed. The MMC is an excellent way of customizing the tools you use most in a single console setting, thus keeping you, the administrator, from having to jump from one utility to another.

574 Chapter 11: Designing a Security Solution for Access Between Networks

FIGURE 11-7

Creating the IP security policy

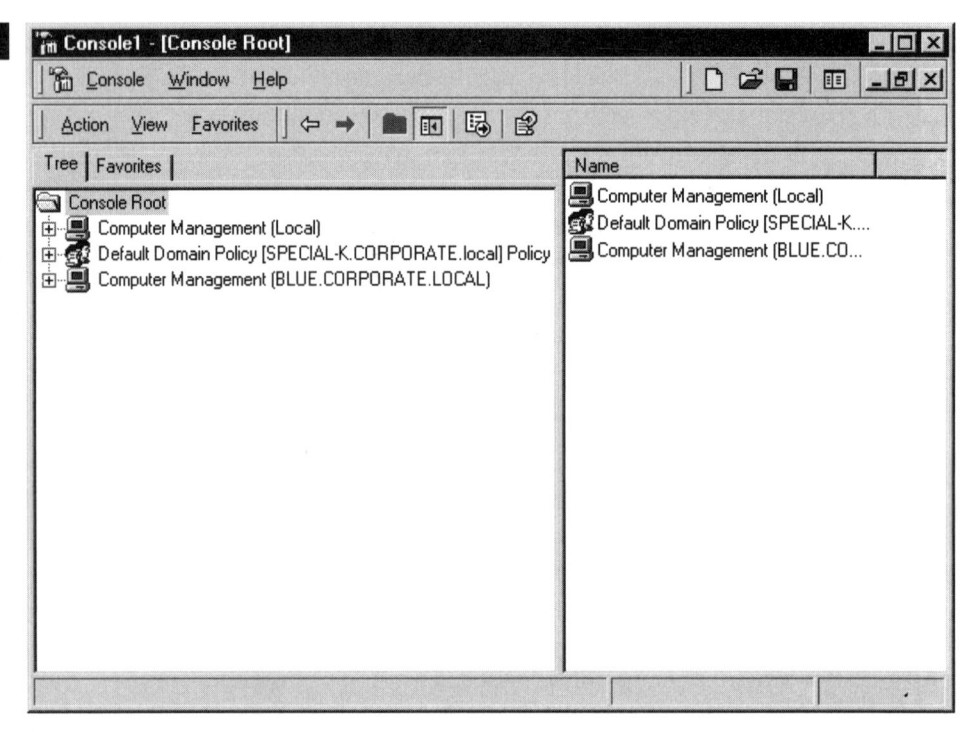

[Screenshot: Console1 - [Console Root] window showing Console Root with Computer Management (Local), Default Domain Policy [SPECIAL-K.CORPORATE.local] Policy, and Computer Management (BLUE.CORPORATE.LOCAL) in the tree pane. Name pane shows Computer Management (Local), Default Domain Policy [SPECIAL-K...., and Computer Management (BLUE.CO...]

Configure the IP Security Monitor To monitor the connections that the IPSec policy will create, we will use IP Security Monitor from our server. Before we create any policies, let's first start and configure IP Security Monitor.

1. To start the IP Security Monitor tool, click Start | Run, and type **ipsecmon** into the Open text box. Click OK.

2. Click Options in the IP Security Monitor tool, and change the default value for Refresh Seconds from 15 to 1. Click OK.

3. Click Minimize (just under the Options button) to minimize the IP Security Monitor window. You will use this minimized tool to monitor the policies later.

Before configuring the IPSec Authentication Method, Filter List, or Negotiation method, you must first create a new policy.

Creating an IPSec Policy   The following are the steps to create an IPSec Policy.

1. Using our server (for me that is SPECIAL-K), in the left pane of the MMC Console, right-click IP Security Policies on Local Machine, and then click Create IP Security Policy. The IP Security Policy Wizard appears.
2. Click Next.
3. Type a name for your policy, and click Next. We used New IP Security Policy.
4. Clear the Activate the Default Response Rule check box, and click Next.
5. Make sure that the Edit Properties check box is selected (it is by default), and click Finish.
6. In the Properties dialog box for the policy you have just created, ensure that the Use Add Wizard check box in the lower-right corner is selected. Click Add to start the Security Rule Wizard.
7. Click Next to proceed through the Security Rule Wizard.
8. Select This Rule Does Not Specify a Tunnel (selected by default) and then click Next.
9. Select the option button for All Network Connections (selected by default) and click Next.

Now we must configure the IKE authentication, which indicates how the computers are going to trust each other. As mentioned earlier, IKE in Windows 2000 supports three authentication methods: public/private keys using certificates, Kerberos v5.0, and pre-shared key (password). For our exercise we will use a pre-shared key for authentication. This is a password that the server and the client in our situation must know.

exam
Watch   ***IKE is not used to encrypt data. It is only used during negotiation.***

Configure the Authentication Mode In Figure 11-8 we will select Use This String to Protect the Key Exchange. For our example we are using ELVIS as the password. This will need to be set up on the other machine as well.

IP Filters and Creating a List In Windows 2000, filtering can be applied to different security policies on different computers. It is IP filters that will determine what actions to take. These actions are based upon the destination and protocol of individual IP packets.

Perform the following steps to set up the IP Filter List:

1. In the IP Filter List dialog box, click Add. An empty list of IP filters is displayed. Give your filter a name that is descriptive to you.

2. Make sure that the Use Add Wizard check box is selected and then click Add. This will start the IP Filter Wizard, shown in Figure 11-9.

FIGURE 11-8

Choosing the authentication method

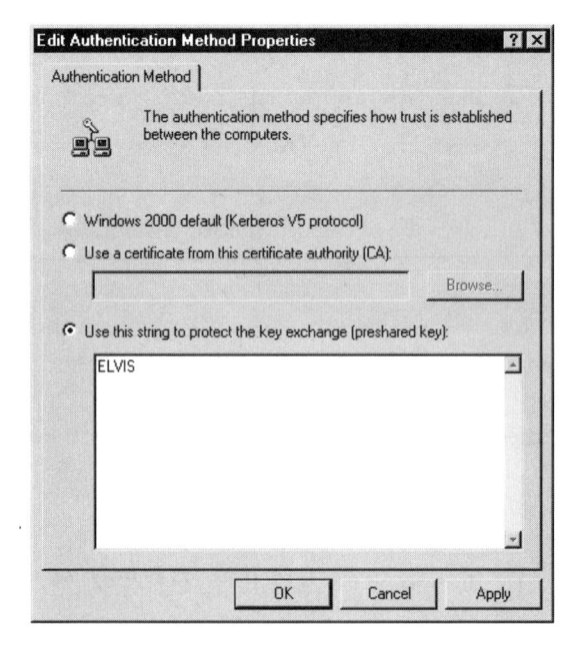

Design an IPSec Solution **577**

FIGURE 11-9

IThe IP Filter Wizard Welcome screen

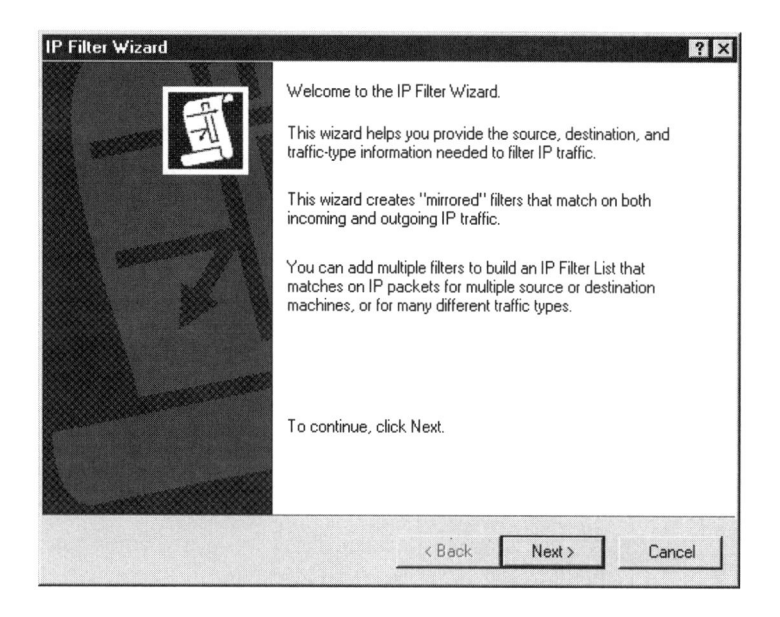

3. Click Next.
4. Accept My IP Address as the default source address, as shown in Figure 11-10. Click Next.

FIGURE 11-10

IP Traffic Source

578 Chapter 11: Designing a Security Solution for Access Between Networks

5. Select a specific IP address from the list, then type the workstation's IP address. Click Next.

6. Accept protocol type Any.

7. The next screen should have the Edit Properties check box cleared (which it is by default). Click Finish.

8. Click OK to leave the IP Filter List dialog box, shown in Figure 11-11, and return to the New Rule Wizard.

9. Select the radio button next to the new IP filter that you created, as shown in Figure 11-12.

10. Select Next.

Security Levels We have just finished configuring both the input and output filters for matching IP packets. Now we must configure the action that is to take

FIGURE 11-11

IP Filter List dialog box

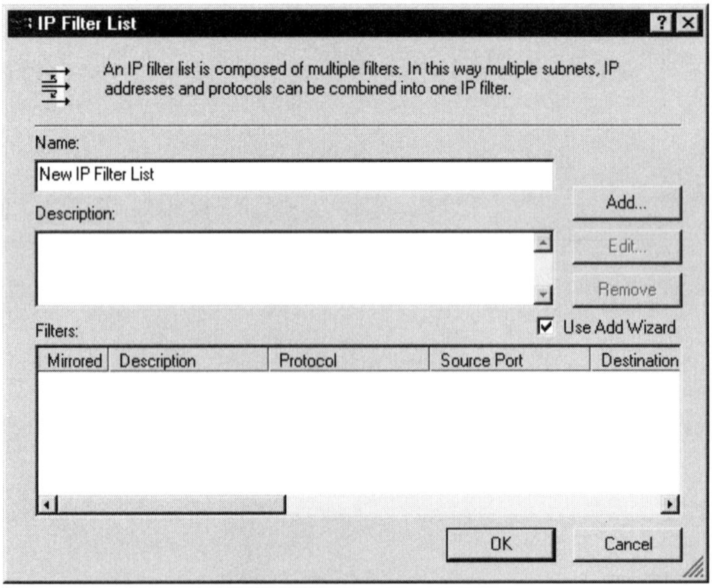

FIGURE 11-12

Choosing the filter you just created

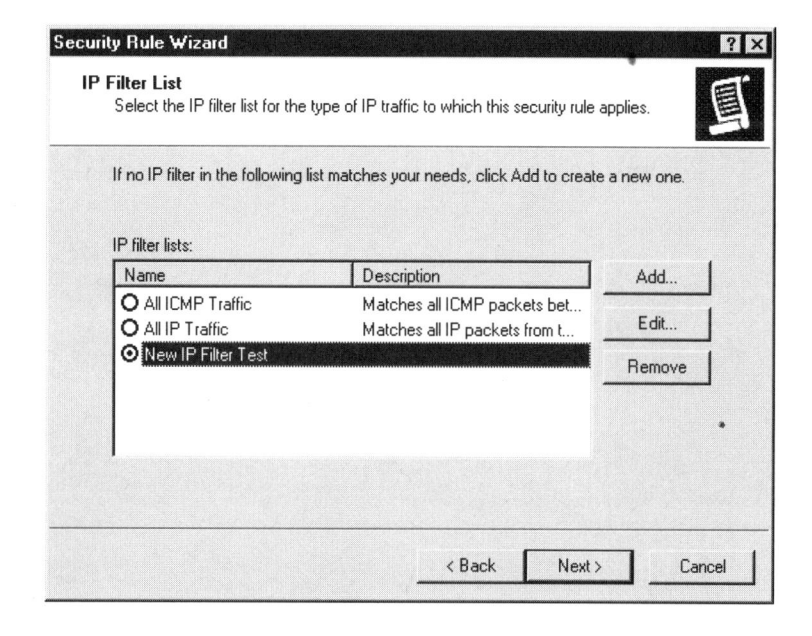

place for those packets. We have the choice of permitting, blocking, or securing the packets that match the filters. If we choose to use the action Permit, this will let the packets go in the clear, so to speak—in other words, not secured. Some situations in which we might want to do this are when we want to permit traffic types of DNS, Simple Network Management Protocol (SNMP), Simple Mail Transfer Protocol (SMTP), or even Internet Control Message Protocol (ICMP). We can also permit traffic to specific destinations: for example, DHCP servers, the default gateway, or other non-IPSec systems. We can also choose to use the setting Fall Back to Unsecured Communication. This allows us to revert to unsecured communication with a destination by going back to clear text if the destination does not reply to the IKE request.

Configuring the Filter Action Now we will configure the filter action, which is to be applied to the IP packets that meet our rules that we specified earlier.

FIGURE 11-13

Selecting the filter action for our rule

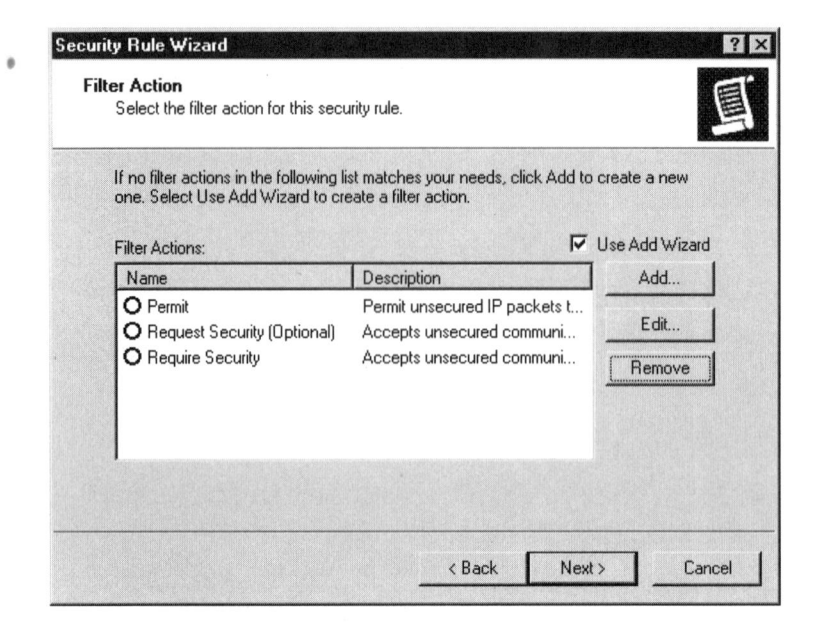

1. As shown in Figure 11-13, select the Use Add Wizard check box, then click Add.
2. In the next screen we will choose to proceed through the Wizard.
3. As shown in Figure 11-14, we must name this filter action. Choose a name that is descriptive to you.
4. Select Negotiate Security, shown in Figure 11-15, then click Next.

Design an IPSec Solution 581

FIGURE 11-14

Choosing a filter action name

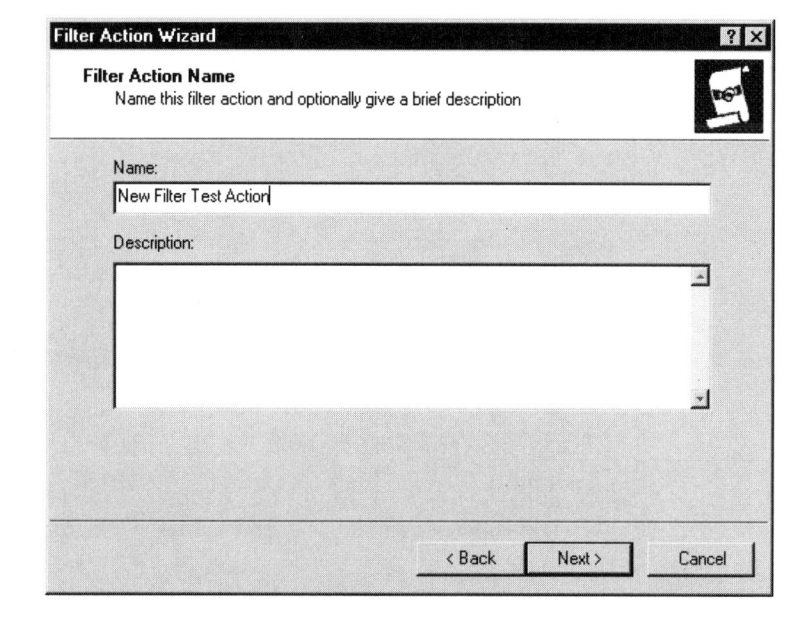

FIGURE 11-15

Selecting the filter action behavior

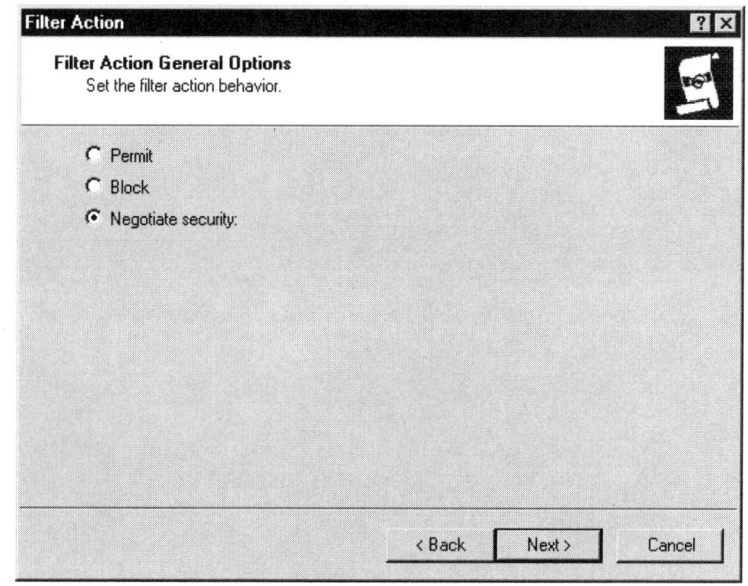

582 Chapter 11: Designing a Security Solution for Access Between Networks

5. Select Do Not Communicate with Computers That Do Not Support IPSec, as shown in Figure 11-16. Click Next.

6. On the list of security methods, choose whichever method you would like to test. For this exercise, we select High. Note that High corresponds to ESP, whereas Medium is equivalent to Authentication Header (AH).

7. After clicking Next, be sure that the Edit Properties box is cleared. After this, click Finish.

8. In the Filter Action dialog box, select the radio button next to the IP action filter that you just created. In Figure 11-17, you see how this looks for our scenario.

9. Click Next. Verify that the Edit Properties box is not selected, then click Finish.

10. On the Properties page that is now showing, click Close.

FIGURE 11-16

Choosing not to communicate with non-IPSec computers

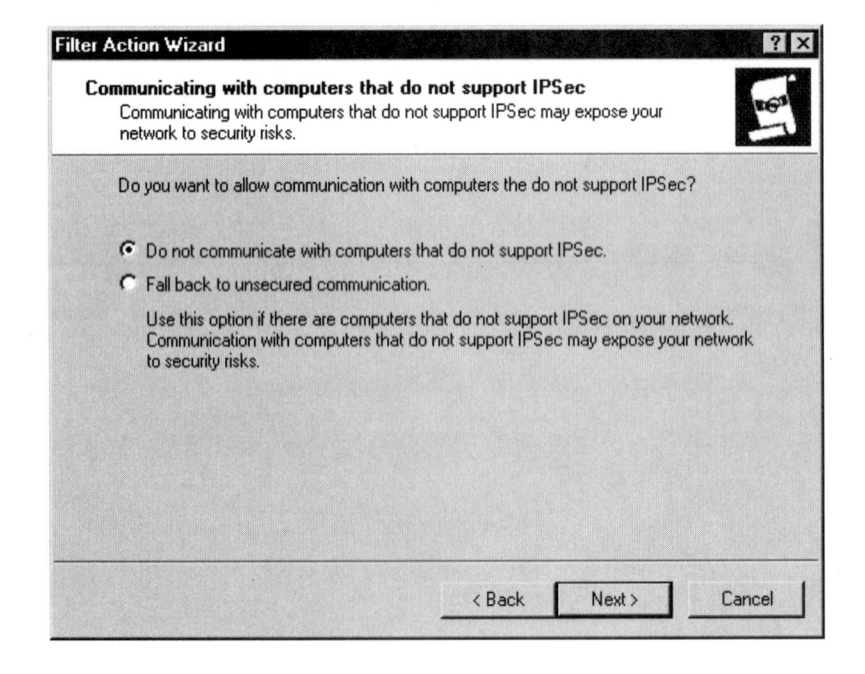

FIGURE 11-17

Choosing our newly created IP filter action

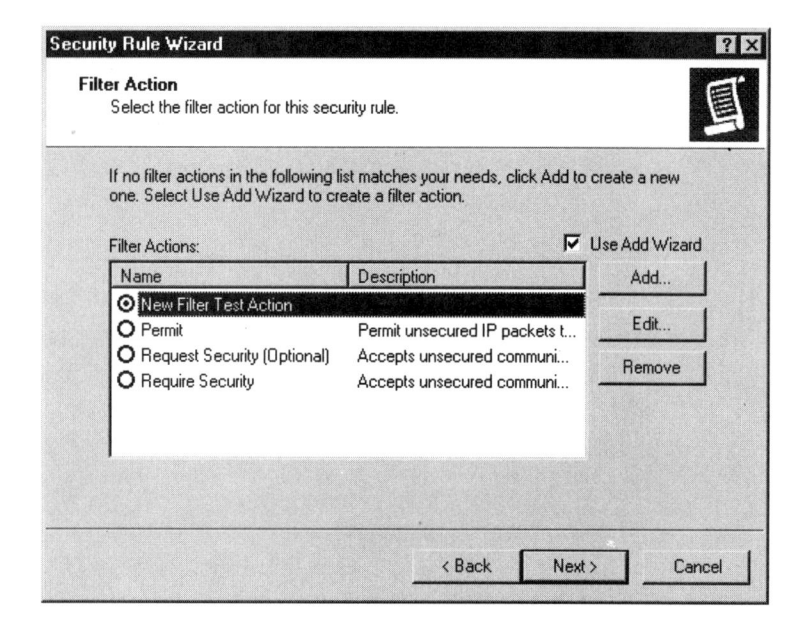

[Screenshot of Security Rule Wizard - Filter Action dialog showing filter actions list with "New Filter Test Action" selected, along with Permit, Request Security (Optional), and Require Security options]

We have now configured the filter action that is to be used during negotiations with our workstation and we have successfully configured an IPSec policy. Before testing our policy, we must do the same thing for our workstation or our test will fail.

Testing your IPSec Policy

It's important to always test your IPSec policy. To do so, perform the following steps:

1. In the left pane of the MMC console, select IP Security Policies on Local Machine. Note that in addition to the three built-in policies, the policy you just configured is listed in the right pane.
2. Right-click your policy, and then click Assign from the context menu. The status in the Policy Assigned column should change from No to Yes. Do this step on both machines before continuing.

FIGURE 11-19

IP Security Monitor

Policy Name	Security	Filter Name	Source Address	Dest. Address
{0874AA1C-7A54-4F96-AF...	ESP DES/CBC HMAC MD5	No Name	SPECIAL-K.CO...	BLUE

IPSEC Statistics
- Active Associations: 1
- Confidential Bytes Sent: 91,330
- Confidential Bytes Received: 294,772
- Authenticated Bytes Sent: 104,992
- Authenticated Bytes Received: 311,552
- Bad SPI Packets: 0
- Packets Not Decrypted: 0
- Packets Not Authenticated: 0
- Key Additions: 2

ISAKMP/Oakley Statistics
- Oakley Main Modes: 2
- Oakley Quick Modes: 2
- Soft Associations: 0
- Authentication Failures: 0

IP Security is enabled on this computer.

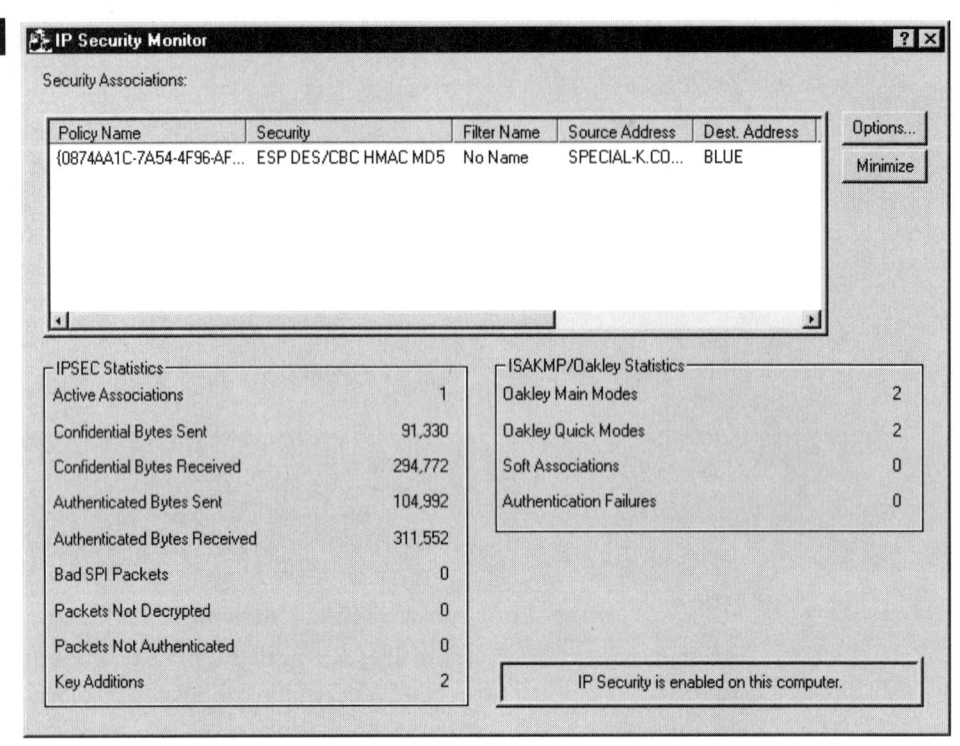

3. Open a command prompt window, and type **ping** *<workstation name>*. You should receive four Negotiating IP Security responses. Repeat the command, and you should receive four successful ping replies.

4. Restore the IP Security Monitor window (which you minimized earlier) that is shown in Figure 11-18. You should see details of the Security Association that is currently in use between your two computers, as well as statistics on the number of Authenticated and Confidential bytes transmitted among others. Minimize this window again.

5. In the left pane of the MMC console, select Computer Management | System Tools | Event Viewer | Security. In the security log, you should see event 541, which notes the establishment of an IPSec security association (SA), as shown in Figure 11-19.

6. Repeat Step 3 to unassign the Partner policy, and return both computers to their previous states. This time, when you right-click the policy, click Unassign.

IPSec Encryption Scheme

With IPSec, there are two choices of security service: Authentication Header (AH), and Encapsulating Security Payload (ESP). AH allows authentication of the sender of data, but it does not provide privacy. ESP supports both authentication of the sender and encryption of the data as well. The information that is associated with each of these services is inserted into the packet in a header that follows the IP packet header. IPSec can be used in two modes: *tunnel mode,* which puts an existing IP packet inside a new IP packet and is sent to a tunnel end point in the IPSec format; and *transport mode,* which secures an existing IP packet from source to destination.

exam
 ⓦatch
Remember that IPSec is used to maintain integrity and secrecy of data in transit on end-to-end systems and that the data can be accessed only by authenticated users.

FIGURE 11-19

Event 541 successful IKE

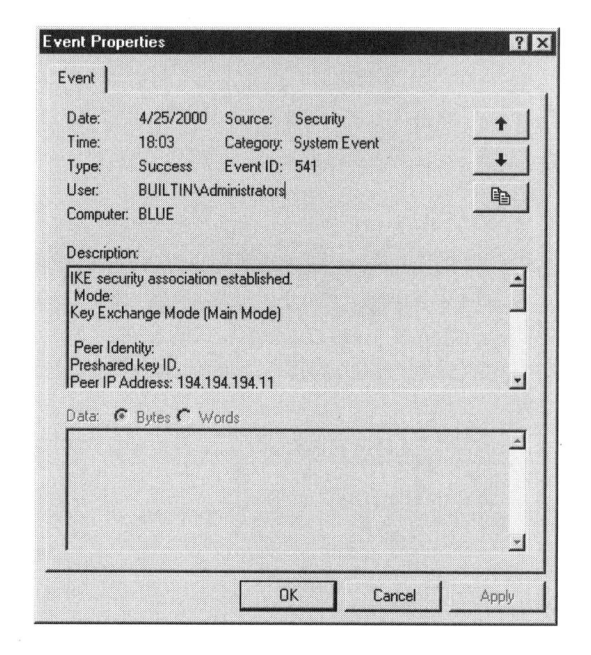

SCENARIO & SOLUTION

Over what UDP port does IKE take place?	UDP 500
Name three authentication methods supported by IKE.	Public/private key signature using certificates, Kerberos v5.0, and pre-shared passwords.
IP filters are responsible for what?	IP filters determine what actions to take when a certain criterion is met.
What utility can you use to look at statistics that pertain to IPSec?	IP Security Monitor (also known as IPSecmon)

IPSec Management Strategy

Typically, you want your IPSec management strategy to remain as simple as possible without compromising the security of the data that it is set to insure. How stringent you need to be will decide your strategy. You may want to set up your network so that all of the machines on the network require communications with IPSec, or you may want to enable IPSec communications when needed but revert to the default where protection is not applied.

Negotiation Policies

Negotiation policies will determine the security that an administrator wants to include for each type of communication scenario for the entire enterprise. In Windows 2000 this is handled by the service named ISAKMP/Oakley. An administrator can choose between services that include confidentiality or those that don't. The setting up of multiple security methods for each negotiation policy is supported. For example, if the first method is not accepted, the service will continue down the list until it finds one that is.

Security Policies

Every individual configuration of Windows IP Security attributes is called a *security policy*. These policies are built on associated negotiation policies and IP filters. An IP security policy can be assigned to the default domain policy, the default local policy, or even a customized policy that you, the administrator, create. Computers in the domain automatically pick up the properties of the default domain and default local policies, which include the IP security policy assigned to that domain policy. Figure 11-20 shows where you can find the IP security policy through the Group Policy console.

CERTIFICATION SUMMARY

In this chapter we discussed in detail the objectives we set at the beginning. We discussed providing secure access to public networks from a private network, where we set up a Windows 2000 server, configured it with RRAS, and set up NAT (network address translation). For the second objective (Provide External Users with Secure Access to Private Network Resources), we covered basic RAS (Remote Access Service) and VPN (virtual private network) setups. In Exercise 11-2, we implemented a Windows 2000 dial-up and VPN server. Our third objective was to provide secure access between private networks. We did this by covering such areas as IPSec, the use of PKIs (public key infrastructures), and created an enterprise root CA server in Exercise 11-3.

We then began on the design objectives of this chapter. The first design objective was to design windows 2000 security for remote access users. We covered this by

FIGURE 11-20

The IP Security Policies view in Group Policy

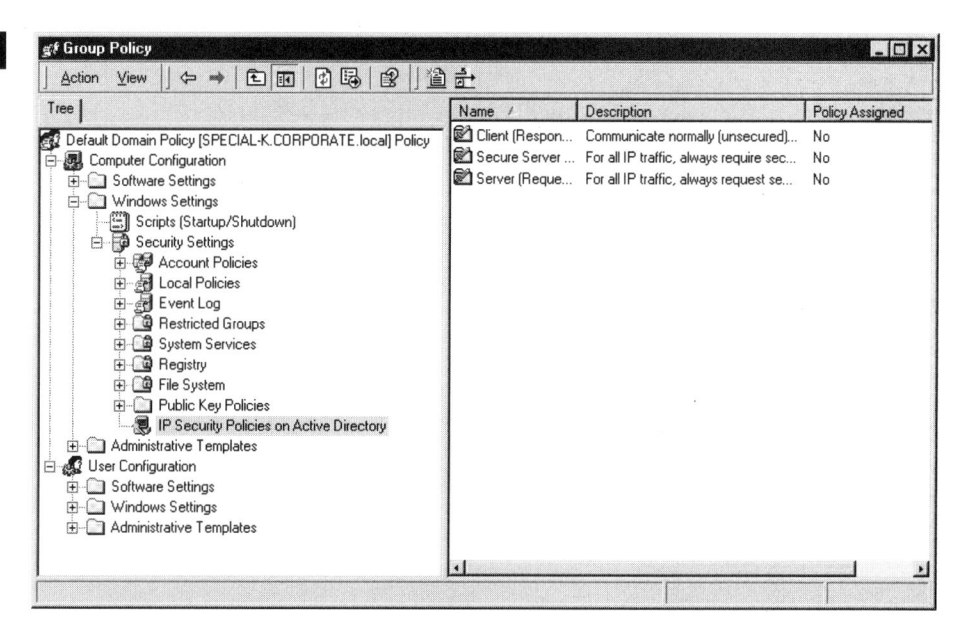

walking through the steps needed in setting up the ability to manage access by policy. We covered the options you had under both mixed mode and native mode. Next, we covered the material needed to design an SMB signing solution. We defined what SMB signing was, and we set up a situation where our servers would only respond to SMB signed packets and not acknowledge those that weren't. We also went over how to design an IPSec solution. Here we covered such areas as what an IKE (Internet Key Exchange) is. We also covered Security Associations and we implemented an IPSec policy. After covering this material in great detail, and working through each of the exercises and the lab at the end of the chapter, you will probably want to skim through the material at least twice before taking the exam. Good luck on the exam.

✓ TWO-MINUTE DRILL

Provide Secure Access to Public Networks from a Private Network

- ❏ **NAT**   Network Address Translation is a protocol used within Windows 2000.
- ❏ **ICS**   Internet Connection Sharing is a feature of Network and Dial-Up tools.

Provide External Users with Secure Access to Private Network Resources

- ❏ **VPN**   Virtual Private Network makes use of public networks such as the Internet to allow access to private internal network resources by encrypting the data. With VPNs, you can use modems, ISDN modems/routers, cable modems, or DSL connection devices.
- ❏ **RAS**   Remote Access Service has been part of Microsoft networking products since LAN Manager. It allows users to dial directly into the network and acts as a remote node.

Provide Secure Access Between Private Networks

- ❏ **CA Enterprise Root Server**   The first CA Server created in a hierarchy for a private network such as a domain or site.
- ❏ **PKI**   Is not one single product, but the culmination of many products in providing security on networks. Makes use of digital signatures.

Design Windows 2000 Security for Remote Access Users

- ❏ **EAP**   Extensible Authentication Protocol, an infrastructure that allows the addition of arbitrary authentication methods such as certificates, one-time passwords, smart cards, and token cards.
- ❏ **RADIUS**   Remote Authentication Dial-In User Service, allows the remote access user authentication, authorization, and accounting data to be maintained in a central location.

- ❑ **IAS** Internet Authentication Service, Microsoft's RADIUS implementation under Windows 2000.
- ❑ **L2TP** Layer-Two Tunneling Protocol encapsulates PPP frames to be sent over IP, X.25, Frame Relay, or ATM networks.
- ❑ **PPTP** Point-to-Point Tunneling Protocol can provide authenticated and encrypted communications between a client and a server, without requiring a PKI.
- ❑ **BAP** Bandwidth Allocation Protocol, a PPP control protocol that is used on a multiprocessing connection to dynamically add and remove links.
- ❑ **BACP** Bandwidth Allocation Control Protocol negotiates the election of a favored peer for a multiprocessing connection.

Design an SMB Signing Solution

- ❑ **SMB** Server Message Block, a protocol developed by Microsoft, Intel, and IBM that defines a series of commands used to pass information between network computers.
- ❑ **CIFS** Common Internet File System, a new name for the SMB protocol that was given by Microsoft.

Design an IPSec Solution

- ❑ **IPSec** IP Security, a protocol that provides authenticity, data integrity, privacy, and anti-replay capabilities.
- ❑ **Security Policy** Each individual configuration of Windows IP security attributes.
- ❑ **Negotiation Policies** Determine the security that an administrator wants to include for each type of communication scenario for the entire enterprise.

SELF TEST

The following questions will help you measure your understanding of the material presented in this chapter. Read all of the choices carefully, as there may be more than one correct answer. Choose all correct answers for each question.

Provide Secure Access to Public Networks from a Private Network

1. When using Windows 2000 Server as a gateway to the Internet, what must the system be configured as when running RRAS?

    A. Member Server

    B. Multi-homed system

    C. Domain Controller

    D. Certificate Authority (CA) Enterprise System

2. Network Address Translation is a _____ in Windows 2000.

    A. Feature

    B. Service

    C. Protocol

    D. Policy

Provide External Users with Secure Access to Private Network Resources

3. To constitute a Virtual Private Network (VPN) _____ and _____ must be implemented across the use of a public network.

    A. Tunneling and RADIUS

    B. Tunneling and data encryption

    C. RADIUS and data encryption

    D. Policies and Logon scripts

592 Chapter 11: Designing a Security Solution for Access Between Networks

4. As the corporate Windows 2000 administrator, you've been assigned the task of setting up your company's first ever VPN server. You have everything you need from your ISP. Now you have to configure it. What must you have in your server to allow it to be a VPN server?

   A. One modem connected to the internal network and a modem connected to the Internet

   B. One NIC connected to the internal network and another NIC connected to the Internet

   C. One modem connected to the internal network and a NIC connected to the Internet

   D. Straight fiber connected to your house

5. Before creating an Enterprise CA, which of the following does not need to exist:

   A. Windows 2000 DNS is installed (required by AD)

   B. Active Directory is installed

   C. The Enterprise Administrator privileges are set on the DNS, Active Directory, and the CA Server

   D. Guest account must be disabled

Provide Secure Access Between Private Networks

6. L2TP is actually a combined development of which two protocols?

   A. TCP/IP and IPX

   B. L2F and PPTP

   C. XNS and NetBEUI

   D. DLC and PPTP

7. Your CIO has addressed an issue about security with you. He says he is concerned about data being picked up off the wire. Although you have three other sites, none of your sites is connected to the Internet. What is the best way to provide the type of security that your CIO demands?

   A. Switch to a peer-to-peer network

   B. Install an Enterprise CA server and create a CA hierarchy throughout all three sites

   C. Make use of Ethernet switches

   D. Force all packets to use L2TP

8. Windows 2000 will allow administrators to manage remote access users via policies in which of the following mode(s)?

    A. Native Mode Only

    B. Enhanced Mode Only

    C. Mixed Mode Only

    D. Both Native and Mixed Mode

Design Windows 2000 Security for Remote Access Users

9. With Windows 2000 setup with a VPN, IPSec in _____ mode is used to secure the data.

    A. Transport mode

    B. Tunnel mode

    C. Enhanced mode

    D. Standard mode

10. You've set up your RRAS server to use NAT, while also configuring your remote clients to use L2TP/IPSec transport mode. You keep getting calls from users who say that they are unable to authenticate. Why?

    A. You forgot to set up the RAS policy for this.

    B. Because of incompatibilities between the Internet Key Exchange (IKE) protocol and NAT, it is not possible for remote clients to use L2TP/IPSec transport mode.

    C. No one has been granted dial-up access rights.

    D. Because OSPF is not configured and there is no policy for it.

11. You share administrator duties with another person who works a different shift than you. The next day you come in, you analyze each of the servers and notice that they are performing noticeably slower. What could be causing this?

    A. The Workstation service has been disabled from each server.

    B. All servers received RAM upgrades two weeks ago.

    C. SMB-signing has been enabled.

    D. A NetWare server is on the network.

Design an SMB-Signing Solution

12. What is one thing SMB-signing can protect against?

    A. DoS Attacks

    B. Man In the Middle attack

    C. Viruses

    D. PING

13. SMB-signing is supported by which operating system(s)?

    A. Windows 98

    B. Windows NT 4.0 service pack 3 or higher

    C. Windows 2000

    D. All of the above

14. What does a security association (SA) refer to?

    A. IKE (Internet Key Exchange)

    B. PKI (Public Key Infrastructure)

    C. IPSec (IP Security)

    D. Lockout policy in Active Directory

Design an IPSec Solution

15. IPSec is used to maintain _____ and security for data in transit on end-to-end systems. The data can be accessed only by _____.

    A. integrity, authenticated machines

    B. systems, passwords

    C. integrity, authenticated users

    D. confidentiality, the administrator

16. _____ policies will determine the security that an administrator wants to include for each type of communication scenario for the entire enterprise.

    A. Group

    B. Negotiation

    C. IKE

    D. TCP/IP

LAB QUESTION

Your corporate network is going through some big changes. Access to the Internet is currently being handled through a Windows NT 4.0 Server running RRAS. The system is quite old and needs replacing. Your company has begun its move to Windows 2000 and thus all new servers must be configured with this operating system. The Director of IT has informed the entire IT staff that all traffic on the network will be digitally signed and that a CA hierarchy must be created and that all measures should be taken to prevent the hashing of passwords on the internal network. You are asked to use a Windows 2000 Server as your router to the Internet and you must implement NAT. You have been assigned a static IP address by your ISP. It is 190.73.35.112, and your subnet mask is 255.255.255.0. Your intranet is made up of a single subnet, and you are currently using the address scheme 10.1.1.0, with the subnet mask set to 255.255.0.0. Your director also assigns you the task of setting up the company's first ever implementation of a VPN. You are given four capable servers do all of this. What are the steps you would follow to accomplish this procedure?

SELF TEST ANSWERS

Provide Secure Access to Public Networks from a Private Network

1. ☑ **B.** Multi-homed system. For the system to be a "gateway" it must have a dedicated connection to the Internet and a dedicated connection to the intranet. This is usually done by installing two NICs in the system. One pointing out (Internet), and one pointing in (intranet).
   ☒ **A** and **C** are incorrect because server role has nothing to do with whether a Windows 2000 Server can be a gateway. The issue is can it connect to both networks. An Internet gateway, though, can be either a member server or domain controller. **D** is incorrect because in the above question there is nothing that states that any packets have to be digitally signed.

2. ☑ **C.** NAT (Network Address Translation) is a protocol.
   ☒ **A** is incorrect because by definition NAT is a protocol; it can even be considered a Feature, but on ALL Microsoft exams, you will be asked to choose the best answer; in this case A is not. **B** is incorrect because NAT is not a service by itself; it is part of RRAS. **D** is incorrect because NAT is a protocol, so it cannot be a policy.

Provide External Users with Secure Access to Private Network Resources

3. ☑ **B.** Tunneling and data encryption. The use of BOTH tunneling across a public network and data encryption to access a private network.
   ☒ **A** and **C** are incorrect because RADIUS is an authentication method for users; it has nothing to do with encrypting data. **D** is incorrect because the use of or implementation of policies and logon scripts is not needed.

4. ☑ **B.** The NIC connected to the Internet is where the VPN clients will communicate to get access to resources within the corporate intranet. The NIC connected to the internal network is our communication channel to our resources. VPN clients are unaware of its specifications.
   ☒ **A** is incorrect because Windows 2000 Server does not support the use of two modems for the setting up of a VPN. **C** is incorrect because the interface to the intranet MUST be a NIC. **D** is incorrect because straight fiber would do nothing in setting up a VPN.

5. ☑ **D.** This is set by default on Windows 2000 Servers and has nothing to do with the setup process of an Enterprise CA.
   ☒ **A, B,** and **C** all must be in place to create the CA. DNS must be installed, so that Active Directory can be. Also Enterprise Administrator privileges must be set to allow for configuration.

Provide Secure Access Between Private Networks

6. ☑ **B.** With L2F originally coming from Cisco and PPTP coming mostly from Microsoft, the IETF requested a protocol capable of what both could do individually, hence the creation of L2TP.
☒ **A** and **C** are incorrect because these protocols are mainly used as transports at their respective levels. **D** is incorrect because DLC is a protocol that would be tunneled, not one that tunnels. Plus it is used to communicate on SNA type networks and many dedicated network print devices (such as Hewlett-Packard's JetDirect Cards).

7. ☑ **B.** With this major component of a PKI, you can force all traffic to be digitally signed, therefore making it more difficult to de-crypt.
☒ **A** is incorrect because it lacks the security your organization needs to ensure that all packets are valid. **C** is not the best answer although one could argue for the use of VLAN's (Virtual LAN's) and with each server on its own port, packets can still be falsified, which would leave a large security gap. **D** is not the correct answer because in Windows 2000 L2TP is a tunneling protocol; it does not guarantee the validity or authenticity of a packet.

8. ☑ **D.** Native mode by nature allows users to be managed solely with policies, whereas in Mixed mode users must individually be granted access rights for remote access; then administrators can manage users via policies.
☒ **A** is incorrect because with some tweaking, mixed mode can be made to support this also. **B** is incorrect because there is no enhanced mode. **C** is incorrect because Native Mode by nature allows the managing of remote access users via policies.

Design Windows 2000 Security for Remote Access Users

9. ☑ **A.** Windows 2000 uses IPSec transport mode for securing data.
☒ **B** is incorrect because IPSec Tunnel mode is *not* designed to be used for VPN's and, for that reason, it isn't able to secure the data. **C** is incorrect because there is no existing enhanced mode for Windows 2000. **D** is incorrect because there is no existing standard mode for Windows 2000.

10. ☑ **B.** Remember our exam watch on this exact issue? It is because L2TP/IPSec cannot be passed through NAT.
☒ **A** is incorrect because you have to enable RRAS to even set up NAT. So the service is on. **C** is not the best answer because we are running more into a technical incompatibility as opposed to a missed step in the setup procedure. **D** is incorrect because OSPF has nothing to do with clients getting authenticated on the network. It is a link-state routing protocol.

598 Chapter 11: Designing a Security Solution for Access Between Networks

11. ☑ C. Remember that if SMB-Signing is enabled it will cost approximately 10-15% processor utilization. This has no effect on the speed of the network, just extra CPU cycles.
☒ A is incorrect because disabling the Workstation service should only affect the Server in situations where an administrator is using a server as a client. In normal production mode, this is not the case as typically the SERVER service is primarily dominant in this situation. B is incorrect because adding RAM should increase performance but since this was already done two weeks prior, we know this has no bearing on our server performance issue. D is incorrect because a NetWare Server typically should have no influence on our Windows 2000 server. The only situation where this could be an issue is if we are using GSNW (Gateway Services for NetWare) and our clients on the network are going through our Windows 2000 Server to access NetWare services. Since this is NOT explicitly specified in the question, then this answer is incorrect.

Design an SMB-Signing Solution

12. ☑ B. SMB-signing supports mutual authentication, which closes this attack. It also supports message authentication, which prevents active message attacks. It provides this authentication by placing a digital security signature into each SMB, which is then verified by both the client and the server.
☒ A is incorrect because the reason behind using SMB-signing has nothing to do with not allowing denial of service attacks. It was originally designed to "verify" the authentication of SMB's. One could possibly argue that this would disable the use of DoS attacks, but in all Microsoft exams they will ask you for the "best" answer. In this situation it's Man in the Middle. C is incorrect because viruses do not infect SMBs (at least, not yet). D is incorrect because PING never makes use of SMBs.

13. ☑ D. SMB-signing is supported by Windows 98, NT4.0 (with service pack 3 or higher), and Windows 2000.

14. ☑ A. Security Association is the term Microsoft has given to its Internet Key Exchange.
☒ B is incorrect because a PKI (Public Key Infrastructure) encompasses implementations of security methodologies. C is incorrect because IPSec deals with the encrypting of the data inside a packet. D is incorrect because it deals with policies and not "negotiations" between systems.

Design an IPSec Solution

15. ☑ A. Remember that IPSec is used to maintain data integrity. IPSec applies to machines and not users. Users could use machines that are making use of IPSec and never know it.

☒ **B, C,** and **D** are incorrect, because, once again, IPSec is used for data integrity with encryption, and since access only applies to machines, the use of passwords is not needed in the same domain.

16. ☑ **B.** It is Negotiation policies that determine the security that an administrator wants to include.
☒ **A** is incorrect because it applies to Sites and OUs and not communications. **C** is incorrect because IKE (Internet Key Exchange) is a process, which Microsoft calls SA for public keys. **D** is incorrect because TCP/IP as a protocol does not influence security for communication scenarios.

LAB ANSWER

You may want to use the exercises within the chapter as points of reference in completing the tasks. Each will walk you step by step through the processes needed to complete the tasks.

1. Examine the diagram of your existing network configuration to the Internet, as shown in Figure 11-21.
2. Begin setting up and installing the first DC for Windows 2000; this machine will run all five FSMOs (described in Chapter 6; it will do this by default) and set up DNS.
3. Set up and install the new Enterprise CA Server.
4. Set up and install the first new RRAS server; set up the routing along with NAT.
5. Set up the last box to be a VPN server.
6. Enable SMB-signing.

FIGURE 11-21

Existing Network connection to the Internet

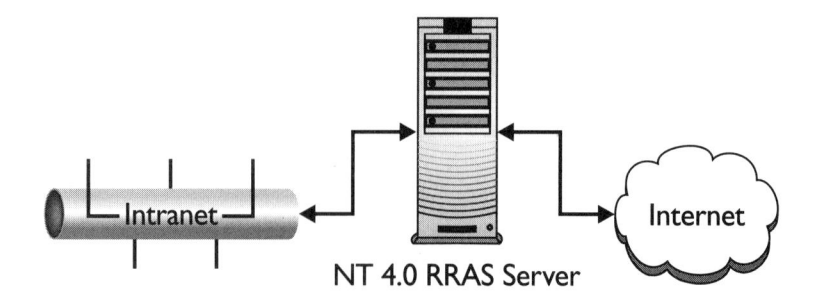

Intranet — NT 4.0 RRAS Server — Internet

A

About the CD

This CD-ROM contains the CertTrainer software. CertTrainer comes complete with ExamSim, Skill Assessment tests, CertCam movie clips, the e-book (electronic version of the book), and Drive Time. CertTrainer is easy to install on any Windows 98/NT/2000 computer and must be installed to access these features. You may, however, browse the e-book directly from the CD without installation.

Installing CertTrainer

If your computer CD-ROM drive is configured to autorun, the CD-ROM will automatically start up upon inserting the disc. From the opening screen you may either browse the e-book or install CertTrainer by pressing the Install Now button. This will begin the installation process and create a program group named "CertTrainer". To run CertTrainer use START | PROGRAMS | CERTTRAINER.

System Requirements

CertTrainer requires Windows 98 or higher and Internet Explorer 4.0 or above and 600MB of hard disk space for full installation.

CertTrainer

CertTrainer provides a complete review of each exam objective, organized by chapter. You should read each objective summary and make certain that you understand it before proceeding to the SkillAssessor. If you still need more practice on the concepts of any objective, use the In Depth button to link to the corresponding section from the Study Guide or use the CertCam button to view a short .AVI clip illustrating various exercises from within the chapter.

Once you have completed the review(s) and feel comfortable with the material, launch the SkillAssessor quiz to test your grasp of each objective. Once you complete the quiz, you will be presented with your score for that chapter.

ExamSim

As its name implies, ExamSim provides you with a simulation of the actual exam. The number of questions, the type of questions, and the time allowed are intended to be an accurate representation of the exam environment. You will see the following screen when you are ready to begin ExamSim:

When you launch ExamSim, a digital clock display will appear in the upper left-hand corner of your screen. The clock will continue to count down to zero unless you choose to end the exam before the time expires.

There are three types of questions on the exam:

- **Multiple Choice**   These questions have a single correct answer that you indicate by selecting the appropriate check box.
- **Multiple-Multiple Choice**   These questions require more than one correct answer. Indicate each correct answer by selecting the appropriate check boxes.
- **Simulations**   These questions simulate actual Windows 2000 menus and dialog boxes. After reading the question, you are required to select the appropriate settings to most accurately meet the objectives for that question.

Saving Scores as Cookies

Your ExamSim score is stored as a browser cookie. If you've configured your browser to accept cookies, your score will be stored in a file named "History". If your browser is not configured to accept cookies, you cannot permanently save your scores. If you delete this History cookie, the scores will be deleted permanently.

E-Book

The entire contents of the Study Guide are provided in HTML form, as shown in the following screen. Although the files are optimized for Internet Explorer, they can also be viewed with other browsers including Netscape.

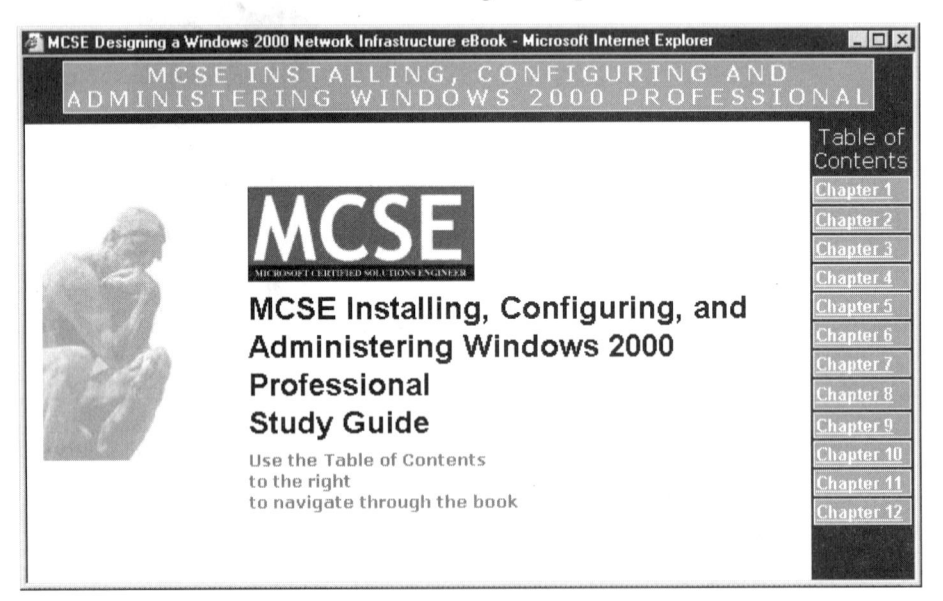

CertCam

CertCam .AVI clips provide detailed examples of key certification objectives. These clips walk you step-by-step through various system configurations and are narrated by Thomas Shinder, M.D., MCSE, MCT. You can access the clips directly from the CertCam table of contents (shown in the following screen) or through the CertTrainer objectives.

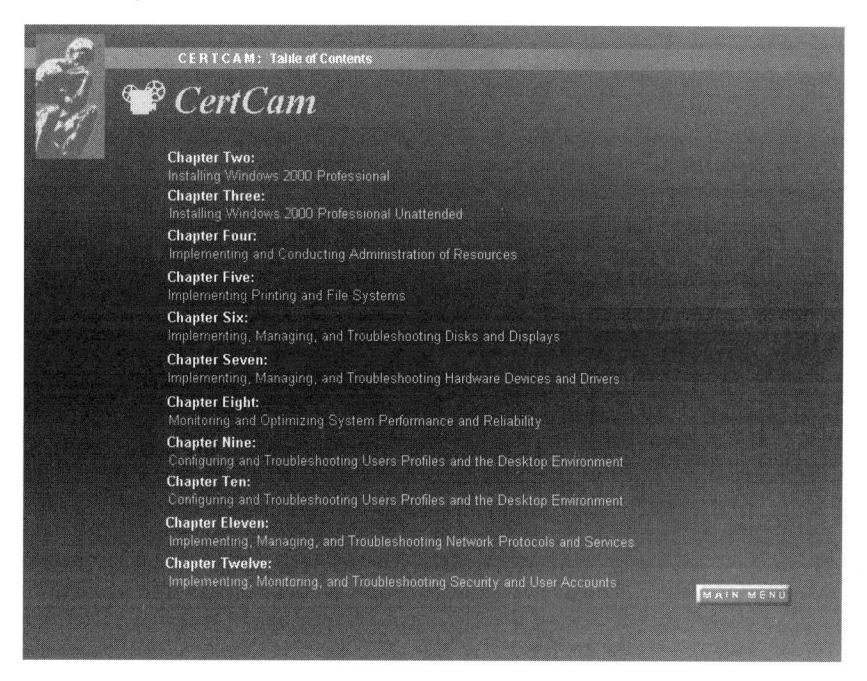

The CertCam .AVI clips are recorded and produced using TechSmith's Camtasia Producer. Since .AVI clips can be very large, ExamSim uses TechSmith's special AVI Codec to compress the clips. The file named **tsccvid.dll** is copied to your Windows\System folder when you install CertTrainer. If the .AVI clip runs with audio but no video, you may need to re-install the file from the CD-ROM. Browse to the "bin" folder, and run TSCC.EXE.

DriveTime

DriveTime audio tracks will automatically play when you insert the CD-ROM into a standard CD-ROM player, such as the one in your car or stereo. There is one track for each chapter. These tracks provide you with certification summaries for each chapter and are the perfect way to study while commuting.

Help

A help file is provided through a help button on the main CertTrainer screen in the lower right hand corner.

Upgrading

A button is provided on the main ExamSim screen for upgrades. This button will take you to www.syngress.com where you can download any available upgrades.

B

About the Web Site

At Access.Globalknowledge, the premier online information source for IT professionals (http://access.globalknowledge.com), you'll enter a Global Knowledge information portal designed to inform, educate, and update visitors on issues regarding IT and IT education.

Get *What* You Want *When* You Want It

At the Access.Globalknowledge site, you can:

- Choose personalized technology articles related to your interests. Access a news article, a review, or a tutorial, customized to what you want to see, regularly throughout the week.

- Continue your education, in between Global courses, by taking advantage of chat sessions with other users or instructors. Get the tips, tricks, and advice that you need today!

- Make your point in the Access.Globalknowledge community by participating in threaded discussion groups related to technologies and certification.

- Get instant course information at your fingertips. Customized course calendars show you the courses you want, and when and where you want them.

- Obtain the resources you need with online tools, trivia, skills assessment, and more!

All this and more are available now on the Web at http://access.globalknowledge.com. Visit today!

MCSE
MICROSOFT CERTIFIED SYSTEMS ENGINEER

Glossary

Access Control Entry (ACE) An Access Control List (ACL) is a list of who has permission to an object and what that permission is. The granular permission in ACL is called an ACE.

Access Control List (ACL) Servers use ACLs to control access to resources on the network, whether they reside on a Windows NT server or a Windows 2000 server. These ACLs are contained on the object, and that object may or may not be in Active Directory. An example of an object not contained in Active Directory is a file sitting in a directory on a file server. ACLs are attached to that file that state who can access the file and what they can do with it. An ACL is a list of who has permission to an object and what that permission is.

Account Lockout Policy The Account Lockout Policy dictates the behavior for locking and unlocking user accounts.

ACE *See* Access Control Entry.

ACL *See* Access Control List.

ACPI *See* Advanced Configuration and Power Interface.

Active Directory The Active Directory is implemented on Windows 2000 domain controllers, and the directory can be accessed from Windows 2000 Professional as an Active Directory client. The Active Directory arranges objects—including computer information, user and group information, shared folders, printers, and other resources—in a hierarchical structure, in which domains can be joined into trees (groups of domains that share a contiguous namespace). Trees can be joined into forests (groups of domain trees that share a common schema, configuration, and global catalog).

Active Directory Service This service provides the means for locating the Remote Installation Services (RIS) servers and the client computers on the network. The RIS server must have access to the Active Directory.

Active Directory Services Interface (ADSI) This is a set of Component Object Model (COM) interfaces that enables Windows 9*x*, Windows NT, and Windows 2000 applications to access Active Directory and other directory services.

Add Printer Wizard　All clients running a version of the Windows operating system (Windows 2000, Windows NT, Windows 98, and Windows 95) can use the Add Printer Wizard to create a printer entry on the client. This Add Printer Wizard can create and share a printer on a print server. The Windows 2000 version of the Add Printer Wizard has more options than the wizard in other versions of Windows, but many of the same methods can be used to get the printer set up on the client.

Administration　The word *administer* is generally used as a synonym for *manage,* which in turn means to exert control. One of the many enhancements to Windows 2000—both the Professional and Server incarnations—is the ability Microsoft has given administrators to apply the degree of control desired, in a flexible and granular manner.

ADSI　*See* Active Directory Services Interface.

Advanced Configuration and Power Interface (ACPI)　ACPI combines Plug and Play (PnP) capability with Power Management, and places these functions under complete control of the operating system.

Advanced Power Management (APM)　An Intel/Microsoft application programming interface (API) allowing programs to indicate their requirements for power to regulate the speed of components.

Alerts　Alerts allow some action to be performed when a performance counter reaches a particular threshold. A common action is to log the event in the application event log. You can also send a network message to a specified computer. You can have the alert start a performance log to start logging when the alert occurs. And finally, you can configure the alert to start a program.

Analysis　Analysis is the process of comparison, contrast, diagnosis, diagramming, discrimination, and/or drawing conclusions.

Analysis phase　During the analysis stage, you put together the information gathered during phase one and draw conclusions based on the totality of the data. In the analysis phase, you determine what the problems are.

Answer file   An answer file is a file containing the information you would normally have to key in during the setup process. Answer files help automate the installation process as all the queries presented to you during installation are answered by the answer files. With careful planning, you can prepare answers that eliminate the possibility of incorrect answers typed in by the person performing the installation, thus reducing the chances of setup failure. You can use the Setup Manager wizard to create a customized answer file. This technique minimizes the chances of committing syntax-related errors while manually creating or editing the sample answer files.

API   *See* Application Programming Interface.

APIPA   *See* Automatic Private Internet Protocol Addressing.

APM   *See* Advanced Power Management.

AppleTalk   The AppleTalk protocol suite was developed by Apple Computer for use in its Macintosh line of personal computers. AppleTalk is a local area networking system that was developed by Apple Computer Inc. AppleTalk networks can run over a variety of networks that include Ethernet, FDDI, and Token Ring as well as Apple's proprietary media system LocalTalk. Macintosh computers are very popular in the education and art industries, so familiarity with the way they communicate using their native protocol is very useful.

AppleTalk printing device   Another type of remote printer is the AppleTalk printing device. Like a Transmission Control Protocol/Internet Protocol (TCP/IP) printer, an AppleTalk printer can be connected directly to an AppleTalk network or shared across the network through an AppleShare print server. Like the TCP/IP printers, a large number of modern, high-capacity PostScript printers can be configured to communicate with an AppleTalk network as well as a TCP/IP network. In fact, many Hewlett-Packard LaserJet printers have JetDirect cards that will speak TCP/IP and AppleTalk at the same time.

Application   A program designed to perform a specific function directly for the user or for another application program. An application would be, for example, word processors, database programs, graphics/drawing programs, Web browsers, e-mail programs.

Application Programming Interface (API) A set of routines used by a program to request and carry out lower level services performed by the computer's operating system or other component, which provides the program with a way to communicate with the system.

Application Service Provider (ASP) ASPs are companies that manage applications and provide organizations with application hosting services. Analysts expect the ASP market will be a six billion-dollar industry by the year 2001. The application-hosting model offers organizations the option of outsourcing application support and maintenance.

ASP *See* Application Service Provider.

Assessment and Evaluation Phase Often forgotten, the last and very important phase is the assessment and evaluation phase. In this phase, you test the security plan you've set in place and determine whether you have accomplished your goals, and whether the cost (both monetary and otherwise) of the higher security level is justified by the benefits to the company.

Asymmetric Encryption Two different but corresponding keys (called a key pair) are used; one—the public key—is used to encrypt the data and is not kept secret but is published to all wishing to send an encrypted message to the owner. The second key—the private key—is known only by the owner and is used to decrypt data that was encrypted with the corresponding public key. Also called public key encryption.

Auditing Windows 2000 gives the ability to audit security-related events, track access to objects and use of user rights, and detect attempted and successful access (authorized and unauthorized) to the network. Auditing is not enabled by default, but once enabled, a security log is generated that provides information in regard to specific activities performed on the computer.

Authentication The process of validating the identity of a user or a device such as a server or router. There are a number of different methods of authenticating identity, including Kerberos, NTLM, RADIUS, and others.

Authentication Header (AH) An AH allows authentication of the sender of data, but it does not provide privacy.

Automatic Private Internet Protocol Addressing (APIPA) APIPA, or Automatic Client Configuration, is a new feature initially available in Windows 98. The feature has been extended to Windows 2000 and allows Dynamic Host Configuration Protocol (DHCP) client computers to self-configure their IP addressing information in the event a DHCP server is not available when the computer issues a DHCPDISCOVER message. It also allows self-configuration when it senses that it has been moved from a previous network via Windows 2000 media sensing capabilities.

Backup Domain Controller (BDC) A backup file or copy of the Primary Domain Controller (PDC). Periodically, the BDC is synchronized with the PDC.

Backup Logs Windows Backup generates a backup log file for every backup job. These files are the best place to review the backup process in case some problem is encountered by the program. The backup log is a text file that records all the events during the backup process.

BACP *See* Bandwidth Allocation Control Protocol.

Bandwidth Allocation Control Protocol (BACP) Bandwidth Allocation Control Protocol (BACP) is a Point-to-Point Protocol (PPP) network control protocol that negotiates the election of a favored peer for a multiprocessing connection. If both ends of the connection issue a connection request at the same time, then the connection request of the favored peer is performed.

Bandwidth Allocation Protocol (BAP) Bandwidth Allocation Protocol (BAP) is a PPP control protocol that is used on a multiprocessing connection to dynamically add and remove links.

BAP *See* Bandwidth Allocation Protocol.

Basic Encryption Uses a 40-bit Microsoft Point-to-Point Encryption (MPPE) key. This is a good option for servers working as Virtual Private Network (VPN) servers. The Point-to-Point Tunneling Protocol (PPTP) protocol is also available at this level. Security is bumped up to a 56-bit key if the Layer Two Tunneling Protocol (L2TP) protocol is used.

Basic Input/Output System (BIOS)   A set of programs encoded in ROM on IBM PC-compatible computers programs handle startup operations such as Power On Self Test (POST) and low-level control for hardware such as disk drives, keyboards, etc.

BDC   *See* Backup Domain Controller.

BIOS   *See* Basic Input/Output System.

Boot   The process of loading an operating system into the computer's memory (RAM) so those applications can be run on it.

Boot ROM   A boot ROM is a chip on the network adapter that helps the computer boot from the network. Such a computer need not have a previously installed operating system. The BIOS of the computer that has a PXE-based boot ROM must be configured to boot from the network. Windows 2000 Server RIS supports PXE ROM versions 99 or later.

Bottleneck   A bottleneck in computer terms is also a component of the system as a whole that restricts the system from operating at its peak. When a bottleneck occurs, the component that is a bottleneck will have a high rate of usage and other components will have a low rate of usage. A lack of memory is a common cause of bottleneck when your computer doesn't have enough memory for the applications and services that are running.

Branch Office Model   The branch office model is one in which there is a primary office or headquarters and multiple small branch offices that are distributed across a region. The main difference between this and a regional model is that the connectivity that is employed is typically on-demand LAN connectivity. Each site has a LAN where the primary connectivity with the main office is accomplished through a modem, DSL, or cable modem connection to an ISP utilizing either PPTP or L2TP to create a secure VPN connection.

Business Model   A business model refers to the ways in which a company conducts its business.

CA   *See* Certificate Authority.

CAL   *See* Client Access License.

CAPI   *See* CryptoAPI.

Centralized Model   This model consolidates administrative control of group policies. A single team of administrators is responsible for managing all Group Policy Objects (GPOs) no matter where they are. This is usually applied by giving all the top-level Organizational Unit (OU) administrators full control to all GPOs no matter where they are located. They give each second-level OU administrator Read permission only to each GPO. You can also decentralize other resources or keep all resources centralized, depending on the environment.

Centralized Organization   A centralized organization gives very little autonomy to units within the organization. Most decisions are made at the corporate offices, and units are expected to abide by those decisions. The military is a good example of a centralized organization. Centralized organizations are often said to be command-and-control style organizations.

Certificate   A message that has a digital signature that is associated with the private key of a trusted third party, and confirms that a particular public key belongs to the party (user or device) that claims to own it.

Certificate Authority (CA)   An authority/organization that produces digital certificates with its available public key. A Certificate Authority (CA) is a public key certificate issuer (for example, Verisign). To use a public key certificate, you must trust the issuer (CA). This means that you have faith in the CA's authentication policies. The CA is used for doing things such as authorizing certification authenticity, revoking expired certificates, and responding to certification requests. Windows 2000 offers an alternative to a third-party CA. You can become a CA within your own Intranet. Thus you can manage your own certificates rather than relying on a third-party Certification Authority.

Certificate Service   Provides security and authentication support, including secure e-mail, Web-based authentication, and smart card authentication.

Challenge Handshake Authentication Protocol (CHAP) A protocol used for authentication over a Point-to-Point Protocol (PPP) connection. The Challenge Handshake Authentication Protocol verifies the identity of the peer, using a three-way handshake. The authenticator sends a challenge message to the peer. The peer returns the user name and an MD5 hash of the challenge, the session ID, and the client's password. The authenticator then checks this response, and if the values match, the authentication is acknowledged; if not, the connection is ended. CHAP provides protection against playback attack because the challenge value changes with every message. Because the password is never sent unencrypted over the network or link, it is considered very difficult to crack.

Change Permission This permission allows users the ability to change permissions on files and folders without giving them the Full Control permission. You can also use this permission to give a user or group access to modify permissions on file or folder objects without giving them the ability to have complete control over the object.

Child Domains Domains connected to the root on the tree are referred to as child domains.

Cipher An algorithm used to encrypt text to make it unreadable to unauthorized persons.

Cipher Command The cipher command is another way to encrypt and decrypt data. You can use it from the command line and it has many switches, so that you can define exactly what you want to have done. The Cipher.exe command syntax is simply CIPHER, followed by the switches that you would like to use, followed by the path and directory/file name. The most common switches are the /E switch (encrypts the specified directories) and the /D switch (decrypts the specified directories). You can also use wildcards with the cipher command.

CIW *See* Client Installation Wizard.

Client Access License (CAL) The CAL allows clients to access the Windows 2000's network services, shared folders, and printers. There are two types of CAL modes: Per Seat and Per Server. It is important to understand the difference between the two modes: Per Seat and Per Server. When you use the Per Seat mode, each computer that accesses the server must have a CAL. The Per Server mode requires a CAL for each connection to the server. This is a subtle but significant difference. In addition, the CAL allows clients to access the Windows 2000 Server's network services, shared folders, and printers. The licensing modes are the same as under Windows NT 4.0.

Client Installation Wizard (CIW) When a client computer boots using either the Remote Boot Disk or the PXE-based Boot ROM, it tries to establish a connection to the Remote Installation Services (RIS) server. If the RIS server is pre-configured to service the RIS clients, it helps the client get an Internet Protocol (IP) address from the Dynamic Host Configuration Protocol (DHCP) service. The CIW is then downloaded from the RIS server. This wizard has four installation options. The options that are presented to the user depend on the group policy set in the Active Directory. A user may get all four options, or may not get any of the options starting an automatic setup.

Cloning *See* Disk Imaging/Cloning.

Comprehension The process of distinguishing between situations, discussing, estimation, explaining, indicating, paraphrasing, and giving examples.

Computer Account A computer account is an account that is created by a domain administrator and uniquely identifies the computer on the domain. A newly created account is used so that a computer may be brought into a Windows 2000 Domain.

Configuration Configuration of an operating system involves specifying settings that will govern how the system behaves.

Container Object Container objects can contain other objects. A special type of container object you can create in the Active Directory is the Organizational Unit (OU).

Containers Containers are used to describe any group of related items, whether they are objects, containers, domains, or an entire network.

Control Panel Accessibility Options These are options which include StickyKeys, FilterKeys, ToggleKeys, SoundSentry, ShowSounds, High Contrast, MouseKeys, and SerialKeys.

Cooperative Multitasking   An environment in which an application relinquishes its use of the computer's Central Processing Unit (CPU) so that another application can use the CPU.

Copy Backup   This type of backup simply copies the selected files. It neither looks for any markers set on the files nor does it clear them. The Copy backup does not affect the other Incremental or Differential backup jobs and can be performed along with the other types of backup jobs.

CryptoAPI (CAPI)   CryptoAPI (CAPI) architecture is a collection of tasks that permit applications to digitally sign or encrypt data while providing security for the user's private key data.

Cryptography   The study of creating and deciphering encoded or encrypted messages.

Daily Backup   This type of backup does not use any markers to back up selected files and folders. The files that have changed during the day are backed up every day at a specified time. This backup will not affect other backup schedules.

Data Backup   A backup and disaster protection plan is an essential part of a network administrator's duties. Windows 2000 provides a built-in Backup utility used to back up data to tape or file, or to create an Emergency Repair Disk (ERD). An ERD can be used to repair a computer with damaged system files.

Data Compression   Windows 2000 offers the capability of compressing data on a file-level basis, so long as the files and folders are located on an NT File System (NTFS) formatted partition or volume. Compression saves disk space; however, NTFS compression cannot be used in conjunction with file encryption.

Data Confidentiality   The ability to encrypt data before it is transferred over the network so that it cannot be read by someone eavesdropping or "tapping" the network.

Data Encryption Standard (DES)   A method of cryptography that uses a secret (private) key, originated by IBM and later adopted by the U.S. government.

Data Link Control (DLC)   DLC is a non-routable protocol used for connecting to IBM mainframes and some network-connected laser printers.

DC   *See* Domain Controller.

Debugging Mode   This is the most advanced startup option of all. To use this option you will need to connect another computer to the problematic computer through a serial cable. With proper configuration, the debug information is sent to the second computer.

Decentralized Model   This model is appropriate for companies that rely on delegated levels of administration. They decentralize the management of Group Policy Objects (GPOs), which distributes the workload to a number of domains. To apply this model, simply give all Organizational Unit (OU) administrators full control of their respective GPOs.

Decentralized Organization   In these organizations, units within the company have most of the decision-making authority. The parent company may exist only to provide common infrastructure needs for the units. Companies are often organized in this way to improve both their flexibility and their response to changing market conditions. Holding companies and cartels like OPEC are good examples of decentralized organizations.

Dedicated Print Server   A dedicated print server is a Windows 2000 server whose only role is to provide printing services. The server does not provide directory space for users other than storage for spooled print jobs. It does not provide authentication services, does not host database services, does not act as a Domain Name System (DNS) server, and so on. A dedicated print server can host several hundred printers and print queues, however. Though it may not be obvious, the printing process does have an impact on the performance of the server providing the printing services. An environment with a large number of printers or print jobs should strongly consider using at least one dedicated print server.

Defragmentation   The task of finding fragmented files and moving them into contiguous space is called defragmentation.

Denial of Service Attacks   The server is flooded with numerous requests that use all the bandwidth or resources so that the server cannot communicate.

Deny Permissions   Unlike the Allow permission, the Deny permission overrides all other permissions set for a file or folder. If a user is a member of one group with a Deny Write permission for a folder and is a member of another group with an Allow Full Control permission, the user will be unable to perform any of the Write permission tasks allows because it has been denied. The Deny permission should be used with extreme caution, as it can actually lock out all users, even administrators, from a file or folder. The proper way to remove a permission from a user or group on a file or folder is to uncheck the Allow permission for that user or group, not to check the Deny permission.

DES   *See* Data Encryption Standard.

Design Phase   The design phase is where you put forth a solution or solutions to the problems identified in phase two. How can you best address the issues within the parameters of your organization's budget, philosophy, and priorities? There may be more than one possible solution, and you will need to assess the pros and cons of each and decide on a plan of action. It is a good idea to also have in place a contingency plan if Plan A does not work.

Dfs   *See* Distributed File System.

DHCP   *See* Dynamic Host Configuration Protocol.

Differential Backup   The differential backup checks and performs a backup of only those files that are marked. It does not clear the markers after the backup, which means that any consecutive differential backups will back up the marked files again. When you need to restore from a differential backup, you will need the most current full backup and the differential backup performed after that.

Digest Authentication (DA)   DA prompts a user of a browser for an ID and a password. The ID and password are protected in transit from the server to the browser by a hash—created from the user ID and password and coupled with the server's public ID. DA can only be used on servers running Windows 2000; earlier versions of Windows or other operating systems do not have DA integration, so it cannot be used.

Digital Signatures These are message digests that are attached to a document, and used to verify the identity of the sender and the fact that the data in the document has not been tampered with.

Digital Subscriber Line (DSL) There are many variants of digital subscriber line (xDSL). All versions utilize the existing copper loop between a home and the local telco's Central Office (CO). Doing so allows them to be deployed rapidly and inexpensively. However, all DSL variants suffer from attenuation, and speeds drop as the loop length increases. Asymmetrical DSL (ADSL) and Symmetrical DSL (SDSL) may be deployed only within 17,500 feet of a CO, and Integrated Services Digital Network emulation over DSL (IDSL) will work only up to 30,500 feet. All DSL variants use Asynchronous Transfer Mode (ATM) as the data-link layer.

Direct Memory Access (DMA) DMA is a microprocessor capable of transferring data between memory units without the aid of the Central Processing Unit (CPU). Occasionally, built-in circuitry can do this same function.

Directory A directory is a database that contains information about objects and their attributes.

Directory Service The directory service is the component that organizes the objects into a logical and accessible structure, and provides for a means of searching and locating objects within the directory. The directory service includes the entire directory and the method of storing it on the network.

Directory Services Restore Mode This startup mode is available on Windows 2000 Server domain controller computers only. This mode can be used to restore the SYSVOL directory and Active Directory on the domain controller.

Discover A Dynamic Host Configuration Protocol (DHCP) client begins the lease process with a DHCPDISCOVER message. The client broadcasts this message after loading a minimal Transmission Control Protocol/Internet Protocol (TCP/IP) environment. The client does not know the address of the DHCP server, so it sends the message using a TCP/IP broadcast, with 0.0.0.0 as the source address and 255.255.255.255 as the destination address. The DHCPDISCOVER message contains the client's network hardware address, its computer name, a list of DHCP options the client supports, and a message ID that will be used in all messages between the client and server to identify the particular request.

Disk Compression   Allows you to compress folders, subfolders, and files to increase the amount of file storage, but it slows down access to the files.

Disk Defragmenter   Disk Defragmenter can analyze your volumes and make a recommendation as to whether or not you should defragment it. It will also give you a graphical display showing you the fragmented files, contiguous files, system files and free space. Disk Defragmenter does not always completely defragment free space; instead, it often moves it into just a few contiguous areas of the disk, which will still improve performance. Making the free space one contiguous space would have little added benefit.

Disk Imaging/Cloning   The deployment of a new operating system is one of the most challenging and time-consuming tasks that a network administrator has to perform. The disk duplication methods are particularly useful when you need to deploy Windows 2000 Professional on a large number of computers. This is also known as disk imaging or cloning. These tools make the rollout fast and easy.

Disk Quota   Windows 2000 comes with a disk quota feature that allows you to control users' disk consumption on a per user/per partition basis. To begin setting disk quotas for your users, right-click any partition in either Windows Explorer or the My Computer object. Click Properties and then click the Quota tab. Also, a disk quota allows you to limit the amount of disk space used by each user.

Distributed File System (Dfs)   The Windows 2000 Distributed File System provides you a method to centralize the organization of the shared resources on your network. In the past, shared resources were most often accessed via the Network Neighborhood applet, and users would have to wade through a number of domains and servers in order to access the shared folder or printer that they sought. Network users also had to remember where the obscure bit of information was stored, including both a cryptic server name and share name. The Distributed File System (Dfs) allows you to simplify the organization of your network resources by placing them in central shares accessed via a single server. Also, the Dfs allows you to create a central share point for shared resources located through the organization on a number of different servers.

Distribution Server This is a server on which the Windows 2000 installation files reside. When you install the operating system over the network, the client machine does not need a CD-ROM drive. The first requirement for network installation is a distribution server that contains the installation files. The distribution server can be any computer on the network to which the clients have access.

DLC *See* Data Link Control.

DMA *See* Direct Memory Access.

DNS *See* Domain Name System.

Domain A collection of connected areas. Routing domains provide full connectivity to all end systems within them. Also, a domain is a collection of accounts and network resources that are grouped together using a single domain name and security boundary. Domains harbor all objects on a network, where objects are defined as users, computers, printers, and anything else that can attach to the network. Windows 2000 networks can be based on one domain or several.

Domain Controller (DC) Domain controllers validate logons, participate in replication of logon scripts and policies, and synchronize the user account database. This means that domain controllers have an extra amount of work to perform. Since the Terminal Server already requires such heavy resources, it is not a good idea to burden a Terminal Server with the extra work of being a domain controller. Also, all user accounts, permissions, and other network details are all stored in a centralized database on the domain controllers.

Domain Local Groups Domain Local Groups are used for granting access rights to resources such as file systems or printers that are located on any computer in the domain where common access permissions are required. The advantage of Domain Local Groups being used to protect resources in that a member of the Domain Local Group can come from both inside the same domain and from outside as well.

Domain Name System (DNS)   Because the actual unique Internet Protocol (IP) address of a web server is in the form of a number difficult for humans to work with, text labels separated by dots (domain names) are used instead. DNS is responsible for mapping these domain names to the actual Internet Protocol (IP) numbers in a process called resolution. Sometimes called a Domain Name Server.

Domain Naming Master   This is the domain controller that oversees the addition or removal of domains within the forest. Like the schema master, this is a forest-wide role.

Domain Restructure   Domain restructure, or domain consolidation, is the method of changing the structure of your domains. Restructuring your domains can allow you to take advantage of the new features of Windows 2000, such as greater scalability. Windows 2000 does not have the same limitation as the Security Accounts Manager (SAM) account database in Windows NT. Without this limitation, you can merge domains into one larger domain. Using Windows 2000 Organizational Units (OUs), you have finer granularity in delegating administrative tasks.

Domain Tree   A domain tree is a hierarchical collection of the child and parent domains within a network. The domains in a domain tree have contiguous namespaces. Domain trees in a domain forest do not share common security rights, but can access one another through the global catalog.

Driver Signing   One of the most frustrating things about Windows operating systems is that any software vendors can overwrite critical system level files with their own versions. Sometimes the vendor's version of a system level file is buggy or flawed, and it prevents the operating system from functioning correctly, or in the worst case, prevents it from starting at all. Windows 2000 uses a procedure called Driver Signing that allows the operating system to recognize functional, high-quality files approved by Microsoft. With this seal of approval, you should be confident that installing applications containing signed files will not disable your computer. Windows 98 was the first Microsoft operating system to use digital signatures, but Windows 2000 marks the first Microsoft operating system based on NT technology to do this.

DSL *See* Digital Subscriber Line.

Dynamic Disks Dynamic disks introduce conceptual as well as technical changes from traditional basic disk structure. Partitions are now called volumes, and these can be created or changed without losing existing data on the disk. Recall that when using basic disks, you must first create primary partitions (up to a maximum of four), then extended partitions (a maximum of one) with logical drives. Dynamic disks allow you to create volume after volume, with no limit on the number or type that can exist on a single disk; you are limited only by the capacity of the disk itself.

Dynamic Host Configuration Protocol (DHCP) A software utility that is designed to assign Internet Protocol (IP) addresses to clients and their stations logging onto a Transmission Control Protocol/Internet Protocol (TCP/IP) and eliminates manual IP address assignments.

EAP *See* Extensible Authentication Protocol.

EDI *See* Electronic Data Interchange.

EFS *See* Encrypting File System.

Electronic Data Interchange (EDI) EDI is the computer-to-computer electronic exchange of business documents using standard formats that are widely recognized both nationally and internationally. The use of standardized data formats allows organizations to exchange common business documents without having to customize their hardware or software system for each organization they do business with.

Encapsulating Security Payload (ESP) With IPSec, there are two choices of security service: Authentication Header (AH), and Encapsulating Security Payload (ESP). An AH allows authentication of the sender of data, but it does not provide privacy. ESP supports both authentication of the sender and encryption of the data as well.

Encrypting File System (EFS) Unlike Windows NT 4.0, Windows 2000 provides the Encrypting File System (EFS) that allows you to encrypt and decrypt data on a file-by-file basis without the need for third-party software, as long as it is stored on an NTFS formatted partition or volume. EFS is based on public key cryptography.

Encryption Scrambling of data so as to be unreadable; therefore, an unauthorized person cannot decipher the data.

ESP *See* Encapsulating Security Payload.

Ethernet A networking protocol and shared media (or switched) Local Area Network (LAN) access method linking up to 1K nodes in a bus topology.

Evaluation Evaluation is the process of assessing, summarizing, weighing, deciding, and applying standards.

Extended Partitions Although extended partitions cannot be used to host operating systems, they can store other types of data and provide an excellent way to create more drives above the four-partition limit. Extended partitions do not represent one drive; rather, they can be subdivided into as many logical drives as there are letters in the alphabet. Therefore, one extended partition can contain several logical drives, each of which appears as a separate drive letter to the user.

Extensible Authentication Protocol (EAP) EAP allows the administrator to "plug in" different authentication security providers outside of those included with Windows 2000. EAP allows your organization to take advantage of new authentication technologies including "smart card" logon and Certificate-based authentication.

FAT *See* File Allocation Table.

Fault Tolerance Fault tolerance is high-system availability with enough resources to accommodate unexpected failure. Fault tolerance is also the design of a computer to maintain its system's performance when some internal hardware problems occur. This is done through the use of back-up systems. Fault tolerance is not a replacement for regular backups. Instead, fault tolerance provides a higher level of availability of network services and data in the event of failure.

FEK *See* File Encryption Key.

File Allocation Table (FAT) A FAT is an area on a disk that indicates the arrangement of files in the sectors. Because of the multi-user nature of Terminal Server, it is strongly recommended that the NTFS file system be used rather than the FAT file system. FAT does not offer file and directory security, whereas with NTFS you can limit access to subdirectories and files to certain users or groups of users.

File Allocation Table 16 (FAT16) The earlier version of the FAT file system implemented in MS-DOS is known as FAT16, to differentiate it from the improved FAT32.

File Allocation Table 32 (FAT32) FAT32 is the default file system for Windows 95 OSR2 and Windows 98. The FAT32 file system was first implemented in Windows 95 OSR2, and was supported by Windows 98 and now Windows 2000. While FAT16 cannot support partitions larger than 4GB in Windows 2000, FAT32 can support partitions up to 2TB (Terabytes) in size. However, for performance reasons, the creation of FAT32 partitions is limited to 32GB in Windows 2000. The second major benefit of FAT32 in comparison to FAT16 is that it supports a significantly smaller cluster size—as low as 4K for partitions up to 8GB. This results in more efficient use of disk space, with a 15 to 30 percent utilization improvement in comparison to FAT16.

File Encryption Key (FEK) A random key called a file encryption key (FEK) is used to encrypt each file and is then itself encrypted using the user's public key. At least two FEKs are created for every encrypted file. One FEK is created with the user's public key, and one is created with the public key of each recovery agent. There could be more than one recovery agent certificate used to encrypt each file, resulting in more than two FEKs. The user's public key can decrypt FEKs created with the public key.

File Transfer Protocol (FTP)   An Internet protocol allowing the exchange of files. A program enables the user to contact another computer on the Internet and exchange files.

Firewall   Either hardware or software that provides a security boundary or barrier between two networks by filtering incoming and outgoing packets.

FireWire   Also known as IEEE 1394. An Apple/Texas Instruments high-speed serial bus allowing up to 63 devices to connect; this bus supports hot swapping and isochronous data transfer.

Forest   A forest is a grouping of one or more domain trees that do not share a common namespace but do share a common schema, configuration, and global catalog; in fact, it forms a noncontiguous (or discontiguous) namespace. The users in one tree do not have global access to resources in other trees, but trusts can be created that allow users to access resources in another tree.

Forward Lookup Query   A forward lookup query occurs when a computer needs to get the Internet Protocol (IP) address for a computer with an Internet name. The local computer sends a query to a local Domain Name System (DNS) name server, which resolves the name or passes the request on to another server for resolution.

FQDN   *See* Fully Qualified Domain Name.

FSP   *See* Full Service Provider.

FTP   *See* File Transfer Protocol.

Full Service Provider (FSP)   FSPs offer multilayer suites of help that are sandwiched between a company's application and the data center. The service is a packaged solution of hardware, software, and hosting facilities. As an extra safety measure, the service providers guarantee 100 percent uptime with 24x7 checking on the security, backup, and hosting of the Web site. The strategy for FSP business solutions for growing enterprises is to free companies from the headaches of managing back-end infrastructure so they can focus on their core business. FSPs provide storage and networking equipment, software, bandwidth allotment, and round-the-clock technical support, with help from blue-chip suppliers.

Fully Qualified Domain Name (FQDN)   A full site name of a system rather than just its host name. The FQDN of each child domain is made up of the combination of its own name and the FQDN of the parent domain. The FQDN includes the host name and the domain membership of that computer.

Gateway   In networking, gateway refers to a router or a computer functioning as one, the "way out" of the network or subnet, to get to another network. You also use gateways for software that connects a system using one protocol to a system using a different protocol, such as the Systems Network Architecture (SNA) software (allows a Local Area Network (LAN) to connect to an IBM mainframe). You can also use Gateway Services for NetWare used to provide a way for Microsoft clients to go through a Windows NT or Windows 2000 server to access files on a Novell file server.

GC   *See* Global Catalog.

Global Catalog (GC)   The GC holds a replica of every object in Active Directory, but it only includes some of the objects' attributes—those most often used in search operations. The GC allows users and administrators to find directory information without having to know which server or domain actually contains the data.

Global Catalog (GC) Server   The GC server is a domain controller that contains a partial replica of every domain in Active Directory. Generally, a user must have access to a global catalog server to successfully log on to the network because the global catalog is needed to determine what groups the user belongs to.

Global Groups   Global Groups are used for combining users who share a common access profile based on job function or business role. Typically organizations use Global Groups for all groups in which membership is expected to change frequently. These groups can have as members only user accounts defined in the same domain as the Global Group.

Globally Unique IDentifier (GUID)   The Globally Unique IDentifier (GUID) is a unique numerical identification created at the time the object is created. An analogy would be a person's social security number, which is assigned once and never changes, even if the person changes his or her name, or moves.

GPC   *See* Group Policy Container.

GPO   *See* Group Policy Object.

GPT   *See* Group Policy Template.

Graphical User Interface (GUI)   An overall and consistent system for the interactive and visual program that interacts (or interfaces) with the user. GUI can involve pull-down menus, dialog boxes, on-screen graphics, and a variety of icons.

Group Policy   Group Policy provides for change management and desktop control on the Windows 2000 platform. You are familiar with the control you had in Windows NT 4.0 using System Policies. Group Policy is similar to System Policies but allows you a much higher level of granular configuration management over your network. Some of the confusion comes from the change of names applied to different groups in Windows 2000. You can apply Group Policy to sites, domains, and organizational units. Each of these represents a group of objects, so Group Policy is applied to the group of objects contained in each of these entities. Group Policy cannot be directly applied to Security Groups that are similar to the groups you are used to working with in Windows NT 4.0. However, by using Group Policy Filtering, you can successfully apply Group Policy to individual Security Groups.

Group Policy Container (GPC)   The Active Directory object Group Policy Containers (GPCs) store the information for the Folder Redirection snap-in and the Software Deployment snap-in. GPCs do not apply to local group policies. They contain component lists and status information, which indicate whether Group Policy Objects (GPOs) are enabled or disabled. They also contain version information, which ensures that the information is synchronized with the Group Policy Template (GPT) information. GPCs also contain the class store in which GPO group policy extensions have settings.

Group Policy Object (GPO)   After you create a group policy, it is stored in a Group Policy Object (GPO) and applied to the site, domain, or Organizational Unit (OU). GPOs are used to keep the group policy information; essentially, it is a collection of policies. You can apply single or multiple GPOs to each site, domain or OU. Group policies are not inherited across domains, and users must have Read permission for the GPO that you want to have applied to them. This way, you can filter the scope of GPOs by adjusting who has read access to each GPO.

Group Policy Template (GPT)   The subset of folders created on each domain controller that store Group Policy Object (GPO) information for specific GPOs are called Group Policy Templates (GPTs). GPTs are stored in the SysVol (System Volume) folder, on the domain controller. GPTs store data for Software Policies, Scripts, Desktop File and Folder Management, Software Deployment, and Security settings. GPTs can be defined in computer or user configurations. Consequently, they take effect either when the computer starts or when the user logs on.

GUI   *See* Graphical User Interface.

GUID   *See* Globally Unique IDentifier.

HAL   *See* Hardware Abstraction Layer.

Hardware Abstraction Layer (HAL)   The Windows NT's translation layer existing between the hardware, kernel, and input/output (I/O) system.

Hardware Compatibility List (HCL)   The Hardware Compatibility List is published by Microsoft for each of its operating systems, and is updated on a monthly basis. There is a copy of the HCL on the Windows 2000 Professional CD, located in the Support folder and named Hcl.txt.

Hardware Profile   A hardware profile is a set of instructions that tell your computer how to boot the system properly, based on the setup of your hardware. Hardware profiles are most commonly used with laptops. This is because laptops are frequently used in at least two different settings: stand-alone and in a docking station on a network. For example, when the laptop is being used at a docking station, it requires a network adapter. However, when the laptop is used away from the network, it does not. The hardware profile dialog manages these configuration changes. If a profile is created for each situation, the user will automatically be presented these choices on Windows startup.

Hash   A mathematical calculation applied to a string of text, resulting in a string of bits of a fixed size, which cannot be done in reverse to arrive back at the original source data.

HCL   *See* Hardware Compatibility List.

HKEY_CLASSES_ROOT   Contains information used for software configuration and object linking and embedding (OLE), as well as file association information.

HKEY_CURRENT_CONFIG   Holds data about the current hardware profile that is in use.

HKEY_CURRENT_USER   Has information about the user who is currently logged on.

HKEY_LOCAL_MACHINE   Stores information about the hardware, software, system devices, and security information for the local computer.

HKEY_USERS   Holds information and settings for the environments of all users of the computer.

HTML   *See* HyperText Markup Language.

HTTP   *See* HyperText Transfer Protocol.

HyperText Markup Language (HTML)   The format used to create documents viewed on the World Wide Web (WWW) by the use of tags (codes) embedded within the text.

HyperText Transfer Protocol (HTTP)   HTTP is an Internet standard supporting World Wide Web (WWW) exchanges which creates the definitions of Universal Resource Locators (URLs) and their retrieval usage throughout the Internet.

IAS   *See* Internet Authentication Services.

ICS   *See* Internet Connection Sharing.

IDE *See* Integrated Drive Electronics.

Identity Interception Unauthorized access is gained by using the valid credentials of someone else.

IIS *See* Internet Information Service.

Impersonation The ability of an unauthorized person to present credentials that appear to be valid.

Implementation Phase The implementation phase is the phase in which you actually put the plan into action. Implementation may require hiring outside personnel, or you may be able to implement your plan with your current IT staff.

Inbound Connection Inbound connections are those where access to the intranet or resources within the intranet are being accessed by users outside of it. These users could be dialing in using a modem and connecting directly to the intranet or they could make use of an existing public network, such as the Internet, to gain access to resources within. Either way, security must be in the forefront of any such implementation.

Incremental Backup This backup process is similar to the Differential backup, but it clears the markers from the selected files after the process. Because it clears the markers, an incremental backup will not back up any files that have not changed since the last incremental backup. This type of backup is fast during the backup but is very slow while restoring the files. One needs the last full backup and all of the subsequent incremental backups to fully restore data. The positive side of this backup type is that it is fast and consumes very little media space.

Indexing Service Provides indexing functions for documents stored on disk, allowing users to search for specific document text or properties.

Industry Standard Architecture (ISA) A PC's expansion bus used for peripherals plug-in boards.

Infrastructure An underlying base or foundation for an organization or system.

Infrastructure Master There is an infrastructure master for each domain, and it updates the group-to-user references when group members are changed.

Inheritance When you nest an Organizational Unit (OU) within another OU, by default, the properties of the parent OU flow down the hierarchy. This is called inheritance. These properties can consist of security or Group Policies. Inheritance allows an object in an OU to inherit the permissions applied to the OU or parent object. In most cases, the parent object is an OU. One of the advantages and disadvantages of inheritance is that it can be blocked. Inheritance lets a given Access Control Entry (ACE) propagate from the container where it was applied to all children of the container. Inheritance can be combined with delegation to grant administrative rights to a whole subtree of the directory in a single operation.

Integrated Drive Electronics (IDE) Drive An IDE drive is a hard disk drive for processors containing most controller circuitry within the drive. IDE drives combine Enhanced System Device Interface (ESDI) speed with Small Computer System Interface (SCSI) hard drive interface intelligence.

Integrated Services Digital Network (ISDN) Integrated Services indicates the provider offers voice and data services over the same medium. Digital Network is a reminder that ISDN was born out of the digital nature of the intercarrier and intracarrier networks. ISDN runs across the same copper wiring that carries regular telephone service. Before attenuation and noise cause the signal to be unintelligible, an ISDN circuit can run a maximum of 18,000 feet. A repeater doubles this distance to 36,000 feet.

International Model In this model, a global enterprise does business in more than one country and perhaps has offices in different nations as well. In addition, a company is operating with an international business model if it has operations that are located in more than one country. The company will have business operations that will consist of a Worldwide Headquarters, possibly divisional headquarters that are based around the country or continent that is being serviced, as well as offices, production and distribution facilities located to take advantage of the economic advantages of being in multiple international locations.

Internet Authentication Services (IAS) IAS performs authentication, authorization, and accounting of dial-up and Virtual Private Networking (VPN) users. IAS supports the Remote Access Dial-In User Service (RADIUS) protocol.

Internet Connection Sharing (ICS) ICS can be thought of as a less robust version of Network Address Translation (NAT). ICS uses the same address translation technology. ICS is a simpler version of NAT useful for connecting a few computers on a small Local Area Network (LAN) to the Internet or useful for a remote server through a single phone line and account.

Internet Information Service (IIS) Windows NT web browser software that supports Secure Sockets Layer (SSL) security protocol from Netscape. IIS provides support for Web site creation, configuration, and management, along with Network News Transfer Protocol (NNTP), File Transfer Protocol (FTP), and Simple Mail Transfer Protocol (SMTP).

Internet Packet eXchange (IPX) Novell NetWare's built-in networking protocol for Local Area Network (LAN) communication derived from the Xerox Network System protocol. IPX moves data between a server and/or workstation programs from different network nodes. Sometimes called an Internetnetwork Packet eXchange.

Internet Protocol Security (IPSec) IPSec is a new feature included in Windows 2000 and provides for encryption of data as it travels between two computers, protecting it from modification and interpretation if anyone were to see it on the network.

Internet Service Provider (ISP) The organization allowing users to connect to its computers and then to the Internet. ISPs provide the software to connect and sometimes a portal site and/or internal browsing capability.

Internetworking Internetworking refers to connecting two or more networks. This concept is the foundation of the global Internet, as well as private large enterprise networks. With Internet connectivity becoming a necessity rather than a luxury, and most major (and many, many minor) companies "on the net," it is important to know how to secure your internal, private LAN from unauthorized access originating on the public network to which it is connected.

Interrupt ReQuest (IRQ)   An electronic signal that is sent to the computer's processor requiring the processor's attention. Also, a computer instruction designed to interrupt a program for an Input/Output (I/O).

IPSec   *See* Internet Protocol Security.

IPX   *See* Internet Packet eXchange.

IRQ   *See* Interrupt ReQuest.

ISA   *See* Industry Standard Architecture.

ISDN   *See* Integrated Services Digital Network.

ISP   *See* Internet Service Provider.

Kerberos   Kerberos v5 is the default network authentication protocol for Windows 2000. Kerberos is not a new protocol that Microsoft invented as it has been used in the UNIX world for several years. Microsoft has chosen to implement Kerberos network authentication in Windows 2000 to enhance security since network servers and services need to know that the client requesting access is actually a valid client. Kerberos is based on tickets containing client credentials encrypted with shared keys. Connections to application and file servers are faster when Kerberos authentication is used since the Kerberos server only needs to examine the credentials supplied by the client to determine if access is allowed. The same credentials supplied by the client can be utilized for the entire network logon session. Kerberos authentication also provides authentication for both the client and server sides. Trusts are another area that the use of Kerberos is beneficial. Kerberos is the basis for transitive domain trusts, and Windows 2000 uses transitive trusts by default with other Windows 2000 domains.

Knowledge   Knowledge is the very lowest level of learning. It is, of course, important that a network administrator have this knowledge. Knowledge involves the processes of defining, location, recall, recognition, stating, matching, labeling, and identification.

L2TP   *See* Layer Two Tunneling Protocol.

Last Known Good Configuration This mode starts the system using the configuration that was saved in the registry during the last system shutdown. This startup option is useful when you have changed some configuration parameters and the system fails to boot. When you use this mode to start the system, all changes that were made after the last successful logon are lost. Use this option when you suspect that some incorrect configuration changes are causing the system startup failure. This mode does not help if any of the installed drivers have been corrupted or any driver files are deleted by mistake.

Layer Two Tunneling Protocol (L2TP) L2TP offers better security through the use of IPSec and creates Virtual Private Networks (VPNs). Windows 2000 uses L2TP to provide tunneling services over Internet Protocol Security (IPSec)-based communications. L2TP tunnels can be set up to traverse data across intervening networks that are not part of the VPN being created. L2TP is used to send information across intervening and nonsecure networks.

LDAP *See* Lightweight Directory Access Protocol.

Legend The legend displays information about the counters that are being measured. It is the set of columns at the bottom of System Monitor.

Life Cycle The phase that a business will progress through when implementing a change from the beginning to the end of use is known as the life cycle. Depending on the topic there are various phases that a process goes through until it begins to repeat itself again. Products tend to go through various stages such as new technology, state of the art; advanced; mainstream; mature; and obsolete.

Lightweight Directory Access Protocol (LDAP) A simplified Directory Access Protocol (DAP) accessing a computer's directory listing. LDAP is able to access to X.500 directories.

Line Printer Daemon (LPD) LPD is the server process that advertises printer queues and accepts incoming print submissions, which are then routed to the print device.

Line Printer Remote (LPR) LPR is a process that spools a print job to a remote print spool that is advertised by the Line Printer Daemon (LPD).

Link Parameter Negotiation An Agreement between the client and the server on the size of the packets as well as how they are framed.

Local Model The local model is the "mom and pop" corner store model, in which all or most business comes from members of the immediate neighborhood or community, or within a city.

Local Policy A group policy stored locally on a Windows 2000 member server or a Windows 2000 Professional computer is called a local policy. The local policy is used to set up the configuration settings for each computer and for each user. Local policies are stored in the \%systemroot%\system32\grouppolicy folder on the local computer. Local policies include the auditing policy, user rights and privilege assignment, and various security options.

Local Printer A print device that is directly attached, via a parallel or serial cable, to the computer that is providing the printing services. Drivers for the print device must reside on the computer that connects to the printer.

Local User Profiles (Local Profiles) Local user profiles are kept on one local computer hard drive. When a user initially logs on to a computer, a local profile is created for them in the \%systemdrive%\Documents and Settings\<username> folder. When users log off the computer, the changes that they made while they were logged on will be saved to their local profile on that client computer. This way, subsequent logons to that computer will bring up their personal settings. When users log on to a different computer, they will not receive these settings, as they are local to the computer in which they made the changes. Therefore, each user that logs on to that computer receives individual desktop settings. Local profiles are ideal for users who only use one computer. For users that require access to multiple computers, the Roaming profile would be the better choice.

LogicalDisk Object The LogicalDisk object measures the transfer of data for a logical drive (i.e., C: or D:) or storage volumes. You can use the PhysicalDisk object to determine which hard disk is causing the bottleneck. Then, to narrow the cause of the bottleneck, you can use the LogicalDisk object to determine which, if any, partition is the specific cause of the bottleneck. By default, the PhysicalDisk object is enabled and the LogicalDisk object is disabled on Windows 2000 Server.

LPD   *See* Line Printer Daemon.

LPR   *See* Line Printer Remote.

Macro Viruses   Macros are small programs that run inside other programs; for example, macros can be written to automate commonly used functions in Microsoft Word and other word processing programs. A macro virus uses this capability to invade a system and cause damage or gain unauthorized access to data.

Malicious Code   This is a method of attacking a network by embedding ActiveX, VBScript, or a Java applet in a Web page or e-mail message. When the page or message is executed, it will provide the intruder with a way to access information on the network which he or she is not authorized to access.

Management Model   An important facet of the overall business model is the company's management model. How does the "chain of command" work within the company? Is management paternalistic, where control emanates from one person who may see him or herself as a benevolent dictator? Is the management style more team-oriented, in which upper level employees run the operation (management by committee)?

Mandatory Roaming Profiles   Mandatory roaming profiles are mandatory user profiles the user cannot change. They are usually created to define desktop configuration settings for groups of users in order to simplify administration and support. Users can make changes to their desktop settings while they are logged on, but these changes will not be saved to the profile, as Mandatory profiles are read-only. The next time they log on, their desktop will be set back to the original Mandatory profile settings.

Man-in-the-Middle Attacks   An intruder intercepts packets in transit and changes the security credentials to administrator, thereby allowing administrative functions on the server.

Masquerading This is where an unauthorized user uses the IP address of a trusted system account or device.

Master File Table (MFT) The MFT stores the information needed by the operating system to retrieve files from the volume. Part of the MFT is stored at the beginning of the volume and cannot be moved. Also, if the volume contains a large number of directories, it can prevent the free space from being defragmented.

Master Image After configuring one computer with the operating system and all the applications, Sysprep is run to create an image of the hard disk. This computer serves as the master or model computer that will have the complete setup of the operating system, application software, and any service packs. This hard disk image is the master image and is copied to a CD or put on a network share for distribution to many computers. Any third-party disk-imaging tool can then be used to replicate the image to other identical computers.

MCSE *See* Microsoft Certified Systems Engineer.

Message Queuing Service Provides a communication infrastructure and a development tool for creating distributed messaging applications. Such applications can communicate across heterogeneous networks and with computers that might be offline. Message queuing provides guaranteed message delivery, efficient routing, security, transactional support, and priority-based messaging.

MFT *See* Master File Table.

Microsoft Certified Systems Engineer (MCSE) An engineer who is a technical specialist in advanced Microsoft products, specifically NT Server and NT Workstation.

Microsoft Challenge Handshake Authentication Protocol (MC-CHAP) The Microsoft Challenge Handshake Authentication Protocol is similar to CHAP but is considered more secure. As with CHAP, the authenticator sends a challenge to the peer. The peer must return the user name and an MD4 hash of the challenge string, the session ID, and the MD4-hashed password. This sort of design manipulates a hash of the MD4 hash of the password, and provides an additional level of security because it allows the authenticator to store hashed passwords instead of clear-text passwords.

Microsoft Management Console (MMC) The MMC provides a standardized interface for using administrative tools and utilities. The management applications contained in an MMC are called Snap-ins, and custom MMCs hold the Snap-ins required to perform specific tasks. Custom consoles can be saved as files with the .msc file extension. The MMC was first introduced with NT Option Pack. Using the MMC leverages the familiarity you have with the other snap-ins available within MMC, such as SQL Server 7 and Internet Information Server 4. With the MMC, all your administrative tasks can be done in one place.

Mini-Setup Wizard The purpose of this wizard is to add some user-specific parameters on the destination computer. These parameters include: End-user license agreement (EULA); Product key (serial number); Username, company name, and administrator password; Network configuration; Domain or workgroup name; and, Date and time zone selection.

Mirror Set In a mirror set, all data on a selected partition or drive are automatically duplicated onto another physical disk. The main purpose of a mirror set is to provide fault tolerance in the event of missing or corrupt data. If one disk fails or contains corrupt files, the data is simply retrieved and rebuilt from the other disk.

Mirrored Volume Like basic disks, dynamic disks can also be mirrored, and are called mirrored volumes. A continuous and automatic backup of all data in a mirrored volume is saved to a separate disk to provide fault tolerance in the event of a disk failure or corrupt file. Note that you cannot mirror a spanned or striped volume.

Mirroring Also called RAID 1. RAID 1 consists of two drives that are identical matches, or mirrors, of each other. If one drive fails, you have another drive to boot up and keep the server going.

Mixed Mode When in Mixed Mode, the domain still uses master replication with a Windows 2000 PDC. The Windows NT Backup Domain Controllers (BDCs) replicate from the Windows 2000 server, as did the Windows NT Primary Domain Controller (PDC). When you are operating in Mixed Mode, some Windows 2000 functionality will not be available. You will not be able to use group nesting or transitive trusts. Mixed Mode is the default mode.

MMC *See* Microsoft Management Console.

NAT *See* Network Address Translation.

National Model In the national model, the company does business all over the country, but rarely or never conducts business outside the national boundaries. The company will have business operations that will consist of a corporate headquarters, regional offices, and production and distribution facilities located in multiple regions of a country.

Native Mode Native Mode allows only Windows 2000 domain controllers to operate in the domain. When all domain controllers for the domain are upgraded to Windows 2000 Server, you can switch to Native Mode. This allows you to use transitive trusts and the group-nesting features of Windows 2000. When switching to Native Mode, ensure you no longer need to operate in Mixed Mode, because you cannot switch back to Mixed Mode once you are in Native Mode.

NDS *See* NetWare Directory Service.

NetBEUI *See* NETwork Basic Input/Output System Extended User Interface.

NetBIOS *See* Network Basic Input/Output System.

NetWare Directory Service (NDS) NDS (created by Novell) has a hierarchical information database allowing the user to log on to a network with NDS capable of calculating the user's access rights.

Network Address Translation (NAT) With NAT, you can allow internal users to have access to important external resources while still preventing unauthorized access from the outside world.

Network Basic Input/Output System (NetBIOS) A program in Microsoft's operating system that links personal computers to a Local Area Network (LAN).

Network Two or more computers connected together by cable or wireless media for the purpose of sharing data, hardware peripherals, and other resources.

Network Authenticator A network authenticator is a special packet that contains information that is unique to the sender or client—and incidentally, one of the most important aspects of network security. By authenticating a user you give that user rights within the network. When it is done properly, authenticating once will get the user through your network without any hitches—the user can go about his or her normal work and not be interrupted by needing to authenticate again for access to certain areas of the network with higher security.

NETwork Basic Input/Output System Extended User Interface (NetBEUI) The transport layer for the Disk Operating System (DOS) networking protocol called Network Basic Input/Output System (NetBIOS).

Network Interface Card (NIC) A board with encoding and decoding circuitry and a receptacle for a network cable connection that, bypassing the serial ports and operating through the internal bus, allows computers to be connected at higher speeds to media for communications between stations.

Network Layer Protocol Negotiation The act of negotiating and obtaining a valid IP address.

Network Printer A print device that has a built-in network interface or connects directly to a dedicated network interface. Both workstations and servers can be configured to print directly to the network printer, and the network printer controls its own printer queue, determining which jobs from which clients will print in which order. Printing clients have no direct control over the printer queue and cannot see other print jobs being submitted to the printer. Administration of a network printer is difficult. Drivers for the print device must reside on the computer that connects to the printer.

NIC *See* Network Interface Card.

Nondedicated Server A nondedicated print server is a Windows 2000 server that hosts printing services in addition to other services. A domain controller, database server, or Domain Name System (DNS) server can provide printing services as well, but should be used only for a smaller number of printers or for printers that are not heavily used. Anyone setting up a nondedicated print server should monitor the performance of the printing process and the other tasks running on the server and be prepared to modify the server configuration if the performance drops below acceptable levels.

Nonmandatory Roaming Profiles Roaming user profiles are stored on the network file server and are the perfect solution for users who have access to multiple computers. This way their profile is accessible no matter where they log on in the domain. When users log on to a computer within their domain, their Roaming profile will be copied from the network server to the client computer and the settings will be applied to the computer while they are logged on. Subsequent logins will compare the Roaming profile files to the local profile files. The file server then copies only any files that have been altered since the user last logged on locally, significantly decreasing the time required to log on. When the user logs off, any changes that the user made on the local computer will be copied back to the profile on the network file server.

Normal Backup This is the most common type and is also known as a full backup. The Normal backup operation backs up all files and folders that are selected irrespective of the archive attributes of the files. This provides the easiest way to restore the files and folders but is expensive in terms of the time it takes to complete the backup job and the storage space it consumes. The restore process from a Normal backup is less complex because you do not have to use multiple tape sets to completely restore data.

NT File System (NTFS) The NT File System (with file names up to 255 characters) is a system created to aid the computer and its components recover from hard disk crashes. NTFS v5 also provides support for the Encrypting File System.

NT LAN Manager (NTLM) NTLM was the default authentication system in Windows NT 4.0 and is backward compatible with Windows 2000 for networks that run earlier versions of the operating system (OS).

NTFS   *See* NT File System.

NTLM   *See* NT LAN Manager.

NWLink IPX/SPX/NetBIOS Compatible Transport Protocol (NWLink)   Microsoft's implementation of Novell's Internet Packet eXchange/Sequenced Packet eXchange (IPX/SPX) protocol stack, required for connecting to NetWare servers prior to version 5. NWLink can also be used on small networks that use only Windows 2000 and other Microsoft client software. NWLink is a Network Driver Interface Specification (NDIS) compliant, native 32-bit protocol. The NWLink protocol supports Windows sockets and NetBIOS.

ODBC   *See* Open DataBase Connectivity.

Offer   After the Dynamic Host Configuration Protocol (DHCP) server receives the DHCPDISCOVER message, it looks at the request to see if the client configuration request is valid. If so, it sends back a DHCPOFFER message with the client's network hardware address, an IP address, a subnet mask, the length of time the lease is valid, and the IP address of the server that provided the DHCP information. This message is also a Transmission Control Protocol/Internet Protocol (TCP/IP) broadcast, as the client does not yet have an Internet Protocol (IP) address. The server then reserves the address it sent to the client so that it is not offered to another client making a request. If there are more than one DHCP servers on the network, all servers respond to the DHCPDISCOVER message with a DHCPOFFER message.

Open DataBase Connectivity (ODBC)   A database programming interface that allows applications a way to access network databases.

Open Systems Interconnection (OSI) Model   This is a model of breaking networking tasks into layers. Each layer is responsible for a specific set of functionality. There are performance objects available in System Monitor for analyzing network performance.

Operations Master   This is a domain controller that takes on the role of handling a single master operation.

Organizational Chart The Organizational Chart is a logical description of the structure of a business organized by groups, divisions and, often, individuals. This structure is depicted in the context of who performs the work and who manages the workers and who manages the managers, etc. Equally important is how each business unit, division, department, etc., fits into the "Big Picture" of how the business as a whole operates.

Organizational Units (OUs) OUs in Windows 2000 are objects that are containers for other objects, such as users, groups, or other organizational units. Objects cannot be placed in another domain's OUs. The whole purpose of an OU is to have a hierarchical structure to organize your network objects. You can assign a group policy to an OU. Generally, the OU will follow a structure from your company. It may be a location, if you have multiple locations. It can even be a department-level organization. Also, OUs are units used to organize objects within a domain. These objects can include user accounts, groups, computers, printers, and even other OUs. The hierarchy of OUs is independent of other domains.

OSI *See* Open Systems Interconnection.

OU *See* Organizational Units.

Outbound Connections Connecting to and accessing private network resources through the Internet or some other public network is where Virtual Private Networks (VPNs) take over. This allows the administrator to centrally maintain security from outbound connections while also allowing users to make use of local Internet Service Providers (ISPs). This prevents the users from having to make long distance calls and racking up very large phone bills.

Paging When enough memory is not available for the running applications, pages of memory can be swapped from physical memory to the hard disk too much and slow the system down. This is also known as paging because pages of memory are swapped at a time. Windows 2000 separates memory into 4KB pages of memory to help prevent fragmentation of memory. Swapping can even get bad enough that you can hear your hard disk running constantly.

Paging File A file on the hard disk (or spanning multiple disks) that stores some of the program code that is normally in the computer's RAM. This is called virtual memory, and allows the programs to function as if the computer had more memory than is physically installed.

Password   A string of characters (text, numbers, or symbols) that is kept private and used to authenticate a user's identity.

Password Authentication Protocol (PAP)   A simple authentication method used over Point-to-Point Protocol (PPP) connections, which is less secure than Challenge Handshake Authentication Protocol (CHAP).

Password Policy   A password policy regulates how your users must establish and manage their passwords. This includes password complexity requirements and how often passwords must change. There are several settings that can be used to implement a successful password policy. You can enforce password uniqueness so those users cannot simply switch back and forth between a few easy to remember passwords. This can be set to low, medium, or high security. With low security, the system remembers the user's last 1–8 passwords (it is your choice as administrator to decide how many); with medium, it remembers the last 9–16 passwords; with high, it remembers the last 17–24 passwords.

PCMCIA   *See* Personal Computer Memory Card International Association.

PDC   *See* Primary Domain Controller.

Peer-to-Peer Network   A workgroup is also referred to as a peer-to-peer network, because all the computers connected together and communicating with one another are created equal. That is, there is no central computer that manages security and controls access to the network.

Performance Logging   Performance logging has many features. The data collected are stored in a comma-delimited or tab-delimited format, which allows for exportation to spreadsheet and database applications for a variety of tasks such as charting and reports. The data can also be viewed as collected. You can configure the logging by specifying start and stop times, the name of the log files, and the maximum size of the log. You can start and stop the logging of data manually or create a schedule for logging. You can even specify a program to run automatically when logging stops. You can also create trace logs. Trace logs track events that occur rather than measuring performance counters.

Permissions Inheritance By default, all permissions set for a folder are inherited by the files in the folder, the subfolders in the folder, and the contents of the subfolders. When the permissions on a folder are viewed in the Security tab of the file or folder Permissions window, inherited permissions are indicated with a gray check box.

Personal Computer Memory Card International Association (PCMCIA) An interface standard for plug-in cards for portable computers; devices meeting the standard (for example, fax cards, modems) are theoretically interchangeable.

Physical Memory Physical memory is the actual Random Access Memory (RAM) on the computer. When the physical memory becomes full, the operating system can also use space on the hard disk as virtual memory. When memory becomes full, rather than locking up the computer, the operating system stores unused data on the hard disk in a page file (also called paging or swap file). Data are swapped back and forth between the hard disk and physical memory as needed for running applications. If memory is needed that is in virtual memory, it is swapped back into physical memory.

Physical Security Physical security consists of protecting the network's physical assets (servers, workstations, cable, hubs, and so on) from intruders.

PhysicalDisk Object The PhysicalDisk object measures the transfer of data for the entire hard disk. You can use the PhysicalDisk object to determine which hard disk is causing the bottleneck. By default, the PhysicalDisk object is enabled and the LogicalDisk object is disabled on Windows 2000 Server.

PKI *See* Public Key Infrastructure.

Plug and Play (PnP) A standard requiring add-in hardware to carry the software to configure itself in a given way supported by Microsoft Windows 95. Plug and Play can make peripheral configuration software, jumper settings, and Dual In-line Package (DIP) switches unnecessary. PnP allows the operating system to load device drivers automatically and assign system resources dynamically to computer components and peripherals. Windows 2000 moves away from this older technology with its use of Kernel-mode and User-mode PnP architecture. PnP auto-detects, configures, and installs the necessary drivers in order to minimize user interaction with hardware configuration. Users no longer have to tinker with IRQ and I/O settings.

PnP *See* Plug and Play.

Point-to-Point Protocol (PPP)   A serial communication protocol most commonly used to connect a personal computer to an Internet Service Provider (ISP). PPP is the successor to Serial Line Internet Protocol (SLIP) and may be used over both synchronous and asynchronous circuits. Also, PPP is a full-duplex, connectionless protocol that supports many different types of links. The advantages of PPP made it de facto standard for dial-up connections.

Point-to-Point Tunneling Protocol (PPTP)   One of two methods of creating a Virtual Private Network with Windows 2000. PPTP allows corporations to extend their own corporate network through private tunnels over the Internet without the use of expensive private leased lines.

Policy Inheritance   Group policies have an order of inheritance in which the policies are applied. Local policies are applied first, then group policies are applied to the site, then the domain, and finally the Organizational Unit (OU). Policies applied first are overwritten by policies applied later. Therefore, group policies applied to a site overwrite the local policies and so on. When there are multiple Group Policy Objects (GPOs) for a site, domain, or OU, the order in which they appear in the Properties list applies. This policy inheritance order works well for small companies, but a more complex inheritance strategy may be essential for larger corporations.

Ports   A channel of a device that can support single point-to-point connections is known as a port. Devices can be single port, as in a modem.

Power Options   Power options entail the computer hardware power usage and are dependent on the particular hardware. Power options include Standby and Hibernation modes. Standby mode turns off the monitor and hard disks to save power. Hibernation mode turns off the monitor and disks, saves everything in memory to disk, turns off the computer, and then restores the desktop to the state in which you left it when the computer is turned on.

PPP   *See* Point-to-Point Protocol.

PPTP   *See* Point-to-Point Tunneling Protocol.

Preboot eXecution Environment (PXE)   The PXE is a new Dynamic Host Configuration Protocol (DHCP)-based technology used to help client computers boot from the network. The Windows 2000 Remote Installation Services (RIS) uses the PXE technology along with the existing Transmission Control Protocol/Internet Protocol (TCP/IP) network infrastructure to implement the RIS-based deployment of Windows 2000 Professional. The client computer that has the PXE-based ROM uses its Basic Input/Output System (BIOS) to contact an existing RIS server and get an Internet Protocol (IP) address from the DHCP server running on the network. The RIS server then initializes the installation process on the client computer.

Preemptive Multitasking   An environment in which timesharing controls the programs in use by exploiting a scheduled time usage of the computer's Central Processing Unit (CPU).

Primary Domain Controller (PDC)   Performs NT security management for its local domain. The PDC is periodically synchronized to its copy, the Backup Domain Controller (BDC). Only one PDC can exist in a domain. In an NT 4.0 single domain model, any user having a valid domain user account and password in the user accounts database of the PDC has the ability to log onto any computer that is a member of the domain, including MetaFrame servers.

Primary Domain Controller (PDC) Emulator   This domain controller (DC) emulates a Windows NT PDC if there are Windows NT Backup Domain Controllers (BDCs) in the domain, processing password changes and replicating the information to the BDCs. If the domain operates in native mode, with only Windows 2000 DCs, the PDC emulator receives preferential replication of password changes performed by other DCs, serving as a sort of clearinghouse for password medications.

Primary Domain Name System (DNS) Server   The Primary DNS server maintains the master copy of the DNS database for the zone. This copy of the database is the only one that can be modified, and any changes made to its database are distributed to secondary servers in the zone during a zone transfer process. The server can cache resolution requests locally so a lookup query does not have to be sent across the network for a duplicate request. The primary server contains the address mappings for the Internet root DNS servers. Primary servers can also act as secondary servers for other zones, as described below.

Primary Partitions   Primary partitions are typically used to create bootable drives. Each primary partition represents one drive letter, up to a maximum of four on a single hard disk. One primary partition must be marked as active in order to boot the system, and most operating systems must be loaded on a primary partition to work.

Print Device   The hardware that actually does the printing. A print device is one of two types as defined in Windows 2000: local or network-interface. A local print device connects directly to the print server with a serial or parallel interface. A network-interface print device connects to the printer across the network and must have its own network interface or be connected to an external network adapter.

Print Driver   A software program used by Windows 2000 and other computer programs to connect with printers and plotters. It translates information sent to it into commands that the print device can understand.

Print Server   A print server is a computer that manages printing on the network. A print server can be a dedicated computer hosting multiple printers, or it can run as one of many processes on a nondedicated computer.

Printer Permissions   Printer permissions are established through the Security tab in the printer's Properties dialog. The security settings for printer objects are similar to the security settings for folder shares.

Private   A digital code that can be used to decrypt information which works in conjunction with a corresponding public key.

Protocols   Protocols are sets of rules that computers use to communicate with one another. Protocols usually work together in stacks, so called because in a layered networking model, they operate at different layers or levels. These protocols govern the logic, formatting, and timing of information exchange between layers.

Public Key   A digital code used to encrypt information, which is then decrypted by a private key.

Public Key Cryptography   A public key, published and made widely available, is used to encrypt data and a corresponding private key, kept secret, is used for decryption.

Public Key Encryption   The public key is used to encrypt the data and is not kept secret but is published to all wishing to send an encrypted message to the owner.

Public Key Infrastructure (PKI)   A PKI is a system of digital certificates, certificate authorities, and other registration authorities that verify and authenticate the validity of each party involved in an electronic transaction.

Publishing Resources   Resources, such as folders and printers, which are available to be shared on the network, can be published to the Active Directory. The resources are published to the directory and can be located by users, who can query the directory based on the resource's properties (for example, to locate all color printers).

PXE   *See* Preboot eXecution Environment.

QoS   *See* Quality of Service.

Quality of Service (QoS) Admission Control   Admission control allows you to control how applications are allotted network bandwidth. You can give important applications more bandwidth, less important applications less bandwidth.

RADIUS   *See* Remote Authentication Dial-In User Service.

RAID *See* Redundant Array of Inexpensive Disks.

RAS *See* Remote Access Service.

RDP *See* Remote Desktop Protocol.

Recovery Agent The recovery agent restores the encrypted file on a secure computer with its private recovery keys. The agent decrypts it using the cipher command line and then returns the plain text file to the user. The recovery agent goes to the computer with the encrypted file, loads the recovery certificate and private key, and performs the recovery. It is not as safe as the first option because the recovery agent's private key may remain on the user's computer.

Recovery Console The Recovery Console is a new command-line interpreter program feature in Windows 2000 that helps in system maintenance activities and resolving system problems. This program is separate from the Windows 2000 command prompt.

Redundant Array of Inexpensive Disks (RAID) Although mirroring and duplexing are forms of RAID, most people think of RAID as involving more than two drives. The most common form of RAID is RAID-5, which is the striping of data across three or more drives, providing fault tolerance if one drive fails. For the best disk performance, consider using a SCSI RAID (Redundant Array of Independent Disks) controller. RAID controllers automatically place data on multiple disk drives and can increase disk performance. Using the software implementation of RAID provided by NT would increase performance if designed properly, but the best performance is always realized through hardware RAID controllers.

Redundant Array of Inexpensive Disks 5 (RAID-5) Volume A RAID-5 volume on a dynamic drive provides disk striping with parity, and is similar to a basic stripe set with parity. This disk configuration provides both increased storage capacity and fault tolerance. Data in a dynamic RAID-5 volume are interleaved across three or more disks (up to 32 disks), and parity information is included to rebuild lost data in the event of an individual disk failure. Like a spanned or striped volume, a RAID-5 volume cannot be mirrored.

Regional Model   A company is operating with a regional business model if it has operations that are not merely local to a metropolitan area. The company will have business operations that are located in multiple parts of a state or a country.

Registry   The Registry is the hierarchical database that stores operating system and application configuration information. It was introduced in Windows 9x and NT and replaced much of the functionality of the old initialization, system, and command files used in the early versions of Windows (.ini, .sys, and .com extensions). The registry is also a Microsoft Windows program allowing the user to choose options for configuration and applications to set them; it replaces confusing text-based .INI files.

Relationships Model   Another consideration involved in analyzing the business requirements of your organization hinges on the company's relationships with the outside world—business partners, vendors, and customers. This is especially important if the company wishes to make information available to some or all of these through direct access to the company's network.

Remote   The word "remote" can take on a number of different meanings depending on the context. In the case of an individual computer, the computer you are sitting in front of is sometimes referred to as being "local" while any other computer is considered "remote." In this context any machine but your own is considered a remote computer. In discussions related to network configuration and design, "remote" may refer to segments and machines that are on the far side of a router. In this context, all machines on your physical segment are considered "local" and machines located on other physical segments are referred to as remote.

Remote Access Policy   Remote access policies allow you to create demand-dial connections to use specific authentication and encryption methods. In Windows NT versions 3.5x and Windows NT 4.0, authorization was much simpler. The administrator simply granted dial-in permission to the user. The callback options were configured on a per-user basis.

Remote Access Service (RAS)   Remote Access Service is a built-in feature of the Microsoft NT operating system. It allows users to dial establish a connection to an NT network over a standard phone line. Remote Access allows users to access files on a network or transfer files from a remote PC, over a Dial-Up Networking connection. The performance of transferring files over a dial-up connection is very similar to the performance you would get if you were downloading a file from the Internet.

Remote Authentication Dial-In User Service (RADIUS)   A client/server protocol used for authentication of dial-in clients that allows centralized authentication and control of remote users.

Remote Desktop Protocol (RDP)   Remote Desktop Protocol (RDP) is the application protocol between the client and the server. It informs the server of the keystrokes and mouse movement of the client and returns to the client the Windows 2000 graphical display from the server. RDP is a multi-channel, standard protocol that provides various levels of compression so that it can adapt to different connection speeds and encryption levels from 40 to 128 bit. Transmission Control Protocol/Internet Protocol (TCP/IP) carries the messages, and RDP is the language in which the messages are written. Both are needed to use Microsoft's implementation of Terminal Services.

Remote Installation Preparation (RIPrep)   RIPrep is a disk duplication tool included with Windows 2000 Server. It is an ideal tool for creating images of fully prepared client computers. These images are the customized images made from the base operating system, local installation of applications such as Microsoft Office, and customized configurations.

Remote Installation Preparation (RIPrep) Wizard   The RIPrep wizard enables the network administrator to distribute to a large number of client computers a standard desktop configuration that includes the operating system and the applications. This not only helps in maintaining a uniform standard across the enterprise; it also cuts the costs and time involved in a large-scale rollout of Windows 2000 Professional.

Remote Installation Services (RIS)   The RIS, part of Windows 2000 Server, allows client computers to install Windows 2000 Professional from a Windows 2000 Server with the service installed. The Remote Installation Services (RIS) facilitates installation of Windows 2000 Professional remotely on a large number of computers with similar or dissimilar hardware configurations. This not only reduces the installation time but also helps keep deployment costs low. Also, the Windows 2000 Remote Installation Services allow you a way to create an image of Windows 2000 Professional you can use to install Windows 2000 Professional on your network client systems. This image actually consists of the installation files from the Windows 2000 Professional CD-ROM.

Remote Local Printer   A print device connected directly to a print server but accessed by another print server or by workstations. The queue for the print device exists on the server, and the print server controls job priority, print order, and queue administration. Client computers submit print jobs to the server and can observe the queue to monitor the printing process on the server. Drivers for the print device are loaded onto the client computer from the print server.

Remote Network Printer   A network printer connected to a print server that is accessed by client workstations or other print servers. Like the remote local printer, the printer queue is controlled by the print server, meaning that the client computers submit their print jobs to the print server, rather than to the print device directly. This allows for server administration and monitoring of the printer queues. Drivers for the print device are loaded onto the client computers from the print server.

Replay Attack   An attack in which the unauthorized user records the exchange of packets between an authorized user and the server, and plays it back later.

Replication Service   Distributes directory data across the enterprise network.

Repudiation   The identity of the sender cannot be verified.

Request   After the client receives the DHCPOFFER message and accepts the Internet Protocol (IP) address, it sends a DHCPREQUEST message out to all Dynamic Host Configuration Protocol (DHCP) servers indicating that it has accepted an offer. The message contains the IP address of the DHCP server that made the accepted offer, and all other DHCP servers release the addresses they had offered back into their available address pool.

Reverse Lookup Query   A reverse lookup query resolves an Internet Protocol (IP) address to a Domain Name System (DNS) name, and can be used for a variety of reasons. The process is different, though, because it makes use of a special domain called in-addr.arpa. This domain is also hierarchical, but is based on IP addresses and not names. The sub-domains are organized by the *reverse* order of the IP address. For instance, the domain 16.254.169.in-addr.arpa contains the addresses in the 169.254.16.* range; the 120.129.in-addr.arpa domain contains the addresses for the 129.120.*.* range.

RID Master   The RID master is a domain-wide role, and this domain controller (DC) allocates relative ID sequences to the domain controllers in its domain. A RID is a unique security identifier assigned each time a user, group, or computer object is created.

RIPrep   *See* Remote Installation Preparation.

Rollback Strategy   As with any upgrade, problems can sometimes require going back to the previous state. This possibility also applies to upgrading your domain to Windows 2000. You need to create a plan to "roll back" your network to its previous state if the upgrade to Windows 2000 fails.

Routing and Remote Access Service (RRAS)   Within Windows NT, a software routing and remote access capability combining packet filtering, Open Shortest Path First (OSPF) support, etc.

RRAS   *See* Routing and Remote Access Service.

Safe Mode   Safe Mode starts Windows 2000 using only some basic files and device drivers. These devices include monitor, keyboard, mouse, basic VGA video, CD-ROM, and mass storage devices. The system starts only those system services that are necessary to load the operating system. Networking is not started in this mode. The Windows background screen is black in this mode, and the screen resolution is 640 by 480 pixels with 16 colors.

Safe Mode with Command Prompt This option starts the operating system in a safe mode using some basic files only. The Windows 2000 command prompt is shown instead of the usual Windows desktop.

Safe Mode with Networking This mode is similar to the Safe Mode, but networking devices, drivers, and protocols are loaded. You may choose this mode when you are sure that the problem in the system is not due to any networking component.

SAM *See* Security Accounts Manager.

Schema A set of rules which defines the classes of objects and attributes contained in the directory, the constraints and limits on instances of these objects, and the format of their names.

Schema Master The domain controller (DC) designated as schema master controls updates and modifications to the schema. This role is forest wide, because a common schema is shared by all domains in a forest. There can be only one schema master in the forest, and changes to the schema can be made only through that machine.

Scripted Method This method for Windows 2000 Professional installation uses an answer file to specify various configuration parameters. This is used to eliminate user interaction during installation, thereby automating the installation process. Answers to most of the questions asked by the setup process are specified in the answer file. Besides this, the scripted method can be used for clean installations and upgrades.

SCSI *See* Small Computer System Interface.

Secondary Domain Name System (DNS) Server Secondary DNS servers provide fault tolerance and load balancing for DNS zones. Secondary servers contain a read-only copy of the zone database that it receives from the primary server during a zone transfer. A secondary server will respond to a DNS request if the primary server fails to respond because of an error or a heavy load. Since secondary servers can resolve DNS queries, they are also considered authoritative within a domain, and can help with load balancing on the network. Secondary servers can be placed in remote locations on the network and configured to respond to DNS queries from local computers, potentially reducing query traffic across longer network distances. While there can be only one primary server in a zone, multiple secondary servers can be set up for redundancy and load balancing.

Secret Key   A digital code or password shared by two parties, used for both encryption and decryption of messages.

Secret Key Encryption   When two parties use the same shared secret key to encrypt and decrypt data.

Secure Sockets Layer (SSL)   A protocol that provides security at the socket level and is used for securing Web access.

Security Accounts Manager (SAM)   The Security Accounts Manager (SAM) is the portion of the Windows NT Server registry that stores user account information and group membership. Attributes that are specific to Terminal Server can be added to user accounts. This adds a small amount of information to each user's entry in the domain's SAM.

Security Groups   The Windows 2000 Security Groups allow you to assign the same security permissions to large numbers of users in one operation. This ensures consistent security permissions across all members of a group. Using Security Groups to assign permissions means the access control on resources remains fairly static and easy to control and audit. Users who need access are added or removed from the appropriate security groups as needed, and the access control lists change infrequently.

Security Templates   Windows 2000 comes with several predefined Security Templates. These templates address several security scenarios. Security Templates come in two basic categories: Default and Incremental. The Default or Basic templates are applied by the operating system when a clean install has been performed; they are not applied if an upgrade installation has been done.

Segment   In discussions of Transmission Control Protocol/Internet Protocol (TCP/IP), segment often refers to the group of computers located on one side of a router, or sometimes a group of computers within the same collision domain.

Sequenced Packet eXchange (SPX)   The communications protocol (from NetWare) used to control network message transport.

Server   The word "server" can take on a variety of different meanings. A server can be a physical computer. A server can also represent a particular software package. For example, Microsoft Exchange 2000 is a mail and groupware Server application. Often, server applications are just referred to as "servers," as with mail servers. The term "server" is also used to refer to any computer that is currently sharing its resources on the network. In this context, all computers, whether Windows $3x$ or Windows 2000, can be servers on a network.

Server Message Block (SMB) Signing   SMB signing requires that every packet in the stream be verified. Enabling SMB signing can result in decreased performance on the server. This may be an acceptable tradeoff in an environment where sensitive data is subject to attack, but is a side effect of which you should be aware if your network's functions require optimum performance.

Service Level Agreement (SLA)   The SLA is a document that is created by the Information Technology (IT) department that describes the roles and responsibilities of the IT department, outlines the scope of services to be performed, and attempts to set expectations for the end user.

Service Pack   A service pack typically contains bug fixes, security fixes, systems administration tools, drivers, and additional components. Microsoft recommends installing the latest service packs as they are released. As a new feature in Windows 2000, you do not have to reinstall components after installing a service pack.

Setup Manager   The Setup Manager is the best tool to use when you have no idea of the answer file syntax or when you do not want to get into the time-consuming task of creating or modifying the sample answer file. When you choose to use the Setup Manager for unattended installations, you need to do a lot of planning beforehand. It is understood that you will not be using Setup

Manager for automating installations on one or two computers; that would be a waste of effort. Setup Manager is useful for mass deployments only.

SETUPACT.LOG   The Action log file contains details about the files that are copied during setup.

SETUPAPI.LOG   This log file contains details about the device driver files that were copied during setup. This log can be used to facilitate troubleshooting device installations. The file contains errors and warnings along with a time stamp for each issue.

SETUPCL.EXE   The function of the SETUPCL.EXE file is to run the Mini-Setup wizard and to regenerate the security IDs on the master and destination computers. The Mini-Setup wizard starts on the master computer when it is booted for the first time after running SysPrep.

SETUPERR.LOG   The Error log file contains details about errors that occurred during setup.

SETUPLOG.TXT   This log file contains additional information about the device driver files that were copied during setup.

Shared Folders   Sharing folders so that other users can access their contents across the network is easy in Windows 2000, as easy as right-clicking on the folder name in Windows Explorer, selecting the Sharing tab, and choosing Share This Folder. An entire drive and all the folders on that drive can be shared in the same way.

Shared Folders Permissions   As only folders, not files, can be shared, shared folder permissions are a small subset of standard NT File System (NTFS) permissions for a folder. However, securing access to a folder through share permissions can be more restrictive or more liberal than standard NTFS folder permissions. Shared folder permissions are applied in the same manner as NTFS permissions.

Shared Printers   The process for sharing a printer attached to your local computer is similar to that for sharing a folder or drive. If the users who will access your printer will do so from machines that don't run the Windows 2000 operating system, you will need to install drivers for the other operating system(s).

Shared Resource   A shared resource is a device, data, or program that is made available to network users. This can include folders, files, printers, and even Internet connections.

Simple Network Management Protocol (SNMP)   A standard for managing hardware devices connected to a network, approved for Unix use, that lets administrators know, for example, when a printer has a paper jam or is low on toner.

Simple Volume   A simple volume is a volume created on a dynamic disk that is not fault tolerant, and includes space from only one physical disk. A simple volume is just that—it is a single volume that does not span more than one physical disk, and does not provide improved drive performance, extra capacity, or fault tolerance. One physical disk can contain a single, large simple volume, or several smaller ones. Each simple volume is assigned a separate drive letter. The number of simple volumes on a disk is limited only by the capacity of the disk and the number of available letters in the alphabet.

Single-Instance-Store (SIS) Volume   When you have more than one image on the Remote Installation Services (RIS) server, each holding Windows 2000 Professional files, there will be duplicate copies of hundreds of files. This may consume significant hard drive space on the RIS server. To overcome this problem, Microsoft introduced a new feature called the Single-Instance-Store, which helps in deleting all the duplicate files, thus saving on hard drive space.

Single Master Operation   This is an operation in which a single domain controller is in charge of a particular operation for a period of time.Single

Sign-on   The ability of users to provide one username and password to access all authorized network resources rather than having to be authenticated separately for multiple servers and applications.

SIS   *See* Single-Instance-Store.

Site Server Internet Locator Server (ILS) Service   This service supports Internet Protocol (IP) telephony applications. Publishes IP multicast conferences on a network, and can also publish user IP address mappings for H.323 IP telephony. Telephony applications, such as NetMeeting and Phone Dialer in Windows Accessories, use Site Server ILS Service to display user names and conferences with published addresses. Site Server ILS Service depends on Internet Information Services (IIS).

SLA   *See* Service Level Agreement.

Small Computer System Interface (SCSI)   A complete expansion bus interface that accepts such devices as a hard disk, CD-ROM, disk drivers, printers, or scanners.

Smart Card   A device similar to a credit card, which contains an embedded chip (also called a token) that stores digital certificates and is used for authentication. By adding a chip to the card, it becomes a smart card with the power to serve many different uses. As an access-control device, smart cards protect personal and business data so that only the appropriate users are granted access.

SMB   *See* Server Message Block.

SMP   *See* Symmetric Multiprocessing.

SMS   *See* Systems Management Server.

SNA   *See* Systems Network Architecture.

Snap-ins   The management applications that are contained in an Microsoft Management Console (MMC) are called snap-ins, and custom MMCs hold the snap-ins required to perform specific tasks.

SNMP   *See* Simple Network Management Protocol.

Social Engineering Attack   This is the term used for breaking into a network by simply "outwitting" employees and convincing them to reveal their passwords. Often the intruder pretends to be with the company's IT department and tells the users that he is verifying their password or that there is a problem with their network account.

Spanned Volume   A spanned volume is similar to a volume set in NT 4.0. It contains space from multiple disks (up to 32), and provides a way to combine small "chunks" of disk space into one unit, seen by the operating system as a single volume. It is not fault tolerant. When a dynamic volume includes the space on more than one physical hard drive, it is called a spanned volume. Spanned volumes can be used to increase drive capacity, or to make use of the leftover space on up to 32 existing disks. Like those in a basic storage volume set, the portions of a spanned volume are all linked together and share a single drive letter.

SPX   *See* Sequenced Packet eXchange.

Stack   A data structure in which the first items inserted are the last ones removed, unlike control structure programs that use the Last In First Out (LIFO) structure.

Static Internet Protocol (IP) Address   A static IP address allows users to use a domain name that can be translated into an IP address. The static IP address allows the server to always have the same IP address, so the domain name always translates to the correct IP address. If the address was assigned dynamically and occasionally changed, users might not be able to access the server across the Internet using the domain name.

Stripe Set   The term "striping" refers to the interleaving of data across separate physical disks. Each file is broken into small blocks, and each block is evenly and alternately saved to the disks in the stripe set. In a two-disk stripe set, the first block of data is saved to the first disk, the second block is saved to the second disk, and the third block is saved to the first disk, and so on. The two disks are treated as a single drive, and are given a single drive letter.

Stripe Set with Parity   A stripe set with parity requires at least three hard disks, and provides both increased storage capacity and fault tolerance. In a stripe set with parity, data is interleaved across three or more disks, and includes parity (error checking) information about the data. As long as only one disk in the set fails, the parity information can be used to reconstruct the lost data. If the parity information itself is lost, it can be reconstructed from the original data.

Striped Volume   Like a stripe set in NT 4.0, a striped volume is the dynamic storage equivalent of a basic stripe set and combines free space from up to 32 physical disks into one volume by writing data across the disks in stripes. This increases performance but does not provide fault tolerance. A striped volume improves drive performance and increases drive capacity. Because each data block is written only once, striped volumes do not provide fault tolerance.

Striping Striping is when the data are striped across the drives and there is parity information along with the data. The parity information is based on a mathematical formula that comes up with the parity based on the data on the other drives.

Strong Encryption Uses a 56-bit DES key. There are 72 quadrillion possible combinations—this is to say that strong encryption is fairly safe.

Subnetting The process of taking one TCP/IP network address range (Class A, B, or C) and dividing it into two or more ranges.

Subsidiary Model A subsidiary model is one in which there exists a parent company that owns in whole or in part other companies. The core business that each subsidiary services can be completely different or subsidiaries can be in competition with each other. A company that has a subsidiary model will typically choose to implement Active Directory (AD) with multiple domains in a single tree. The reasons for this are that each subsidiary will probably want to retain complete control over their environment. With the creations of multiple domains each subsidiary can maintain it own autonomy. They are able to deploy their own set of requirement for their users.

Symmetric Multiprocessing (SMP) SMP is a system in which all processors are treated as equals, and any thread can be run on any available processor. Windows 2000 also supports processor affinity, in which a process or thread can specify which set of processors it should run on. Application Programming Interfaces (APIs) must be defined in the application.

Synthesis The process of design, formulation, integration, prediction, proposal, generalization, and show relationships.

SYSPREP.INF SYSPREP.INF is an answer file. When you want to automate the Mini-Setup wizard by providing predetermined answers to all setup questions, you must use this file. This file needs to be placed in the %Systemroot%\Sysprep folder or on a floppy disk. When the Mini-Setup wizard is run on the computer on which the image is being distributed, it takes answers from the SYSPREP.INF file without prompting the user for any input.

System Monitor The System Monitor is part of this Administrative Tools utility, and allows you to collect and view data about current memory usage, disk, processor utilization, network activity and other system activity. System Monitor allows you to collect information about your hardware's performance as well as network utilization, and can be used to measure different aspects of a computer's performance on one's own computer or on other computers on the network.

System Policy The system policy editor is used to provide user and computer configuration settings in the Windows NT registry database. The system policy editor is still used for the management of Windows 9*x* and Windows NT server and workstations and stand-alone computers using Windows 2000.

System Preparation (Sysprep) SysPrep provides an excellent means of saving installation time and reducing installation costs. Sysprep is the best tool to copy the image of a computer to other computers that have identical hardware configurations. It is also helpful in standardizing the desktop environment throughout the organization. Since one Sysprep image cannot be used on computers with identical hardware and software applications, you can create multiple images when you have more than one standard. It is still the best option where the number of computers is in hundreds or thousands and you wish to implement uniform policies in the organization.

Systems Management Server (SMS) This Windows NT software analyzes and monitors network usage and various network functions.

Systems Network Architecture (SNA) Systems Network Architecture (SNA) was developed by IBM in the mainframe computer era (1974, to be precise) as a way of getting its various products to communicate with each other for distributed processing. SNA is a line of products designed to make other products cooperate. In your career of designing network solutions, you should expect to run into SNA from time to time because many of the bigger companies (i.e., banks, healthcare institutions, government offices) bought IBM equipment and will be reluctant to part with their investment. SNA is a proprietary protocol that runs over SDLC exclusively, although it may be transported within other protocols, such as X.25 and Token Ring. It is designed as a hierarchy and consists of a collection of machines called nodes.

Take Ownership Permission This permission can be given to allow a user to take ownership of a file or folder object. Every file and folder on an NT File System (NTFS) drive has an owner, usually the account that created the object. However, there are times when ownership of a file needs to be changed, perhaps because of a change in team membership or a set of new responsibilities for a user.

Task-based Model This model is appropriate for companies in which administrative duties are functionally divided. This means that this model divides the management of Group Policy Objects (GPOs) by certain tasks. To apply this model, the administrators that handle security-related tasks will also be responsible for managing all policy objects that affect security. The second set of administrators that normally deploy the companies' business applications will be responsible for all the GPOs that affect installation and maintenance.

TCO *See* Total Cost of Operation.

TCP/IP *See* Transmission Control Protocol/Internet Protocol.

Terminal Services In application server mode, Terminal Services provides the ability to run client applications on the server, while "thin client" software acts as a terminal emulator on the client. Each user sees an individual session, displayed as a Windows 2000 desktop. The server manages each session, independent of any other client session. If you install Terminal Services as an application server, you must also install Terminal Services Licensing (not necessarily on the same computer). However, temporary licenses can be issued for clients that allow you to use Terminal servers for up to 90 days. In remote administration mode, you can use Terminal Services to log on remotely and manage Windows 2000 systems from virtually anywhere on your network (instead of being limited to working locally on a server). Remote administration mode allows for two concurrent connections from a given server and minimizes impact on server performance. Remote administration mode does not require you to install Terminal Services Licensing.

TFTP *See* Trivial File Transfer Protocol.

Theory X   Theory X is the so-called traditional model, often used in government agencies, where there is a strict chain of command that employees are expected to follow. Going "over the heads" of superiors is frowned upon, or even formally prohibited, and the structure of the organization is paramilitary in nature. Employees are expected to follow the rules that are handed down from on high.

Theory Y   Theory Y is the modern management theory that offers a kinder, gentler atmosphere in which employee input in decision-making is encouraged or even required. The company presents itself as one big, happy family where each member is equally valued (although not, of course, equally compensated in monetary terms). Creativity is considered a more valuable asset than going "by the book."

Token Ring   A Local Area Network (LAN) specification that was developed by IBM in the 1980s for PC-based networks and classified by the IEEE (Institute of Electrical and Electronics Engineers) as 802.5. It specifies a star topology physically and a ring topology logically. It runs at either four Mbps or 16 Mbps, but all nodes on the ring must run at the same speed.

Total Cost of Operation (TCO) Analysis   The whole idea of TCO analysis is to expose the hidden costs of a product over its projected life cycle.

Transmission Control Protocol/Internet Protocol (TCP/IP)   A set of communications standards created by the U.S. Department of Defense (DoD) in the 1970s that has now become an accepted way to connect different types of computers in networks because the standards now support so many programs.

Trees   Trees are groups of domains that share a contiguous namespace. It allows you to create a hierarchical grouping of domains that share a common contiguous namespace. This hierarchy allows global sharing of resources among domains in the tree. All the domains in a tree share information and resources with a single directory, and there is only one directory per tree. However, each domain manages its own subset of the directory that contains the user accounts for that domain. So, when a user logs into a domain, the user has global access to all resources that are part of the tree, providing the user has the proper permissions.

Trivial File Transfer Protocol (TFTP)　A network application similar to FTP except that it uses User Datagram Protocol (UDP) instead of Transmission Control Protocol (TCP) and provides no mechanism for user authentication or directory visibility.

Trojan Horse　A virus or malicious program is disguised as a harmless program.

Trust　The users in one tree do not have global access to resources in other trees, but trusts can be created that allow users to access resources in another tree. A trust allows all the trees to share resources and have common administrative functions. Such sharing capability allows the trees to operate independently of each other, with separate namespaces, yet still be able to communicate and share resources through trusts.

Trust Relationship　A trust relationship is a connection between domains in which users who have accounts in and log on to one domain can then access resources in other domains, provided they have proper access permissions.

UDF　*See* Unique Database File.

UDP　*See* User Datagram Protocol.

Unattended Method　The unattended method for Windows 2000 Server installation uses the answer file to specify various configuration parameters. This method eliminates user interaction during installation, thereby automating the installation process and reducing the chances of input errors. Answers to most of the questions asked by the setup process are specified in the answer file. In addition, the scripted method can be used for clean installations and upgrades.

UNATTEND.TXT File　The creation of customized UNATTEND.TXT answer files is the simplest form of providing answers to setup queries and unattended installation of Windows 2000. This can be done either by using the Setup Manager or by editing the sample UNATTEND.TXT file using Notepad or the MS-DOS text editor. The UNATTEND.TXT file does not provide any means of creating an image of the computer.

UNATTEND.UDF This file is the Uniqueness Database File, which provides customized settings for each computer using the automated installation.

UNC *See* Universal Naming Convention.

UNICODE UNICODE is a 16-bit character encoding standard developed by the Unicode Consortium between 1988 and 1991 that uses two bytes to represent each character and enables almost all of the written languages of the world to be represented using a single character set.

Uninterruptible Power Supply (UPS) A battery that can supply power to a computer system if the power fails. It charges while the computer is on and, if the power fails, provides power for a certain amount of time allowing the user to shut down the computer properly to preserve data.

Unique Database File (UDF) When you use the WINNT32.EXE command with the /unattend option, you can also specify a Unique Database File (UDF), which has a .UDB extension. This file forces Setup to use certain values from the UDF file, thus overriding the values given in the answer file. This is particularly useful when you want to specify multiple users during the setup.

Universal Groups Universal Groups are used in larger, multi-domain organizations, in which there is a need to grant access to similar groups of accounts defined in multiple domains. It is better to use Global Groups as members of Universal Groups to reduce overall replication traffic from changes to Universal Group membership. Users can be added and removed from the corresponding Global Groups with their account domains, and a small number of Global Groups are the direct members of the Universal Group. Universal Groups are used only in multiple domain trees or forests. A Windows 2000 domain must be in native mode to use Universal Groups.

Universal Naming Convention (UNC) A UNC is an identification standard of servers and other network resources.

Universal Serial Bus (USB)   A low-speed hardware interface (supports MPEG video) with a maximum bandwidth up to 1.5 MBytes per second.

UPS   *See* Uninterruptible Power Supply.

USB   *See* Universal Serial Bus.

User Account   The information that defines a particular user on a network, which includes the username, password, group memberships, and rights and permissions assigned to the user.

User Datagram Protocol (UDP)   A protocol similar to TCP except that it does not provide a guarantee of packet delivery nor does it provide sequencing of packets.

Value Bar   The value bar is positioned below the graph area. It displays data for the selected sample, the last sample value, the average of the counter samples, the maximum and minimum of the samples, and the duration of time the samples have been taken over.

Virtual Private Network (VPN)   A private network configured within or over a public network. Access control and encryption can provide the same security as a private network, while taking advantage of the scale and built-in management facilities of larger public networks. VPNs reduce service costs and long distance/usage fees, lighten infrastructure investments, and simplify Wide Area Network (WAN) operations over time.

Volume Set   The term "volume" indicates a single drive letter. One physical hard disk can contain several volumes, one for each primary partition or logical drive. However, the opposite is also true. You can create a single volume that spans more than one physical disk. This is a good option when you require a volume that exceeds the capacity of a single physical disk. You can also create a volume set when you want to make use of leftover space on several disks by piecing them together as one volume.

VPN   *See* Virtual Private Network.

WDM   *See* Windows32 Driver Model.

Windows 3x   Windows 3*x* changed everything. It was a 16-bit operating system with a user interface that resembled the look and feel of IBM's (at that time not yet released) OS/2, with 3D buttons and the ability to run multiple programs simultaneously, using a method called cooperative multitasking. Windows 3 also provided virtual memory, the ability to use hard disk space to "fool" the applications into behaving as if they had more RAM than was physically installed in the machine.

Windows 9x   In August of 1995, Microsoft released its long-awaited upgrade of Windows, Windows 95. For the first time, Windows could be installed on a machine that didn't already have MS-DOS installed. Many improvements were made: the new 32-bit functionality (although still retaining some 16-bit code for backward compatibility); preemptive multitasking (a more efficient way to run multiple programs in which the operating system controls use of the processor and the crash of one application does not bring down the others that are currently running); and support for filenames longer than the DOS-based eight-character limit.

Windows32 Driver Model (WDM)   The Win32 Driver Model (WDM) provides a standard for device drivers that will work across Windows platforms (specifically Windows 98 and 2000), so that you can use the same drivers with the consumer and business versions of the Windows operating system.

Windows 2000   Microsoft's latest incarnation of the corporate operating system was originally called NT 5, but the name was changed to Windows 2000 between the second and third beta versions—perhaps to underscore the fact that this is truly a *new* version of the operating system, not merely an upgrade to NT.

Windows 2000 Control Panel   The Control Panel in Windows 2000 functions similarly to the Control Panel in Windows 9*x* and NT, except that "under the hood" there are now two locations where information is stored, which is modified by the Control Panel applets. The Control Panel in previous operating systems was a graphical interface for editing Registry information.

Windows Backup   Windows Backup is a built-in Backup and Restore utility, which has many more features than the backup tool provided in Windows NT 4.0. It supports all five types of backup: Normal, Copy, Differential, Incremental, and Daily. Windows Backup allows you to perform the backup operation manually or you may schedule it to run at a later time in unattended mode. Included with the operating system, it is a tool that is flexible and easy to use.

Windows Internet Name Service (WINS)   WINS provides name resolution for clients running Windows NT and earlier versions of Microsoft operating systems. With name resolution, users can access servers by name, instead of having to use Internet Protocol (IP) addresses that are difficult to recognize and remember. WINS is used to map NetBIOS computer names to IP addresses. This allows users to access other computers on the network by computer name. WINS servers should be assigned a static IP address, which allows clients to be able to find the WINS servers. Clients cannot find a WINS server by name because they need to know where the WINS server is in order to translate the name into an IP address.

Windows Internet Name Service (WINS) Name Registration   Each WINS client has one or more WINS servers identified in the network configuration on the computer, either through static assignment or through DHCP configuration. When the client boots and connects to the network, it registers its name and IP address with the WINS server by sending a registration request directly to the server. This is not a broadcast message, since the client has the address of the server. If the server is available and the name is not already registered, the server responds with a successful registration message, which contains the amount of time the name will be registered to the client, the Time To Live (TTL). Then the server stores the name and address combination in its local database.

Windows Internet Name Service (WINS) Name Release   When a WINS client shuts down properly, it will send a name release request to the WINS server. This releases the name from the WINS server's database so that another client can use the name if necessary. The release request contains the WINS name and address of the client. If the server cannot find the name, it sends a negative release response to the client. If the server finds the matching name and address in its database, it releases the name and marks the record as inactive. If the name is found but the address does not match, the server ignores the request.

Windows Internet Name Service (WINS) Name Renewal As with Dynamic Host Configuration Protocol (DHCP), WINS name registrations are temporary and must be renewed to continue to be valid. The client will attempt to renew its registration when half (50 percent) of the Time To Live (TTL) has elapsed. If the WINS server does not respond, the client repeatedly attempts to renew its lease at ten-minute intervals for an hour. If the client still receives no response, it restarts the process with the secondary WINS server, if one is defined. The client will continue attempting to renew its lease in this manner until it receives a response from a server. At that time, the server sends a new TTL to the client and the process starts over.

Windows Internet Name Service (WINS) Proxy Agent A WINS Proxy agent is similar to a Dynamic Host Configuration Protocol (DHCP) Relay Agent. It listens for requests for non-WINS network clients and redirects those requests to a WINS server. A WINS proxy operates in two modes.

Windows Internet Name Service (WINS) Snap-in With the snap-in, you can view the active WINS entries under the Active Registrations folder. In addition, you can supply static mappings for non-WINS clients on the network through the snap-in. To configure a static mapping, select the Active Registrations folder and select New Static Mapping from the Action menu. Once a static mapping is entered into the WINS database, it cannot be edited. If you need to make changes to a static mapping, you must delete and re-create the entry.

Windows NT The NT kernel (the core or nucleus of the operating system, which provides basic services for all other parts of the operating system) is built on a completely different architecture from consumer Windows. In fact, NT was based on the 32-bit preemptive multitasking operating system, OS/2, that originated as a joint project of Microsoft and IBM before their parting of the ways. NT provided the stability and security features that the "other Windows" lacked, albeit at a price, and not only a monetary one; NT was much pickier in terms of hardware support, did not run all of the programs that ran on Windows 9*x* (especially DOS programs that accessed the hardware directly), and required more resources, especially memory, to run properly.

WINNT.EXE Program The WINNT.EXE program is used for network installations that use an MS-DOS network client. The WINNT32.EXE program is used to customize the process for upgrading existing installations. The WINNT32.EXE program is used for installing Windows 2000 from a computer that is currently running Windows 95/98 or Windows NT.

WINS *See* Windows Internet Name Service.

Workgroup   A workgroup is a logical grouping of resources on a network. It is generally used in peer-to-peer networks. This means that each computer is responsible for access to its resources. Each computer has its own account database and is administered separately. Security is not shared between computers, and administration is more difficult than in a centralized domain.

Zones of Authority   The Domain Name System (DNS) name space is divided into zones, and each zone must have one name server that is the authority for the name mapping for the zone. Depending on the size of the name space, a zone may be subdivided into multiple zones, each with its own authority, or there may be a single authority for the entire zone. For instance, a small company with only 200-300 computers could have one DNS server handle the entire namespace.

INDEX

A

Access control, 35, 443-445
Access control entries (ACEs), 297, 320, 443
    blocking inheritance of, 445
    using ACL editor to modify, 403
Access control list (ACL), 54, 297, 320, 443, 454
    adding to, 455
    modifying, 455
    viewing or modifying, 325
Access Control Policy, 51, 54
Access Control Settings dialog box, 206, 327, 460
Access.Globalknowledge site, 608
Account lockout, 172, 414
Account lockout interval, 172
Account lockout policy, 414
Account policies, 414
ACL editor, 402-403
Acquisition plans, company, 107-108
Active Directory (AD)
    concepts, 296-309
    creating an OU in, 69
    directory service, 297
    global catalog, 298-299
    installing, 62-69
    namespaces, 300
    network security support, 296
    physical and logical structures, 301
    replication, 305-306
    restoring on a DC, 474-475
    schema, 242, 298
    schema attributes, 243
    schema definitions, 298
    security and administration, 36
    sites, 301-304
    stamps, 239-240
    structure, 53
    structure chart, 54
    tombstone lifetime, 470
    trust relationships, 299-300
Active Directory chart, 61
Active Directory components, 401
    planning security for, 310-320
    securing, 320-333
Active Directory Domains and Trusts, 250-251
Active Directory Installation Wizard, 62-69, 231-238
Active Directory log, 234
Active Directory Sites and Services, 302-304
Active Directory Users and Computers snap-in, 246, 324, 456
Add Script dialog box, 406
Add Standalone snap-in dialog box, 398, 421
Administration (IT), 114-115
Administrative control, delegating. *See* Delegation of administrative authority
Administrative group (network security), 136, 138-139, 448
Administrative processes, researching, 54-55
Administrative responsibilities, example, 520
Administrative structure design basics, 445-447

677

Administrator account
  categories of recovery, 506
  limiting use of, 166
  object ownership, 444
  roles and responsibilities, 54, 202, 450
Administrator account password, 236
Advanced Attributes dialog box, 356
Advanced Features (Windows 2000),
  enabling, 326
Algorithms (cryptography), 35
Allow Access if Dial-In Permission
  Is Enabled, 551
Allow Inheritable Permissions from Parent...,
  321-322
Analog modem, 540, 557
Analog phone line, 540
Analysis issues (Exam 70-220), 13-21
Analysis phase (security planning), 11
Analyzing business models, 49-95
Analyzing business requirements, 13-16, 97-133
Analyzing company processes, 74-76
Analyzing current information security model,
  152-153, 160-171
Analyzing current physical security model,
  152-159
Analyzing security requirements, 289-349
Analyzing technical requirements, 191-227
Analyzing users' requirements, 135-189
ANI/CLI authorization, 147
Anti-virus software, 210-211
Application groups, 152
Application Programming Interface (API), 204
Application requirements, 149-152, 206-207
Application roles, 150
Application servers, 257-258
Application service providers (ASPs), 104-105,
  204, 206

Application-level encryption, 483
Applications
  in use, 256
  security of existing, 210-211
Apply Group Policy permission, 402
Assessment and evaluation phase (security
  planning), 12
Assets (physical), ownership of, 204
Asymmetric encryption, 35, 369
Asynchronous Transfer Mode (ATM)
  networks, 556
Attributes, object, 296, 298
Audit events, 167
Audit Policy, 407-412, 415
Auditing, 22, 166-167, 407-412
  enabling for object access, 411
  planning a strategy for, 409-411
  success or failure, 412
  viewing results of, 409-410
Auditing entries, inherited, 411
Auditing options, 409
Authentication, 22, 32
  certificate-based, 358-359
  Digest Authentication (DA), 362-363
  Kerberos, 360-361
  NTLM, 361-362
  remote access policy, 565
  smart card, 359, 363-364
Authentication Header (AH), 585
Authentication methods, 22-23, 36,
  358-364, 576
Authentication protocols, 143, 170, 554-559
Authentication service, selecting, 545
Authentication strategy, designing, 357-359
Authoritative restore, 471, 475
Authorized connection, 563
Authorized user access, enabling, 6
Authorized users, 6, 442

Autonomy, management model, 100-101
Average monthly expenses (TCO model), 113

B

BackOffice products, 368
Backing up data, 155-156
Backup devices, 155
Backup domain controller (BDC), 230, 361
Backup Operators group, 470
Backup products, and loss of data, 469
Backup and recovery operations, EFS, 501-508
Backup and recovery tools, 469
Backup and restore rights, 470-471
Backup strategy, 469
Backup utility (Windows 2000), 469-475
    backing up/restoring an encrypted file, 505
    backing up/restoring an encrypted folder, 502-504
    features of, 470
    file system constraints, 471
    moving an encrypted file, 501
Bandwidth, 201
    available, 198-200
    cost of, 71
Bandwidth Allocation Control Protocol (BACP), 559
Bandwidth Allocation Protocol (BAP), 559, 565
Baseline security, 20, 229-287, 290
Basic encryption, 112, 208, 565
Basic security templates (BASIC*.INF), 412-413
Batch files, running, 266
BDC (backup domain controller), 230, 361
Boot configuration, protecting, 471
Boot floppy, fault-tolerant, 468
Boot sector inspection, 478
Bottom line factors (company), 9

Branch office model, 73
Branch site users, data protection for, 168-169
Bridgehead servers, 313
Browse for a Group Policy Object dialog box, 399
Browser certificates, 372
Business. *See* Company (business)
Business classes, 136-140
Business life cycles, 77-81
Business location diagrams, 56
Business models, 14
    analyzing, 49-95
    branch office model, 73
    existing and planned, 99-109
    international, 71-72
    national, 70-71
    regional, 57-61
    subsidiary model, 72-73
Business partnerships, 137
Business requirements, 136-152
    analyzing, 13, 97-133
    for remote access, 56
Business structure, mirroring in OU structure, 447
Business unit, delegation by, 448
Business unit two-tiered structure diagram, 449
Business-to-business transactions, 373
Busmaster controllers, 254

C

Cable modems, 198-200
Cache memory, server performance and, 253
Caching controllers, 254
Callback feature, 146
Case study question format, 13
Case study sample question demo, 13

CD-ROM (with this Guide), 601-606
Central connection points, securing, 17
Centralized administration model, 446
Centralized IT administration, 114-115
Centralized organizations, 100-101
CertCam, 604-605
Certificate Authority (CA), 32, 160, 370, 486, 549
    in online transactions, 371
    PKI with, 373
    sites as their own, 373
    third-party, 373
Certificate Authority hierarchy, 370, 547
Certificate Authority server, 539, 547
Certificate formats, 371-372
Certificate management, 371-372
Certificate Services roles, 370-371
Certificate Services sample policies, 370
Certificate-based authentication, 32, 149, 160, 358-359, 370-373
CertTrainer software
    help file, 606
    installing, 602
    system requirements, 602
Chain of command (business), 15
Change Permissions permission, 326
Change-management process, IT, 116
CHAP (Challenge Handshake Authentication Protocol), 32, 555
Chapter summaries of this Guide, 25-31
Child domains, 102
Child folders, 322
Child object, 321-322
Choice Options Properties window, 376
Cipher command, 32, 488, 497-500
    options, 498
    without parameters, 499

Classes, object, 242, 296, 298, 455
Classes in the schema, 242
Client computers assigned to sites, 301
Client-server communication flow, 76
CMOS settings, server, 155
Common Internet File System (CIFS), 565
Communication channels, security design for, 24-25
Communication flow through a company, 76
Company (business). *See also* Business models
    access control policies, 51, 54
    acquisition plans, 107-108
    bottom line, 9
    branch office model, 73
    communication flow, 76
    customer relationships, 107
    data administrative processes, 54-55
    expansion plans, 213
    geographical scope, 99-100
    growth strategies, 8-9, 110
    hierarchy, 102
    information flow, 75
    international model, 71-72
    IT management structure, 114-119
    management model, 100-101
    national model, 70-71
    network topology, 56
    organization, 102-103
    organizational charts, 50, 52-53, 519
    partnership relationships, 106-107
    priorities, 7-8, 110
    processes, 74-76, 101-102
    products or services, 137
    projected growth, 8-9, 110, 194
    regional model, 57-61
    size of, 193-194
    structure of, 50, 52, 137

subsidiary model, 72-73
technical environment, 192-209
technology infrastructure, 55
tolerance for risk, 112-113
vendor relationships, 103-106
Company management, security planning and, 6-9
Company model, analyzing, 51-74
Company strategies, factors that influence, 15-16, 109-110, 112-114
Compatible (COMPAT*.INF) templates, 307, 413
Computer Management MMC snap-in, 573
Computers (Active Directory objects), 401
Conflict prevention, 239
Conflict resolution, 239
Connect to Domain Controller, 250-251
Connecting RRAS to the Internet, 529-539
Connection protocols, 170
Connections
    authorized, 563
    choices of, 198
    data protection for, 169
    inbound, 559-562
    low-speed, 71
    on-demand, 73
    outbound, 562
    types and speeds, 199
Consolidation mergers, company, 107-108
Consultants, 106
Consulting groups, 106
Container ACL, modifying, 455
Controllers, 253-254
Copper cable, detecting tapping of, 17
Copying or moving encrypted files, 495-496
Core protocol, 24
Cost of implementation, 9

Create Volume Wizard, 469
Cross-domain group-to-user reference, 249
Cryptography, 33, 355
    basics, 35
    levels of, 208
Customer relationships, company, 107
Customized delegation, 333

D

Data administrative processes, researching, 54-55
Data backups, 155-156
Data centers, controlling access to, 154-156
Data confidentiality, 35
Data decryption field (DDF), 484
Data encryption, 355, 482-483, 560. *See also* EFS
Data encryption protocols, 170
Data encryption scenarios, 482-483
Data exchanges, 373
Data files. *See* Files
Data integrity, 35
Data interception, 21
Data manipulation, unauthorized, 294
Data protection, 160-171
Data recovery, 463-481
Data recovery fields (DRFs), 484
Data security, 441-526
Data sensitivity, 214
Database and log locations, 65, 234
Dcpromo.exe, 231
Decentralized IT administration, 115
Decentralized organizations, 100-101
Decision tree, 117
Decision-making process, IT, 80-81, 116

Decrypting a folder on a local machine, 492-493
Decryption, 486-488
Decryption process diagram, 486
Dedicated domain controller templates, 413
Dedicated servers, 253-260
Default-First-Site-Name, 301-302
Define This Policy Setting dialog box, 567
Definitions of terms in this Guide, 609-676
Delegation of administrative authority, 22, 92, 305, 327-333
   and built-in security groups, 462
   combined with inheritance, 444-445
   creating OUs for, 447
   explained, 442
   flexibility of, 447
   full control, 450-451
   of Group Policy object control, 462
   methodology, 448, 450-454
   for an OU, 456-461
   per-object class control, 452-453
   procedures, 454-462
   of sites and services control, 462
   standard vs. customized, 333
   steps for, 328
   strategy for, 442-463
Delegation of Control Wizard, 93-95, 455, 457-458
   at OU level, 333
   options, 328
   using, 329-332
Demand Dial Interface Wizard, 533-538
Demand-dial Internet connection, 532-538
Demilitarized zone (DMZ), 18, 175
Denial of Service (DoS) attacks, 21, 174-175, 293
DES (Data Encryption Standard) encryption, 33, 112, 208, 565
Design, defined, 3
Design exams, purpose of, 3
Design issues (Exam 70-220), 22-25
Design phase (security planning), 11
Designing a security baseline, 229-287
Designing a security solution, 351-389
Designing security, explained, 3
Desktop scenario (Group Policy), 265-267
DHCP clients, 76
DHCP servers, 76, 376, 529
Dial-in access, risks from, 294
Dial-in constraints, remote access policy, 564
Dial-up permissions, 145-146
Dial-up Preferences, 146
Dial-up protocols, 144
Dial-up server, 259-260, 362, 539
Digest Authentication (DA), 362-363
Digiboards, 259, 540
Digital business model, 14
Digital certificates, 32, 149, 160, 358-359, 370-373
Digital signatures, 35, 370
Digital versatile disc (DVD), 209
Direct dial-up connectivity, 144-146
Directory partitions, global catalog, 298
Directory replication, 305-306
Directory services, 256, 297
Disaster recovery, 463-481
Disaster recovery plan, questions to ask, 464
Discretionary access control list (DACL), 297
Disk access time, 254
Disk Management tool, 468
Disk performance, 254
Disk subsystem performance, 253-254
   application server and, 257
   file and print servers and, 258-259
   RAS Server and, 260
Disks, physical access to, 508

Index **683**

Distributed security, 34
Distributing Internet interfaces, 175
Distribution groups, Windows 2000, 23
DNIS (Dialed Number Identification Service), 147
DNS Manager MMC snap-in tool, 374
DNS name, 310
DNS security, 374-375
DNS zone files, 374
Document that defines groups, 51
Domain, 102
Domain audit policies, 409
Domain Controller for a New Domain, 231
Domain controllers (DCs), 230-240, 301
    first, 231-238
    PDC emulator role for, 250-251
    number of, 256
    replication of, 70-71
    roles of, 238, 301
Domain hierarchy, 311
Domain local security groups, 307
Domain name, 300
Domain Name Server (DNS), 232, 300, 374, 376
Domain Naming Master, 242-244, 252
Domain Service Agent (DSA), 240
Domain structure, 138
Domain trees, 102
    creating, 63, 232
    multiple, 73
Domains, 114-115, 139, 353-354
    adding to a forest, 243-244
    multiple, 72-73, 311
    planning, 310-312
    users in, 57
    ways to break up, 353
Downtime, scheduled, 55
DriveTime (audio tracks), 605-606
DSL lines, 198, 201
DVD Consortium worldwide regions, 209
Dynamic disks, 468
Dynamic DNS (DDNS), 76, 374
Dynamic Host Configuration Protocol (DHCP), 76, 376, 529

E

Ease of implementation (security solutions), 9
E-commerce model, 14
EFS (Encrypting File System), 22, 161, 369, 355-357, 481-510
    backup and recovery operations, 501-508
    decryption process diagram, 486
    encrypting a folder using, 356
    encryption on a remote server, 493
    file encryption process diagram, 485
    file recovery process diagram, 487
    limitations of, 483
    overview of, 484-486
    private key, 505
    public key, 369
    recovery policy, 505
    security considerations of, 508-509
    using on a workstation, 509-510
Electronic data interchange (EDI), 103
Electronic purse cards (smart cards), 363
Emergency repair, 475-480
Emergency Repair disk (ERD), 470, 478-480
Emergency repair process, 476-480
Empty recovery policy, 506
Encapsulating Security Payload (ESP), 556, 558, 585
Encrypted Data Recovery Agent (EDRA), 484, 505-506
Encrypted directory, copying, 497

Encrypted files, 162, 507
    attempting to open, 508
    backing up and restoring, 505
    copying or moving, 495-496
    moving between machines, 501
    recoverability of, 484
Encrypted folders, 356
    backing up and restoring, 502-504
    copying between NTFS volumes, 497
    copying or moving, 496
    vs. files, 491
    on a local machine, 488-490
    on a remote server, 494
Encrypting data, 355, 482-483, 560
Encrypting File System. *See* EFS
Encryption, 33, 486-488
    asymmetric, 369
    128-bit, 207
    types of, 35
Encryption levels, 112, 208
Encryption properties, 565
Encryption scheme, IPSec, 585
Encryption Warning dialog box, 491
End users. *See* Users
Enterprise architect, 3
Enterprise CA, 547-550
Enterprise CA server, 547-550
Enterprise CA server setup, 548-550
Enterprise Root CA, creating, 547-550
Equinox cards, 259, 540
Equipment, ownership of, 204
Equipment costs (TCO model), 113
Error Applying Attributes message, 500
Error Copying (or Moving) File, 495-496
ESP (Encapsulating Security Payload), 556, 558, 585
Event Log, 415-416
Event Properties dialog box, 410, 585

Event Viewer, 408
Events to be audited, selecting, 408-409, 411
Everyone category, 141
Exam 70-220, 2-5
    analysis issues, 13-21
    design issues, 22-25
    Microsoft's stated objectives for, 13
    overview of, 13-25
    Windows 2000 vs. NT 4.0, 2-3
ExamSim, 603-604, 606
ExamSim upgrades, 606
Executive group (network security), 136-138
Explicit permissions, 321-322
Extensible Authentication Protocol (EAP), 555
External security and access policies, 139
External security risks, 17-18, 119, 172-175, 295
External trust, 300
Extranets, 148, 203

F

Facilities, physical access to, 153-154
Fast Repair, 477-478
Fatal failures during encryption/decryption, 508
Fault tolerance, components of, 465
Fault tolerant volumes, 465-469
Fault-tolerant boot floppy, 468
F8, pressing when starting Windows 2000, 476
Fiber cable, detecting tapping of, 16-17
56-bit DES encryption, 112, 208, 565
File encryption key (FEK), 484
File encryption process diagram, 485
File and print servers, 258-259
File Recovery enhanced key, 484, 507
File recovery process diagram, 487

File System Security, 418-419
Files. *See also* EFS
    copied and pasted into encrypted folder, 355
    copying or moving encrypted, 495-496
    encrypting, 357
    encrypting/decrypting with cipher, 497-500
    Read Only access to, 326
    recovering, 484
    risks to, 292
    storing on network servers, 161
Filter Action Wizard, 581-582
Financial issues, company, 137
Financial services industry, 111
Firewall products, 211
Firewall screening methods, 211
Firewalls, 33, 211
First domain controller, making, 231-238
Five-year cycle costs (TCO model), 113
Flexible network design, 197
Flexible single master operators (FSMOs), 238, 240-249
Folders
    backing up and restoring encrypted, 502-504
    copying or moving encrypted, 496
    decrypting on a local machine, 492-493
    encrypting on a local machine, 488-490
    encrypting on a remote server, 494
    encrypting using EFS, 356
    encrypting/decrypting with cipher, 497-500
    risks to, 292-293
Forest, 102, 139
    adding a domain to, 243-244
    creating, 63
Frame relay, 199
FSMO roles, 241-249
Full control, delegating, 450-451
Full replica, 305
Full restore, Windows 2000 Professional/Server, 473-474, 476
Full Service Providers (FSPs), 104-105, 204-205

G

Generic Routing Encapsulation (GRE), 559
Geographic model (business), 14
Geographical scope, company, 51-74, 99-100
Global catalog (Active Directory), 298-299
    directory partitions, 298
    replication planning, 314
Global Knowledge information portal, 608
Global security groups, 308
Globally unique identifier (GUID), 240, 394
Glossary of terms in this Guide, 609-676
Group permissions, 326, 333
Group policies
    applying, 401-404
    to assign and run scripts, 405
    associated with an OU, 445
    blocking inheritance of, 403-404
    configuring, 405-407
    enforcing higher-level, 403
    filtering, 402
    guidelines for implementing, 405, 407
    inheritance of, 366, 402
    IP security policy view, 587
    local, 368
    local vs. nonlocal, 394
    naming and saving, 400
    options to disconnect users, 158
    order of applying, 401
    order of inheritance, 366
    overview of, 392-395
    planning, 318-319
    security settings, 319

Group Policy console, 393
Group Policy container (GPC), 394-395
Group Policy Editor (GPE) MMC snap-in, 368, 396-400, 424-425
Group Policy (GP) MMC snap-in, 307-308, 365, 392-393, 568, 573
Group Policy Management Console, 365
Group policy objects (GPOs), 261, 307-308, 365, 393-394
    control delegation, 462
    disabling for SDOU, 404
    planning, 318-319
    settings, 366
Group Policy scenarios, 260-272
    creating OUs for, 263
    Desktop scenario, 265-267
    environment settings, 264
    files installed by, 262
    installing, 261-265
    Kiosk scenario, 270-272
    Laptop scenario, 267-269
    list of, 265
    Low TCO desktop, 272
    user and computer accounts, 264
Group Policy template (GPT), 394-395
Groups. *See* Security groups
Growth (company), 8-9, 110, 194

H

Hard disk failure, 466
Hard drive local data, protecting, 160-165
Hardware configurations, sample network, 286
Hardware device security, 16
Hardware devices, controlling access to, 159
Hardware security, 34-35, 411
Hardware settings, sample network, 281
Hardware upgrades, 212
Hardware-level RAID, 254, 466
Hash (hashing algorithm), 33
HCL (Hardware Compatibility List), 540
Health Information Portability and Accountability Act (HIPAA), 111
Healthcare industry, 111
Hierarchical network elements, 102
Highly secure (HISEC*.INF) templates, 307, 413
Hiring process, steps in, 74
Homogenous network, 200
HTML form of this Guide, 604
Hubs
    controlling access to, 155
    switches more secure than, 17
Human resources, 7, 196
Hypertext Transport Protocol (HTTP), 170

I

Identification badges, 155
Identity interception, 20
IKE authentication
    configuring, 575
    and network address translation (NAT), 557
IKE (Internet Key Exchange) protocol, 25, 556, 568-569
IKE negotiation
    network trace of, 571
    successful, 585
Impersonation, 20
Implementation phase (security planning), 11-12
Inbound connections, 559-562
Incompatibility of equipment or software, 197

Incremental templates, 413
Information flow through a company, 75
Information gathering (security planning), 11
Information security model, analyzing, 152-153, 160-171
Infrastructure master, 248-249
Inheritable permissions, 321
Inheritance
    of auditing entries, 411
    combined with delegation, 444-445
    of Group Policies, 366, 402-404
    order for Group Policies, 366
    of permissions, 320-322, 328
Inspect Startup Environment, 477
Integrated Services Digital Network (ISDN), 539
Interior perimeter, 19
Internal attacks, 153-154
Internal security risks, 18-19, 118, 139, 171-172, 295
International business model, 14, 71-72, 100
International encryption policy, 207
International laws, 207, 209
International links, 72
Internet attacks, types of, 293
Internet Authentication Service (IAS), 550-551, 555
Internet connection for RRAS, 529-539
Internet Connection Server, RAS on, 542-546
Internet Connection Sharing (ICS), 529, 531
Internet interfaces, distributed, 175
Internet Key Exchange. *See* IKE
Internet Protocol Security. *See* IPSec
Internet Service Providers (ISPs), 147, 362, 529
Internetworking, 24
Intersite replication of domain controllers, 71, 313
Intrasite replication of domain controllers, 71, 313-314

IP addresses, 56, 301, 529
    pool of valid, 544
    static, 539
IP Filter List, setting up, 576
IP Filter List dialog box, 578
IP Filter Wizard Welcome screen, 577
IP filters (IPSec), 576-583
IP properties, remote access policy, 564
IP Security Monitor, 574, 584
IP security policies, 586-587
IP security policy view in Group Policy, 587
IP Traffic Source, 577
IPSec filters, 25
IPSec (Internet Protocol Security), 25, 33, 147, 376, 546-547
    communication scenarios, 572
    encryption scheme, 585
    implementation diagram, 570
    information evaluation, 571
    lockdown mode, 569
    lockdown servers, 572-583
    with L2TP, 169
    management strategy, 586
    negotiation policies, 569, 586
    secure servers, 572
    security associations, 572
    security levels, 572
    transport mode, 556, 585
    tunnel mode, 556, 585
IPSec modes, 556, 585
IPSec policies, 32
    creating, 573-583
    testing, 583-584
IPSec solution, designing, 568-587
ISAKMP/Oakley service, 569, 586
ISDN lines, 199
IT administration, 9-10, 114-115
IT administrative structure, 9-10

IT departments
    change-management process, 116
    decision-making in, 80-81, 116
    decision-making process, 116
    eliminating/integrating, 108-109
IT management structure, 114-119
IT planning, overall, 138

J

Janitorial staff, security and, 411

K

Kerberos authentication, 33, 160, 360-361
    vs. NTLM, 108
    v5.0, 568
Kerberos Distribution Center (KDC), 360
Kerberos policy, 414
Key (cryptography), 35
Key pair, 35
Kiosk, how it works, 271
Kiosk scenario (Group Policy), 270-272
Knowledge Base (KB), 309
Knowledge Consistency Checker (KCC), 312

L

LAN sites, 312
LAN topology, 138-139
LAN users, 142-143
LANs (local area networks), 99, 353
    connectivity on-demand, 73
    infrastructure diagram, 59
    secure access within, 547
Laptop, stolen, 482
Laptop scenario (Group Policy), 267-269
Last Known Good Configuration, 476-477
Laws and regulations, 8, 110, 112, 207, 209
Layer 2 Forwarding (L2F), 556
Layer 2 Tunneling Protocol (L2TP), 73,
    147-148, 169, 556, 559
Layers of security, network, 18
Licenses, archiving, 209
Life cycles, business, 77-81
Line of Business (LOB) application, 271
Loadpol.bat file, 263, 266
Local business model, 14, 99
Local Group Policy objects, 368, 394
Local groups, granting resource
    permissions, 455
Local hard drive data, protecting, 160-165
Local policies and event log, 415
Local Security Settings console, 369
Local Site Domain OU (LSDOU), 366
Lockdown servers, IPSec, 572-583
Locking computers, 165
Logical security, 34
Logon hours, restricting, 157-158
Logon hours configuration screen, 157
Logon Properties dialog box, 406-407
Low connection speeds, 71
Low TCO desktop scenario, 272
L2TP (Layer 2 Tunneling Protocol), 73,
    147-148, 556
    with IPSec, 169
    with NAT, 559

M

MACHINESCRIPTS subfolder, 405
Malicious mobile code, 344
Management by Objectives (MBO), 15
Management models (business), 15, 100-101

Index

Managers (company), security planning and, 6-9
Man-in-the-middle attacks, 24, 566
Manipulation, 21
Manual repair, 477-478
Masquerading, 21
Master domain, 56-57
Master and resource domain diagram, 57
MD4 or MD5 hash (of a password), 555
Mean time to failure (MTTF), 466
Memory
    for application servers, 257
    for file and print servers, 258
    for RAS Servers, 259
    server performance and, 253
    for Windows 2000, 200
Memory cards (smart cards), 363
Mergers, company, 107-108
Metropolitan area network (MAN), 100
Microsoft Certificate Services (CS), 370-371
Microsoft Knowledge Base (KB), 309
Microsoft Management Console (MMC), 392
    BackOffice products, 368
    empty, 396
    saving in Author mode, 396-397
    saving in User mode, 396-397
Microsoft Management Console (MMC) snap-ins, 367-368, 393
Microsoft Point-to-Point Encryption (MPPE), 112, 169, 208
Microsoft Proxy Server 2.0, 18
Microsoft Technet site, 309-310
Microsoft Windows Client Strategy, 114
Microsoft Windows 2000 Resource kit, 309
Microsoft's stated objectives for Exam 70-220, 13
Mobile users, data protection for, 167-168
Modem pools, 362

Modify Owner permission, 327, 444
Movetree.exe, 246
MS-CHAP (Microsoft Challenge Handshake Authentication Protocol), 555-556
MS-CHAPv2, 556
Multi-domain model, 312
Multilink connections, remote access policy, 565
Multiple domains, 72-73, 311
Multiple network adapters, 255
Multiple remote access policy profiles, 564
Multiple sites, 353
Multi-master domain structure, 70
Multi-master operations model, 239-240
Multi-master replication, 70-71, 247, 306
Multi-master update, 239
Multiport serial adapters, 540
Multi-serial management devices, 259

N

Namespaces (Active Directory), 300, 310-312
Naming convention for users, 55
NAT (Network Address Translation), 529, 531
    IKE and, 557
    with L2TP, 559
National business model, 14, 70-71
National company, 100
NDIS (Network Driver Interface Specification), 557-558
NDISWAN, 557-558
NetBIOS domain name, 233
Network access methods, 349
Network access server (NAS), 555
Network adapter types, 255
Network adapters, multiple, 255
Network authenticator packet, 358

Network Connection Wizard, 562
Network failure, reasons for, 463-465
Network interface cards (NICs), 260, 375, 529, 541
Network layer, Open Systems Interconnect (OSI), 375
Network logon authentication, 160
Network management, existing and planned, 213-214
Network media security, 16
Network physical model, analyzing, 16-17
Network plan, developing for expansion, 213
Network printers, risks to, 291
Network resources. *See* Resources (network)
Network roles and responsibilities, 202-209
Network diagrams, 282, 287
Network security groups. *See* Security groups
Network security layers, 18
Network security plan, designing, 3-4
Network security support, Active Directory, 296
Network services, 23-24, 36, 256, 374-377
    at international sites, 72
    delegation of control, 462
Network Services Management, 367
Network subsystem performance and capacity, 254-256
    application server and, 258
    file and print servers and, 259
    RAS Server and, 260
Network topology, researching, 56
Network user communities, 136
Networked business model, 14
Networking (Windows 2000), basic concepts, 36
No Override option, 403-404
No recovery policy, 506
Non-authoritative restore, Active Directory, 471, 474

Non-Windows Kerberos realm trust, 300
NT File System (NTFS) encryption, 357
NT LAN Manager (NTLM), 108, 160, 361-362
Ntds.dit file, 298
Ntdsutil command-line tool, 244
    help screen, 249
    running offline, 245
NTFS file system, 161, 357
NTFSv5 format, 161
NTLM authentication, 361-362

O

Object attributes, 296, 298
Object class schema definition, 242, 455
Object classes, 242, 296, 298, 455
Object ownership, 326-327, 444
Objects, 296. *See also* Permissions
    common, 297
    moving between OUs, 453
    security information, 321
On-demand LAN connectivity, 73
128-bit encryption, 207
128-bit encryption laws, 110, 112
One-way trust relationship, 149, 299
Online transactions, CAs and digital certificates, 371
Open Systems Interconnect (OSI) network layer, 375
Operating costs (TCO model), 113
Operating system, single, 159
Operations master roles, 241-249
Operations masters, 240-252
Optical splitter, in fiber cable, 16
Organizational chart (company), 50, 52-53, 60, 519

Organizational structures, analyzing, 99-109
Organizational units. *See* OUs
Originating DSA (Domain Service Agent), 240
OTDR (Optical TDR), 17
OU properties, 459
OU structure
    and business structure, 446-447
    examples, 61, 526
    planning, 318
    steps for creating, 448, 450
OUs (organizational units), 149, 193, 301, 305, 327, 354, 443
    adding to ACLs of, 455
    benefits of using, 194
    characteristics of, 445
    creating in Active Directory, 69
    creating for scenarios, 263
    granting full control of, 445
    moving an object between, 453
    organized by business unit, 318
    organized by physical location, 317
    organized by role, 318
Outages, scheduled, 55
Outbound connections, 562
Outsourcing, benefits and drawbacks of, 115-116
Owner tab, Access Control Settings, 206
Ownership of objects, 326-327, 444
Ownership of resources, 204-206

P

Packet filtering, 18
PAP (Password Authentication Protocol), 33
Parent domain, 102
Parent folders, 322
Parent object, 321-322
Parent-child trust, 299

Partial replica, 305
Partner access methods, 149
Partners (trusted), 141, 148-149, 169
Partnerships, company, 106-107
Pass the hash, 566
Password cracking, 172
Password hashes, 555
Password policies, 159, 162-164, 172, 414
Password-derived encryption keys, 483
Password-protected screen savers, 165
Passwords, 33, 236, 568
Path of tunneled data in VPN client, 557-558
PDC emulator, 246-248, 250-251
PDC (primary domain controller), 70, 230, 361
People principle, 7
Per-domain roles, 241
Per-file file encryption and decryption, 487
Per-folder file encryption and decryption, 487
Per-forest roles, 241
Performance factors, 10
Performance requirements, 200-201
Permission assignment at the group level, 205
Permission compatible with pre-Windows 2000 servers, 67
Permission Entry dialog box, 461
Permissions
    changing, 326
    customizing at a group level, 333
    handling, 205
    inherited, 320-322, 328
    process order, 322
    resetting, 322
    setting, 236, 321
    user, 160
    user vs. group, 326
    viewing, 323-326

Per-object class control, delegating, 452-453
Personal Identification Number (PIN), 156
Physical location, delegation by, 448
Physical network model, analyzing, 16-17
Physical security issues, 34-35, 411
Physical security model, analyzing, 152-159
PKCS certificates, 372
PKI (public key infrastructure), 23, 36, 370, 547
    designing, 369-373
    with third-party CAs, 373
Points of Presence (POPs), 362
Point-to-Point Encryption (MPPE), 112, 169, 208
Point-to-Point Protocol (PPP), 556, 561
Point-to-Point Protocol (PPP) frames, 556
Point-to-Point Tunneling Protocol (PPTP), 73, 147, 556, 559
POL files (Windows NT 4.0), 402
Policy conflict, 366
Power problems, protecting against, 465
PPTP, 73, 147, 556, 559
Pre-shared authentication keys, 568
Primary domain controller (PDC), 70, 230, 361
Primary domain controller (PDC) emulator, 246-248, 250-251
Primary restore, 472, 474
Print servers, 258-259
Printers, risks to, 291
Printing, unauthorized, 214
Private Communications Technology (PCT), 170
Private key, 33
Private networks, 105
    external access to, 539-546
    secure access between, 546-550
Processor cards (smart cards), 363

Processor performance, 200, 253, 257, 258, 260
Product life cycle, 77-80
Products, company, 137
Promiscuous mode, 19
Protocol analyzers, 155
Protocols, number of installed, 255
Proxy Server 2.0, 18
Public key cryptography, 23, 33, 35, 369, 549
Public key infrastructure (PKI), 23, 36, 370, 547
    designing, 369-373
    with third-party CAs, 373
Public Key Policies, 505-506
Public key scheme, EFS, 369
Public key/private key encryption, 369, 549, 568
Public key/private key signature, 568
Public network data protection, 170
Public network users, 148, 170
Public networks
    secure access across, 547
    secure access to, 528-539
Pull replication, 306

Q

Quality of service (QoS), 197-198

R

RADIUS (Remote Authentication Dial-In User Service), 33, 362, 545, 555, 565
RAID (redundant array of inexpensive disks), 254, 466-468
RAID levels, 466-467

RAM (random access memory)
    for application servers, 257
    for file and print servers, 258
    for RAS Servers, 259
    server performance and, 253
RAS (Remote Access Service), 36, 539-540, 550. *See also* RRAS
    basic setup, 540
    connection diagram, 540
    on Internet Connection Server, 542-546
    in mixed mode domain, 552-554
    outsourcing, 362
    and VPN setup, 542-546
RAS Server, 259-260, 362, 539
Read access, 444
Read Group Policy permission, 402
Read Only access, file, 326
Recovery, administrator categories of, 506
Recovery agents, 484-485, 505
Recovery Console, 476-477
Recovery of data, 463-481, 484
Recovery policy
    attempting to bypass or alter, 509
    attempting to remove, 509
    changes to, 509
    default, 507
Redundant power supply, 465
Regback folder, 478
Regional business model, 14, 57-61
Regional company, 99-100
Registry files, repairing, 478
Registry keys, protected by policy, 417
Registry security, 417-418
Registry security template objects, 418
Relationships business model, 15
Relative ID master (RID master) role, 244-246
Relative ID (RID), 244

Remote access
    business requirements for, 56
    user requirements for, 143-148, 167-169, 550-565
Remote access policies, 550-554, 563-565
Remote access policy conditions, 564
Remote access policy profiles, multiple, 564
Remote connections. *See* Connections
Remote Desktop Protocol (RDP), 150
Remote Installation Service (RIS), 375
Remote Procedure Call (RPC) protocol, 243, 313-314
Replay attack, 20
Replicated data, restoring, 471-472
Replication (Active Directory), 70-71, 305-306, 314
    configuring, 316-317
    inter-site, 313
    intra-site, 313-314
    site-based, 312
Replication interval, 315
Replication methods, 306
Replication schedule, 315
Replication transport, 315
Repudiation, 21
Requested but optional servers, 572
Requested and required servers, 572
Resource distribution (company), 195-196
Resource domain, 56-57, 454
Resource and master domain diagram, 57
Resource ownership, 204-206
Resource permissions
    handling, 205
    local groups granting, 455
Resources (network)
    diagrammed, 50
    evaluating security of, 295

new Windows 2000 features for, 309
secure external access to, 539-546
security levels for each, 290-296
Restoring Windows 2000 Professional/Server, 472-474
Restricted Groups, 416-417
Return on Investment (ROI), 113
RID pool, 245-246
RID (relative ID), 244-246
Rights
assigned to groups, 54
assigned intelligently vs. carelessly, 358
RIS security, 375
Risk, company tolerance for, 112-113
Risks, security. *See* Security risks
Roles
operations master, 241-249
delegation by, 449
domain controller, 238, 301
per-forest and per-domain, 241
network, 202-209
Root domain, 102
Routers, controlling access to, 155
Routing, 155, 564
RRAS connection to the Internet, 529-539
RRAS (Routing and Remote Access Service), 143-144, 529, 561-562
RRAS setup wizard, 530-533, 538, 543-545
Runas command, 166

S

Safe Mode, 476
Savepol.bat file, 266
Scalability, network, 196
Scalability goals (company), analyzing, 194
Scheduled downtime and outages, 55

Schema, Active Directory, 242-243, 298, 455
Schema attributes, 243
Schema classes, 242
Schema definition, 455
Schema master (schema operations master), 241-242, 252
Schema updates, 242
Screen savers, password-protected, 165
Scripts
assigning to run at user logon, 406
group policies used to assign and run, 405
SDOU (site domain organizational unit), 394
Secret key encryption, 34-35
Secure access
between networks, 24, 527-600
between private networks, 546-550
for local users, 143
to private networks, 539-546
to public networks, 528-539
Secure channels, 196
Secure networking environment, elements of, 34-35
Secure (SECURE*.INF) templates, 307, 413
Secure servers, IPSec, 572
Secure Sockets Layer (SSL) protocol, 34, 169-170, 372
Secure traffic, 196
Securing Active Directory components, 320-333
Securing the network, 320-333
Security, defined, 3
Security Association (SA), 25, 568
Security auditing, 407-412
Security baseline, 20, 229-287, 290
Security cards (smart cards), 363
Security configuration, within Group Policy, 307

Security Descriptor, 443
Security design, and technical environment, 210-214
Security design for communication channels, 24-25
Security Design exam, 2-5
Security features of Windows 2000, 4, 140
Security fundamentals, 34-35
Security group policies. *See* Group policies
Security groups, 23, 136-142
    assigned rights, 54
    delegation and, 462
    explained, 401
    filtering by, 402
    and OUs, 447
    predefined, 307-308
    strategy for, 365-369
Security host, third-party, 147
Security identifier (SID), 244-245, 326, 443
Security layers, network, 18
Security level for each resource, 290-296
Security levels, 578-579, 290-296
Security log, explained, 408
Security log retention methods, 412
Security Manager, IPSec, 573
Security market, 111
Security Options, 415
Security planning, 6-12
    steps, 10-12
    strategies, 5-10
    structure, 10-12
Security planning team, 6
Security policies. *See also* Group policies
    developing, 210
    IP, 586-587
    placement of, 22

    placement and inheritance of, 352-357
    size and complexity of, 352
    using Security Manager, 573
Security Policy Setting dialog box, 163
Security principal objects, 246, 443
Security requirements analysis, 20-21, 136-152, 289-349
Security rings, 17
Security risks, 118-119, 171-175, 291-296
    analyzing, 17-19
    to network files, 292
    types of, 20-21
Security Rule Wizard, 579-580, 583
Security standards, defining, 109
Security support in Active Directory, 296
Security templates. *See* Templates (security)
Security terminology, 32-34
Select Group Policy Object dialog box, 399
Sensitivity of data, 214
Serial Line Internet Protocol (SLIP), 144
Server services, restoring and reconciling, 474
Servers, 252-260
    CMOS settings, 155
    controlling access to, 154-156
    first domain controller, 231-238
    limiting access to, 165-166
    physically securing, 17
    purchasing, 200
    role of through lifespan, 200
    storing data files on, 161
    use of administrator accounts, 166
Servers and clients, communication flow, 76
Service level agreement (SLA), 77
Service life cycle, 77-78
Service packs, 212
Service policy (for company's users), 204

Services (company), 137
Services (network), 23-24, 36, 256, 374-377
    at international sites, 72
    delegation of control, 462
Sessions configuration, 151
SET (Secure Electronic Transaction)
  certificates, 372
Shared secret, 25
Shared System Volume, 235
Shares, unauthorized access to, 292-293
Shortcut trust, 300
SID (security identifier), 244-245, 326, 443
Signatures, digital, 35, 370
Simple Network Management Protocol (SNMP), 375-377
Single domain model, 312
Single sign-on (for secure networking), 34
Single-master operations, 241
Site domain organizational unit (SDOU), 394
Site links
    cost of, 315
    creating, 303-304
    configuring, 316-317
    planning, 315
Site topology, 312
Site-based replication, planning, 312
Sites, 139
    Active Directory, 301-304
    as their own CAs, 373
    delegation of control, 462
    multiple, 353
    planning, 312-317
Slow international links, 72
Smart cards, 34, 156, 359, 363-364, 485
    controlling access to, 159
    types of, 363
SMB (Server Message Block) protocol, 24

SMB (Server Message Block) signing, 24-25, 565
SMB signing solution
    designing, 565-568
    implementing, 566-567
SMP (symmetric multiprocessing), 253, 257
Snap-ins, MMC, 367-368, 393
Sniffing software, 19
SNMP security, 375-377
Software application groups, 152
Software incompatibility, 197
Software licenses, archiving, 209
Software mirroring, 468
Software packages, hosted online, 206
Software piracy, 209
Software security, 34
Software upgrades, 212
Software-level RAID, 466, 468
SSL (Secure Sockets Layer), 34, 169-170, 372
SSL (Secure Sockets Layer) certificates, 372
Staff group, 141
Stamp of a value, Active Directory, 239-240
Standard delegation, 333
State-based replication, 306
Static IP address, 539
Static pool of IP addresses, 544
Store-and-forward replication, 306
Stored data, encryption of, 482
Strong encryption, 112, 208, 565
Strong passwords, 159, 172
    components of, 164
    requiring, 162-164
Strongest encryption, 565
Subnets. *See* Sites
Subsidiary model, 72-73
Support, ownership of, 204
Switches, vs. hubs, 17

Symmetric encryption, 35
Symmetric multiprocessing (SMP), 253, 257
System files, verifying, 478
System Integrators (SI), 205
System Policies, 396
System Policy Editor, 396
System processor, 200, 253, 257, 258, 260
System Services Security, 419-420
System State, backing up, 470-471
Systems
    availability of, 55
    security of existing, 210-211
    unbootable, 508-509
    user access to, 201-202
Systems management, existing and planned, 213-214
SYSVOL folder, 66, 234, 239

T

Take Ownership permission, 327, 444
Talent shortage, 196
Tapping and stealing data, 16-17
Task, delegation by, 94, 449
Tasks to Delegate page, 94
TCO model for security strategy, 113
TCO (total cost of operations), 113-114
TCP/IP protocol, 56, 150, 558
TDR (Time Domain Reflectometer), 17
Technical environment
    existing and planned, 19-20, 192-209
    security design and, 210-214
Technical group (network security), 136, 139-140
Technical point of view of security planning, 9-10
Technical requirements of security
    analyzing, 19-20, 191-227
    of applications, 206-207
    handling in-house, 205
Technical support structure, analyzing, 212-213
Technology infrastructure, researching, 55
Template Security Policy Setting dialog box, 418, 423
Templates (security), 55, 165, 307, 412-425
    applying to OU policy, 424
    configuring, 414-423
    creating and applying, 423-425
    creating and configuring, 421-423
    table of, 413
    types of, 412-413
    using, 420-423
Terminal Services, 150-152, 377
Terminal Services Profile configuration, 151
Terminal Services security, 377
Terms in this Guide, glossary of, 609-676
Theory X, 15
Theory Y, 15
Third-party certificates, 149, 373
Third-party security host, 147
Token, 34
Total Quality Management (TQM), 15
Transactions, CAs and digital certificates in, 371
Transit internetwork, 561
Tree-root trust, 299
Trees (domain), 102
    creating, 63, 232
    multiple, 73
Triple DES (3DES) encryption, 565
Trojan horse attacks, 21, 173, 294
Trust relationship, 34, 299-300

Trusted for delegation (computer), 493-495, 501
Trusted partners, 141, 148-149, 169
Tunneling protocols, 170, 561
Two-tiered business unit structure diagram, 449
Two-way transitive trusts, 299
Type 1 certificate, 372
Type 2 certificate, 372

U

Unauthorized access, 6
    dial-in, 294
    to local data, 482
    to network printers, 291
    to shares, 292-293
Unauthorized manipulation of data, 294
Unbootable system, 508-509
Universal security groups, 308
Unrestricted access, 482
Upgrades, existing and planned, 212
UPS (uninterruptible power supply), 465
User Account options, Active Directory, 167
User applications, 149-152
User certificates and keys, changes to, 509
User class, 296
User communities, 136, 140-141
User Datagram Protocol (UDP), 556
User dial-in settings, 563-564
User logon, assigning a script run at, 406
User logon hours, restricting, 157-158
User object, 297
User permissions, 160, 326
User Properties Dial-in tab, 145
User Rights Assignment, 415
User Rights policy, 158-159
User vs. group permissions, 326

Users
    access to data and systems, 201-202
    access to work areas, 157
    affect of security on, 7, 214
    analyzing requirements of, 135-189
    authorized, 442
    copying/moving encrypted files, 495
    distribution of in the company, 194-195
    educating, 35
    encrypting shared files, 495
    explained, 7
    location of, 142-149
    naming convention for, 55
    number of, 255-256
    object ownership, 444
    remote access security for, 550-565
    roles and responsibilities of, 202-203
    service policy for, 204
    in a single ADS domain, 57
    technical group working with, 140
    unfairly mistrusted, 7
    workspace security, 156-159
Users (Active Directory objects), 401
Users and Computers snap-in, 246, 324, 456
Users Computers or Groups page, 93
Users group, 141
Users or Groups page, 94
USERSCRIPTS subfolder, 405

V

Vendors
    authorized to work on equipment, 155
    company relationships with, 103-106
Virtual Network, 541
Virus detection software, 210-211

Viruses, 173-174, 210-211, 294
Voice over IP (VoIP), 197
VPN client, 561
VPN server or gateway, 541, 561
VPNs (virtual private networks), 103, 105, 143, 147, 539-540
    basic setup, 541
    connecting to, 562
    connection components, 561
    logical and physical design diagram, 541
    logical view diagram, 560
    path of tunneled data in, 557-558
    and RAS setup, 542-546

W

WAN site link, 312
Wide area networks (WANs), 100, 353
    secure access within, 547
    topology of, 138-139
    users on, 143
Windows Components Wizard, 549
Windows Explorer, using to encrypt a folder, 488-490

Windows 2000
    distributed services, 376
    enabling Advanced Features, 326
    new and improved security features, 4, 140, 309
    TCO of, 113-114
Windows 2000 magazine, 309
Windows 2000 Professional/Server, full restore, 473-474
Windows 2000 Resource kit, 309
Working documents, 50-51
Workstation security, 156-159
Write access, 444

X

X.509 certificates, 372
XML (Extensible Markup Language), 103

Z

Zero lockout count, 248

Custom Corporate Network Training

Train on Cutting Edge Technology We can bring the best in skill-based training to your facility to create a real-world hands-on training experience. Global Knowledge has invested millions of dollars in network hardware and software to train our students on the same equipment they will work with on the job. Our relationships with vendors allow us to incorporate the latest equipment and platforms into your on-site labs.

Maximize Your Training Budget Global Knowledge provides experienced instructors, comprehensive course materials, and all the networking equipment needed to deliver high quality training. You provide the students; we provide the knowledge.

Avoid Travel Expenses On-site courses allow you to schedule technical training at your convenience, saving time, expense, and the opportunity cost of travel away from the workplace.

Discuss Confidential Topics Private on-site training permits the open discussion of sensitive issues such as security, access, and network design. We can work with your existing network's proprietary files while demonstrating the latest technologies.

Customize Course Content Global Knowledge can tailor your courses to include the technologies and the topics which have the greatest impact on your business. We can complement your internal training efforts or provide a total solution to your training needs.

Corporate Pass The Corporate Pass Discount Program rewards our best network training customers with preferred pricing on public courses, discounts on multimedia training packages, and an array of career planning services.

Global Knowledge Training Lifecycle Supporting the Dynamic and Specialized Training Requirements of Information Technology Professionals

- Define Profile
- Assess Skills
- Design Training
- Deliver Training
- Test Knowledge
- Update Profile
- Use New Skills

College Credit Recommendation Program The American Council on Education's CREDIT program recommends 53 Global Knowledge courses for college credit. Now our network training can help you earn your college degree while you learn the technical skills needed for your job. When you attend an ACE-certified Global Knowledge course and pass the associated exam, you earn college credit recommendations for that course. Global Knowledge can establish a transcript record for you with ACE, which you can use to gain credit at a college or as a written record of your professional training that you can attach to your resume.

Registration Information

COURSE FEE: The fee covers course tuition, refreshments, and all course materials. Any parking expenses that may be incurred are not included. Payment or government training form must be received six business days prior to the course date. We will also accept Visa/MasterCard and American Express. For non-U.S. credit card users, charges will be in U.S. funds and will be converted by your credit card company. Checks drawn on Canadian banks in Canadian funds are acceptable.

COURSE SCHEDULE: Registration is at 8:00 a.m. on the first day. The program begins at 8:30 a.m. and concludes at 4:30 p.m. each day.

CANCELLATION POLICY: Cancellation and full refund will be allowed if written cancellation is received in our office at least six business days prior to the course start date. Registrants who do not attend the course or do not cancel more than six business days in advance are responsible for the full registration fee; you may transfer to a later date provided the course fee has been paid in full. Substitutions may be made at any time. If Global Knowledge must cancel a course for any reason, liability is limited to the registration fee only.

GLOBAL KNOWLEDGE: Global Knowledge programs are developed and presented by industry professionals with "real-world" experience. Designed to help professionals meet today's interconnectivity and interoperability challenges, most of our programs feature hands-on labs that incorporate state-of-the-art communication components and equipment.

ON-SITE TEAM TRAINING: Bring Global Knowledge's powerful training programs to your company. At Global Knowledge, we will custom design courses to meet your specific network requirements. Call 1 (919) 461-8686 for more information.

YOUR GUARANTEE: Global Knowledge believes its courses offer the best possible training in this field. If during the first day you are not satisfied and wish to withdraw from the course, simply notify the instructor, return all course materials, and receive a 100% refund.

In the US:
CALL: 1 (888) 762-4442
FAX: 1 (919) 469-7070
VISIT OUR WEBSITE:
www.globalknowledge.com
MAIL CHECK AND THIS FORM TO:
Global Knowledge
Suite 200
114 Edinburgh South
P.O. Box 1187
Cary, NC 27512

In Canada:
CALL: 1 (800) 465-2226
FAX: 1 (613) 567-3899
VISIT OUR WEBSITE:
www.globalknowledge.com.ca
MAIL CHECK AND THIS FORM TO:
Global Knowledge
Suite 1601
393 University Ave.
Toronto, ON M5G 1E6

REGISTRATION INFORMATION:

Course title _____

Course location _____ Course date _____

Name/title _____ Company _____

Name/title _____ Company _____

Name/title _____ Company _____

Address _____ Telephone _____ Fax _____

City _____ State/Province _____ Zip/Postal Code _____

Credit card _____ Card # _____ Expiration date _____

Signature _____

LICENSE AGREEMENT

THIS PRODUCT (THE "PRODUCT") CONTAINS PROPRIETARY SOFTWARE, DATA AND INFORMATION (INCLUDING DOCUMENTATION) OWNED BY THE McGRAW-HILL COMPANIES, INC. ("McGRAW-HILL") AND ITS LICENSORS. YOUR RIGHT TO USE THE PRODUCT IS GOVERNED BY THE TERMS AND CONDITIONS OF THIS AGREEMENT.

LICENSE: Throughout this License Agreement, "you" shall mean either the individual or the entity whose agent opens this package. You are granted a non-exclusive and non-transferable license to use the Product subject to the following terms:

(i) If you have licensed a single user version of the Product, the Product may only be used on a single computer (i.e., a single CPU). If you licensed and paid the fee applicable to a local area network or wide area network version of the Product, you are subject to the terms of the following subparagraph (ii).

(ii) If you have licensed a local area network version, you may use the Product on unlimited workstations located in one single building selected by you that is served by such local area network. If you have licensed a wide area network version, you may use the Product on unlimited workstations located in multiple buildings on the same site selected by you that is served by such wide area network; provided, however, that any building will not be considered located in the same site if it is more than five (5) miles away from any building included in such site. In addition, you may only use a local area or wide area network version of the Product on one single server. If you wish to use the Product on more than one server, you must obtain written authorization from McGraw-Hill and pay additional fees.

(iii) You may make one copy of the Product for back-up purposes only and you must maintain an accurate record as to the location of the back-up at all times.

COPYRIGHT; RESTRICTIONS ON USE AND TRANSFER: All rights (including copyright) in and to the Product are owned by McGraw-Hill and its licensors. You are the owner of the enclosed disc on which the Product is recorded. You may not use, copy, decompile, disassemble, reverse engineer, modify, reproduce, create derivative works, transmit, distribute, sublicense, store in a database or retrieval system of any kind, rent or transfer the Product, or any portion thereof, in any form or by any means (including electronically or otherwise) except as expressly provided for in this License Agreement. You must reproduce the copyright notices, trademark notices, legends and logos of McGraw-Hill and its licensors that appear on the Product on the back-up copy of the Product which you are permitted to make hereunder. All rights in the Product not expressly granted herein are reserved by McGraw-Hill and its licensors.

TERM: This License Agreement is effective until terminated. It will terminate if you fail to comply with any term or condition of this License Agreement. Upon termination, you are obligated to return to McGraw-Hill the Product together with all copies thereof and to purge all copies of the Product included in any and all servers and computer facilities.

DISCLAIMER OF WARRANTY: THE PRODUCT AND THE BACK-UP COPY OF THE PRODUCT ARE LICENSED "AS IS." McGRAW-HILL, ITS LICENSORS AND THE AUTHORS MAKE NO WARRANTIES, EXPRESS OR IMPLIED, AS TO RESULTS TO BE OBTAINED BY ANY PERSON OR ENTITY FROM USE OF THE PRODUCT AND/OR ANY INFORMATION OR DATA INCLUDED THEREIN. McGRAW-HILL, ITS LICENSORS, AND THE AUTHORS MAKE NO GUARANTEE THAT YOU WILL PASS ANY CERTIFICATION EXAM BY USING THIS PRODUCT. McGRAW-HILL, ITS LICENSORS AND THE AUTHORS MAKE NO EXPRESS OR IMPLIED WARRANTIES OF MERCHANTABILITY OR FITNESS FOR A PARTICULAR PURPOSE OR USE WITH RESPECT TO THE PRODUCT. NEITHER McGRAW-HILL, ANY OF ITS LICENSORS, NOR THE AUTHORS WARRANT THAT THE FUNCTIONS CONTAINED IN THE PRODUCT WILL MEET YOUR REQUIREMENTS OR THAT THE OPERATION OF THE PRODUCT WILL BE UNINTERRUPTED OR ERROR FREE. YOU ASSUME THE ENTIRE RISK WITH RESPECT TO THE QUALITY AND PERFORMANCE OF THE PRODUCT.

LIMITED WARRANTY FOR DISC: To the original licensee only, McGraw-Hill warrants that the enclosed disc on which the Product is recorded is free from defects in materials and workmanship under normal use and service for a period of ninety (90) days from the date of purchase. In the event of a defect in the disc covered by the foregoing warranty, McGraw-Hill will replace the disc.

LIMITATION OF LIABILITY: NEITHER McGRAW-HILL, ITS LICENSORS NOR THE AUTHORS SHALL BE LIABLE FOR ANY INDIRECT, SPECIAL OR CONSEQUENTIAL DAMAGES, SUCH AS BUT NOT LIMITED TO, LOSS OF ANTICIPATED PROFITS OR BENEFITS, RESULTING FROM THE USE OR INABILITY TO USE THE PRODUCT EVEN IF ANY OF THEM HAS BEEN ADVISED OF THE POSSIBILITY OF SUCH DAMAGES. THIS LIMITATION OF LIABILITY SHALL APPLY TO ANY CLAIM OR CAUSE WHATSOEVER WHETHER SUCH CLAIM OR CAUSE ARISES IN CONTRACT, TORT, OR OTHERWISE. Some states do not allow the exclusion or limitation of indirect, special or consequential damages, so the above limitation may not apply to you.

U.S. GOVERNMENT RESTRICTED RIGHTS: Any software included in the Product is provided with restricted rights subject to subparagraphs (c), (1) and (2) of the Commercial Computer Software-Restricted Rights clause at 48 C.F.R. 52.227-19. The terms of this Agreement applicable to the use of the data in the Product are those under which the data are generally made available to the general public by McGraw-Hill. Except as provided herein, no reproduction, use, or disclosure rights are granted with respect to the data included in the Product and no right to modify or create derivative works from any such data is hereby granted.

GENERAL: This License Agreement constitutes the entire agreement between the parties relating to the Product. The terms of any Purchase Order shall have no effect on the terms of this License Agreement. Failure of McGraw-Hill to insist at any time on strict compliance with this License Agreement shall not constitute a waiver of any rights under this License Agreement. This License Agreement shall be construed and governed in accordance with the laws of the State of New York. If any provision of this License Agreement is held to be contrary to law, that provision will be enforced to the maximum extent permissible and the remaining provisions will remain in full force and effect.

GET CERTIFIED WITH HELP FROM THE EXPERTS

MCSE Windows® 2000 Study Guide

A COMPLETE STUDY PROGRAM BUILT UPON PROVEN INSTRUCTIONAL METHODS

Self-study features include:

Expert advice on how to take and pass the test:

"You will need to know how to design and plan the placement of security policies for sites, domains, and OUs, and how to control (force or block) inheritance of policies by child containers from the parent containers in which they reside."

Step-by-Step Certification Exercises focus on the specific skills most likely to be on the exam. The **CertCam** icon guides you to diagrams with descriptive audio that demonstrates this skill set on CD-ROM.

Special warnings that prepare you for tricky exam topics:

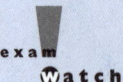

"You will need to understand the concepts of virtual private networks and how companies can leverage the wide availability and low cost of connections to ISPs. You will need to know how to create a VPN and configure Windows 2000 as an on-demand router."

MCSE Designing Windows 2000 **On The Job** notes present important lessons that help you work more efficiently:

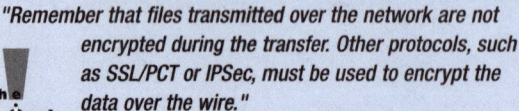

"Remember that files transmitted over the network are not encrypted during the transfer. Other protocols, such as SSL/PCT or IPSec, must be used to encrypt the data over the wire."

Two-Minute Drills at the end of every chapter quickly reinforce your knowledge and ensure better retention of key concepts:

"EFS prevents the leaking of key information to page files and ensures that all copies of an encrypted file, even if moved, remain encrypted on Windows 2000 NTFS partitions."

Scenario & Solution sections lay out problems and solutions in a quick-read format. For example:

If I have a network running both Windows NT 4.0 and Windows 2000, which authentication system is recommended?

Because Kerberos is not backward compatible with Windows NT 4.0, you will have to run NTLM.

More than 190 realistic practice questions with answers help prepare you for the real test.

If a domain administrator chooses to delete recovery policy at the domain level (thereby removing all recovery certificates from the policy), what is the effect of this action?

- **A.** A. Users will not be able to encrypt additional files on computers in the domain.
- **B.** Users will still be able to encrypt files on computers in the domain.
- **C.** Local administrators will need to add recovery agents to the recovery policy on the local computer before users will be able to encrypt additional files.
- **D.** All files on domain computers will automatically become decrypted and no future encryption will be able to occur.

☑ **B.** If the domain recover policy is deleted (effectively establishing "no policy"), then users can continue encrypting files as before, except recovery policy will be enforced by the default recovery policy defined on the local computer. The default recovery policy on the local computer lists the local administrator as the sole recovery agent.

☒ **A** is incorrect because the default local recovery policy still exists. **C** is incorrect because the default local recovery policy becomes the new recovery policy. **D** is incorrect because all previously-encrypted files will remain encrypted with recovery information from the old domain recovery policy. As these files are modified, they will be re-encrypted with the local recovery policy information.